ENDLESS HOLOCAUSTS

Endless Holocausts

Mass Death in the History of the United States Empire

David Michael Smith

MONTHLY REVIEW PRESS
New York

Copyright © 2023 by David Michael Smith
All Rights Reserved

Library of Congress Cataloging-in-Publication Data
available from the publisher.

ISBN paper: 978-1-58367-9890
ISBN cloth: 978-1-58367-9906

Typeset in Minion Pro

MONTHLY REVIEW PRESS, NEW YORK
monthlyreview.org

5 4 3 2 1

Contents

Acknowledgments | 7

Introduction | 9

CHAPTER 1 The Indigenous Peoples Holocaust | 16

CHAPTER 2 The African American Holocaust | 57

CHAPTER 3 The Workers Holocaust | 97

CHAPTER 4 From Colonial Wars to Global Holocausts | 122

CHAPTER 5 The Holocausts of Pax Americana I | 169

CHAPTER 6 The Holocausts of Pax Americana II | 210

CHAPTER 7 Other Holocausts at Home and Abroad | 258

Notes | 290

Index | 507

for Rona

Acknowledgments

I am deeply grateful to all the researchers who responded to my inquiries and shared their expertise while I was writing this book. Many thanks to Mikaela Morgane Adams, Jeffrey S. Adler, Fred Anderson, George Reid Andrews, Andy Baker, Francisco Balderrama, Douglas A. Blackmon, Peter K. Brecke, D. Brian Burghart, Donald S. Burke, Colin G. Calloway, E. Ann Carson, Stephen K. Cusick, James P. Daughton, James Downs, Douglas R. Egerton, James Fenske, Elsa Gelpi, Dina Gilia-Whitaker, Arline Geronimus, Erik Gilbert, Thavolia Glyph, Peter C. Gøtzsche, Sandra Elaine Greene, Gerald Horne, Robert Gudmestad, Joseph Hanlon, Jeffrey Hilgert, Joseph E. Inikori, Robin D. G. Kelley, Martin Klein, Bruce Lanphear, Patrick Manning, Emily Marquez, Stephen Majeski, Keith Meyers, Joseph Miller, Vicente Navarro, Jeffrey Ostler, Gary Potter, Robert Proctor, Daniel T. Reff, George Andrews Reid, Richard Reid, Rebecca Reindel, Andrés Reséndez, Javier Rodriguez, Nigel Rollins, Randolph Roth, Francisco A. Scarano, Michael Schroeder, Nancy Shoemaker, David Stark, David A. Swanson, Lauren MacIvor Thompson, Russell Thornton, Fred A. Wilcox, and Brian Glyn Williams.

It is worth emphasizing that none of these researchers is responsible for the analysis and conclusions in this book, and the responsibility for any errors is entirely mine. I also want to thank Greg Broyles,

Angelita Chapa, Patty Harlan, Folko Mueller, Paul Mullan, Tracy Orr, Pat Thompson, and Fred A. Wilcox for reading and providing feedback on various chapters. My greatest debt is to Rona E. Smith, my wife, who encouraged me to write this book, read earlier versions of the chapters, and shared important ideas for improving them. It is no exaggeration to say that this book would not have been written without Rona's steadfast support.

Introduction

For generations, capitalists, politicians, and pundits have promoted the doctrine of U.S. exceptionalism. Scores of millions of people in this country have embraced what Christian Appy has called "the central tenet of American national identity—the broad faith that the United States is a unique force for good in the world, superior not only in its military and economic power, but in the quality of its government and institutions, the character and morality of its people, and its way of life."[1] To be sure, many Indigenous people, people of African descent, workers, and others have not accepted this "broad faith," but its reach and endurance has been widely recognized. However, as Sidney Lens pointed out half a century ago, U.S. exceptionalism has always been "a myth of morality," and "America the benevolent . . . does not exist and never has existed."[2] In the 1960s and 1970s, mass movements against racism and the wars in Southeast Asia exposed this myth to tens of millions of people. In the decades that followed, the deteriorating conditions of workers, growing inequality, increasingly dysfunctional governance, wars in Iraq and Afghanistan, the persistence of police brutality, the opioid crisis, and climate change further undermined this dogma. More recently, the resurgence of white supremacy, the erosion of U.S. primacy in the

10   ENDLESS HOLOCAUSTS

world, the transformation of the Republicans into a far-right party, the rise of Donald Trump, the hundreds of thousands of preventable COVID-19 deaths, and the fascist-led attack on Congress on January 6, 2021, have led many more people to abandon their illusions about this country.

That the United States is a colonialist and imperialist country—an empire—can hardly be questioned. The conquest and near-extermination of several hundred Indigenous nations by European and U.S. settlers provided the land on which the contiguous United States was built, and Native peoples continue to live in colonial conditions, deprived of sovereignty and self-determination. The United States also colonized Liberia, Alaska, Hawaii, Puerto Rico, Guam, the eastern Samoan Islands, the Philippines, the U.S. Virgin Islands, and the Northern Mariana Islands. Panama, which Washington carved out of Colombia to build a transoceanic canal, and Cuba were U.S. protectorates for decades. The United States recognized the independence of Liberia in 1847 and the Philippines in 1946 and admitted Alaska and Hawaii as states in 1959 but refused to relinquish the Panama Canal Zone until 1999 and still occupies forty-five square miles of land and water at Guantánamo Bay, Cuba.

Today the United States officially includes not only the fifty states and the District of Columbia but also 574 federally recognized Indigenous nations, the commonwealths of Puerto Rico and the Northern Mariana Islands, the inhabited territories of Guam, American Samoa, and the U.S. Virgin Islands, and nine uninhabited islands and atolls in the Pacific and the Caribbean.[3] Residents of Washington, DC, the commonwealths, and the inhabited territories do not have full representation in Congress. Indeed, as the U.S. Department of the Interior has stated, the commonwealths and inhabited territories are areas "in which the United States Congress has determined that only selected parts of the United States Constitution apply."[4] The people of American Samoa are not even recognized as U.S. citizens. The "freely associated states" of the Federated States of Micronesia, the Republic of the Marshall Islands, and the Republic of Palau are U.S. protectorates.[5]

INTRODUCTION   11

In addition to its long history of conquest and colonization, the United States has always energetically exploited other peoples' resources, markets, and labor. The enslaved labor of people of African descent fueled early U.S. economic development and the Industrial Revolution. By the 1820s, U.S. merchants were shipping opium from Turkey to China so they could sustain imports of tea, spices, porcelain, and nankeen. As Greg Grandin has noted, the Monroe Doctrine of 1823 "announced to European empires that Latin America fell under Washington's exclusive sphere of influence."[6] In the mid-nineteenth century, the mounting need to export surplus products led the U.S. Empire to threaten and use violence against China, Japan, and Korea. In the last quarter of the century, intensifying industrial development and agricultural production contributed to unprecedented economic growth. By the 1890s, U.S. businesses were shipping steel, iron, oil, and agricultural machinery to foreign markets, and the export of capital had begun. During that decade, the United States replaced Britain as the world's largest economy. In 1895, Secretary of State Richard Olney, referring to South America, claimed that "the United States is sovereign on this continent."[7] In stark contrast, after acquiring most of Spain's colonies in 1898, the United States demanded an "Open Door" for U.S. trade and investment in China and did not even consult its government.

The U.S. Empire's imperatives of expansion and accumulation have dramatically grown in the era of modern imperialism, and so has its exploitation of the resources, markets, and labor of people in other countries. As Grandin has explained, in the early decades of the twentieth century "American corporations and financial houses came to dominate the economies of Mexico, the Caribbean, Central America, as well as large parts of South America."[8] To protect its investments and promote its interests, the empire militarily intervened in the Mexican Revolution of 1910 and invaded and occupied Nicaragua, Haiti, and the Dominican Republic.

Industry, agriculture, and trade grew significantly when the United States funded and armed, and then joined the Entente Powers during the First World War. Afterward, the United States invaded Soviet

Russia, supported the Guomindang regime in China, and welcomed European fascism as a bulwark against communism—entering the Second World War only because the Axis powers threatened its own imperialist interests. By 1945, the United States had become the wealthiest and most powerful empire in the world. Since then, the imperium has vigorously sought to obtain the oil, strategic materials, and other resources it requires and to keep, in the words of Harry Magdoff, "as much as possible of the world open for trade and investment by the giant multinational corporations."[9]

These imperatives led to unrelenting confrontation with the Soviet Union and other socialist states—at horrific human expense. The later collapse of most of these states, which occurred partly because of U.S. actions over the decades, made the world a more dangerous place as the empire found itself to be the sole superpower and moved to establish its presence in those and other lands. Since 1945, the United States has fought devastating large-scale wars in Korea, Vietnam, Laos, Cambodia, Iraq (twice), and Afghanistan. It has launched proxy wars on four continents, routinely attacked countries, overthrown and installed governments, destroyed popular movements, assassinated foreign leaders, engaged in economic sabotage, and supported its allies' violent domestic repression and acts of war against other nations. The only country to ever use atomic bombs, the United States has deployed nuclear weapons around the world, developed ominous plans "to win a nuclear war," and brought humanity to the brink of nuclear holocaust on several occasions.[10] Today, the empire has a network of client states encompassing about 40 percent of the world's countries, about eight hundred foreign military bases, and more than 200,000 military personnel and contractors deployed in about 140 countries.[11] But the rise of China, the return of Russia, and the mounting economic, social, and political crises at home make clear that the United States' "unipolar moment" is already fading.[12]

Although there have long been activists and writers willing to challenge the myth of U.S. exceptionalism, new scholarly work in recent decades has powerfully illuminated some of the ugliest dimensions of U.S. history and contemporary society. This research has significantly

INTRODUCTION 13

contributed to the literature on settler colonialism and genocide against Indigenous people, white supremacy and the oppression of Black people, U.S. imperialism and its perpetual wars, the uniquely high level of violence in this country, and other grave threats to public health. However, a great deal more must be said about the almost unimaginable loss of life resulting from U.S. capitalism, colonialism, and imperialism over the centuries. Although there has been considerable debate over the size of the Indigenous population in the Western Hemisphere before 1492, an estimate of the total number of deaths caused by colonialism and genocide throughout the present-day United States has not yet been published. Writers have expressed different views on the overall loss of life caused by the transatlantic slave trade, but an assessment based on historical information about each stage of that dreadful saga has not yet been developed. The *Maafa*, or great disaster, was only the beginning of five centuries of brutality and injustice experienced by people of African descent.[13]

The scourge of fatal workplace injuries and occupational diseases that accompanied the Industrial Revolution and continues today has received only limited scholarly attention. But there is ample historical and contemporary evidence that vast numbers of workers perished from occupational injuries and diseases in the past century and a half.

Although there is now a remarkable literature on U.S. imperialism, the total number of deaths in U.S. wars, military interventions, and other hostile actions abroad is still not known. Similarly, the cumulative human costs of other forms of state and social violence, the profit-driven proliferation of dangerous drugs and other unsafe consumer products, the automobile-centered transportation system, the commodified and often dangerous health care system, and environmental pollution in this country have not been gauged. This author knows of no study that comprehensively surveys all these forms of mass deaths and demonstrates their centrality and significance in U.S. history and contemporary U.S. society.

This book aims to help fill these gaps in the critical, counter-hegemonic literature on the United States. I argue that the prehistory, formation, expansion, and global ascendancy of the U.S. Empire have required endless holocausts at home and abroad. I also develop informed and reasonable, if rough or very rough, estimates of the loss of life in each one. The Oxford English Dictionary defines "holocaust" as "destruction or slaughter on a mass scale," and an unrelenting, endless succession of such catastrophes lies at the heart of U.S. history and U.S. society today.[14] Far from being occasional, unfortunate exceptions to an otherwise benevolent or benign historical record, different kinds of large-scale annihilation of human life have made this country what it is. Indeed, though most capitalists, politicians, and pundits will never admit it, these endless holocausts have been indispensable in the rise of the wealthiest and most powerful imperium in the history of the world. Tragically, they have also resulted in the deaths of almost unimaginable numbers of people from the European colonial period to the present.

In this book, I examine diverse holocausts for which the U.S. Empire is responsible or shares responsibility. Some of these mass deaths have resulted and continue to result from large-scale violence, which is often viewed as "the intentional use of physical force or power."[15] The holocausts suffered by Indigenous peoples, people of African descent, and the victims of U.S. militarism worldwide have involved widespread carnage, to be sure. But even in these cases, many fatalities have occurred because of disease, starvation, and related causes. Other forms of mass deaths have not been engendered by violence as traditionally defined. Instead, they are large-scale instances of what Frederick Engels viewed as "social murder," that is, deaths caused by deprivation of the "necessaries of life" and the imposition of conditions in which people cannot survive.[16] These various kinds of social murder are not inevitable but are rooted in U.S. capitalism. In the following chapters, I explore mass deaths resulting from both far-reaching violence and social murders.

Chapter 1, "The Indigenous Peoples Holocaust," analyzes the near-annihilation of Native peoples in the lands that became the United States, from the early sixteenth century to the present. Chapter 2, "The African American Holocaust," assesses the catastrophic human costs of the transatlantic slave trade, slavery, and subsequent anti-Black

INTRODUCTION   15

oppression in this country. Chapter 3, "The Workers Holocaust,"
investigates the mass deaths from workplace injuries, occupational
diseases, and anti-labor violence since the mid-nineteenth century.
Chapter 4, "From Colonial Wars to Global Holocausts," examines
the immense human toll of U.S. wars, military interventions, and
support for repression and fascism abroad through the end of the
Second World War. Chapter 5, "The Holocausts of Pax Americana I,"
explores the enormous loss of life in other countries resulting from
U.S. imperialism between 1945 and 1980. Chapter 6, "The Holocausts
of Pax Americana II," analyzes the extensive carnage in other countries brought about by U.S. imperialism since 1980. Chapter 7, "Other
Holocausts at Home and Abroad," investigates the stunning number
of U.S. lives lost because of the U.S. Empire's wars and other forms
of violence as well as the mass deaths caused by dangerous drugs,
tobacco, unsafe consumer products, automobiles, the health care
system, and pollution.

Altogether, I estimate that the U.S. Empire is responsible or shares
responsibility for close to 300 million deaths. The almost incon-
ceivable loss of life in these endless holocausts arguably makes this
country exceptional, though in a strikingly different way than its
apologists intend. As this book makes clear, this succession of catastrophes will continue as long as the imperium exists. And as its
primacy erodes, the U.S. ruling class may act like a "wounded beast"
and commit heinous new crimes against the peoples of the world—
including the people of this country—to maintain as much wealth
and power as possible.[17] Although this book focuses on manifold
forms of mass deaths, it also points to an extraordinary history of
resistance by Indigenous peoples, people of African descent, workers,
people in other nations brutalized by U.S. imperialism, and demo-
cratic-minded people around the world. Everyone who supports the
dismantling of the empire can draw inspiration from this history of
resistance.

1

The Indigenous Peoples Holocaust

Let the white race perish. They seize your land; they corrupt your women; they trample on the ashes of your dead! Back, whence they came, upon a trail of blood, they must be driven. Back! Back, ay, into the great water whose accursed waves brought them to our shores!

—TECUMSEH, ADDRESS IN TUCKAUBATCHEE, 1811

David Stannard has used the expression "American Holocaust" to refer to the historically unprecedented number of deaths caused by European and U.S. settler colonialism in the Western Hemisphere. Stannard has argued that this was "the worst human holocaust the world had ever witnessed."[1] It may also be viewed as the most horrific genocide in history.[2] Some contemporary scholars believe that the Indigenous population of the present-day United States and the hemisphere declined between 90 and 95 percent between 1492 and 1900.[3] As Russell Thornton and other researchers have explained, wars, genocidal violence, enslavement, land expropriation, forced removals and relocations, diseases, destruction of food sources, dietary changes, malnutrition, elimination of traditional ways of life, erasure of identity, and reduced birth rates contributed

THE INDIGENOUS PEOPLES HOLOCAUST

to this cataclysmic demographic collapse in what is today the United States.[4] Although many Indigenous nations have survived and experienced a demographic recovery since 1900, various forms of violence, poor health conditions rooted in colonialism and racism, and related forms of oppression persist, and the Indigenous Peoples Holocaust continues today.[5]

THE AMERICAS BEFORE THE EUROPEANS

As Roxanne Dunbar-Ortiz has emphasized, centuries before the arrival of Cristóbal Colón (Christopher Columbus), the Indigenous nations of the Western Hemisphere had built "great civilizations" whose "governments, commerce, arts and sciences, agriculture, technologies, theologies, philosophies, and institutions were intricately developed."[6] These diverse societies ranged from the Maya of Central America, the Runa (Incas) of western South America, and the Mexicas (Aztecs) of Mexico, to the Haudenosaunees (Iroquois), Tsalagis (Cherokees), Diné (Navajo) in the lands that became the United States. North America was a "continent of nations and federations of nations."[7] Most Native people lived in towns and successfully farmed, while others were nomadic hunters or hunter-gatherers.[8] A sophisticated network of roadways connected different nations and facilitated trade.[9] Although Indigenous peoples in the present-day United States did not have written languages, their laws, poetry, song, dance, and ceremonies articulated their history "in an oral vocabulary more complex than Europe's."[10] Howard Zinn has pointed out that in these lands "human relations were more egalitarian than in Europe."[11]

THE EUROPEAN QUEST FOR WEALTH AND THREAT
TO INDIGENOUS CIVILIZATIONS

An important component of what Lens called "the myth of morality" is the fiction that the settlement of the English colonies that became the United States is largely a story of oppressed people seeking freedom from religious and political persecution.[12] The historical reality is strikingly different. In the first place, as Gerald Horne has pointed out, "The United States is the inheritor of the munificent crimes of not only London but Madrid, too."[13] The Spaniards were the first Europeans to conquer, colonize, and plunder some of the lands that today constitute the U.S. Empire. Some people who settled in the English colonies of North America had indeed experienced repression at home, and many more had suffered extreme privation. Signally, though, their rulers—like those in Spain and the other European countries that laid claim to vast territories in the Western Hemisphere—were primarily interested in the accumulation of wealth and the expansion of state power. It was the quest for gold, silver, and a route to the Far East that could restore trade in silk and spices that led to the initial European invasion of what came to be known as the Americas.[14]

Karl Marx wrote in the first volume of *Capital*: "The discovery of gold and silver in America [and] the extirpation, enslavement, and entombment in mines of the Indigenous population of that continent" were among the "chief moments of primitive accumulation" that gave rise to modern capitalism.[15] After arriving in the Western Hemisphere, the Europeans invoked the "Doctrine of Discovery" to claim these lands. This doctrine was articulated in a series of late fifteenth-century papal decrees and used to justify the conquest and colonization of much of the planet in the centuries that followed.[16] The Europeans' aims brought them into direct, violent conflict with Indigenous peoples in the Americas, as they would in the Pacific islands, Asia, and Africa. But the expropriation of Indigenous lands and the near-extermination of Indigenous peoples became the indispensable foundation for establishing and expanding European colonies and creating and expanding the U.S. Empire.

THE SIZE OF THE INDIGENOUS POPULATION

The island that the Taino (Arawak) people called Guanahani in the present-day Bahamas where Colón landed in 1492 was not heavily

THE INDIGENOUS PEOPLES HOLOCAUST   19

populated. But when his expedition reached the Caribbean island they named Hispaniola, they found tens of thousands of people.[17] In the next several decades, Spanish invaders encountered millions upon millions of Indigenous people in the lands that we know today as Mexico, Central America, and South America.[18] Estimates of the pre-contact Indigenous population in the Western Hemisphere range from a low of 8.4 million made by Alfred Kroeber in 1939 to a high of 145 million made by Henry Dobyns in 1988.[19] Stannard has estimated that approximately 100 million Native people lived in the Americas in 1492, and Ward Churchill has suggested that the number may have been about 125 million.[20] For decades, Russell Thornton estimated that the population in the hemisphere was about seventy-five million, but recently he indicated that the actual number might have been closer to sixty million.[21] In 2019, scientists and geographers studying the ecological impact of the first century of European colonization also estimated that the pre-contact Native population was about sixty million.[22] However, this assessment may be too low, and a rough estimate of sixty-five million for the hemisphere may be prudent.[23]

The Indigenous population of North America north of present-day Mexico was significantly smaller than in lands to the south. However, as William Denevan has shown, even here the landscape was not "primarily pristine, virgin, a wilderness, nearly empty of people."[24] Estimates for what became the coterminous United States range from a low of 720,000 made by Alfred Kroeber in 1939 to a high of fifteen million made by Dunbar-Ortiz in 2014.[25] Douglas Ubelaker has concluded that the pre-contact population in today's contiguous United States was approximately two million.[26] Thornton's view is that more than five million Indigenous people lived here.[27] Although some researchers agree with Ubelaker's estimate, James Wilson has noted that Thornton's estimate is probably "the nearest to a generally accepted figure."[28] In addition, the combined Native populations of Alaska, Puerto Rico, and Hawai'i likely numbered about eight hundred thousand, so the total Indigenous population of the present-day United States was probably close to six million.[29]

20 ENDLESS HOLOCAUSTS

Conquest, Colonization, and Disease

In the 1960s and 1970s, the renewal of Indigenous peoples' struggles for sovereignty and self-determination focused public attention on the catastrophe of settler colonialism. Some commentators sought to deny or minimize the colonizers' genocidal intentions by largely attributing the near annihilation of Native peoples to new diseases.[30] Stannard has criticized this line of argument:

> It is true, in a plainly quantitative sense of body counting, that the barrage of disease unleashed by the Europeans . . . caused more deaths than any other single force of destruction. However, by focusing almost entirely on disease, by displacing responsibility for the mass killing onto an army of invading microbes, contemporary authors increasingly have created the impression that the eradication of those tens of millions of people was inadvertent—a sad, but both inevitable and "unintended consequence" of human migration and progress. . . . In fact, however, the near-total destruction of the Western Hemisphere's Native people was neither inadvertent nor inevitable.[31]

For Stannard, it was the terrible synergy of "microbial pestilence" and "purposeful genocide" that killed so many.

In recent decades, most researchers have acknowledged the impact of smallpox, measles, typhus, and other new diseases on Indigenous populations while emphasizing other aspects of colonialist devastation. Today many investigators reject Dobyns's conclusion that smallpox and other "virgin soil" epidemics swept across North America throughout the sixteenth century.[32] Thornton's view that the early "medical conquest" of Native peoples generally "paved the way" for "military conquests and colonizations" in the present-day United States has also been challenged.[33] It increasingly appears that the widespread transmission of new diseases usually did not precede the invaders but accompanied them.[34] Moreover, David S. Jones explains, "It was the turbulence of colonization and not genetic liability that

THE INDIGENOUS PEOPLES HOLOCAUST

created Indians' devastating susceptibility to imported pathogens."[35] Current documentary and archaeological evidence do not permit final conclusions on the early history of Native depopulation in these lands, the comparative lethality of disease and violence, or the complete dimensions of the demographic collapse. However, it is possible to outline the broad contours of the Indigenous Peoples' Holocaust in this country and develop an informed and reasonable, if rough, estimate of the total loss of life.

APOCALYPSE FROM THE CARIBBEAN TO SOUTH AMERICA

The apocalyptic consequences of the European invasion became clear soon after Colón's arrival on Hispaniola in late 1492.[36] The Spaniards began enslaving thousands of Taino people and forcing them to work in gold mines and on plantations.[37] Bartolomé de Las Casas, a conquistador turned priest, condemned the invaders' widespread murder and torture.[38] Fernández de Oviedo, a conquistador who became the official historian of Spain's Caribbean colonies, admitted that he and his compatriots were responsible for "innumerable cruel deaths . . . as uncountable as the stars."[39] Although some analysts have suggested that smallpox erupted on Hispaniola in 1507, there is little evidence of this.[40] However, violence, enslavement, exhaustion, famine, and disease reduced the island's population to about 250 people by 1540.[41] Colón's lieutenant, Juan Ponce de León, established the Spanish colony on the island of Puerto Rico in 1508 and became its governor. Here, too, violence, slavery, and diseases were catastrophic. When the first recorded smallpox epidemic broke out in the Spanish colonies in 1518, its impact in Puerto Rico was significant. Between twenty to fifty thousand Tainos on the island had died by 1544, the first casualties of European colonialism in the lands that later became part of the U.S. Empire.[42]

Hernán Cortés's invasion of the Mexicas in 1519–1521, Pedro de Alvarado and Cristóbal de Olid's subjugation of most of the Maya in the 1520s, and Francisco Pizarro and Diego de Almagro's conquest of much of the Runa in the 1530s unleashed hell on a much larger scale. Warfare, genocidal violence, enslavement, and famine combined with

22   ENDLESS HOLOCAUSTS

smallpox and other "firestorms of disease" to produce as many as forty million deaths in present-day Mexico, Central America, Peru, and Chile by the late 1560s.[43] Diseases brought by Europeans also killed sizeable numbers of Indigenous people in what are now Colombia, Ecuador, Bolivia, and Brazil.[44] In their 2019 study, the scientists and geographers assessing the environmental effects of European colonization estimated that approximately 56 million Native people died in the Western Hemisphere between 1492 and 1600.[45] These researchers found that this "Great Dying" led to the significant "regrowth of the natural habitat," the removal of vast amounts of carbon dioxide from the atmosphere, and the cooling of the global climate.[46]

EARLY EUROPEAN EXPLORATION AND VIOLENCE IN THE PRESENT-DAY UNITED STATES

During the sixteenth century, European invasion and settlement of the lands that became the United States were much more limited. However, Giovanni Caboto (John Cabot) explored present-day Newfoundland and Labrador, New England, and perhaps Long Island in 1497–98.[47] Hundreds of other European explorers, traders, and adventurers visited the Atlantic and Pacific coasts during the next hundred years and sometimes made contact with Indigenous peoples.[48] In 1501, the Portuguese adventurer Gaspar Corte-Real sailed along the coast of Newfoundland and Maine and kidnapped about fifty Native people.[49] In 1524, the Italian explorer Giovanni da Verrazano sailed along Long Island and later met with a delegation of Wampanoag and Narragansett people. He also encountered the Indigenous peoples of present-day Rhode Island and either the Abnakis or Penobscots of present-day Maine.[50] The following year, the Portuguese explorer Estêvão Gomes visited what is now New England and New York, captured dozens of Native people, and took them to Spain.[51] Verrazano and Gomes also met members of the Powhatan Confederacy when sailing along the coast of present-day North Carolina and Virginia.[52] The Europeans who encountered various Indigenous peoples may well have left deadly pathogens behind.[53]

THE INDIGENOUS PEOPLES HOLOCAUST   23

In 1513, Ponce de León landed on the Atlantic coast of the land he called La Florida. He hoped to enslave Indigenous people and transport them to Caribbean plantations but met with resistance and fled. He returned with two hundred men and arrived near present-day Port Charlotte in July 1521, but the Calusa people repulsed their landing. About eighty Spaniards were killed or died of their wounds, including Ponce de León, and twice as many Calusas may have perished.[54] Smallpox epidemics did not erupt afterward, as some scholars have suggested, but the violence and disruption caused by the Spaniards probably left the Calusas more vulnerable to already existing diseases.[55] In 1526, Lucas Vázquez de Ayllón and several hundred Spaniards, along with about a hundred enslaved African people, established a settlement called San Miguel de Gualdape, possibly at the mouth of the Savannah River near present-day Tybee Roads, Georgia. Vázquez de Ayllón died of illness soon afterward, and the settlement was threatened by inclement weather, food shortages, internal dissension, a revolt by the enslaved Africans, and disease—most likely malaria.[56] After the settlers took over a local Indigenous village and consumed its food supplies, its inhabitants fought back, resulting in the collapse of the settlement and the flight of 150 Spanish survivors.[57]

In May 1528, Pánfilo de Narváez, the Spanish governor of Cuba, landed with about three hundred armed men near present-day Tampa Bay, Florida, searching for gold and other riches. Their ships were destroyed by a hurricane, and resistance by Indigenous peoples, starvation, and illness—perhaps malaria but possibly typhoid, dysentery, or other diseases—wiped out most of the Spaniards. After using rafts to return to the Gulf from the Florida interior, Narváez and many others were lost in a storm. Álvar Núñez Cabeza de Vaca and about eighty compatriots survived but were shipwrecked near Galveston Island in present-day Texas. New bouts of disease killed many of the survivors.[58] Soon afterward, Indigenous people in the area began to die, chiefly from a "dysentery-type disease" that could have been caused by the Spaniards "defecating and urinating in local drinking water or in aquatic areas where Indigenous peoples gathered clams or oysters."[59] The first known epidemic in present-day Texas,

24   ENDLESS HOLOCAUSTS

probably cholera, struck the Karankawa people in 1528.[60] During the
next six years, only Cabeza de Vaca and three others survived near-
starvation and enslavement by Coahuiltecan people as they wandered
through present-day Texas, New Mexico, and Arizona on their long
trek toward Spanish settlements in what is now Mexico.[61]

Spanish Invasions of the Southeast and the Southwest

In May 1539, Hernando de Soto brought about six hundred soldiers,
enslaved Indigenous and African people, two hundred horses, and
three hundred pigs to present-day Tampa Bay. For the next four years,
de Soto's expedition traveled through what is now Florida, Georgia,
the Carolinas, Tennessee, Alabama, Mississippi, Arkansas, Texas, and
Louisiana while looking for gold.[62] As the Spaniards proceeded, they
invaded Native villages, stole their food, and enslaved more people.[63]
They also left a trail of Indigenous bodies in their wake, beginning
with about forty Timucas killed in the battle of Two Lakes in Florida in
September 1539.[64] In October 1540, de Soto's forces killed as many as
three thousand Mobile warriors led by Tascalusa in a battle at Mabila
in present-day Alabama.[65] Fighting in what is today Mississippi and
other areas in 1541–42 resulted in hundreds more Native deaths.[66] De
Soto became ill and died in May 1542. Less than half of his expedition survived and reached Spanish settlements in present-day Mexico
in September 1543.[67] The expedition did not introduce smallpox
or measles, but it resulted in widespread destruction and destabilization, increased local susceptibility to existing diseases, and likely
spread malaria throughout the region.[68] These developments marked
the beginning of a significant decline of the Native population in the
Southeast during the following century and a half.[69]

In July 1540, Francisco Vázquez de Coronado arrived in what is
today New Mexico with about 350 soldiers and about 1,300 Indigenous
allies. They entered the lands of the Pueblo peoples searching for gold
and proceeded to destroy thirteen villages and kill several hundred
inhabitants within a year.[70] Coronado then led his expedition into
what are now Texas, Arizona, Oklahoma, and Kansas but never found

THE INDIGENOUS PEOPLES HOLOCAUST   25

gold and returned to present-day Mexico in 1542. There is no evidence that Coronado's forces brought European diseases with them, but the Spaniards' devastation and disruption, along with the spread of existing diseases, reduced the Pueblo population from about fifty thousand in 1540 to forty thousand during the next six decades.[71] In May 1598, Juan de Oñate brought four hundred Spaniards into the area to establish a permanent settlement and begin the process of colonization. In January 1599, after inhabitants of Acoma resisted, the Spaniards sacked the town, killed about eight hundred people, and enslaved many others.[72] In the winter of 1601, the Spaniards burned three Tompiro towns and killed about nine hundred people.[73] With the onset of colonization, smallpox, measles, and other European diseases also began to appear and soon proved to be devastating.[74]

THE FIRST PERMANENT SPANISH AND ENGLISH SETTLEMENTS

Shortly after French colonizers founded Fort Caroline, near present-day Jacksonville, Florida, in 1564, they began suffering from diseases. As Paul Keaton has remarked, by this time "malaria had likely become endemic in Florida from previous European invasions."[75] The following year, Pedro Menéndez de Avilés led about eight hundred Spaniards in destroying Fort Caroline and establishing St. Augustine as the first permanent European settlement in what is today the continental United States. The Timucuas fought against the Spanish conquest of their lands, and their armed resistance to occupation continued for years. After Menéndez and his forces left a garrison and mission in southwestern Florida, a brief détente with the Calusas ended, and more warfare ensued.[76] Violence, forced tribute and enslavement, destabilization, hunger, and trauma proved to be deeply destructive to Native communities. Soon after St. Augustine was founded, many Indigenous people began dying from a mysterious disease that may have been typhus. Malaria and other existing diseases took a toll as well.[77] Smallpox had also arrived, but what Paul Kelton has called "the limited extent of Spanish colonialism" precluded major outbreaks at the time.[78] Much worse was to come in the next century.

26   ENDLESS HOLOCAUSTS

The English established a colony on Roanoke Island off the coast of what is today North Carolina in 1585, but it did not survive for long. Inadequate food supplies, conflict with local Indigenous people, and disease contributed to this failure and the disappearance of more than a hundred colonizers after 1587.[79] Francis Drake's relief expedition to Roanoke Island the previous year may well have brought typhus, but limited contact with Native inhabitants there likely precluded a catastrophic epidemic.[80] When English settlers founded Jamestown in present-day Virginia in 1607, they encountered the Powhatan Confederacy of perhaps 15,000 people.[81] Another ten thousand or more Indigenous people also lived in the area.[82] Whether Native nations here had suffered massive depopulation from European epidemics in the preceding century is a subject of debate among researchers.[83] But the historical record of death and destruction at the hands of English settlers after 1607 is not in dispute. Ill-supplied and unable to provide for themselves amid terrible drought and bitter winters, the Jamestown colonizers soon faced starvation.[84] Members of the confederacy led by Wahunsonacock (Powhatan) saved the colony by providing food to the settlers. However, the colonizers soon began stealing their corn and attacking their villages.[85]

Early Wars, Enslavement, and Disease in the Southeast

The Powhatans ended trade with the settlers and laid siege to Jamestown, which resulted in 160 deaths from hunger and disease in the winter of 1609–10. Scores of other settlers and Powhatan people were killed in battle before hostilities ended in 1614.[86] An epidemic, possibly related to malnutrition, erupted in 1617 and resulted in many more deaths among Native people than settlers.[87] War broke out again in 1622. Now led by Opechancanough, the confederacy's attacks on several English settlements along the James River left about 350 people dead.[88] The colonizers, in turn, poisoned about two hundred Indigenous people at what was announced as a peace conference in 1624.[89] The following year, the settlers killed about one thousand Pamunkey members of the confederacy and destroyed their town.[90] A

THE INDIGENOUS PEOPLES HOLOCAUST

treaty in 1632 ended the fighting but not for long. In 1644, as the colonizers expanded their domain, Opechancanough's forces attacked them and killed between four hundred and five hundred people.[91] The settlers, now numbering about eight thousand, struck back forcefully, killing Opechancanough and destroying the Powhatan resistance.[92]

The subsequent growth of English settlements in Virginia and Maryland was disastrous for local Indigenous nations. Continuing violence, trauma, starvation, and disease led to many more Native deaths.[93] Conflict with Susquehannock (Conestoga) people and the rebellion against colonial authorities led by Nathaniel Bacon resulted in about three hundred deaths in Virginia in 1676–77.[94] By this time, English settlers had been trading guns and manufactured goods for deerskins and people captured by Native allies for more than two decades.[95] The relentless demand for labor in the Europeans' Atlantic colonies led to the growth of this slave trade.[96] As Kelton has noted, by 1698 "a thriving exchange network linked British colonies and Native communities from the James to the Savannah and from the Atlantic to the Mississippi."[97] The slave trade significantly changed "the social landscape" and the enormously increased "volume of human traffic" provided a new conduit for spreading acute infectious disease.[98] What Kelton calls the Great Southeastern Smallpox Epidemic of 1696 killed tens of thousands of Native people throughout the region by 1700.[99] By the turn of the century, only about two thousand Powhatans and other Indigenous people remained alive in Virginia.[100] The combined horrors of colonialism likely caused more than a hundred thousand Native deaths in the Southeast between 1685 and 1715.[101]

EARLY WARS, ENSLAVEMENT, AND DISEASE IN THE NORTHEAST

In 1608, the French explorer Samuel de Champlain founded Quebec. For almost a century, French traders exchanged "guns, metal and glass goods, brandy, and foodstuffs" for moose hides and, more recently, pelts with the Mi'kmaq nation of what is today Nova Scotia.[102] Dietary change, malnutrition, excessive alcohol consumption, and increased susceptibility to disease had killed thousands—more likely, tens of thousands—of Mi'kmaqs by the early 1610s.[103] The subsequent expansion of the French fur trade with the Wendat (Huron) in present-day Ontario led to the spread of disease and the arming of these Native allies for attacks on the Haudenosaunee confederacy, some of whom lived in what is today New York State. In the 1630s, smallpox killed as many as ten thousand Wendats, and hundreds of others died in battles.[104] About ten thousand Haudenosaunee people also perished from smallpox in the same decade.[105] The Wendats eventually lost their ancestral homelands, and many of them migrated to other lands, including the present-day United States.[106] After the Inoca (Illinois) Confederacy began trading goods and captives with the French, they lost between 7,500 and 17,500 people to calamitous epidemics and war with the Haudenosaunees and Mesquakies (Fox).[107] Many members of these nations also died in wars with the French and their Native allies.[108]

In 1620, English settlers founded Plymouth Colony in present-day Massachusetts. Four years before their arrival, an acute epidemic had killed thousands—perhaps tens of thousands—of Wampanoag, Pawtucket, Abnaki, and Massachuset people along the coast.[109] In 1624, the Dutch established a settlement at New Amsterdam in what is now Manhattan. In 1630, the English founded Massachusetts Bay Colony near present-day Boston. Three years later, a smallpox epidemic devastated the Indigenous nations in the areas near the English settlements and the Pequots and Mohegans in what became Connecticut and the Haudenosaunees in present-day New York State. Tens of thousands of Native people died, as did a much smaller number of settlers.[110] Other diseases followed, as did violent conflicts. After Pequots killed an English trader during a commercial dispute with the Dutch in 1634, Massachusetts Bay Colony leaders refused to accept restitution and exploited the crisis to seize additional Pequot lands. The colonizers launched what Dunbar-Ortiz has called "a hideous war of annihilation."[111] The Pequot War of 1636–37 resulted in 1,500 to 1,800 Native deaths.[112]

Between 1643 and 1645, Dutch settlers sought to exterminate Lenapes (Delawares) and other Indigenous peoples who resisted

THE INDIGENOUS PEOPLES HOLOCAUST

encroachments on their land and refused to pay tribute. Along with English and Mohawk allies, the Dutch killed more than 1,600 Lenapes.[113] In 1675, the Wampanoag chief Metacom led his nation, the Narragansetts, and the Nipmucks in a sustained assault on the English colonies in Massachusetts, Connecticut, and Rhode Island.[114] During what became known as King Philip's War, the settlers recruited Native allies and formed the first ranger forces to engage in "wilderness warfare" against their Indigenous enemies.[115] Colonial officials began paying bounties for the scalps of Native men, women, and children.[116] Metacom's forces threatened the survival of these colonies but were eventually defeated. About six thousand Wampanoag, Narragansett, and Nipmuck people were killed, and about three thousand settlers died before the war finally ended.[117] The historic defeat suffered by these Indigenous peoples opened the door to the expansion of the New England colonies during the next half-century.[118] The ensuing loss of Native peoples' "land base . . . hunting grounds, and fisheries" led to more poverty, malnutrition, and vulnerability to disease.[119] By the end of the century, New England's Indigenous population had declined from at least 70,000 in 1600 to about 12,000.[120]

The Destruction of Native Peoples in Nuevo México and La Florida

Five years after King Philip's War began, the Pueblo peoples in Santa Fe de Nuevo México revolted against the Spanish colonizers. For eight decades, these invaders had subjected the Pueblo to violence and abuse, required tribute or labor from them, promoted the slave trade, and benefited from their impoverishment.[121] During this time, smallpox, typhus, and other diseases had greatly diminished the Native population.[122] When the Pueblo rose up in 1680, they lost about three hundred people but killed about four hundred Spaniards and forced the surviving settlers to flee to El Paso.[123] Nine years later, soldiers led by the Spanish governor attempted to reconquer the region. They destroyed the main village, Tsiya (Zia), and killed about six hundred inhabitants but were not strong enough to reconquer the other towns

30 ENDLESS HOLOCAUSTS

and had to withdraw.[124] However, in 1692, a new Spanish governor returned with three hundred troops, attacked the town of Jemez, and killed eighty-four people.[125] The Spaniards violently repressed other Indigenous resistance and reestablished control of the region by 1696.[126] Only about 15,000 Pueblo people remained alive at the end of the seventeenth century.[127]

In Spanish Florida, the growth of missions and trade proved to be deadly for Indigenous communities in the seventeenth century.[128] The Spaniards did far more than proselytize the many Timucuas, Apalachees, and Guales they reached. As in the Southwest, the Spaniards required tribute and labor by Natives, which, combined with dietary changes, malnutrition, and poor health, reduced their resistance to diseases.[129] At the same time, Spanish colonialism also "removed buffer zones that had previously separated the Timucuas, the Apalachees, and the Guales" and these communities "became links in a chain of supplies traveling to and from St. Augustine," and from other countries and other colonies.[130] This transformation of the "social landscape" in Florida fostered the transmission of European pathogens to Indigenous communities, and the results were devastating.[131] Beginning in 1617, smallpox and other epidemics struck Natives repeatedly, killing perhaps scores of thousands.[132] Decades later, slave raids by English settlers from the Carolina colony and their Indigenous allies struck new blows against the Natives of Florida.[133] By the mid-eighteenth century, the Timucuas, Apalachees, Guales, and other original inhabitants of Florida had been virtually wiped out.[134]

FROM KING WILLIAM'S WAR TO THE YAMASEE WAR

Many Indigenous people died during the four colonial wars fought by England (Britain after the Act of Union in 1707), France, and Spain for control of North America between 1689 and 1763. During King William's War of 1689–97, the first colonial war between the English and the French, between two thousand and six thousand members of the Haudenosaunee Confederacy perished when French and allied

THE INDIGENOUS PEOPLES HOLOCAUST 31

Native forces destroyed their villages during the conflict.[135] Hundreds of other Indigenous peoples allied with France also died.[136] By the time that representatives of forty Indigenous nations met in Montreal in 1701 to end long-standing hostilities among themselves and with the French, war and diseases had already substantially reduced their numbers.[137]

During Queen Anne's War of 1702–1713, which pitted the English against the Spaniards and the French, Native peoples "suffered the greatest."[138] In 1703–1704, English settlers and Muscogee (Creek) allies killed more than 1,100 Apalachee people in Spanish missions in Florida and enslaved several thousand others.[139] As Gary Clayton Anderson has pointed out, the war "left virtually all of Spanish Florida in ruins and the lands of the Indians nearly vacated."[140] In 1712, a contingent of French troops and several hundred Ottawa and Potawatomi fighters near Detroit killed about one thousand Mesquakies and Mascoutens, whom they viewed as potential British allies.[141] By then, the Tuscaroras in North Carolina had begun to fight back against the British settlers who were seizing more of their lands and spreading deadly diseases.

During the Tuscarora War of 1711–13, more than 220 settlers and soldiers and thirty-five Yamasee allies perished.[142] About 1,400 Tuscaroras and allied Corees died, and another thousand were enslaved.[143] Most Tuscarora survivors migrated to New York and became part of the Haudenosaunee Confederacy.[144] The Yamasees, who had already lost many people to smallpox and other epidemics, soon learned that their alliance with the colonizers provided little benefit.[145] After settlers and speculators began taking control of their lands in South Carolina and colonial traders' fraud and brutality mounted, the Yamasees acted to defend themselves. During the Yamasee War of 1715–18, they joined with Muscogees, Catawbas, Apalachees, and other Indigenous peoples to attack colonial settlements. Together, the Indigenous forces killed about four hundred settlers, but about three hundred Yamasees died or were enslaved.[146] Yamasee survivors fled to what is now Georgia and Florida. The massive Indigenous depopulation in the Southeast largely ended the

32   ENDLESS HOLOCAUSTS

British trade in captured Natives and led them to increasingly rely on the labor of enslaved Africans.[147]

NEW FRENCH AGGRESSION FROM THE GREAT LAKES TO MISSISSIPPI

A decade after the Yamasee War, French colonizers and their allies struck new blows against Indigenous people in present-day Wisconsin, Illinois, and Mississippi. Although the Mesquakies had made peace with the French in 1716, the colonizers refused to free enslaved members of their nation or abandon the lucrative slave trade.[148] In turn, the Mesquakies renewed their interference with the French fur trade in the Mississippi Valley and areas to the West.[149] In 1727, the French encouraged their Inoca, Anishinaabe (Ojibway), and Ottawa allies to launch new slave raids against these old enemies, and a new war began.[150] In 1730, French troops and Native fighters massacred about five hundred Mesquakies in what is now Illinois.[151] The following year, another three hundred died at the hands of France's Indigenous allies.[152] In sum, several thousand Mesquakies had died by the early 1730s.[153] The few survivors joined the Sauk people, and both nations then migrated to the land that became Iowa.[154] In present-day Mississippi, war erupted in 1729 when the Natchez people refused the French Louisiana commander's order to abandon their main village so he could expand his plantation. Natchez fighters burned a French fort and killed more than 230 settlers, but the French soon counterattacked with the help of artillery and Choctaw allies. By early 1730, several hundred Natchez people had died, and the survivors were defeated and forced to leave their lands.[155]

NEW EPIDEMICS AND EUROPEAN CONFLICTS OVER NATIVE LANDS

British settlers established the colony of Georgia in 1732. The Spaniards considered this an illegal occupation of their land, and tensions mounted. Before long, both groups of colonizers were appealing to the Tsalagis in Georgia for support. Governor James Oglethorpe's

THE INDIGENOUS PEOPLES HOLOCAUST 33

soldiers and their Indigenous allies began attacking Spanish plantations in northern Florida and killing Native people and escaped enslaved people.[156] At the same time, new waves of disease were decimating Indigenous communities across the continent. In 1731–32, a new smallpox epidemic killed many Haudenosaunees and forced others to migrate and settle near Massachusetts and New Hampshire.[157] In the mid-1730s, smallpox struck the Great Lakes region, killing about two thousand Anishinaabes and about 75 percent of the Arikaras.[158] Smallpox reportedly killed several thousand Tsalagis in the Carolinas in 1738–39.[159] A series of smallpox epidemics also erupted in what is now California and Texas and caused many deaths in the 1730s and the following decades.[160]

KING GEORGE'S WAR AND THE FRENCH AND INDIAN WAR

The War of Jenkins's Ear between Britain and Spain erupted in 1739 and was the prelude to King George's War between Britain and France, 1744–48.[161] These two conflicts were bloody and Indigenous people were not "unscathed in body or goods," though the total number of their deaths in this conflict remains unknown.[162] The French and Indian War of 1754–63, part of the Seven Years' War and the final colonial war between Britain and France, proved disastrous for Indigenous people. Abenakis, Mi'kmaqs, Anishinaabes, Ottawas, Lenapes, Shawnees, Miamis, Wyandots, and other Native nations supported the French, though some of these nations withdrew from the conflict in 1758. Although divided over the war, most Haudenosaunees joined the Catawbas and other Indigenous peoples to back the British.[163] Tsalagis initially fought alongside the British but turned against them after repeated attacks by their ostensible allies.[164] The offering of bounties for scalps in some British colonies encouraged frontiersmen to join local militias and ranger groups and kill as many Native people as possible.[165]

Hundreds of Tsalagis died violently, and many more perished from disease and starvation during the Anglo-Cherokee War of 1760–61, "a distinct conflict within the Seven Years' War."[166] By the mid-1760s, the Tsalagi population had declined by about two thousand during the previous two decades.[167] How many Anishinaabes, Menominees, Potawatomis, and Ho-Chunks (Winnebagos) died in combat is unknown, but more than 750 Catawbas and three hundred Menominees died from the smallpox epidemic, which the French and Indian War helped to spread.[168] The total number of Indigenous deaths from violence or disease during the war likely exceeded three thousand.[169] Britain's victory made it the predominant power in the eastern part of North America. But in the aftermath of the French defeat, the Ottawa chief Obwandiyag (Pontiac) launched a formidable rebellion to prevent British expansion in the Great Lakes region. Potawatomies, Wyandots, Anishinaabes, Kickapoos, Miamis, Senecas, and other local Native nations joined the Ottawas in what was called Pontiac's War.[170] The conflict lasted from 1763 to 1765 and resulted in the deaths of perhaps 2,500 British settlers and soldiers and untold numbers of Native people.[171] Unable to defeat Obwandiyag and his allies, the British negotiated a peace treaty and issued the Proclamation of 1763, which pledged to prohibit colonial settlement west of a line drawn along the Appalachian Mountains.[172]

The Colonization of California, the Pacific Northwest, and Hawai‘i

When the Spaniards established their first mission in San Diego in 1769, the Indigenous population of California was approximately 310,000.[173] This population declined to about 245,000 during the next six decades because of enslavement and violence by the missions, reduction of food supplies, diseases, and physical and social disruptions.[174] The Native population of the Pacific Northwest was approximately 180,000 in the mid-1770s when smallpox appeared, perhaps conveyed by Spanish expeditions landing along the coast.[175] About 25,000 Indigenous people in the area likely died from the disease in the next several years.[176] In the mid-1770s and early 1780s, smallpox also killed an estimated 13,000 Mandans, Hidatsas, and Arikaras

THE INDIGENOUS PEOPLES HOLOCAUST

in the Great Lakes region, approximately 10,000 Native people on the Plains, about 9,000 Pueblo and Nermernuh (Comanche) people in New Mexico, and thousands of other Indigenous people in present-day Texas and Arizona.[177] Thousands of miles away, the arrival of British explorer James Cook in Hawai'i in 1778 unleashed diseases that reduced the population of about 683,000 by almost 485,000 in a little more than four decades.[178]

THE WAR OF INDEPENDENCE AND INDIGENOUS PEOPLES

During the War of Independence from 1775 to 1783, both the insurgents and the British Crown sought support from Native peoples. The Haudenosaunee Confederacy was divided. Most Mohawks, Cayugas, Senecas, and Onondagas joined British and Loyalist troops while Oneidas and Tuscaroras aligned with the insurgents. The Tsalagis were also split, with some backing the Crown and others seeking peace with the rebels. Shawnees, Wyandots, Miamis, Chickasaws, and Choctaws supported the British, but Stockbridge Mohegans and Potawamis fought with the pro-independence forces.[179] Like the previous European colonial wars, the War of Independence was devastating for several Indigenous nations. In 1776–77, colonial militias destroyed dozens of Tsalagi towns and killed hundreds of their people in Tennessee.[180] One hundred or more Haudenosaunee warriors died in a battle against U.S. soldiers in Oriskany, New York, in 1777.[181]

The new U.S. government signed a peace treaty with the Lenapes to obtain their support during the conflict but did not honor it for long, setting an ominous precedent.[182] In 1778, Major General John Sullivan's troops burned dozens of Haudenosaunee towns in New York and killed between 473 and 580 people.[183] The loss of their homes and food supplies led to thousands of other Haudenosaunee deaths.[184] In March 1782, a Pennsylvania militia massacred almost one hundred Lenape people in Gnadenhütten, Ohio, and the colonizers committed other massacres elsewhere.[185] Close to six thousand Indigenous people died because of the War of Independence.[186]

U.S. Expansionism and War in the Old Northwest, Kentucky, and Tennessee

The 1783 Treaty of Paris ended the war and recognized the independence of the United States. But as Dunbar-Ortiz has emphasized, this "did not end military actions against Indigenous peoples but rather was a prelude to unrestrained violent colonization of the continent."[187] Although Russia established a settlement in Alaska in 1784 and Spain still claimed much of North America, it was the United States, "the first new nation" to free itself from European rule, that successfully built a new empire in the following decades.[188]

The newly independent U.S. government immediately demanded land cessions from the Haudenosaunees and Indigenous nations in the Ohio River Valley. In the mid- and late-1780s, large numbers of U.S. settlers moved into the western frontiers of New York and Pennsylvania, the Old Northwest Territory ceded by Britain, the part of Virginia now known as Kentucky, and other areas inhabited by Native peoples.[189] In response to the demands for land cessions and the influx of settlers, about a dozen Indigenous nations formed an alliance to defend themselves and their homes.[190] Although a small number of Native leaders signed concessionary treaties with the U.S. government, most did not, and some began attacking settlers.[191] In 1786–87, U.S. soldiers and militias burned several Indigenous towns and killed hundreds of their people in Ohio country.[192]

By 1789, Miami, Shawnee, and other Native fighters had killed approximately 1,500 settlers in the region.[193] President George Washington ordered a massive military campaign that led to a conflict known as Little Turtle's War, or the Northwest Indian War of 1790–95. In two battles in Indiana Territory in late 1790, the Miamis led by Little Turtle and the Shawnees led by Blue Jacket defeated U.S. forces sent to subdue them, killing more than 180.[194] The following year, a large Native army killed more than six hundred soldiers and militia and about two hundred camp followers at the U.S. post at the Wabash River in Ohio.[195] Indigenous warriors usually prevailed in intermittent

THE INDIGENOUS PEOPLES HOLOCAUST 37

skirmishes during the next two years. But in 1794, General "Mad Anthony" Wayne's troops destroyed Shawnee villages and fields and killed noncombatants along the way.[196] The U.S. forces defeated their adversaries at the Battle of Fallen Timbers near present-day Toledo.[197] All told, the United States lost more than one thousand lives during the conflict, and the Indigenous peoples lost more than three hundred.[198] Most vanquished nations agreed to peace terms in 1795 and sold much of their land to the United States, but Native resistance in the region was not extinguished.[199] Many more Indigenous people had died fighting the settlers in Kentucky and Tennessee from 1787 to 1795.[200]

GROWING THREATS TO NATIVE PEOPLES IN THE EARLY NINETEENTH CENTURY

At the dawn of the nineteenth century, the Indigenous population of the coterminous United States had declined to about 600,000.[201] War and disease took an additional huge toll in the first few decades of the new century. A new smallpox epidemic in 1801–1802 ravaged much of the central part of the continent, killing many Omahas, Poncas, Otos, Arikaras, Hidatsas, Mandans, Crows, and other Natives. The epidemic spread to the Pacific Northwest, New Mexico, and Texas as well, and thousands of Indigenous people died in these areas in the next several years.[202] By this time, as Dunbar-Ortiz explains, land speculators aiming to profit from "sales of occupied Indigenous lands," slave owners requiring "vast swaths of land for cash crops," and settlers seeking new lands fueled a new era of relentless U.S. expansionism.[203] During his two terms as president, Thomas Jefferson threatened violence, authorized bribes, and exploited mounting Native problems with debt and alcohol to obtain about 200,000 square miles of Indigenous lands through thirty-two treaties.[204] Moreover, after purchasing the Louisiana Territory from France in 1803, Jefferson began to support the removal of Native peoples from the southeastern United States to areas west of the Mississippi River.[205]

THE WARS OF 1812

As in the War of Independence, Indigenous people fought on both sides of the War of 1812. More fought alongside British soldiers than with U.S. troops, largely because Washington's unrelenting drive to expel Natives from their lands led to "two parallel wars" between 1810 and 1815—one in the Old Northwest, and one in the Southeast.[206] In the Ohio Country, the Shawnee chief Tecumseh led an alliance that included Miamis, Sauks, Mesquakies, Potawomis, Wyandots, Ho-Chunks, and other Indigenous peoples.[207] Determined to defend their lands, this alliance began to attack U.S. settlements and military forces. In November 1811, soldiers and militia members defeated Tecumseh's forces at Tippecanoe Creek in present-day Indiana. Almost 120 combatants died in the battle.[208] Indigenous fighters killed more settlers in the first half of 1812, but some Native nations were afraid to join his alliance. After the War of 1812 began, Tecumseh aligned with the British. His forces seized Fort Dearborn near present-day Chicago, helped the British capture Detroit, and killed a total of about five hundred U.S. soldiers, militia members, and settlers.[209] But Tecumseh died in the Battle of the Thames in Ontario in October 1813. Thousands of other Indigenous warriors and noncombatants perished in the coming year, while others returned to their homes afterward, concluding that the much larger and better armed U.S. forces could not be defeated.[210]

THE CREEK WAR AND THE INVASION OF FLORIDA

The Creek War of 1813–14 in the Southeast was also a ferocious conflict. Militant Muscogees, called Red Sticks because of their red war clubs, began attacking settlers in Georgia, Alabama, and Tennessee in 1812. They also attacked Muscogee accommodationists aligned with the U.S. government.[211] The Red Sticks found considerable support among the Seminoles and communities of African Americans who had escaped slavery in northern Florida.[212] In August 1813, the Red Sticks destroyed Fort Mims in present-day Alabama, killing as many as three hundred soldiers and settlers while losing as many as two

THE INDIGENOUS PEOPLES HOLOCAUST 39

hundred fighters.[213] Three months later, soldiers and militia members killed about five hundred militant Muscogees in two battles. Between late November 1813 and late January 1814, U.S. forces and Muscogee allies killed another five hundred Red Sticks.[214] In March 1814, General Andrew Jackson's forces killed more than eight hundred Muscogee fighters, women, and children at Tohopeka, or Horseshoe Bend, on the Tallapoosa River in Alabama.[215] Jackson's approval of the murder of noncombatants and mutilation of Native bodies made clear that he was indeed "a genocidal sociopath."[216] Altogether, around two thousand Red Sticks died in combat, and many others died from starvation and disease during the war, while about seven hundred U.S. soldiers and settlers perished.[217] Between 7,500 and 11,000 Native people died because of disease, combat, and related causes in the Wars of 1812.[218] The subsequent peace treaty required the Muscogees—including those allied with the United States—to cede approximately 36,000 square miles in Georgia and Alabama.[219]

As Jeffrey Ostler has noted, the defeat of the Indigenous peoples in the Old Northwest and the Southeast "accelerated the process of western settlement and encouraged ever more aggressive designs on the territory of Native nations."[220] The U.S. government soon turned its attention to the Seminoles, African Americans, and Red Stick refugees in northern Florida. Officials in Washington were determined to crush Indigenous resistance, re-enslave the Black people, and replace the Spanish as the dominant power in Florida.[221] In July 1816, soldiers and sailors and Muscogee allies attacked Negro Fort, a fortress inhabited largely by African Americans and some Seminoles. The destruction of Negro Fort was the opening battle in the First Seminole War of 1816–18 and resulted in more than 270 African American and Seminole deaths.[222] In November 1817, after a few other small but deadly confrontations, the Seminoles killed forty-six soldiers and family members on a boat on the Apalachicola River.[223] In the spring of 1818, Jackson's troops and allies destroyed several Seminole towns, killed about forty Indigenous people in a Red Stick village on the Econfina River, and seized two Spanish forts.[224] Spain ceded Florida to the United States the following year.

40   ENDLESS HOLOCAUSTS

The Forced Removal of Indigenous Peoples from the Eastern United States

Although Russia had established Fort Ross north of San Francisco in 1812 and begun to exploit Native peoples' labor, its reach was quite limited, and it withdrew from the area in 1841.[225] In 1821, the people of Mexico won their independence from Spain, yet this hardly entailed liberation for the Indigenous peoples there.[226] However, the most significant threat to the Native population on the continent continued to come from the expanding U.S. Empire. Dunbar-Ortiz has explained:

> Between 1814 and 1824, three-fourths of present-day Alabama and Florida, a third of Tennessee, a fifth of Georgia and Mississippi, and parts of Kentucky and North Carolina became the private property of white settlers.[227]

Support for the relocation of all Indigenous peoples west of the Mississippi River grew in this country. Southern political leaders wanted Native lands to "build the slave labor empire" and "use enslaved people to produce cotton for global markets."[228] Northern political leaders supported the removal of Indigenous peoples from their region because their "free labor empire" required new lands for "speculators, canal developers, miners, and farmers"—and for "discontented urban workers."[229]

Jackson became president in 1829 and was committed to the expulsion of Natives from their remaining lands in the East. After Congress passed the Indian Removal Act in 1830, approximately 64,000 Choctaws, Muscogees, Seminoles, Tsalagis, and Chickasaws were forcibly relocated from their remaining lands in the Southeast to the Oklahoma Territory and Indian Territory.[230] About 24,000 Wyandots, Ottawas, Ohio Senecas, Potawatomis, Miamis, Sauks, Mesquakies, Ho-Chunks, Shawnees, Anishinaabes, Kickapoos, and other Indigenous peoples were compulsorily removed from their homelands in the North and resettled in various locations west of

THE INDIGENOUS PEOPLES HOLOCAUST 41

the Mississippi River.[231] Although about 85 percent of the Native people in the Southeast were forcibly relocated, only about 50 percent in the North suffered the same fate.[232] Slaveholders believed they needed to deport all Indigenous people from the South, but capitalists, speculators, and farmers in the North could tolerate some Native communities.[233] The forced relocations proved calamitous for virtually all the affected Indigenous peoples.

TRAILS OF TEARS AND DEATH

One Choctaw chief described the removal of his people from Mississippi to present-day Oklahoma in 1831–33 as a "trail of tears and death."[234] Approximately 2,500 Choctaws died from exposure, malnutrition, and disease while being deported or soon afterward.[235] In 1832, a group of Sauks, Mesquakies, and allies led by the Sauk leader Black Hawk fought against their forced relocation from Illinois and Wisconsin. The Black Hawk War lasted several months and resulted in the deaths of as many as six hundred Indigenous people and about seventy U.S. fighters but did not prevent the Natives' removal.[236] The deportation of most Muscogees from Alabama occurred between 1834 and 1836, and Washington relied on state militia members and volunteers to capture or kill those who had fled to southern Alabama and western Florida. Approximately 4,500 Muscogees died during the removal process.[237] In Florida, the Seminoles' resistance to forced removal led to the Second Seminole War between 1835 and 1842. About two thousand soldiers, militia members, and noncombatants died.[238] But the much larger U.S. forces killed about seven hundred Seminoles, deported sizeable groups amid the hostilities, and finally prevailed.[239] As many as 1,300 Seminoles died while being removed from their homeland.[240]

The U.S. government began relocating Tsalagi people from their remaining lands in Georgia and Alabama in 1834, but most of the removal occurred in 1838–39. About two thousand died in internment camps awaiting deportation, and others perished on the trip to what is today northeast Oklahoma.[241] Members of this nation later named the journey *Nunna daul Tsunyi*, which means "The trail where we cried."[242] Approximately five thousand Tsalagis died during the removal or shortly after arrival.[243] The deportation of the Chickasaws in 1838 occurred during a smallpox epidemic and led to as many as six hundred fatalities.[244] Altogether, the removal of the Native nations in the South resulted in more than 14,000 deaths.[245] The forced relocation of the Native nations in the North, which involved considerably smaller numbers of people and took place over two decades, produced about three thousand fatalities.[246] Many more deaths followed the removals. By 1860, the relocated southern Native nations had lost another ten thousand people, and the relocated northern Native nations had lost another nine thousand people.[247] In addition, about three thousand Omahas, Oto-Missourias, Osages, Ioways, and Kanzas (Kaws) who already lived in what Ostler has called "zones of removal" perished between the 1840s and 1860.[248]

Disease, War, and Genocide: The Great Plains, Texas, and California

War and disease brought by the colonizers were also laying waste to Indigenous nations in other parts of the continent. By the 1830s, the Nermernuh population had already declined by approximately twenty thousand in the previous several decades, primarily because of disease.[249] In the early 1830s, as many as ten thousand Pawnees died in an epidemic.[250] Then a massive outbreak of smallpox occurred along the Missouri River between 1836 and 1840 and spread to other regions.[251] The Mandans were almost entirely wiped out, and losses were suffered by Piegans, Blackfeet, Bloods, Akiraras, Hidatsas, Pawnees, Osages, Crows, Assiniboines, Kiowas, Ho-Chunks, and the Sioux peoples.[252] Farther south, the epidemic also killed many Apaches, Nermernuhs, and Cayuses, and reached New Mexico and Texas.[253] Altogether, at least 17,000 Indigenous people, and possibly thousands more, died from smallpox in the central part of the continent between 1836 and 1840.[254] In the 1830s, an outbreak of malaria killed perhaps 18,000 Chinooks and Kalapuyas in present-day Oregon.[255]

THE INDIGENOUS PEOPLES HOLOCAUST 43

The Indigenous population of present-day Texas may have numbered in the hundreds of thousands before the European invasion but was reduced to between forty and fifty thousand by 1830.[256] The spread of new diseases; wars with Spanish, Mexican, and U.S. settlers; malnutrition; and starvation had contributed to much of the depopulation.[257] ,Some Native nations had become extinct or migrated by this time, but others had arrived in the area.[258] In the 1820s and 1830s, hostile settlers forced the Karankawas and Tonkawas out of the lower Brazos and Colorado River valleys, killing about a hundred in the process.[259] In 1836, the rebellion against Mexico by settlers and enslavers from the United States succeeded, and the Republic of Texas was created. Two years later, Texas president Mirabeau Lamar announced a campaign to exterminate or expel Indigenous peoples.[260] The Texas Army and the newly formed Texas Rangers defeated and expelled the Kickapoos in 1838 and the Tsalagis and their allies in 1839. Several hundred Natives died during the fighting and subsequent flight.[261] Caddos and Wichitas were also forced to leave their homelands. In 1839–40, Texas forces attacked the Nermernuhs, Kiowas, and Apaches, killing hundreds and leaving even larger numbers to die from exposure or starvation.[262] Aggression against Natives continued after Texas became part of the United States in 1845.

In California, malaria and smallpox killed about 60,000 Indigenous people in the 1830s and early 1840s.[263] What Sherburne Cook called "endemic disease, armed conflict, and destruction of food supply" caused another 40,000 deaths by the mid-1840s.[264] The gravely reduced Native population of about 145,000 suffered even more catastrophe after the U.S. government, pursuing its putative "manifest destiny," wrested control of California from Mexico during the War of 1846–48.[265] The discovery of gold in 1848 brought about 80,000 new settlers to the territory before it became a state two years later.[266] By 1860, more than 362,000 people lived in California, but the Indigenous population was rapidly declining.[267] As Benjamin Madley has documented, between 1846 and 1873, soldiers, militia members, vigilantes, and individuals killed between 9,492 and 16,094 Native people "and probably many more."[268] Madley has rightly described

44   ENDLESS HOLOCAUSTS

these intentional killings as "an American genocide."[269] This horrific violence, the destruction of villages and food supplies, forced relocations, enslavement, and diseases resulted in approximately 115,000 Indigenous deaths during this period. The Achumawi, Atsugewi, Klamath, Ataxum (Luiseño), Maidu, Modoc, Nongatl, Paiute, Pomo, Shasta, Tolowa, Wintu, Wiyot, Yana, Yuki, Yurok, and other peoples sustained grave losses. By 1873, only about 30,000 Native people remained alive in California.[270]

INDIGENOUS RESISTANCE IN THE SOUTHWEST AND THE PACIFIC NORTHWEST

In the decade and a half before the Civil War, other Native peoples languished because of conquest and colonization. When U.S. soldiers and settlers arrived in the New Mexico Territory in 1846, Pueblo and Diné people opposed them. U.S. troops and artillery quickly crushed the new Pueblo Revolt in Taos, killing about two hundred Indigenous people.[271] Hundreds more died when smallpox struck the area again in 1852.[272] Diné fighters in present-day Arizona and New Mexico engaged U.S. forces in small-scale combat between 1846 and 1860, and hundreds on both sides were killed.[273] In present-day Oregon and Washington, the influx of settlers led to massacres and mounting violence in the late 1840s and the early 1850s.[274] Measles, smallpox, and other diseases further decimated the Indigenous population there in the 1850s.[275] During the Rogue River War of 1855–56, Takelmas, Tutunis, and their allies fought the invaders in southern Oregon but were defeated. About 250 Indigenous people and about a hundred settlers and soldiers died in the conflict.[276] In the mid- and late-1850s, U.S. troops also fought Lakotas (Sioux) in present-day Wyoming; Nermernuhs and Kiowas in Texas, Oklahoma, and Kansas; and the remaining Seminoles in Florida. Hundreds more died in these confrontations.[277]

THE CIVIL WAR AND NEW WARS AGAINST INDIGENOUS PEOPLES

During the Civil War of 1861–65, the U.S. government fought against

THE INDIGENOUS PEOPLES HOLOCAUST 45

not only southern secessionists but also western Indigenous peoples who impeded the consolidation of its continental empire.[278] Washington's wars against the Apaches and Yavapais in Arizona and New Mexico began in 1861 and continued for the next twenty-five years. In the first decade alone, more than 1,750 Apaches, Yavapais, and allies were killed, and more than 450 U.S. soldiers and settlers lost their lives.[279] In Minnesota in 1862, Dakota (Sioux) warriors led by Taoyetaduta (Little Crow) began attacking the settlers taking their farmland, forcing them onto small reservations, and condemning them to hunger.[280] The Dakotas killed an estimated eight hundred settlers and soldiers in just a few months while losing perhaps 150 of their own people.[281] A large U.S. military force soon suppressed the uprising, and President Abraham Lincoln authorized the hanging of thirty-eight Dakotas in December 1862, the largest mass execution in U.S. history.[282] Several hundred others died of starvation and disease while being relocated from Minnesota to the Dakota Territory in 1863.[283] During the next two years, when U.S. troops pursued and engaged Dakota and Lakota combatants, as many as seven hundred Indigenous people and 110 soldiers and settlers died.[284]

By the fall of 1862, Shoshones, Paiutes, and Bannocks had been attacking settlers along the Oregon and California Trails for a decade, and the U.S. government acted to defend its westward expansion.[285] In January 1863, a California militia massacred approximately 350 Shoshones in their village on the Bear River in Idaho, and hostilities ended later that year.[286] But the larger, deadlier Snake War began several months later, and the Paiutes, Shoshones, and Bannocks fought U.S. forces in southwestern Idaho, central and southeastern Oregon, northwestern Nevada, and northeastern California.[287] Approximately a thousand Indigenous people and two hundred settlers and soldiers were killed before the war ended five years later.[288] By the late 1860s, more than two thousand people had died because of conflicts in Oregon in the previous two decades.[289] In 1863–64, a regiment led by Kit Carson finally ended the resistance of the Diné people in Arizona and New Mexico. U.S. soldiers killed about three hundred fighters, burned their crops, and killed their livestock.[290] With many people "freezing and starving," the majority of Diné surrendered.[291] More than eight thousand Diné people were forced to march three hundred miles to the Bosque Redondo reservation in eastern New Mexico. About two hundred people died during the relocation, and approximately three thousand died at Bosque Redondo, mainly from disease and malnutrition.[292] Those who survived were allowed to return to their ancestral lands in 1868.

After silver was discovered in traditional Indigenous hunting grounds in Colorado, the state government acted to forcibly remove local nations. In 1864, the Colorado Cavalry massacred at least 137 Tsetchestahase (Cheyenne) people and twenty-six Arapahos at Sand Creek, Colorado, which began the Cheyenne War.[293] The Sand Creek Massacre led to a large mobilization of Lakota, Tsetchestahase, Arapaho, Kiowa, and Nermernuh warriors against U.S. and Confederate forces across the plains from the Dakota Territory to Texas.[294] From 1866 to 1868, Lakota Chief Mahpíya Lúta (Red Cloud) led the resistance against the construction of U.S. forts in Wyoming. The fighting resulted in the deaths of more than 240 U.S. people and more than 125 Natives.[295] The U.S. government subsequently abandoned the forts, which the Lakotas and Tsetchestahases then burned. In November 1868, Lieutenant Colonel George Armstrong Custer and soldiers under his command massacred more than one hundred Tsetchestahases living on a reservation near the Washita River in what is now Oklahoma.[296] More than 1,100 Native people, soldiers, and settlers had perished during the Cheyenne War by the end of the decade.[297]

From the Piegan War to the Sioux War

In the summer and fall of 1869, Piegans killed fifty-six white miners in the Montana Territory, and the U.S. Army quickly took revenge.[298] In January 1870, soldiers massacred 173 Piegans in a village near the Marias River.[299] In April 1871, U.S. and Mexican civilians and Indigenous allies massacred 144 Apaches at Aravaipa in the Arizona Territory.[300] Renewed resistance by the Apaches and Yavapais in present-day Arizona, New Mexico, and northern Mexico led to the

THE INDIGENOUS PEOPLES HOLOCAUST

deaths of more than two hundred Indigenous people and more than five hundred U.S. and Mexican soldiers and settlers during the next several years.[301] The Red River War of 1874–75 erupted in response to U.S. settlers slaughtering buffalo herds on the southern Plains. Tsetchestahase, Kiowa, and Nermernuh fighters conducted raids in western Kansas, north Texas, and New Mexico before being defeated by the U.S. Army and Texas Rangers. More than eighty Indigenous fighters and dozens of noncombatants were killed, and about two hundred settlers, soldiers, and Texas Rangers died.[302] As Micheal Clodfelter noted, "The Red River War effectively ended frontier warfare on the southern Plains."[303] A quarter-century later, the U.S. Census listed only 470 Native people in Texas.[304]

In 1874, gold was discovered in the Black Hills of present-day South Dakota, and an influx of settlers and miners ensued. When the Lakota people refused to sell their sacred hunting grounds to the federal government, soldiers launched "preemptive strikes" to seize control of those lands.[305] Thus began the Sioux War of 1876–77. When the Lakota people and their Tsetchestahase allies left their reservations to defend these lands, U.S. troops confronted them, and a series of violent encounters ensued. Dozens of Indigenous and U.S. combatants died in the first skirmishes.[306] In June 1876, Tatanka Yotanka (Sitting Bull) and Tasunke Witco (Crazy Horse) led Lakota warriors, along with Tsetchestahase and Arapaho fighters, in a massive assault on Custer's troops near the Little Bighorn River in southeastern Montana Territory. More than 260 soldiers, including Custer, and as many as one hundred Indigenous fighters perished.[307] However, U.S. soldiers prevailed in the smaller battles that followed, and scores more Native people died.[308] The Indigenous peoples' resistance was overcome and the United States took possession of the Black Hills. Tatanka Yotanka and some Lakotas fled to Canada. Tasunke Witco surrendered in May 1877 and was killed in detention a few months later.[309]

FROM THE NEZ PERCE WAR TO THE LAST APACHE WAR

That same year, many Nimi'ipuu (Nez Perce) people in Oregon refused the U.S. demand to move to a reservation in the Idaho Territory. Chief Joseph led several hundred warriors, women, and children on a 1,700-mile journey to Canada, where they hoped to find refuge.[310] They fought soldiers and settlers intermittently as they traversed Idaho, Wyoming, and Montana. Approximately two hundred soldiers and settlers died, and more than two hundred Nimi'ipuu people perished along the way before they surrendered and were deported.[311] In 1878, seventy-eight Bannocks and Paiutes and about forty soldiers and settlers died in battles in Oregon and Idaho.[312] By the end of the century, only 35,000 to 40,000 Indigenous people remained alive in the Pacific Northwest, a decline of at least 140,000 since the mid-1770s.[313] U.S. military actions against the Tsetchestahase people in Kansas and Nebraska in 1878–79 and against the Nuu-ci (Ute) people in northwestern Colorado in 1879 led to scores of additional deaths.[314] Between 1881 and 1886, Nana and Goyaale (Geronimo) led Apache warriors into combat against U.S. and Mexican troops in Arizona, New Mexico, and northern Mexico. An estimated 630 fighters and noncombatants perished in the conflict.[315] After the destruction of buffalo by U.S. forces, approximately six hundred Niitsitapi (Blackfoot) people starved in the northern Plains during the winter of 1883–84.[316]

The Ghost Dance Movement and the Massacre at Wounded Knee

By the late 1880s, Indigenous peoples in the United States had almost been annihilated. Largely confined to reservations, surviving Natives continued to suffer because of poverty, disease, the destruction of traditional ways of life, and the erasure of identity. Increasingly, white people forcibly took Indigenous children from their families and sent them to boarding schools that aimed to "kill the Indian and save the man."[317] Amid such misery and hopelessness, Natives on dozens of reservations participated in a religious resistance movement known as the Ghost Dance. Initiated by a Paiute mystic named Wovoka in Nevada, this movement urged them to perform the Ghost

THE INDIGENOUS PEOPLES HOLOCAUST 49

Dance, which, as Dunbar-Ortiz observed, "promised to restore the Indigenous world as it was before colonialism, making the invaders disappear and the buffalo return."[318] Many Lakota and Dakota people embraced the Ghost Dance, and Tatanka Yotanka, who had returned from Canada five years after the Battle of the Little Bighorn, strongly supported it.[319]

U.S. government officials feared that the Ghost Dance movement might lead to the renewal of armed resistance by Indigenous peoples.[320] As a result, U.S. and allied forces moved against Tatanka Yotanka and against Natives still living outside reservations, who were derided as "fomenters of disturbance."[321] Following government orders, Lakota police at the Standing Rock reservation in South Dakota attempted to arrest Tatanka Yotanka in December 1890 and fatally shot him when his supporters resisted.[322] Seven Ghost Dancers and six police also died in this incident.[323] Numerous Lakotas fled their reservations, and soldiers were dispatched to force their return. On December 29, 1891, U.S. troops massacred as many as three hundred Lakota men, women, and children at Wounded Knee.[324] This infamous atrocity marked the end of major Indigenous opposition to conquest and colonization. However, some limited but deadly skirmishes occurred during the next three decades.

THE END OF ARMED INDIGENOUS RESISTANCE

In 1898, Anishinaabes on the Leech Lake reservation in Minnesota killed six soldiers and a Native police officer who were protecting loggers cutting pine logs on their land.[325] In 1907, a dispute over the dipping of sheep turned into a confrontation near Fort Defiance, Arizona, which left three Diné dead and a dozen others sent to military prison.[326] Two years later, allegations of theft of a wagon of smoked meat in Hickory Ground, Oklahoma, led to local deputies killing several Muscogees and their African American neighbors. Two deputies also died in the conflict.[327] In 1911, a group of Paiutes left their reservation in Nevada and killed four settlers. A posse tracked down the Paiutes and killed nine of them, suffering one fatality.[328]

50 ENDLESS HOLOCAUSTS

In 1914–15, Paiute and Nuu-ci people fought briefly against settlers and Diné policemen in Utah and Colorado before surrendering to soldiers. A total of six people died.[329] In 1918, a band of Yaquis briefly fought U.S. forces in Bear Valley, Arizona, resulting in the death of the Yaqui leader.[330] In 1923, Chief Posey led a small number of Paiute and Nuu-ci people in another conflict with settlers in Utah. The Native fighters were defeated, and Chief Posey later died from wounds suffered in battle.[331]

The Nadir of the Native Population and Demographic Recovery

The Indigenous population in this country reached its nadir during the last decade of the nineteenth century. The Census Bureau reported that the number of Native people in the coterminous United States was approximately 237,000 in 1900.[332] The Apalachee, Calusa, Erie, Guale, Karankawa, Massachuset, Mobile, Susquehannock, Timucua, Tompiro, Wappinger, Yahi Yana, Yamasee, Yazoo, and other Indigenous nations had been driven to extinction.[333] By 1900, only about 28,000 Indigenous people remained in Alaska, and by 1920 just under 24,000 Native people were alive in Hawai'i .[334] As noted earlier in this chapter, the Tainos of Puerto Rico had been all but wiped out by the mid-sixteenth century. Thus, in the lands that became the United States, the Native population of about six million in 1492 was reduced to less than 300,000 at the dawn of the twentieth century.[335]

Finally, the Native population in this country and the hemisphere began to grow again in the early twentieth century.[336] In 2018, the U.S. Census Bureau identified almost 6.8 million people as American Indians and Alaska Natives.[337] There are also more than 560,000 Native Hawaiians living in this country.[338] As Thornton has pointed out, the demographic recovery of the Native population in the United States has been significant, but "much of the increase in the number of American Indians" in recent decades "was a result of changing racial definitions from one census to another."[339] Today, at least 54 million Indigenous people live throughout the Western Hemisphere.[340]

THE INDIGENOUS PEOPLES HOLOCAUST 51

The Indigenous Peoples Holocaust Continues

Although the "Indian Wars" have ended, the Indigenous Holocaust has not.[341] Various forms of violence have continued to destroy Native lives. Thousands of Indigenous men served in the U.S. armed forces during the twentieth century, and many lost their lives in the empire's wars abroad. At least 360 Native Americans and possibly hundreds more died in action in the First World War. Approximately 550 perished in the Second World War. About 104 died in the Korean War, and about 226 were killed in the Vietnam War. At least three died in the Persian Gulf War, approximately thirty perished in the Afghanistan War, and about forty-three died in the Iraq War.[342]

Between 1900 and 2006, there were fifty-eight executions of Indigenous persons, bringing the official total since 1639 to 464.[343] In the 1920s, white racists murdered scores of Osage people in Oklahoma in a far-reaching criminal conspiracy after the discovery of oil on their reservation earned them scores of millions of dollars.[344] In the late 1960s and early 1970s, renewed Native resistance led to the occupation of Alcatraz Island and Wounded Knee and efforts to defend Lakota people against corrupt tribal leaders supported by the federal government.[345] Washington and its allies were responsible for the deaths of more than sixty Indigenous activists fighting for sovereignty and self-determination during this period.[346]

Today police kill about twenty Indigenous people each year, a per capita rate that exceeds that of African Americans.[347] Native people are now incarcerated at four times the rate of non-Hispanic whites, and scores die each year in jails and prisons.[348] Homicide rates are about four times higher for Indigenous peoples than for non-Hispanic white people.[349] Untold thousands of Indigenous women have gone missing in the past several decades, many of whom were murdered.[350] And Native people have the highest suicide rate in the United States.[351]

Vastly larger numbers of Indigenous people have perished since 1900 as a result of diseases, deprivation, and other perils inherent in the "colonial condition" and institutionalized racism.[352] At the beginning of the twentieth century, the mortality rate among Native peoples in the coterminous United States was about 58 percent higher than that of the white population.[353] The forced enrollment of scores of thousands of Native children in assimilationist boarding schools continued well into the twentieth century, and as many as 40,000 died from inadequate food and clothing, disease, and abuse, exposure after escaping, and related causes.[354] In 1916, approximately 60 percent of all Indigenous children died within the first five years of life.[355] At least eight thousand Indigenous people died from the Spanish flu in the continental United States in 1918–19.[356] In 1924, a new federal law recognized Indigenous people as citizens but did not guarantee their right to vote or significantly improve their lives.[357] Hundreds of Diné men who mined uranium in the western United States between the 1940s and the 1980s died from radiation exposure.[358] Native fatalities caused by residing near abandoned uranium mines, toxic dumps, and other environmental dangers have not been counted but are likely considerable.[359]

In 1957, data on five leading causes of death among Natives indicated that their excess mortality rate was more than 60 percent.[360] Although the creation of the Indian Health Service led to some improvements in the 1960s and 1970s, limited funding for medical services has contributed to deteriorating conditions for Indigenous peoples since then.[361] In the first decades of the twenty-first century, the mortality rate among Indigenous peoples in the continental United States is about 46 percent higher than that of non-Hispanic whites, and the mortality rate among Native Hawaiians is more than 40 percent higher than that of whites.[362] Indigenous infants are twice as likely to die in their first year as white infants.[363] Native children between the ages of one and four years die at almost three times the rate of other children.[364] Indigenous people die from diabetes, chronic liver disease and cirrhosis, and accidents at least three times the national rate, and their rate of deaths from heart disease, influenza and pneumonia, and tuberculosis exceeds that of the general population.[365]

MEASURING SOCIAL MURDERS SINCE THE 1930s

The vast numbers of Native deaths that occur each year because of

THE INDIGENOUS PEOPLES HOLOCAUST   53

disease, deprivation, and related conditions should be understood as social murders. As Engels wrote in 1845:

> When society places hundreds of proletarians in such a position that they inevitably meet a too early and an unnatural death, one which is quite as much a death by violence as that by the sword or bullet; when it deprives thousands of the necessaries of life, places them under conditions in which they cannot live—forces them, through the strong arm of the law, to remain in such conditions until that death ensues which is the inevitable consequence—knows that these thousands of victims must perish, and yet permits these conditions to remain, its deed is murder just as surely as the deed of the single individual.[366]

The federal government did not collect mortality statistics for the entire United States until 1933, Indigenous deaths have not always been recorded, and many Native decedents have been misidentified as members of another racial or ethnic group.[367] Nonetheless, available information on mortality rates and estimates of the total number of Native deaths since the 1930s makes it possible to estimate the minimum number of excess deaths during this period.

The concept of "excess" deaths refers to the difference between the actual number of Native deaths and the number of deaths that would have occurred if Natives experienced the same death rate as whites.[368] The Centers for Disease Control and Prevention have estimated that approximately 329,000 Native deaths occurred in the continental United States and Alaska between 1999 and 2019.[369] About 46 percent of this total, more than 151,300, were excess deaths. If the same excess death rate is applied to the approximately 362,000 Indigenous people who were alive in the coterminous United States and Alaska in 1930 but, with rare exceptions, died before 1999, it appears that there were over 166,500 excess deaths in this cohort.[370] In sum, at least 317,000 excess Indigenous deaths have occurred in the continental United States since 1930. This estimate is quite conservative because it uses the more recent 46 percent excess mortality rate and does not include

54   ENDLESS HOLOCAUSTS

the excess deaths of Native Hawaiians during this period. Uncounted thousands of additional excess deaths must have occurred in the first three decades of the twentieth century.

THE DANGER OF CULTURAL GENOCIDE

As late as the mid-1970s, about 25 percent of Native children were routinely taken away from their parents and placed in foster or adoptive homes or boarding schools.[371] As in previous generations, white authorities sought to promote assimilation, not the welfare of the children.[372] Between 1970 and 1976, physicians sterilized about 25 percent of Indigenous women of childbearing age.[373] As Brianna Theobald has remarked, "Some of these procedures were performed under pressure or duress, or without the women's knowledge or understanding."[374] About sixty of the 175 Native languages still in use in 1998 disappeared in the next two decades.[375] More recently, state and federal officials have violated the lands and traditional ways of life of the Lakota people to build the Dakota Access Pipeline in South Dakota and done the same to the Carrizo/Comecrudo nation to build sections of Trump's border wall in South Texas.[376] Racist stereotypes of Native peoples continue to permeate the media, and some professional and college sports teams continue to use racist names and mascots.[377]

However, there is growing public awareness of the Indigenous Peoples Holocaust. Thousands of people from diverse backgrounds joined the water protectors at Standing Rock in 2016–17.[378] And by 2019, seven states and more than 130 cities were honoring Indigenous Peoples' Day instead of Columbus Day.[379] One poll indicated that 79 percent of college students support this change.[380] Ironically, these positive developments come amid mounting evidence of the assimilation of Native peoples into the society that almost exterminated them. The 2010 census revealed that 44 percent of those labeled American Indians and Alaska Natives reported multiracial ancestry.[381] Approximately 62 percent of those identifying as Native Hawaiian also claim mixed heritage.[382] In addition, almost 60 percent

THE INDIGENOUS PEOPLES HOLOCAUST   55

of Indigenous people in this country are marrying people from different national, racial, and ethnic groups.[383] More than 70 percent now live in metropolitan areas.[384] As Thornton has warned, "If these trends continue, both the genetic and tribal distinctiveness of the total Native American population will be greatly lessened."[385]

COUNTING THE DEAD

How many people have perished in the Indigenous Peoples Holocaust in the present-day United States during the past five centuries? The total number of Native people who died in these lands because of invasion, conquest, colonialism, and related forms of oppression will never be known. Nonetheless, an informed and reasonable estimate can be advanced. If the Native population in what later became the coterminous United States was more than five million in 1492 and declined to about 237,000 in 1900, the loss of Indigenous lives in this country would initially appear to be around five million people. However, as Thornton has emphasized,

> Such a population decline implies not only that some 5 million American Indians died during the 400 years but also that, in fact, many times the approximate figure of 5 million died, as new but ever numerically smaller generations of American Indians were born, lived, and died.[386]

In his books and articles, Thornton has not estimated the total number of Native deaths in this country, but he has recently suggested that perhaps twelve million Indigenous deaths occurred in the present-day coterminous United States between 1492 and 1900.[387]

To this staggering number must be added almost 800,000 deaths in Puerto Rico, Alaska, and Hawai'i by 1900 and well over 300,000 excess deaths in the continental United States since the 1930s.[388] In sum, the Indigenous Peoples Holocaust in what is now the United States may be estimated to have taken more than thirteen million lives, and it continues today. This horrific toll is only a small portion of the number of Native deaths throughout the Western Hemisphere since 1492. In addition to the approximately fifty-six million who died throughout the Americas by 1600, millions more died in "new but ever numerically smaller generations" during the next three centuries.[389] Still others have perished because of state violence or social murders since 1900. It may be roughly estimated that between seventy million and eighty million Indigenous people have died because of colonialism, racism, and capitalism in the Western Hemisphere.[390] Tragically, the Indigenous Peoples Holocaust in this country was only the first of the endless holocausts that have made the U.S. Empire what it is today.

2

The African American Holocaust

What, to the American slave, is your Fourth of July? I answer: a day that reveals to him, more than all other days in the year, the gross injustice and cruelty to which he is the constant victim. To him, your celebration is a sham; your boasted liberty, an unholy license; your national greatness, swelling vanity.

—FREDERICK DOUGLASS,
ADDRESS IN ROCHESTER, NEW YORK, 1852

In the early sixteenth century, the massive decline of the Indigenous population in the Western Hemisphere forced the European colonizers to begin importing captive people from Africa to labor for them.[1] Marx observed in *Capital* that, like the oppression of Indigenous people in the Americas, "the conversion of Africa into a preserve for the commercial hunting of black-skins" was one of the "chief moments of primitive accumulation" that made capitalist production possible.[2] For 350 years, the wealth produced by enslaved Black people enriched Europe and its colonies, including the lands that became the United States. This wealth helped fuel the Industrial Revolution, fostered the global ascendancy of these regions, and contributed to the "Great Divergence" between wealthy and poor nations.[3]

As David Brion Davis has emphasized, the transatlantic slave trade "ranks as one of history's greatest crimes against humanity."[4] The *Maafa* resulted in a catastrophic loss of life in Africa, the Americas, and the present-day United States.[5] Vast numbers of Black people born in this country and other parts of the Western Hemisphere died because of the brutality and harshness of life under slavery.[6] Many more have perished in the United States since the end of slavery because of various forms of white supremacist violence, poor health conditions rooted in racism, convict labor, mass incarceration, criminal homicides, participation in imperialist wars, and related forms of oppression.[7] Despite some important social and political progress in the twentieth century, the African American Holocaust continues today.

Africa Before the Europeans

In 1500, Africa was home to a population of perhaps one hundred million people who lived in many different kingdoms, states, and tribes.[8] Significant achievements in science, mathematics, engineering, and architecture occurred in ancient Egypt long before the rise of Greece and Rome.[9] Other large, highly developed African societies arose later: Kush, Axum, Ghana, Mali, Songhai, and Kongo among them.[10] As Henry Louis Gates Jr. has pointed out, "The first iron technology in the world was developed in Africa."[11] Like many Indigenous peoples in North America, African farmers were skilled and productive.[12] The continent was well endowed in natural resources, its diverse regions were traversed by trade routes, and commerce fostered by sub-Saharan and Arab merchants was significant.[13] Gold exports from West Africa, Ghana, Mali, and Songhay helped promote economic development in Europe in the fourteenth and fifteenth centuries.[14] Although many African peoples did not have written languages, their distinctive oral communications and histories were highly effective.[15] Other African peoples had been using written languages for thousands of years.[16] By the fourteenth century, the Islamic madrassa, known as the University of Sankore in Timbuktu, was a prominent center of learning that housed an extraordinary library.[17]

THE AFRICAN AMERICAN HOLOCAUST

Slavery was traditional and widespread in Africa. Alexander Ives Bortolot has explained that "private land ownership was largely absent from precolonial African societies, and slaves were one of the few forms of wealth-producing property an individual could possess."[18] Ruling elites and tribal groups generally fought to extend their control over people and resources, and enslavement through war and raids was a long-standing characteristic of African life.[19]

As various researchers have remarked, enslaved people in Africa were traditionally given some rights, and their treatment generally was not as heinous as that suffered by those who were forcibly transported to other lands.[20] Nonetheless, it was still bondage.[21] The Arab slave trade, which began in the seventh century and lasted 1,200 years, forcibly transported between nine million and twelve million Africans to Muslim North Africa, the Arabian Peninsula, islands in the Indian Ocean, and the Indian subcontinent.[22]

THE BEGINNING OF THE TRANSATLANTIC SLAVE TRADE

Portuguese traders began shipping African captives to Europe in 1444, chiefly for use as domestic servants.[23] By the end of the fifteenth century, the Portuguese were transporting Black people to the Atlantic islands off the western coast of Africa.[24] Shortly after papal decrees articulated the "Doctrine of Discovery," new Vatican edicts and a treaty between Spain and Portugal gave Spain the exclusive right to explore and trade with the "new world"—except for present-day Brazil—and gave Portugal the exclusive right to explore and trade with Africa and other non-Christian regions of the "old world."[25] These two countries would dominate the transatlantic slave trade for the next century and a half.[26] Spain began sending enslaved Africans from Europe to Hispaniola in 1501.[27] As the large-scale depopulation of Indigenous peoples in the Americas unfolded and the colonizers' need for enslaved labor grew, Madrid contracted with Lisbon to deliver Africans to the Caribbean.[28] In 1526, the Portuguese transported enslaved people from Africa directly to the Caribbean for the first time.[29] In the years that followed, Portugal transported millions of Black people to various colonies in the Western Hemisphere.[30] Many died in Africa during Portuguese military interventions to establish colonies and dominate local states.[31] In the following centuries, a much larger number perished as the Netherlands, Britain, France, Denmark, Sweden, Brandenburg (Prussia), the United States, and Brazil joined in the transatlantic slave trade.[32] While traditional African slavery and the Arab slave trade continued, the transatlantic trade fostered the transformation of slavery into a mode of production on much of the continent.[33] Martin Klein observed: "Slave trading and slave production became the most important economic activities for many African states."[34]

A Dutch ship's delivery of about twenty Africans to the English colony of Jamestown, Virginia, in 1619 is widely but incorrectly regarded as the origin of slavery in what is today the United States. More than a century earlier, in 1512, the Spaniards had begun transporting enslaved Africans from Europe to Puerto Rico.[35] Vázquez de Ayllón brought about a hundred of the enslaved to his ill-fated settlement in present-day Georgia in 1526, and their revolt helped to bring about its collapse.[36] In 1528, an enslaved African named Estevanico survived Narváez's doomed voyage to present-day Tampa Bay and accompanied Cabeza de Vaca and two other survivors on their arduous six-year journey to Spanish settlements in what is now Mexico.[37] In May 1539, Black people held in bondage accompanied de Soto's expedition in what is today the southeastern United States.[38] After the first permanent Spanish city was founded in St. Augustine in 1565, slave labor played a major role in the economic development of Spanish Florida.[39] British colonists initially treated Black people like indentured servants, but race-based slavery developed within a few decades.[40] The Dutch began importing African captives to New Amsterdam (New York City) in 1626.[41] As labor shortages grew and the limits of indentured European servants became clearer, the British began transporting larger numbers of Africans to their colonies in the Caribbean and on the North American mainland.[42] The French began importing African captives to the Louisiana Territory in 1710.[43] Paul Lovejoy has noted, "In the Americas, the primary purpose of slave

THE AFRICAN AMERICAN HOLOCAUST

61

labor was the production of staple commodities—sugar, coffee, tobacco, rice, cotton, gold, and silver—for sale on world markets."[44]

THE NUMBER OF AFRICANS FORCIBLY TRANSPORTED TO THE AMERICAS

Various researchers have estimated that between fifteen and twenty million Africans were forcibly deported to the Western Hemisphere between 1501 and 1867.[45] However, in *The Atlantic Slave Trade: A Census*, a seminal work published in 1969, Philip Curtin critically interrogated these appraisals and developed a significantly lower estimate. Curtin calculated that approximately 9.5 million Africans had been imported to the Western Hemisphere and acknowledged that this assessment was only "within a range of possibility" and subject to revision.[46] Curtin also said that perhaps 12 to 15 percent of those transported from Africa had died during the Middle Passage across the Atlantic Ocean.[47] This meant that about eleven million Africans had originally been deported from their continent.[48] Many scholars have praised Curtin for rejecting previous larger estimates based on speculation and developing estimates based on concrete historical information such as shipping records, supply records, and port and colony documents.[49] However, debate and controversy over the number of enslaved and transported Africans did not subside. Ibrahima Baba Kake has criticized "revisionists" like Curtin, who, when writing about the transatlantic slave trade, "minimize both its scale and its consequences."[50] The Guyanese scholar and activist Walter Rodney famously argued:

> Any figure of Africans imported into the Americas which is narrowly based on surviving records is bound to be low because there were so many people at the time who had a vested interest in smuggling slaves (and withholding data).[51]

In addition, Joseph E. Inikori has challenged Curtin's data and methodology, pointing out that the records Curtin studied did not

62   ENDLESS HOLOCAUSTS

include information on all slave ship voyages and suggested that the number of people forcibly removed from Africa could be much higher than he estimated.[52] In the decades following the publication of Curtin's book, new information about previously unknown slave ship voyages was discovered, and a great deal of new research has been conducted on the transatlantic slave trade.

More recently, David Eltis and David Richardson, working with a database that includes information on about 35,000 known transatlantic slave voyages, have estimated that about 12.5 million Africans were forcibly transported to the Western Hemisphere between 1500 and 1867.[53] Eltis and Richardson have found that approximately 1.8 million died during the Middle Passage, and about 10.7 million arrived alive.[54] The deaths on the voyage were largely the result of disease, malnutrition, dehydration, violence, physical abuse, despair, and suicide.[55] As many as 100,000 died in revolts aboard slave ships or on African coasts.[56] Other deaths occurred when slave ships sank.[57] Some researchers consider the work by Eltis and Richardson to be the gold standard on the transatlantic slave trade.[58]

In contrast, Inikori, Yves Benot, and Nelly Schmidt have offered estimates of total deportations ranging from fifteen to eighteen million.[59] These writers may prove to be right in the future. As Lovejoy wrote about Curtin's allowance for adjustments to his own estimate, "The cautious historian expects that upward revision is more probable than downward."[60] Nonetheless, the Eltis-Richardson estimate of 12.5 million provides a helpful, if conservative, starting point for assessing the horrific loss of life associated with the transatlantic slave trade.

Over the centuries, most Black captives were transported to Brazil and the Caribbean.[61] Eltis and Richardson have estimated the number directly transported from Africa to mainland North America over the centuries to be only around 391,000.[62] In addition, approximately 72,000 Africans were brought to mainland North America from the Caribbean, especially Jamaica and Barbados, between 1619 and 1807.[63] About fifty thousand Black people were also transported to Puerto Rico.[64] In sum, more than half a million Africans arrived in the

THE AFRICAN AMERICAN HOLOCAUST

present-day United States.[65] They represented a little over 5 percent of the total number brought to the Western Hemisphere and were primarily disembarked in the Carolinas-Georgia area, the Chesapeake, the northern United States, and the Mississippi-Florida area.[66]

ESTIMATES OF DEATHS IN THE TRANSATLANTIC SLAVE TRADE

The death toll from the transatlantic slave trade in Africa, the Western Hemisphere, and the lands that became the United States was nothing less than a holocaust. Curtin has pointed out:

> The cost of the slave trade in human life was many times the number of slaves landed in the Americas. For every slave landed alive, other people died in warfare, along the bush paths leading to the coast, awaiting shipment, or in the crowded and unsanitary conditions of the Middle Passage. Once in the New World, still others died on entering a new disease environment.[67]

Rodney has also contended that the overall mortality figure would be many times the millions landed alive outside of Africa.[68] As Johannes Postma has remarked, Black people caught up in the slave trade "found death at every stage of their ordeal and, on the average, must have had a very short life expectancy."[69]

A century ago, W. E. B. Du Bois wrote that approximately fifty million Africans died in their native lands or "on the high seas" during the transatlantic slave trade.[70] Woodrow Borah has estimated that thirty million died in Africa or during the Middle Passage.[71] Stannard has concluded that the total number of Africans who died in all stages of the transatlantic slave trade was between thirty million and sixty million.[72] In contrast, other researchers have acknowledged the significant loss of life during the Middle Passage but eschewed efforts to estimate the total number of deaths resulting from this extraordinary crime against humanity. Curtin, for example, believed that "most of these losses are not measurable."[73] Herbert S. Klein and Stanley L. Engerman insisted that because scholars do not have the same kinds

64 ENDLESS HOLOCAUSTS

of records for other stages of the slave trade as they do for the Middle Passage, "we cannot answer questions about the overall mortality in the transatlantic slave trade."[74] Indeed, Klein has criticized "some recent scholars" for their "quite extraordinary figures" on the total number of African deaths.[75]

These conclusions by Curtin, Klein, and Engerman are unpersuasive. The 1.8 million deaths that occurred during the Middle Passage are clearly the best-documented fatalities of the transatlantic slave trade, and, indeed, comparable records do not exist for the much larger numbers of deaths that occurred in the other stages of the *Maafa*. Nonetheless, there is considerable historical information and contemporary research on the African wars and raids that produced most captives for the slave trade, the forced marches of captives from the interior to the coast, their imprisonment in barracoons while waiting to be forced onto slave ships, the period between their arrival in the Western Hemisphere and their transfer to slaveholders, their so-called seasoning in the Americas, and their subsequent experience of servitude. If one begins with the well-documented number of people forcibly taken out of Africa, works back through the prior stages of their captivity, and then considers the Middle Passage and subsequent stages of captivity and enslavement in the Western Hemisphere, it is possible to develop informed and reasonable estimates of the total loss of African lives associated with the transatlantic slave trade.

Deaths on Marches to Slave Forts and in Barracoons

The approximately 12.5 million people transported from Africa were the survivors of a much larger group that suffered grievous losses while marching from the point of capture to the slave forts on the West African coast and while awaiting transportation to the Americas. The distance traveled in many marches was often hundreds of miles and, in some cases, over a thousand miles. The time required to complete these marches ranged from weeks to months.[76] The captives were generally barefoot and chained together, and they were often required

THE AFRICAN AMERICAN HOLOCAUST   65

to carry heavy loads as they marched.[77] The rigor of these forced marches, exposure to new disease environments and epidemics, dietary change, and the psychological impact of enslavement combined to produce many deaths.[78] Often captives who fell ill were killed or left to die along the way. Human skeletons were frequently found along the routes by those who followed.[79] When captured Africans arrived at the slave forts on the coast, they faced new dangers from diseases brought by the Europeans, the harshness of imprisonment in barracoons for months or even a year, and inadequate food and water. Captives who were not accepted by the European slave traders were sometimes executed or left to die.[80]

Patrick Manning's estimate that four million captives died while still in Africa is far too low.[81] The British abolitionist Thomas Fowell Buxton estimated in 1839 that approximately half of all captured Africans died before leaving the continent.[82] Some contemporary researchers have reached similar conclusions. Charles Johnson, Patricia Smith, and colleagues also concluded that about half of those captured "never even made it to the slave ships."[83] Joseph C. Miller has estimated that about 50 percent of the Africans captured in the continent's interior died during the long march to the Angolan coast or while imprisoned in barracoons.[84] Jan Hogendorn has estimated that about 50 percent of those captured in Central Sudan perished on the journey to coastal West Africa.[85] If, as Eltis and Richardson have maintained, about 12.5 million Africans were deported from their homeland, and if this number represented only about half of those enslaved, then it may be estimated that approximately 25 million Africans were originally captured, and 12.5 million of them died between capture and embarkation.[86]

DEATHS IN WARS AND RAIDS

Many other deaths resulted from the wars and raids that captured people who were later sold to European, U.S., and Brazilian slave traders.[87] Some armed conflicts were undoubtedly motivated more by political considerations than the drive to obtain and sell slaves.[88]

But the development of the transatlantic slave trade fueled the proliferation of wars and raids, and they became endemic in much of West and Central Africa.[89] With the spread of firearms acquired from slave traders, the attacks also became more lethal.[90] Many died while resisting capture, and many who fled the fighting later died from disease or starvation because their crops, livestock, and homes had been destroyed.[91] In addition, many enslavers died from armed resistance or diseases that spread through troop concentrations.[92] Lovejoy has noted: "Deaths at the point of enslavement had a significant impact on the demography of the trade, but there is little information on the scale of such deaths."[93]

Although some prominent researchers have expressed the view that it is not possible to estimate the total number of these deaths,[94] there is sufficient historical information to develop a rough appraisal of this loss of life.[95] The British abolitionist Thomas Cooper estimated in 1787 that "for one slave procured, ten at least are slaughtered."[96] Such a large ratio of captures to deaths surely did not occur everywhere in West and Central Africa for the duration of the transatlantic slave trade. The prominent eighteenth-century slave trader John Newton wrote: "Though they do not bring legions into the field, their wars are bloody. I believe the captives reserved for sale are fewer than the slain."[97] In 1839, Buxton estimated that at least one to two Africans were killed for each one captured and enslaved.[98] The nineteenth-century German explorer Gustav Nachtigal found that Bornu raiders lost three or four people to deaths and escapes for each captive taken.[99] More recent research by Dennis D. Cordell has indicated that deaths at the point of capture in Central Africa ranged from 10 to 60 percent.[100] Miller has estimated that "overall loss rates in raids or wars" approximated 50 percent in Angola during most of the transatlantic slave trade but dramatically declined "late in the history of the trade" as enslavement through judicial and commercial processes became more typical.[101] Adu Boahen, Jacob F. Ade Ajayi, and Michael Tody emphasize that "as many people were killed as were caught" in these wars and raids, and Michaela Alfred-Kamara has reached the same conclusion.[102]

THE AFRICAN AMERICAN HOLOCAUST 67

Total Deaths in Africa and on the Middle Passage

If about 80 percent of the twenty-five million Africans captured during more than three and a half centuries were seized in wars and raids, and if at least one African died for each one captured in this way, the number of deaths in wars and raids was approximately twenty million. This may well be a conservative estimate of those killed at the point of capture, and it does not include the deaths from disease or starvation suffered by survivors or the deaths among the aggressors.[103] When these twenty million fatalities are added to the estimated 12.5 million who died between capture and transport to the Western Hemisphere, it appears that a total of at least 32.5 million people perished in Africa because of the transatlantic slave trade. When the 1.8 million deaths during the Middle Passage are added to the deaths in Africa, the total number is 34.3 million, which is close to Borah's estimate of thirty million Africans lost in their homeland and on slave ships.

Deaths After Arrival and During Seasoning

More death awaited the approximately 10.7 million captured Africans who survived the Middle Passage. After reaching the Americas, slave ships often remained in harbors for weeks before the captives were sold to local slaveholders. About 5 percent of the Black people who arrived alive perished from diseases or other causes before they left the ships.[104] What Lorena S. Walsh has described as "the only extant North American quantitative study" found that 5.4 percent of Africans brought to Virginia between 1710 and 1718 perished before being sold.[105] The loss of 5 percent of African captives shortly after arrival in the Western Hemisphere amounted to approximately 535,000 additional deaths and left about 10,165,000 Africans alive.

Significantly more perished during "seasoning," the period of one to three years in which newly enslaved people began arduous physical labor and tried to become acclimated to their new environment. Slaveholders' violence and abuse, exposure to new diseases, overwork, harsh labor conditions, and suicide resulted in a mortality rate that has

68 ENDLESS HOLOCAUSTS

been estimated at between 33 percent and 50 percent during seasoning.[106] In the study reviewed by Walsh, almost one-third of the Black
people enslaved by one Virginia planter between 1733 and 1742 died
within three years.[107] If about one-third of newly enslaved people died
during the seasoning process, that amounts to more than 3.35 million
deaths, leaving approximately 6.8 million alive.

Subsequent Premature Deaths of Enslaved People

Many of the enslaved who survived seasoning later died prematurely
as a result of their enslavement. Many enslaved people who worked
on Caribbean sugar plantations perished within eight to ten years,
and most who labored in Brazil's gold mines died within ten to twelve
years.[108] Death rates among the enslaved in the Caribbean and Brazil
were higher than in the present-day United States, primarily because of
poorer diets and the more rapid spread of disease in tropical environments.[109] But as Walsh has remarked, "Here 'lower' is indeed a relative
term, one that describes something less than complete demographic
catastrophe, but that tends to obscure exceedingly foreshortened
life chances throughout much of coastal North America."[110] Walsh
has pointed out that the death rates in rice-growing districts in the
Carolinas may have resembled those in sugar-producing areas in the
Caribbean.[111] In Walsh's review "less than half" of the enslaved people
in her study were alive after a decade.[112] For Walsh, records of slave-
holdings with "proportionally few survivors . . . in the older age groups"
suggest "dismally limited life chances" for most enslaved Africans.[113]
Individuals in their early fifties were often described as "very old,"
and those in their sixties "were rare indeed."[114] Of the approximately
6.8 million enslaved people who remained alive after seasoning, it can
be estimated that about 50 percent of them—3.4 million people—perished as the result of bondage within ten to fifteen years of arrival in the
Western Hemisphere.

The Human Toll of the Transatlantic Slave Trade

When the deaths during the Middle Passage, the interval between

THE AFRICAN AMERICAN HOLOCAUST   69

arrival and sale to slaveholders, the seasoning process, and the following decade are added together, the total is more than nine million. Thus, an estimate of the total loss of life in the transatlantic slave trade can be advanced. When the more than nine million deaths in the Middle Passage and the Americas are added to the approximately 32.5 million deaths in Africa, it appears that a total of more than 41.5 million people lost their lives as a direct result of the slave trade. For every person who arrived alive in the Western Hemisphere, more than three had perished in Africa, and almost 70 percent of those who survived the Middle Passage were no longer alive a decade and a half later. This estimate of more than 41.5 million African deaths falls below the estimate of fifty million by Du Bois but exceeds the low-end estimate of 30 million deaths by Stannard. Future research may well disclose an even larger human toll. As only a little more than 5 percent of all captive Africans were sent to the present-day United States, it can be said that this part of the slave trade was associated with the deaths of more than two million people.[115]

THE AFRICAN AMERICAN POPULATION IN
THE EIGHTEENTH CENTURY

The *Maafa* was only the beginning of the African American Holocaust. The number of Black people forcibly transported to the lands that later became the United States remained small during most of the seventeenth century but grew to about 28,000 by 1700.[116] In 1730, the African American population was more than 91,000, and by 1750, it had increased to about 236,000.[117] By 1770, there were about 460,000 people of African descent in these lands, about two-thirds native-born.[118] By the end of the eighteenth century, more than one million Black people were in the newly independent United States. About 80 percent had been born there, and almost 90 percent were enslaved.[119] What demographers call "natural reproduction" distinguished the enslaved population in the present-day United States from its counterparts in the Caribbean and Brazil.[120] Nonetheless, extremely high mortality rates persisted among people transported from Africa, and

70   ENDLESS HOLOCAUSTS

slavery exacted a grave toll among native-born Black people throughout the eighteenth century.

The Murder, Torture, and Abuse of Enslaved People in the Eighteenth Century

Untold numbers of enslaved people were killed outright or died from physical abuse by slaveholders or overseers. Tom Costa has noted, in Virginia in 1705, "A sweeping new law allowed planters to discipline enslaved people to death or, in some cases, to kill runaways without penalty."[121] This law also permitted the dismemberment of enslaved people who were deemed "incorrigible."[122] Some other British colonies passed similar laws.[123] Johnson, Smith, and colleagues have pointed out,

> It was not uncommon to see a man's, woman's, or child's back crisscrossed with raw scars, not uncommon to see Africans hobble about with missing feet, to see a ragged stump where a hand should be. It was not uncommon to see their eyes swollen shut, their hands bound in rusty iron contraptions, their bones broken. It was not uncommon to hear that someone alive was now dead, someone who had dared to stand tall before his master and say, in his own language, *No. No more.*[124]

Moreover, as Derek N. Kerr has observed: "Countless fugitive slaves were killed in pursuit with no written records of their deaths occurring," and others likely died from exposure, starvation, or disease during their flight from bondage.[125]

Eighteenth-Century Resistance and Rebellions by Enslaved People

The horrors of slavery led to numerous acts of resistance, efforts to organize rebellions, and—occasionally—major uprisings in the colonies that later became the United States.[126] The first uprisings against

THE AFRICAN AMERICAN HOLOCAUST 71

the British in Virginia occurred in 1663 and 1687. They were suppressed and their leaders were put to death.[127] An uprising in Newton, Long Island, in 1708 resulted in the deaths of seven whites and the subsequent execution of four Africans.[128] A rebellion in New York City in 1712 led to the deaths of at least nine whites and the execution of twenty-one enslaved people.[129] A planned uprising in Charleston in 1720 was discovered before it occurred, and at least several Black people were hanged or burned alive.[130] A large planned rebellion in Norfolk and Princess Anne counties in Virginia in 1730 was similarly crushed before it broke out, and four Africans were put to death.[131] The discovery of imminent uprisings in New Orleans in 1730 and 1732 led to the execution of more than a dozen insurgents by the French colonial authorities.[132] The Stono Rebellion in South Carolina in 1739 resulted in the deaths of twenty-five settlers and fifty enslaved people.[133] Rumors of a "Great Negro Plot" in New York City in 1741 led to the execution of about thirty-four people, including four white abolitionists.[134] In 1767 in Alexandria, Virginia, enslaved Africans poisoned their overseers, and several rebels were executed.[135] In 1774 in St. Andre's Parish, Georgia, several people held in bondage killed four colonists. At least two of the insurgents were burned alive afterward.[136]

FLIGHT FROM BONDAGE DURING THE WAR OF INDEPENDENCE

During the British colonists' War of Independence between 1775 and 1783, some nine thousand to ten thousand African Americans—free and enslaved—served in the revolutionary army, navy, state militias, or non-combat capacities.[137] How many of these lives were lost during the war is unknown because surviving records did not identify U.S. casualties by race.[138] Signally, after Lord Dunmore, the Royal Governor of Virginia, issued a proclamation in late 1775 promising freedom to enslaved people who would support British forces, as many as 60,000 fled to the British army lines.[139] As Gary B. Nash has pointed out, this was the largest rebellion by Black people up to this point in North American history.[140] Thousands of the enslaved fought with the British forces or performed labor for them.[141] Perhaps 25,000

72 ENDLESS HOLOCAUSTS

who had sought British protection died of smallpox and other diseases during the war.[142] Others were recaptured by U.S. slaveholders. When the fighting ended, 15,000 or more Blacks left North America with the British.[143] However, many remained enslaved by departing Loyalists, and thousands who relocated to the British Caribbean islands died because of yellow fever and hurricanes in the late 1780s.[144]

THE SUPPRESSION OF SLAVE RESISTANCE AND REBELLIONS AFTER INDEPENDENCE

In 1786, militia members and Catawba allies destroyed a maroon community with a population of about a hundred in Bell Isle, Georgia. The escapees had taken food from local plantations, defended themselves with arms, and sparked fears of a large uprising among slaveholders. The assault on the community killed up to a dozen people, and one of its leaders was subsequently executed.[145] In 1792, six enslaved African Americans attacked a member of a slave patrol in Northampton County, Virginia. Three of the assailants were quickly apprehended and executed.[146] The next year, three Blacks were executed in Albany, New York, for setting fire to several buildings.[147] In 1795, dozens of enslaved people revolted in Point Coupee Parish in then-Spanish Louisiana. About twenty-five died in the uprising, and about twenty-five more were captured and executed.[148] That same year, escapees killed an overseer near Wilmington, North Carolina. Slave patrols subsequently killed five escapees; four more were captured and executed.[149] As many as twenty-two Blacks and whites died in armed conflicts in Prince William County and Southampton County, Virginia, in 1797 and 1799.[150] In addition to 621 executions for various reasons during the eighteenth century, hundreds of African Americans died in acts of resistance, efforts to organize uprisings, and rebellions against slavery.[151]

SOCIAL MURDERS IN THE EIGHTEENTH CENTURY

Africans transported to the present-day United States as well as their

THE AFRICAN AMERICAN HOLOCAUST

descendants perished in vast numbers in the eighteenth century. The descendants of enslaved people generally experienced childhoods with inadequate nutrition, decades of hard labor, various forms of abuse and neglect, the frequent loss of family and friends, stress caused by unrelenting racism, and poor health conditions.[152] Despite the paucity of records, it is possible to estimate the minimum number of social murders of native-born enslaved African Americans.[153] About half of those born into slavery in the nineteenth century died before the age of five—twice the mortality rate of the white population—and it is likely that this excess death rate was approximately the same in the eighteenth century.[154] For each of the 720,000 native-born enslaved African Americans alive at the end of the eighteenth century, about the same number died in their first five years. If enslaved children had experienced the same mortality rate as white children at this time, their death toll would have been about 360,000. This rough estimate of a minimum of 360,000 excess deaths is likely conservative because it does not account for excess deaths of enslaved African American adults and because the life prospects of free African Americans were not necessarily better.[155]

THE AFRICAN AMERICAN POPULATION IN THE NINETEENTH CENTURY

The nineteenth century witnessed significant growth of the African American population. By 1860, more than 4.4 million Black people lived in the United States. Almost all were native-born, and almost 90 percent were enslaved.[156] The African American population increased to almost nine million by the end of the nineteenth century.[157] Between 1774 and 1804, all the northern states moved to abolish slavery, though it did not entirely disappear there until around 1840.[158] After the War of Independence, the United States joined the ranks of slave-trading countries. Eric Foner has emphasized:

> In the run-up to [the War of Independence], Congress banned the importation of slaves as part of a broader non-importation

74   ENDLESS HOLOCAUSTS

policy. . . . Inspired by the ideals of the Revolution, most of the
newly independent American states banned the slave trade. But
importation resumed to South Carolina and Georgia, which had
been occupied by the British during the war and lost the largest
number of slaves.[159]

Although the transatlantic slave trade was increasingly recognized
as a crime against humanity and even some southern states passed legislation banning participation, South Carolina and Georgia imported
approximately a hundred thousand African captives between 1783
and 1807.[160] Notwithstanding the outlawing of the slave trade that
began in 1808, approximately fifty thousand Black people were
brought to this country in the decades that followed.[161] The *Clotilda*,
the last slave ship to reach the United States, arrived in 1860 in Mobile
Bay, Alabama.[162]

U.S. Participation in the Illegal Slave Trade with Cuba and Brazil

Some U.S. capitalists, slaveholders, and politicians were deeply
involved in the illegal trafficking of Africans to Cuba and Brazil.[163]
Between 1790 and 1867, more than 780,000 African captives arrived in
Cuba.[164] Between 1800 and 1850, approximately 2.1 million arrived in
Brazil.[165] Dale T. Graden has explained: "The transatlantic slave trade
of the first half of the nineteenth century flourished partially due to
the involvement of U.S. merchants and the capital of U.S. investors."[166]
From 1815 to 1860, as many as a thousand U.S.-built ships, sold or
leased to "known slave traders," carried more than one million Black
people to Cuba and Brazil.[167] Dry foods, alcohol, muskets, gunpow-
der, and other vital provisions made in the United States and Europe
were sold to slave depots on the west coast of Africa. U.S. consuls
and naval officers provided diplomatic cover for the illegal trafficking
and helped slave ships evade capture by British naval patrols.[168] As a
result, the United States was partly responsible for roughly 3.7 million

THE AFRICAN AMERICAN HOLOCAUST   75

deaths in Africa, Cuba, and Brazil during the illegal transatlantic slave trade.[169] As Stephen Chambers has noted, complicity in the suffering and servitude of Africans forcibly transported to Cuba and Brazil enriched many U.S. capitalists and slaveholders and contributed to the expansion of the U.S. Empire.[170]

THE SECOND MIDDLE PASSAGE

During the first half of the nineteenth century, about one million Blacks were forcibly relocated from the Upper South—Maryland, Virginia, and Kentucky—to the Deep South—Alabama, Mississippi, and Louisiana.[171] The number of enslaved people involved in this "second Middle Passage" far exceeded the number of captives originally brought from Africa to mainland North America.[172] As Ira Berlin has pointed out, this process was driven by "a seemingly insatiable demand for cotton and an expanding market for sugar."[173] Edward E. Baptist has explained that cotton "was the key raw material during the first century of the industrial revolution" and "the returns from the cotton monopoly powered the modernization of the rest of the American economy."[174] During the first two decades of the century, slaveholders moving west and south brought most of the people they had enslaved with them.[175] Over time, a massive slave trade developed as enslavers in the Upper South contracted with "a new group of merchants whose sole business became the trade in human beings."[176] About two-thirds of those deported to the Deep South were victims of this new internal slave trade.[177] Many enslaved people were transported by flatboats, steamboats, and trains, and many were forcibly marched.[178] The longest part of this "Slave Trail of Tears" stretched for a thousand miles, and coffles. men in chains, often walked for ten hours a day or more, marshaled by slave drivers with guns and whips.[179] Berlin has emphasized that this "second Middle Passage" continued until the Civil War began and was "traumatic and often deadly."[180] Uncounted thousands died from violence, exhaustion, exposure, and diseases.[181]

Murder, Torture, and Abuse of Enslaved People in the Nineteenth Century

Although slaveholders often claimed that economic self-interest precluded the abuse of enslaved people, the writings of Frederick Douglass, Sojourner Truth, Solomon Northup, Harriet Jacobs, and others have eloquently attested to the horrors of bondage.[182] The American Anti-Slavery Society reported in 1839 that the enslaved were

> frequently flogged with terrible severity, have red pepper rubbed into their lacerated flesh, and hot brine, spirits of turpentine, etc. poured over the gashes to increase the torture . . . they are often stripped naked, their backs and limbs cut with knives, bruised and mangled by scores and hundreds of blows with the paddle, and terribly torn by the claws of cats . . . they are often hunted with blood hounds and shot down like beasts, or torn in pieces by dogs . . . they are often suspended by the arms and whipped and beaten till they faint, and when revived by restoratives, beaten again till they faint, and sometimes till they die . . . their ears are often cut off, their eyes knocked out, their bones broken, their flesh branded with red hot irons . . . they are maimed, mutilated, and burned to death over slow fires.[183]

The number of enslaved people murdered outright or who died because of beatings, floggings, or torture during the nineteenth century is unknown but was undoubtedly substantial.[184] Another kind of grotesque abuse occurred when gynecology pioneer J. Marion Sims and other white surgeons performed experimental surgery on enslaved Black women and infants without consent or anesthesia.[185]

Flight from Bondage Before the Civil War

From 1830 until 1860, between thirty thousand and 150,000 people of African descent escaped from servitude.[186] Sometimes they were

THE AFRICAN AMERICAN HOLOCAUST   77

aided by the Underground Railroad, which Foner has described as "an interlocking series of local networks."[187] Many eventually found freedom in the Northeast or in Canada. But many others were captured and either killed or harshly punished and returned to bondage. Still others perished from exposure, disease, starvation, or racist violence.[188] Beginning in the 1820s, the American Colonization Society, supported by slaveholders, other white supremacists, and the U.S. government, transported between 12,000 and 13,000 African Americans to its new colony in Liberia.[189] About 4,500 had been born free, and the rest had been "emancipated from slavery on the condition that they leave the country."[190] Approximately two thousand died on the way to Liberia or shortly after arrival, primarily because of disease.[191]

NINETEENTH-CENTURY RESISTANCE AND REBELLIONS BY ENSLAVED PEOPLE

More than a thousand African Americans perished during the nineteenth century because they participated in acts of resistance, efforts to organize uprisings or rebellions against slavery, or because they formed maroon communities.[192] Hundreds of enslaved people planned to join Gabriel's Rebellion near Richmond, Virginia, in 1800, but they were betrayed, and the uprising was crushed before it began. Gabriel Prosser and approximately thirty-four others were executed.[193] Other substantial revolts were suppressed in rural Virginia and North Carolina in 1802, and at least fifty-two Black people were put to death afterward.[194] Inspired by the successful Haitian Revolution of 1804, more than five hundred enslaved people participated in a highly organized rebellion in the German Coast region near New Orleans in present-day Louisiana in 1811. U.S. soldiers and slaveholders' militia drowned the rebellion in blood, killing or executing sixty-six insurgents at the site of the battle.[195] Other participants in the uprising were tried and executed later, and the total number of African American deaths was likely about one hundred.[196] After the War of 1812 began, about four thousand Black people escaped bondage in Virginia and Maryland and sought refuge with the British forces,

78   ENDLESS HOLOCAUSTS

who promised them freedom and resettlement. Some of the newly emancipated African Americans joined the British Colonial Marines, fought against the U.S. Army, and participated in the burning of the White House.[197]

In 1816, a plot to burn slaveowners' homes and launch an uprising near Camden, South Carolina, was betrayed and thwarted. Six leaders of the planned rebellion were executed.[198] Around the same time, state militia destroyed two maroon communities in that state, killing or capturing all their members.[199] The destruction of Negro Fort in northern Florida by U.S. forces in 1816 resulted in more than 270 African American and Seminole deaths.[200] Three years later, a conspiracy to set fire to buildings in Augusta, Georgia, and ignite a rebellion was disclosed to local authorities and suppressed. Afterward, several insurgents were put to death.[201] In 1822, Denmark Vesey, who was born into bondage but had purchased his freedom, planned a rebellion in Charleston, South Carolina. Hundreds of enslaved African Americans joined him, but a few participants betrayed them. Vesey and thirty-six enslaved people were subsequently condemned and executed.[202] The following year, militias destroyed maroon communities in Norfolk County, Virginia, and near Pineville, South Carolina, killing some Black people at the time and executing others afterward.[203] In 1826, seventy-seven African Americans transported down the Ohio River by enslavers for sale in the Deep South escaped confinement, killed five white men on the boat, and fled to Indiana. All of them were later captured, and five were executed.[204]

In 1829 and 1830, fires thought to be set by enslaved people destroyed or partly destroyed buildings in Alabama, Georgia, Kentucky, South Carolina, Louisiana, and Maryland.[205] An 1829 rebellion in a coffle being brought south from Maryland resulted in two enslavers' deaths in Virginia and six African Americans' subsequent capture and execution.[206] An 1830 assault by North Carolina militia killed as many as sixty Blacks who had escaped slavery and were reportedly planning an uprising.[207]

In 1831, scores of enslaved people and a few free African Americans supported Nat Turner's Rebellion in Southampton County, Virginia.

THE AFRICAN AMERICAN HOLOCAUST 79

The insurgents killed fifty-seven slaveholders and their family members before the uprising was crushed.[208] Virginia militia and racist mobs responded by killing more than a hundred Black people, many of whom were not involved in the rebellion.[209] In addition, Turner and about nineteen other insurgents were executed.[210] In 1837, after plans for a rebellion near Alexandria, Louisiana, were betrayed, nine enslaved people and three free African Americans were executed, and seven other enslaved people were killed by vigilantes.[211] In 1848, seventy-five armed enslaved people fled Fayette County, Kentucky, intending to reach freedom. However, battles with white pursuers resulted in two deaths, and three leaders of the escape were hanged.[212]

As mounting tensions over slavery moved the country closer to civil war, enslaved people's resistance and efforts to organize rebellions continued, and panic among slaveholders and other white people mounted.[213] In 1856, the discovery of a planned uprising in Colorado County, Texas, led to the severe whipping of two hundred African Americans, the subsequent death of two from their wounds, and the execution of three reported leaders.[214] That same year, Tennessee authorities discovered that enslaved ironworkers were preparing for a rebellion, hanged nine at the Cumberland River Iron Works, and executed nineteen more in Dover.[215] In 1858, near Coffeeville, Mississippi, an armed slave revolt on the plantation owned by the widow of former President James K. Polk was violently suppressed.[216] In 1859, five African Americans joined John Brown, two of his sons, and other white abolitionists in the historic raid on the arsenal at Harpers Ferry, Virginia (now West Virginia). Ten of the participants were killed or died from injuries, and several others, including Brown, were executed.[217] Brown was prescient when he wrote, "The crimes of this guilty land will never be purged away, but with blood."[218] The following year, Alabama officials killed at least twenty-five African Americans and four whites suspected of planning an uprising in four towns.[219] Between mid-1861 and mid-1863, pro-slavery forces in Mississippi executed as many as two hundred African Americans whom they viewed as subversive.[220]

MILITARY SERVICE AND FLIGHT FROM BONDAGE DURING THE CIVIL WAR

During the Civil War between 1861 and 1865, approximately half a million enslaved people escaped to freedom and sought protection behind U.S. military lines.[221] This was undoubtedly the largest slave rebellion in the history of the United States. Although President Abraham Lincoln initially opposed military service by African Americans, high Union casualties and the need for more troops led him to reverse his position by late 1862. Subsequently, more than 200,000 Black men, most of them escaped enslaved people, served in the U.S. Army and Navy during the conflict.[222] As Lincoln later said, "Without the military help of the Black freedmen, the war against the South could not have been won." [223] But they paid a heavy price for their service. About ten thousand died in combat or from injuries, another thirty thousand died from infections and diseases, and almost thirty thousand more were reported as missing.[224] Confederate General Nathan Bedford Forrest's troops massacred almost three hundred Black troops after they surrendered at Fort Pillow, Tennessee, in 1864.[225] That same year, Confederate soldiers executed scores of African American prisoners of war at Saltville, Virginia.[226] Other Black people also suffered greatly during the Civil War and its aftermath. In New York City in 1863, racist whites outraged by the draft, wealthy men's evasion of military service, and competition for jobs with African Americans rioted for several days. Although official records listed about a hundred fatalities, approximately five hundred people—mainly African Americans—died.[227] Racist riots in Boston and Detroit resulted in more Black deaths.[228]

As James Downs has pointed out, the Civil War also brought about "the largest biological crisis of the nineteenth century."[229] Many more Union and Confederate soldiers died from diseases than from combat, and the half-million African Americans who had fled slavery suffered more than anyone. Downs has explained:

Disease and sickness had a more devastating and fatal effect

THE AFRICAN AMERICAN HOLOCAUST 81

on emancipated slaves than on soldiers since ex-slaves often lacked the basic necessities to survive. Emancipation liberated bondspeople from slavery, but they often lacked clean clothing, adequate shelter, proper food, and access to medicine in their escape toward Union lines.[230]

Many died while traveling to U.S. military camps, and many others died after arriving.[231] Smallpox, dysentery, pneumonia, and other diseases claimed the lives of 150,000 or more formerly enslaved people during the Civil War.[232] Approximately 350,000 other African Americans perished from disease in the years following the Confederate surrender at Appomattox in 1865.[233]

THE RACIST REIGN OF TERROR AGAINST RECONSTRUCTION

The postwar project of reconstructing a more egalitarian social order in the South initially achieved a great deal. Between 1865 and 1870, new amendments to the U.S. Constitution outlawed slavery, promised all persons due process and equal protection of the laws, and extended voting rights to African American men.[234] Black men and white allies were elected to local, state, and federal offices. The southern Republicans promoted integration, public education, and tax reform.[235] However, as Douglas R. Egerton has emphasized, "White Democrats, an electoral minority in every southern state after the war, engaged in racial terrorism to restore the prewar social order."[236] In 1866, racist mobs killed forty-six Blacks and two whites in Memphis and thirty-seven Blacks and three white allies in New Orleans.[237] In 1868, white supremacists murdered about two hundred African Americans in Opelousas, Louisiana.[238] Throughout the South, many more died in smaller local attacks by mobs, small groups of vigilantes, and individuals, including racist police and deputies.[239] In 1871, the Southern States Convention of Colored Men held in Columbia, South Carolina, reported that twenty thousand Blacks and white allies had been killed since the beginning of Reconstruction.[240] In 1873, a white militia killed as many as 150 African Americans in Colfax,

Louisiana.[241] The following year, racists killed sixteen Black men in Trenton, Tennessee.[242]

In 1883, white supremacists overthrew the biracial local government in Danville, Virginia, and killed several African Americans.[243] In 1886, an attack at the courthouse in Carroll County, Mississippi, left twenty-three Blacks dead.[244] The next year, the state militia and white vigilantes murdered more than a hundred striking African American sugar workers and supporters in Thibodaux, Louisiana.[245] In 1892, racists attacked three Black co-owners of the People's Grocery in Memphis. When the victims of the assault fought back, they were arrested, jailed, and then lynched.[246] In 1895, hundreds of unionized white dockworkers in New Orleans were laid off and replaced by non-unionized African Americans. The white workers launched an armed assault against the Black dockworkers and killed at least six of them.[247] In 1898, a mob of about two thousand committed to restoring white supremacist rule in Wilmington, North Carolina, violently overthrew the biracial local government and murdered about sixty African Americans.[248] Three decades after Appomattox, Robert Smalls, who escaped slavery, became a Union war hero, and served as a member of the U.S. House of Representatives, reported that 53,000 African Americans had been murdered.[249] Egerton has noted that Smalls's estimate is "entirely plausible."[250] This number of victims dwarfs the 2,600 people of African descent who were legally executed during the nineteenth century.[251]

MASS INCARCERATION AND CONVICT LABOR

What Douglas A. Blackmon has called "slavery by another name" deprived many African American men of their freedom—and even their lives—for several decades after the end of the Civil War.[252] Between the 1870s and the late 1920s, several hundred thousand Black men were unjustly imprisoned after being convicted of charges such as "illegal voting," changing jobs without the permission of a white employer, vagrancy, bigamy, and sexual relations with white women.[253] Blackmon has emphasized,

THE AFRICAN AMERICAN HOLOCAUST

Repeatedly, the timing and scale of surges in arrests appeared more attuned to rises and dips in the need for cheap labor than any demonstrable acts of crime. Hundreds of forced labor camps came to exist, scattered throughout the South—operated by state and county governments, large corporations, small-time entrepreneurs, and provincial farmers. . . . Where mob violence or the Ku Klux Klan terrorized black citizens periodically, the return of forced labor as a fixture in Black life ground pervasively into the daily lives of far more African Americans.[254]

The proliferation of convict labor on public projects and the leasing of Black prisoners to privately owned factories, mines, plantations, lumber camps, and other businesses led to many fatalities. Some of these deaths resulted from industrial accidents, overwork, poor nutrition, and inadequate medical care, while others were murdered by overseers or other incarcerated men.[255] Blackmon has cautioned that more research must be done before the total number of fatalities can be reliably estimated.[256] But the number of deaths likely ran into the tens of thousands over six decades.[257]

THE RESTORATION OF WHITE SUPREMACIST RULE IN THE SOUTH

Egerton has observed that by the end of the nineteenth century "unremitting clandestine violence" had ended "the first progressive era in the nation's history," and the restoration of white supremacist rule in the South largely had been achieved.[258] Lynchings and other racially motivated murders, which often occurred "in the presence of or with the complicity of law enforcement," had become a heinous way to terrorize and subjugate African Americans.[259]

The combination of widespread convict labor and the super-exploitation inherent in sharecropping and tenant farming meant that the vast majority of Blacks in the South would live in conditions of "involuntary de facto servitude" for generations to come.[260] New state laws, state constitutions, and local government measures deprived most Black men of the right to vote, hold public office, and serve on juries. African Americans were generally denied due process and equal protection of the laws, and a rigid new system of racial segregation was developed.[261] Real freedom remained an aspiration but not a reality for almost nine million people.

Social Murders in the Nineteenth Century

Although the African American population significantly expanded during the nineteenth century, so did the excess deaths attributable to poor nutrition, hard labor, abuse and neglect, the loss of family and friends, stress caused by racism, and poor health. As with the previous century, it is possible to estimate the minimum number of excess deaths suffered by native-born enslaved African Americans in the nineteenth century. For each of the approximately 3.9 million enslaved people alive in 1860, about the same number died in their first five years. If enslaved children had experienced the same mortality rate as white children during this time, their death toll would have been about 1.95 million. Like the appraisal of excess deaths among native-born enslaved African Americans for the previous century, this is likely a conservative estimate because it does not account for excess deaths of enslaved Black adults and because the life prospects of free Blacks were not necessarily better than those of enslaved people.[262]

The African American Population Since 1900

During the twentieth century, the African American population dramatically expanded. It grew from just under nine million in 1900 to more than fifteen million in 1950.[263] It was more than 26.6 million in 1980 and about 36.5 million in 2000.[264] By 2019, the population had reached more than 48 million.[265] Black people have achieved some important social and political progress during the past 120 years but continue to suffer in many ways from systemic, institutionalized racism.[266] Various forms of white supremacist violence and abuse, a new wave of mass incarceration, the disproportionate impact of criminal homicides, participation in U.S. wars abroad, excess mortality

THE AFRICAN AMERICAN HOLOCAUST   85

rates, and related forms of oppression have taken a terrible toll on Blacks in the United States since 1900. Ironically, even larger numbers have perished because of white supremacy than in previous centuries.

MURDERS BY MOBS, VIGILANTES, AND POLICE IN THE FIRST HALF OF THE TWENTIETH CENTURY

The routinized murder of African Americans by white mobs, vigilantes, and police continued apace during the first decade of the twentieth century. In 1900, a confrontation between white police officers and a Black man in New Orleans led to the deaths of at least a dozen African Americans and seven whites.[267] In 1906, racist crowds in Atlanta killed two dozen Black people; several whites also died.[268] In 1908, hate-filled whites in Springfield, Illinois, murdered seven African Americans.[269] In 1910, whites killed as many as two hundred Black people in the Slocum Massacre in East Texas.[270] In 1917, white mobs in East St. Louis, Missouri, attacked African Americans who were migrating from southern states in search of jobs. As many as 250 Blacks died.[271] The same year, African American soldiers at Fort Logan in Houston participated in an armed uprising after enduring abuse from local police officers and other white people. Sixteen white police officers and civilians, along with four insurgents, were killed during the uprising, and nineteen Black soldiers were executed afterward.[272]

In 1918, racist whites rioted in Philadelphia after an African American moved into a largely white neighborhood. One Black and three whites died.[273] The worst racist violence of the period occurred between April and November 1919, which James Weldon Johnson called the "Red Summer" because of the bloodshed throughout the country.[274] In April, the death of two white police officers in a shootout in Carswell Grove, Georgia, led to lynching and attacks that took the lives of several Black people.[275] In July, white mobs began attacking African Americans in Washington, DC, after police released a Black man accused of harassing a white woman. About forty people died in the conflict.[276] A week later in Chicago, the death of a young African

American man at a segregated beach led to armed conflict and the deaths of twenty-three Blacks and fifteen whites.[277] In August, thirty to forty people died in Knoxville, Tennessee, when whites attacked an African American neighborhood after failing to find and lynch a biracial man accused of murdering a white woman.[278] In September in Elaine, Arkansas, whites massacred 237 African Americans who were trying to organize a union for sharecroppers.[279] Altogether, the "Red Summer" of 1919 resulted in several hundred deaths in dozens of cities and towns.[280] But as Jesse J. Holland has explained, "Red Summer also marked a new era of Black resistance to white injustice, with African Americans standing up in unprecedented numbers and killing some of their tormentors."[281]

In 1920, in Ocoee, Florida, Ku Klux Klan members and supporters killed as many as sixty African Americans to prevent them from voting and drive them off their land.[282] The following year in Tulsa, after a young Black man was charged with assaulting a young white woman, about seventy-five armed African Americans marched to the local courthouse to prevent a lynching. A crowd of about fifteen hundred whites confronted them, shots were fired, and several people were killed. Thousands of whites then went on a rampage, burned and looted Black businesses and homes, and killed as many as three hundred African Americans.[283] In 1922, three Black men in Kirven, Texas, were burned alive, and as many as twenty-seven other Black people were killed following the murder of a young white woman.[284] In 1923, racist mobs burned down the African American town of Rosewood, Florida. At least eight people, Black and white, died during the violence.[285] In 1925, an independent Detroit newspaper reported that police shot fifty-five Blacks, some of whom died, in the first half of the year alone.[286]

In 1935 and 1943, African Americans participated in what James Boskin has called "protest riots" in Harlem, damaging property and looting stores in reaction to injustice.[287] The first occurred after false rumors spread that a young Black shoplifter had been brutally beaten; three people died. The second erupted after a police officer shot and wounded a young Black soldier; at least five people died.[288] More

THE AFRICAN AMERICAN HOLOCAUST 87

traditional anti-Black riots led to thirty-four deaths in Detroit and three deaths in Beaumont, Texas, in 1943.[289] In 1946, dozens of white supremacists shot to death George W. Dorsey, his pregnant wife, Mae Murray Dorsey, Roger Malcom, and his wife, Dorothy Malcom, in rural Walton County, Georgia.[290] In 1948, several white men killed Isaiah Nixon, a Black veteran, after he defied threats and voted in a local primary election in Georgia.[291] By 1950, the number of African Americans lynched since the turn of the century had grown to almost two thousand.[292]

VIGILANTE AND STATE VIOLENCE IN THE SECOND HALF OF THE TWENTIETH CENTURY

Although large-scale massacres such as in Slocum, East St. Louis, Elaine, and Tulsa declined after the midcentury, significant racist violence persisted. White supremacist vigilantes continued to murder Black people, and as public pressure mounted on the federal government and state governments to rein in mob violence, racist policing played an increasingly important role in their subjugation.[293] Repression mounted in the 1950s and 1960s as African Americans organized to end segregation and obtain voting rights in the South. Approximately 125 civil rights activists and supporters perished at the hands of racists during these decades.[294] These activists included voting rights organizers Henry and Henriette Moore, who died when their home in Florida was bombed on Christmas night, 1951, and Reverend George Lee, killed in Mississippi in 1955.[295] The murder of fourteen-year-old Emmett Till in Mississippi in 1955 horrified much of the nation.[296] The killing of truck driver Willie Edwards Jr. by Ku Klux Klan members in Alabama in 1957 was similarly tragic but less widely noticed.[297] Herbert Lee, who was helping Black people register to vote, was killed in Mississippi in 1961.[298] Medgar Evers, the state leader of the NAACP, was assassinated in the same state in 1963.[299] Addie Mae Collins, Denise McNair, Carole Robertson, and Cynthia Wesley, all young Black girls, died when racists bombed the Sixteenth Street Baptist Church in Birmingham the same year.[300] Ku Klux

88 ENDLESS HOLOCAUSTS

Klan members, including local deputies, murdered civil rights activists James Chaney, an African American, and Jewish New Yorkers Andrew Goodman and Michael Schwerner, in Mississippi in 1964.[301] Even as vigilante and police murders continued in the South, the murder and mistreatment of Black people by police in other parts of the country sparked protest riots and uprisings during much of the 1960s. In Harlem in 1964, a white off-duty officer's killing of a fifteen-year-old young Black man resulted in demonstrations, street disturbances, and the death of a second Black man.[302] Soon afterward, in Rochester, New York, outrage over police officers' use of dogs during an arrest of an African American led to a riot in which four people died.[303] In Alabama in 1965, state troopers beat and shot to death Jimmie Lee Jackson while he was protecting a civil rights march in Marion, and neo-Nazis murdered Willie Brewster in Anniston.[304] Also, in 1965, Malcolm X was killed in Harlem by individuals who may have had ties to the FBI and the New York Police Department.[305] The same year, in the Watts neighborhood in Los Angeles, an altercation following a traffic stop by the California Highway Patrol sparked a six-day uprising that claimed thirty-four, almost entirely Black, lives.[306]

The African American freedom movement forced Congress to pass the Civil Rights Act of 1964 and the Voting Rights Act of 1965. The following decades witnessed the dismantling of *de jure* segregation, significant Black enfranchisement in the South, and the election of thousands of African Americans to government offices. However, white supremacist violence did not cease. In 1966, a racist gas station owner killed student civil rights activist Samuel Leamon Younge Jr. in Tuskegee, Alabama.[307] In 1967, reports that Newark, New Jersey, police had beaten a Black cab driver led to unrest and the deaths of twenty-six people, mostly African Americans.[308] Two weeks later, in Detroit, a police raid on an after-hours bar in the Black community ignited an uprising in which forty-three people died.[309] In February 1968, state police killed three young Black men at South Carolina State University in Orangeburg during a protest against segregation.[310] Two months later, Dr. Martin Luther King Jr. was assassinated

THE AFRICAN AMERICAN HOLOCAUST 89

in Memphis. More than forty people died in the subsequent riots in over one hundred cities.[311] Whether the alleged shooter who was convicted and imprisoned acted alone or was part of a conspiracy involving the FBI, Memphis police, and white supremacists who publicly called for King's death remains unknown today.[312] The FBI and local police killed at least thirty-four members of the Black Panther party by the early 1970s.[313] By 1971, at least 228 people had died in more than 750 riots in the previous seven years.[314]

The suppression of the prisoners' uprising at Attica, New York, in 1971 resulted in thirty-nine deaths.[315] The same year, two people died during protests against racism in Wilmington, North Carolina.[316] In 1972, a sheriff's deputy killed two Black students at a protest at Southern University in Baton Rouge, Louisiana.[317] In 1979, neo-Nazis and Klan members killed five Black, Latino, and white communists at a demonstration in Greensboro, North Carolina.[318] After a jury acquitted four police officers in the beating death of Arthur McDuffie in 1980, riots erupted in Miami, and eighteen people died.[319] Ku Klux Klan members lynched Michael Donald in Mobile, Alabama, in 1981.[320] The Philadelphia police killed eleven people when they bombed the home of the African American MOVE group in 1985.[321] Three years later, neo-Nazis killed Mulugeta Seraw, an Ethiopian immigrant, in Portland, Oregon.[322] In 1992, after a jury acquitted four police officers in the beating of Rodney King, an uprising in Los Angeles resulted in more than fifty deaths.[323] A police killing sparked a riot in St. Petersburg, Florida, in 1996.[324] Virulent white supremacists killed James Byrd near Jasper, Texas, in 1998.[325] Major protests occurred after the police killed Amadou Diallo in New York City in 1999.[326]

RACIST EXECUTIONS IN THE TWENTIETH CENTURY

More than four thousand African Americans were convicted of capital crimes and executed during the twentieth century.[327] Not only was the death penalty disproportionately meted out to Black people, but many of these convictions and executions were patently unjust, and

90   ENDLESS HOLOCAUSTS

the ultimate punishment continued to be what Noel A. Cazenave has called "a lethal form of racial terrorism and control."[328] Thomas Griffin, Meeks Griffin, and two other Black men were executed for the murder of a white man in South Carolina in 1915 after being framed by another suspect.[329] Fortune Ferguson was thirteen years old when he was executed for rape in Florida in 1927.[330] George Tinney Jr. was fourteen years old when he was executed for murder in South Carolina in 1944.[331] Lena Baker was executed in Georgia in 1945 because she killed a white man in self-defense after he kidnapped and assaulted her.[332] Tommy Lee Walker was executed for rape and murder in Texas in 1954 based on a coerced confession.[333] William Tines was put to death for rape in Tennessee in 1960 after being convicted by a tainted jury without substantial evidence of guilt.[334] Willie Darden was executed for murder in Florida in 1988 despite credible alibi evidence emerging after his trial.[335] Despite overwhelming evidence of mental illness, Ricky Ray Rector was executed for murder in Arkansas in 1992 after Governor Bill Clinton refused to grant clemency.[336] Brian Baldwin was executed for murder in Alabama in 1999 after being convicted solely because of a confession obtained through beatings and torture.[337]

TWENTIETH-CENTURY MEDICAL EXPERIMENTS ON AFRICAN AMERICANS

Racist medical experiments also destroyed other African American lives in the twentieth century. From 1932 until 1972, the U.S. government was responsible for the infamous Tuskegee experiment, in which four hundred Black male patients diagnosed with syphilis were left untreated. At least 128 men died from the disease or related complications.[338] In the early 1950s, the Central Intelligence Agency and the U.S. Army conducted experiments that deliberately exposed African Americans in Florida to swarms of mosquitoes carrying yellow fever and other diseases.[339] In the 1950s and 1960s, Black prisoners in Pennsylvania, Ohio, and Louisiana were used as research subjects to test pharmaceuticals and personal hygiene products.[340] Between 1960

THE AFRICAN AMERICAN HOLOCAUST   91

and 1972, a University of Cincinnati radiologist exposed two hundred cancer patients, three-fourths of them African Americans, to previously discredited total body radiation. Dozens of patients died of radiation poisoning.[341] Two decades later, Columbia University researchers injected young Black people with Fenfluramine, which Harriet A. Washington has identified as "half of the deadly, discontinued weight loss drug Fen-Phen," to test the hypothesis about the genetic origins of violence.[342]

RACIST VIOLENCE IN THE TWENTY-FIRST CENTURY

Although capital punishment has become less common in recent years, Black people are still put to death disproportionately.[343] Strikingly, Shaka Sankofa (Gary Graham), executed in Texas in 2000, and Troy Davis, executed in Georgia in 2011, were not guilty of the crimes for which they were condemned.[344] Today, Black people are about three times more likely to be killed by law enforcement officers than white people.[345] Even a short list of high-profile police killings of African Americans since 2000 is not that short. The dead include Timothy Thomas in Cincinnati in 2001; Corey Ward in Atlanta in 2002; Kendra James in Portland, Oregon, and Michael Pleasence in Chicago in 2003; Timothy Stansbury in New York City in 2004; James Brissette, Roland Madison, and Henry Glover in New Orleans in 2005; Sean Bell in New York City in 2006; David Willis in Savannah in 2007; Aaren Gwenn in North Chicago in 2008; Oscar Grant in Oakland in 2009; Aiyana Mo'Nay Stanley-Jones in Detroit in 2010; Kenneth Chamberlain Sr. in White Plains, New York, in 2011; Alan Blueford in Oakland and Ramarley Graham in the Bronx in 2012; Deon Williams in Little Rock in 2013; Michael Brown in Ferguson, Missouri, Ezell Ford in Los Angeles, Tamir Rice in Cleveland, and Akai Gurley and Eric Garner in New York City in 2014; Freddie Gray in Baltimore and Walter Scott in North Charleston, South Carolina, in 2015; Alton Sterling in Baton Rouge and Philando Castile in St. Paul, Minnesota, in 2016; Aaron Bailey in Indianapolis and Jordan Edwards in Balch Springs, Texas, in

2017; Stephon Clark in Sacramento and Botham Jean in Dallas in 2018; Elijah McClain in Aurora, Colorado, and Atatiana Johnson in Fort Worth in 2019; Breonna Taylor in Louisville, George Floyd in Minneapolis, Rayshard Brooks in Atlanta, and Jonathan Price in Wolfe City, Texas, in 2020; and David Lee Tovar in San Jose, Jamal Sutherland in North Charleston, South Carolina, and Daunte Wright in Brooklyn Center, Minnesota, in 2021.[346]

Law enforcement officers shot to death approximately 244 African Americans in 2020.[347] Other Black people died that year because they were restrained, beaten, or tasered by police or fatally injured by police vehicles.[348] Many of those killed were not armed with guns, and some of those who were armed were not threatening anyone when they died at the hands of police.[349] Most Black deaths caused by law enforcement officers over the decades are far from reasonable.[350] Although police records in the United States have always been incomplete and unreliable, it is likely that the total number of unnecessary and preventable killings of African Americans by police since the mid-nineteenth century runs into the tens of thousands.[351]

Brazen white supremacist vigilantes have also continued to murder African Americans during the past twenty years. The dead include Garry Lee near Pittsburgh in 2000; Eric Taylor in Massilon, Ohio, in 2002; as many as four people in New Orleans in 2005; Stephen Johns in Washington, D.C., and Selma Goncalves and Arlindo DePina Goncalves in Boston in 2009; Reginald Clark in Eureka, California, in 2010; James Craig Anderson in Jackson, Mississippi, in 2011; Trayvon Martin in Sanford, Florida, and Jordan David in Jacksonville, Florida, in 2012; nine parishioners at Emanuel African Methodist Episcopal Church in Charleston, South Carolina, in 2015; Larnell Bruce Jr. in Portland, Oregon, in 2016; Richard Collins III in College Park, Maryland, and Timothy Caughman in New York City in 2017; MeShon Cooper in Shawnee, Kansas, and Vickie Lee Jones and Maurice Stallard in Louisville, Kentucky, in 2018; Quentin Hicks in St. Petersburg, Florida, in 2019; Ahmaud Arbery in Brunswick, Georgia, in 2020; and Henry Tapia in Belmont, Massachusetts, in 2021.[352]

THE AFRICAN AMERICAN HOLOCAUST

A NEW WAVE OF MASS INCARCERATION

A new wave of mass incarceration began in the mid-1970s, and the prisoner population dramatically expanded from around 300,000 to more than two million thirty years later.[353] President Richard Nixon's desire to target African Americans and white hippies inspired his call for a "war on drugs" and his demand to get "tough on crime."[354] The number of prisoners doubled during the presidency of Ronald Reagan in the 1980s.[355] For decades, both Republican and Democratic politicians supported extremely long sentences for drug-related offenses and other crimes.[356] Black people have been disproportionately arrested, convicted, and incarcerated in what Michelle Alexander has called the "New Jim Crow."[357]

Alexander has persuasively argued that this mass incarceration is a racial caste system; other researchers have contended that the government's class-based targeting of poor people explains the hugely disproportionate impact on African Americans.[358] Today the United States has less than 5 percent of the world's population but almost 25 percent of its prisoners.[359] Mass incarceration has proved deadly for many Blacks. Between 1981 and 2018, several thousand African American inmates died from suicide, homicide, accidents, and other non-natural causes in U.S. prisons and jails.[360] Many other Black prisoners have died because of inadequate medical care.[361]

ROUTINE CRIMINAL HOMICIDES

Vast numbers of African Americans have been the victims of routine criminal homicides. As Randolph Roth has pointed out, homicide rates in the rural South soared in the late 1880s and 1890s. In those years, the South surpassed the Southwest as the most homicidal region in the United States. In addition, homicide rates among Blacks surpassed those among whites in both the North and the South. They remain higher to this day.[362]

Between 1900 and 2019, more than 1.5 million homicides occurred in this country, and Black people have suffered disproportionately from this enduring epidemic of social violence.[363]

Between 1980 and 2013 alone, there were approximately 262,000 homicides of African American men and hundreds of thousands of others occurred in the first eight decades of the twentieth century.[364] Several thousand Black men, women, and children continue to be murdered each year, and homicide is the leading cause of death among young Black men.[365]

African American Deaths in Imperialist Wars

Participation in U.S. wars abroad has taken a smaller but still tragic toll among African American soldiers, Marines, sailors, and Air Force personnel. In the First World War two hundred Black troops served in the racially segregated U.S. Allied Expeditionary Force, primarily in supply and labor units. Almost eight hundred died in combat, and more died from wounds, diseases, and related causes.[366] About 500,000 African Americans served overseas in the still-segregated armed forces in the Second World War. More than seven hundred died in combat, and more died from other causes.[367] The first racially integrated military units in U.S. history appeared during the Korean War, and between 3,200 and 5,000 Black service members died during this conflict.[368] More than 7,200 African Americans died in the Vietnam War.[369] More than 640 African Americans lost their lives in the Afghanistan War and the Iraq War.[370] Black armed forces members have perished in other U.S. wars and military interventions. The number of Black veterans who have died from suicide, alcoholism, or drug abuse after their experiences in war has never been counted but is likely substantial.

Social Murders Since 1900

By far, the most significant human toll for African Americans since 1900 has been the staggering number of excess deaths, or social murders, caused by poor health conditions rooted in racism.[371] Despite some important improvements in health and health care, Blacks continue to suffer from massive racial disparities. Today African

THE AFRICAN AMERICAN HOLOCAUST 95

American infants are more than twice as likely to die as white infants.[372] As Linda Villarosa has noted, this is "a racial disparity that is actually wider than in 1850."[373] The maternal mortality rate for Black women is three to four times higher than the rate for white women.[374] African American death rates from cardiovascular disease, cancer, diabetes, trauma, HIV, and COVID-19 also are higher than the rates for white people.[375] The much higher levels of hunger, poverty, unemployment, low-wage work, inadequate housing, residential segregation, community disinvestment, neighborhood violence, and exposure to environmental pollution experienced by Black people contribute to poorer health and more precarious life prospects.[376] Unequal access to health care and unequal treatment by doctors and other medical personnel also have profoundly harmful effects on many African Americans.[377]

What Mary R. Jackman and Kimberlee A. Shauman have called "the chronic, everyday injuries of racial discrimination and economic inequality" experienced by Black people are integrally linked to many serious health problems and vast numbers of premature deaths.[378]

Javier M. Rodriguez, Arline T. Geronimus, John Bound, and Danny Dorling have explained:

> Racialization and its subsequent environmental, material, and health care constraints shape exposure to everyday challenges and coping options. Repeated and high-effort coping with social disadvantage and the contingencies of stereotyped social identity are now thought to contribute to a cumulative physiological toll across the life-course, or weathering.... Weathering reflects stress-mediated physiological damage and dysregulation across body systems. These can result in a relatively steeper age-gradient increase in high allostatic load, adverse health outcomes including early onset of hypertension, diabetes, and disability, and excess death from young through middle adulthood.[379]

In recent decades, researchers have been able to use the increasing amount of available related data to estimate the total number of excess deaths among African Americans. Robert S. Levine and his colleagues have concluded that approximately four million excess Black deaths occurred between 1940 and 2000.[380] Rodriguez, Geronimus, Bound, and Dorling have estimated 2.7 million excess deaths among Blacks between 1970 and 2004.[381] More recently, Jackman and Shauman estimated almost 7.7 million excess deaths among African Americans in the twentieth century.[382] They also reported that well over one million such deaths happened between 2000 and 2014.[383] In addition, almost 400,000 excess deaths likely occurred between 2015 and 2020.[384] In sum, it appears that there have been more than nine million social murders among African Americans since 1900.

COUNTING THE DEAD

How many people of African descent have perished during the prehistory, formation, expansion, and global ascendancy of the U.S. Empire? As with the Indigenous Peoples Holocaust, the exact numbers will never be known. Again, the available historical information provides the basis for an informed and reasonable, if rough, estimate. The importation of African captives to the lands that became the United States, participation in the illegal transatlantic slave trade, various forms of white supremacist violence, poor health conditions rooted in racism, convict labor, mass incarceration, criminal homicides, participation in imperialist wars, and related forms of oppression have resulted in considerably more than 18 million Black deaths during the past five centuries. Moreover, this staggering number was only part of the broader holocaust that befell people of African descent who perished because of the transatlantic slave trade, slavery, and various forms of post-slavery oppression in the Western Hemisphere. It may well be that the total loss of Black lives in Africa and the Americas was comparable to the total loss of Indigenous lives—approximately seventy to eighty million—over the centuries.[385] Like the Indigenous Peoples Holocaust in the present-day United States, the African American Holocaust continues today.

3

The Workers Holocaust

Never has [the worker] been speeded up to the present pitch, nor thrown upon the industrial scrap heap so early as too old and exhausted for further use. Never has industry crippled and killed so many of those seeking to earn a livelihood on the land and with the machinery which others possess.

—SOLON DE LEON,
THE AMERICAN LABOR YEAR BOOK, 1929

Indigenous peoples and people of African descent have suffered the most brutal forms of subjugation in the lands that became the United States. Vast numbers of other laborers from diverse national backgrounds have experienced less horrific but nonetheless harsh and sometimes deadly forms of exploitation. In the seventeenth and eighteenth centuries, the lives of indentured servants were often "nasty, brutish, and short."[1] In the nineteenth century, the Industrial Revolution profoundly transformed U.S. society but at an enormous human cost. The development of steamboats and railroads, the growth of manufacturing and mining, and the rise of giant factories contributed to unprecedented economic expansion.[2] By 1870, most of the laboring population had become workers, selling their labor

98   ENDLESS HOLOCAUSTS

power to employers in exchange for wages.[3] While the exploitation of workers has generated unprecedented wealth for the capitalist class and made possible the global ascendancy of the U.S. Empire, it has also produced a veritable holocaust. Workplace injuries and occupational diseases—new kinds of social murder—have claimed staggering numbers of lives for more than a century and a half.[4] In addition, workers in the United States have endured the "bloodiest and most violent labor history of any industrial nation in the world."[5] U.S. capitalists and government officials have been responsible for the deaths of many workers in other countries as well.[6] Notwithstanding some significant labor reforms in the twentieth century, the Workers Holocaust continues today.

INDENTURED SERVITUDE IN THE ENGLISH COLONIES

The English companies and settlers that colonized North America soon recognized the need for more labor, and indentured servitude originated as a solution to this problem.[7] Destitute people in England, Scotland, Ireland, and Germany who hoped for better lives in the colonies signed contracts agreeing to perform unpaid labor, usually for four to seven years, in exchange for passage.[8] England also deported tens of thousands of prisoners, who performed the first form of convict labor in these lands.[9] Between 1630 and 1680, 50,000 of the 75,000 European immigrants to the Chesapeake Bay colonies were indentured servants.[10] About half of the approximately 450,000 Europeans who voluntarily came to the English (later British) colonies before the War of Independence were indentured.[11] Overwork, inadequate nutrition, and disease killed many of them, and suicides were not uncommon.[12] Steven Mintz and Sara McNeil noted: "Half of all white servants in the Chesapeake colonies of Virginia and Maryland died within five years of their arrival."[13] Occasionally, indentured servants who rebelled against their employers or fled servitude were put to death. More frequently, those who displeased their employers were whipped or beaten.[14] After the beginning of the eighteenth century, the predominance of indentured servants diminished, and labor by

THE WORKERS HOLOCAUST 99

enslaved people of African descent became more common, but the practice continued for another hundred years.[15]

DEATHS ON CANALS, STEAMBOATS, AND TRAINS, 1820s–1860s

As the Industrial Revolution unfolded in the first half of the nineteenth century, early economic development projects undertaken by state governments and private companies took an awful human toll. In the 1820s, as many as a thousand workers, mainly Irish immigrants, perished from malaria, other diseases, and construction accidents while building the Erie Canal in New York State.[16] In the mid-1830s, as many as eight thousand Irish immigrant workers died because of harsh labor conditions and a yellow fever epidemic during the construction of the Pontchartrain Canal in New Orleans.[17] Hundreds of other workers, chiefly immigrants, died from cholera, other diseases, and workplace accidents during the construction of the Chesapeake and Ohio Canal from Washington, DC, to Cumberland, Maryland, between 1828 and 1850.[18] Hundreds died from cholera while building the Wabash and Erie Canal in Indiana in 1849–50.[19] About two hundred died from the same disease while working on the St. Mary's Canal in Michigan in 1854.[20] In addition, steamboat tragedies caused by boiler explosions occurred regularly. The *Helen McGregor* exploded at the New Orleans dock and killed more than forty workers and other people in 1830.[21] The *Pulaski* blew up off the coast of North Carolina in 1838, resulting in about a hundred deaths.[22] The *Lucy Walker* exploded on the Ohio River near New Albany, Indiana, and killed at least fifty people in 1844.[23] The worst steamboat tragedy occurred in 1865 when approximately 1,800 people died when the boilers on the *Sultana* exploded on the Mississippi River near Memphis.[24]

As Mark Aldrich has emphasized, "Death rode the rails," too.[25] Aldrich has pointed out that "the slaughter of railroad employees began almost as soon as the first lines were built," and the same can be said for passengers.[26] The first railroad fatality occurred in 1832 when one of four people thrown from a train car near Quincy,

100   ENDLESS HOLOCAUSTS

Massachusetts, died.[27] A derailment on the Boston and Worcester train in 1847 killed six passengers.[28] About 913 workers, passengers, and other people died in New York railroad accidents between 1850 and 1852.[29] The frequency of fatal train disasters soon increased.[30] In 1853, 11 major collisions and derailments resulted in 121 deaths, and smaller accidents were "far more numerous."[31] In 1855, twenty-three people died when a train derailed near Burlington, New Jersey.[32] About sixty-six people died in a head-on train accident at Camp Hill, Pennsylvania, in 1856.[33] The mounting number of fatalities among railroad workers, passengers, and others led to the new "accidents, railroad" category in the 1860 census, which listed 599 deaths for the preceding year.[34] Work and travel on railroads was significantly more dangerous in the United States than Britain.[35] When a U.S. company undertook the construction of the Panama Railroad in Colombia, between six thousand and twelve thousand workers from Colombia, Jamaica, China, Ireland, and other countries died between 1850 and 1855.[36]

The Perils of Manufacturing and Mining, 1820s-1860s

In the early nineteenth century, textile mills became one of the first major industries in this country, "producing ready-made clothing from slave-harvested cotton."[37] M. T. Anderson has described the early mills as "the beating heart of America's mass-production infancy."[38] Initially centered in New England, these mills primarily employed young women, who were paid low wages for long hours of difficult work. Textile workers were particularly susceptible to byssinosis, or brown lung disease, caused by exposure to cotton dust in poorly ventilated workplaces. They were also vulnerable to tuberculosis, other respiratory disorders, and accidental dismemberment.[39] Although many employees recognized these workplace hazards, their principal demand during strikes in Paterson, New Jersey, in 1835 and in Pittsburgh in 1845 was the reduction of the twelve-hour workday.[40] In 1845, women textile workers in Lowell, Massachusetts, forced the state legislature to hold hearings on the issue of weekly work hours,

THE WORKERS HOLOCAUST   101

but the proceedings yielded no immediate benefits.[41] Textile workers' deaths caused by occupational diseases and fatal accidents were not investigated until much later. However, in 1860 the country's attention turned to Lawrence, Massachusetts, when the Pemberton textile mill collapsed and killed 145 workers.[42]

The production of iron began during the colonial period and grew during the first half of the nineteenth century in Pennsylvania, New York, and northern New Jersey. The nation's increasing need for power for "steam engines, furnaces, and forges" fostered the expansion of coal mining—and its dangers—in the first half of the nineteenth century.[43] Between 1839 and 1859, eight mine explosions in Virginia and Pennsylvania led to about 176 deaths.[44] By the 1850s and 1860s, doctors in coal mining areas had begun to recognize the deadly effects of "miner's consumption" or "miner's asthma" among patients who labored in the earth.[45] An 1858 study indicated that the average chance of a Pennsylvania miner surviving for a dozen years was less than 50 percent.[46]

Other major industrial accidents began to occur in the United States before the Civil War. In 1850, the boiler in a hat manufacturing plant in New York City exploded and killed sixty-three workers.[47] The following year, scores of workers died in a fire at a factory in Philadelphia.[48] In 1854, seventeen workers perished in an explosion at an ammunition manufacturing plant in New York City.[49] Another kind of danger emerged when police killed two tailors during a strike of three hundred workers in New York City in 1850 and police killed two railroad workers during a strike in Portage, New York, in 1851.[50]

The Transportation of Chinese Laborers to the Americas

As the illegal transatlantic slave trade declined in the mid-nineteenth century, labor shortages worsened in the Americas. The need for many new workers was also pressing in some parts of Southeast Asia and Africa. Between the mid-1840s and the mid-1870s, the United States joined Britain, Spain, Peru, Portugal, and France in transporting approximately 750,000 impoverished Chinese laborers to work in

102   ENDLESS HOLOCAUSTS

different countries.[51] U.S. ships brought as many as 350,000 Chinese men to work on tobacco, coffee, and sugar plantations in Cuba, on cotton and sugar plantations and in guano pits of Peru, and on plantations in other nations.[52] Robert J. Schwendinger has explained that these workers were procured "through deception, widespread kidnappings, and under the pretext of legitimate labor contracts."[53] Often they were crowded into barracoons in Chinese cities while awaiting transportation and whipped if they tried to escape.[54] Once aboard the ships, they suffered from inadequate nutrition, virtually nonexistent sanitary facilities, and violence by crew members.[55]

Between 1847 and 1859, more than 7,500 Chinese workers died on U.S. ships traveling to Cuba, and uncounted others perished on U.S. ships going to Peru and other countries.[56] After arrival in the Caribbean and South America, the workers transported by U.S. and European vessels often labored under extremely harsh conditions and were treated as if they were enslaved. More than two-thirds of the 100,000 to 150,000 Chinese workers who arrived in Peru died there, and many of the 150,000 who arrived in Cuba lost their lives as well.[57] U.S. capitalists shared responsibility for the deaths of scores of thousands.[58] In 1862, Congress outlawed U.S. participation in the sordid trade, but it continued illegally for more than another decade.[59]

INDUSTRIAL ADVANCES IN THE 1860s

The military exigencies of the Civil War required increased industrial development in the Union. As Benjamin T. Arrington has pointed out, "The Northern railroad companies boomed during the conflict."[60] Other Northern industries such as weapons manufacturing, iron production, leather goods, and textiles "grew and improved as the war progressed."[61] The growing use of reapers, threshing machines, and horse-drawn planters boosted Northern agricultural production.[62] The Union's industrial strength played a key role in its victory over the Confederacy.[63] The loss of life during the Civil War and its aftermath was horrific, and rapid industrialization in the following decades led to an unprecedented number of deaths and grievous injuries in

THE WORKERS HOLOCAUST   103

workplaces.[64] In 1867, a train derailment near Angola, New York, killed forty-two employees and passengers.[65] The same year, a boiler explosion in Philadelphia killed twenty-eight people.[66] "Hundreds, perhaps thousands" of Chinese immigrant workers perished while building the final segment of the Transcontinental Railroad between Omaha and Sacramento before it was completed in 1869.[67] That same year, about 179 miners died in an explosion at the Avondale coal mine in Pennsylvania, and forty-five workers died in a flash fire at the Yellow Jacket silver mine in Nevada.[68] Reflecting the growing death toll in workplaces, new categories of "mining accidents," "injuries by machinery," and accidents from "falling bodies" were added to the 1870 census.[69]

"AN INDUSTRIAL ACCIDENT CRISIS OF WORLD-HISTORICAL PROPORTIONS," 1870–1900

In the decades after the Civil War, the expansion of railroads, mining, textile mills, ironworks, steel mills, factories, and mechanized production dramatically changed the United States. The wealth created by industrial workers, largely appropriated by the capitalist class, helped the country become an increasingly important economic power in the world.[70] But by the 1870s and 1880s, the United States was experiencing what John Fabian Witt has called "an industrial accident crisis of world-historical proportions."[71] In the twenty-five years before the First World War, more than 75,000 railroad workers were killed on the job.[72]

Almost 43,000 miners lost their lives while working between 1884 and 1912.[73] Some seven thousand workers died in boiler explosions in various industries between 1883 and 1907.[74] Thousands perished in the timber industry over the decades.[75] Thousands of Chinese American workers died from overwork, disease, and exposure while performing various kinds of labor in the western United States.[76] Growing numbers of workers in other industries died as well. In 1878, a dust explosion at the Washburn flour mill in Minneapolis killed eighteen workers.[77] In the following decade, fatal accidents in steel

104 ENDLESS HOLOCAUSTS

mills and other industrial workplaces accounted for about 20 percent of all male deaths in Pittsburgh.[78] In Costa Rica, about five thousand workers employed by a U.S. company perished while building a major railroad in the mid-1880s.[79]

As the number of fatal occupational injuries soared and pressure on government by labor advocates grew, some state agencies began to investigate the dangers in workplaces. Reports by the Ohio Bureau of Labor Statistics in 1881 and 1883 starkly depicted the grim reality, summarized more than a century later by the U.S. Department of Labor:

> A boiler in a steam engine running a threshing machine exploded, killing three men and scalding a young boy. One man was thrown 80 feet through the air to his death; another had his head blown off, which landed grotesquely in a basket. A buzz-saw operator got caught in his machine and lost an arm and a leg. A year earlier he had lost his right arm in the same manner. An engineer trying to oil machinery while it was in motion was killed when his head was caught against a post by a heavy fly wheel, "grinding out his brains." A boy in a printing house working at a press tried to straighten out an improperly placed sheet of paper and had several fingers crushed when he did not get his hand out of the way in time.[80]

The Minnesota Bureau of Labor Statistics reported similar tragedies in 1892.[81]

By the 1880s, the mounting wave of workplace deaths and injuries had aroused the grief and outrage of many people throughout the country.[82] In 1889, President Benjamin Harrison told Congress that railroad workers faced "a peril of life and limb as great as that of a soldier in time of war."[83] In 1891, the New Jersey Bureau of Statistics of Labor and Industry reported that "the destruction of human life is much greater in the peaceful pursuits of industry than in war, and if it were possible to enumerate them, it will be found far greater than during the four years of destruction in the late Civil War."[84] The rate of

THE WORKERS HOLOCAUST   105

fatal occupational injuries in the United States in the nineteenth century was significantly higher than in Britain, Germany, and France.[85] However, the federal government did not issue comprehensive national statistical reports on workplace deaths for another century, and state agencies did not provide accurate, reliable estimates of industrial accident rates.[86] Uncounted hundreds of thousands likely died in workplace accidents between 1850 and 1880. Eric Foner has estimated that approximately 35,000 workers died on the job annually between 1880 and 1900—a total of 700,000 for these two decades alone.[87]

The Growth of Occupational Diseases, 1870–1900

Occupational diseases also increasingly endangered workers. As textile mills spread across the country, so did brown lung disease and other respiratory diseases.[88] "Miner's consumption" was gradually acknowledged as the most common cause of death among older miners.[89] Workers who breathed tiny particles of mineral ore, rock, or sand—what David Rosner and Gerald Markowitz have called "deadly dust"—often developed silicosis.[90] This disease resulted in the deaths of not only miners but also quarry workers, foundry workers, nail manufacturing plant employees, granite cutters, brick workers, ceramic workers, glass workers, sandblasters, and other laborers.[91] In addition, many coal miners developed coal workers' pneumoconiosis, better known as black lung disease.[92] Silicosis and black lung disease would cut short the lives of hundreds of thousands of coal miners during the next century.[93] Lead poisoning also became a grave problem. As many as thirty thousand cases of lead poisoning may have occurred among miners and other workers in the lead deposits in Utah between 1870 and 1900.[94] Workers in lead smelters, white lead factories, battery manufacturing plants, and other factories, along with painters, often became ill or died from lead poisoning.[95] Many men and women also contracted tuberculosis in garment sweatshops and other workplaces.[96] As Christopher C. Sellers has noted, "The explosion of industrial policyholders between the late 1870s and

106   ENDLESS HOLOCAUSTS

1900—from 11,000 to 3.5 million—partly reflected worker anxiet-
ies about the financial impact of occupational diseases on themselves
and their families."[97] Reliable statistics on deaths from occupational
diseases in the late nineteenth century do not exist, but this loss of life
was likely also enormous.[98]

Anti-Labor Violence, 1870–1900

By the late nineteenth century, workers also faced potential death
or serious injury when they engaged in collective action to obtain
a shorter work week, higher wages, and safer working conditions.
During this period, the repression of workers by police officers,
soldiers, company security agents, and private militias was often
deadly. More than a hundred people died during the Great Railroad
Strike of 1877.[99] Twenty Irish American miners—the famous "Molly
Maguires"—were hanged in Pennsylvania between 1877 and 1879 on
charges of murdering mine superintendents and foremen.[100] In early
May 1886, amid a national strike and other labor actions demanding
the eight-hour day, police killed several workers at the McCormick
Harvester Works in Chicago. The next evening, as local workers
protested in Haymarket Square, a bomb was thrown into the police
ranks, killing several officers. Four anarchists were wrongfully executed for the bombing, and a fifth condemned prisoner committed
suicide.[101] May First later became an international workers holiday.[102]
In 1886, nine people died in the Southwest Railroad Strike.[103] The following year the state militia and vigilantes massacred more than a
hundred striking African American sugar workers and supporters in
Thibodaux, Louisiana.[104] Nine workers and seven Pinkerton agents
died in the Homestead Steel Strike in Pittsburgh in 1892.[105] During
the national Pullman Strike of 1894, about thirty people were killed.[106]

"The Industrial Slaughterhouse," 1900–1930

In the early years of the twentieth century, "The United States was
in the fifth decade of an accident crisis like none the world had ever

THE WORKERS HOLOCAUST 107

seen and like none any Western nation has seen since."[107] U.S. capitalists' drive for what the contemporary observer C. H. Mark called "international industrial supremacy" and domination of global markets produced a "stupendous loss" of life.[108] As a series of massive workplace disasters occurred, the *Cleveland Citizen* lamented that the United States had become an "industrial slaughterhouse."[109] In 1900, a coal mine explosion in Scoville, Utah, killed at least two hundred workers.[110] In 1902, 112 miners died in a gas and dust explosion at the Rolling Mill mine in Johnstown, Pennsylvania.[111] Another coal mine explosion in Fraterville, Tennessee, killed 216 workers the same year.[112] In 1903, 169 workers died in a mine explosion in Hanna, Wyoming.[113] In 1905, a boiler explosion at the Grover Shoe Factory in Brockton, Massachusetts, killed fifty-eight people.[114] Between mid-1906 and mid-1907, 546 workers died in industrial accidents in Allegheny County, Pennsylvania, alone.[115] In 1907, 362 workers died in a coal mine explosion in Monongah, West Virginia.[116] The same year, 239 workers died in the Darr Mine disaster in Rostraver, Pennsylvania.[117] Forty-three workers died between 1908 and 1913 while building the Los Angeles Aqueduct.[118] In 1909, sixty-seven workers died because of a fire during the construction of a water intake tunnel for the City of Chicago.[119]

In 1910, coal mine explosions in Mulga and Palos, Alabama, took 124 lives.[120] Also in 1910, 259 miners died in the Cherry Mine coal fire in Illinois, and a fire in a textile factory in Newark, New Jersey, killed 26 workers.[121] In 1911, 146 young women workers died in a fire at the Triangle Shirtwaist Factory in New York City.[122] That same year, 128 miners—primarily African American convict laborers—died in a mine explosion in Littleton, Alabama.[123] A different kind of tragedy occurred on Christmas Eve in 1913, when seventy-three people, mostly children of striking copper miners, died in a stampede at the Italian Hall in Calumet, Michigan, after a strikebreaker yelled "Fire!"[124] In 1917, 168 miners died in an explosion at the Speculator mine in Butte, Montana.[125] The following year, an explosion at a munitions depot near Sayreville, New Jersey, resulted in about one hundred deaths.[126] In 1919, twenty-one people died when a giant

108 ENDLESS HOLOCAUSTS

molasses tank in Boston burst.[127] In 1924, an explosion at a mine in Castle Gate, Utah, killed 172 workers, and an ammonium nitrate explosion at a nitration plant near New Brunswick, New Jersey, killed 20 workers.[128] The United States continued to have far more major industrial accidents than any other country until well into the twenty-first century.[129]

The deaths resulting from these major calamities were only a small portion of the horrific loss of life in U.S. workplaces. In 1907 alone, almost 12,000 workers, passengers, and others died in railroad accidents.[130] That year, more than 3,200 coal miners died on the job.[131] Witt has emphasized:

> Indeed, accidents were the leading cause of death among workers in hazardous industries as diverse as railroads, mining, metalwork, rubber work, shipping and canals, quarries, telegraph and telephones, electric lighting, brick- and tile-making, and terra-cotta work.[132]

By this time, untold thousands of workers had also died on the job in logging, woodworking, paper mills, meatpacking, painting, glass working, construction, oil, and other industries.[133] I. M. Rubinow, a leading contemporary advocate for social insurance and health care for workers, described the scale of industrial deaths in the early twentieth century as "vastly greater" in the United States "than in any European country."[134] Labor leaders on both sides of the Atlantic condemned the much higher numbers of fatal occupational injuries here.[135]

Many more non-fatal industrial accidents also occurred each year. Arthur Reeves estimated in 1907 that there were about 500,000 workplace injuries each year.[136] The following year, William H. Tolman estimated that approximately five million injuries had occurred in industrial and other accidents between 1897 and 1907.[137] Today, some analysts believe that the annual number of serious industrial accidents in the early twentieth century may have been 700,000 or more.[138] Although most injuries sustained in these accidents were not

THE WORKERS HOLOCAUST 109

fatal, they contributed to the widespread recognition that the United States had become what one historian called the "land of disasters."[139] Workplace deaths and other industrial accidents became one of the most important social and political issues in the country, and awareness of the dangers of occupational diseases gradually increased.[140] Responding to workers' agitation and public outrage, President Theodore Roosevelt advocated the creation of workers' compensation programs in 1907, and most states established some version of these during the next decade.[141] More than a hundred years later, however, these programs remain shamefully inadequate.[142]

WORKERS' DEATHS IN OTHER COUNTRIES, 1900–1930

U.S. capitalists' pursuit of profits also resulted in the deaths of many workers in other countries. In 1904, a year after Roosevelt engineered the creation of the new country of Panama and secured its independence from Colombia, his administration began construction on the Panama Canal. More than 5,600 workers, mainly men of color, died while building the canal before it was completed in 1914.[143] Between 1907 and 1912, approximately six thousand workers from several nations died while building the Madeira-Mamore railroad in Brazil for a U.S. company.[144] Around the same time, as many as thirty thousand enslaved Indigenous laborers in the then-Peruvian Amazon died from exhaustion, exposure, disease, starvation, and violence while producing rubber for export to New York and London.[145] Thousands of miles away, Thomas Fortune Ryan, Daniel Guggenheim and other U.S. financiers invested in mining, rubber, and agricultural interests in Congo in 1906, providing half the capital for the major Belgian mining corporation Forminière.[146] They were not involved in the enslavement, exploitation, and violence that killed approximately ten million Congolese in King Leopold's so-called Free State.[147] But they were deeply complicit in the deaths of countless thousands of workers from brutal work conditions, physical abuse, forced relocations, disease, and political repression in the following decades.[148] Beginning in 1917, U.S. capital and technical expertise significantly contributed

110   ENDLESS HOLOCAUSTS

to the industrial development of South Africa, the ruthless white
exploitation of Black labor, and the deaths of thousands of miners
and other workers.[149]

ESTIMATES OF WORKPLACE DEATHS IN THE UNITED STATES, 1900–1930

Marc Linder has remarked, "No one in the early twentieth century
knew how many industrial soldiers were being mortally wounded
each year in the United States."[150] At the time, the federal government's limited collection of mortality data and state agencies' reliance
on employer self-reporting made it difficult to accurately assess the
enormous loss of life.[151] But as the carnage on railroads and in mines,
mills, factories, and other workplaces mounted, so did public pressure to count the number of workers who died each year on the job.
When industry analysts, government officials, academics, labor advocates, and journalists began estimating the annual human toll, they
developed widely divergent estimates. In 1908, Frederick L. Hoffman
of the Prudential Life Insurance company estimated that as many
as 17,500 deaths that year resulted from "dangerous industries or
trades."[152] The same year, a journalist estimated annual occupational
fatalities to be about 35,000.[153] In 1910, Columbia University profes-
sor Henry Rogers Seager estimated that industrial accidents caused
approximately 30,000 deaths each year.[154] The new National Safety
Council, dominated by business interests, found that between 18,000
and 21,000 fatal occupational injuries occurred in 1912.[155] Workers'
compensation expert E. H. Downey estimated about 35,000 annual
workplace deaths that year.[156]

Hoffman estimated that approximately 25,000 lives were lost in
the workplace in 1913.[157] In 1914, Carl M. Hansen of the Workmen's
Compensation Service Bureau in New York reported that between
40,000 and 45,000 workers were dying on the job each year.[158] In 1915,
the U.S. Commission on Industrial Relations informed Congress that
about 35,000 industrial deaths had occurred the previous year.[159] In
1924, Carl Hookstadt of the U.S. Bureau of Labor Statistics estimated

THE WORKERS HOLOCAUST

that more than 21,000 fatal job accidents were occurring annually.[160] Also in 1924, Downey estimated that the annual loss of life was approximately 25,000.[161] The National Safety Council estimated that about 20,000 workers lost their lives on the job in 1929.[162] In contrast, the *American Labor Year Book 1929* estimated that about 35,000 workers had died in workplaces that year.[163] The precise numbers of fatal occupational injuries in the United States between 1900 and 1930 will never be known, but the largest contemporary appraisals were almost certainly closer to the truth than other assessments. It may be estimated that approximately 35,000 workplace deaths occurred each year during the first two decades of the twentieth century, and approximately 30,000 occurred annually during the 1920s. In sum, a total of about one million workers likely died on the job between 1900 and 1930.

DEATHS FROM OCCUPATIONAL DISEASES, 1900–1930

Brown lung disease, silicosis, black lung disease, and lead poisoning among workers increased between 1900 and 1930.[164] Tuberculosis contracted in workplaces also continued to produce many fatalities, though the rate of fatal infections eventually decreased.[165] In addition, miners and workers in shipbuilding, manufacturing, construction, and the oil industry exposed to asbestos often developed and perished from asbestosis, better known as white lung disease, or from lung cancer or mesothelioma.[166] Stonecutters often became ill and died from respiratory diseases.[167] Workers involved in manufacturing or processing tin, rubber, leather, explosives, and paints were increasingly exposed to benzene and often developed and died from aplastic anemia.[168] Hatmakers became ill from mercury poisoning and sometimes died as a result.[169] Furriers lost their health and sometimes their lives from mercury poisoning, other harmful chemicals, and dust.[170] The proliferation of chemicals endangered workers in other industries as well.[171] Watchmakers died from radium poisoning.[172] Cigar and tobacco workers suffered and sometimes perished from heart and lung diseases caused by workplace conditions.[173]

112   ENDLESS HOLOCAUSTS

Gerald N. Grob has argued that "it is virtually impossible to generalize about the role of industrial disease as a factor in total mortality at the turn of the century."[174] However, the first National Conference on Industrial Diseases, held in Chicago in 1910, acknowledged the growing significance of occupational illnesses while lamenting the lack of reliable statistics on related mortality and morbidity.[175] At the time, it was difficult to quantify the number of deaths from occupational diseases, partly because the causes listed on death certificates were not always accurate and partly because less than 60 percent of the states reported annual deaths from all causes to the Census Bureau.[176] Nonetheless, the available historical information suffices for developing estimates of annual deaths caused by occupational illnesses. In 1913, Emery R. Hayhurst described tuberculosis as "the principal terminal occupational disease" and found it to be the "leading cause of death in 110 of the 140 groups of occupations surveyed." [177] Hayhurst estimated that almost 37,000 workers in these occupations perished in 1909 alone.[178] To this number must be added the deaths from tuberculosis contracted in workplaces in the remainder of the country and deaths from brown lung disease, silicosis, black lung disease, and lead poisoning. A conservative estimate is that the annual death toll from work-related diseases in 1900 was approximately 50,000 and that this number gradually increased over the decades to the better documented but still conservative estimate of 100,000 annual deaths in 1970.[179] Approximately 1.8 million workers likely perished from work-related diseases in the first three decades of the twentieth century.[180]

ANTI-LABOR VIOLENCE, 1900–1940

The violent repression of strikes and other labor actions also continued to exact a dreadful human toll between the turn of the century and the Second World War. Forty-two people died during a strike for the eight-hour day in Colorado in 1903–1904.[181] At least twenty-one people died in the Teamsters strike in Chicago in 1905.[182] In 1906, a contingent of Arizona Rangers helped Mexican police

THE WORKERS HOLOCAUST

brutally suppress a strike by workers at a U.S.-owned copper mine at Cananea in Sonora.[183] About thirty-six people lost their lives during the violence.[184] Thirty-one people died during a streetcar strike in San Francisco in 1907, and at least twelve workers died in a strike against a railroad car manufacturer in McKees Rock, Pennsylvania, in 1909.[185] Two men trying to organize cigar workers were lynched in Tampa in 1910, and police shot to death one worker during the strike at the steel mill in Bethlehem, Pennsylvania, the same year.[186] Approximately fifty people died in the coal miners' strike in the Paint Creek-Cabin's Creek area in West Virginia in 1912–13.[187] Two workers died during the Lawrence Textile Strike in Massachusetts in 1912.[188] In 1914 in Ludlow, Colorado, National Guard troops killed sixty-six men, women, and children at a tent camp housing more than a thousand striking coal miners and family members who had been evicted from their company-owned homes.[189] Several other people also died during the strike.[190]

By the time of the Ludlow Massacre, as many as eight hundred workers had died during labor actions in the previous four decades.[191] Several hundred more perished in the quarter-century after Ludlow. In 1915, private security guards killed six striking workers at an oil plant in Bayonne, New Jersey, and Joe Hill, an organizer for the Industrial Workers of the World, was framed for murder and executed in Utah.[192] In 1916, three steelworkers died during a strike in Youngstown, Ohio, and a miner was killed during a strike on the Mesabi iron ore range in Minnesota.[193] The same year, five IWW members were shot to death, and at least six others drowned when they came by boat to Everett, Washington, to support a strike by shingle-makers.[194] In 1917, IWW organizer Frank Little was lynched in Butte, Montana.[195] In 1919, five people died during a strike by streetcar conductors and motormen in Charlotte, North Carolina and four organizers for the International Timber Workers Union were murdered in their office in Bogalusa, Louisiana.[196] Racist whites killed 237 African Americans trying to organize a union for sharecroppers in Elaine, Arkansas, that year.[197] At least twenty-two workers died in the Great Steel Strike of 1919.[198] In contrast, no one died in the Seattle General Strike the same year.[199]

114   ENDLESS HOLOCAUSTS

In 1920, state troopers killed about sixteen black and white coal miners during a strike in Walker County, Alabama, strikebreakers killed seven people during a streetcar strike in Denver, and five longshoremen died during a strike in Philadelphia.[200] The United Mine Workers' efforts to organize coal miners in West Virginia in 1920–22 met with fierce resistance, which led to the Matewan Massacre, the assassination of a pro-union sheriff, an intermittent guerrilla war, and ten thousand armed miners fighting state police and deputies in the Battle of Blair Mountain. As many as 150 workers died during those two years.[201] In 1922, three coal miners died in Herrin, Illinois, during the national strike called by the UMW, and their comrades killed twenty company guards and strikebreakers.[202] In 1924, fourteen sugar plantation workers and three police officers died during a strike in Hanapepe, Kauai Hawai'i.[203] Three years later, Colorado state police fatally shot six coal miners during a strike at the Columbine Mine in Serene.[204] In 1928, when a massive strike crippled United Fruit Company operations in Colombia, company pressure and U.S. government threats resulted in the Colombian army crushing the labor action, and approximately one thousand workers died.[205]

As the Great Depression ravaged the United States, there was a historical upsurge of labor activism. Sixteen people were killed during the miners' strike in Harlan County, Kentucky, in 1931–32.[206] Police murdered six Black Alabama Sharecroppers Union members during the same period.[207] Several unionists and others died during the San Francisco General Strike and broader West Coast Waterfront Strike of 1934.[208] Also in 1934, two workers died in a strike against an auto parts plant in Toledo, Ohio, four people were killed during a Teamsters' strike in Minneapolis, and seven textile workers died in Honea Path, South Carolina, during a national strike.[209] During the Pacific Northwest Lumber strike the following year, police and armed strikebreakers killed three workers in Humboldt County, California.[210] More than a hundred workers were killed during labor actions across the country between 1933 and 1936.[211] Approximately thirty steelworkers and others died in Chicago and Youngstown during the Little Steel Strike in 1937.[212] Twenty-eight members of

THE WORKERS HOLOCAUST 115

the National Maritime Union lost their lives during strikes in Texas, Louisiana, and other states between 1936 and 1938.[213] In the decades that followed, company and state violence against workers in labor actions significantly declined but did not disappear.[214]

WORKPLACE DEATHS AND DEATHS FROM OCCUPATIONAL DISEASES, 1930–1970

The frequency of major industrial disasters and the annual number of fatal occupational injuries slowly declined after 1930, but the significant loss of life from workplace accidents and occupational diseases remained a central feature of U.S. capitalism. As many as 1,500 workers who helped construct the Hawk's Nest Tunnel to carry the New River through Gauley Mountain in West Virginia in 1930–31 died of acute silicosis in what has been called this country's "worst industrial disaster."[215] More than a hundred workers died building the Hoover Dam in Colorado between 1931 and 1936.[216] About eighty died during the construction of the Grand Coulee Dam in Washington between 1933 and 1942.[217] An oil well explosion in St. George, Utah, killed ten workers in 1935.[218] As the Second World War raged, there were numerous industrial casualties on the home front. In 1944, a munitions explosion at the Naval Ammunition Depot at Port Chicago, California, killed 320 workers.[219] That same year, a natural gas tank explosion and fire in Cleveland left 131 people dead.[220] From 1942 until 1945, the U.S. government paid the Brazilian government to transport workers to the Amazon to tap rubber for wartime production under perilous conditions. Twenty-five thousand workers died from disease, lack of medical care, and attacks by wild animals.[221] By the end of 1945, almost 85,000 coal miners had been killed in accidents since the new century began.[222]

The number of Congolese workers who died from exposure to radiation after mining uranium for export to the United States between 1942 and 1960 may never be known.[223] At least two thousand workers who mined uranium in the western United States between the 1940s and the 1980s, including many Diné people, perished from

116   ENDLESS HOLOCAUSTS

radiation-related causes.[224] More than 33,000 U.S. nuclear weapons plants employees have died from exposure to radiation since 1945.[225] In 1947, at least 581 workers and local residents died in Texas City, Texas, when an explosion occurred as ammonium nitrate was being loaded onto a ship.[226] Measured in terms of immediate deaths, this was the worst industrial accident in U.S. history.[227] That same year, 111 workers died in an explosion at a coal mine in Centralia, Illinois.[228] In 1950, thirty-one dockworkers and others lost their lives when munitions detonated on barges and trains at the Raritan River Port in South Amboy, New Jersey.[229] The following year, 119 workers died in an explosion at a coal mine near West Frankfurt, Illinois.[230] In 1956, a fire at a refinery near Sunray, Texas, led to the deaths of nineteen firefighters.[231] In 1959, a flood in a coal mine in Jenkins Township, Pennsylvania, killed twelve workers, and eight people died when an oil tanker exploded and burned in the Houston ship channel.[232]

In 1960, a chemical plant explosion in Kingsport, Tennessee, killed sixteen workers.[233] In 1965, a gas explosion in a missile silo at an Air Force base near Searcy, Arkansas, killed fifty-three people.[234] In 1968, seventy-eight workers died in a mine explosion in Farmington, West Virginia.[235] Amid the political upheavals of the late 1960s, labor activists demanded legislative reforms to reduce fatal occupational injuries and deaths from occupational diseases. Under intense public pressure, President Richard Nixon signed the Occupational Safety and Health Act of 1970. This law established an agency of the same name within the U.S. Department of Labor "to assure safe and healthful working conditions for working men and women by setting and enforcing standards and by providing training, outreach, education and assistance."[236] Strikingly, the Act did not establish a mechanism for accurately counting the annual number of work-related deaths.[237] In 1972, *The President's Report on Occupational Safety and Health* estimated that 14,000 workers were dying on the job each year, and about 2.2 million disabling accidents were occurring annually.[238] *The President's Report* also estimated that as many as 100,000 people were dying each year from occupational diseases, and 390,000 new cases were developing annually.[239] National Safety Council statistics

THE WORKERS HOLOCAUST   117

published since then have indicated that more than 620,000 fatal occupational injuries occurred between 1930 and 1970, and this estimate almost certainly did not include all workplace deaths.[240] Between 1930 and 1970, more than 3.3 million people likely died from work-related diseases.[241]

"The Continuing Death Roll of Industry," 1970–1990

Since 1970, the Occupational Safety and Health Act and other new legislation promoting mine safety and worker protections have helped reduce fatal occupational injuries in the United States. However, as David Rosner has pointed out, "There is a continuing 'death roll of industry.'"[242] The same year OSHA became law, an explosion at a coal mine in Hyden, Kentucky, killed thirty-eight workers.[243] In 1971, an explosion at a chemical plant in Camden County, Georgia, resulted in twenty-nine deaths.[244] In 1972, a coal slurry impoundment dam in Logan County, West Virginia, burst and killed 125 people.[245] Ninety-one silver miners died in a fire at the Sunshine Mine between the cities of Wallace and Kellogg in Idaho the same year.[246] At least sixty workers died while building the World Trade Towers in lower Manhattan before they opened in 1973.[247] Half a world away, the massive U.S. military presence in Thailand during the Vietnam War fostered the significant growth of prostitution and sex trafficking, which contributed to almost 600,000 deaths there from Acquired Immunodeficiency Syndrome between 1984 and 2008.[248] In 1976, an explosion and fire at a grain elevator in Houston killed nine workers.[249] In 1977, eighteen workers died in a flash fire at a grain elevator in Galveston.[250] The collapse of a partially constructed cooling tower at a power plant in Willow Island, West Virginia, killed fifty-one workers in 1978.[251]

In 1983, an explosion in an unlicensed fireworks factory killed eleven employees.[252] In 1984, seventeen workers died in an explosion at an oil refinery in Romeoville, Illinois.[253] The same year, a gas leak at the Union Carbide pesticide plant in Bhopal, India, became the worst industrial disaster in world history.[254] Exposure to methyl isocyanate, the toxic gas used to make the pesticides, killed about seven thousand

118   ENDLESS HOLOCAUSTS

people in the first three days and about 25,000 people since the incident.[255] In 1988 in Henderson, Nevada, a chemical plant explosion resulted in two deaths.[256] Also in 1988, 167 workers lost their lives in a gas explosion on a U.S. company's oil platform in the North Sea, and seven oil workers died in a refinery explosion or Norco, Louisiana.[257] In 1989, a gas explosion at a refinery in Pasadena, Texas, killed twenty-three workers, and an explosion on the battleship USS *Iowa* off the coast of Puerto Rico claimed the lives of forty-seven sailors.[258] As of 1990, more than ten thousand workers were still dying on the job every year.[259] National Safety Council data have indicated that more than 250,000 fatal occupational injuries occurred between 1970 and 1990, and this may well have been an undercount.[260]

Many more workers died from occupational diseases during these two decades. Some researchers have estimated that the annual number of deaths from work-related diseases declined to between fifty and seventy thousand between 1970 and 1990.[261] Other analysts and labor advocates have insisted that the loss of life each year remained approximately 100,000 during this period.[262] Milan Stone of the AFL-CIO Industrial Union Department testified in a Congressional hearing in 1985:

> The exposed worker populations include . . . 3 million workers exposed to benzene with a risk of leukemia up to five times greater than normal; 2.5 million workers exposed to asbestos, many with a risk of lung cancer five times greater than normal; 1.5 million workers exposed to arsenic, many of whom have a risk of lung cancer two to five times greater than normal; 725,000 workers exposed to chromium and chromate pigments, some with a risk of cancer five to nine times greater than normal; 1.4 million workers exposed to nickel, some of a risk of cancer 5–10 times greater than normal. Examples of other noncarcinogenic but nevertheless dangerous workplace exposures include 89 agents of heart disease . . . 1 million workers exposed to silica dust at risk of lung disease; and 800,000 workers exposed to cotton dust at risk of brown lung disease. . . . Some 100,000 die

THE WORKERS HOLOCAUST

and another 1 million may be disabled each year from occupational disease.[263]

The higher estimate is surely more accurate yet still conservative.[264] It is likely that at least two million workers died from occupational diseases between 1970 and 1990.

WORKPLACE DEATHS AND DEATHS FROM OCCUPATIONAL DISEASES, 1990–2020

Since 1990, the annual number of fatal occupational injuries has declined, but many workers continue to die on the job each year. In 1990, a chemical plant explosion in Channelview, Texas, killed seventeen workers.[265] The next year, twenty-five workers perished in a fire at a food processing plant in Hamlet, North Carolina.[266] Also in 1991, an explosion at a nitro-paraffin plant in Sterlington, Louisiana, killed eight workers.[267] In 1993, a fire at a Thai factory producing toys for U.S. companies killed 188 workers.[268] In 1998, a series of explosions at a grain elevator and storage facility in Haysville, Kansas, killed seven people.[269] In 1999, an explosion at a power plant in an automobile production complex in Dearborn, Michigan, resulted in six deaths.[270] In 2005, fifteen workers died in an explosion at a refinery in Texas City, Texas.[271] In 2006, twelve workers died in a coal mine explosion at Sago, West Virginia, and three died in a gas explosion in a gear manufacturing plant in Milwaukee.[272] Later that year, an explosion at a coal mine in Holmes Mill, Kentucky, killed five workers.[273] In 2007, two collapses at a mine in Crandall Canyon, Utah, resulted in nine deaths.[274] The following year, an explosion at a sugar refinery in Port Wentworth, Georgia, killed fourteen people, and a crane collapse in New York City killed six workers and a tourist.[275] From 2008 through 2017, 1,566 fatal occupational injuries reportedly occurred in the oil-and-gas drilling industry and related businesses.[276]

In 2010, a power plant explosion killed five workers in Middletown, Connecticut, and a coal mine explosion claimed twenty-nine lives in Montcoal, West Virginia.[277] Eleven workers died when the Deepwater

Horizon drilling rig in the Gulf of Mexico blew up the same year.[278] In 2011, a grain elevator explosion killed six workers in Atchison, Kansas.[279] In 2013, fifteen people died in an explosion at a fertilizer storage facility in West, Texas.[280] In recent years, the transfer of production to low-wage countries has enabled the U.S. Empire to outsource large-scale workplace disasters.[281] In 2010, a fire at a textile factory supplying U.S. and other multinational corporations killed at least twenty-seven workers near Dhaka, Bangladesh.[282] Nine employees of Foxconn, the electronics manufacturer that supplies several U.S. companies, committed suicide in China because of harsh working conditions the same year.[283] In 2012, a fire at a textile factory near Dhaka resulted in 112 deaths, and a fire in a clothing plant in Karachi, Pakistan, killed almost three hundred workers. Both businesses produced apparel for Walmart.[284] In 2013, approximately 1,130 people died when the Rana Plaza building, which housed garment factories supplying global brands, collapsed near Dhaka.[285] Later that year, an explosion at a factory in Ciudad Juarez, Mexico, which produced candy for U.S. companies, killed seven workers.[286] Today cobalt mining in the Democratic Republic of the Congo for U.S. and other companies leads to frequent accidental deaths and the risk of hard-metal lung disease.[287]

In 2019, about 5,333 workers died on the job in the United States.[288] Statistics from the National Safety Council and the Bureau of Labor Statistics indicate that almost 170,000 fatal occupational injuries occurred between 1990 and 2018.[289] Although 3.5 million new accidents and illnesses were officially reported in 2017, the AFL-CIO has contended that the annual number is actually between 7 million and 10.5 million.[290] Since 1990, some analysts have reported that between fifty and sixty thousand people die each year from work-related diseases.[291] For years, the AFL-CIO included similar appraisals in its annual *Death on the Job* report while warning that many occupational diseases are undetected for years and are often "misdiagnosed and poorly tracked."[292] Other investigators have concluded that the annual toll remains about 100,000, and still others have offered estimates of 200,000 to 300,000.[293] In the most recent editions of *Death on the Job*,

THE WORKERS HOLOCAUST

the AFL-CIO has estimated the annual number of deaths from occupational diseases to be approximately 95,000, and this is arguably still a conservative appraisal.[294] In sum, between 1990 and 2020, approximately three million people likely died from occupational diseases.

COUNTING THE DEAD

As with the Indigenous Peoples Holocaust and the African American Holocaust, the total number of people who have perished in the Workers Holocaust in the United States can only be estimated. The available historical information makes possible an informed and reasonable, if rough, estimate of the terrible loss of life. Since 1880, almost 13 million workers have suffered fatal occupational injuries or died from occupational diseases in this country.[295] To this number must be added the deaths of indentured servants in the colonial period; Chinese workers transported by U.S. ships to Cuba, Peru, and other countries; U.S. railroad company employees in Central and South America; laborers hired by the United States to build the Panama Canal; rubber workers in the Amazon; miners in Congo; sex workers in Thailand; and other workers employed by U.S. companies or their suppliers in various countries. When these deaths are included, the total loss of life may be close to 13.5 million. Like the Indigenous Holocaust and the African American Holocaust, the Workers Holocaust continues today.

4

From Colonial Wars to Global Holocausts

*I will not abandon my resistance until the . . . pirate invaders . . .
assassins of weak peoples . . . are expelled from my country. . . . I will
make them realize that their crimes will cost them dear. . . . There
will be bloody combat. . . . Nicaragua shall not be the patrimony
of imperialists. I will fight for my cause as long as my heart beats.*
— AUGUSTO CÉSAR SANDINO,
MESSAGE TO MEXICO CITY, 1928

The United States did not become the most powerful empire on the planet until the end of the Second World War, but its long history of wars, military interventions, and other destructive actions had already taken a dreadful human toll. The European colonial wars had left Britain as the predominant power in eastern North America, but thirteen colonies subsequently waged a successful War of Independence and became the United States. This "first new nation" then fought against France, the Barbary states, and Britain to advance its economic interests.[1] The acquisition of Florida, the annexation of Texas, and the war against Mexico substantially expanded the continental U.S. Empire.[2] In the mid-nineteenth century, the United States threatened and used violence against China, Japan, and Korea to obtain markets and began to seize islands in the Pacific and

FROM COLONIAL WARS TO GLOBAL HOLOCAUSTS 123

Caribbean.[3] The Civil War preserved the Union and ended non-penal slavery but at horrific human expense. In the following decades, the United States took control of Alaska, Hawaii, and other Pacific islands and militarily intervened in more than a dozen countries.[4] The empire fought the war of 1898 and the war against the Philippines to acquire new colonies, helped crush the Boxer Rebellion in China, engineered the creation of Panama, intervened in the Mexican Revolution, and occupied Nicaragua, Haiti, and the Dominican Republic.[5] Support for the Entente Powers during the First World War made the United States deeply complicit in this "imperial bloodbath."[6] Participation in the invasion of Soviet Russia and support for the Guomindang regime in China contributed to millions more deaths.[7] And the United States' extensive economic relations with fascist Italy, Nazi Germany, and militarist Japan—along with its political accommodation and appeasement of these countries—made it partly responsible for the unprecedented carnage of the Second World War.[8]

THE COLONIAL WARS IN NORTH AMERICA

Four wars involving Britain, France, and Spain and their colonies occurred in and near North America between 1689 and 1763. These wars for empire were part of much broader conflagrations centered in Europe and resulted in many deaths. King William's War of 1689–97 pitted the British against the French in North America and did not significantly alter the existing balance of power on the continent. Less than a thousand British and French colonists perished in the conflict, but hundreds of Native people allied with France and between two thousand and six thousand Haudenosaunees allied with Britain died.[9] During Queen Anne's War of 1702–13, Britain fought against Spain and France. The theater of war ranged from the St. Lawrence River in Canada to the island of Guadaloupe in the Eastern Caribbean. As Micheal Clodfelter has observed, this conflict "was waged half-heartedly and was interrupted frequently by long lulls."[10] More than 1,800 European soldiers, sailors, and colonists perished from Canada to the Caribbean.[11] About two thousand Apalachees, Mesquakies,

124 ENDLESS HOLOCAUSTS

and Macoutens also died.[12] The treaty that ended the war recognized British control of Acadia (Nova Scotia) and the Hudson Valley in New York.

Disputes over the new colony of Georgia and trade with South America led to the War of Jenkins's Ear between Britain and Spain in 1739.[13] A much larger war involving these two empires and other nations erupted in Europe the next year. Fighting in Georgia and Florida was limited, but 8,500 British and colonial troops died in a disastrous attack on the Spanish port city of Cartagena, Colombia, in 1741.[14] This conflict was the prelude to King George's War of 1744–48, which began when Britain and France fought over the boundaries of Acadia and northern New England. The battles there and in New York, like the hostilities in the U.S. Southeast, did not produce any major political changes. But in addition to an unknown number of deaths among Indigenous people, more than 14,000 British, French, and Spanish people died in and near North America.[15]

The French and Indian War of 1754–63 began when Britain and France sought to build a fort at the same location near present-day Pittsburgh. Different Indigenous nations fought alongside the two empires. Within two years, this conflict had become part of a war waged by several European countries on five continents. After some early French victories, the British and their Native allies seized Fort Duquesne near Pittsburgh and French strongholds in Nova Scotia and captured Quebec in 1759 and Montreal in 1760. Significant fighting occurred along the frontier as far south as South Carolina, and the related Anglo-Cherokee War of 1760–61 also took many lives.[16] In 1763, the Treaty of Paris ceded Canada and Florida to Britain and Louisiana to Spain. More than forty thousand people, including more than three thousand Indigenous people, had died on or near the continent.[17]

THE WAR FOR INDEPENDENCE

Britain's predominance in eastern North America was short-lived because subsequent actions by King George III and Parliament sparked

FROM COLONIAL WARS TO GLOBAL HOLOCAUSTS   125

mounting dissatisfaction in the thirteen colonies. Although the ensuing War of Independence is often depicted as a heroic struggle for freedom and democracy, the historical reality is much less sanguine. The Proclamation of 1763 limiting expansion into Native lands west of the Appalachians, the levying of onerous new taxes to retire war debts and fund imperial protection, and concern about what appeared to be declining British support for slavery stoked the flames of rebellion among various segments of the colonial population.[18] The capitalists and slaveholders who led the rebellion were chiefly interested in protecting and increasing their wealth and power. They looked down on the masses of small farmers and urban dwellers but were compelled to enlist their support for the revolutionary cause.[19] Although some of the common people who came to support independence hoped for egalitarian and democratic reforms, others were more interested in claiming new lands in the West for themselves.[20] Armed struggle began in 1775 when colonial militia resisted British troops' efforts to confiscate munitions in the rebellious colony of Massachusetts. The following year, the Second Continental Congress declared the independence of the United States of America.

John Adams later estimated that one-third of the colonists supported independence, one-third were "averse to the revolution," and one-third were neutral.[21] The Continental Army and colonial militias did most of the fighting for independence, but they and the British both relied on alliances with various Indigenous nations.[22] Although nine to ten thousand African Americans served with the revolutionary forces, as many as sixty thousand enslaved people fled to the British lines after Lord Dunmore promised emancipation early in the war. Thousands took up arms for Britain, and others performed labor for its forces.[23] Auxiliary troops from several German states also fought with the British and Loyalist forces. In the first years of the conflict, revolutionary forces suffered serious defeats in Canada, New York, and New Jersey. The Continental Army went on to win important battles in Trenton and Princeton, and its decisive victory in Saratoga, New York, in late 1777 helped persuade France to enter into an alliance with the new United States.[24] Spain joined the war against

126   ENDLESS HOLOCAUSTS

Britain in 1779, and Holland followed the next year. Although the conflict centered on British North America, the European belligerents also fought some battles in the Caribbean, Gibraltar, and India.[25] Only French and Spanish military intervention and economic assistance enabled U.S. forces to win the war.[26] More than 130,000 people died because of the conflict before the Treaty of Paris recognized the independence of the United States in 1783.[27]

Progressive reforms sparked by the revolution were limited.[28] "Modest, but only modest, gains" were made in voting rights, which generally continued to be limited to white men who met property or taxpaying qualifications.[29] Pennsylvania and the New England states approved the abolition of slavery, but this was gradual in most cases.[30] Mounting domestic crises were soon frightening the ruling elites. The new national government could not tax or repay those who had loaned it money during the Revolution. Nor could the government regulate currency, maintain a standing army, or override state legislatures influenced by large crowds of common people. Popular opposition to creditors' confiscation of indebted farmers' lands, imprisonment for debt, and harsh economic conditions exploded, and Shays's Rebellion in western Massachusetts raised the specter of armed rebellion against the national government.[31] In response, in 1787, a small group of capitalists, slaveholders, and politicians promulgated a new constitution that created a stronger national government with the authority to tax, repay public debts, regulate currency and interstate commerce, maintain a standing army, and suppress "insurrections" and "domestic violence."[32] The new constitution dramatically strengthened protections for property and wealth and ensured they would be beyond the reach of popular majorities.[33] As Michael Parenti has explained, it was "a constitution for the few."[34]

ENVISIONING EMPIRE

Even before the Constitution of 1787 was ratified, U.S. political leaders began to anticipate the expansion of the United States. George Washington described the new nation as "our infant empire."[35] For

FROM COLONIAL WARS TO GLOBAL HOLOCAUSTS 127

Washington, "However unimportant America may be considered at present . . . there will assuredly come a day, when this country will have some weight in the scale of Empires."[36] Alexander Hamilton believed that the United States was "the embryo of a great empire."[37] He envisioned an imperium throughout the entire Western Hemisphere when he advocated "erecting one great American system, superior to the control of all transatlantic force or influence, and able to dictate the terms of the connection between the old and the new world."[38] Thomas Jefferson wrote, "Our confederacy must be viewed as the nest from which all America, North and South, is to be peopled."[39] He hoped that the Spanish Empire could hold on to its colonies "until our population can be sufficiently advanced to gain it from them piece by piece."[40] John Jay argued that the United States should aspire to the power and prestige of the British Empire: "We have heard much of the fleets of Britain, and the time may come, if we are wise, when the fleets of America may engage attention."[41] Niall Ferguson has pointed out that "there were no more self-confident imperialists than the Founding Fathers themselves."[42]

WARS AGAINST FRANCE AND THE BARBARY STATES

Although France had been the new nation's closest ally during the War of Independence, tensions developed between the two countries within a decade. After the French Revolution began in 1789, most wealthy people in the United States were horrified by the social upheaval and challenges to property and inequality.[43] As Secretary of the Treasury, Hamilton urged President Washington to pursue closer ties with Britain, the world's leading economic power.[44] When war broke out between France and Britain in 1793, the United States abrogated its treaty of alliance with Paris, proclaimed its neutrality, and continued to trade with both countries. In response, both Britain and France seized U.S. ships, and Britain impressed U.S. sailors.[45] In 1798, the new nation fought a brief undeclared naval war against France. The logic of empire, not French interference with shipping, led to the "Quasi War." U.S. officials viewed the maintenance of trade with

128 ENDLESS HOLOCAUSTS

Britain as essential for economic development, and London quietly agreed to remove forts in the Old Northwest that impeded new U.S. settlements.[46] U.S. leaders also hoped that war with France might become "a vehicle for seizing Louisiana, the two Floridas, and parts of Latin America from Spain."[47] The naval conflict with the French resulted in about 150 deaths and ended with a diplomatic agreement in 1800.[48]

By this time, the nascent U.S. Empire was increasingly seeking opportunities for trade in far-flung parts of the world, and its merchant ships were traversing the Mediterranean. State-sponsored piracy was widespread in the area, and European countries paid an annual tribute to the Barbary States of Tripoli, Tunis, Algiers, and Morocco to guarantee the safety of their ships. The United States also paid tribute for fifteen years but fell behind in its payments; newly inaugurated President Jefferson wanted to end the practice.[49] After the ruler of Tripoli demanded larger payments and declared war on the United States, the First Barbary War of 1801 to 1805 ensued. U.S. leaders wanted to establish freedom of the seas as a recognized international principle and expand profitable commerce for their country.[50] After initial naval engagements failed to produce results, the United States assembled a substantial mercenary army and plotted to replace the government of Tripoli with a friendlier regime—both firsts in U.S. history.[51] In 1805, the ruler in this city-state agreed to end attacks on U.S. ships and was allowed to remain in power, but the U.S. government still had to pay a ransom for the release of captured citizens.[52] Approximately a thousand people, mainly North Africans, died in the conflict.[53]

THE ACQUISITION OF THE LOUISIANA TERRITORY
AND THE WAR OF 1812

Early in his presidency, Jefferson acquired the vitally important port city of New Orleans. Agricultural produce, pelts, and finished goods from the western part of the United States were often transported on the Mississippi River and stored in the city before being shipped to

FROM COLONIAL WARS TO GLOBAL HOLOCAUSTS 129

markets.[54] Since 1763, Spain had controlled the Louisiana Territory, which "stretched from the Gulf of Mexico to Canada, and from the Mississippi River to the Rocky Mountains."[55] Spain had allowed U.S. vessels free passage and the right to store cargo in New Orleans, but this arrangement ended when Spain ceded the entire Louisiana Territory to France in 1802.[56] Concerned that Napoleon would deploy French troops to secure New Orleans and threaten U.S. commerce, Jefferson in 1803 sent representatives to Paris to negotiate the purchase of the city. At the time, French forces were desperately trying to crush the Haitian Revolution, and Napoleon urgently needed money for another war against Britain. U.S. diplomats were pleasantly surprised to learn that the First Consul of France was prepared to sell the entire Louisiana Territory, and they agreed to pay $15 million for the 828,000 square miles.[57] The Louisiana Purchase nearly doubled the size of the United States.[58] Neither the Indigenous people nor the people of African descent who lived there were asked how they felt about this "real estate transaction."[59] Jefferson dispatched troops to New Orleans to suppress local resistance to U.S. annexation, preserve slavery, assert authority over Indigenous people, and defend against foreign intervention.[60]

The War of 1812 is often depicted as a "Second War of Independence," but the conflict resulted from Washington's quest for new markets and territory.[61] The economic imperative of exporting surplus agricultural products had become clear.[62] While the Napoleonic Wars raged in Europe, exports to British and French markets produced what Sidney Lens has called an unprecedented "economic bonanza" for the United States.[63] However, the belligerents' economic warfare inevitably ensnared this country, as it had in the previous decade. Both France and Britain began seizing U.S. ships, the British continued to impress U.S. sailors, and occasional naval hostilities erupted.[64] In 1807, Congress passed the Embargo Act prohibiting trade with all foreign countries. The new law led to a severe economic depression, widespread public discontent, and growing sectional differences.[65] Congress replaced the Embargo Act with a more limited prohibition of trade with Britain and France in 1809, but concerns

130   ENDLESS HOLOCAUSTS

about British naval power continued, and expansionist sentiment led to growing calls for the conquest of Canada and the Floridas.[66] In 1810, U.S. nationals who had settled in West Florida rebelled against the Spanish authorities there, and two years later, President James Madison dispatched troops to seize portions of Spanish East Florida.[67] The persistence of disputes with Britain and mounting land hunger led to war in 1812.[68] The conflict was a "total and monumental failure" for the United States.[69] Not only did British forces capture and burn the White House, but when the fighting ended in 1815, the United States had won no new territory and no guarantee of an end to British naval interference.[70] Control of much of East Florida reverted to Spain.[71] The war had claimed close to forty thousand U.S., British, and Indigenous lives.[72]

Continental Expansion and Overseas Interventions, 1815–1830

In the decades that followed, the United States continued to expand its continental empire and increasingly pursued markets and resources around the world. A large naval force deployed by Madison in 1815 killed scores of people in the brief Second Barbary War, which finally ended interference with U.S. ships by North African states.[73] In 1818, Jackson invaded East Florida, defeated the Spanish, and battled local Indigenous people in the First Seminole War. Spain ceded the Florida Territory to the United States the next year.[74] By the early 1820s, trade with China was bolstering the U.S. economy despite the absence of any bilateral treaty. U.S. merchants were shipping furs, Spanish silver dollars, sandalwood, and ginseng to the Middle Kingdom— along with opium from Turkey.[75] Although the British dominated the odious trade, the United States accounted for 20 to 30 percent of opium imports to China.[76] In late 1821, U.S. colonists began arriving in present-day Texas with the approval of the newly independent Mexican government. While authorities there hoped this arrangement would deter U.S. expansionism, many of the settlers looked forward to annexation by Washington at some point.[77] That same year,

FROM COLONIAL WARS TO GLOBAL HOLOCAUSTS 131

the American Colonization Society established the colony of Liberia for formerly enslaved African Americans.[78] In 1823, President James Monroe declared, "The American continents . . . are henceforth not to be considered as subjects for future colonization by any European powers."[79] As Paul L. Atwood has noted, the Monroe Doctrine unambiguously signaled that the U.S. Empire would do "what it insisted Europeans could not."[80]

Between 1822 and 1825, U.S. naval vessels repeatedly engaged pirates in or near Cuba. The pirates' chief offense was raiding Spanish slave ships and selling Black captives at prices much lower than those charged by wealthy U.S. citizens in Cuba.[81] In 1824, two hundred Marines attacked the town of Fajardo in Puerto Rico for sheltering pirates and insulting U.S. officers.[82] In 1827, the U.S. Navy attacked Greek pirate vessels that had interfered with merchant ships.[83] In 1831–32, it used force to free three seal-hunting ships seized by an Argentinian official for unauthorized intrusion on the Malvinas Islands.[84] Hundreds of people died because of U.S. actions in these four countries.[85] In 1832, after pirates plundered a merchant ship and killed three crew members near Kuala Batu in Sumatra, a U.S. naval vessel killed about 150 pirates in the area and then burned the town, killing more than 300 civilians.[86] This was the first U.S. military attack in Asia. Washington also sent armed forces to Argentina in 1833 and Peru in 1835–36, ostensibly to protect U.S. lives and property during unrest.[87] Subsequent attacks on Kuala Batu and Mukki in Sumatra and in Fiji, Samoa, and Drummond's Island killed scores, if not hundreds, of people.[88] Some U.S. actions followed aggression by local pirates or opposition to U.S. merchants or explorers. But implicit in this pattern of military intervention, as Lens has observed, was "the notion that strong powers have the right to violate the sovereignty of weak powers when they feel that the interests of their nationals are affected."[89]

THE ACQUISITION OF HALF OF MEXICO AND
THE OPENING OF CHINA

Presidents John Quincy Adams and Andrew Jackson tried to purchase the area now known as Texas from Mexico in the 1820s and early 1830s but were unsuccessful.[90] Yet mounting tensions between U.S. colonists and the Mexican government foreshadowed crisis and conflict. Many settlers had come from the southern United States and had brought enslaved people with them. When the Mexican government enforced its prohibition of slavery in Coahuila y Tejas and outlawed further immigration from the United States in 1830, most settlers were outraged.[91] The rise of the new centralist government under President Antonio López de Santa Anna further infuriated them. In 1835, the colonists launched an armed rebellion against their adopted country. Although they proclaimed their love of freedom and opposition to tyranny, their insurgency was largely motivated by the government's actions on slavery and new immigration.[92] The rebellion lasted six months and led to more than 2,200 deaths and the creation of the Republic of Texas, an independent country that officially enshrined white supremacy and slavery in its new constitution.[93] Although many citizens of the new country hoped to become part of the United States, sectional differences over the expansion of slavery and fear of a potential war with Mexico delayed the U.S. annexation of Texas for nine years.

When Britain fought China in the First Opium War in 1839–42, the United States did not join the conflict. But U.S. merchants temporarily took over much of the opium trade until the end of the war.[94] Britain's victory led to a treaty recognizing its right to continue the opium trade, providing access to five port cities, and granting other concessions. The United States was determined to obtain a treaty with the same rights and concessions, and President John Tyler's administration named U.S. Representative Caleb Cushing as envoy to China.[95] Cushing informed Washington that "fleets and armies" would be required to compel acquiescence, and he arrived with four warships in China in 1844.[96] Although Emperor Mianning had already contemplated the advantages of treaties affording other countries the same privileges as Britain, he did not appoint an imperial ambassador to meet with Cushing for months.[97] Cushing told a local Chinese official that refusal to receive a foreign ambassador could

FROM COLONIAL WARS TO GLOBAL HOLOCAUSTS 133

be considered grounds for war by some nations, and a U.S. warship's twenty-one-gun salute near Canton was likely viewed as "a less-than-subtle suggestion of gunboat diplomacy."[98] It was "under the shadow of their guns and Cushing's threats of a second war" that the Chinese government agreed to a treaty with the United States.[99]

The United States annexed Texas as its twenty-eighth state in 1845. The following year, President James Polk negotiated a treaty in which Britain ceded much of the Oregon Territory. The eleventh president launched a war against Mexico after its government refused to sell California to the United States. Frederick Douglass, U.S. Representative Abraham Lincoln, and many others in the United States opposed the conflict.[100] But Polk's war was supported by southern politicians and planters who desired the expansion of slavery and by northern and western interests, which shared John O'Sullivan's view that it was "our manifest destiny to overspread the continent allotted by Providence for the free development of our yearly multiplying millions."[101] By early 1848, the United States had won the war. As many as 64,000 people, primarily Mexicans, died during the conflict.[102] Mexico was forced to give up its claims to Texas and cede territory that later became the states of California, Nevada, and Utah, along with large parts of present-day Arizona and New Mexico and smaller parts of what are now Colorado and Wyoming.[103] The Mexican Cession of 1848 cost Mexico 55 percent of its national territory.[104] The U.S. Empire now reached "from sea to shining sea."[105]

OVERSEAS INTERVENTIONS AND THE OPENING OF JAPAN, 1850–1860

Although the Americo-Liberians declared their country's independence in 1847, Washington did not grant them diplomatic recognition for another fifteen years. In the decades that followed, the United States did not develop close economic ties with Liberia, but its frequent military interventions kept the Americo-Liberian elite in power and effectively made the country a protectorate.[106] By the middle of the nineteenth century, U.S. whalers and missionaries had

134   ENDLESS HOLOCAUSTS

come to play an important role in Hawai'i, and some were already calling for annexation by Washington.[107] Some U.S. officials, slaveholders, and capitalists wanted to annex Spanish Cuba, and Polk was willing to pay up to $100 million for the island.[108] After Madrid refused to part with its colony, southern slaveholders financed two filibuster expeditions led by former Spanish military officer Narciso López to foment revolution and seize power. His invasions of Cuba in 1850 and 1851 were a total failure and resulted in the deaths of several hundred people.[109] Spanish forces apprehended and executed López in Havana in 1851.[110] That same year, the USS *Dale* arrived at Johanna Island off the coast of Africa and demanded the release of a U.S. whaling ship captain imprisoned for an unauthorized supply stop there the previous year. After the *Dale* bombarded the island's main fort, the captain was freed, and the local authorities signed a commercial treaty with the United States.[111] Three years later, the residents of Greytown, Nicaragua, tried to arrest a commercial U.S. ship captain and the U.S. ambassador after the captain murdered a local fishing boat owner. In response, a U.S. naval vessel bombarded and destroyed Greytown, though no loss of life was reported.[112]

In the 1850s, the U.S. objective of obtaining guano for fertilizer led to the acquisition of Howland Island, Baker Island, Jarvis Island, and Johnston Atoll in the Pacific Ocean and Navassa Island in the Caribbean.[113] Over time, Washington claimed more than one hundred islands under the Guano Islands Act, though it eventually abandoned most of these claims.[114] Keenly aware of the growing need for new markets and resources, Commodore Matthew Perry wrote in 1852 that "our people must naturally be drawn into the contest for empire."[115] Several years earlier, Japan had rejected a U.S. effort to obtain a commercial treaty. For Perry, both "the honor of our nation" and "the interest of our commerce" required that the Land of the Rising Sun open itself to trade and business relations with the U.S. Empire.[116] In 1853, Perry arrived in Japan with four warships and a letter from President Millard Fillmore demanding the establishment of economic relations. However, the Japanese politely declined. The next year, Perry returned with nine warships, and Japanese officials

FROM COLONIAL WARS TO GLOBAL HOLOCAUSTS 135

felt compelled to allow the United States to open a diplomatic office and access two ports where its ships could be refueled with coal. However, Japan did not open its markets to this country until complete diplomatic relations were established and a formal commercial treaty was signed four years later.[117]

Despite the continued British presence in Nicaragua, U.S. interest in the country remained strong. After the acquisition of California and the discovery of gold there, the commercial value of a canal across Central America greatly increased; Nicaragua was one possible site for this project. Some influential U.S. leaders even supported the annexation of the country.[118] In 1855, a California business owner whose mining interests in Nicaragua were imperiled by local unrest hired an adventurer named William Walker to intervene in the conflict and protect his investments. After arriving with several dozen men in Nicaragua, Walker seized power, made himself dictator, reestablished slavery, and persuaded President Franklin Pierce to recognize his government.[119] Walker was strongly backed by some capitalists and was viewed as a hero by Southern slaveowners, but his confiscation of Cornelius Vanderbilt's property in Nicaragua led the railroad and shipping magnate to financially support armies from Costa Rica, El Salvador, Guatemala, and Honduras committed to ousting Walker.[120] These armies defeated the adventurer's forces, and he was forced to flee Nicaragua in 1857. Walker tried unsuccessfully to return to Nicaragua later that year and in 1858 and 1860. In his last attempt, he was captured in Honduras and executed. Walker's invasions had resulted in the deaths of approximately ten thousand people.[121]

In 1854, the United States sent warships to China, ostensibly to protect its interests during the Taiping Rebellion, a civil war between 1850 and 1864 that killed between twenty and forty million people.[122] When Chinese government forces occupied the Westerners' racetrack in Shanghai, U.S. and British troops attacked them. Approximately three hundred Chinese soldiers died in the assault, and two U.S. military personnel were killed.[123] Britain and the United States became angry over mounting Chinese opposition to the existing treaties, and both empires sought even larger concessions.[124] After Britain

136 ENDLESS HOLOCAUSTS

launched the Second Opium War on a flimsy pretext in 1856, U.S. sailors and Marines landed in Canton and destroyed five ports on the Pearl River, killing as many as five hundred Chinese defenders.[125] France joined Britain in the prosecution of the war, but the United States soon pledged to remain neutral. However, in 1859 U.S. naval forces assisted British vessels engaged in an unsuccessful attack on forts at Taku, leaving 450 British and French military personnel dead or wounded.[126] After the Chinese surrendered in 1860, the United States benefitted from "hitchhiking imperialism" again when it won expanded commercial rights in the Middle Kingdom.[127] In the decades that followed, trade did not increase as much as some U.S. merchants expected. U.S. imports of opium declined, but Christian missionaries continued to arrive. Washington would maintain a military presence in China until the People's Republic was founded in 1949.[128]

THE CIVIL WAR IN THE UNITED STATES

By 1860, the mounting sectional economic and political tensions over slavery had become irreconcilable. The wealth produced by enslaved Black people was the primary means of primitive accumulation facilitating the rise of industrial capitalism in the lands that became the United States.[129] For generations, the entire U.S. economy had been deeply implicated in this ongoing crime against humanity. But the growing incompatibility of Northern capitalists' need for "free labor" and Southern slaveholders' need to expand the "peculiar institution" westward arguably made the Civil War inevitable.[130] Founded in 1854, the Republican Party embraced the former and opposed the latter, and its candidate, Abraham Lincoln, was elected president in November 1860.[131] Soon afterward, the Southern states began to secede and formed the Confederate States of America, which was committed to preserving slavery and white supremacy. In April 1861, the Confederacy began the Civil War by attacking and defeating federal forces at Fort Sumter, South Carolina. The federal government's original objective was preserving national unity, not the immediate or near-term abolition of slavery.[132] But within two years, the growing

FROM COLONIAL WARS TO GLOBAL HOLOCAUSTS 137

casualties, the unpopularity of the conflict and military conscription, and the need to enlist African American troops transformed the Union's war efforts into a crusade "to make men free."[133]

In May 1865, the last major Confederate army unit surrendered, and the Civil War ended. A Confederate sympathizer had assassinated Lincoln the previous month, and the human costs of the war were enormous: the Superintendent of the 1870 Census estimated that at least 850,000 men had died during the conflict.[134] But the destruction of records made it difficult to assess the extent of Confederate losses, and after 1900 the loss of life in the war was widely estimated to be about 620,000.[135] In 2011, the demographer J. David Hacker announced that new microdata samples from censuses between 1850 and 1880 indicated that as many as 850,000 people died because of the war.[136] In 2012, historian Jim Downs pointed out that Hacker's new computations did not include the deaths of enslaved people killed by soldiers or the much larger number of African American deaths from disease in the Union camps to which half a million had fled.[137] As Downs emphasized, "If former slaves were included in this figure, the Civil War death toll would likely be over a million casualties."[138]

THE ACQUISITION OF ALASKA AND OVERSEAS INTERVENTIONS, 1860–1880

At the same time the U.S. government was fighting against the Confederacy, it continued to wage war on Indigenous peoples at home and to intervene in other countries. After the Emperor of Japan ordered an end to trade with the West and the expulsion of foreigners in 1863, the United States joined Britain, France, and the Netherlands to force Japan to allow foreign shipping in the Straits of Shimonoseki. The USS *Wyoming* sank two Japanese vessels, killing at least forty Japanese sailors and losing five military personnel in the process.[139] The next year, the *Wyoming* was part of a larger Western fleet that decisively defeated Japanese resistance and resulted in additional deaths.[140] In 1865, Washington sent troops to the Department of Panama in Colombia, putatively to protect U.S. property and lives during civil strife.[141] In the decade and a half that followed, the U.S. Empire acquired more territory, pursued new foreign markets and resources, and increasingly sent its armed forces to intervene in other countries around the world.

In 1866, the *General Sherman*, a heavily armed merchant ship, attempted to compel Korea to trade with the United States. The crew defied Korean orders to leave, kidnapped a local official, and killed a dozen people before being wiped out.[142] In 1867, Washington purchased Alaska and the Aleutian Islands from Russia and took formal possession of Midway Island in the Pacific. During the last half of the decade, U.S. military forces also intervened in China, Mexico, Nicaragua, Japan, Uruguay, and Colombia on the pretext of defending national interests.[143] In 1869, President Ulysses Grant and many members of Congress wanted to annex Santo Domingo to acquire naval ports, project military power, and defend a possible future canal across Nicaragua. But the treaty of annexation failed to secure a two-thirds majority in the Senate. As Robert Kagan has acknowledged, some political leaders could not countenance "adding the darker-skinned population of Dominicans to the already large population of African-Americans."[144] Like Polk, Grant also wanted to purchase Cuba from Spain, but this never happened, partly because other officials did not think the island's population could be assimilated and partly for other political reasons.[145] The Grant administration deployed troops to Mexico and Colombia on multiple occasions, ostensibly to protect U.S. property and citizens.[146]

Rapidly intensifying industrial development and agricultural production in the post–Civil War years contributed to what Fareed Zakaria has called "a truly stunning pace" of U.S. economic growth.[147] Leading capitalists, politicians, and military leaders increasingly recognized the dependence of the U.S. economy on the unceasing acquisition of new foreign markets and resources.[148] They viewed the "bottomless markets of Asia" as indispensable for the future of the empire, even as they sought to expand their reach in the Caribbean, Central America, and South America.[149] In 1871, five U.S. warships sailed to Korea to exact revenge for the *General Sherman* incident and force the Hermit Kingdom to accept commercial relations. U.S.

FROM COLONIAL WARS TO GLOBAL HOLOCAUSTS 139

forces killed about 350 people but failed to secure an agreement with the Korean government.[150] A commercial treaty with Korea was not signed for more than a decade.[151] By 1874, U.S. capitalists had come to dominate economics and politics in Hawai'i, and troops were deployed to suppress protests against the election of a new king friendly to U.S. business interests.[152] In 1877, the United States acquired Pago Pago in Samoa and later used its port as a coaling station and naval base.[153]

OVERSEAS INTERVENTIONS, 1880–1890

In 1879, a nationalist rebellion erupted in Egypt. Many Egyptians opposed the British and French colonial presence and a local government that accepted European control of the Suez Canal. In 1882, after about fifty Europeans were killed in rioting, British warships and gunboats bombarded Alexandria, and British troops attacked Egyptian positions. More than 2,100 Egyptians were killed, as were more than one hundred British soldiers.[154] About 150 U.S. sailors and Marines were deployed early in the conflict and they became the first foreign troops to enter the center of Alexandria. The number of Egyptians killed by U.S. forces is unknown but was likely substantial.[155] In 1885, amid civil war in Colombia, Marines guarded the assets of the U.S.-owned Panama Railroad and helped armed men organized by a French canal company to apprehend and execute at least fifty-eight people accused of looting.[156] Washington sent six hundred Marines and sailors to reopen the railroad and secretly instructed the naval commander to identify possible sites for naval bases.[157] One New York journalist embedded with U.S. forces described the Colombians as "savages" and reported that "almost every night, the American pickets shoot a few of the outlaws."[158]

In 1887, a group composed primarily of U.S. businessmen and politicians who supported the annexation of Hawai'i forced King Kalākaua to relinquish most of his power and accept voting reforms that ended the dominance of the Native majority.[159] Members of a militia aligned with the annexationists compelled the king's acceptance of the "Bayonet Constitution" at gunpoint.[160] Two years later,

140   ENDLESS HOLOCAUSTS

U.S. troops landed in Hawai'i to help suppress a popular rebellion that sought to rescind this constitution, bring Princess Lili'uokalani to the throne, and restore Indigenous rule.[161] Several insurgents died, chiefly at the hands of the pro-U.S. militia.[162] In 1888, six years after a commercial treaty had been signed with Korea, troops landed there to safeguard U.S. citizens during political unrest.[163] U.S. capitalists hoped to exploit the Hermit Kingdom's gold mines and other mineral wealth and were eventually able to do so for decades.[164] Germany tried to gain control of all the Samoan islands by installing an ally as king in 1887. However, Samoans successfully repulsed the German forces that landed the following year. A powerful typhoon destroyed some of the German, U.S., and British warships on the scene in 1889. Fifty-one U.S. military personnel and three times that number of Germans died in the storm.[165] Soon afterward, the three empires reached an agreement to divide control of the islands among them.[166]

    In 1888, as an insurgency challenged a new government in Haiti, the United States demanded a naval base and authority to diplomatically represent the country in Europe. After the Haitian government rejected this demand, Washington provided arms, ammunition, transportation, and naval support to the rebels.[167] When the Haitian government seized a U.S. merchant ship that was supporting the insurgents, the Secretary of State sent warships to secure the captured vessel's return.[168] With Washington's significant assistance, the insurgency was victorious, and its leader became the new president of Haiti. The number of Haitian deaths during this rebellion remains unclear even today, but U.S. officials were deeply complicit in this tragedy. Ironically, under pressure from the Haitian people, the new government also refused U.S. entreaties for a naval base, even after Washington sent its most powerful ships to Port-au-Prince.[169]

THE ACQUISITION OF HAWAI'I AND OVERSEAS INTERVENTIONS,
1890–1898

During the 1880s and 1890s, the size and strength of the U.S. economy reached new heights. The United States surpassed Britain in

FROM COLONIAL WARS TO GLOBAL HOLOCAUSTS   141

manufacturing in 1885 and became the largest steel producer in the world.[170] By 1890, this country consumed more energy than Britain.[171] Within a few years, the United States replaced Britain as the world's largest economy.[172] In addition to their ongoing agricultural exports, U.S. businesses had begun to ship steel, iron, oil, and agricultural machinery to foreign markets.[173] The export of capital had begun as well.[174] In the 1890s, many political and business leaders followed Frederick Jackson Turner in believing that the end of the frontier in North America required new forms of expansionism abroad.[175] As Washington pursued predominance in the Western Hemisphere and a significant role in Asia and the Pacific, support grew for developing a large modern navy to facilitate its increasingly global commerce.[176] This entailed the increased need for far-flung coaling and naval stations, so by the end of the decade, the empire would acquire vital new territories in the Caribbean, Asia, and the Pacific.

U.S. military forces were sent to Argentina to protect business interests in 1890 and uphold claims to Navassa Island in the Caribbean in 1891.[177] U.S. and British naval forces boarded and expelled dozens of merchant ships suspected of seal poaching near the Aleutian Islands in 1891.[178] When civil war broke out in Chile the same year, Washington did not send troops to fight for the pro-U.S. government, but dispatched warships to prevent the delivery of arms to the insurgents. U.S. forces also cut the rebels' international telegraph line, shared information on their troop movements with the regime, and provided asylum to government officials after the insurgents won the war.[179] The United States was partly responsible for the loss of more than six thousand lives in this conflict.[180] After the civil war ended, deep resentment of Washington's intervention and a deadly bar fight between U.S. sailors and Chileans in Valparaiso almost led to war between the two countries.[181]

In 1893, Queen Lili'uokalani, who had ascended to the Hawaiian throne after her brother's death, moved to restore Native power and concentrate authority in her hands. U.S. business owners and politicians quickly overthrew her with the approval and support of the U.S. ambassador. At the ambassador's request, 160 Marines landed to

142   ENDLESS HOLOCAUSTS

assist the insurgents and protect the new government.[182] The settlers named Sanford Dole as president and requested annexation by the United States. President Benjamin Harrison wanted Hawai'i because of its strategic location, the importance of the military base established at Pearl Harbor, and the islands' sugar and rice.[183] However, political opposition at home prevented the ratification of an annexation treaty.[184] The next president, Grover Cleveland, bluntly admitted that the new government in Hawai'i "owes its existence to an armed invasion by the United States. By an act of war . . . a substantial wrong has been done."[185] Nonetheless, five years after the coup, President William McKinley won congressional approval for the islands' annexation despite strong opposition from most Native Hawaiians.[186]

Although the overthrow of the Queen of Hawai'i was virtually bloodless, Washington's intervention in the Brazilian Civil War of 1893–95 was not. In defense of a friendly regime and growing commercial interests in the country, the United States sent warships to break the insurgents' blockade of Rio de Janeiro, threatened to fire on rebel vessels, and provided vital supplies to the government.[187] Washington's support for the regime was decisive in defeating the insurgency and contributed to the deaths of between ten and twelve thousand people.[188] The United States also sent troops to Nicaragua four times in the 1890s.[189] Washington was committed to protecting a "projected isthmian canal route," defending the U.S. banana export business there, and replacing the British as the dominant imperialist power in the country.[190] The number of Nicaraguans who died during these interventions was never recorded.

In 1895, the U.S. government successfully demanded that Britain submit to arbitration in its dispute with Venezuela over the boundaries of British Guiana. Britain's claims were almost completely affirmed later, but Secretary of State Richard Olney declared: "Today the United States is sovereign on this continent and its fiat is law upon the subjects to which it confines its interposition."[191] That same year, Senator Henry Cabot Lodge boasted, "We have a record of conquest, colonization, and territorial expansion unequaled by any people in the nineteenth century."[192] And the century had not ended yet.

FROM COLONIAL WARS TO GLOBAL HOLOCAUSTS   143

The War of 1898 and the War Against the Philippines

After the Cuban War of Independence began in 1895, reports of Spanish atrocities and Cuban deaths aroused sympathy among many people in the United States. However, U.S. investors were generally more concerned with protecting their business interests in Cuba and restraining revolutionary forces that included many poor and Black people.[193] Some business owners and policymakers clamored for a war against Madrid that would deliver Cuba and the Philippines and other Spanish colonies into U.S. hands.[194] The United States had been an empire since its birth, but its emergence in 1898 as the world's leading economic power led to a brutal new chapter in its history. As a *Washington Post* editorial proclaimed early that year:

> A new consciousness seems to have come upon us—the consciousness of Strength—and with it a new appetite, the yearning to show our strength. . . . Ambition, interest, land hunger, pride, the mere joy of fighting, whatever it may be, we are animated by a new sensation. We are face-to-face with a strange destiny. The taste of Empire is in the mouth of the people even as the taste of blood in the jungle.[195]

In contrast, many socialists, workers, and progressive intellectuals opposed war against Spain and imperialism in general.[196]

When Spain proved unable to end the rebellion in Cuba, the United States moved closer to war. McKinley dispatched the U.S. battleship *Maine* to Havana, sending a clear message of disapproval of Spanish actions on the island. In February 1898, a mysterious explosion sank the ship and killed 260 members of its crew.[197] A hastily called investigation in the United States suggested the explosion had been caused by a mine, though the explosion likely resulted from internal causes.[198] Two months later, Congress declared war on Spain. The United States struck Spanish forces in the Philippines in late April and in Cuba in May, took possession of Guam and Wake Island in June, and invaded Puerto Rico in July. Spain was quickly defeated, an

144   ENDLESS HOLOCAUSTS

armistice was signed in August, and a peace treaty was approved in December.[199] U.S. victory over Spain did not lead to sovereignty and self-determination for Madrid's former possessions. Instead, Puerto Rico, Guam, and the Philippines became U.S. colonies, and Cuba became a U.S. protectorate.[200] Washington also annexed Wake Island. The War of 1898 substantially enlarged the U.S. Empire, and Secretary of State John Hay called the conflict "a splendid little war."[201] However, the conflict resulted in more than 22,000 deaths.[202]

The resistance to U.S. authority was limited in Cuba and Puerto Rico, but the people of the Philippines continued to fight for independence. Washington sent more than 126,000 troops to impose control, but the conquest of the Philippines required a much longer and bloodier war than the one just concluded.[203] U.S. soldiers soon became notorious for killing Filipino freedom fighters in combat, torturing and executing prisoners, murdering vast numbers of civilians of all ages, and engaging in rape.[204] Cholera and other diseases took a great many lives, as did hunger and privation in concentration camps into which many Filipinos were herded.[205] U.S. troops' war crimes, crimes against humanity, virulent racism, and complete disregard for human life led one analyst to describe the war against the Philippines as "America's first Vietnam."[206] Other analysts have pointed out that the United States was doing to the Filipinos on a larger scale exactly what it had done to Indigenous peoples at home.[207] Although the main revolutionary army led by Emilio Aguinaldo was defeated in 1902, other Filipino forces continued to fight the United States, and the Moro resistance in the southern part of the country was not defeated until 1913.[208] The first large-scale U.S. imperialist war in Asia exacted a catastrophic human toll. As many as one million Filipinos perished from war, genocidal violence, disease, and famine.[209]

THE ACQUISITION OF EASTERN SAMOA AND SUPPRESSION OF
REBELLION IN CHINA

At the same time the U.S. Empire was laying waste to the Philippines, it was engaging in other military interventions in Asia and the

FROM COLONIAL WARS TO GLOBAL HOLOCAUSTS   145

Americas. In 1899, the decade-old tripartite protectorate in Samoa disintegrated as different chieftains fought to control the islands. U.S. and British forces intervened and killed scores of Samoans.[210] Washington assumed control of the eastern islands and annexed American Samoa the following year.[211] Also in 1899, popular opposition to foreign domination of China erupted. Although Washington had insisted on a "Closed Door" policy in Latin America for three-quarters of a century, it had demanded an "Open Door" and equal access to Chinese markets and was part of the International Settlement at Shanghai.[212] The insurgents known in the West as the Boxers killed about thirty thousand Chinese Christians and several hundred missionaries and other foreign nationals.[213] Widespread support for the rebellion led Empress Cixi to embrace their cause, but the imperialists refused to let the Chinese people determine their own future. U.S. troops joined armed contingents from seven other countries in crushing the uprising in 1900–1901.[214] U.S. forces also participated in the pillaging of Beijing and the extraction of humiliating new commercial concessions from the Chinese government.[215] Hundreds of soldiers from the imperialist countries and local allies died fighting the Boxers and Chinese government forces.[216] Tens of thousands of insurgents, Chinese government forces, and Chinese civilians died at the hands of U.S. and other foreign troops.[217]

INTERVENTION IN COLOMBIA AND THE CREATION OF PANAMA

Between 1899 and 1902, U.S. troops repeatedly intervened on behalf of Colombia's conservative government during the civil war known as the War of a Thousand Days.[218] Washington was increasingly anxious to obtain a treaty allowing the construction of a canal in the Department of Panama, where much of the conflict was being fought. When liberal insurgents were on the verge of seizing the important city of Colón, the government sought U.S. assistance to keep the Panama Railroad open. The commander of the nearby U.S. gunboat *Iowa* subsequently threatened the insurgents with the deployment of Marines, preventing an insurgent victory there at the time.[219] When

146 ENDLESS HOLOCAUSTS

the rebels later gained control of most of Panama, the government requested Washington's intervention again, and U.S. Marines prevented the rebels from capturing Colón and Panama City. The United States deployed troops on railroad cars and a U.S. naval commander informed the insurgents that only U.S. troops could occupy or use the railroad.[220] These actions were decisive in defeating the insurgency, and the rebels were forced to sign a peace treaty aboard the USS *Wisconsin*.[221] About 120,000 people had perished in the civil war, and although the Colombian belligerents bore primary responsibility for most of these deaths, Washington had also contributed to this massive loss of life.[222]

Shortly after the civil war in Colombia ended, the U.S. government began to press Bogotá for a canal treaty. The conservative-dominated Colombian Senate appreciated Washington's support during the recent conflict but found the terms of the proposed treaty inadequate and unanimously rejected it.[223] President Theodore Roosevelt's administration openly castigated the Colombian government for its decision, and U.S. newspapers called for secession or revolution in Panama.[224] As Howard Zinn has explained, in late 1903, Roosevelt "engineered a revolution against Colombia and created the 'independent' state of Panama to build and control the Canal."[225] U.S. troops prohibited Colombian soldiers from using the railroad to reach Panama City, and U.S. warships on both sides of the isthmus prevented the Colombian armed forces from suppressing the revolution.[226] Washington quickly recognized the new nation and soon had a treaty establishing U.S. control of a ten-mile-wide Panama Canal Zone and allowing U.S. intervention to protect the canal.[227] As Lars Schoultz has emphasized, "The United States had seized control over the single most valuable piece of Latin America's territory."[228] Roosevelt later reportedly boasted that "I took the Canal Zone."[229] The Panama Canal was built between 1904 and 1914 at great human expense. The new nation remained a U.S. protectorate until 1939, and U.S. control of the Canal Zone was not relinquished until 1999.[230]

FROM COLONIAL WARS TO GLOBAL HOLOCAUSTS   147

New Interventions and Occupations in the Western Hemisphere

In a presidential address in 1904, Roosevelt announced that the U.S. government had the authority to exercise "an international police power" in countries in the Western Hemisphere that were guilty of "chronic wrongdoing or impotence."[231] The United States had been intervening in the Caribbean, Mexico, Central America, and South America for almost a century, and the so-called Roosevelt Corollary to the Monroe Doctrine sought to legitimize future imperialist actions.[232] Privately, Roosevelt wrote that he eschewed "the desire for aggrandizement" but insisted, "It is our duty, when it becomes absolutely inevitable, to police these countries in the interest of order and civilization."[233] Roosevelt soon decided that Caribbean and Central American countries' inability to repay foreign loans justified U.S. intervention. The United States took control of finances in the Dominican Republic in 1904.[234] In 1908, the U.S. Navy provided vital assistance to a coup in Venezuela led by Vice President Juan Vicente Gómez. For the next twenty-seven years, Gómez and his supporters butchered many people but maintained Washington's support by granting massive concessions to Standard Oil of New Jersey, Gulf Oil Company, Royal Dutch Shell, and other Western oil companies.[235] In 1910, Marines landed in Nicaragua to help insurgents overthrow the government. The new regime immediately allowed U.S. banks to take control of the country's national bank, customs collections, and railroads.[236] The empire was moving to consolidate its domination of the Americas.[237]

After taking control of Cuba, the U.S. government required the island's new constitution to recognize its authority to militarily intervene on the island as necessary and to acquire territory for a naval base. Most U.S. troops withdrew in 1902, and the following year Washington leased forty-five square miles of land and water for a naval base at Guantánamo Bay.[238] In the first two decades of the new

148   ENDLESS HOLOCAUSTS

century, the United States deployed troops to Cuba three times to maintain friendly regimes and suppress popular opposition. One of those interventions occurred in 1912 when U.S. soldiers helped crush an uprising by Cuban sugar workers of African descent. Between three thousand and six thousand lives were lost during the rebellion.[239] That same year, U.S. armed forces intervened in Panama and Honduras and invaded Nicaragua to support the weak new conservative government it had previously helped bring to power.[240] The occupation of Nicaragua continued until 1933. More than two thousand people died during the initial invasion, and many more died in subsequent years.[241] After Washington repeatedly demanded that Haiti surrender control of its customs collection, Marines landed there in 1914, took half a million dollars out of the national bank, and delivered it to the National City Bank in New York.[242] The United States invaded Haiti the next year and occupied that country until 1934. Approximately 15,000 Haitians died, many in combat against U.S. troops and the Haitian *Garde* they established, and many others in forced labor camps built by the occupiers.[243]

The United States invaded the Dominican Republic in 1916 amid insurgency and financial instability and occupied that country until 1924. More than eleven hundred Dominicans died at the hands of U.S. forces.[244] Eventually, widespread resistance and armed struggle forced the invaders to leave Nicaragua, Haiti, and the Dominican Republic.[245] At the same the United States was invading and occupying these three countries it was assuming broad powers over Liberia's finances and military force as well, reinforcing its status as "a virtual colony."[246] Still deeply impoverished a decade later, Liberia agreed to lease up to one million acres to Firestone Rubber Company for ninety-nine years.[247] In 1917, Washington purchased what became known as the U.S. Virgin Islands from Denmark.

Intervention in the Mexican Revolution

When the people of Mexico rose up against the thirty-four-year-old dictatorship of José de la Cruz Porfirio Díaz Mori in 1910, U.S.

FROM COLONIAL WARS TO GLOBAL HOLOCAUSTS 149

capitalists and government officials reacted with trepidation. U.S. banks and businesses owned vast amounts of Mexico's land and controlled most of its oil, minerals, and railroads.[248] The previous year, President William Howard Taft had met with Díaz in El Paso and had subsequently written, "It is inevitable in case of a revolution or internecine strife that we should interfere."[249] When Francisco Ignacio Madero González led the uprising against Díaz and forced him into exile, the Taft administration and leading business interests feared that the revolution could jeopardize these investments.[250] Madero, who was elected president in 1911, came from a wealthy family and was no radical. He aimed to develop a liberal democratic state and reconcile the interests of the old and new sections of the capitalist class.[251] However, Madero's government was unable to pacify the former supporters of the Díaz dictatorship or suppress the popular struggle for agrarian and social transformation led by the forces of Emiliano Zapata Salazar and Francisco "Pancho" Villa.[252] As a result, Washington repeatedly intervened in Mexico during the next decade to support friendly forces, limit the changes brought about by the revolution, and safeguard U.S. economic interests.

Taft's ambassador to Mexico helped former Díaz supporters and other conspirators organize the overthrow of Madero and his replacement by General Victoriana Huerta in 1913.[253] This putsch led to the execution of Madero and many other deaths and sparked a new wave of armed resistance among liberal bourgeois reformists and more revolutionary-minded urban workers and rural laborers.[254] When it became clear that Huerta favored British, not U.S., oil interests, President Woodrow Wilson turned against him. After initially embracing Villa, Wilson began supporting the reformists led by José Venustiano Carranza de la Garza.[255] In 1914, U.S. warships prevented the delivery of arms shipments to Huerta's forces at Veracruz and Tampico. The warships shelled Veracruz, killed hundreds of people, occupied the city for seven months, and enabled the reformists to reach Mexico City before Zapata's forces could.[256] General Smedley Butler later acknowledged that he had "helped make Mexico, especially Tampico, safe for American oil interests."[257] Huerta was ousted,

150 ENDLESS HOLOCAUSTS

and Carranza's growing military campaign against the armies of Zapata and Villa earned him U.S. withdrawal from Veracruz, diplomatic recognition, arms and ammunition, and renegotiation of debts in 1915.[258] As Niall Ferguson has explained: "The Carranza regime was nothing if not a product of American policy."[259] After Washington stopped shipping arms to Villa, he attacked Columbus, New Mexico. General John J. Pershing invaded Mexico with six thousand soldiers in 1916. Villa was never captured, but a year of intermittent conflict significantly weakened his forces.

By 1917, Carranza's support for reforms in the new Mexican constitution and the deepening split between urban and rural laborers produced what James Cockcroft has called "a triumph for the liberal wing of bourgeois democracy."[260] The two most prominent leaders of the movement for revolutionary social change were assassinated in the years that followed. Carranza's agents killed Zapata on the way to what was supposed to be a peace conference in 1919. Both the Mexican government headed by Alvaro Obregón, Carranza's successor, and the U.S. government were involved in the murder of Villa in 1923.[261] The elimination of Villa appears to be one of the conditions Washington demanded in exchange for recognition of the Obregón regime.[262] Between 1910 and 1920, almost two million people died during the Mexican Revolution, and the United States was deeply complicit in this carnage.[263] Moreover, policymakers were willing to take other military actions to safeguard capitalist interests in Mexico. In 1919–20, U.S. military analysts developed "Special Plan Green," which called for an invasion of Mexico to "protect" its oil fields or confront problems along the border. The plan envisioned the eventual replacement of occupying troops by a "native Mexican constabulary."[264] Signally, "Special Plan Green" remained on the shelf until 1942, when Mexico entered the Second World War on the Allies' side.[265]

THE U.S. ROLE IN THE FIRST WORLD WAR

The U.S. Empire also shared responsibility for the unprecedented global holocaust that contemporaries called the Great War. Oliver

FROM COLONIAL WARS TO GLOBAL HOLOCAUSTS   151

Stone and Peter Kuznick explained that "Europe was awash in imperial rivalries" as the new century unfolded.[266] Germany's growing industrial, financial, and military strength posed a significant challenge to Britain, and the rising continental power sought to acquire new colonies in Africa to rival those of London and Paris. All three countries wanted to obtain new lands and oil in West Asia from the declining Ottoman Empire, while the Austro-Hungarian Empire and the Russian Empire competed for power in the Balkans.[267] The assassination of Austrian Archduke Franz Ferdinand and his wife, Sophie, by a Serbian nationalist in Sarajevo in July 1914 led to the outbreak of hostilities. But it was not the cause of the war between the Central Powers—Austria-Hungary, Germany, and Turkey—and the Entente Powers—Britain, France, Italy, Russia, and Japan. As Vladimir Lenin wrote, this was an imperialist war, "an annexationist, predatory war of plunder on the part of both sides; it was a war for the division of the world, for the partition and repartition of colonies and spheres of influence of finance capital."[268] Wilson told his ambassador to Britain that the cause of the war was "England's having the earth and Germany's wanting it."[269] Wilson "carefully omitted the fact that the corporate and political elites of the United States wanted it too."[270] Years later, the president publicly admitted that this had been "a commercial and industrial war."[271]

In August 1914, soon after the war began, Wilson issued a proclamation of neutrality. He declared that the United States would remain "impartial in thought as well as in action."[272] Two years later, his reelection campaign emphasized the slogan: "He kept us out of war."[273] Yet as Atwood explained, "Wilson merely pretended neutrality while his policies were carrying the country inexorably into the war."[274] In fact, the United States strongly supported the Entente during most of the conflict. Five months after the war began, J. P. Morgan and Company became the sole authorized financial agent for Britain and France in the United States. Over time, Morgan arranged about $3 billion in contracts with exporters.[275] Lens observed that "the United States became the Allied source for food; raw materials such as copper, iron ore, zinc, cotton, lumber, wool, oil; as well as munitions." [276] The value

152   ENDLESS HOLOCAUSTS

of annual U.S. munitions exports rose from $6 million in 1914 to $1.7 billion between January 1916 and March 1917, and the E. I. du Pont de Nemours company provided the Entente with 40 percent of their ammunition during the war.[277] The United States also provided essential financial assistance. Morgan loaned Britain and France $500 million in 1915 alone, and U.S. bank loans to the Entente eventually totaled $2.5 billion.[278] While death and destruction swept across Europe and parts of Asia, the Pacific, and Africa, the U.S. economy dramatically recovered from the deep recession of 1913–14, and its industry, agriculture, and trade expanded in a historically unprecedented manner.[279]

By early 1917, the Entente faced a gravely deteriorating military and economic situation, mutinies among French troops, and mounting demands in Russia for an end to the war.[280] German submarines were increasingly successful at sinking military and merchant ships near Britain and the Entente's dwindling collateral and gold progressively limited its ability to make vital purchases in the United States.[281] In March 1917, U.S. Ambassador to Britain Walter Hines Page warned the State Department that the dramatic reduction of Entente orders and transatlantic trade would produce an economic panic in this country.[282] U.S. officials and capitalists feared that the loss of access to war materials and other goods would lead to the Entente's defeat, the inability of Britain and France to repay their loans, catastrophic financial losses for Morgan and other U.S. banks and businesses, and the weakening of the entire economy.[283] Hines advised, "It is not improbable that the only way of maintaining our preeminent trade position and averting a panic is by declaring war on Germany."[284] Other officials warned that a victorious, dominant Germany might close European markets to U.S. products and threaten growing U.S. hegemony in the Western Hemisphere.[285] In addition, Wilson now wanted a major role in shaping the postwar international order to ensure that it promoted U.S. interests and contained the threat of workers' revolutions in other countries.[286]

In April 1917, Wilson asked Congress for a declaration of war and obtained it. Germany's renewed attacks on U.S. ships delivering

FROM COLONIAL WARS TO GLOBAL HOLOCAUSTS   153

supplies to the Entente and German aspirations for an alliance with Mexico merely provided a pretext for Wilson's action.[287] As he later told the Senate Foreign Relations Committee, the United States would have entered the war even "if Germany had committed no act of injustice against our citizens."[288] Nor did the United States go to war because "the world must be made safe for democracy."[289] None of the belligerents were very democratic, and Wilson's racism, anti-worker politics, and military interventions in the Americas made clear he was no advocate of democracy.[290] Ferguson has remarked that after the United States officially entered the war, "it was Morgan as much as Britain which was bailed out."[291] Washington directly loaned the Entente Powers vast sums. U.S. banks and businesses made even greater profits, and the U.S. economy grew faster.[292] The arrival of U.S. forces in Europe helped to turn the tide of battle, and an armistice was signed in November 1918.[293] Unlike the other warring countries, the United States emerged from the conflagration much richer and stronger than before. It had become a creditor nation, and New York City had replaced London as the world's financial center.[294] After taking over British, German, and other investments, Washington had become "the unchallenged monarch of the Western hemisphere."[295] Indeed, the U.S. Empire was now a major imperialist power. Approximately thirty million people had died in this "imperial bloodbath."[296]

THE INVASION OF SOVIET RUSSIA

Many workers around the world welcomed the October Revolution in Russia in 1917.[297] But the ruling classes of the leading capitalist countries shared Winston Churchill's determination to "strangle the Bolshevik infant in its cradle."[298] U.S. Secretary of State Robert Lansing wrote that the communists' commitment "to make the ignorant and incapable mass of humanity dominant on the earth" threatened the "existing social order and all countries."[299] In August 1918, the United States and thirteen other nations invaded Soviet Russia. About twelve thousand U.S. soldiers were deployed to

154 ENDLESS HOLOCAUSTS

Vladivostok and Archangel, where they killed Bolsheviks and their allies and supported counterrevolutionary White Russian forces and other foreign troops.[300] Washington shipped rifles, machine guns, and other military supplies worth hundreds of millions of dollars to the White armies. The United States also sent them food, clothing, and other so-called humanitarian aid, while workers and peasants starved in large numbers.[301] The masses of Russian workers and peasants rallied to the Bolshevik cause, and by 1919, the White armies had suffered devastating losses and were entirely dependent on foreign aid.[302] Washington withdrew the last of its troops in 1920 but provided substantial aid to the Polish militarists' invasion of Soviet Russia that same year.[303] The counterrevolution was defeated by late 1922. About nine million people died during the civil war and related famine, and the United States significantly contributed to this ghastly loss of life.[304]

WASHINGTON WELCOMES FASCISM IN ITALY

Workers' uprisings inspired by the October Revolution erupted in Germany, Hungary, Finland, and other European countries but were violently suppressed. In Italy, during the Biennio Rosso of 1919–20, Italian workers seized factories, poor farmers occupied rural estates, mass strikes and demonstrations grew, and armed struggle between militant workers and fascists began.[305] In the two years that followed, fascist fighters backed by industrialists and large landowners killed several thousand communists, socialists, anarchists, and others.[306] Officials in Washington bemoaned the Italian government's inability to crush the workers' movement and generally welcomed the fascist leader Benito Mussolini's rise to power in 1922.[307] Many of these officials agreed with the boast of Italy's ambassador to Washington that his was "the first nation to have the courage to conquer Bolshevism."[308] Prominent political leaders, major business interests, the Catholic Church, the American Legion, and a considerable number of citizens in the United States soon came to support fascism in Italy.[309] By 1930, Washington had favorably resolved Italy's war

FROM COLONIAL WARS TO GLOBAL HOLOCAUSTS 155

debt, and U.S. companies had loaned Italy more than $460 million and invested another $400 million in the country.[310] U.S. arms and military supplies flowed to the fascist dictatorship despite its violent domestic repression and killing hundreds of thousands of people in colonized Libya.[311] *Time* and *Fortune* were "unabashed supporters of Mussolini."[312] The *New York Times*, the *Washington Post*, the *Wall Street Journal*, and other major U.S. publications praised Mussolini for rescuing Italy from revolution and chaos.[313]

Supporting Dictatorship and Preventing Revolution in the Americas

Between 1927 and 1933, U.S. occupation forces killed about five thousand Nicaraguans during the rebellion led by Augusto Sandino.[314] Before withdrawing its troops, the United States created the Nicaraguan National Guard and appointed Anastasio Samoza García as its leader. Four years later, Washington supported Samoza's seizure of power, which ushered in four decades of dynastic rule that killed approximately fifteen thousand people.[315] U.S. officials did not bring Rafael Trujillo to power in the Dominican Republic in 1930 but soon began sending weapons and money to his military dictatorship. Support for Trujillo continued during the next three decades while as many as sixty thousand Dominicans and Haitians died at the hands of the regime.[316] In 1932, the U.S.-backed military dictator in El Salvador, General Maximiliano Hernández Martínez, oversaw *La Matanza*, the massacre of thirty thousand Pipil people and communists.[317] In 1934, even as U.S. troops withdrew from Haiti, officials in Washington pressured Colonel Fulgencio Batista y Zaldívar to overthrow the new president of Cuba, Ramón Grau San Martín, who had criticized U.S. colonialism and promised "Cuba for the Cubans."[318] Batista ruled for several years through puppet presidents, spent some time away from politics, and then returned to power. By the time the Cuban Revolution triumphed twenty-five years later, well over twenty thousand people had died at the hands of Batista and his henchmen.[319]

156   ENDLESS HOLOCAUSTS

Backing the Guomindang Regime in China

The U.S. government recognized Jiang Jieshi's new Guomindang regime in China in 1928. During the next decade, Washington provided significant support to the dictatorship despite its harsh repression and campaign to exterminate the Chinese Communist Party forces vying for control of the country.[320] U.S. companies developed the country's civilian aviation, electrical industry, and telephone system. Washington provided a substantial loan to purchase wheat and cotton and purchased a massive quantity of Chinese silver to help stabilize its currency.[321] Although U.S. officials wanted to expand investments and influence in the Middle Kingdom, most wanted to avoid provoking Japan. Washington enjoyed a much larger commercial relationship with Tokyo, had long recognized its substantial interests in China, and wanted to accommodate Japanese expansion in mainland Asia. This posture continued after Japanese troops seized Manchuria in 1931, attacked Shanghai in 1932, and took control of much of northern China.[322] Like fascist Italy and Nazi Germany, the United States was more interested in helping the Guomindang consolidate power and kill communists than assisting with the ouster of Japanese forces. U.S. companies sold Jiang airplanes, tanks, guns, munitions, and other military equipment, and U.S. nationals trained Chinese air force pilots who bombed communist-held areas.[323] The civil war was suspended in 1937, when dissent among the nationalists forced Jiang to accept the communists' proposal for a united front against Japan. About two million people had died in what turned out to be only the first part of the Chinese Civil War.[324]

The U.S. Welcome of Nazism in Germany

A sizeable number of U.S. government officials and capitalists welcomed Adolf Hitler's appointment as Chancellor in Germany in 1933. David F. Schmitz has noted that the State Department never praised Hitler "in the same manner as it did Mussolini," partly because of Germany's "greater military potential" and concern about possible

FROM COLONIAL WARS TO GLOBAL HOLOCAUSTS   157

Nazi aggression, and partly because of the Nazis' virulent anti-Semitism.[325] But U.S. ambassador to Germany Frederic Sackett spoke for many when he stated, "From the standpoint of stable political conditions, it is perhaps well that Hitler is now in a position to wield unprecedented power."[326] Sackett and others feared that the failure of the Nazi regime would "open the door to communism in Germany."[327] George Gordon, the U.S. *chargé d'affaires* in Berlin, viewed Hitler as the leader of a "moderate" section of the Nazi Party, "which appeal[s] to all civilized and reasonable people."[328] U.S. ambassador to Italy Breckinridge Long urged President Franklin Roosevelt to meet Nazi demands for resources and territorial expansion to prevent war.[329] Long argued that while German domination of Europe would be "hard and cruel," it would be preferable to the "westward progress of Russia."[330] The Roosevelt administration shared this perspective, viewing the Nazi Reich as another right-wing dictatorship that could serve as a bulwark against communism while maintaining normal economic relations with other major imperialist powers.[331] During the next several years, the Roosevelt administration sought to accommodate and appease the Nazis and refused to publicly criticize them when they imprisoned communists and socialists, banned labor unions, murdered hundreds of German Jews in the *Kristallnacht*, annexed Austria, and invaded part of Czechoslovakia.[332]

Many U.S. companies had made large investments in Germany and entered business partnerships with German firms in the 1920s, and continued to do business there after the Nazis came to power.[333] Jacques R. Pauwels remarked, "The German dictator and his fascist ideas were particularly liked and admired by the owners, managers, and shareholders of those American enterprises."[334] U.S. business investments in Germany totaled about $475 million by late 1941.[335] Major U.S. investors included DuPont, General Motors, Ford, Standard Oil of New Jersey, Texas Oil Company, General Electric, International Business Machines, International Telephone and Telegraph, Union Carbide, Westinghouse, Goodrich, Singer, Eastman Kodak, and Coca-Cola.[336] Brown Brothers Harriman, Union Banking Corporation, Chase National Bank, National City Bank of New York,

J. P. Morgan, and Dillon, Read and Company provided banking services for the Reich.[337] As Bradley W. Hart has pointed out, "It was not just profit motives and business opportunities that drove American corporate bosses into the arms of the Nazis."[338] Henry Ford, William Randolph Hearst, Irénée DuPont, Alfred Sloan, Torkild Rieber, Sosthenes Behn, and other major capitalists were "motivated by genuine affinities for Nazism."[339] Many people in the United States opposed Hitler, but Charles Lindbergh, Father Charles Coughlin, the German American Bund, and the Silver Legion mobilized support for the Nazis.[340] Some U.S. newspapers criticized Hitler's mounting repression at home and aggression abroad, but Hearst newspapers, the Associated Press, the *National Geographic*, and other publications presented positive appraisals of Hitler's regime.[341]

The Invasion of Ethiopia and the Fascist Coup in Greece

After Mussolini's forces invaded Ethiopia in 1935, Washington condemned the aggression and ended arms sales to Italy but rejected British and French calls for an oil embargo.[342] Instead, U.S. companies significantly increased their exports of oil, copper, iron, and other materials to Italy, which were necessary for its conquest of Ethiopia.[343] Some policymakers justified this direct economic support for the Italian invasion as necessary to avoid alienating Mussolini and preventing Il Duce from launching a broader war in Europe.[344] The lives of Ethiopians did not matter much more in Washington than they did in Rome. More than 760,000 people died in this colonialist war and occupation, and vital economic support for Italy made the United States partly responsible for this massive loss of life.[345] When the fascist general Ioannis Metaxas overthrew the republic and assumed dictatorial powers in Greece in 1936, U.S. officials welcomed this development as another blow against communism.[346] The next year, a State Department report presented a class-based analysis of fascism:

> When there is suffering, the dissatisfied masses, with the example of the Russian revolution before them, swing to the Left. The

FROM COLONIAL WARS TO GLOBAL HOLOCAUSTS 159

rich and middle classes, in self-defense, turn to Fascism. . . . It must succeed or the masses, this time reinforced by the disillusioned middle classes, will again turn to the Left.[347]

Policymakers' fear of a "turn to the Left" drove many U.S. business and political leaders to help ensure that fascism succeeded in European countries.[348]

SUPPORT FOR THE FASCIST INSURGENCY IN SPAIN

When Spaniards abolished the monarchy and established a republic in 1931, U.S. policymakers voiced concern that this was the first step toward radical social change.[349] After five years of political turbulence and a new election that significantly strengthened republicans and leftists, General Francisco Franco and the Spanish army launched a fascist insurgency. State Department officials, business owners, and U.S. Catholic Church leaders who had opposed the republic's progressive reforms voiced support for the uprising.[350] Deep political divisions among anti-fascist forces hampered the struggle against the insurgents, and Italy and Germany sent more than eighty thousand military personnel along with airplanes, tanks, and other military aid to Franco's forces.[351] The Soviet Union provided military and economic aid to the Spanish government, and the International Brigades of volunteers from other countries fought alongside republican forces. Many people in the United States supported the Spanish government but the Roosevelt administration, citing the Neutrality Acts, refused to send weapons to Madrid.[352]

However, as in Ethiopia, the United States was hardly neutral. General Motors, Ford, and Studebaker sold the fascists twelve thousand trucks, almost three times the number provided by Italy and Germany, and Firestone sold them tires.[353] The Texas Oil Company ended its relationship with the Spanish government and shipped oil instead to Franco's forces, largely on credit. This company, Standard Oil of New Jersey, Shell, and other U.S. firms provided three-quarters of the oil, gasoline, and aviation fuel required by the fascists.[354]

DuPont sold Germany forty thousand bombs to use in Spain.[355] Washington's denial of arms to Madrid and U.S. companies' economic support helped Franco's forces to prevail in 1939.[356] As one official in the fascist regime later explained, "Without American petroleum and American trucks and American credit, we could never have won the Civil War."[357] Roosevelt later expressed regret for his position on Spain, but his change of heart came too late.[358] Approximately half a million people died in the civil war and its aftermath, and the fascist victory in Spain paved the way for the outbreak of the Second World War in Europe.[359]

U.S. Imperialism and the Origins of the Second World War

For the past seventy-five years, the Second World War has been routinely depicted as the "Good War."[360] Most people in the United States have been taught to believe that Washington entered this war to defend freedom and democracy against the aggression of the Axis Powers. But this is a myth, as Zinn, Atwood, Pauwels, and other researchers have emphasized. The Second World War was just as deeply rooted in imperialist rivalries as the First World War, although Germany's invasion of the Soviet Union made the defense of the world's first socialist state a genuinely progressive, anti-imperialist struggle.[361] The United States' significant economic relations with fascist Italy, Nazi Germany, and militarist Japan and its political accommodation and appeasement of these countries—even after they invaded other countries and killed vast numbers of people—made the U.S. Empire deeply complicit in the destruction wrought.[362] Only when the Japanese Empire and the Nazi Reich threatened U.S. economic interests in Asia and Europe did Washington move toward war. Atwood points out that the United States entered the war "to preserve the mainstay of American foreign policy—the Open Door to the resources, markets, and labor power of the territories that were threatened with closure."[363] People worldwide welcomed every new blow struck against the Axis Powers, but the U.S. Empire fought to advance its own interests and subjugate competing empires.[364]

FROM COLONIAL WARS TO GLOBAL HOLOCAUSTS   161

Although U.S. officials accepted Japan's conquest of vast stretches of China in the early 1930s, they gradually became concerned by Tokyo's unmistakable intention to take control of Asian resources and markets dominated by the Western empires.[365] Still, U.S. policymakers and capitalists valued the lucrative commercial relations with Japan. The sale of aircraft, trucks, machine tools, oil, steel, scrap iron, and other products generated substantial profits for U.S. businesses but also decisively contributed to the growing power of Tokyo's war machine. Indeed, what David Bradley has called Japan's "Western-style military-industrial complex" was built with oil and steel largely imported from the United States.[366] V. G. Kiernan has pointed out that Japan's devastating invasion of China in 1937, which marked the beginning of the Second World War in Asia, relied "very largely on oil and steel bought from America."[367] As many as 800,000 Chinese people died at the hands of Japanese troops by the end of that year.[368] Washington condemned the invasion, and some policymakers began to develop contingencies for a future war against Tokyo.[369] Nonetheless, U.S. firms continued to do business with Japan while its Imperial Army killed millions more in China during the next few years. U.S. companies sent Japan more than 57 percent of its imported war materials in 1938 and provided about 80 percent of its oil until mid-1941.[370]

However, Japan's plans for further expansion and the development of a "Greater East Asia Co-Prosperity Sphere" were increasingly problematic for the U.S. Empire. In the mid-1930s, more than half of all raw materials imported into the United States came from Asia.[371] Washington would not allow Tokyo to interfere with the Open Door policy.[372] In 1939, the United States ended its commercial treaty with Japan, moved its Pacific fleet from San Diego to the Pearl Harbor naval base in Hawai'i, and strengthened its air and naval forces in the Philippines.[373] Roosevelt knew he was forcing Japan to choose between permanent subordination to the United States and Britain or go to war.

After the Pacific Fleet commander warned that Tokyo would view recent U.S. military actions in the Pacific as a dangerous provocation,

162   ENDLESS HOLOCAUSTS

Roosevelt said, "Sooner or later, the Japanese would commit an overt act against the United States, and the nation would be willing to enter the war."[374] In the summer of 1941, after Japan invaded the resource-rich French colony of Indochina, the United States froze its assets there and cut off shipments of oil, scrap iron, and technology.[375] In late November 1941, the U.S. government gave Japan an ultimatum to withdraw its troops from China and Indochina, knowing its rulers would not comply.[376] Less than two weeks later, Japanese forces attacked Pearl Harbor, killing more than 2,400 military personnel and civilians. As Atwood has explained, this was the "spark" but "not the cause" of the U.S. entry into the Second World War.[377]

U.S. capitalists also played a crucial role in Germany's rearmament and its subsequent wars of aggression and crimes against humanity. Brown Brothers Harriman and the Union Banking Corporation bought and shipped gold, steel, coal, fuel, and U.S. treasury bonds to Hitler's regime.[378] General Motors and Ford manufactured many of the tanks, motor vehicles, and airplanes without which the *blitzkriegs* could not have occurred.[379] Standard Oil and Texaco sold the Germans oil and airplane fuel, which were indispensable for the war effort.[380] ITT sold the Nazis not only telephones, switchboards, radio equipment, field communication sets, and radar equipment but also "fuses for artillery shells" and "ingredients for the rocket bombs that fell on London."[381] Charles Higham has noted: "Without this supply of crucial materials, it would have been impossible for the German Air Force to kill American and British troops, for the German army to fight the Allies, for England to have been bombed, or for Allied ships to have been attacked at sea."[382] IBM sold the Nazis punch-card technology, which was used to identify, track, imprison, and execute Jews and other enemies of the Reich.[383] As Edwin Black has pointed out, "The infamous Auschwitz tattoo began as an IBM number."[384] Some U.S. businesses continued to meet German military needs even after war between the two countries began.[385]

Although existing U.S. investments in Germany were increasingly profitable, overall trade between the two countries declined, and Berlin ended its most favored nation agreement with Washington.[386]

FROM COLONIAL WARS TO GLOBAL HOLOCAUSTS 163

U.S. officials gradually began to fear potential German domination of Europe, the part of the world where the U.S. Empire was most heavily invested. Continental autarky would deny the United States access to essential markets, resources, and labor and facilitate the production of low-cost goods by the Reich and its vassal states. This was unacceptable to U.S. ruling circles, as were prospects for expanded German influence in oil-rich West Asia and South America.[387] After the Nazis invaded Poland in September 1939 and Britain and France declared war, Roosevelt announced that the United States would not enter the conflict. But he quickly persuaded Congress to revise the Neutrality Acts so the United States could provide weapons and financial assistance to Britain.[388] In 1940, Congress instituted the first peacetime military conscription in U.S. history, began constructing military aircraft and ships on a massive scale, and adopted the Lend-Lease Act. In 1941, U.S. naval forces began assisting British warships and engaging German vessels in the North Atlantic.[389] After Congress declared war on Japan in December 1941, Germany issued its own declaration of war on the United States, and Congress quickly reciprocated.

How the U.S. Empire Fought "The Good War"

Notwithstanding its lofty proclamations, the Roosevelt administration joined the war against the Axis Powers to promote the interests of the U.S. Empire. Gabriel Kolko has explained, "The American economic war aim was to save capitalism at home and abroad."[390] U.S. political and business leaders aimed to defeat the economic threat posed by Japan and Germany, emerge as the preeminent empire on the planet, "Americanize" the global economic system, ensure greater access to foreign resources and markets, and contain the threats of socialism and decolonization.[391] Barely one month after the United States entered the war, the director of the Council on Foreign Relations wrote that U.S. forces must secure areas "strategically necessary for world control" after victory.[392] In May 1942, the Council's Security Subcommittee of the Advisory Committee on Postwar Foreign Policy,

164   ENDLESS HOLOCAUSTS

which was working closely with the State Department, emphasized the need to develop "a mental view toward world settlement after this war which will enable us to impose our own terms, amounting perhaps to a Pax Americana."[393]

Although Washington found itself in an alliance with the Soviets, its long-standing willingness to work with fascists and opposition to communists shaped its conduct during the war. After U.S. troops defeated the Vichy French forces in North Africa in 1942, they installed the fascist collaborator Admiral Francois Darlan as ruler.[394] In 1943, after U.S. and British troops invaded Sicily and the Fascist Grand Council deposed Mussolini, Washington approved the retention of power by the fascist collaborators King Victor Emmanuel and Marshal Pietro Badoglio.[395]

Signally, the Soviet Union did most of the fighting against the Nazis.[396] Despite repeated promises to Soviet leader Joseph Stalin, Roosevelt joined British prime minister Winston Churchill in refusing to open a second front against the Germans in Western Europe until June 1944. It was not military constraints but the willingness to let the communist-led country bear the brunt of the war against Germany that explained the two-and-a-half year delay in launching this front.[397] This delay contributed to the loss of millions of Soviet soldiers and civilians.[398] The United States and Britain finally decided to invade Normandy in June 1944 because the Red Army was inexorably advancing toward victory over the Nazis, and neither Washington nor London could countenance the communists becoming the sole liberators of Western Europe.[399]

After communist-led resistance forces drove German occupation forces out of Greece in 1944, Churchill installed a new provisional regime and demanded that the prewar fascist collaborator King George II be returned to the throne.[400] In December 1944 and January 1945, British troops and local allies crushed a popular uprising against the new government and the prospective return of the monarch, resulting in thousands of deaths.[401] Despite initial misgivings, Roosevelt largely supported Churchill's actions and shared his objective of containing the communists in Greece.[402] The U.S.

FROM COLONIAL WARS TO GLOBAL HOLOCAUSTS 165

government backed bourgeois opposition forces instead of popular resistance forces led by communists in several other occupied countries.[403] To ensure its economic predominance in the postwar world, Washington engineered the Bretton Woods agreement in 1944, which established a new global monetary system centered on the U.S. dollar and created the institutions that became the U.S.-dominated International Monetary Fund and World Bank.[404]

The Roosevelt administration's claim that it was fighting for freedom and democracy was belied by its actions at home. Although people of color and women played an important role in the war effort, white supremacy and male domination remained firmly entrenched. African Americans still suffered from racist oppression and remained unable to vote throughout the South. U.S. military forces were rigidly segregated during the war.[405] The Red Cross even separated the blood donations of Blacks and whites.[406] Some Mexican American service members killed abroad could not be buried in white cemeteries at home.[407] In addition, Roosevelt's Executive Order 9066 authorized the imprisonment of 120,000 U.S. citizens and residents of Japanese descent.[408] Racist war propaganda promoted a "profound hatred" toward all people in Japan, depicting them as "vermin, cockroaches, rattlesnakes, and rats."[409] Washington's long-standing refusal to accept Jewish refugees continued throughout most of the war. Only about 21,000 were admitted to the United States and some members of the House of Representatives "spewed anti-Semitic vitriol" in opposing proposals to allow more to enter the country. Socialists who opposed participation in the war were imprisoned, and other dissenters were sometimes beaten, tortured, or killed by mobs.[410] The United States was certainly not a fascist dictatorship, but it shared, to a degree, some of the vile features of the Axis Powers it fought against.

Washington and London were willing to kill an extraordinary number of civilians during the conduct of the war. The "strategic" bombing of Japanese and German cities between 1943 and 1945 resulted in approximately one million civilian deaths.[411] In April 1945, Hitler committed suicide as the Soviets entered Berlin, and German

166 ENDLESS HOLOCAUSTS

armies began surrendering. The following month, while the Allied Powers celebrated the end of the war in Europe, French forces killed about forty-five thousand Algerians and seven thousand Tunisians demanding independence.[412] Washington shared responsibility for these atrocities because it had "saved the North African possessions for France and had re-established French domination over them," and had provided the weapons, equipment, and training used by the French forces.[413]

In August 1945, U.S. airplanes dropped atomic bombs on Hiroshima and Nagasaki. As many as 210,000 civilians died immediately or in the following months.[414] Scores of thousands more died from radiation poisoning in later years.[415] The atomic bombings were not needed to end the war in the Pacific; the Japanese government was already moving toward surrender. Instead, the new U.S. president, Harry Truman, wanted to intimidate the Soviet Union and demonstrate his willingness to use this new weapon to advance U.S. interests in the postwar world.[416] In mid-August, the U.S. government announced the partition of Korea and moved to occupy South Korea to prevent a popular communist movement from coming to power.[417] Truman also demanded that Japanese forces in Asia and the Pacific surrender to "politically acceptable military forces," not "local leftist-led Resistance movements."[418]

THE UNITED STATES BECOMES THE MOST POWERFUL EMPIRE IN
THE WORLD

On September 2, 1945, Japan's formal surrender ended the Second World War. Eighty million people had died in the global holocaust, and much of Europe and Asia was devastated.[419] However, the United States had achieved its objective of becoming the most powerful empire in the world.[420] The challenges to the prewar international order by Japan, Germany, and Italy had been defeated. The British and French empires were economically crippled, and though they would recover, they would lose most of their colonies and never regain their former power.[421] The Soviet Union, which

FROM COLONIAL WARS TO GLOBAL HOLOCAUSTS   167

had liberated much of Europe from the Nazi Reich, had suffered the greatest loss of life and widespread devastation. In stark contrast, the United States sustained fewer casualties and far less damage than the other belligerents. It had also become the wealthiest country in the world.[422] War production had finally brought the Great Depression to an end and generated extraordinary profits and capital accumulation.[423]

Industrial production had increased about 15 percent annually during the war, and exports more than doubled.[424] By the end of the war, the United States produced 50 percent of the world's goods and services and held 75 percent of the world's invested capital and 67 percent of global gold reserves.[425] A member of Britain's House of Lords observed that the United States "has been left by the war rich beyond her dreams."[426] In addition, Washington now dominated an "Americanized" global economic system and was also the only country with atomic weapons. Walter Lippmann wrote: "What Rome was to the ancient world, America is to be to the world of tomorrow."[427] He showed no awareness of the bloodshed and brutality that had been required to maintain Pax Romana—or would be necessary to maintain Pax Americana.

COUNTING THE DEAD

U.S. wars, military interventions, and other destructive actions between 1775 and 1898 resulted in almost 1.3 million deaths, most of which occurred in the Civil War. The global expansion and gradual ascendancy of the U.S. Empire between 1898 and 1945 led to an extraordinary escalation of carnage and destruction. The war against the Philippines, the intervention in the Mexican Revolution, and the invasion of Soviet Russia implicated Washington in approximately 12 million deaths. U.S. support for the Guomindang regime in China, fascist Italy's colonization of Libya and war against Ethiopia, and the fascist insurgency in Spain contributed to about 3.5 million fatalities. The United States also shared responsibility for 110 million lives lost in the First and Second World Wars. Altogether, the U.S. Empire was responsible or shared responsibility for approximately 127 million deaths between 1775 and 1945. Tragically, many would die at the hands of the United States, its client states, and allied forces in the decades that followed the Second World War.

5

The Holocausts of Pax Americana I

*We were waging a people's war—à la manière Vietnamienne.
America's sophisticated arms, electronic devices, and all the rest
were to no avail in the end. In war there are the two factors—
human beings and weapons. Ultimately, though, human beings
are the decisive factor. Human beings! Human beings!*

—GENERAL Võ NGUYÊN GIÁP,
INTERVIEW WITH STANLEY KARNOW, 1990

Although the United States emerged from the Second World War as the world's preeminent empire, its plans for a Pax Americana faced formidable challenges. The Soviet Union would recover from its wartime devastation, communist-led revolutions were beginning in other countries, and scores of colonized nations were demanding independence. U.S. officials and capitalists worried that these developments could jeopardize their access to markets and resources and undermine economic and political stability at home.[1] During the next thirty-five years, the U.S. Empire expanded its economic penetration of other countries, developed a large system of client states, and established a vast network of military bases worldwide.[2] Supporters have long claimed that the postwar liberal international order generally preserved peace and promoted prosperity. But Sidney Lens was right to note that Pax Americana is "global imperialism [that] unfolded from the inner logic of America's new status," and its consequences have been catastrophic for most of the globe.[3] Since 1945 the United States has fought several major wars, launched proxy wars, routinely attacked countries, overthrown and installed governments, destroyed popular movements, assassinated foreign leaders, engaged in economic sabotage, and supported its allies' violent domestic repression and acts of war against other nations.[4] The only country to use atomic bombs, the United States deployed nuclear weapons around the world, developed ominous plans "to win a nuclear war," and brought humanity to the brink of a nuclear holocaust on several occasions.[5] By 1980, the holocausts of Pax Americana resembled the global horrors that a reasonable observer might have expected from a fascist victory in the Second World War.[6]

U.S. DOMINATION OF THE NEW UNITED NATIONS ORGANIZATION

The United States dominated the new United Nations organization from its founding in 1945, as it did the global economic institutions created at Bretton Woods.[7] Even before the war ended, U.S. policymakers planned to use the UN to help implement the new Pax Americana.[8] As Phyllis Bennis explained, although U.S. diplomats talked about "peace and justice and internationalism," in fact, "Washington's agenda was power."[9] Only fifty-one nations signed the UN Charter, and thirty-five of them were aligned with the United States.[10] The vast majority of nations in Asia, Africa, and Latin America—still colonized or dependent—were not represented in the Security Council or the General Assembly.[11] U.S. policymakers ensured that the five permanent members of the Security Council—the United States, Britain, France, China, and the Soviet Union—would have veto power and control the organization.[12] China would be represented by the Guomindang, which resumed its war against the communists, and Washington expected Jiang to support its positions and initiatives.[13] With four out

THE HOLOCAUSTS OF PAX AMERICANA I 171

of five votes among the Security Council's permanent members, U.S. officials hoped to limit any challenge by the Soviet Union. The United States also took control of the islands of Micronesia, which were formerly held by Japan and now considered the UN Trust Territory of the Pacific Islands.[14] Decades later, the Northern Mariana Islands became a U.S. commonwealth. The "freely associated states" of the Federated States of Micronesia, the Republic of the Marshall Islands, and the Republic of Palau became U.S. protectorates.

INTERVENTION IN THE CHINESE CIVIL WAR

In the weeks following the atomic bombing of Hiroshima and Nagasaki, U.S. generals left armed Japanese troops in control of parts of China to help prevent the communists from taking power there. Sixty thousand U.S. troops were already in the country, and Washington deployed fifty thousand more to stop the People's Liberation Army from seizing Beijing, secure the coastal cities, and safeguard strategic sites.[15] U.S. forces engaged the communists in combat and transported half a million nationalist soldiers to fight them.[16] After efforts to broker a peace agreement failed, Washington withdrew some troops but continued to support Jiang's forces. The United States equipped and trained thirty-nine Guomindang army divisions, providing about $3 billion in cash, arms, ammunition, and military equipment.[17] U.S. officials knew that Jiang's forces were irredeemably corrupt, lacked popular support, and would likely be defeated, but backed them until shortly before the communist victory in 1949.[18] As Mao Zedong proclaimed on September 21, "The Chinese people have stood up!"[19] But more than six million combatants and civilians died in this second phase of the Chinese Civil War.[20] After Jiang and his troops fled to Taiwan, the Truman administration supported their strikes against the mainland city of Sungmen, which resulted in as many as 2,500 deaths in 1950.[21] During the next decade, the CIA organized and financed numerous assaults on the People's Republic by Guomindang troops resettled in northern Burma. Tens of thousands of people died in these attacks.[22]

172   ENDLESS HOLOCAUSTS

Military Government and Right-Wing Dictatorship in South Korea

Communists had led the main resistance to the Japanese occupation in Korea and were the most popular political force in the country.[23] But in September 1945, a month after partitioning the nation, the United States sent more than 75,000 troops to establish a military government in the south.[24] They destroyed the fledgling Korean People's Republic being formed by "people's committees," protected the land-owning elite's wealth and power, and allowed right-wing Koreans to mobilize for "a kind of home-grown fascism."[25] In contrast, the Soviet military administration in North Korea helped local communists create a new socialist-oriented state committed to ending colonialism, landlordism, and class exploitation.[26] In 1948, Washington installed Syngman Rhee, an anti-communist U.S. resident for almost forty years, as leader of the Republic of Korea. Kim Il Sung, who had fought with Chinese communist forces against the Japanese, became the leader of the Democratic People's Republic of Korea in the North.[27] Jon Halliday and Bruce Cumings have pointed out that from 1945 to 1950, "mass popular resistance" culminating in "armed guerilla resistance" challenged the U.S. military government and the new Rhee dictatorship.[28] At least 100,000 people died in this struggle, a harbinger of what was to come in Korea.[29]

Support for European Colonialism in Vietnam and Indonesia

When the people of Vietnam proclaimed their independence after the Japanese surrender in September 1945, they cited portions of the U.S. Declaration of Independence. They appealed to Truman to recognize their new government.[30] Instead, Washington financially and militarily supported France's efforts to reconquer its former colony. The United States provided $2.6 billion in aid to Paris between 1950 and 1954 alone, eventually subsidizing about 80 percent of the costs of the war.[31] U.S. military assistance included airplanes, tanks, and hundreds of thousands of rifles and machine guns.[32] U.S. personnel also

THE HOLOCAUSTS OF PAX AMERICANA I   173

built airfields, ports, and highways for the French, and the CIA's Civil Air Transport transported French troops and supplies.[33] When French troops were facing their final defeat at Dien Bien Phu in 1954, President Dwight Eisenhower even offered Paris two atomic bombs to use.[34] The French government declined this offer and recognized that its colonial war against the people of Vietnam was ending. Approximately 850,000 people, primarily Vietnamese, died during this war.[35]

Although officials in Washington said they endorsed an eventual transition to self-rule in the Dutch East Indies, they did not recognize Indonesia's declaration of independence in 1945. Instead, the United States supported the Netherlands during most of its intermittent war to reconquer Indonesia during the next four years.[36] Theodore Friend has pointed out that the Dutch were U.S. allies, and "anticommunism in Europe was more important to the States than anticolonialism in Asia."[37] The Truman administration had what Bradley R. Simpson has called "the same ambivalence about the fitness of Indonesians for self-government as it did for Vietnam."[38] Washington provided more than $1 billion in aid to The Hague between 1945 and 1949. The Dutch used almost half of that amount to maintain its armed forces in Indonesia and fight the independence movement.[39] It was not until late 1948, after the Dutch violated a second cease-fire and the Indonesian government crushed a communist uprising, that the United States decided to accept Indonesian independence.[40] A year later, the Netherlands formally recognized the new nation's sovereignty. As many as 200,000 people died in the war.[41]

SUPPORT FOR EUROPEAN COLONIALISM IN MADAGASCAR AND MALAYA

When the Magalasy people's struggle for independence from France erupted in Madagascar in 1947, U.S. officials supported its violent suppression. Washington feared communist influence in this colony and the postwar government in Paris.[42] After prime minister Paul Ramadier fired the communists in his cabinet for criticizing French repression in Madagascar, the United States sent massive

174 ENDLESS HOLOCAUSTS

new shipments of grain to France, and the World Bank approved a new $500 million loan for the country.[43] As Douglas Little has noted, even after reports of widespread French massacres, executions, and torture reached Washington, officials "appear to have been relieved that France was on the road to a quick victory in Madagascar."[44] The United States sent France an additional $150 million while the details of economic reconstruction aid were still being worked out.[45] By the spring of 1948, most of the independence fighters had been defeated. As Little has emphasized, "The Ramadier regime may have provided the firepower to crush the revolt, but the Truman administration provided the economic and moral support without which such victory would have been neither quick nor cheap."[46] Approximately 90,000 Magalasy people perished in the struggle.[47]

When communist-led guerrillas launched a war of independence in the British colony of Malaya in 1948, London resolved to crush the uprising as quickly as possible. Britain deployed scores of thousands of troops and local security forces to defend its colony, yet fighting continued for about a decade. Some accounts of the "Malayan Emergency" have emphasized that the United States did not become involved in this war, and, indeed, Washington did not dispatch soldiers to join the conflict.[48] However, the Second World War had left Britain almost bankrupt, and only massive U.S. loans made its counterinsurgency in Malaya possible.[49] Although Washington initially hesitated to provide arms to the British troops and their local allies, as Phillip Deery has acknowledged, within a few years, "U.S.-made weaponry" was being effectively used against the insurgents.[50] A decade later, the war was effectively over. Britain had prevailed, partly because of financial and military assistance from the United States and partly because London agreed to independence for its colony. More than eleven thousand people, mainly insurgents and their supporters, had been killed.[51]

Postwar Crises in Iran and the Philippines

During the Second World War, Britain and the Soviet Union occupied

THE HOLOCAUSTS OF PAX AMERICANA I   175

Iran, with the approval of the United States, to prevent the country and its oil from being captured by Germany. The three countries had agreed to share oil concessions as repayment after the war, but Washington later reneged and rejected Soviet economic claims. In 1946, when Soviet troops remained in northern Iran pending resolution of the dispute, Truman threatened to drop atomic bombs on its wartime ally. The Soviets withdrew and catastrophe was averted, but the United States had set an ominous precedent.[52] That same year, Washington finally granted independence to the Philippines on the condition that U.S. businesses and citizens would have "equal rights" to develop Filipino natural resources and operate Filipino public utilities.[53] The United States also obtained a ninety-nine-year lease for twenty-three military bases.[54] Manuel Roxas, who had collaborated with the Japanese, was installed as the first president of the Philippines.[55] The communist-led guerrilla movement Hukbalahap, which had fought against the Japanese, now demanded land reform, industrialization, and social change. Ten Huks were elected to Congress but were denied their seats, and vicious state repression followed.[56] After the Huks launched an armed struggle against the government in 1948, Washington sold Manilla more than $200 million of military equipment and supplies and trained its troops.[57] CIA officials ran the successful campaign of presidential candidate Ramon Magsaysay in 1953.[58] By the time the insurgency ended in 1954, more than twelve thousand had lost their lives.[59]

INTERVENTION IN THE GREEK CIVIL WAR

Even before a fraudulent plebiscite approved the return of King George II to Greece in 1946, the right-wing regime and its allies had unleashed an unrelenting wave of violence against communists and "all democratic, liberal, and republican elements."[60] A few months after Greek anti-fascists resumed armed struggle, London informed Washington that it could no longer afford a significant military presence in Greece or substantial aid to the embattled regime. The United States responded by announcing the deceptive and dangerous Truman Doctrine,

176 ENDLESS HOLOCAUSTS

pledging assistance to "free peoples who are resisting subjugation by armed minorities or outside pressure."[61] Washington spent hundreds of millions of dollars to provide combat aircraft, naval patrol vessels, artillery, napalm bombs, rifles, communications equipment, and other supplies to the Greek government.[62] Hundreds of U.S. military personnel developed battle plans for the Greek army, trained its soldiers and sailors, and embedded with regime units.[63] As Oliver Stone and Peter Kuznick have reported, U.S. advisers used the conflict to "test tactics, some new and some old," such as napalm attacks on villages, mass executions, torture, mass imprisonment of combatants' family members, the destruction of unions, and press censorship.[64] Washington's intervention was decisive in bringing about the insurgents' surrender in 1949.[65] A total of about 158,000 Greeks died in the civil war.[66]

Safeguarding Capitalism in Europe and Latin America

In 1948, the United States began spending billions of dollars through the Marshall Plan to help rebuild Western European countries and ensure that they remained capitalist societies and became U.S. client states.[67] That same year, the CIA paid millions of dollars to conservative politicians and conducted a massive covert propaganda campaign to prevent communists from winning national elections in Italy.[68] Such interference in Italian elections continued for the next twenty-five years.[69] Also in 1948, the murder of a prominent liberal leader in Colombia and the government's brutal suppression of the ensuing popular uprising led to almost two decades of bloody civil war known as *La Violencia*. The United States provided extensive financial and military support for the government, including the sale of combat aircraft and infantry training.[70] Two hundred thousand Colombians lost their lives in the conflict in the next two decades.[71] Before 1948 ended, Washington backed the overthrow of a progressive government in Costa Rica, which resulted in two thousand deaths, and supported a military coup against the first democratically elected president of Venezuela, which produced a dictatorship that went on to kill hundreds of people.[72]

THE HOLOCAUSTS OF PAX AMERICANA I   177

The Creation of a Zionist State in Palestine

Amid escalating terrorist attacks by Jewish settlers against British colonial authorities and indigenous Palestinians, the United States government supported the United Nations' creation of a Zionist state in Palestine in 1947.[73] Although the world was learning more about the scope of the *Shoah*, officials in Washington remained opposed to large-scale Jewish immigration to the United States.[74] There were differences of opinion in Washington about the creation of Israel. Still, prominent policymakers and military leaders recognized the advantage of a European colonial settler state with a pro-Western orientation and an ability to help defend U.S. access to Arab oil and U.S. bases in the region.[75] In 1948, Washington recognized Israel after its unilateral declaration of independence. This proclamation of statehood and the subsequent seizure of additional Palestinian land sparked massive resistance and led to a brief but bloody war with several Arab countries. Twenty-one thousand people, chiefly Palestinians and other Arabs, died during the war, and roughly 800,000 Palestinians were forced to leave their ancestral homeland.[76] The *Nakba*, or catastrophe, was followed by more than seven decades of occupation, wars, brutality, immiseration, and betrayals by ostensible allies. More than 120,000 Palestinians, other Arabs, and Israelis have died in the wars and conflicts involving the Zionist state since its creation.[77] Other Palestinian refugees have died from malnutrition or preventable disease in various countries since 1948, but their numbers have never been counted. A year after the first Arab-Israeli war, the CIA helped right-wing Syrian soldiers overthrow the democratically elected government.[78]

The Creation of the FRG and NATO

In 1949, U.S. officials oversaw the creation of the Federal Republic of Germany, preferring a pro-capitalist regime in the wealthier western part of the country to a unified but non-aligned nation that might elect a leftist government.[79] The German Democratic Republic came

178   ENDLESS HOLOCAUSTS

into being soon afterward with the support of the Soviet Union. Former Nazis played a prominent role in the new FRG during the next few decades. One chancellor, one president, and twenty-five cabinet ministers had been members of Nazi organizations.[80] Ex-Nazis also assumed important positions in the new state's Foreign Ministry, Finance Ministry, and police and intelligence agencies.[81] In contrast, the GDR underwent a far-reaching "de-Nazification" process.[82]

Also in 1949, Washington and its European allies formed the North Atlantic Treaty Organization, the United States' first peacetime military alliance. Notwithstanding its rhetoric about a commitment to peace and democracy, NATO's purpose from the outset was to confront the Soviet Union and the new socialist-oriented governments of Central and Eastern Europe and "contain" the spread of communism on the continent.[83] U.S. officials also viewed the new alliance as a way to institutionalize military cooperation among its client states in Europe.[84] By this time, Washington was organizing covert armed actions by right-wing émigrés against Albania and Ukraine, which resulted in hundreds of deaths.[85]

War in Korea

When war broke out in Korea in June 1950, U.S. political leaders and journalists depicted it as communist aggression. In fact, this was a "civil and revolutionary war," as Halliday and Cumings have emphasized, largely caused by Washington's partition of the peninsula, its installation of a right-wing regime in Seoul, widespread violence against communists in the South, and the Rhee government's increasing attacks on the North.[86] Soon after the war began, North Korean troops captured Seoul, and U.S. generals began considering the use of atomic bombs.[87] Washington obtained UN approval for war while the Soviets were boycotting the Security Council over its exclusion of the new revolutionary government in China, but the United States provided most of the soldiers, military equipment, and funding.[88] U.S. troops drove the North Koreans back across the Thirty-eighth Parallel and helped South Korean forces kill vast

THE HOLOCAUSTS OF PAX AMERICANA I 179

numbers of communist guerrillas and civilians.[89] After Pyongyang fell and U.S. soldiers moved toward the Yalu River, China entered the war, helped the North Koreans recapture their capital, and forced U.S. troops to retreat.[90] In late 1950, Truman publicly threatened to drop atomic bombs on the North but by mid-1951, the war had become a stalemate.[91] By the time an armistice based on the prewar division of the country was signed in 1953, approximately five million people had died.[92]

THE CIA COUP IN IRAN

After Iran's prime minister Mohammad Mossadegh won parliamentary approval for the nationalization of the British-controlled oil industry in 1951, the United States began planning to overthrow him. The young Shah, a constitutional monarch, was forced to leave the country after the government discovered he was collaborating with the coup plotters.[93] In 1953, the CIA, with British support, used mercenaries, mobs, religious extremists, and other Iranians on its payroll to oust Mossadegh.[94] Hundreds of the supporters of the democratically elected Iranian government were killed during the putsch.[95] The Shah returned to Iran and assumed dictatorial powers. As Stone and Kuznick have noted, "Five U.S. oil companies now received 40 percent ownership of the new consortium established to develop Iranian oil."[96] During the next quarter-century, Washington provided airplanes, weapons, ammunition, other military equipment, as well as extensive financial aid, to the Shah's regime. At least ten thousand Iranians died at the hands of his soldiers and dreaded secret police before he was overthrown in 1979.[97]

SUPPORT FOR FASCISM IN SPAIN AND APARTHEID IN SOUTH AFRICA

The same year as the Iranian coup, the United States signed the Pact of Madrid with fascist Spain, which promised significant military and economic aid in exchange for the establishment of U.S. Air Force and

180 ENDLESS HOLOCAUSTS

naval bases.[98] Washington provided more than $1 billion in military assistance to Franco's dictatorship during the following decade.[99] The Spanish government's harsh repression of political opponents continued during these years but did not deter the United States from maintaining close ties.[100] Also in the early 1950s, Washington had come to depend on apartheid South Africa's uranium, chromium, and other resources, as well as its fierce anti-communism and ability to help safeguard the important commercial sea shipping lane off the Cape of Good Hope.[101] Washington sold weapons and military equipment to Pretoria, trained some of its soldiers, and loaned it money to modernize its railroads, roads, and harbors.[102] IBM sold South Africa the technology that made possible the infamous "Pass Laws," used to regulate the movement of Blacks and facilitate the forced resettlement of more than three million individuals.[103] Ford and General Motors sold Pretoria vehicles and replacement parts used by military and police forces to keep the Black majority subjugated.[104]

BACKING FEUDAL REPRESSION IN ETHIOPIA

During the early 1950s, Washington began to develop a close relationship with Emperor Haile Selassie's repressive feudal regime in Ethiopia. In exchange for allowing the United States to operate a major communications center at Kagnew Station in Asmara, access other ports, and use the country's airspace, the Ethiopian government received substantial economic and military assistance.[105] Washington armed, equipped, and trained Selassie's soldiers and police with some help from other countries, provided counterinsurgency advisers, and deployed several thousand military personnel to Ethiopia.[106] Over time, Washington assumed what V. G. Kiernan has called "a big part in the running of things" in Ethiopia.[107] U.S. policymakers viewed the country as a geopolitically and strategically important asset in the Cold War and were generally unconcerned with the widespread exploitation, poverty, and despair.[108] Not surprisingly, many Ethiopians came to resent and oppose not only the Selassie regime but also the United States.[109]

THE HOLOCAUSTS OF PAX AMERICANA I 181

The CIA Coup in Guatemala

In 1954, the United States overthrew the democratically elected government of Guatemala.[110] With broad popular and legislative support, President Jacobo Arbenz announced the nationalization of 40 percent of United Fruit Company's property.[111] Secretary of State John Foster Dulles, CIA Director Allen Dulles, and other officials had close personal business ties to United Fruit and began recruiting rightwing Guatemalan army officers for a coup.[112] After discovering the plot, Arbenz denounced imperialism and purchased weapons from Czechoslovakia, which led to dire U.S. warnings about communism and Soviet domination of the Central American country.[113] U.S. pilots then bombed the nation's largest military base and the government radio station while the CIA led 150 right-wing Guatemalan soldiers, exiles, and mercenaries from various countries in an invasion from Honduras and Nicaragua.[114] Arbenz was forced from power, and as many as nine thousand people were arrested, many of them tortured and killed.[115] Washington installed Colonel Carlos Castillo Armas as the new president. During the next six decades, the United States provided vital economic support for a succession of right-wing regimes and armed, trained, and advised troops who killed approximately 250,000 Guatemalans.[116]

U.S. Imperialism Replaces French Colonialism in Vietnam

After a historic defeat at Dien Bien Phu in 1954, France sought a face-saving way to leave Vietnam. Led by Ho Chi Minh and the communists, the Viet Minh enjoyed widespread support, controlled most of the country, and were widely expected to come to power.[117] In Geneva, diplomats from several countries agreed on a plan for a transition to independence. Vietnam would be temporarily divided, the Viet Minh would withdraw to the North, the French would withdraw to the South, and national elections would be held in two years. However, the United States and the French puppet Bao Dai refused to sign the Geneva Accords.[118] The following year, the Eisenhower administration installed Ngo Dinh Diem as the new ruler in the South and supported him as his forces murdered thousands of Viet Minh militants.[119] In 1956, Washington and Saigon canceled the scheduled national elections after Eisenhower was informed that 80 percent of the country's population would vote for Ho Chi Minh.[120] Washington's support for a regime that its chief CIA agent on the ground described as "fascistic" and its refusal to allow the most popular political force to govern the country led to the renewal of insurgency in South Vietnam.[121]

Support for French Colonialism in Algeria

The United States backed France during the Algerian War of Independence that began in 1954. Washington advocated steps toward limited self-rule for the colony and occasionally criticized France's handling of the insurrection.[122] But as Miloud Barkaoui has argued, U.S. officials chiefly sought to "manage the colonial status quo," backing France's bloody counterinsurgency "as long as it did not threaten Western interests in the region and did not open the way for Soviet penetration of North Africa."[123] In NATO meetings, U.S. diplomats approved the French deployment of hundreds of thousands of troops to Algeria.[124] Washington armed the French troops and equipped them with airplanes, helicopters, heavy trucks, and other equipment.[125] As Kiernan has observed, helping the French obtain large loans meant that "America was in fact helping it to carry on this colonial war too."[126] The United States also opposed or abstained from UN resolutions recognizing Algeria's right to self-determination.[127] The strength of the Algerian insurgents, mounting opposition at home, and growing international pressure eventually forced France to end the war. Algeria gained its independence in 1962, but as many as 1.5 million people had died in the conflict.[128]

The Invasion of Egypt and Intervention in Hungary

After Egyptian President Gamal Nasser nationalized the Suez Canal

THE HOLOCAUSTS OF PAX AMERICANA I   183

in 1956, Britain, France, and Israel invaded Egypt to regain Western control and oust the nationalist leader. Global opposition and the prospect of Soviet intervention led the White House to oppose the invasion, but the U.S. military commander of NATO threatened to use nuclear weapons against Moscow if the Soviets attacked the invaders.[129] Washington's allies were forced to withdraw, and Egypt retained control of the canal, but as many as 3,250 people died in the conflict.[130] That same year, the United States supported an armed insurrection against the socialist government in Hungary.[131] Washington's Radio Free Europe urged Hungarians to fight, offered tactical advice to the anti-communist forces, and led listeners to believe that U.S. military assistance was imminent.[132] The United States could not risk a major war with the Warsaw Pact nations in Hungary, but the CIA dispatched agents to help organize the insurgency.[133] Soviet troops ended the rebellion and helped bring a new Hungarian communist-led government to power, but approximately 2,500 Hungarians and 700 Soviets died in the fighting.[134]

Washington's Secret War in Tibet

In the last half of the 1950s, the United States launched a secret war in Tibet. When the People's Republic of China extended its control to Tibet in 1951, it did not immediately overthrow the traditional feudal order there but began to slowly implement progressive social reforms.[135] Even gradual changes were unacceptable to the ruling elite, however, which had long relied on slavery, serfdom, and savage repression to maintain its wealth and power.[136] In 1956, the CIA began airlifting anti-communist Tibetans it had trained and equipped to attack the People's Liberation Army in the region.[137] Intermittent but deadly conflict followed during the next few years. In 1959, U.S.-backed Tibetan rebels launched a major uprising in the capital of Lhasa. Most Tibetans did not join or support the rebels.[138] China quickly suppressed the rebellion, consolidated its control over Tibet, and outlawed slavery and serfdom in the years that followed.[139] More than 130,000 Tibetans and Chinese had died during the conflict by

184   ENDLESS HOLOCAUSTS

1959.[140] U.S. support for clandestine armed operations in the region
continued until 1973.[141]

Sustaining Friendly Regimes in Haiti and Lebanon

By 1958, Francois "Papa Doc" Duvalier had become a brutal dictator in Haiti. Nonetheless, Washington trained his soldiers and secret
police, sent troops to crush an insurgency, and generally tolerated his
excesses because of his strident anti-communism.[142] When he died
thirteen years later, the U.S. government approved the succession
of his son Jean-Claude "Baby Doc" and dispatched naval vessels to
"assure order and discourage exile infiltration."[143] As many as sixty
thousand Haitians died under the Duvaliers.[144] Washington was also
deeply complicit in the deaths that occurred during the civil war in
Lebanon in 1958. The United States had replaced France as the main
imperialist power there, and the CIA had funded the election of a pro-
Western Christian president and allied parliamentary deputies who
opposed the anti-imperialist politics of the growing Muslim population.[145] The 1958 civil war occurred because of widespread opposition
to the president's desire to seek an unconstitutional second term and
his close ties to Washington.[146] Eisenhower's deployment of 14,000
troops and dozens of naval vessels to Lebanon ended the conflict,
but four thousand people had already died.[147] A new president was
elected, but U.S. influence and intervention contributed to a more
devastating civil war fifteen years later.[148]

U.S. Subversion from Iraq to Congo

Reformist military officers overthrew the pro-Western monarchy in
Iraq in 1958. Only the threat of a Soviet military response prevented
the United States and Turkey from invading the new republic.[149] The
CIA subsequently tried but failed to assassinate the new Iraqi prime
minister Abd al-Karim Qasim.[150] At the same time, the Eisenhower
administration attempted to oust the non-aligned government in
Indonesia headed by the popular former independence movement

THE HOLOCAUSTS OF PAX AMERICANA I 185

leader, Sukarno.[151] The CIA organized and armed thousands of dissident troops and mercenaries and provided B-26 bombers, fighters, and transport airplanes for air support.[152] The coup was defeated, but several hundred people died in the process.[153] Washington may not have "fomented" or "guided" the military overthrow of the government in Turkey in 1960, but as Ömer Aslan has explained, it "underwrote the coup financially, politically and militarily."[154]

That same year, U.S. troops stationed in Ethiopia helped defeat a coup against the Selassie dictatorship.[155] As many as two thousand Ethiopians died or were wounded in the uprising.[156] In the autumn of 1960, the United States and Belgium organized and financed a military coup that ousted Patrice Lumumba, the newly independent Congo's prime minister, and brought army officer Joseph-Désiré Mobutu and allied politicians to power. Washington and Brussels were also deeply implicated in the subsequent execution of Lumumba in early 1961.[157] During the next four years, Washington sent CIA operatives, soldiers, military trainers, and airplane pilots to help Mobutu and his soldiers wipe out progressive Congolese forces.[158] More than 100,000 were killed during this period.[159] Also in 1961, Washington organized, financed, and armed the dissidents who assassinated its longtime but increasingly erratic and unpopular ally, Trujillo, in the Dominican Republic.[160]

ACTS OF WAR AGAINST CUBA

In 1959, revolutionaries led by Fidel Castro ousted the Batista dictatorship in Cuba. Six decades of U.S. domination and financial and military support for right-wing rule had ended, but five thousand people had died in the armed struggle.[161] In early 1960, the Eisenhower administration began bombing sugarcane fields and factories in Cuba.[162] In March 1960, the CIA was involved in bombing the French ship *La Coubre*, which was transporting arms and ammunition to Havana. More than a hundred people died in the attack.[163] During the next several decades, more than 3,400 Cubans perished in acts of state terrorism organized or supported by Washington.[164]

186 ENDLESS HOLOCAUSTS

In the autumn of 1960, Eisenhower launched an embargo against the new government of Cuba, which continues to the present day. During the past six decades, Washington's harsh restrictions on food and medicine imports, along with other punishing strictures, have contributed to the deaths of thousands of Cubans.[165] In April 1961, President John Kennedy authorized the invasion of Cuba by a small army of right-wing émigrés organized, armed, and trained by the CIA.[166] U.S. military airplanes destroyed or disabled half of the small Cuban air force. Three days later, after the invaders landed at Playa Giron, the Bay of Pigs, revolutionary forces rallied to defeat them. Approximately 300 people, including 114 invaders and 4 U.S. pilots, were killed, and the defeat was a public humiliation for the Kennedy administration.[167]

Support for Portuguese Colonialism in Africa

When Angolan guerrillas began fighting for independence from Portugal in 1961, the Kennedy administration announced its support for decolonization and self-determination. But such a dramatic change in long-standing U.S. foreign policy was largely rhetorical.[168] Washington prioritized the Portuguese dictatorship's participation in NATO and the U.S. military base in the Azores islands over Angolan independence and national sovereignty. As the national liberation struggle grew in Angola and similar struggles began in Guinea and Mozambique, the United States supported Portugal.[169] U.S. business investments significantly increased in these colonies, particularly in resource-rich Angola.[170] U.S. military support for Portugal was indispensable for these colonialist wars. As Kiernan has noted, Portugal fought "largely with American or NATO weapons during the next thirteen years."[171] Washington also provided aircraft and helicopters to the Portuguese for its counterinsurgency and trained its officers in the United States.[172] More than 135,000 people, overwhelmingly Africans, died during these wars for independence.[173] At the same time, U.S. officials searched for Angolan fighters with whom they could do business in the future.[174]

THE HOLOCAUSTS OF PAX AMERICANA I   187

New Interventions in Vietnam, British Guiana, and Cuba

By 1961, the insurgency led by the National Liberation Front threatened to topple the U.S.-backed regime in South Vietnam. Kennedy increased the number of U.S. military advisers there from 800 to 16,000 and authorized U.S. pilots to fly combat missions against the insurgents.[175] Between 1962 and 1964, the CIA financed and organized strikes, protests, and other actions to oust Prime Minister Cheddi Jaggan in British Guiana (now Guyana) because of his demand for independence and socialist politics.[176] Hundreds of people died in the violence, and a party supported by the CIA defeated Jaggan's party in the next election.[177] In October 1962, the Cuban Missile Crisis erupted. After Washington discovered that the Soviet Union was deploying nuclear missiles on the island, it launched a naval blockade and threatened Moscow. The crisis brought the world to the edge of nuclear war, but the Soviets agreed to remove the missiles in exchange for the United States removing its missiles from Turkey and pledging not to attack Cuba again.[178] However, a few weeks later, a team of émigrés dispatched by Washington blew up a Cuban industrial plant and killed four hundred workers.[179]

Support for Apartheid South Africa

A CIA agent helped the South African government capture African National Congress leader Nelson Mandela in 1962, which led to his imprisonment for twenty-seven years and undermined the liberation struggle in that country.[180] In 1963, two years after the South African police massacred sixty-nine Black protesters in Sharpeville, the Kennedy administration announced an embargo on the sale of weapons and military equipment that could be used for internal repression. However, the U.S. government continued to sell helicopters, missiles, submarines, and torpedoes to the racist regime.[181] Washington also continued its nuclear collaboration and sharing of military intelligence with Pretoria.[182] U.S. business investments in South Africa and trade between the two countries remained

188   ENDLESS HOLOCAUSTS

substantial.[183] At the end of the 1960s, the CIA provided "advice and assistance" in the creation of Pretoria's infamous Bureau of State Security.[184] Thus, despite its rhetorical condemnation of white supremacist rule and limited military embargo, Washington continued to support the apartheid government despite its ongoing repression of the Black majority and its murder of hundreds of people during this decade.[185]

Backing Coups in Ecuador, Iraq, and Vietnam

In a commencement address at American University in June 1963, President Kennedy denied that the United States was presiding over "a Pax Americana enforced on the world by American weapons of war."[186] But just four months earlier, the CIA had helped Baath Party and other anti-communist military officers in Iraq overthrow the Qasim regime. Qasim had begun limiting U.S. and European oil concessions, played a leading role in the creation of the Organization of the Petroleum Exporting Countries, and had grown closer to the Iraqi left.[187] The young Saddam Hussein, an important contributor to the putsch, was already on the U.S. payroll.[188] Qasim was executed and the CIA provided the names of Iraqi communists and labor militants to the new government, which then murdered as many of them as possible.[189] More than eight thousand died in the aftermath of the coup, and moves toward the nationalization of Iraqi oil ended.[190] In July 1963, a month after Kennedy's commencement address, the CIA supported a military coup that overthrew the president of Ecuador, who was viewed as too friendly toward communism.[191] The coup resulted in several deaths. Another hundred people later perished in a successful struggle to oust the junta that had taken power.[192] In November 1963, as the NLF extended its control and land reform in parts of South Vietnam, Kennedy approved the overthrow of the despised Diem regime, and U.S. officials worked with South Vietnamese generals to plan the coup.[193] Diem and his brother were executed during the putsch. Ironically, Kennedy himself was assassinated a few weeks later.

THE HOLOCAUSTS OF PAX AMERICANA I 189

SUPPORT FOR REPRESSION IN PANAMA, URUGUAY, AND BRAZIL

In early 1964, protests erupted in Panama over popular demands to fly the nation's flag inside the U.S. Canal Zone. U.S. troops violently suppressed the protests, leading to the deaths of twenty-two students.[194] The crisis eventually led to negotiations in which Washington agreed to relinquish control of the Canal Zone at the end of the century.[195] That same year in Uruguay, CIA and other U.S. operatives began to help security forces fight, capture, torture, and kill Tupamaro communist insurgents. At least 350 guerrillas, soldiers, police, and civilians died in the conflict during the next eight years.[196] Also in 1964, the United States helped right-wing military officers overthrow the democratically elected reformist government of João Goulart in Brazil. The CIA had secretly funded his opponents in local elections, financed street demonstrations, launched a mass anti-government propaganda campaign, encouraged the putschists, and promised U.S. military support if needed.[197] The dictatorship that followed the ouster of Goulart killed more than four hundred Brazilians during the next two decades.[198]

THE U.S. WAR AGAINST VIETNAM

By 1964, 23,000 U.S. military advisers were deeply involved in planning and executing attacks on the NLF in South Vietnam and the Democratic Republic of Vietnam.[199] In August of that year, President Lyndon Johnson falsely accused the DRV of unprovoked attacks on U.S. naval vessels in the Gulf of Tonkin, and then won congressional approval for the expanded use of military force in the country.[200] Washington began bombing North Vietnam and deployed thousands of Marines to South Vietnam in March 1965. By the end of that year, 185,000 U.S. military personnel had been sent to crush the communist-led insurgency.[201] By 1968, more than half a million U.S. troops were on the ground in Vietnam.[202] Amid peace talks in Vietnam and a tightening race for president at home, Republican candidate Richard Nixon secretly promised more concessions to South

190   ENDLESS HOLOCAUSTS

Vietnamese officials if he won the election. Those officials withdrew from the negotiations, Nixon became president, and the carnage continued.[203] However, the U.S. invasion, the relentless bombing, and the threats of nuclear attacks could not defeat the NLF and the Democratic Republic of Vietnam.[204] The indefatigability of the Vietnamese liberation fighters, intense public opposition to the war at home, and mounting rebellion within the U.S. armed forces led to the withdrawal of the United States from Vietnam in 1973.[205] Two years later, the country was reunited and became the Socialist Republic of Vietnam. More than 5.3 million Vietnamese people had died because of the U.S. war.[206]

The U.S. War Against Laos

Washington's savage opposition to communism also resulted in the ghastly loss of life in countries adjacent to Vietnam. By 1964, the United States had organized three coups in Laos to defend the Royal Lao government and prevent the communist-led Pathet Lao from coming to power.[207] The CIA had also fielded a "Secret Army" of Hmong Laotians, Thais, South Vietnamese, other Asians, and U.S. Special Forces to fight against the intermittent insurgency.[208] After right-wing politicians backed by the CIA replaced the neutralist government in April 1964, the Pathet Lao's armed struggle grew in strength and became quite formidable. Because its "Secret Army" could not defeat the communists and their allies, Washington escalated its ostensibly "Secret War" to massive sustained bombing of Laos in 1965.[209] The large-scale carnage continued for eight years, but the Pathet Lao won the war and seized state power in 1975. About one million people in Laos had died by then.[210]

The U.S. War Against Cambodia

As the wars in Vietnam and Laos expanded after 1964, Prince Norodom Sihanouk of Cambodia sought to maintain his country's neutrality. During the previous decade, Sihanouk had rebuffed U.S. pressures to

THE HOLOCAUSTS OF PAX AMERICANA I 191

join its anti-communist crusade and defeated U.S. plots to overthrow him.[211] Although he opposed the use of Cambodian territory by the NLF and the DRV, he also opposed incursions by the United States and its allies. In 1969, President Richard Nixon authorized the secret bombing of Cambodia to destroy or cripple Vietnamese liberation forces based there.[212] The next year, U.S. military personnel helped right-wing Cambodian politicians overthrow Sihanouk and install a pro-U.S. government.[213] In May 1970, Nixon ordered the invasion of Cambodia. The widespread devastation and death resulting from the U.S. bombing and invasion led many Cambodians to support the Khmer Rouge's fight against the invaders.[214] DRV troops helped to free parts of Cambodia, and the exiled Sihanouk's backing for the Khmer Rouge increased its popularity. Approximately 800,000 people had died in the U.S. war in Cambodia by 1975 when the Khmer Rouge came to power.[215] And Washington shared responsibility with the new rulers for the approximately 1.7 million deaths from starvation, disease, and executions that followed.[216]

U.S. BASES AND COUNTERINSURGENCY IN THAILAND

The conservative authoritarian regime in Thailand became a U.S. client state around 1950 and enthusiastically cooperated with Washington's anti-communist project in Southeast Asia.[217] By 1964, the United States was turning Thailand into a virtual military base for its war in Vietnam, and about fifty thousand troops were eventually deployed there.[218] A small communist insurgency began in 1965 and demanded U.S. withdrawal and a new government in Thailand.

William Blum has pointed out that Washington "financed, armed, equipped, and trained police and military units in counterinsurgency, significantly increasing their numbers."[219] U.S. military personnel also transported Thai government forces to battlefields and participated in combat operations against the guerrillas.[220] During the insurgency, perhaps ten thousand guerrillas, regime soldiers, and civilians died.[221] The Thai government survived, and the communists did not come to power as they did in Vietnam, Laos, and Cambodia. But the massive

192   ENDLESS HOLOCAUSTS

U.S. military presence in Thailand in the 1960s and 1970s led to the huge growth of prostitution and sex trafficking, which contributed to almost 600,000 AIDS-related deaths in the decades that followed.[222]

INVASION OF THE DOMINICAN REPUBLIC AND SUPPORT FOR DICTATORSHIP IN ZAIRE

In April 1965, more than forty thousand U.S. soldiers invaded the Dominican Republic to prevent the return of Juan Bosch to power. Military officers had ousted the reform-minded president two years before, and a massive popular movement subsequently sought to restore him to office.[223] Four thousand Dominicans died during the invasion, and more than three thousand others died at the hands of the U.S.-backed regime during the next decade.[224] Also in 1965, Mobutu cast aside allied politicians and established a dictatorship in Congo. Mobutu's ascendancy signaled the United States' replacement of Belgium as the preeminent imperialist power in the country he renamed Zaire.[225] Mobutu stole billions of dollars in government revenues and killed uncounted thousands of political opponents during his thirty-two-year dictatorship.[226] But he was an ally against African socialism. Although he nationalized mining industries, he sold some Zairean minerals to the United States and kept all of them "out of Soviet hands."[227] Washington provided massive economic and military aid to the Mobutu dictatorship, trained its troops, and helped crush rebellions in the late 1970s.[228] President George H. W. Bush later praised Mobutu as "our best friend in Africa."[229]

THE MASSACRE OF COMMUNISTS IN INDONESIA

Beginning in October 1965, the U.S. government supported a year-long reign of terror against communists and their allies in Indonesia. Despite the failure of its attempted coup seven years earlier, Washington had not abandoned its aim of overthrowing Prime Minister Sukarno. Indeed, the United States had subsequently played

THE HOLOCAUSTS OF PAX AMERICANA I   193

a larger role in financing, arming, and training Indonesian military forces and increasingly urged its leaders to oust Sukarno and prevent one of the largest communist parties in the world from coming to power.[230] U.S. officials worked to promote a confrontation between the army and the communists, and these efforts eventually succeeded.[231] In October 1965, a group of junior officers sympathetic to the communists detained several anti-communist generals, who were subsequently killed. More than five decades later, this episode remains a mystery. It may have been a botched action approved by the communist leader Dipa Nusantara Aidit, who aimed to expose an army plot against his party and Sukarno. If so, it was undertaken without the knowledge of his party's central committee. Alternatively, the incident may have been a subterfuge planned by anti-communist military leaders to obtain a pretext for the destruction of the communists and the overthrow of Sukarno.[232]

With Washington's enthusiastic backing, the right-wing generals moved to wipe out the communists and limit Sukarno's authority before deposing him. With the assistance of anti-communist militias and mobs, the Indonesian army proceeded to kill as many as one million communists, allies, and other people during the next twelve months.[233] The United States provided weapons, communications equipment, clothing, food, money, and supplies to the army during its extermination campaign.[234] U.S. officials also gave the army the names of about five thousand communists and checked them off as reports of their deaths were received.[235] Howard Federspiel of the State Department admitted: "No one cared, as long as they were communists, that they were butchered. No one was getting very worked up about it."[236] Washington was thus deeply involved in what the *New York Times* called "one of the most savage mass slaughters of modern political history."[237] Sukarno was formally removed from office in March 1967, and General Suharto, who had collaborated with the Japanese occupiers during the Second World War, came to power.[238] The Suharto dictatorship murdered thousands more Indonesians in the decades that followed.[239]

The Coup in Ghana and Counterinsurgency in Peru, Bolivia, and Colombia

In 1965–66, CIA operatives and military advisers trained, organized, and directed a counterinsurgency operation in Peru that resulted in the deaths of more than one hundred Marxist guerrillas.[240] In 1966, the CIA played a decisive role in the military coup in Ghana that overthrew President Kwame Nkrumah, a powerful critic of Western neo-colonialism.[241] Twenty-seven people died during the coup.[242] Two years earlier, Washington had backed a military coup in Bolivia and the new regime's violent suppression of militant tin miners. The United States provided more weapons and more training for the Bolivian army and took over a large part of Bolivian intelligence services after a communist insurgency began.[243] Between 1964 and 1968, several hundred Bolivians died at the hands of the government.[244] In 1967, CIA agents were directly involved in the capture and execution of Che Guevara in Bolivia.[245] In Colombia, after new communist guerrilla groups emerged in the mid-1960s, the United States increased its financial and military assistance to the army and police. Washington spared no expense to maintain friendly Colombian governments in power and facilitate the killing of as many insurgents as possible.[246] More than 250,000 people died in the conflict during the next five decades.[247]

Backing the Coup in Greece

In April 1967, one month before national elections, a group of right-wing military officers overthrew the Greek government and formed a military junta. U.S. intelligence and military personnel stationed in Greece had met repeatedly with the plotters and encouraged them to prevent the re-election of George Papandreou, the former reformist prime minister, or take drastic action if he was elected.[248] Papandreou had been critical of U.S. domination of his country, and CIA agents had helped bribe Greek politicians to oust him two years before.[249] He was expected to win back his office in May 1967, but the new junta canceled the elections. The leader of the junta, George Papadopoulos,

THE HOLOCAUSTS OF PAX AMERICANA I 195

was "an avowed fascist and admirer of Adolf Hitler" who had collaborated with the Nazi occupation during the Second World War and been on the CIA payroll for fifteen years.[250] The United States quickly recognized the new regime and, after a brief cessation of arms sales, increased its military and financial assistance to Greece.[251] The dictatorship imprisoned and tortured thousands of people and killed scores of others during the next seven years.[252] The junta's support for a Greek Cypriot extremist coup on the island in 1974 sparked a Turkish invasion of the island and a brief war that killed 7,400 people and led to a permanent partition of the island.[253]

Support for Israel in the Six-Day War

In late May 1967, President Johnson gave Israel the green light for its 1967 war of aggression against Egypt, Jordan, and Syria.[254] The Zionist forces benefited from the significant economic and military assistance they had previously received from Washington.[255] Tel Aviv's victory over its Arab neighbors in the Six-Day War resulted in 19,000 deaths, the considerable expansion of its borders, and much greater oppression of the Palestinians.[256] More than 5,500 people, mainly Egyptian soldiers and civilians, perished because of Israeli air strikes, artillery shelling, and commando raids in the subsequent "War of Attrition" in 1969–70.[257] Washington substantially increased its shipment of weapons and other military equipment to Israel in the years that followed.[258] At the same time, the Palestine Liberation Organization, a broad national front of resistance organizations, was gaining popular support in occupied Palestine and the diaspora.[259] Fifteen hundred miles away, U.S. advisers and soldiers provided critical support for the Ethiopian regime's violent suppression of Eritrean insurgents between 1967 and 1970, which resulted in approximately two thousand deaths.[260]

U.S. Complicity in the Biafran War

After protracted ethnic conflict, two coups, and the massacre of thirty

196 ENDLESS HOLOCAUSTS

thousand people, the Igbo of eastern Nigeria announced the independence of Biafra in 1967.[261] The federal government, dominated by Hausa-Fulani and Yoruba people, refused to recognize Biafra, where almost two-thirds of Nigeria's oil was produced.[262] Although the former British colony was in London's "sphere of influence," Gulf Oil became Nigeria's second-largest oil producer, and other U.S. businesses invested heavily in the country.[263] When the civil war broke out, the U.S. government announced that it would not sell weapons to either side, but its declaration of neutrality was a self-interested lie.[264] Washington continued to endorse a unified Nigeria and train federal troops in the United States.[265] While pretending to support an arms embargo, U.S. officials quietly backed the shipment of British weapons and military equipment to Lagos.[266] Washington ended economic aid programs in Biafra but continued them elsewhere in Nigeria, and U.S. oil companies significantly expanded their investments in federally controlled areas.[267] At home, increasing public awareness of the holocaust in Biafra sparked major humanitarian relief efforts, but Washington downplayed the Nigerian regime's responsibility for most of the deaths.[268] In 1970, the Biafra independence movement was defeated. Between one million and three million people, chiefly Igbo, had died.[269] In the years to come, the United States replaced Britain as the dominant imperialist power in Nigeria.[270]

Another Coup in Iraq and New Counterinsurgency in the Philippines

In 1968, the CIA was deeply involved in organizing another coup in Iraq, which enabled the Baath Party to oust its coalition partners.[271] Although the putsch itself was bloodless, the new regime executed scores of political opponents in the following months and killed hundreds more during the next decade.[272] Saddam Hussein soon became the second most powerful person in the new regime.[273] In 1969, Washington backed President Ferdinand Marcos in the Philippines with money and weapons when he launched major military campaigns against the communist New People's Army, the successor to the Huks,

THE HOLOCAUSTS OF PAX AMERICANA I   197

and the Moro Muslim insurgency in the southern part of the country.[274] U.S. support continued despite Marcos's declaration of martial law in 1972, and by the mid-1980s, his regime had received more than one billion dollars in military aid.[275] After the assassination of the reformist politician Benigno Aquino in 1983, popular opposition to Marcos mounted, and he was forced to flee the Philippines in 1986. His regime had murdered more than three thousand political opponents and critics, not including armed guerillas.[276] Significant U.S. financial and military assistance has continued to flow to Manilla, making the U.S. Empire deeply complicit in the deaths of close to 200,000 communist and Muslim insurgents in the past half-century.[277]

Washington's Role in Black September

In September 1970, the Popular Front for the Liberation of Palestine, an organization belonging to the PLO, hijacked three planes in its continuing struggle against the Zionist occupation of their homeland. At the same time, the PFLP and other Palestinian militants in Jordan began calling for the overthrow of King Hussein, who nervously sought support from Washington.[278] Still mired in war in Southeast Asia and facing political and logistical constraints in West Asia, the United States could not dispatch combat troops to save Hussein.[279] But Nixon persuaded the king to unleash his army against the Palestinians, assured him of Washington's support, publicly threatened U.S.-Israeli military intervention, and sent the entire Sixth Fleet and two additional naval vessels to within one hundred miles of the coast of Lebanon.[280] After Syrian troops came to defend the Palestinian fighters from the Jordanian army's onslaught, Nixon persuaded Israel to help save Hussein, but this turned out to be unnecessary.[281] Syria decided against providing air support for its troops or the Palestinians. While Hussein met with growing derision in the Arab world, President Nasser of Egypt brokered a cease-fire between the king and the PLO.[282] Approximately 3,500 Palestinians and other Arabs died during what came to be known as Black September, and Hussein expelled the PLO a year later.[283]

198   ENDLESS HOLOCAUSTS

Counterinsurgency in Yemen and Coups in Turkey and Bolivia

By 1971, Washington was sending economic assistance and military advisers to the Yemen Arab Republic to help suppress a leftist insurgency and overthrow the neighboring People's Democratic Republic of Yemen.[284] The following year, a brief war between the two countries claimed at least two hundred lives.[285] In Turkey, amid mounting communist and worker militancy—and a ferocious right-wing backlash—the CIA played a central role in planning and executing a military coup in 1971.[286] This putsch has been called a "coup d'état by communiqué" because it was accomplished by a memorandum from military leaders to the prime minister demanding a new civilian government, not the typical deployment of tanks and troops in the streets that had become part of modern Turkish history.[287] With eleven different prime ministers in the decade that followed, economic and political instability increased. Thousands died in continuing clashes between the left and right in Turkey.[288] The United States continued to provide arms and military equipment to Ankara except for a ban between 1975 and 1978 following the Turkish invasion of Cyprus.[289] Washington also provided extensive financial, military, and logistical support to General Hugo Banzer Suárez's overthrow of a ten-month-old progressive regime in Bolivia in 1971.[290] More than a hundred people died in the coup, and the new Banzer dictatorship killed thousands of leftists, workers, and peasants during the next seven years.[291]

Sustaining Dictatorship in Uganda

After Britain and Israel helped Idi Amin seize power in Uganda in 1971, U.S. officials quickly recognized the new government. London, Tel Aviv, and Washington had opposed the previous president's plans to nationalize 60 percent of Uganda's largest industries, businesses, and banks.[292] Amin's foreign patrons were encouraged by his declaration of commitment to private enterprise and his denationalization of several British companies.[293] But Amin soon turned against

THE HOLOCAUSTS OF PAX AMERICANA I 199

Britain and Israel after they refused to sell him advanced jet fighters and other sophisticated military equipment. He expelled Israelis and Asians from Uganda, obtained combat aircraft from Libya, embraced the Palestinians, and routinely murdered people because of ethnic, religious, and political differences.[294] Washington periodically condemned some of Amin's actions and placed restrictions on economic and military assistance but continued to back his regime. The CIA and other U.S. agencies provided Amin with bombs, weapons, and military equipment; trained his troops and police; and participated in some military operations on his behalf against rebels in Uganda.[295] Approximately 300,000 people died at the hands of Amin's forces before he was deposed in 1979.[296]

Support for Pakistan in the Bangladesh War

Pakistan became a U.S. client state several years after it gained its independence from Britain.[297] West Pakistan was separated from East Pakistan by more than a thousand miles of Indian territory and harshly exploited this part of the country.[298] But Pakistan's anti-communism led Washington to view it as an outpost of "Western defense."[299] In the country's first national elections in March 1971, a party supporting autonomy won the most votes in East Pakistan, but the military rulers in Islamabad delayed the convening of the new national assembly and declared martial law.[300] Troops from West Pakistan and local allies began massacring Bengalis in the East, and a civil war broke out.[301] Pakistani soldiers and their supporters killed indiscriminately for the next nine months, often with U.S. weapons.[302] Washington energetically backed Islamabad and sent more weapons, ammunition, military equipment, and economic assistance.[303] After ten million Bengalis fled to India, New Delhi entered the war in December 1971. Nixon sent the Seventh Fleet's Task Force 74 to the Bay of Bengal and threatened to land troops, but Soviet naval vessels arrived to defend India.[304] A global war was averted, Pakistan was defeated, and the new nation of Bangladesh was born. Although estimates vary widely, it appears that at least one million people died in the war.[305]

200   ENDLESS HOLOCAUSTS

Backing the Racist Regime in Rhodesia

In 1971, Nixon signed a new law restoring the importation of chromium ore from Rhodesia. These imports had ended four years before after the Johnson administration implemented UN sanctions against Ian Smith's white-minority government.[306] Although many people in the United States supported sanctions and other measures to isolate the racist regime, some capitalists and politicians still backed Rhodesia, highlighting the profitability of business investments there and warning of the threat of African socialism.[307] In addition, some U.S. companies provided economic aid to Salisbury, the CIA provided intelligence to the Rhodesian army, and U.S. mercenaries fought alongside its soldiers.[308] U.S. support prolonged the life of the racist regime and increased the number of casualties in the country.[309] But the strength of the armed liberation struggle and the political constraints on U.S. support forged by domestic and global opposition led to the final defeat of white minority rule in 1980. Approximately fifty thousand people perished in the struggle for freedom in the land now known as Zimbabwe.[310]

Complicity in Repression in Burundi and Uruguay

After a rebellion failed in Burundi in 1972, the predominantly Tutsi army began killing large numbers of the Hutu majority.[311] U.S. officials criticized the slaughter and called on other African countries to intervene. However, Washington refused to consider an embargo on Burundi's coffee exports, 80 percent of which went to the United States.[312] Within four months, between 100,000 and 200,000 Hutus died.[313] In 1973, military officers took control of the government in Uruguay. U.S. diplomats expressed concerns about the new junta's closure of the national legislature and other repressive measures, but nonetheless U.S. military aid and training for the new regime continued for another three years.[314] Even after Congress ended direct military support, it agreed to let the regime purchase weapons in the United States.[315] About 180 people died at the hands of

THE HOLOCAUSTS OF PAX AMERICANA I

201

the dictatorship, and many more were tortured during the next decade.[316]

OVERTHROW OF THE POPULAR UNITY GOVERNMENT IN CHILE

In September 1973, Chilean military leaders recruited, financed, and supported by the United States overthrew the democratically elected Popular Unity government of Salvador Allende Gossens.[317] For a decade, Washington had funded and organized political opposition and propaganda to prevent socialist advances in Chile.[318] In 1970, the Nixon administration provided weapons and money to right-wing military officers to prevent Allende's election. The conspirators assassinated General René Schneider Chereau, the commander-in-chief of the Chilean army, but failed to launch a coup.[319] After Allende became president in November 1970, his coalition promoted progressive social reforms as part of a democratic road to socialism.[320] In 1971, the Chilean National Congress nationalized U.S. copper companies and took control of ITT.[321] At the same time, the U.S. government worked with business interests and international financial institutions to "make the economy scream" and undermine popular support for Allende.[322] The CIA instructed its agents in Chile to "induce as much of the military as possible, if not all, to take over and displace the Allende government."[323] The Chilean president and scores of others died in the September 1973 coup. More than four thousand people were murdered or disappeared during the US.-backed dictatorship of General Augusto Pinochet in the fifteen years that followed.[324]

SUPPORT FOR ISRAEL IN THE YOM KIPPUR WAR

When Egypt, Syria, and other Arab countries attacked Israel in October 1973, the Zionist state fought back with many weapons, artillery, tanks, and airplanes provided by the United States.[325] After Tel Aviv suffered early losses, Washington immediately sent more weapons and military equipment and expanded its naval presence in the eastern Mediterranean.[326] The Soviet Union provided military

202   ENDLESS HOLOCAUSTS

supplies and technicians to the Egyptians and Syrians and deployed ships to the region.[327] After the direction of the war changed, the Soviets persuaded the United States to help arrange a cease-fire, but the Israelis violated the agreement and continued to batter Egyptian forces.[328] When Washington declined Moscow's proposal for a joint peacekeeping force, Soviet airborne divisions prepared for possible deployment to West Asia, and the Nixon administration placed U.S. nuclear forces on high alert.[329] But Secretary of State Henry Kissinger told a news conference that the present conflict did not "justify the unparalleled catastrophe that a nuclear war would represent."[330] A nuclear holocaust was avoided, and the Yom Kippur War ended. More than 21,000 soldiers and civilians died during this conflict.[331]

The Conquest of East Timor and the Proxy War in Angola

After the historic defeat of the U.S. Empire in Southeast Asia, domestic opposition to militarism limited its ability to launch large-scale invasions during the next decade and a half. Despite the "Vietnam Syndrome," Washington continued to organize proxy wars, overthrow governments, support client states' wars, and conduct smaller invasions. In 1975, President Gerald Ford and Secretary of State Kissinger met with Suharto in Jakarta and approved his plans to invade East Timor and make it part of Indonesia.[332] The Indonesian invasion began the day after Ford and Kissinger left Jakarta.[333] Two hundred thousand East Timorese people died in the war.[334] Also in 1975, a year after a leftist soldiers' rebellion toppled the dictatorship in Portugal, Angola and Mozambique became independent nations. The Ford administration provided weapons and training for pro-Western rebels fighting the leftist Popular Movement for the Liberation of Angola (MPLA) for control of the country. The United States also paid mercenaries to join the rebels and supported South African troops' attacks on the MPLA.[335] After the MPLA won, Congress prohibited further intervention in Angola, but the CIA illegally shipped weapons to South Africa, which were almost certainly used in Angola.[336] Scores of thousands died there during the next several years.[337]

THE HOLOCAUSTS OF PAX AMERICANA I   203

Intervention in the Lebanese Civil War

In 1975, a calamitous civil war broke out in Lebanon. The right-wing Maronite Christians, who had long dominated the government with Washington's backing, opposed the "democratic redistribution of power" to the growing Muslim majority and their allies.[338] A coalition of Muslims, Druze, nationalists, and leftists known as the Lebanese National Movement demanded significant political and social change, including an end to collaboration with the U.S. Empire.[339] After the armed conflict began, PLO fighters who had taken refuge in Lebanon after their expulsion from Jordan supported this coalition.[340] Afraid that a new government in Lebanon would oppose U.S. interests in the region, Washington quietly provided military and financial support to the Maronites and their Phalangist militia.[341] As the civil war continued over the next fifteen years, the United States supported attacks, invasions, and occupations by the Syrians and Israelis to limit change in Lebanon and drive the PLO out of the country.[342] U.S. troops also deployed to Beirut, briefly and disastrously.[343] Washington eventually acceded to some important if limited reforms in Lebanon, but the PLO was forced to leave the country. The total loss of life during the Lebanese civil war exceeded 168,000.[344]

The Coup in Argentina and Operation Condor

In 1976, right-wing generals in Argentina overthrew the government led by Isabel Martínez de Perón and began murdering leftists and other political opponents. Some U.S. politicians condemned the junta's repression, but Kissinger personally assured leaders that he approved their actions and urged them to end the problem of "terrorism" as quickly as possible.[345] After Jimmy Carter became president in 1977, he often invoked human rights rhetoric, but U.S. foreign policy did not significantly change. U.S. military and economic assistance to the Argentine junta continued until late 1978.[346] When the junta was ousted seven years later, it had killed approximately thirty thousand people.[347] In the last half of the 1970s, 75 percent of Latin America's

204 ENDLESS HOLOCAUSTS

peoples lived under military dictatorships backed by Washington.[348] The right-wing regimes of Argentina, Bolivia, Brazil, Chile, Paraguay, and Uruguay participated in Operation Condor, which involved the coordinated murder of dissidents and critics abroad. J. Patrice McSherry has pointed out that U.S. officials "aided and facilitated Condor operations as a matter of secret but routine policy."[349] More than 13,000 people were assassinated in foreign countries where they had sought refuge, including the United States.[350]

SUBVERSION AND VIOLENCE IN JAMAICA

In the last half of the 1970s, Washington also conducted a campaign of sabotage and violence that led to the electoral defeat of Michael Manley, the social democratic prime minister of Jamaica.[351] Manley wanted to buy out majority ownership in U.S. and other multinational corporations mining Jamaican bauxite. He also established diplomatic relations with the Soviet Union and Cuba and supported the new Angolan government.[352] The United States ended economic aid to Jamaica and shipped weapons to opposition forces. The CIA helped organize assassinations, bombings, and arson by Manley's opponents; financially supported the main opposition party; acquired paid operatives within the armed forces and police; recruited middle-class Jamaicans into anti-government organizations; coordinated strikes by workers; and supported an unrelenting propaganda campaign by the island's major newspaper.[353] Some aluminum companies left Jamaica or reduced production, the tourist industry was devastated, and political violence soared. Manley lost his bid for re-election in 1980. More than eight hundred people perished because of political violence that year.[354] Another thousand died at the hands of the police in the new U.S.-supported regime of Edward Seaga during the next several years.[355]

DEFENDING DICTATORSHIP IN NICARAGUA

By 1977, the Sandinista National Liberation Front was leading a popular revolution against the regime of Anastasio Somoza Debayle

THE HOLOCAUSTS OF PAX AMERICANA I 205

in Nicaragua. Washington had supported the Somoza family dictatorship for decades, but the Nicaraguan masses wanted to end the repression, corruption, and poverty fostered by the regime.[356] As the Sandinista forces gained growing public support for the armed struggle against the government, the United States supplied weapons, ammunition, and other military equipment to Somoza's army and police.[357] U.S. officials also unsuccessfully sought to have the Organization of American States intervene in the conflict.[358] The revolution succeeded in driving Somoza from power in 1979, but between forty and fifty thousand people died during the struggle.[359] After the Sandinistas were in power, Carter authorized the CIA to fund and organize political opposition to their new government.[360]

DEFENDING DICTATORSHIP IN IRAN

Jimmy Carter celebrated New Year's Eve 1977 with the murderous Shah of Iran in Tehran. The president praised the Shah's regime as "an island of stability in one of the most troubled areas of the world."[361] Neither Carter nor the CIA recognized the depth of popular opposition to the Shah or the strength of the developing insurgency.[362] Thirteen months later, a mass uprising forced the Shah to flee the country, and Ayatollah Ruhollah Khomeini was greeted by millions when he returned from exile.[363] Soon afterward, Iranians voted to establish an Islamic Republic, and later that year, they voted to approve a constitution for the new government.[364] After the Shah went to the United States for medical treatment, Iranians demanded that he be returned to face trial for his crimes. Washington's refusal to meet this demand led to Iranian students' detention of U.S. Embassy staff in Tehran for more than a year and the continued deterioration of relations between the two countries. The United States launched an embargo of Iranian oil and seized Iranian financial assets in this country.[365]

A NEW CLIENT STATE IN SOMALIA

In mid-1977, President Mohammed Siad Barre of Somalia ordered

206   ENDLESS HOLOCAUSTS

the invasion of the ethnic Somali Ogaden region of Ethiopia. The invasion failed within several months, in part because the Soviets disavowed their former ally and supported the new leftist government in Ethiopia.[366] After the Somali forces were defeated, Barre forged a new alliance with Washington. U.S. forces were granted permission to use Somali military bases, and his regime would serve as a counterweight to the new Ethiopian government.[367] In exchange, the United States provided hundreds of millions of dollars of economic and military assistance to Somalia.[368] Saudi Arabia, Italy, and other U.S. allies also sent large amounts of arms, military equipment, and money to the Barre regime.[369] At the same time, Washington pushed IMF demands for privatization of state enterprises, ending agricultural price controls, and reduced government spending, which crippled the Somali economy.[370] U.S. officials remained silent when Barre's forces killed thousands of opponents and exacerbated clan rivalries in the years that followed.[371] Officials in Washington and capitalists on Wall Street undoubtedly appreciated the Somali government's agreement that Conoco, Amoco, Chevron, and Phillips could explore and exploit oil and natural gas in two-thirds of the country's territory.[372]

WASHINGTON'S PROXY WAR IN AFGHANISTAN

After a pro-socialist party overthrew the government of Afghanistan in 1978, the United States sought to destroy the new regime. Although the new rulers were deeply divided and faced substantial opposition, they abolished usury, eliminated peasant debts, began land reform, and built hundreds of schools and medical clinics.[373] They outlawed child marriage and marriages arranged "in exchange for money or commodities" and began teaching women to read.[374] The Carter administration responded by working closely with Pakistan, Saudi Arabia, and other countries to field an army of "holy warriors" to overthrow the new government. During the next decade, Washington spent about $3 billion and provided extensive CIA support for its new proxy army, which included the Al-Qaida fighters led by the Saudi religious extremist Osama bin Laden.[375] The National

THE HOLOCAUSTS OF PAX AMERICANA I 207

Security Adviser Zbigniew Brzezinski later boasted of the administration's success in forcing the Soviets to intervene in 1979.[376] The counterrevolutionary war backed by the United States and its allies was decisive in weakening the regime in Kabul, and the presence of Soviet troops galvanized opposition among the extremists. The pro-socialist government fell in 1992, and the Taliban came to power four years later. Between 1.5 million and 1.8 million people died during the war.[377] Washington experienced catastrophic blowback when Al-Qaida operatives attacked U.S. targets on September 11, 2001.[378]

Backing Repression in Yemen, Turkey, and South Korea

By 1979, U.S. weapons, military equipment, and military advisers were playing an increasingly important role in the Yemen Arab Republic's continuing efforts to end a leftist insurgency and overthrow the People's Democratic Republic of Yemen.[379] Another brief war between the two countries broke out that year and left at least five hundred dead.[380] Washington continued to train and arm paramilitary forces that destroyed bridges, committed other acts of sabotage, and killed people of Yemen during the next several years.[381] In 1980, Washington supported yet another military coup in Turkey, resulting in scores of executions and hundreds more deaths over the next three years.[382] Also in 1980, when workers and students rose against the South Korean dictatorship in Kwangju, the U.S.-led military command released Korean troops to violently suppress the rebellion. Between two thousand and three thousand people died during the uprising.[383]

A New Client State in Liberia

By the late 1970s, Washington was alarmed by the Liberian government's friendly relations with socialist countries, and the CIA began to support political opposition groups in its former colony and longtime protectorate. In 1980, U.S. policymakers welcomed a military coup in Liberia led by Master Sergeant Samuel Doe.[384] Washington helped

208   ENDLESS HOLOCAUSTS

the staunchly anti-communist Doe form a new governing junta and deployed U.S. troops already in the country to help maintain order.[385] U.S. advisers were assigned to several government ministries, and the regime agreed to make major financial decisions only with their approval.[386] Doe also granted permission for the United States to use its airports and naval ports and pledged his support for Washington's foreign policy. In return, Washington provided about $500 million in military and economic aid during the next five years. U.S. officials accepted Doe filling most offices with members of his minority Krahn ethnolinguistic group, rigging national elections, and murdering thousands of Gios, Manos, and other people.[387] Over time, however, Doe's growing equivocation on arrangements with the U.S government and long-standing privileges for Firestone led to growing disapproval and declining support from Washington.[388]

The New Persian Gulf Doctrine

In the aftermath of the revolutions in Afghanistan and Iran, the U.S. Empire moved to reassert its dominance in West Asia. Carter announced in his State of the Union address in 1980 that any attempt by an outside power to gain control of the Persian Gulf or impede the flow of oil would be viewed as an assault on the vital interests of the United States.[389] Carter made clear that Washington would defend these interests "by any means necessary, including military force."[390] As in the case of the Monroe Doctrine, the prohibition against foreign intervention in the region did not apply to the United States. The so-called Carter Doctrine, which has been reaffirmed by presidents from Reagan to Obama, set the stage for dramatically expanded and much more destructive U.S. intervention in West Asia and beyond.[391]

Counting the Dead

Between 1945 and 1980, major U.S. wars in Korea, Vietnam, Laos, and Cambodia killed twelve million people. Washington also shared responsibility for the 1.7 million people who died during the rule of

THE HOLOCAUSTS OF PAX AMERICANA I   209

the Khmer Rouge, and the U.S. proxy war in Afghanistan led to the deaths of at least 1.5 million. U.S. support for the Guomindang in the second phase of the Chinese civil war, for the French campaign to reconquer Vietnam, for the anti-communist exterminations in Indonesia, for the Nigerian government during the Biafran War, and for the Pakistani government during the Bangladesh War implicated Washington in the deaths of almost 11 million people. Other U.S. military actions and support for repression abroad caused or contributed to millions of additional fatalities. Altogether, the U.S. Empire was responsible or shared responsibility for approximately 29 million deaths during the first thirty-five years of Pax Americana. Both major parties and virtually all politicians in the United States consistently supported Washington's leadership in the liberal international order throughout this period. But scores of millions worldwide continued to oppose U.S. imperialism and its endless holocausts.

6

The Holocausts of Pax Americana II

Some may have believed that the rise of the empire to the status of the sole superpower, with a military and technological might with no balancing pole anywhere in the world, would frighten or dishearten the Cuban people. Yet today they have no choice but to watch in amazement the enhanced courage of this valiant people. We . . . are prepared to defend our homeland and our Revolution with ideas and with weapons to our last drop of blood.
—FIDEL CASTRO, ADDRESS IN HAVANA, 2003

By 1980, the U.S. Empire was exploiting the resources, markets, and labor of much of the planet. The empire had acquired more than fifty client states, established several hundred military bases in other countries, and deployed hundreds of thousands of soldiers, Marines, sailors, and air force personnel in scores of nations.[1] The vast wealth, extraordinary military power, and far-reaching political domination of the United States had made it the most formidable imperium in history.[2] Although the empire had suffered a historic defeat in Vietnam, Ronald Reagan's inauguration as president in January 1981 signaled "the restoration of America's global military power" and "resurgent American expansionism."[3] In the four decades that followed, the United States was responsible or

THE HOLOCAUSTS OF PAX AMERICANA II   211

shared responsibility for a staggering loss of life in new wars, proxy wars, military interventions, and other destructive actions abroad.[4] U.S. complicity in the collapse of most socialist states also produced an enormous human toll.[5] In the first two decades of the twenty-first century, however, neither neoconservatives' efforts to create a "New American Century" nor neoliberals' endeavors to shore up Pax Americana were able to stop the erosion of U.S. primacy in an increasingly multipolar world.[6] The election of Donald Trump on a virulently racist and authoritarian "America First" platform in 2016 both reflected and contributed to mounting crises at home and the diminution of hegemony abroad.[7] Trump's brazen national chauvinism, repudiation of the postwar liberal international order, mishandling of the COVID-19 pandemic, encouragement of far-right forces, and incitement of an unprecedented insurrection marked a historic inflection point in the decline of the U.S. Empire. So, too, did Washington's defeat and humiliation in Afghanistan.

The U.S. Role in the War Between Iraq and Iran

During his 1980 campaign, Reagan criticized the Carter administration for its inability to free the U.S. Embassy staff held in Tehran.[8] However, both presidential candidates found it expedient to offer some support to the Islamic Republic. The Carter administration publicly offered to deliver $300 million to $500 million in weapons previously purchased by the Shah's regime in exchange for releasing the hostages.[9] To prevent an "October surprise" that could help Carter win re-election, Reagan campaign officials secretly met with Iranian representatives in Madrid. As Oliver Stone and Peter Kuznick explained, "The details are murky and impossible to confirm," but it appears that the campaign officials offered to allow Israel to send U.S. weapons to Iran in exchange for holding the hostages until after the election.[10] Tehran accepted Reagan's proposal, the hostage crisis continued to undermine Carter's popularity, and Reagan won the election. Kai Bird has noted, "The hostages were inexplicably released minutes after Reagan was sworn in as president."[11] Soon afterward,

212   ENDLESS HOLOCAUSTS

the new administration approved Israel's shipment of U.S. arms and spare parts to the Islamic Republic, and this arrangement continued for several years.[12]

Two months before the U.S. election, Iraq invaded Iran. Now led by Saddam Hussein, Iraq initially achieved important battlefield victories, but the flow of U.S. weapons helped Iran "turn the tide."[13] However, when Iranian troops began moving toward Basra in mid-1982, the Reagan administration secretly abandoned its public commitment to neutrality and resolved to prevent Iraq from losing the war.[14] Although arms continued to be sent to Iran, U.S. officials were determined to cripple the regime and prevent it from threatening client states Saudi Arabia, Kuwait, and Jordan.[15] Baghdad had ended diplomatic relations with Washington during the Six-Day War in 1967, and the Nixon administration had deplored Baghdad's nationalization of its oil in 1972. But now, intense hostility toward the Islamic Republic led the United States to favor Iraq in the war while preventing either country from becoming strong enough to dominate the Persian Gulf.[16]

In 1982, Reagan authorized the sale of aircraft, helicopters, weapons, and other military equipment to Iraq through third countries.[17] The CIA also began to provide essential military intelligence to Hussein's regime and continued to do so throughout most of the war.[18] The administration authorized U.S. companies to sell anthrax, other biological agents, and ingredients for chemical weapons to Baghdad.[19] A CIA-front organization in Chile sold Iraq cluster bombs.[20] Nonetheless, in 1983 the Reagan administration provided the Islamic Republic the names of Soviet agents and collaborators in the country, which led to the execution of two hundred people.[21] In 1985, Reagan secretly authorized the sale of anti-tank and anti-aircraft weapons to Tehran to continue financing his proxy war in Nicaragua.[22] The United States also provided battlefield intelligence to Tehran.[23] Between 1986 and 1988, the U.S. government increased its military operations in the Persian Gulf, began flagging and escorting Kuwaiti oil tankers through the Gulf, and then launched a brief "undeclared yet bloody naval and air war" against the Islamic

THE HOLOCAUSTS OF PAX AMERICANA II   213

Republic.[24] In April 1988, after a Navy ship hit an Iranian mine in the Persian Gulf, the United States crippled six Iranian vessels and destroyed two Iranian oil rigs, killing more than fifty people.[25] In July 1988, the USS *Vincennes* shot down an Iranian civilian airplane in Iranian airspace, killing all 290 passengers and crew members.[26] The next month, Tehran accepted a UN peace resolution, and the war with Baghdad ended. The U.S. Empire had assisted both sides in the carnage, however unequally, and significantly contributed to the loss of about one million lives.[27]

SUPPORT FOR RIGHT-WING REGIMES AND COUNTERREVOLUTIONARIES IN LATIN AMERICA

After becoming president, Reagan increased U.S. support for the dictatorships in Guatemala, Chile, Argentina, and other Latin American countries.[28] During Reagan's first two years in office, the Guatemalan regime killed 100,000 peasants with weapons and ammunition provided by the United States.[29] Washington also expanded assistance to the government of Peru, which was fighting the Shining Path and Túpac Amaru insurgencies.[30] Determined to roll back socialist-oriented regimes, Reagan pressured international financial institutions to withhold loans from the new Sandinista government in Nicaragua and organized a proxy army of counterrevolutionary émigrés to sabotage and strike as much of the country as possible.[31] The Contras destroyed schools and hospitals, tortured and murdered supporters of the new regime, and ravaged the economy.[32] After Congress cut off funds for this unpopular war, Reagan's second secret arms deal with the Iranians provided new funds for the Contras.[33] This illegal arrangement was exposed, scandal ensued, and Washington abandoned its proxy army. But years of bloodshed and economic dislocations led to the Sandinistas' electoral defeat in 1990.[34] As many as 50,000 people died in the conflict.[35]

The United States used Honduras as a staging ground for attacks by the Contras, and the people of that country suffered greatly. Honduran soldiers armed, equipped, trained, and advised by Washington,

214 ENDLESS HOLOCAUSTS

killed hundreds of suspected leftists and other innocent people during the 1980s.[36] The CIA trained the infamous Battalion 316 in torture techniques and provided Honduran troops with the necessary tools.[37] At the same time, the Reagan administration's massive military and economic support enabled the right-wing regime in El Salvador to escape defeat at the hands of a popular insurgency led by the Farabundo Marti National Liberation Front.[38] The United States spent more than $4 billion on weapons, military equipment, and other assistance for the government and trained thousands of its troops at Fort Benning in Georgia and in Panama.[39] Raymond Bonner reported that the Reagan administration also sent advisers "to help the Salvadoran military fight its dirty war."[40] Three U.S. soldiers died after guerrillas shot down their helicopter, which was running arms to government troops.[41] Eventually, the perseverance of the revolutionary forces, a military stalemate, and the decline of U.S. aid for the Salvadoran government led to peace talks and an end to the conflict in 1992. Approximately 90,000 Salvadorans had perished by then.[42]

INTERVENTION IN CHAD AND LEBANON

Soon after Reagan became president, the CIA developed a long-term plan to overthrow Muammar al-Qaddafi in Libya.[43] In 1982, Washington sought to weaken him by overthrowing an allied government in neighboring Chad. The CIA organized, financed, and provided weapons and technical support to an insurgency led by Hissen Habré. The insurgency ousted the Chadian regime, and Habré established a dictatorship that killed approximately 40,000 people during the eight years that followed.[44] Also in 1982, the Reagan administration financially and militarily supported Israel's invasion of Lebanon during that country's devastating civil war.[45] U.S. and Israeli intervention in the conflict on behalf of right-wing Lebanese forces contributed to the devastating human toll. The Israeli invasion alone led to 21,000 deaths over three years.[46] In 1983, after 1,800 Marines were deployed to support the Lebanese government, the bombing of a barracks killed 241 U.S. troops, and Reagan withdrew the remainder soon afterward.[47]

THE HOLOCAUSTS OF PAX AMERICANA II 215

THE INVASION OF GRENADA AND SUPPORT FOR REACTION IN SRI LANKA

In 1983, the United States invaded the tiny island nation of Grenada and overthrew the left-leaning government shortly after its leader, Maurice Bishop, died in an internal power struggle. Scores of Grenadians, Cubans, and U.S. troops died during the invasion.[48] During much of the civil war that raged in Sri Lanka between 1983 and 2009, the United States joined India and other countries to support the Sinhalese-led government, whose historic mistreatment of the Tamil minority was well known. Washington trained Columbo's troops, gave the government a naval command and control system, provided a used Coast Guard ship and tactical support, and shared military intelligence with the regime.[49] More than 100,000 people died before the Tamil insurgency was finally crushed.[50] More than a decade after the end of the civil war, Sri Lanka continues to be ravaged by ethnic oppression and authoritarian rule.[51]

OPPOSITION TO LIBERATION IN ANGOLA, MOZAMBIQUE, NAMIBIA, AND SOUTH AFRICA

By the early 1980s, the African National Congress's armed struggle against the apartheid regime in South Africa was growing, as was the global condemnation of white minority rule. However, U.S. investment and trade with South Africa had increased dramatically during the previous decade and Reagan praised Pretoria as a strategic ally that could not be abandoned.[52] The CIA provided covert support to the South Africans, mercenaries, and allied forces fighting to overthrow the new socialist-oriented government in Angola and defeat the armed struggle for the liberation of Namibia.[53] Congress renewed direct military aid to pro-Western rebels in Angola, and the devastating war there took many more lives.[54] In Mozambique, the insurgency sponsored by South Africa and right-wing organizations in the United States killed many people. It was so widely condemned that the Reagan administration could not

216 ENDLESS HOLOCAUSTS

directly support it.[55] So Washington wielded powerful economic weapons against Maputo instead. Amid widespread starvation and malnutrition, the U.S. government eliminated food shipments to Mozambique for a few years. It then used the renewal of food aid, economic assistance, and IMF structural adjustments to destroy the new government's socialist aspirations.[56]

Under mounting pressure from African Americans, civil rights advocates, students, and workers, Congress approved comprehensive economic sanctions against South Africa over Reagan's veto in 1986.[57] UN sanctions followed, and the armed struggles in South Africa and Namibia continued. International pressure grew on Pretoria to withdraw its soldiers from Namibia and negotiate a transition to Black majority rule at home. In 1990, Namibia became independent, and Nelson Mandela was released from prison in South Africa. Four years later, the first democratic election in South African history brought Mandela and the African National Congress to power. By then, the wars in Angola and Mozambique had ended, but Washington had been deeply complicit in the enormous loss of life in these countries. Approximately 21,000 people died at the hands of the apartheid regime in South Africa.[58] At least 25,000 died during the struggle for the liberation of Namibia.[59] More than one million died in Angola, and between one and two million died in Mozambique.[60]

Overthrowing the Government in Ethiopia

During the early 1980s, Washington reduced and then eliminated food aid to Ethiopia during a terrible famine.[61] The devastation was compounded by the Tigrayan, Eritrean, and other armed rebellions against the Ethiopian government and problems with the regime's agricultural policy.[62] Approximately one million people died because of the famine.[63] As citizens in the United States became aware of this tragedy, they pressured the Reagan administration to join international relief efforts.[64] New global and U.S. assistance undoubtedly saved a great many lives.[65] However, much of the money ended up in the hands of insurgents.[66] In addition, Washington had begun

THE HOLOCAUSTS OF PAX AMERICANA II   217

providing anti-communist groups opposed to the Ethiopian government with CIA advisers and financial assistance since 1981.[67]

U.S. officials also launched an Amharic-language Voice of America radio program, which contributed to undermining the government.[68] It soon became clear that the Tigrayan and Eritrean forces were the most formidable opponents of the regime, but the Reagan administration did not want to back them because they were led by Marxists.[69] However, as the global crisis of socialism deepened and these insurgents began to abandon their ideological roots, the United States provided them with tactical support, military intelligence, and other assistance.[70] When the government collapsed in the spring of 1991, Washington assumed a "de facto advisory role" for the victorious rebels. The United States now had the power to shape the country's destiny.[71] In 1991, Tigrayan, Eritrean, and other insurgents succeeded in ousting the regime, and the new government looked to Washington for guidance and support.[72] More than 350,000 people died during the civil war.[73]

NUCLEAR ESCALATION IN EUROPE AND AGGRESSION AGAINST LIBYA

In 1983, Washington's bellicose drive to maintain military superiority over Moscow led to the phased deployment of new intermediate-range nuclear missiles in Europe, despite global opposition. The deployment made the world a more dangerous place, and stagnation in the Soviet economy would make it hard to match the U.S. escalation, much less undertake desperately needed economic and political reforms at home.[74] In March 1986, U.S. jets destroyed three or four Libyan ships and attacked two of the country's anti-aircraft sites.[75] The following month, after accusing Libyan agents of bombing a Berlin nightclub frequented by U.S. soldiers, Washington bombed Tripoli and Benghazi in an attempt to assassinate Qaddafi and terrorize his people.[76] Scores of people, almost entirely civilians, died in the attacks and the victims included a young daughter of Qaddafi.[77] The UN General Assembly subsequently condemned the U.S. bombing.[78]

218 ENDLESS HOLOCAUSTS

In 1989, U.S. naval airplanes shot down two Libyan jet fighters flying over the Mediterranean Sea.[79] Washington also supported Israel's violent suppression of the first Palestinian intifada between late 1987 and 1993, in which more than two thousand people died.[80]

Backing Repression in Somalia, Liberia, and Sierra Leone

In Somalia, the U.S.-backed Barre regime murdered approximately 200,000 members of the Isaaq clan between 1987 and 1989.[81] Civil war broke out in 1989, and 50,000 Somalis, mainly civilians, had died by early 1990.[82] Barre was overthrown in 1991, but a new government could not be established amid the continuing armed struggle among various warlords and clans.[83] This violence and anarchy was, in part, the legacy of U.S. involvement and exacerbated the human toll of the drought and famine that ravaged Somalia in 1992.[84] Approximately 350,000 additional deaths occurred by late 1992.[85] In Liberia, the U.S. government and the Firestone rubber company supported a rebellion that began in 1989 and led to the ouster and execution of President Doe the next year.[86] U.S. intelligence agencies had long-standing ties with insurgent leader Charles Taylor, whose forces eventually won the ensuing civil war in Liberia and invaded Sierra Leone to take control of its diamond reserves.[87] Taylor became president of Liberia in 1997, but Washington eventually turned against him. After six years, he was forced out of office and was subsequently convicted in The Hague of war crimes and crimes against humanity.[88] But by then, Taylor and his U.S. patrons shared responsibility for about 250,000 deaths in Liberia and Sierra Leone.[89]

The Invasion of Panama

In 1989, President George H. W. Bush ordered the invasion of Panama to capture the military ruler Manuel Noriega and bring him to the United States to face charges of drug trafficking. Noriega had been on the CIA payroll for most of the previous two decades, and his long history of drug trafficking, money laundering, corruption,

THE HOLOCAUSTS OF PAX AMERICANA II   219

and political murders had generally been tolerated.[90] He also allowed U.S. bases in Panama to support Washington's wars in El Salvador and Nicaragua and train Contras there.[91] But the Bush administration decided that his future usefulness as an asset was limited and deployed 15,000 troops to join the 12,000 already in Panama to overthrow him.[92] Bush's insistence that this action was necessary to save U.S. lives in Panama was widely rejected, and the Organization of American States condemned the invasion.[93] Between three and four thousand Panamanians died while defending their country.[94] Noriega spent most of the rest of his life in prison in the United States and France.

THE FIRST U.S. WAR AGAINST IRAQ

In 1990, Kuwait's extraction of millions of barrels of oil from the disputed Rumaila field on the border with Iraq led to mounting tensions.[95] After U.S. Ambassador April Glaspie told Hussein that Washington had "no opinion" on the issue, Iraqi troops invaded and occupied Kuwait in August 1990.[96] Unalterably opposed to Iraq now controlling 20 percent of the world's oil, the Bush administration launched a war against the Hussein regime, deploying more than half a million troops to the region. The United States also conducted a massive bombing campaign against Iraqi forces in Kuwait and military sites and civilian infrastructure in Iraq.[97] Bush's objectives were to punish the impudent former U.S. ally, restore the Al Sabah monarchy in Kuwait, safeguard the royal family in Saudi Arabia, establish a permanent military presence in the region, and ensure continued Western access to oil in the region.[98] With the Soviet Union collapsing and unable to take effective countermeasures, the U.S. Empire's war plans won UN approval and garnered support from more than two dozen countries.[99] Most of the U.S.-led ground operations and bombardment occurred in January and February 1991, forcing Hussein's troops to return to Iraq and producing widespread carnage and destruction. More than 3,400 Kuwaitis died during Hussein's invasion, and the loss of Iraqi lives was far greater.[100] More than 200,000

220   ENDLESS HOLOCAUSTS

Iraqis, half of them women and children, died because of the war.[101]
Subsequent economic sanctions against Iraq resulted in more than
half a million deaths, primarily of children and women, by 1995.[102]

THE 1991 COUP IN HAITI

In 1991, five years after popular opposition ousted "Baby Doc"
Duvalier, Jean-Bertrand Aristide became the first democratically
elected president in the history of Haiti. Washington had backed a
more conservative candidate and opposed the new president's proposals for a minimum wage increase, a social security program, and land
reform.[103] The Haitian army and police, still funded and supported by
the United States, overthrew Aristide after only nine months in office.
Some coup leaders were on the CIA payroll, and U.S. intelligence officers were in the Haitian military headquarters during the coup.[104] The
Bush administration formally denounced Aristide's ouster but quietly
backed the new Haitian regime, which murdered between four and
five thousand Aristide supporters and other people during the next
three years.[105] In 1994, after the massive refugee crisis fueled by this
violence became an international issue, the UN authorized a U.S.-
led intervention to restore Aristide to power. However, U.S. officials
limited Aristide's term in office, forced him to forgo major reforms,
and insisted that supporters of the dictatorship must be viewed as the
legitimate opposition in Haiti.[106]

COUNTERINSURGENCY IN TURKEY AND PERU

By the early 1990s, Washington had been providing Turkey with aircraft, helicopters, tanks, weapons, and other military equipment used
against the continuing Kurdish insurgency for a decade.[107] The United
States sold approximately $15 billion in weapons to Ankara between
1980 and 1999.[108] Almost forty thousand Kurds and Turks had perished by 1999, and more would die in the decades that followed.[109]
In the early 1990s, under the pretext of combating drug trafficking,
the Bush administration began training Peruvian soldiers and police,

THE HOLOCAUSTS OF PAX AMERICANA II   221

which had a long history of human rights abuses, to fight the resilient Shining Path and Túpac Amaru guerrillas.[110] Public U.S. assistance was briefly suspended after Peruvian president Alberto Fujimori assumed dictatorial powers in 1992, but covert aid was uninterrupted, and the CIA helped capture the Shining Path leader later that year.[111] The armed struggle against the government has greatly diminished in the past two decades but continues intermittently to this day, as does U.S. counterinsurgency assistance.[112] Peru's total number of related deaths has been conservatively estimated at more than 69,000.[113]

U.S. COMPLICITY IN THE COLLAPSE OF THE SOVIET UNION

Profound domestic economic and political problems played a central role in the abandonment of socialism by the leadership of the Communist Party of the Soviet Union in the late 1980s and the subsequent collapse of the world's first socialist state in 1991. So, too, did the unwinnable arms race, unrelenting military threats, sabotage, subversion, and propaganda for which the U.S. Empire was largely responsible.[114] Thus anti-communist leaders in both Washington and Moscow shared the responsibility for approximately 150,000 deaths in the nationalist wars and uprisings in Georgia, Azerbaijan, Armenia, Russia, and other former Soviet republics after 1991.[115] Many U.S. officials, advisers, and capitalists energetically promoted what came to be known as "shock therapy"—the rapid privatization of state and collective enterprises, the creation of a new capitalist class, and the elimination of social protections and state services.

The results were catastrophic for most people in Russia, the former Soviet republics, and the former socialist countries of Central and Eastern Europe.[116] Seumas Milne has emphasized that "far from opening the way to emancipation, these changes led to beggary for most citizens, ushering in the most cataclysmic peacetime economic collapse of an industrial country in history."[117] Milne explained:

Under the banner of reform and the guidance of American-prescribed shock therapy, perestroika became catastroika.

222   ENDLESS HOLOCAUSTS

Capitalist restoration brought in its wake mass pauperization and unemployment; wild extremes of inequality; rampant crime; virulent antisemitism and ethnic violence; combined with legalized gangsterism on a heroic scale and precipitous looting of public assets.[118]

Life expectancy in Russia dropped precipitously.[119] By 2001, as many as three million excess deaths had occurred.[120] Eight years later, the number of excess deaths had risen to almost seven million.[121] Similar but smaller-scale tragedies occurred in some other nations that experienced "shock therapy."[122] Not surprisingly, most people in Russia and former Soviet states continue to tell pollsters that they regret the destruction of socialism and the breakup of the Soviet Union.[123] The end of food aid that accompanied the collapse of Soviet socialism also contributed to the loss of hundreds of thousands of lives during a terrible famine in North Korea between 1995 and 2000.[124]

INTERVENTION IN SOMALIA

In late 1992, after the massive loss of life in Somalia brought on by drought, famine, and civil war had begun to abate, the U.S. government began deploying 28,000 troops as part of a UN mission to safeguard international food shipments and other humanitarian assistance. Both the outgoing Bush administration and the incoming administration of Bill Clinton were chiefly concerned with helping create a central government in Somalia that could honor the country's contracts with Conoco, Amoco, Chevron, and Phillips for the exploration and exploitation of oil and natural gas.[125] Although some Somalis appreciated foreign assistance in food deliveries, many others resented the United States because of its previous backing of the Barre regime.[126] When U.S. soldiers began attacking various Somali clans to support a pro-Western warlord's claim to power, significant combat and massive casualties ensued. In 1993, Somali fighters shot down two Black Hawk helicopters, killed eighteen U.S. soldiers, and dragged some of their bodies through the streets of Mogadishu.

THE HOLOCAUSTS OF PAX AMERICANA II   223

Clinton withdrew U.S. forces early in 1994, but by then several thousand Somalis had died because of the military intervention and the country was more unstable than ever.[127]

Wars Against Serbia

The United States had long sought to restore capitalism in the multinational socialist state of Yugoslavia.[128] Significant borrowing from international financial institutions in the 1980s led to the IMF's imposition of structural adjustments, and economic problems in Yugoslavia had mounted by the early 1990s.[129] Deteriorating social conditions and intense pressure by the United States and its NATO allies fueled the rise of nationalism in the six republics and led to the disintegration of the country and a series of wars.[130] Substantial direct intervention by U.S. military forces, the CIA, and NATO helped Croatians and Bosnian Muslims defeat the Serbs in the Bosnia-Herzegovina War of 1992–95, which resulted in as many as 150,000 deaths.[131] U.S. forces subsequently began secretly training and supplying the Kosovo Liberation Army of Albanian Kosovars, which killed 1,500 Serbs in its struggle for independence in 1998 alone.[132] The following year, the United States led the NATO bombing of Serbia on the pretext of defending the Kosovars from genocide.[133] Twenty-five hundred Serbs and Kosovars died as a result.[134] Washington then deployed several thousand troops to Kosovo as part of a UN peacekeeping force and later supported its declaration of independence from Serbia.[135]

Growing U.S. Intervention in Africa

Notwithstanding the global crisis of socialism and President Bush's proclamation of "a New World Order" in 1990, the U.S. Empire continued to face substantial challenges.[136] The imperative to obtain vital resources, new markets, and cheap labor remained relentless.[137] And the bombing of the World Trade Center in 1993, which left six people dead, reflected what Helen C. Epstein has called "the growth of anti-Western sentiments" in West Asia and East Africa.[138] Africa became

224 ENDLESS HOLOCAUSTS

increasingly important to U.S. policymakers for both reasons, and Washington found new allies in President Yoweri Museveni of Uganda and his chief of military intelligence, the Rwandan-born Tutsi exile Paul Kagame.[139] Although Museveni's forces had killed scores of thousands of Ugandans to seize and maintain power, Washington began providing significant military and economic aid to his regime.[140] In contrast, the U.S. government disapproved of the Hutu-majority government in Rwanda, which had ousted the Tutsi-minority monarchy and brought considerable progress for many Rwandans.[141] By 1990, Washington had succeeded in pressuring President Juvénal Habyarimana to privatize state enterprises, reduce government spending, and implement other IMF structural agreements.[142] And U.S. officials were demanding that Rwanda accept the return of Tutsi exiles from Uganda, where they had lived for decades.[143]

Support for the Invasion of Rwanda

While Washington was loudly condemning Iraq's invasion of Kuwait in 1990, it was quietly supporting Uganda's invasion of Rwanda. The invaders were mainly Tutsi exiles who had been part of Museveni's army, and some had been trained in the United States.[144] U.S. officials wanted a new, friendlier Rwandan government to help the Ugandan regime unlock Central Africa's mineral resources for Western capitalist exploitation.[145] But Belgian, French, and Zairean troops helped the Rwandans fend off the invaders, now rebranded as the Rwandan Patriotic Front, who retreated and began a guerrilla war.[146] Edward Herman and David Peterson noted: "Paul Kagame and the RPF were creatures of U.S. power from their origins in Uganda in the 1980s."[147] Kagame left a U.S. Army training course at Fort Leavenworth, Kansas, to assume command of the invaders.[148] During the next three and a half years, Washington nearly doubled its aid to Uganda.[149] In 1991, Washington sold Kampala ten times more weapons than in the previous four decades, knowing that many would be transferred to the RPF.[150] At the same time, U.S. officials demanded that Habyarimana add RPF leaders to his government and army, though they knew the

THE HOLOCAUSTS OF PAX AMERICANA II

invaders aimed to restore Tutsi minority rule in Rwanda.[151] More than ten thousand Rwandans died in the conflict, but the signing of the Arusha Accords in 1993 appeared to signal the arrival of peace.[152]

THE GENOCIDAL CIVIL WAR IN RWANDA

Keenly aware that upcoming elections would not restore Tutsi minority control of Rwanda, Kagame ordered the assassination of the nation's president. Both Habyarimana and Cyprien Ntarymira, the Hutu president of Burundi, died when the Rwandan leader's airplane was shot down in April 1994.[153] Within one to two hours of the plane going down, the RPF launched a new military offensive against the Rwandan government.[154] In response to the assassinations and the associated RPF assault, extremist Hutus began killing Tutsis and mobilizing the population to participate in the slaughter.[155] The RPF also engaged in widespread slaughter, primarily of Hutus but also of Tutsis.[156] Rwandan officials pleaded for help from the United Nations, but the Clinton administration insisted on the withdrawal of most peacekeepers already in the country.[157] Backed by the United States and Uganda, the RPF captured the capital of Kigali in July 1994. Soon afterward, Washington extended diplomatic recognition to Kagame's new Tutsi minority regime, sent economic aid, and deployed troops to train the newly renamed Rwandan Patriotic Army.[158] Years later, Clinton apologized for his "inaction" during the Rwandan holocaust, but this was as dishonest as his policy had been.[159] Washington had helped bring Kagame to power in Rwanda and was deeply complicit in the horrific loss of lives among both Hutus and Tutsis. Former UN general secretary Boutros Boutros-Ghali believed that "the genocide in Rwanda was one hundred percent the responsibility of the Americans."[160]

Most Western accounts of the Rwandan holocaust have focused exclusively on the 500,000 to one million Tutsis and moderate Hutus who died at the hands of the Hutu extremists between April 1994 and July 1994.[161] However, the Tutsi forces led by Kagame killed the same number of Hutus and moderate Tutsis during these four months .[162]

226   ENDLESS HOLOCAUSTS

More than a million Hutus, most of whom had not been involved in the killings, sought refuge in eastern Zaire.[163] The new Tutsi minority regime in Rwanda continued to kill thousands of Hutus during the last half of 1994 and throughout 1995.[164] Some of the Hutu mass murderers who had fled to Zaire launched attacks on the RPA across the border and organized to overthrow the Tutsi regime in their homeland. But most Hutu exiles, predominantly women and children, were concerned with survival, not insurgency.[165] Nonetheless, in October 1996, units of Kagame's RPA, equipped by the Pentagon and trained by U.S. Special Forces, attacked Hutu refugee camps in Zaire, forced hundreds of thousands to return to Rwanda, and killed as many as 260,000 people.[166]

The Invasion of Zaire

In November 1996, Museveni's Ugandan army joined the RPA in a full-scale invasion of Zaire supported by the United States. After the end of the Cold War, the long-standing World Bank and IMF economic support for the Mobutu regime ended amid growing domestic opposition.[167] Washington now wanted far greater access to the country's cobalt, copper, gold, diamonds, coltan, and other resources.[168] U.S. officials were also concerned about Mobutu's ties with Sudan and the prospect of unfriendly nations obtaining Zairean resources.[169] The Clinton administration began demanding Mobutu's resignation a year before the invasion but was repeatedly rebuffed.[170] When Museveni's and Kagame's troops invaded Zaire, they served as proxy armies for the U.S. Empire. Washington had trained both armies, provided the Ugandans with arms, and sent the Rwandans weapons and military equipment through Uganda and other countries.[171] The U.S. government and U.S. companies provided vital military intelligence to the invaders, and a small contingent of U.S. Special Forces fought alongside the invaders in Zaire.[172]

Although Washington and its allies depicted the invasion as a civil war, the Ugandans and Rwandans created Laurent Désiré Kabila's Alliance of Democratic Forces for the Liberation of Congo-Zaire

THE HOLOCAUSTS OF PAX AMERICANA II 227

and did much of the fighting on its behalf.[173] The giant U.S. company Bechtel "became first in line to win contracts" after providing Kabila with satellite intelligence during the rebellion.[174] A month before ousting Mobutu, Kabila approved a $1 billion mining contract with American Mineral Fields, a multinational corporation headquartered in Clinton's hometown, Hope, Arkansas.[175] In May 1997, Mobutu was forced to flee the country, and Kabila came to power in what became known as the Democratic Republic of the Congo. In the years to come, the new ruler would open up as much of the country's mineral wealth as possible to U.S. and other Western exploitation.[176]

PLUNDER AND GENOCIDE IN THE DEMOCRATIC REPUBLIC OF THE CONGO

In 1998, Kabila became estranged from his Ugandan and Rwandan allies and ordered their troops to leave his country. Museveni and Kagame refused and instead launched a new invasion of the DRC and began working with about a dozen Congolese opposition groups with the shared aim of toppling Kabila.[177] Washington continued to train Kagame's troops until shortly before the invasion and dispatched a military and diplomatic team to the Rwanda-Congo border when it began. The U.S. government had lost hope in Kabila and did not waver in its support of its Ugandan and Rwandan proxies.[178] Once again, Washington deployed a small number of troops into Congo.[179] However, Angola, Zimbabwe, and other African countries intervened to defend the new regime in Kinshasa.[180] Although Kabila maintained power in the capital and some other regions, the invaders and allied militias took control of vast stretches of eastern Congo. During the next five years, Ugandan and Rwandan forces and their local partners transported billions of dollars in gold, diamonds, coltan, timber, elephant tusks, and other resources out of Congo.[181] A UN report in 2002 identified eighty-five U.S., Canadian, and European corporations that were profiting from the looting of the country by Kabila, the Ugandans, the Rwandans, and their allies.[182]

In 2001, Kabila was assassinated, and his son Joseph came to power in Kinshasa. In 2003, a peace treaty between the DRC government and its major adversaries was signed, and Ugandan and Rwandan troops withdrew. Although the level of violence has significantly declined since then, intermittent armed struggle between the regime and Congolese militias allied with Kampala or Kigali has turned the country into what reporter Jeff Gettleman has called "a never-ending nightmare."[183] The plunder of Congo has continued, albeit on a smaller scale than before, and in recent years Western domination of its mining industry has declined.[184] In 2018, Kabila agreed to leave office, but the subsequent presidential election was widely regarded as fraudulent.[185] Today the masses in the DRC remain impoverished and unable to benefit from their country's extraordinary resources, while U.S. policy has handsomely rewarded those who have invaded and pillaged their land. More than 5.4 million people died because of war, disease, and starvation in the DRC between 1998 and 2008, and many thousands more have died since then.[186] As an independent Ugandan newspaper concluded, "The U.S. and the West bear responsibility for the deaths of the Congolese people."[187] Glen Ford has explained that "the United States has financed and given overall direction to the worst genocide since World War Two in the Democratic Republic of Congo."[188]

Backing the Regime—and Rebels—in Sudan

After a second civil war began in Sudan in 1983, Washington provided significant military assistance to support the government against southern insurgents.[189] But U.S. policy changed after a new regime came to power in 1989 and then supported Iraq during the Gulf War and allowed bin Laden to seek refuge there.[190] Soon afterward, the U.S. government began paying Uganda to provide military training and equipment to the insurgents fighting against Khartoum.[191] In 1996, the Clinton administration began sending communications equipment and other ostensibly non-lethal military equipment to the rebels through Uganda, Ethiopia, and newly independent Eritrea.[192] Museveni's soldiers also fought alongside the insurgents in Sudan and against Ugandan rebels based there.[193] Small contingents of U.S. troops

THE HOLOCAUSTS OF PAX AMERICANA II   229

were reported to be fighting for the rebels in Sudan as well.[194] After Al-Qaida attacked U.S. embassies in Kenya and Tanzania in 1998, killing 224 people, Clinton ordered strikes against a purported chemical weapons plant in Sudan and military training camps in Afghanistan, where bin Laden had moved two years before.[195] In fact, the Al-Shifa facility in Sudan, a pharmaceutical plant with no ties to Al-Qaida or chemical weapons, was destroyed by U.S cruise missiles.[196] Only one person died in the strike, but thousands of Sudanese likely perished in the following years because the plant was never rebuilt, and they were unable to obtain life-saving medications.[197]

New Rulers and New Violence in Indonesia and Ethiopia

Just as the U.S. Empire ousted Mobutu in Zaire when he had outlived his usefulness, it drove General Suharto from power in Indonesia in 1998.[198] Suharto had resisted structural adjustments demanded by the IMF and was slowly losing control of his country. U.S. officials made clear to Indonesian military leaders that it was time for Suharto to go.[199] After students and workers began to demand democratic reforms, the army unleashed a wave of violence against them and against the country's Chinese minority.[200] Twelve hundred people died, and Suharto, who was out of the country, was persuaded to resign.[201] The following year, Washington backed the new Indonesian regime's killing of as many as five thousand people demanding independence in East Timor.[202] In 1998–2000, border skirmishes between the new Ethiopian government dominated by the Tigrayans and its former ally Eritrea erupted into a ferocious war. Although the United States did not actively intervene in this conflict, both sides used military equipment that Washington had provided in past years.[203] About 100,000 people died in the war.[204]

The Bombing of Iraq and Counterinsurgency in Colombia

In 1998–2000, the Clinton administration bombed Iraq after Hussein's forces contested the no-fly zones established over northern and

230 ENDLESS HOLOCAUSTS

southern Iraq after the Gulf War. The bombing led to as many as 2,300 fatalities.[205] Although U.S. officials claimed they wanted to undermine Hussein's weapons of mass destruction programs, their actual motive was destabilization of the Iraqi regime.[206] In 1999, congressional approval of Plan Colombia ostensibly signaled that the rationale for supporting the government there had evolved from traditional anti-communism to a war on drugs. However, most of the substantially increased U.S. assistance was destined for Colombian troops fighting the continuing insurgency led by the Revolutionary Armed Forces of Colombia and the National Liberation Army.[207] In the years that followed, large numbers of people continued to die in what had become the longest civil war in Latin American history.

Repression in Palestine and the Expansion of NATO

In 2000, Al-Qaida forces attacked the USS *Cole* off the coast of Yemen, killing seventeen sailors.[208] Curiously, the U.S. government did not retaliate by striking at bin Laden, then based in Afghanistan. Years later, Clinton said he could not have approved a military action that might have killed hundreds of noncombatants, but his foreign policy record in Africa and Asia made this explanation unconvincing. [209] When the second Palestinian *intifada* erupted in 2000, Washington once again energetically backed Israel.[210] More than four thousand people, primarily Palestinians, died during the next five years.[211] Despite prior U.S. commitments made by Reagan and Bush, Clinton energetically promoted the eastward expansion of NATO, beginning with the Czech Republic, Hungary, and Poland.[212] In the years that followed, the U.S. Empire's growing encirclement of post-Soviet Russia led to deepening tensions and the outbreak of a new kind of Cold War.[213]

September 11, 2001, and the Invasion of Afghanistan

Scores of millions in the United States considered George W. Bush's inauguration in January 2001 as illegitimate because of the aborted vote recount in Florida and the U.S. Supreme Court intervention that

THE HOLOCAUSTS OF PAX AMERICANA II   231

made him president.[214] Yet he wasted no time pursuing an even more belligerent foreign policy than Clinton. Neoconservatives associated with the Project for a New American Century openly proclaimed that the United States should dominate as much of the planet as possible in the twenty-first century and prevent the emergence of any significant rival power.[215] PNAC also brazenly endorsed preemptive war against nations that challenge the United States.[216] The Bush administration began planning for a potential war against Hussein's regime and taking control of Iraq's vast oil resources shortly after taking office early in 2001.[217] In the summer of 2001, U.S. diplomats offered Afghanistan's Taliban "a carpet of gold" if they would surrender bin Laden and allow an oil and natural gas pipeline to be built in their country—and threatened "a carpet of bombs" if they refused.[218] Al-Qaida's subsequent attacks on the United States on September 11, 2001, which resulted in 2,977 deaths, may well have been sparked by Washington's threats.[219]

The subsequent invasion of Afghanistan toppled the Taliban government, but in more than nineteen years of war, U.S. and allied forces could not defeat the ensuing insurgency. Responding to intense pressure from Washington, the government of Pakistan fought some Taliban combatants who sought refuge there and some allied domestic militants. But it is no secret that Pakistani intelligence and military officials traditionally supported the Taliban and favored its inclusion in a new Afghan government.[220] A decade after Al-Qaida's strikes against the United States, Special Forces dispatched by Obama assassinated bin Laden in Pakistan. Although relatively few people in the world mourned the death of the Al-Qaida leader, more than 220,000 people died in Afghanistan, and more than 80,000 people died in Pakistan during Washington's so-called War on Terror in these countries by 2013.[221]

THE FAILED COUP IN VENEZUELA AND NEW INTERVENTION IN THE PHILIPPINES

In April 2002, conservative military officers and business leaders

232 ENDLESS HOLOCAUSTS

in Venezuela launched an ill-fated coup against the democratically elected, anti-imperialist president Hugo Chávez. U.S. officials denied that his ouster was a coup, endorsed the "change of government," and extended diplomatic recognition to the wealthy capitalist who declared himself the new president.[222] Although Washington denied complicity in the putsch, officials had met repeatedly with some of the plotters and sent money to them.[223] The State Department's Inspector General later admitted that "U.S. assistance programs provided training, institution building, and other support to individuals and organizations understood to be actively involved in the brief ouster of the Chávez government."[224] U.S. naval vessels off the coast of Venezuela assisted the coup participants with signals intelligence and communications jamming.[225] More than a hundred people died during the coup, but the masses rallied around Chávez and returned him to power within two days.[226] Also in 2002, a decade after requiring the withdrawal of all U.S. military personnel, the government of the Philippines allowed one thousand troops to return to help fight the "war on terror" against a Muslim insurgency. The following year, Washington sent another two thousand soldiers to fight a different Muslim force.[227] Some of these ostensible enemies were not connected to Al-Qaida or had only loose ties with bin Laden's network, but the deployments were the first step toward a renewed U.S. military presence in its former colony.[228]

THE SECOND U.S. WAR AGAINST IRAQ

In 2002–2003, the Bush administration subjected the U.S. public to an intense propaganda campaign to legitimize a new war against Iraq.[229] U.S. officials wanted to bring Iraqi oil back into international markets, create a new client state, weaken regional opposition to Israel, and expand U.S. power in West Asia.[230] Bush, Vice President Richard Cheney, and other officials falsely claimed that Hussein was developing weapons of mass destruction and had close ties to Al-Qaida.[231] As the U.S. Empire prepared for war, people across the planet forged the largest antiwar movement in history. Twelve million participated in global protests on February 15, 2003.[232] The invasion of Iraq ordered

THE HOLOCAUSTS OF PAX AMERICANA II   233

by Bush the following month blatantly violated the UN Charter prohibiting wars of aggression but drew support from both major political parties and, briefly, the U.S. public.[233] U.S. and allied troops quickly overthrew Hussein and placed a U.S. viceroy in charge of the country. Washington later installed a pro-Western regime that executed Hussein and other former Iraqi leaders and invited foreign oil corporations to invest in Iraq.[234] However, the invasion and occupation resulted in catastrophic destruction, greatly exacerbated religious sectarianism, and sparked armed resistance from various sections of Iraqi society. In 2008, Bush had to accede to the new government's demand that U.S. troops withdraw from Iraq within three years.[235] By 2011, more than a million people had died because of the war.[236]

THE "WAR ON TERROR" IN YEMEN AND SOMALIA

The Bush administration began authorizing drone attacks in Yemen and Somalia, as well as in Pakistan, in 2002. Close to five hundred people died in these attacks during Bush's two terms in office.[237] U.S. officials claimed that these were precision strikes directed at known terrorists, but many of those who perished had not been involved in attacks on the United States or were noncombatants.[238] Bush did not repeat his father's deadly mistake of sending tens of thousands of troops to Somalia, but the United States and Ethiopia deployed small numbers of commandos and hired local warlords to capture or assassinate Al-Qaida members and other individuals suspected of being terrorists.[239] These actions exacerbated many Somalis' hatred for the United States and Ethiopia and significantly strengthened the extremist factions in the Union of Islamic Courts movement, a broad coalition that many Somalis increasingly viewed as preferable to the warlords who had been pillaging the country for more than a decade.[240]

THE 2004 COUP IN HAITI AND FURTHER EXPANSION OF NATO

In 2004, after Aristide had been elected to a second term as president

234 ENDLESS HOLOCAUSTS

of Haiti, disbanded the army, and demanded massive reparations from France for colonialism and slavery, the Bush administration supported an armed rebellion that forced him to resign and leave the country.[241] Bush sent U.S. Marines to Haiti, ostensibly to maintain order until UN peacekeepers could arrive.[242] In the two years that followed, the police, former soldiers, and paramilitary forces murdered approximately four thousand Aristide supporters and other people in the greater Port-au-Prince area.[243] During this period, another four thousand people died at the hands of criminals in the same area.[244] Thousands of miles away, Washington continued to encircle and escalate tensions with post–Soviet Russia by bringing Bulgaria, Romania, Slovakia, Slovenia, Lithuania, Latvia, and Estonia into NATO. Croatia and Albania followed a few years later.[245] And in 2004, U.S. government agencies and political organizations spent tens of millions of dollars to help elect a pro-Western candidate as president of Ukraine.[246]

The U.S. Role in the Creation of South Sudan

Although the Sudanese government led by Omar al-Bashir disavowed Al-Qaida and international terrorism after the September 2001 attacks on the United States, Washington increased its financial assistance to the rebels fighting Khartoum and made clear that it supported self-determination for the southern part of the country.[247] Two decades of war and intermittent famine had devastated much of Sudan, and U.S. and UN sanctions against the regime were punishing. Washington worked to mobilize international public opinion against Khartoum, especially after a new insurgency erupted in Darfur in 2003, leading to more deaths.[248] In 2005, the Sudanese government signed a peace agreement with the main rebel army that promised autonomy and a referendum on independence for southern Sudan. Although some fighting continued, the United States sent vast amounts of humanitarian aid to the country during the next several years.[249] In 2011, South Sudan became an independent country. As Mark Landler observed, the new nation was "in many ways an American creation, carved out

THE HOLOCAUSTS OF PAX AMERICANA II 235

of war-torn Sudan in a referendum largely orchestrated by the United States, and its fragile institution nurtured with billions of dollars in American aid."[250] More than two million people had died in the civil war since 1983.[251] Significant U.S. aid to the government before 1990 and to the rebels afterward had made Washington deeply complicit in this ghastly human toll.

THE U.S. PROXY WAR AGAINST SOMALIA

In 2006, the Union of Islamic Courts defeated an alliance of Somali warlords backed and financed by the United States, gained control of Mogadishu, and quickly expanded its authority to much of central and southern Somalia.[252] The warlord alliance, which previously hoped to become the country's permanent government, was not interested in working with the UIC, which they falsely depicted as made up entirely of terrorists.[253] In December 2006, the U.S. government approved and sponsored Ethiopia's invasion of Somalia and the overthrow of the first relatively stable and popular government that the nation had known in decades. As Jeremy Scahill has pointed out, this was "a classic [U.S.] proxy war."[254] Since coming to power in Addis Ababa and remaining in office with Washington's help, Meles Zenawi's pro-Western regime had killed hundreds of domestic opponents, and it did not hesitate to attack Somalia on behalf of its patron.[255]

U.S. military airplanes bombed suspected terrorist targets and a U.S. naval vessel fired Tomahawk missiles that killed at least one fighter identified as a member of Al-Qaida.[256] A small group of U.S. soldiers was already in Somalia before the invasion. More U.S. troops entered the country with the Ethiopians and established a permanent military presence there.[257] Washington provided satellite and other intelligence to both the Ethiopian soldiers and the Kenyan troops guarding their border with Somalia, and CIA agents worked closely with both allies.[258] U.S.-trained Ugandan troops and other African Union Mission forces also entered the country.[259] The invasion succeeded in ousting and fragmenting the UIC, but approximately twenty thousand died before the Ethiopian occupation ended in early

236 ENDLESS HOLOCAUSTS

2009.[260] This ostensibly counterterrorist war significantly fueled the growth of Al-Shabab and other extremists and paved the way for more violent conflicts, humanitarian crises, and deaths in Somalia.[261]

Support for Repression from Mexico to Palestine

Bush was concerned about the "pink tide" of socialist-oriented and social democratic governments elected in several Latin American countries throughout his tenure as president.[262] In 2008, Washington tried but failed to bring about a coup against Evo Morales in Bolivia.[263] That same year, the U.S. government launched the Mérida Initiative in Mexico, a putative crime-fighting program modeled on Plan Colombia that dramatically increased support for military and police forces long known to be guilty of murder, torture, and corruption.[264] Since then, about 300,000 people have been murdered or have disappeared in Mexico, many of them at the hands of those recipients of U.S. aid.[265] Also in 2008, the Bush administration tried to bring Georgia and Ukraine into NATO but was blocked by Germany and France.[266] Washington's provision of weapons, military equipment, military training and related aid to Georgia encouraged its August 2008 attack on largely Russian South Ossetia, which resulted in about six hundred deaths.[267] The U.S. government also supported Israel's brief but bloody war against Gaza in 2008–2009, which killed more than 1,400 people.[268]

Expansion of the "War on Terror"

Repudiation of the Iraq War and Bush's militarism by a majority of people in the United States contributed to the election of Barack Obama as president in November 2008.[269] Major sections of the capitalist class supported Obama, viewing him as the candidate who would be most able to repair Washington's global image and advance the interests of the U.S. Empire in an increasingly multipolar world.[270] Obama vowed to end the wars in Iraq and Afghanistan but also pledged to vigorously prosecute the "War on Terror" and back U.S. allies across the

THE HOLOCAUSTS OF PAX AMERICANA II   237

planet. Soon after his inauguration in January 2009, Obama began authorizing new drone strikes against reputed terrorists in Pakistan, but civilians were among the first casualties.[271] During the next eight years, there were ten times as many drone strikes as there had been during the Bush years.[272] Approximately 3,800 people, many of whom were not combatants, died in such attacks in Pakistan, Yemen, and Somalia.[273] Obama eventually boasted to his aides that he had become "really good at killing people."[274] One famous victim was the U.S. citizen Anwar al-Awlaki, an important propagandist for Al-Qaida who was never charged with a terrorism-related crime.[275] He was killed in a drone strike in Yemen in 2011, and his sixteen-year-old son and eight-year-old daughter died in subsequent U.S. attacks.[276]

Notwithstanding his campaign promises, Obama increased the number of U.S. soldiers deployed in Afghanistan from 50,000 to 100,000 in 2009, even as other NATO countries withdrew or reduced their presence.[277] However, fierce if intermittent combat continued throughout much of the country. Tens of thousands of people continued to die directly or indirectly because of the war, just as they had during the Bush administration.[278] Although relatively few Al-Qaida militants remained in Afghanistan, the Taliban fought U.S. and allied troops to a virtual stalemate and gradually regained control over wide sections of the country.[279] By the end of his second term, Obama had reduced the number of U.S. soldiers there to less than ten thousand but had not been able to bring the war to a successful conclusion. By 2015, Washington was compelled to support peace talks between the Afghan regime and the Taliban, though these efforts failed to end the fighting.[280]

The Putsch in Honduras and the Failed Putsch in Ecuador

In 2009, right-wing military officers overthrew the reformist government of Jose Manuel Zelaya in Honduras. The Obama administration may not have approved the coup in advance, but U.S. military advisers in Honduras almost certainly encouraged it.[281] Most of the top generals involved in the putsch had trained in the United States, and the U.S. Embassy's defense attaché met with the coup leader the night before his forces ousted Zelaya.[282] As Dana Frank has emphasized, "It is unlikely they would have perpetrated a coup without U.S. approval."[283] The Obama administration refused to endorse Zelaya's return and instead supported the new government.[284] Since 2009, the repressive regime and allied vigilantes in that country have killed thousands of political opponents and other people.[285] In 2010, police officials with a long history of working with U.S. intelligence agencies tried but failed to overthrow President Rafael Correa in Ecuador. There is no evidence of Washington's involvement in this attempted coup, but the plotters were undoubtedly encouraged by U.S. support for the Honduran putsch the previous year.[286]

Civil War, Drought, and Famine in Somalia

The U.S.-Ethiopian invasion of Somalia ended in early 2009, but armed conflict continued between the weak pro-Western Somali government and allied warlords and Al-Shabab and other forces radicalized by decades of foreign intervention.[287] Only a few months into his presidency, Obama shipped forty tons of weapons and ammunition to the Somali regime despite its widespread unpopularity and the desertion of most of its troops.[288] Madeline Bunting has pointed out that Somalia being "sucked into the war on terror" by Washington led to another calamity.[289] A terrible drought and famine in 2010–12, exacerbated by the civil war, led to almost 260,000 deaths, yet another tragedy in Somalia for which the U.S. government shared responsibility.[290] A new pro-Western government was formed in 2012, and U.S. troops, mercenaries, and African Union Mission soldiers continued to conduct ground operations against Al-Shabab while U.S. drones continued to kill both insurgents and civilians.[291]

The War Against Libya

In 2011, the United States, Britain, France, and other countries

THE HOLOCAUSTS OF PAX AMERICANA II 239

launched a war against Libya, where armed rebels were trying to overthrow Qaddafi's regime.[292] After Washington and its allies falsely claimed the Libyan ruler was about to commit genocide, the United Nations authorized military action to protect civilians.[293] However, the Obama administration's actual objective was regime change. It was the Western war against Libya that led to the massive loss of life there.[294] The Obama administration authorized bombing Libyan military installations and troops to support the rebels and provided at least $1 billion in weapons and cash—and CIA assistance—to the insurgents.[295] U.S. naval vessels shot down missiles that the regime fired at the insurgents, and U.S. Airborne Warning and Control planes provided much of the battle management for the war.[296] After the regime fell and the insurgents killed Qaddafi, Secretary of State Hillary Clinton boasted: "We came, we saw, he died."[297] Nick Turse, Henrik Moltke, and Alice Speri reported in the years that followed: "Libya collapsed into chaos and militia-fueled insecurity, allowing terrorist groups to flourish and the so-called Islamic State to take over the Mediterranean coastal city of Sirte."[298] Fighting between armed political groups backed by different countries continues today, and U.S. drone strikes alone have killed more than a thousand combatants and several hundred civilians.[299] Washington bears substantial responsibility for the war-related deaths of more than 43,000 in Libya since 2011.[300] In addition, amid widespread chaos and corruption, Libya has become the "dominant transit point" for refugees and migrants trying to reach Europe from Africa. More than 20,000 people have drowned in the Mediterranean Sea since 2014.[301]

THE RISE OF THE ISLAMIC STATE

As the deadline for the U.S. withdrawal from Iraq approached in 2011, Obama increasingly worried about the instability of the country and the growing influence of Iran. Notwithstanding his vow to end the U.S. presence in Iraq, he proposed leaving thousands of soldiers there, but most Iraqis wanted the occupation to end, and Prime Minister Nuri al-Maliki rejected the request.[302] As U.S. combat

240 ENDLESS HOLOCAUSTS

forces left the country, Obama declared that the war had been a "success" and that Washington was leaving behind "a sovereign, stable, and self-reliant Iraq."[303] At the same time, a group that called itself Al-Qaida in Iraq was gaining strength and recruiting fighters embittered by the U.S. invasion.[304] Members of this group launched the organization that came to be known as the Islamic State. During the next three years, this new movement savagely but skillfully exploited the weakness of the Iraqi regime and challenged the Assad government in Syria. By 2014, the Islamic State had gained control of vast stretches of Iraq and Syria and proclaimed a caliphate. Later that year, Baghdad allowed Washington to deploy 1,500 troops to help train Iraqi forces to fight them.[305] The United States also began to bomb Islamic State positions in Iraq.[306] Although the Obama administration had not hesitated to work with other religious extremists in the region, it could not countenance a caliphate opposed to the U.S. Empire and attacking sites in the United States and Europe. In confronting the Islamic State, Washington was engaging an enemy that its own actions had helped create.[307]

The War Against Syria

In the spring of 2011, while peaceful demonstrations in Syria called for political reforms, armed rebels killed dozens of soldiers and bombed a Baath Party building in Daraa.[308] The government of Bashar al-Assad harshly repressed the protests and fought back against the insurgency.[309] Washington had long supported the ouster of the Syrian regime and, in August 2011, imposed economic sanctions on the country and demanded that Assad give up power.[310] From the outset, the armed insurgency was led by Sunni religious extremists committed to overthrowing the secular Alawite regime.[311] Thousands of fighters from other countries soon came to Syria, mostly through Turkey, and joined the growing war to topple Assad and establish a new Islamist government.[312] Al-Qaida supporters in Syria launched their first bombing campaign against the regime in late 2011 and founded the Jabhat Al-Nusra Front several weeks later.[313] By then, the

THE HOLOCAUSTS OF PAX AMERICANA II 241

United States, with British help, was transporting Libyan small arms from Benghazi depots to the anti-Assad forces, with Turkey, Saudi Arabia, and Qatar paying for the shipments.[314] Washington later helped these countries obtain weapons for the Syrian insurgents from Central Europe.[315]

In August 2012, the Defense Intelligence Agency reported that Al-Qaida and its allies were "the major forces driving the insurgency in Syria."[316] The DIA approvingly anticipated the prospect of a "Salafist principality in eastern Syria and an Al-Qaida-controlled Islamic state in Syria and Iraq."[317] A few months later, U.S. military personnel began secretly training Syrian insurgents to use anti-tank and anti-aircraft weapons they were receiving from Turkey, Saudi Arabia, and Qatar.[318] Washington claimed that it was helping the so-called Free Syrian Army, a group of secular and moderate rebels. But as Aron Lund has explained, this was "a sprawling leaderless resistance of local fighters who shared only some common goals and an assemblage of FSA-inspired symbols."[319] Al-Nusra and other religious extremists initially declared that they belonged to the same resistance, and rare FSA military advances were followed by the imposition of Sharia and widespread human rights abuses.[320] Turkey, Saudi Arabia, and Qatar initially provided financial and military support for several anti-Assad militias.[321] But as Al-Nusra and allied groups proved to be the most organized and capable fighters and eclipsed other insurgents in 2012–13, these governments increasingly favored them.[322]

In 2013, the United States began directly arming FSA fighters and other insurgents that the CIA described as "relatively moderate" Islamists.[323] But these groups were defeated by the regime or by al-Nusra and its allies or chose to unite with Al-Qaida's increasingly powerful Syrian affiliate. Vast amounts of weapons and military equipment provided by the United States ended up in the hands of the forces that Washington was ostensibly fighting in the global "war on terror."[324] Also in 2013, many members of Al-Nusra left to join the Islamic State, which split from Al-Qaida.[325] Now there were two strong international jihadi groups seeking to overthrow the Syrian government. Obama considered airstrikes against the regime after alleging it had used chemical weapons, but he eventually agreed to a Russian plan in which Assad gave up his stockpiles.[326] Later that year, Washington sold approximately $1 billion in anti-tank weapons to Saudi Arabia for use by the Syrian insurgents. Most of these weapons were delivered to various extremists in 2013–14.[327] But the growing strength of the Islamic State led the U.S. government to begin bombing its positions in Syria in 2014.[328] The Obama administration sent hundreds of troops to train and assist the secular Kurdish-led Syrian Democratic Forces fighting the Islamic State in 2015.[329]

By this time, more than 20,000 foreign fighters, their Syrian counterparts, and the weapons and other assistance provided by the United States and its allies had begun to threaten the survival of the Assad regime.[330] Responding to Assad's request for support, Russia deployed aircraft, troops, and other military assets to Syria in September 2015.[331] Along with the Russians, Iranian and Lebanese Hezbollah forces helped the Syrian government gradually defeat most insurgents, recapture a great deal of territory, and stabilize much of the country during the next three years.[332] Although the Obama administration continued to call for Assad to relinquish power, the threat posed by the Islamic State forced U.S. officials to prioritize the bombing of caliphate targets and the deployment of hundreds of additional soldiers to help the SDF in 2016.[333] The campaign to destroy the caliphate in Iraq and Syria would end, and the broader war against Syria would wind down after Obama left office. But massive military and financial support for extremists and other insurgents in Syria made the United States deeply complicit in the deaths of approximately 600,000 people during the conflict.[334]

A New Attack on Gaza and the Coup in Egypt

In 2012, another U.S.-backed Israeli attack on Gaza claimed more than 150 lives.[335] Also in 2012, a year after mass demonstrations ousted Egypt's authoritarian ruler Hosni Mubarak, Mohamed Morsi became the first democratically elected president in the country's history, and the Muslim Brotherhood won a plurality of seats in

THE HOLOCAUSTS OF PAX AMERICANA II 243

parliament.[336] In 2013, massive demonstrations against the new president erupted throughout Egypt, drawing Mubarak supporters, critics of the Brotherhood's "political dominance," and young people angry about the declining economy.[337] U.S. officials pressured Morsi to bring opposition leaders into the government, leaving him president "at least in name, if not in power."[338] When Morsi refused, Washington backed a military coup by General Abdel Fattah al-Sisi and his troops. As one of the deposed and imprisoned president's advisers remarked, "Nobody who knows Egypt is going to believe a coup could go forward without a green light from the Americans."[339]

The Obama administration issued public statements expressing concern about the ouster of Morsi but pointedly refused to recognize it as a coup. Under U.S. law, such a recognition would have required an end to all military assistance to Egypt.[340] Washington withheld planned shipments of aircraft, missiles, and tanks to Cairo for eighteen months but gradually normalized relations with the new Sisi regime and resumed the sale of weapons and the training of Egyptian troops.[341] Sisi's restoration of the old authoritarian political system led to the worst violence in modern Egyptian history and fueled the growth of the Islamic State and other anti-government forces. In the eight months following the coup, the regime's forces killed more than 2,500 Egyptians, and another six hundred died at the hands of extremists.[342] During the next five years, the armed conflict and government political repression resulted in approximately five thousand additional deaths.[343]

THE CIVIL WAR IN SOUTH SUDAN

In 2013, two years after Washington had "helped midwife the birth of this new nation," South Sudan erupted into civil war.[344] President Salva Kiir, a Dinka, had fired Vice President Riek Machar, a Nuer. Kiir then canceled upcoming elections after Machar announced he would seek the presidency, and government troops loyal to Kiir began massacring the Nuers.[345] Similar violence against Dinkas by Machar's supporters followed, and soon much of the country was experiencing

244 ENDLESS HOLOCAUSTS

vicious ethnic cleansing, the killing of noncombatants, and huge numbers of people fleeing their homes.[346] UN experts noted that Kiir's forces have been "the main belligerent" during this war, but the United States continued to support them during the next five years.[347] The Obama administration ended direct military assistance to Juba but blocked an international arms embargo for years while quietly endorsing Uganda's deployment of troops and provision of weapons, airplanes, and helicopters to assist the Kiir regime.[348] Although Exxon Mobil ended its exploration plans in South Sudan in 2014 because of the violence, Washington hoped the restoration of peace would enable U.S. companies to gain some access to South Sudan's immense oil resources, which are currently dominated by China.[349] Five years after the civil war began, Washington finally agreed to support a UN arms embargo and issued sanctions against the oil companies doing business in South Sudan.[350] By that time, more than 380,000 people had died because of the conflict, and significant violence continued despite a new peace accord.[351]

THE COUP IN UKRAINE

In February 2014, State Department officials and CIA agents helped right-wing Ukrainians in parliament and neo-Nazis in the streets overthrow the democratically elected president, Viktor Yanukovych. Anxious to bring this culturally and politically divided country into the European Community and NATO, Washington played a central role in transforming protests against Yanukovych into political violence and ousting him from office in violation of Ukraine's constitution.[352] At least one hundred people died during the protests and coup, and open fascists assumed some prominent leadership positions in the new government while their compatriots began attacking pro-Russian Ukrainians in the south and east of the country.[353] Armed resistance against the new far-right regime began almost immediately in those areas. Moscow sent troops to back the resistance and reclaimed the historically Russian territory of Crimea with the support of most of its inhabitants.[354] During the next eight years, the

THE HOLOCAUSTS OF PAX AMERICANA II   245

simmering low-intensity conflict in eastern Ukraine led to fourteen thousand deaths. After the United States rejected its demand to end NATO's eastward expansion, Russia invaded Ukraine in February 2022, resulting in tens of thousands of deaths within three months.[355]

Support for Israeli Aggression, Sanctions Against Iran and Venezuela

In July 2014, Israel attacked Gaza again and killed more than 2,200 people, mainly noncombatants.[356] As Medea Benjamin and Nicolas J. S. Davies have pointed out, the continuing provision of massive financial and military assistance makes the United States "complicit in the atrocities Israel commits."[357] Although the Obama administration occasionally criticized Israeli policies, it pledged in 2016 that Washington would provide about $38 billion in aid during the next decade.[358] In stark contrast, the United States and other nations imposed draconian economic sanctions against Iran for several years.[359] Although these punitive measures ostensibly aimed at preventing the Islamic Republic from developing nuclear weapons, the CIA and other intelligence agencies informed Congress that there was no current evidence of such a program.[360] The sanctions crippled the Iranian economy; restrictions on exports of civilian airplane parts and licensing for medicine exports have been linked to reports of deaths there.[361] The Joint Comprehensive Plan of Action on Iran's nuclear energy program was eventually signed in 2015, and some sanctions were lifted. But U.S. officials insisted that "the military option" would still be "on the table" if the agreement broke down.[362] That same year, Obama declared that left-leaning Venezuela was a significant threat to U.S. national security and imposed economic sanctions on several of its leaders.[363]

The War Against Yemen

A popular insurgency led by Houthi rebels, largely Shias, began in Yemen in 2014 and overthrew the pro-U.S., pro-Saudi regime in

246 ENDLESS HOLOCAUSTS

early 2015. Soon afterward, Saudi Arabia and other Sunni Arab states launched a war against the Houthis and their allies. The Saudi-led coalition has waged an unrelenting bombing campaign, maintained an air and naval blockade, and deployed ground troops to Yemen.[364] The United States became deeply involved in the war from the outset by selling military aircraft, jet fuel, bombs, weapons, and other military equipment to the Saudis; by helping them choose targets to strike in Yemen; by refueling their aircraft; and by sending an advisory mission to their operational headquarters.[365] In late 2016, as casualties mounted and the scope of the catastrophe in Yemen became increasingly clear, Obama decided to forgo the planned sale of some precision munitions guidance systems and reduce some intelligence-sharing operations with the Saudis. But other significant U.S. military support for the Saudi war continued.[366]

Obama's Neoliberal Legacy in Foreign Affairs

As Cornel West has emphasized, Obama proved to be a neoliberal politician who was just as committed to the defense and expansion of the U.S. Empire as his predecessors had been.[367] Obama's actions in Iraq and Afghanistan; his military strikes against ostensible enemies in Pakistan and Somalia; his undeclared wars in Libya, Syria, and Yemen; his backing of Israeli attacks against Gaza; his support for coups in Honduras, Egypt, and Ukraine; his aid to the regime in South Sudan; and his approval of sanctions against Iran and Venezuela contributed to an enormous number of deaths. Obama also dramatically increased the U.S. military footprint in Africa, establishing dozens of bases and outposts and developing close military ties with several governments.[368] Moreover, although Washington and Moscow signed a New Strategic Arms Reduction Treaty and Obama reduced the U.S. nuclear stockpile by more than twelve hundred weapons, he refused to commit the United States to "No First Use" of weapons of mass destruction.[369] He also approved plans for a comprehensive modernization of U.S. nuclear weapons and delivery systems that would violate existing international arms treaties and cost about $1 trillion

THE HOLOCAUSTS OF PAX AMERICANA II · 247

during the next thirty years.[370] As Glen Ford has suggested, "Barack Obama may go down in history as the most effective—and deceptive—imperialist of them all."[371]

TRUMP'S "AMERICA FIRST" IMPERIALISM

Thomas Meaney and Stephen Wertheim have observed that Donald Trump's "America First" approach to foreign relations was a "radical American imperialism" that "does not so much break with tradition as bring forward some of its most retrograde but persistent elements."[372] Every president since the end of the Second World War has recognized the importance of maintaining close relations with Western client states and invoking the rhetoric of freedom, democracy, and human rights while prioritizing the interests of the U.S. Empire and presiding over imperialist wars, military interventions, and other hostile actions abroad.[373] In stark contrast, Trump repudiated the postwar liberal international order by promoting brazen national chauvinism, endorsing unilateralism, equivocating on NATO's doctrine of collective defense, scorning other global institutions and treaties, and enthusiastically embracing authoritarian rulers.[374] Ironically, although his foreign policy decisions led to numerous deaths in other countries and potentially could have led to catastrophic regional wars or global nuclear conflagrations, the human toll during his tenure turned out to be considerably less than that of his two immediate predecessors.

TRUMP AND NUCLEAR WEAPONS: "PRETTY DAMN SCARY"

As a candidate, Trump repeatedly asked a foreign policy expert why the United States cannot use its nuclear weapons and refused to rule out their use in West Asia or Europe.[375] After Trump entered the White House, former Director of National Intelligence James Clapper warned that his access to the nuclear codes was "pretty damn scary."[376] The refusal of the United States and eight other nuclear powers to sign the new UN Treaty on the Prohibition of Nuclear Weapons in July 2017 was unfortunate but hardly surprising.[377] As president, Trump

248 ENDLESS HOLOCAUSTS

initially wanted a "tenfold increase in the nuclear arsenal," but his advisers helped him understand this was politically impossible.[378] Nonetheless, he became the first president in decades to abandon the objective of reducing weapons of mass destruction, and he authorized the development and deployment of new kinds of nuclear warheads and missiles.[379] After withdrawing the United States from the nuclear agreement with Iran, Trump withdrew from the Intermediate-Range Nuclear Forces Treaty and the Open Skies Treaty. He refused to extend the New Strategic Arms Reduction Treaty.[380] Insisting that "the United States must have dominance in space," he launched a new branch of the armed forces, the U.S. Space Force.[381] Trump's actions to maintain U.S. military superiority sparked a new arms race with Russia and China and heightened the danger of nuclear proliferation and nuclear war.[382]

NORTH KOREA: FROM "FIRE AND FURY" TO "FALLING IN LOVE"

Perhaps because of prior business ties and Kremlin support for his election, Trump was substantially less aggressive toward Russia than his predecessors.[383] However, during his first year in office, he took a belligerent and dangerous posture toward North Korea. In August 2017, Trump threatened to unleash "fire and fury" against Pyongyang.[384] In a speech to the UN General Assembly, he threatened to "totally destroy" the nation of 25 million people.[385] Soon afterward, Senator Bob Corker warned that Trump's reckless threats against other countries could place the United States "on the path to World War III."[386] Indeed, these actions brought the world much closer to the possibility of nuclear war in 2017 and early 2018 than the U.S. public generally realizes.[387] After Kim Jong Un was satisfied that recent advances in his country's nuclear weapons program would deter a U.S. attack, he embraced a diplomatic resolution of the crisis. Kim and Trump met three times, and the U.S. president said they "fell in love."[388] Negotiations between Pyongyang and Washington did not produce agreements on denuclearization of the Korean Peninsula or a treaty

THE HOLOCAUSTS OF PAX AMERICANA II 249

finally ending the Korean War. After Trump refused to lift existing sanctions against his country, Kim rejected a proposal for additional meetings. But at least the peril of nuclear war had abated. Strikingly, some Democratic politicians and pundits who castigated Trump for his reckless threats against North Korea later criticized him for negotiating with Kim without preconditions or prior concessions.[389]

MOUNTING TENSIONS WITH CHINA

China's growing economic strength, military power, and diplomatic reach had stoked U.S. fears of diminishing hegemony during the Obama administration. During the 2016 campaign, Trump accused China of "raping" the United States by engaging in unfair trade practices, intellectual property theft, and currency manipulation.[390] After becoming president, he initially appeared to welcome a diplomatic resolution of issues with President Xi Jinping. But Trump soon assumed a much more aggressive posture. He imposed major tariffs on Chinese products, ordered substantial restrictions on access to U.S. technology, and authorized other measures against Chinese businesses.[391] These actions did not improve the trade balance or bring jobs back to the United States, but they angered and alienated the Chinese government.[392] Even more alarming, the Trump administration repeatedly deployed warships and other naval vessels to parts of the South China Sea that China has claimed as its territory, resulting in several potentially dangerous confrontations.[393] Washington also developed closer ties with Taiwan and sold weapons to its government on at least eleven different occasions in recent years, infuriating PRC leaders.[394] Since 2018, the risk of a major military confrontation over the South China Sea or Taiwan has significantly increased. The prospect of a cataclysmic, even nuclear, war between the two countries is no longer unthinkable.[395] Trump's racist characterization of COVID-19 as "the China virus" and "Kung-flu," his attempts to scapegoat the People's Republic for virus deaths in the United States, and his issuance of sanctions

The Persistence of the "War on Terror"

After assuming office, Trump authorized only a handful of drone strikes against Pakistan but significantly increased the number of these attacks in Yemen and Somalia.[397] More than twelve hundred people died in U.S. aerial attacks there during the first three years of Trump's presidency.[398] At least several hundred others perished in Somalia because of U.S. and allied ground operations against Al-Shabab forces.[399] Trump also approved troop deployments and military assistance to other African nations he has derided as "shithole countries."[400] In Nigeria, insurgencies by Boko Haram and a group called the Islamic State in West Africa Province posed a serious challenge to the federal government. Dismissing long-standing concerns about the brutality and corruption of the Nigerian army, the Trump administration sold combat aircraft, weapons, and military equipment to Abuja and deployed U.S. military personnel to train its soldiers.[401] By 2019, approximately 350,000 people, primarily children, had died in the conflict, mainly because of starvation and disease.[402] Although the religious extremists have killed indiscriminately, the Nigerian army and allied militias are responsible for more than half of the violent deaths, and many of their victims have been civilians, too.[403] The United States also sent troops to join in putative counterterrorism operations in Cameroon, Kenya, Mali, Mauritania, Uganda, Niger, and Tunisia despite grave problems with regime, ethnic, or gender violence in these countries.[404] Like his predecessors, Trump was not concerned that U.S. intervention often fuels the growth of extremist forces.[405] His administration's pledge to increase investment in Africa, which aimed to counter China's presence on the continent, was never fulfilled. He eventually planned to reduce or end military deployments there.[406] In December 2020, Trump ordered the withdrawal of most U.S. forces from Somalia. Although about a hundred U.S. military personnel remained to support the government, Al-Shabab was "at its strongest in years."[407]

THE HOLOCAUSTS OF PAX AMERICANA II 251

CONTINUING THE WAR AGAINST YEMEN

In May 2017, Trump chose Saudi Arabia, one of the world's most repressive countries but a longtime U.S. ally, as his first foreign destination after becoming president. He later boasted that the Saudis had committed to purchasing hundreds of billions of dollars in U.S. weapons and military equipment, but this claim turned out to be greatly exaggerated.[408] However, the visit signaled closer relations with Riyadh and stronger support for the Saudi-led war in Yemen. The Trump administration resumed the sale of precision guidance munitions systems to the Saudis and the sharing of military intelligence related to the conflict.[409] Washington deployed commandos to Yemen to help locate and destroy rebel missile caches and launch sites.[410] The United States also launched air and ground strikes against al-Qaida fighters who emerged in Yemen because of the carnage caused by the war.[411] However, the U.S.-backed coalition sometimes recruited or "cut deals" with these fighters, effectively placing Washington "on the same side" with them.[412] Not even the murder and dismemberment of the U.S. resident and journalist Jamal Khashoggi by Saudi agents in Istanbul in 2018 could weaken Trump's embrace of the House of Saud.[413] In April 2019, Congress passed a historic resolution that invoked the War Powers Act and called for an end to U.S. involvement in the conflict.[414] However, Trump vetoed the resolution, falsely claiming it violated his constitutional authority as commander in chief.[415] By December 2020, approximately 233,000 people had died because of the war in Yemen.[416] After his inauguration as president, Joseph Biden promised to help end this conflict, but his administration continued to sell weapons and military equipment to the Saudis, and the carnage in Yemen continued.[417]

THE END OF THE U.S. WAR IN AFGHANISTAN

Although Trump had criticized the US wars in Afghanistan, Iraq, and Syria during his presidential campaign, he deployed thousands of additional troops to these countries during his first year in office.[418]

Trump also significantly increased aerial bombardment—and civilian casualties—in Afghanistan.[419] At a July 2017 meeting, Trump told his advisers that the United States should demand a share of Afghanistan's enormous mineral wealth as compensation for backing his regime.[420] Afghan President Ashraf Ghani later agreed to work with U.S. companies to explore and extract minerals.[421] In October 2018, the Afghan government signed contracts with the U.S.-based Centar company to develop two sites with copper and gold deposits.[422] The U.S. Geological Survey also signed a letter of intent to assist with resource development and marketing.[423] The deteriorating military situation soon jeopardized these arrangements, however. The Afghan government was widely reviled as corrupt, the Taliban controlled much of the country, and Trump was no more successful than his predecessors in changing these realities.[424] In late 2018, U.S. officials began negotiating directly with the Taliban without the participation of the Kabul regime. The Trump administration and the insurgents signed a peace agreement in February 2020. In exchange for the Taliban's promise to prohibit Al-Qaida operations in areas they control and to seek a peaceful accommodation with the Afghan government, Washington committed to withdrawing its troops from the country.[425] Most U.S. military personnel had departed by November 2020, and Trump announced a further reduction at that time.[426] In the summer of 2021, Biden withdrew the remaining U.S. military personnel from Afghanistan, and the Taliban came to power within days. More than 100,000 Afghans have died as a result of the war since 2013.[427]

The Destruction of the Caliphate in Iraq and Syria

Trump embraced Obama's commitment to defeating the Islamic State, continued bombing its positions in Iraq and Syria, and expanded U.S. ground operations in Syria.[428] Like Obama, Trump showed little concern for the resulting casualties in these countries. The airstrikes and other military actions against the Islamic State authorized by the two presidents killed not only scores of thousands of their fighters but also

THE HOLOCAUSTS OF PAX AMERICANA II 253

tens of thousands of noncombatants.[429] In other respects, Trump's "radical American imperialism" in Iraq and Syria differed from his predecessors. On two occasions in 2017, Trump told Iraq's then-prime minister Haider al-Abadi that Washington should be compensated with oil for supporting his government.[430] Al-Abadi pointed out that U.S. companies had already obtained significant interests in Iraq's oil industry.[431] Trump finally gave up on the idea, but when he made a surprise visit to U.S. troops in Iraq in December 2018, he did not meet with the new Iraqi leader, Adil Abdul-Mahdi.[432] In Syria, Trump authorized the bombing of government military bases in 2017 and 2018 after Assad's forces allegedly used chemical agents.[433] U.S. troops also killed about one hundred Russian military contractors fighting for the Syrian government after they reportedly entered protective zones for the SDF in early 2018.[434] However, Trump abandoned the long-standing U.S. objective of ousting the Assad regime and stopped training and arming anti-Assad insurgents.[435]

In Iraq, most ground operations against Islamic State forces were conducted by Popular Mobilization forces—militias largely trained, equipped, and led by Iran—and Kurdish Peshmerga fighters.[436] In Syria, most of the fighting on land was done by the Assad government and its Russian, Iranian, and Lebanese allies, though the SDF also played an important role.[437] By December 2017, Islamic State forces had been defeated in Iraq. More than 120,000 people, predominantly noncombatants, had died in the continuing conflicts in Iraq since 2012.[438] In December 2018, with only one small area of Syria still under Islamic State control, Trump proclaimed victory.[439] However, his announcement that he would withdraw the two thousand U.S. troops in Syria met with blistering bipartisan opposition, and he agreed to maintain a smaller force in the country.[440] In February 2019, Trump's declaration that he wanted to keep troops in Iraq "to watch Iran" sparked widespread outrage and demands for U.S. withdrawal.[441] Eight months later, he betrayed the SDF forces when he allowed Turkish troops to enter northern Syria, kill hundreds of fighters and civilians, and drive them out of the region.[442]

By mid-2020, U.S. and SDF forces had reconciled and were extracting oil in northeastern Syria and transporting it by trucks to Iraq.[443] When Trump announced his intention to withdraw some troops from Iraq in November 2020, members of Congress from both parties demanded that Washington maintain a robust military presence there and in Syria.[444]

Aggression Against Iran

Trump was not the first U.S. official to claim that Iran is "the leading state sponsor of terror," a spurious accusation belied by the long history of U.S. imperialism, Israeli settler colonialism, and Saudi support for Al-Qaida and other religious extremists.[445] But Trump took a much more aggressive posture toward the Islamic Republic than Obama throughout his term as president. In May 2018, Trump withdrew the United States from the Joint Comprehensive Plan of Action on Iran's nuclear energy program and reinstated punishing economic sanctions against Tehran.[446] By effectively limiting the importation of medical supplies and humanitarian goods, those sanctions have contributed to the deaths of thousands of people in Iran.[447] In addition, Trump backed Israeli military attacks on Iranian forces in Syria and encouraged Jerusalem and Riyadh to ally against Tehran.[448] His National Security Advisor in 2018–19, John Bolton, had long called for bombing Iran and bringing about regime change.[449] In June 2018, Trump threatened to make Iran "suffer consequences the likes of which few throughout history have ever suffered before," and in May 2019, he threatened to bring about "the official end of Iran."[450]

In January 2020, a U.S. drone killed Iranian General Qassim Suleimani and several Iraqi militia leaders in Baghdad, an action condemned throughout much of West Asia and beyond.[451] Trump asked senior advisers in mid-November 2020 for options on military strikes against Iran's main nuclear site at Natanz.[452] Although he was dissuaded by advisers' warnings on the risk of a regional war, he likely gave a "go-ahead" for the Israeli assassination of Iran's top nuclear scientist later that month.[453]

THE HOLOCAUSTS OF PAX AMERICANA II   255

The Enthusiastic Embrace of Authoritarian Rulers

Trump's curious affinity for Vladimir Putin has been widely noted, but the Russian leader was not the only autocrat to whom the U.S. president was drawn. Military, financial, and political support for right-wing regimes and movements has long been a central feature of U.S. foreign policy. Trump, however, was distinctive among modern presidents in his open, enthusiastic embrace of authoritarian rulers in client states. He backed Filipino president Rodrigo Duterte's "War on Drugs," which has led to approximately 30,000 extrajudicial murders.[454] Trump called Egyptian President Sisi "my favorite dictator" and continued the flow of weapons and cash that has enabled his regime to kill thousands of people in the past several years.[455] Trump described himself as "a big fan" of Turkish President Recep Tayyip Erdogan despite Ankara's deadly intervention in Syria and the mass imprisonment of Kurds and other political opponents at home.[456] Trump endorsed the reelection of pro-U.S. Honduran President Juan Orlando Hernández in November 2017 despite electoral fraud and the murder of dozens of people protesting against it.[457] The United States has also continued to fund and arm the right-wing Colombian government, whose supporters have been responsible for killing more than 850 former guerrillas and social justice activists between 2016 and 2019.[458]

Backing Coups in Venezuela and Bolivia

In stark contrast, the Trump administration sought to oust the Venezuelan government of Nicolás Maduro by imposing new, harsher economic sanctions and a de facto embargo on Venezuelan oil. During the Trump years, U.S. officials also financially supported right-wing opposition groups, deployed CIA agents to encourage a military coup, officially recognized a right-wing opposition legislator as president, and placed Venezuelan financial assets in the United States under his control.[459] In addition, Trump repeatedly declared that U.S. military intervention in Venezuela remains "an option."[460] The Maduro government survived the coup effort because many Venezuelans and the armed forces continued to support the Bolivarian Revolution.[461] But U.S. sanctions caused more than 40,000 deaths in Venezuela in 2017–18, and armed conflict between the U.S.-backed opposition and the government led to at least two hundred deaths.[462]

In Bolivia in November 2019, the military and police forced the newly reelected leftist President Evo Morales to leave office. The Trump administration quickly recognized the new regime installed by the putschists. Claiming that the election had been marred by fraud, Washington renewed long-suspended financial aid to Bolivia, and the CIA and State Department provided political advice to the new government while it killed scores of people protesting against the coup.[463] Those fraud claims were soon disproved, and new elections in October 2020 returned Morales's Movement Toward Socialism to power.[464]

Counting the Dead

Between 1980 and 2020, two U.S. wars and sanctions in Iraq and the U.S. war in Afghanistan killed more than two million people. Washington's proxy wars in Angola, Mozambique, Rwanda, Democratic Republic of Congo, and Syria resulted in roughly nine million deaths. U.S. military intervention, support for client states and rebels, and related famines in Sudan, South Sudan, Somalia, Ethiopia, and Nigeria cost the lives of another five million people. The U.S. Empire's role in the collapse of most socialist regimes made it partly responsible for well over seven million deaths. Other U.S. military interventions and hostile actions abroad caused or contributed to millions of additional fatalities. Altogether, the empire was responsible or shared responsibility for the deaths of more than 25 million people during the past forty years of Pax Americana. This total is in addition to the massive ongoing loss of life in the Indigenous Peoples Holocaust, the African American Holocaust, the Workers Holocaust, and the other holocausts at home and abroad to be examined in chapter 7. Today the Biden administration hopes to revitalize the liberal

THE HOLOCAUSTS OF PAX AMERICANA II

international order, rebuild relationships with its client states, impede the rise of China, and thwart the return of Russia. But the erosion of U.S. primacy will continue, and the possibility that the ruling class will act like a "wounded beast" and commit heinous new crimes means that the entire planet may be entering the most dangerous chapter in its history.

7

Other Holocausts at Home and Abroad

Violence continues to sustain the U.S. Empire in never-ending wars that have killed and displaced millions this century. Part of the consequences of this permanent state of violence is seen most recently in El Paso, Dayton, and Gilroy. . . . The high rates of murder and the increasing number of mass shootings in the United States are indicative of a society engulfed in fears fueled by racism, xenophobia, misogyny, militarism, and growing inequalities in income, wealth, and power.
—HOWIE HAWKINS, "THE U.S. CULTURE OF VIOLENCE IS REAPING WHAT IT HAS SOWN," 2019

Consider the companies that knowingly market unsafe products, everything from cars to medications to toys; consider the multinational firms that knowingly sell addictive and injurious tobacco products here and abroad . . . that kill hundreds of thousands every year in the United States alone. Many more people sustain injury, loss, and death from the doings of corporate America than from street crime. There is no social formation more profoundly immoral than a big capitalist corporation.
—MICHAEL PARENTI, *AMERICA BESIEGED*, 2001

OTHER HOLOCAUSTS AT HOME AND ABROAD   259

In addition to the holocausts inflicted on Indigenous people, people of African descent, workers, and the victims of U.S. wars, military interventions, and hostile actions in other countries, the U.S. Empire has been responsible for other kinds of mass death at home and abroad. This country's long history of armed conflicts has resulted in an enormous number of U.S. military and civilian fatalities.[1] White mob and vigilante violence, police murders, political repression, incarceration, and government actions against migrants have taken a terrible human toll.[2] Along with these forms of carnage, widespread homicides and suicides have made the United States the world's most violent advanced capitalist society.[3] Far-right and other extremist violence have proved deadly for many people, as well.[4] Various forms of large-scale social murder continue to occur today, claiming far greater numbers of lives. The profit-driven proliferation of dangerous drugs, tobacco, automobiles, and other unsafe consumer products has led to horrific human costs in this country and other nations.[5] Unconscionable medical experimentation, the failure to address public health crises, limited access to quality health care, and often dangerous medical treatments have produced mass death as well.[6] Moreover, the U.S. Empire's sordid record of environmental pollution has killed vast multitudes of people and now threatens the future of the planet.[7]

U.S. Deaths in the Empire's Wars

The main victims of the empire's wars have generally been people in other lands, but U.S. military personnel and noncombatants have also paid a heavy price. Twenty-six thousand members of the Continental Army and state militias died fighting for the new United States during the War of Independence.[8] Twenty thousand U.S. soldiers died during the War of 1812.[9] Just under 14,000 U.S. troops perished during the Mexican War, and more died later from diseases contracted during the war.[10] The total number of deaths in the Civil War likely exceeded one million.[11] In 1894, the Census Bureau estimated that 19,000 white people had died in the wars that nearly annihilated Indigenous peoples, and this was probably an underestimate.[12] Approximately 6,000 U.S. troops died during the War of 1898, almost entirely because of disease in the war zone and in training camps at home.[13] Another 4,200 soldiers died during the bloody war against the people of the Philippines between 1899 and 1913.[14] Although Washington did not officially enter the First World War until April 1917, more than 120,000 U.S. troops lost their lives in this "imperial bloodbath."[15]

More than 400,000 U.S. soldiers, sailors, and other military personnel died in the Second World War.[16] Almost 37,000 members of the U.S. Armed Forces died in the Korean War.[17] More than 58,000 perished in the Vietnam War, but the total number of U.S. deaths caused by this conflict was far larger.[18] A roughly equivalent number of Vietnam veterans died later from the effects of exposure to Agent Orange, the deadly herbicide widely used by the United States during the war.[19] And a similar number of Vietnam veterans have committed suicide since returning home.[20] About 380 U.S. military personnel died in the Gulf War of 1990–91.[21] More than 2,400 U.S. troops lost their lives in the Afghanistan War.[22] Over 4,500 died in the Iraq War.[23] Uncounted hundreds of U.S. nationals working as mercenaries and military contractors have also died in the conflicts in Afghanistan and Iraq.[24] U.S. combatants and other U.S. nationals have also died in smaller-scale military operations from the "Quasi War" fought primarily off the East Coast and in the Caribbean between 1798 and 1800 to the current military interventions in Syria, Somalia, Yemen, and other countries. Altogether, well over 1.8 million people of the United States have perished in this country's wars since 1775.

Other White Mob and Vigilante Violence in the Nineteenth Century

The most horrific examples of white mob and vigilante violence in the nineteenth century may have been the genocide against Indigenous people in midcentury California and the mass terror against people of African descent in the South after the Civil War. Such violence has been primarily used against Native and Black people, but it has also

OTHER HOLOCAUSTS AT HOME AND ABROAD 261

been directed against other people of color, immigrants, religious minorities, dissidents, and radicals. Bigots killed seventeen Mormons in Missouri in 1837 and murdered Mormon leader Joseph Smith and his brother Hyrum in Illinois in 1844.[25] A pro-slavery mob fatally shot the abolitionist Elijah Lovejoy in 1837 in Illinois.[26] Anti-Catholic violence claimed more than forty-five people in Philadelphia in 1844 and in St. Louis a decade later.[27] About thirty people died in violence initiated by the nativist Know Nothing Party in Baltimore in 1856.[28] More than fifty people died in the conflict between pro-slavery and anti-slavery forces in "Bleeding Kansas" between 1855 and 1860.[29]

In the second half of the century, white mobs and vigilantes murdered several hundred Mexican Americans in Texas, California, Arizona, New Mexico, Wyoming, Nebraska, and other states.[30] Racists killed as many as three hundred Chinese immigrants in California, Washington, Colorado, and Wyoming between the 1850s and the 1880s.[31] More than sixty Catholics and Protestants perished in the Orange Riots in New York City in 1870–1871.[32] Bigots killed several Mormons in Georgia, Tennessee, and Utah in the 1880s.[33] Mobs hanged and shot to death eleven Italian Americans in New Orleans in 1891 and murdered several others in Louisiana in the following years.[34] Anti-Semitic vigilantes lynched Leo Frank in Atlanta in 1913.[35]

POLICE MURDERS AND POLITICAL REPRESSION IN THE NINETEENTH CENTURY

The first police departments were created in Boston in 1838, New York City in 1845, and Chicago in 1851 and were intended to protect capitalist property and maintain social control over the rapidly growing immigrant population.[36] The police departments that emerged in Southern cities evolved from the slave patrols created to apprehend escapees, punish those who violated plantation rules, and to deter or respond to resistance.[37] Gary Potter has explained: "Early American police departments shared two primary characteristics: they were notoriously corrupt and flagrantly brutal."[38] Police officers in some

262   ENDLESS HOLOCAUSTS

cities injured and even killed people by "clubbing" them with batons or nightsticks, and the growing use of handguns led to more deaths.[39] Reports of wrongful killings began to emerge soon after the establishment of police departments. As previously noted, police killed two tailors during a strike in New York City in 1850 and two railroad workers during a strike in Portage, New York, in 1851.[40] Cincinnati police killed a protester in 1853, and a New York City police officer fatally shot an unarmed man fleeing arrest in the back in 1858.[41] Public complaints about the police mounted, and the phrase "police brutality" first appeared in the *Chicago Daily Tribune* in 1872.[42] The exact number of routine police homicides in the United States in the nineteenth century will probably never be known. But law enforcement officers were responsible for some of the more than 50,000 deaths of African Americans in the South in the three decades after the Civil War.[43] Police were prominently involved in many of the murders of Mexican Americans in the second half of the century.[44] And they were responsible for many of the hundreds of deaths of workers engaged in strikes and other labor actions between 1870 and 1900.[45]

POLICE MURDERS AND POLITICAL REPRESSION, 1900–1950

Strikingly, the federal government failed to maintain comprehensive national records of police homicides throughout the twentieth century.[46] In the early part of the century, most local law enforcement agencies did not maintain reliable records on these deaths, either.[47] Jeffrey S. Adler has pointed out that police in Chicago and New Orleans appear to have counted the number of people they killed. Chicago police reportedly killed 248 people between 1900 and 1920 and another eighty-nine in 1926–27.[48] New Orleans police reportedly killed fifty-nine people in fourteen years between 1925 and 1945.[49] Whether the records in these two cities are truly comprehensive is far from clear, and much less is known about police homicides in New York, Philadelphia, St. Louis, Boston, Baltimore, and most other cities and towns across the country. More is known about law enforcement agents' involvement in infamous episodes of racist violence and

OTHER HOLOCAUSTS AT HOME AND ABROAD   263

political repression during this period. During the First Red Scare that began in 1919, the federal government arrested about ten thousand leftists, imprisoned more than four hundred, and deported more than five hundred, yet few deaths occurred in the process.[50]

In contrast, law enforcement officers and vigilantes killed between two and three thousand Mexican Americans in South Texas in 1915–16 after a small armed rebellion had led to the deaths of about fifty white people.[51] In 1918, Texas Rangers, soldiers, and white cattlemen shot to death fifteen men and boys of Mexican descent at Porvenir in West Texas.[52] In addition, police were complicit in many of the several hundred African American deaths during the "Red Summer" of 1919 and in many of the lynchings and other racist murders that occurred in the first half of the twentieth century.[53] Law enforcement officers were also responsible for many of the several hundred workers' deaths during strikes and other labor actions between 1900 and the late 1930s.[54]

In 1931, a federal commission issued the *Report on Lawlessness in Law Enforcement*, which criticized "physical brutality" but failed to adequately assess the scope and significance of police murders.[55] Law enforcement officers throughout the country continued to kill workers of all backgrounds while disproportionately targeting African Americans and other people of color.[56] Police also continued to act against dissidents and radicals, though deaths brought about by political repression paled in comparison with routine police homicides. In 1927, the state of Massachusetts executed Italian immigrants and anarchists Nicola Sacco and Bartolomeo Vanzetti for a murder they did not commit.[57] Police killed three people at a communist-led protest against the eviction of a family in Chicago in 1931.[58] Police in Dearborn, Michigan, killed four people at a communist-led protest by unemployed workers in 1932.[59] That same year, police in Washington, DC, killed two individuals who were part of the Bonus Army, a group of more than 20,000 unemployed veterans demanding immediate payment of promised bonuses for serving in the First World War.[60] Between 1935 and 1937, police violence against Puerto Rican nationalists resulted in twenty-eight deaths.[61] Although data on routine

264 ENDLESS HOLOCAUSTS

police killings between 1900 and 1949 are fragmentary, it may be conservatively estimated that the annual number of police homicides in the first half of the twentieth century was around two hundred. This indicates a total of about ten thousand such deaths between 1900 and 1949, to which must be added more than three thousand deaths of Blacks, Mexican Americans, and workers in the special episodes of repression during this period.

Police Murders and Political Repression, 1950–2000

The Census Bureau and other federal agencies finally began to collect data on police killings in 1949, but their estimates omitted about 50 percent of the fatalities.[62] Close to five hundred people were dying each year at the hands of law enforcement officers in the 1950s.[63] And the annual number of police homicides significantly increased in the following decades. By the first half of the 1970s, police were killing more than seven hundred people each year and the human toll continued to climb, but government statistics still excluded half the deaths.[64] Black people bore the brunt of state and vigilante violence during the 1950s and 1960s. Police and vigilantes murdered about 125 civil rights activists and supporters, and the police and FBI killed at least thirty-four Black Panthers.[65] More than two hundred people—primarily African Americans—lost their lives during the "protest riots" of the 1960s.[66] Law enforcement agents killed other people as well. Police, FBI agents, and National Guard troops killed dozens of people in the nationalist rebellion in Puerto Rico in 1950.[67] After the Second Red Scare began in 1947, ten or twelve thousand people lost their jobs, a few hundred Marxist-Leninists were imprisoned, and the Communist Party was almost destroyed.[68] The execution of Julius and Ethel Rosenberg in 1953 for espionage smeared communists as Soviet spies, but they were not the only fatalities. More than ten leftists and progressives committed suicide as life under McCarthyism grew more repressive; at least three died from "the stress of the investigations and blacklists," and a few were murdered.[69]

National Guard troops killed Allison Krause, Jeffrey Miller, Sandra

OTHER HOLOCAUSTS AT HOME AND ABROAD   265

Scheuer, and William Knox during antiwar protests at Kent State University in Ohio in 1970.[70] That same year, police killed journalist Ruben Salazar and two other people during the Chicano Anti-War Moratorium in Los Angeles.[71] Government agents and allied tribal forces killed more than sixty Indigenous activists in the 1970s.[72] In 1974, after exposing radioactive contamination at a Kerr-McGee nuclear fuel plant in Oklahoma, Karen Silkwood died in a mysterious car accident on her way to meet a reporter.[73] In 1976, a CIA agent working with the Pinochet dictatorship organized the assassination of former Chilean diplomat Orlando Letelier and his colleague Ronni Moffitt in Washington, DC.[74] The FBI and local police were complicit in the murders of five communists by Klan members and neo-Nazis in Greensboro, North Carolina in 1979.[75] Puerto Rican independence activist Angel Rodríguez-Cristóbal was mysteriously murdered in his federal prison cell in Florida in 1979.[76] Philadelphia police killed eleven people when they bombed the home of the African American MOVE group in 1985.[77] In 1993, when federal agents tried to search the Branch Davidian compound near Waco, Texas, and arrest its leader David Koresh on firearms charges, the ensuing gun battle killed four agents and six cult members. After unsuccessfully seeking the surrender of Koresh and his followers for fifty-one days, the FBI used tear gas to try to force them out of the compound. Fires broke out on the property, and Koresh and seventy-five other Branch Davidians died.[78]

In the last quarter of the twentieth century, police continued to kill African Americans, Indigenous people, Latinos, Asian Americans, and people of European descent with alarming regularity. Thousands upon thousands died, and by the end of the 1990s, the police were killing close to nine hundred people each year.[79] Some of the most prominent African American victims during this period are listed in chapter 2. Some of the most prominent non-Black victims were Santos Rodriguez in Dallas in 1973; Joe Campos Torres in Houston in 1977; Luis Baez in New York in 1979; Jeff Cordova and Juan Luis Garcia in Longmont, Colorado, in 1980; Leonard Zuchel in Denver in 1985; Manuel Diaz in Los Angeles in 1987; Carmen Coria in

Perth Amboy, New Jersey, in 1988; Anthony Baez, Anthony Rosario, and Hilton Vega in New York in 1994; Kuanchung Kao in Sonoma County, California, in 1997; and Abelino Montoya in Las Vegas, New Mexico, in 1998.[80] Data from the Census Bureau and other federal agencies indicate a total of just under 13,000 police homicides between 1949 and 1992, and extrapolations for 1993–99 indicate the official total between 1949 and 1999 was just under 15,000 deaths.[81] Because government estimates included only half the officer-involved killings in the 1950s, it may be estimated that approximately 30,000 police homicides occurred in the second half of the twentieth century, to which must be added hundreds more in the special episodes of repression during this period.

POLICE MURDERS AND POLITICAL REPRESSION IN THE TWENTY-FIRST CENTURY

In the absence of sustained mass movements for social justice, violent political repression in the United States has been more limited during the past four decades. However, some high-profile killings have occurred. FBI agents shot to death Filiberto Ojeda Ríos, a fighter for Puerto Rican independence, in 2005.[82] Police killed anti-fascist activist Willem van Spronsen after he threw incendiary devices at ICE vehicles and buildings at a detention center in Tacoma, Washington, in 2019.[83] U.S. Marshals assassinated anti-fascist activist Michael Reinoehl, who was suspected of killing a right-wing activist, near Olympia, Washington, in 2020.[84] As always, vastly larger numbers have died because of routine police violence. And although law enforcement officers have continued to kill African Americans at a much higher rate than other demographic groups, thousands upon thousands of others have also perished at their hands in the first two decades of the twenty-first century. Some of the most prominent non-Black victims during this period were Bich Cau Thi Tran in San Jose in 2003; Rigoberto Alpizar in Miami in 2005; Alvin Faitasi Itula in Salt Lake City in 2006; Michael Cho in La Habra, California, in 2007;

OTHER HOLOCAUSTS AT HOME AND ABROAD   267

Steven Paul Crowels in Tulsa in 2009; Brian Claunch in Houston in 2012; Alex Nieto in San Francisco in 2014; Brandon Stanley in East Bernstadt, Kentucky, in 2016; Dennis Tuttle and Rhogena Nicholas in Houston; Li Xi Wang in Chico, California, in 2019; Erik Salgado in Oakland, California, in 2020; and Joseph Johnson in Idaho Falls, Idaho, in 2021.[85]

Amid the widespread demonstrations sparked by the police killings of Michael Brown, Eric Garner, and Tamir Rice in 2014, the public learned that the federal government still did not have comprehensive national statistics on police homicides.[86] By this time, the Mapping Police Violence project and the Fatal Encounters project had begun tracking officer-involved deaths.[87] In 2015, the *Washington Post* and the *Guardian* also started counting the number of people who died at the hands of police each year.[88] These investigations soon confirmed that half of the people killed in interactions with police were not included in federal government databases in 2013–15.[89] Under growing public pressure, the U.S. Department of Justice's Bureau of Justice Statistics reported that approximately twelve hundred people had been killed by law enforcement officers between June 2015 and May 2016.[90] The federal government's commitment to tracking annual police killings soon faltered, but other researchers continued their work. The *Washington Post* found that officers shot to death almost one thousand people annually between 2015 and 2018.[91] This estimate does not include individuals police have killed with Tasers, batons, their hands or knees, or police vehicles. The Mapping Police Violence project has reported that almost eleven hundred people die each year because of police actions.[92] The Fatal Encounters database has indicated an average annual number of well over fourteen hundred deaths and a total of more than 31,000 deaths since 2000.[93]

U.S. law enforcement officers kill many more people each year than their counterparts in other advanced capitalist countries.[94] The vast majority of these deaths are unnecessary and preventable.[95] Researchers with Mapping Police Violence have emphasized that the majority of all police killings in 2020 could have been avoided.[96] As the editors of the *Houston Chronicle* have pointed out, "Even for the

268   ENDLESS HOLOCAUSTS

ones killed while armed, the mere presence of a gun can't be considered the sole justification for the use of government-sponsored lethal force."[97] Despite the paucity, incompleteness, and unreliability of official records, it can be roughly estimated that law enforcement officers have killed a minimum of nearly eighty thousand people—and possibly many more—since the mid-nineteenth century.

INCARCERATION DEATHS

Approximately sixteen thousand people have been officially executed since the beginning of the British colonial period, and it is widely recognized today that many of them were innocent.[98] However, many more people have died because of various kinds of incarceration in the United States. About two thousand Tsalagis perished in internment camps awaiting deportation to Oklahoma in 1838, and approximately three thousand Diné died while interned at Bosque Redondo in eastern New Mexico in 1864–67.[99] Tens of thousands of men, primarily African Americans, likely died while performing convict labor in harsh and dangerous conditions in southern states between the 1870s and the late 1920s.[100] During the Second World War, the U.S. government's internment of approximately 120,000 people of Japanese descent exacted a substantial human toll. Military guards killed at least seven and possibly more internees accused of trying to escape.[101] More than eighteen hundred died from diseases in the camps, and many of these deaths were at least partly attributable to harsh conditions and inadequate health care.[102] The impact of physical deprivation and psychological trauma on internees lasted for decades after the camps closed. Survey information developed by one researcher indicated that former internees had more than twice the risk of cardiovascular disease, cardiovascular mortality, and premature death than other people.[103] The number of premature deaths among Japanese Americans, at least partly caused by the internment experience, may have run into the thousands in the decades following the end of the Second World War.[104]

The new wave of mass incarceration that began in the mid-1970s

OTHER HOLOCAUSTS AT HOME AND ABROAD 269

increased the U.S. prisoner population from about 300,000 to more than two million.[105] With less than 5 percent of the world's population, this country holds almost 25 percent of its prisoners.[106] The disproportionate impact of mass incarceration on Blacks and Latinos is widely recognized today, but far less attention has been paid to the many deaths of prisoners. More than 10,000 prisoners died from suicide, homicide, "accidents," and other non-natural causes in U.S. prisons and jails between 1981 and 2000.[107] More than 12,000 died of non-natural causes between 2000 and 2018.[108] Local jail and state and federal prison authorities are responsible for these deaths and many of the thousands of fatalities resulting from diseases.[109] A 2017 study concluded that many prisoners' deaths could be prevented if adequate medical care were provided in their institutions.[110]

GOVERNMENT ACTIONS AGAINST MIGRANTS

From its first years, the U.S. government encouraged immigration so there would be enough people to settle the lands forcibly taken from Indigenous people and perform the labor required for capitalist economic development. However, historically racist federal immigration law largely excluded people of color from migrating to the United States until the mid-1960s.[111] Repressive government actions against migrants have taken a considerable human toll over time. During the first half of the twentieth century, hundreds of thousands of people arriving at Ellis Island were detained, sometimes for months, and more than 120,000 of them were deported to their home countries.[112] During the Great Depression in the 1930s, the government deported about one million people of Mexican descent.[113] About 60 percent of them were U.S. citizens.[114] Hundreds of people died while being deported.[115] In 1939, the United States turned away a ship carrying about nine hundred Jewish refugees from Nazi Germany. More than 250 of them later perished in the *Shoah*.[116] Also in 1939, Congress rejected a bill allowing 20,000 German Jewish children to come to this country. Many of these children almost certainly perished in the years that followed.[117] Between the mid-1940s and the mid-1950s, the U.S.

270 ENDLESS HOLOCAUSTS

government deported approximately one million Mexican migrants who were not part of the Bracero temporary worker program.[118] This second mass deportation led to hundreds of deaths.[119] Since 1994, the militarization of the southern border has contributed to as many as ten thousand migrant deaths.[120] Since 2004, almost 200 migrants have died after being detained, and more than 130 more have died after being deported.[121]

HOMICIDES

The status of the United States as the most violent advanced capitalist society in the world is well deserved, but unsurprising given its history of settler colonialism, slavery, white supremacy, class exploitation, imperialist wars, and misogyny. Strikingly, routine homicides and suicides have taken a much greater human toll than state, mob, and vigilante violence for more than a century. The historical and contemporary legitimation of violence and broad access to firearms contribute to current homicide rates far higher than those in Canada, Western Europe, and Japan.[122] Hundreds of mass shootings, not motivated by racism or political extremism, occur each year at restaurants, theaters, schools, workplaces, and other venues, and they have become an ugly but prominent feature of life in this society.[123] Twenty-two people died at a McDonald's restaurant in San Ysidro, California, in 1984.[124] Twenty-four died at a Luby's restaurant in Killeen, Texas, in 1991.[125] Thirty-two people lost their lives at Virginia Tech University in Blacksburg, Virginia, in 2007.[126] Twenty children and six adults perished at Sandy Hook Elementary School in Newtown, Connecticut, in 2012.[127] Sixty people died at a country music fair in Las Vegas, Nevada, in 2017.[128] Twenty-six were shot to death at a church in Sutherland Spring, Texas, the same year.[129] Mass shootings involving fewer fatalities occur almost every day.[130]

However, deaths resulting from mass shootings account for only a small percentage of gun murders each year.[131] In 2020, approximately 19,400 homicides occurred, mostly through firearms violence.[132] Blacks suffer disproportionately from this public health crisis.[133]

OTHER HOLOCAUSTS AT HOME AND ABROAD 271

Although the large annual number of homicides is clearly a major public health problem, federal legislation effectively precluded using federal funds for the scientific study of this issue between 1996 and 2019.[134] The number of routine homicides in the late eighteenth century and the nineteenth century may have run into the hundreds of thousands, not including the killing of Indigenous people, enslaved Black people, the deaths during the Civil War and Reconstruction, and the murders of Mexican Americans and Chinese Americans.[135] Available if incomplete records indicate that well over 1.5 million homicides occurred in this country between 1900 and 2020.[136]

SUICIDES

Although suicides are not as widely publicized as homicides, they have been even more common during the past 120 years. The suicide rate in the United States is higher than in any other advanced capitalist country and has significantly increased in recent decades;[137] 44,834 people took their own lives in 2020.[138] About half of all annual suicides involve the use of a firearm.[139] The suicide rate is most pronounced among Indigenous people and veterans of the U.S. armed forces.[140] Yet during the past twenty years, suicide rates have substantially increased among middle-aged rural white residents with a high school education or less.[141] As Anne Case and Angus Deaton have argued, these suicides have been fueled by long-term declines in economic opportunities, wages, and social support systems and are an important portion of the "deaths of despair" that have raised the overall mortality rate in this country.[142] At the same time, youth suicide rates have grown dramatically since 2007, and over 6,800 people between the ages of ten and twenty-four killed themselves in 2018.[143] Well over 2.6 million people have died by their own hands since 1900.[144]

OTHER RACIST AND FAR-RIGHT VIOLENCE SINCE 1970

In addition to the continuing murders of African Americans, far-right extremists and other racists have claimed many other victims

272   ENDLESS HOLOCAUSTS

since 1970. Amid mounting protests for inclusion and equality at the University of Colorado in Boulder, six Chicano activists were killed by car bombs in 1974. The assassins have never been identified.[145] In 1982, two white racists in Michigan beat Vincent Chin, a Chinese American, to death.[146] In 1984, members of The Order, a neo-Nazi organization, assassinated Jewish radio host Alan Berg in Denver.[147] During the 1980s, a right-wing émigré group killed eleven journalists, publishers, and activists who advocated U.S. recognition of the communist-led government of Vietnam.[148] In 1992, white supremacist Randy Weaver killed a deputy marshal while resisting arrest for firearms violations in Ruby Ridge, Idaho. Weaver's wife and son were also killed.[149] In 1993–94, anti-choice activists murdered two doctors and a bodyguard at abortion clinics in Pensacola, Florida.[150] Neo-Nazis Timothy McVeigh and Terry Nichols killed 168 men, women, and children when they bombed a federal office building in Oklahoma City in 1995.[151] Far-right extremist Eric Rudolph killed one person when he bombed the Centennial Olympic Park in Atlanta in 1996 and two people at an abortion clinic in Birmingham in 1998.[152] A self-described "sovereign citizen" killed two state troopers, a judge, and a local newspaper editor in Colebrook, New Hampshire, in 1997.[153] The next year, homophobes murdered Matthew Shepard near Laramie, Wyoming.[154] Also in 1998, neo-Nazis killed two antiracist activists in Las Vegas.[155]

Shortly after Al-Qaida attacked U.S. targets in September 2001, a member of a white supremacist organization seeking vengeance murdered a Pakistani American and an Indian American in Texas.[156] In 2003, "sovereign citizens" killed two police officers in South Carolina, and in 2004 individuals angry over the seventy-six deaths resulting from the federal government's siege against the Branch Davidian religious community in Waco, Texas, killed a bank guard in Tulsa, Oklahoma.[157] A white supremacist killed a police officer in Arkansas in 2006, and anti-government extremists murdered two other officers in Woodburn, Oregon, in 2008.[158] Also in 2008, a white supremacist killed two members of a Unitarian congregation in Knoxville, Tennessee.[159] During the first half of 2009, an

OTHER HOLOCAUSTS AT HOME AND ABROAD   273

anti-immigrant activist murdered two immigrants in Pima County, Arizona, an anti-choice extremist killed a doctor who performed abortions while he was at church in Wichita, Kansas, and a white supremacist killed a security guard at the Holocaust Memorial Museum in Washington, DC.[160] In 2010, an anti-tax protester killed himself and another person when he flew a small plane into a building that housed Internal Revenue Service offices in Austin, Texas.[161] That same year, two white supremacists killed four people in Washington, Oregon, and California.[162]

In 2012, a racist skinhead murdered six Sikhs at a temple in Oak Creek, Wisconsin, and a group of "sovereign citizens" killed two sheriff's deputies in LaPlace, Louisiana.[163] The same year, an anti-government extremist killed a Transportation Security Administration worker at the Los Angeles International Airport.[164] In 2014, a neo-Nazi murdered three people outside a Jewish community center and retirement home in Overland Park, Kansas, and a right-wing extremist married couple killed two police officers and a third person before being shot dead in Las Vegas, Nevada.[165] In 2015, a white supremacist killed two people at a movie theater in Lafayette, Louisiana, and then himself.[166] Later that year, an anti-abortion extremist killed three people at a Planned Parenthood clinic in Colorado Springs, Colorado.[167] After armed "sovereign citizens" and militia members seized a national wildlife refuge in Harney County, Oregon, in 2016, one of them was shot dead by state police officers.[168] Later that year, a white supremacist murdered an Arab American man in Tulsa, Oklahoma.[169]

Donald J. Trump's virulently racist campaign and presidency contributed to a significant increase in hate crimes, and some of them were deadly.[170] In February 2017, a white man making anti-immigrant remarks killed an Indian engineer at a bar in Olathe, Kansas.[171] In May 2017, a neo-Nazi who had converted to Islam murdered two fascist roommates in Tampa, Florida, and a white supremacist killed two men on a train in Portland, Oregon, after they objected to his harassment of two Muslim women.[172] In August 2017, a neo-Nazi attending the "Unite the Right" rally in Charlottesville, Virginia, killed Heather

274 ENDLESS HOLOCAUSTS

Heyer when he drove his car into a crowd of anti-fascist counter-demonstrators.[173] In December 2017, a neo-Nazi murdered his girlfriend's mother and father in Reston, Virginia.[174] In January 2018, another neo-Nazi stabbed to death a young gay Jewish man in Orange County, California.[175] In February 2018, a former student known for his white supremacist views murdered seventeen people at a high school in Parkland, Florida.[176] The same month, a "sovereign citizen" killed a police officer in Henry County, Georgia.[177] In April 2018, a "sovereign citizen" killed four people at a restaurant in Nashville.[178] In October 2018, a virulent anti-Semite murdered eleven people during services at the Tree of Life synagogue in Pittsburgh in October.[179] In November 2018, a misogynist, racist extremist shot dead two people at a yoga studio in Tallahassee in November.[180]

In March 2019, a QAnon follower killed a reputed mob boss in New York.[181] In April 2019, a neo-Nazi and his wife murdered an elderly man in Tucson and stole hundreds of his firearms.[182] That month, after setting a fire at a mosque in another town, a white supremacist killed a woman at a synagogue in Poway, California.[183] In July 2019, a young white supremacist and misogynist killed three people at a garlic festival in Gilroy, California.[184] In August 2019, a racist who parroted Trump's language about an immigrant "invasion" of the United States murdered twenty-three people at a Walmart in predominantly Latino El Paso, Texas.[185] In February 2020, a white supremacist fatally shot a police officer in Kimberly, Alabama.[186] In March, an anti-government extremist killed a police officer north of Ely, Nevada.[187] In May 2020, two far-right Boogaloo adherents gunned down a federal security officer at a court in Oakland, California.[188] In July 2020, a misogynist attacked the home of a federal judge and killed her son.[189]

That same month, a right-wing U.S. Army sergeant killed an anti-fascist demonstrator in Austin, Texas.[190] In August 2020, a racist white teenager shot two people to death at a protest against police brutality in Kenosha, Wisconsin.[191] In January 2021, the fascists and other Trump supporters who attacked Congress in an attempt to stop the certification of Biden's electoral victory were responsible for the deaths of one police officer and four of their own people.[192] Four other

OTHER HOLOCAUSTS AT HOME AND ABROAD

officers committed suicide in the aftermath of the failed insurrection.[193] In March 2021, a white man killed six Asian American women and two other people at Atlanta area spas.[194] The following month, a white man who had browsed white supremacist websites killed four Sikhs and four others at a FedEx facility in Indianapolis.[195] Despite denials by Trump and most other Republicans, it has become clear that white supremacists and other far-right individuals constitute the most dangerous terrorist threat in the United States today.[196] Between 1990 and 2020, right-wing extremists and other racists killed about seven hundred people in this country.[197]

OTHER EXTREMIST VIOLENCE

During the past three decades, mounting opposition to the U.S. Empire, its client states, its wars in Muslim countries, and its support for Israel have led to unprecedented attacks on the United States by religious extremists and other people. Al-Qaida forces led by bin Laden turned against its former ally and benefactor after the United States stationed troops in Saudi Arabia, the "land of the two holiest sites," in 1990.[198] In 1993, the first bombing of the World Trade Center in New York City by men with ties to Al-Qaida resulted in six deaths.[199] The same year, a Pakistani man angry about U.S. policy toward Palestine shot to death two CIA employees at the agency's Langley, Virginia, headquarters.[200] In 1995, disciples of bin Laden killed five U.S. military personnel in Saudi Arabia.[201] A year later, Al-Qaida declared war on the United States.[202] In 1998, its attacks on U.S. embassies in Kenya and Tanzania killed 240 people, including twelve U.S. nationals.[203] In 2000, bin Laden's forces killed seventeen U.S. sailors when they bombed the USS *Cole* in the port of Aden in Yemen.[204] After Afghanistan's Taliban refused to surrender bin Laden and Washington threatened them with "a carpet of bombs" in the summer of 2001, Al-Qaida operatives flew hijacked airplanes into the World Trade Center and the Pentagon.[205] Another hijacked airplane crashed in rural Pennsylvania after passengers fought back. Altogether, 2,977 people died on September 11, 2001.[206]

276 ENDLESS HOLOCAUSTS

Although far-right and other racist attacks have claimed more victims since then, religious extremists have also killed many people. In 2006, a Pakistani American opposed to the U.S. role in West Asia killed a woman at the Jewish Federation Center in Seattle.[207] In 2009, an Al-Qaida supporter killed a soldier at a military recruiting office in Little Rock, Arkansas. A U.S. Army captain shot thirteen soldiers at Fort Killeen in Texas because he opposed "illegal and immoral aggression against Muslims" in Afghanistan and Iraq.[208] In 2013, two Chechen immigrants opposed to these U.S. wars set off bombs at the Boston Marathon that killed two people and then shot to death a local police officer.[209] An Islamic State adherent killed four people in New Jersey and Washington in 2014.[210] A Kuwaiti American murdered four Marines and one sailor at a military recruiting office in Chattanooga, Tennessee, in 2015.[211] That same year, a married couple with ties to the Islamic State killed fourteen co-workers in San Bernardino, California.[212] In 2016, an Islamic State supporter murdered forty-nine people at the Pulse nightclub in Orlando, Florida.[213] In 2017 another Islamic State adherent killed eight people when he drove his truck into a crowded bicycle lane in New York City.[214] In 2019, a Saudi Air Force cadet inspired by Al-Qaida killed three people while training with the U.S. military in Pensacola, Florida.[215] In the past two decades, religious extremists have been responsible for approximately 141 deaths.[216]

The Profit-Driven Proliferation of Dangerous Drugs

During the past two centuries, the profit-driven proliferation of dangerous drugs has led to an immense number of deaths at home and abroad. By the 1830s, the United States accounted for 20 to 30 percent of opium imports to China and took over much of this trade during the First Opium War in 1839–42.[217] Although U.S. imports of opium to China declined after the Second Opium War of 1856–60, the United States shared significant responsibility for the drug trade and its catastrophic results.[218] Tens of millions of Chinese people became addicted to opium in the nineteenth century, and related deaths likely numbered in the millions.[219] In the United States, widespread

OTHER HOLOCAUSTS AT HOME AND ABROAD 277

use of "Mrs. Winslow's Soothing Syrup," which contained morphine and alcohol, killed thousands of children in the second half of the nineteenth century and the early twentieth century.[220] During the Civil War, injured or ill soldiers in both armies consumed "massive amounts" of opium and, more rarely, morphine, and many became addicted.[221] Decades after the war ended, doctors massively overprescribed morphine and other opiates for pain relief to veterans and affluent women.[222] Smoking opium also increased, particularly among Chinese immigrants and poor white urban men.[223] Approximately 300,000 people were addicted to these drugs by the late nineteenth century, and thousands, perhaps tens of thousands, died because of their addiction between the 1870s and the 1920s.[224]

By the beginning of the twentieth century, cocaine and heroin were viewed as important new medicines and legally sold without prescription. But as public understanding of the addictiveness and other harms of these drugs grew, pressure mounted on the government to address the problem. New laws outlawed heroin and prohibited the non-medical use of opium, morphine, and cocaine.[225] However, during the Prohibition era of 1920–33, the federal government ordered the poisoning of industrial alcohols to deter theft by bootleggers, which resulted in as many as ten thousand deaths.[226] In 1937, at least 107 people died after using an antibiotic known as Elixir Sulfanilamide, a calamity that led Congress to create the Food and Drug Administration.[227] In the 1950s, pharmaceutical companies and doctors promoted amphetamines for weight control, depression, and anxiety, and barbiturates for insomnia, anxiety, and anesthesia.[228] The abuse of these drugs led to many thousands of fatalities in the following decades.[229] A massive underground industry trafficking illegal drugs also arose. The resurgence of heroin and cocaine in the 1960s and 1970s, and the crack cocaine epidemic of the 1980s and 1990s, resulted in more than 150,000 deaths.[230] During the Cold War, U.S. support for drug-dealing syndicates and armies in Europe, Asia, Central America, and the Caribbean contributed to countless other deaths.[231] More recently, an epidemic of drug overdose deaths resulting from prescribed opioids, illegally manufactured fentanyl and methamphetamine, and heroin has fueled what Mike Stobbe has described as "the most widespread and deadly drug crisis in the nation's history."[232] During the year ending in April 2021, more than 100,000 people perished from overdoses, bringing the total number of deaths since 1999 to close to one million.[233] The rate of overdose fatalities in the United States is much higher than in other advanced capitalist societies.[234] These, too, are an important part of what Case and Deaton call "deaths of despair," which contribute to increasing mortality in this country.[235]

TOBACCO: THE GOLDEN HOLOCAUST

In the twentieth century, the extraordinary expansion of the tobacco industry, cigarette smoking, and nicotine addiction led to an unimaginable loss of life in the United States and other countries. Even after doctors and scientists began warning of the grave health hazards associated with smoking and exposure to secondhand smoke in the 1950s, the drive for profits led tobacco companies to deny that their products were life-threatening, and consumption continued to grow.[236] The result has been what Robert N. Proctor has called the "Golden Holocaust."[237] It may be roughly estimated that close to 28 million have died because of smoking or exposure to secondhand smoke in the United States, and another 480,000 people perish because of tobacco each year.[238] Another five to ten million people have perished in other countries because of U.S. tobacco products, and millions more have died abroad because of tobacco products developed by multinational corporations in which U.S. companies were involved.[239] Although U.S. companies now have a smaller share of the global tobacco market than they did in the past, they contribute annually to many of the approximately eight million tobacco-related deaths around the world.[240]

THE HUMAN COSTS OF AUTOMOBILES

For more than a century, the automobile and oil industries, their

OTHER HOLOCAUSTS AT HOME AND ABROAD   279

lobbyists, and their political allies have promoted the production and marketing of automobiles at the expense of public transportation systems.[241] As a result, today public transit is relatively limited in this country, and people are much more dependent on cars, sport utility vehicles, and trucks than in other advanced capitalist societies.[242] Over time, this automobile-centered transportation system has contributed to economic and racial discrimination, social isolation, obesity, and air pollution.[243] This dependence on automobiles has also led to innumerable accidents. Early on, cars were not designed with many safety features in mind, and while public pressure forced manufacturers to make important improvements, some vehicles continued to be, in Ralph Nader's words, "unsafe at any speed."[244] Major design flaws, shoddy manufacturing, defective parts, and industry cover-ups proved fatal for more than four thousand drivers and passengers in Chevrolet's Corsair and Cobalt; Ford's Pinto, Explorer, and Bronco; various General Motors pickup trucks; Daimler-Chrysler Jeeps, Suzuki Samurai, and other vehicles since the 1960s.[245] However, most automobile deaths have occurred because drivers have exceeded speed limits, been exhausted or intoxicated, or failed to use seatbelts, car seats, or booster seats.[246] The rate of automobile fatalities is much greater here than in other advanced capitalist societies. Close to forty thousand people perish each year on U.S. highways, streets, and roads.[247] Between 1899 and 2019, more than 3.8 million died because of vehicular accidents in this country.[248]

Other Unsafe Consumer Products

Since the 1970s, the aggressive marketing of infant formula to women in low- and middle-income countries has resulted in the deaths of millions upon millions of babies. Many of these deaths have occurred because women did not have access to clean water to mix with infant formula. Other deaths have happened because women could not afford the product and diluted it.[249] Although the Swiss multinational corporation Nestlé and other foreign companies bear much responsibility for this staggering loss of life, so do Abbott Laboratories, Kraft Heinz, and

Mead Johnson of the United States.[250] Defective and dangerous consumer products also result in an enormous loss of life here each year. These products include furniture, all-terrain vehicles, lawn mowers, generators, heaters, televisions, kitchen appliances, dryers, lamps, power tools, pools, hot tubs, clothes, toys, strollers, infant bibs, and household cleaning products.[251] Unsafe consumer products are implicated in the deaths of more than 25,000 people each year.[252] Although significant progress has been made in ensuring food safety during the past century, three thousand people continue to die annually because of foodborne diseases.[253] In addition, processed foods "loaded up with salt, sugar, fat, strange additives, and refined grains and bereft of naturally occurring nutrients and antioxidants" contribute to about 310,000 deaths each year from heart disease, strokes, hypertension, diabetes, obesity, and other largely preventable medical conditions.[254]

UNCONSCIONABLE MEDICAL EXPERIMENTATION

Unconscionable medical experimentation in the twentieth century killed close to two hundred African Americans and many other people at home and abroad.[255] In 1905–1906, U.S. occupation forces in the Philippines killed at least seventeen prisoners by inducing beriberi or injecting them with cholera. In the following decades, various medical experiments by doctors led to additional deaths.[256] Two years after the Second World War ended, U.S. scientists infected thousands of Guatemalan sex workers, soldiers, psychiatric patients, and prisoners with syphilis, gonorrhea, and chancroid in experiments testing the efficacy of penicillin.[257] The resulting deaths have never been definitively counted, but at least seventy-one infected psychiatric patients died during the experiments.[258] The U.S. government also sponsored radiation experiments on several thousand hospital patients, disabled children, pregnant women, prisoners, and Alaska Natives between 1944 and 1974.[259] The number of people who perished because of these experiments remains unknown today.

Between 1946 and 1962, the U.S. government deployed as many as 400,000 soldiers and sailors near atmospheric nuclear tests in the

OTHER HOLOCAUSTS AT HOME AND ABROAD 281

Marshall Islands and Nevada.[260] Clyde Haberman explained that these service members were used as "guinea pigs in studies of how combat troops might stand up in a war fought with nuclear arms."[261] Many of them later developed cancer and other diseases, and in 1988 the federal government began providing special benefits to "atomic veterans" suffering from different kinds of cancer "presumptively" caused by exposure to radiation.[262] In 1995, President Clinton publicly apologized for these reprehensible experiments.[263] By 2019, more than 4,600 veterans had been approved for benefits, but more than 3,500 other applications had been denied.[264] Scientific research on the effects of nuclear testing on soldiers and sailors has been limited and has produced mixed results. But exposure to radiation likely contributed to thousands of premature deaths among veterans.[265]

The Failure to Address Public Health Crises

The scourge of gun violence and the opioid epidemic are not the only public health crises that the U.S. government has failed to adequately address. More than a hundred thousand women lost their lives in this country because they did not have the right to safe, legal abortions until the U.S. Supreme Court's *Roe v. Wade* decision in 1973.[266] In the 1980s, the Reagan administration embraced a "concerted policy of non-action" on the Acquired Immunodeficiency Syndrome epidemic, and the subsequent Bush administration was still largely passive on HIV/AIDS.[267] By 1995, more than 300,000 people had died from AIDS.[268] Although the Clinton administration took action to address this epidemic at home, it joined pharmaceutical companies and other Western governments in blocking access to inexpensive medication to treat AIDS in African and Caribbean countries. Under intense public pressure, Clinton eventually changed course, but years of U.S. obstruction contributed to the deaths of untold millions of people.[269]

After the September 2001 attack in lower Manhattan, scientists warned that local residents faced significant air hazards, but authorities insisted that the area was safe.[270] More than two thousand people later died from exposure to toxins, more than fifty thousand New Yorkers are now ill with related diseases, and thousands of additional deaths are expected in the future.[271] Many of the approximately 1,800 Hurricane Katrina deaths in New Orleans in 2005 occurred because of the Bush administration's indifference to poor and Black residents.[272] Many of the roughly 4,600 Hurricane Maria deaths in Puerto Rico in 2017 resulted from the Trump administration's indifference to poor and Latino residents.[273] Until recently, the federal government has been doing "next to nothing" to combat the ongoing opioid epidemic.[274] Between February 2020 and May 2022, one million people perished from COVID-19 in the United States, considerably more than the loss of lives during the 1918–20 influenza pandemic.[275] A substantial portion of these deaths occurred because Trump refused to acknowledge the scope of the crisis and take effective action based on science, and many of his supporters refused to get vaccinated or wear masks.[276] Homelessness is an ongoing public health crisis in the United States. About half a million people lack permanent shelter, and approximately 13,000 die on the streets each year.[277]

LIMITED ACCESS TO QUALITY HEALTH CARE

Because private insurance remains the dominant form of coverage in the United States, health care generally remains a commodity, a product made to be sold for profit.[278] As a result, health care continues to be unavailable or unaffordable for millions. As Roosa Tikkanen and Melinda K. Abrams have emphasized, "The U.S. has worse access to primary care, prevention, and chronic disease management compared to peer nations."[279] Indigenous people and Blacks disproportionately suffer from inadequate access to quality health care, but many others face the same problem. Today approximately 37 million people do not have health insurance, and 68,000 die each year because they do not receive the medical care they need.[280] Another 41 million do not have adequate access to health care and have to forgo doctor visits, medical treatment, and prescription drugs because of costs not covered by their insurance.[281] About 25 percent of adults have reported that

OTHER HOLOCAUSTS AT HOME AND ABROAD 283

they or a family member have postponed care for a serious medical condition because of cost.[282] In one 2019 poll, 13 percent—about 34 million people—reported that a family member or friend died in the past five years due to being unable to afford treatment for a condition.[283] Although the per capita expenses of the health care system in the United States far exceed those in any other advanced capitalist country, public health there is significantly poorer than in most of those other nations.[284] The United States has higher maternal mortality rates, higher infant mortality, higher rates of deaths from preventable diseases, higher rates of chronic diseases, and lower longevity rates.[285] The disparities based on race and class are striking, and it is well known today that individuals' prospects for good health and long life vary drastically by zip code.[286]

MEDICAL ERRORS, IATROGENIC INFECTIONS, AND "DEADLY MEDICINES"

The actual delivery of health care in this country is often dysfunctional and even dangerous. Various kinds of grave medical errors not infrequently lead to death.[287] These mistakes include failure to review the medical record, failure to order appropriate tests and address abnormal results, failure to diagnose diseases, delayed diagnosis, incorrect diagnosis, unnecessary surgeries, "wrong site/wrong procedure" surgeries, injuries caused by surgeries, errors related to anesthesia, inadequate follow-up after treatment, communication errors, and other mistakes.[288] Medical error rates are significantly higher in the United States than in other advanced capitalist countries.[289] In addition, iatrogenic infections, that is, infections resulting from hospital or outpatient treatment, often prove to be fatal, too.[290] Peter C. Gøtzsche has argued that the pharmaceutical industry's "morally repugnant disregard for human lives," corporate domination of the Food and Drug Administration, and the incompetence or complicity of many physicians have sustained a "hugely lethal" epidemic of "deadly medicines."[291]

In the late 1980s, anti-arrhythmic drugs produced by Upjohn and other companies killed fifty thousand people each year.[292] In the late 1990s and early 2000s, Pfizer's hypertension drugs led to approximately forty thousand deaths from heart failure.[293] Between 1999 and 2004, Merck's Vioxx, which was prescribed for arthritis and chronic pain, doubled the risk of heart attacks and caused as many as 120,000 deaths.[294] Eli Lilly's anti-psychotic Zyprexa had killed 200,000 people worldwide by 2007 and is still on the market today.[295] Pfizer's Celebrex, which has been prescribed for arthritis and chronic pain, contributed to approximately 75,000 deaths worldwide by 2004 and remains on the market.[296] Perdue Pharma, other pharmacological companies, the FDA, and many doctors share responsibility for the aggressive marketing, poor regulation, and over-prescription of highly addictive opioids, which have claimed almost one million lives since 1999.[297]

During the past two decades, doctors, scientists, and other analysts have sought to measure the loss of life caused by medical errors, iatrogenic infections, and "deadly medicines." This endeavor has produced widely varying assessments of annual fatalities, considerable controversy, and more than a little vitriol. Researchers' estimates range from 22,000 to more than 780,000 avoidable deaths each year.[298] Some studies have focused on patients' deaths in hospitals, while others have included deaths from outpatient treatment. There are also significantly different views on the loss of life caused by using prescription drugs as directed by doctors. Gøtzsche has estimated that the annual toll from "deadly medicines" exceeds 200,000, and other analysts have reached similar conclusions.[299] Based on current research findings, it may be conservatively estimated that 400,000 people die each year from iatrogenic causes.[300] Adverse reactions to U.S. medicines have also resulted in vast numbers of deaths in poorer countries during the past several decades.[301]

POLLUTION DEATHS IN THE UNITED STATES

Between the 1830s and the 1870s, cholera, a disease that is primarily spread by contaminated water, killed between two hundred thousand and three hundred thousand people.[302] Tens of thousands continued

OTHER HOLOCAUSTS AT HOME AND ABROAD 285

to die of cholera and typhoid, another water-borne disease, each year in the early twentieth century.[303] Between 1870 and 1910, as growing numbers of urban workers were forced to live in tenements and work in crowded factories with poor sanitation and limited light, tuberculosis claimed three to four million lives.[304] The construction of water treatment facilities, new medicines, and other public health improvements dramatically reduced deaths from infectious diseases.[305] However, during the first half of the twentieth century, tens of thousands of children died from exposure to lead paint.[306] Moreover, the "smoke of great cities" produced by coal power plants and coal-powered factories and the air pollution resulting from the use of other fossil fuels in power plants, factories, and automobiles led to widespread and often lethal air pollution.[307]

Toxic air inversions resulted in at least twenty deaths in Donora, Pennsylvania, in 1948 and more than seven hundred deaths in New York City between 1953 and 1966.[308] Radioactive fallout from nuclear weapons testing in Nevada between 1951 and 1963 spread across much of the country, resulting in at least 145,000 fatalities and possibly many more.[309] Hundreds of Diné men who mined uranium between the 1940s and the 1980s perished from radiation exposure, and other Indigenous people have died because they lived near abandoned uranium mines, toxic dumps, and similar environmentally dangerous sites.[310] Although important new laws passed by Congress in the 1960s and 1970s reduced some atmospheric contaminants, enormous numbers of people continued to die from long-term exposure to air pollution in the years that followed. Devra Davis has estimated that more than one million people perished needlessly from air pollution in the last two decades of the twentieth century, but this appraisal is far too low.[311] Despite the progress achieved, at least 200,000 people die from air pollution each year.[312] Thus, the total number of deaths since 1980 may be close to eight million.

By 1980, there were more than 400,000 toxic waste sites and 500,000 abandoned mines across the nation.[313] Only a tiny fraction of these hazardous areas were designated as Superfund cleanup sites under new federal legislation passed that year. Although these sites have been linked to increased cancer risk, most of them still await remediation today.[314] In recent years, lead contamination of water in Flint, Michigan, and Newark, New Jersey, has been widely publicized.[315] Less well known is that 400,000 people die each year because of various kinds of exposure to lead in water, soil, and air.[316] Carcinogenic hexavalent chromium is found in the tap water supplied to more than 200 million residents, and as many as 110 million drink water containing perfluoroalkyl or polyfluoroalkyl substances, which are also carcinogenic.[317] Arsenic, radioactive elements, and other toxic substances also contaminate water supplies and soil in the United States.[318] Most analysts have refrained from estimating the number of deaths caused by water and soil pollution, but at least half of the annual lead-related deaths result from exposure to toxic water or soil.[319] So even in the absence of reliable data about the loss of life caused by other poisons, it may be conservatively estimated that at least eight million people died from water and soil pollution between 1980 and 2020.[320]

Grave new dangers have emerged with the proliferation of chemicals in foods, consumer goods, and other commodities; the mass production of plastics; and the expanded use of pesticides.[321] Most of the hundred thousand chemicals used commercially today have not been adequately tested for toxicity and long-term harm.[322] It is increasingly clear that there is a causal, if complex, connection between some chemicals and the unprecedented "epidemic of cancer" and skyrocketing cancer deaths that has been developing in the United States since 1940.[323] Scientists have found that chemicals used in some food dyes, baking ingredients, preservatives, and other food additives are carcinogenic.[324] Vinyl chloride, used to make plastics for construction and hundreds of consumer products, is also carcinogenic.[325] So are at least two phthalates found in detergents, adhesives, shower curtains, and personal care products.[326] It is not yet known how many of the 600,000 cancer deaths each year are caused or partly caused by chemicals, but approximately 100,000 annual deaths are likely caused by exposure to phthalates.[327] As Davis has lamented, "It seems that cancer has become the price of modern life."[328]

OTHER HOLOCAUSTS AT HOME AND ABROAD   287

Pollution Deaths in Other Countries

The U.S. Empire is also responsible for a substantial, if difficult to quantify, portion of the estimated nine million environmental contamination deaths in other countries each year.[329] Air and water pollution generated in the United States crosses national boundaries, often with deleterious effects on people in distant lands.[330] In addition, as Vandana Shiva has emphasized, the "outsourcing of manufacturing" by U.S. and other corporations to low-wage, low-regulation countries "is also outsourcing of pollution."[331] Because U.S. companies have relocated a significant amount of production to China, they are complicit in some of the approximately one million annual pollution deaths there.[332] Massive U.S. exports of petroleum coke, a dirty fuel waste product, to India contribute to the atmospheric contamination that claims more than one million lives each year.[333] Exxon Mobil and Chevron share responsibility for the massive oil spills in Nigeria, which poison water and soil and lead to the deaths of approximately sixteen thousand infants each year.[334] U.S. exports of hazardous pesticides contribute to more than 200,000 annual deaths in other countries.[335] No one knows how many people in other countries perish each year because of exposure to lead paint, asbestos products, plastics, other toxic commodities, and hazardous waste exported from the United States, but the number is almost certainly large.[336]

Global Warming and Climate Change

Justin Gillis and Nadja Popovich point out that the United States has been the "biggest carbon polluter in history" and bears more responsibility than any other country for the "excess carbon dioxide that is heating the planet."[337] During the past two decades, global warming and the unprecedented climate change it is producing have led to higher temperatures, increasingly severe heat waves, wildfires, droughts, storms, and floods in parts of the world.[338] These developments have resulted in the spread of malaria, dengue fever, and other communicable diseases, along with increasing hunger, malnutrition,

288   ENDLESS HOLOCAUSTS

and diarrhea, mainly in poorer countries.[339] It has been conservatively estimated that between three and four hundred thousand
people are already dying each year because of climate change, and
the future appears even more ominous.[340] As David Wallace-Wells has
warned, global warming and climate change threaten to make parts
of the planet "close to uninhabitable" and other parts "horrifically
inhospitable" in the coming decades.[341] Higher temperatures, more
dangerous and frequent heat waves, the spread of deserts and loss of
soil, growing scarcity of clean water, widespread famine and diseases,
the destruction of cities by rising sea levels, worsening pollution, economic and social collapse, mass migrations, and wars arising from
these catastrophic developments could endanger the lives of billions
of people in the coming decades.[342]

Counting the Dead

The various kinds of state and social violence surveyed in this chapter have exacted terrible human costs, yet different forms of social
murder have taken a significantly higher toll. The total number of
U.S. deaths caused by wars; mob, vigilante, police, and extremist
violence; incarceration; and homicides and suicides is considerably
more than six million.[343] The total number of U.S. deaths resulting
from drug overdoses, tobacco use, the automobile-centered transportation system, other dangerous consumer products, medical
experimentation, government failures to address public health crises,
limited access to health care, iatrogenic causes, and environmental
pollution is close to sixty million.[344] The empire is also responsible for
more than five million fatalities from U.S. tobacco products in other
countries and shares responsibility for at least three million deaths
resulting from climate change since 2010.[345]

In sum, it may be that these holocausts at home and abroad
have taken the lives of more than 74 million people. Moreover, this
appraisal is conservative because it does not include the uncounted
millions who perished because of nineteenth-century U.S. imports
of opium into China, twentieth-century tobacco products made by

OTHER HOLOCAUSTS AT HOME AND ABROAD 289

multinational tobacco companies with U.S. investors, U.S. exports of infant formula and "deadly medicines" to poor countries, the U.S. refusal to allow inexpensive AIDS drugs to be manufactured in Africa in the 1990s, and U.S. contributions to global air pollution. When the mass deaths surveyed in this chapter are considered along with those of Indigenous peoples, people of African descent, workers, and the peoples of other lands, it becomes inescapably clear that as long as it exists, the U.S. Empire will continue to produce endless holocausts.

Notes

Introduction

1. Christian Appy, "America's Not a Force for Good: The Truth About Our Most Enduring—and Harmful—National Myth," *Salon*, March 29, 2015, www.salon.com/2015/03/29/americas_not_ a_force_for_good_ the_truth_about_our_most_enduring_and_harmful_national_myth/.
2. Sidney Lens, *The Forging of the American Empire* (Chicago: Haymarket Books, 2003), chap. 1.
3. Office of Insular Affairs, U.S. Department of the Interior, "Definitions of Insular Area Political Organizations," https://www.doi.gov/oia/islands/politicatypes; and National Congress of American Indians, "Tribal Nations and the United States: An Introduction," February 2020, https://www.ncai.org/resources/ncai_publications/tribal-nations-and-the-united-states-an-introduction. More than two hundred other Indigenous nations have not been federally recognized. See Eilis O'Neill, "Unrecognized Tribes Struggle Without Federal Aid During Pandemic," NPR report, April 17, 2021, https://www.npr.org/2021/04/17/988123 599/unrecognized-tribes-struggle-without-federal-aide-during-pandemic.
4. Office of Insular Affairs, "Definitions of Insular Area Political Organizations."
5. *United States' Interests in the Freely Associated States: Hearings Before the Comm. on Energy and Natural Resources*, 116th Congress (July 23, 2019) (statement of Douglas Domenich, Assistant Secretary, Insular and International Affairs, U.S. Department of the Interior), https://www.doi.gov/ocl/freely-associated-states.

NOTES TO PAGES 11–15   291

6. Greg Grandin, *Empire's Workshop: Latin America, the United States, and the Rise of the New Imperialism* (New York: Henry Holt, 2006), 83.

7. Richard Olney, quoted in Walter LaFeber, *The New Empire: An Interpretation of American Expansion, 1860–1898* (Ithaca, NY: Cornell University Press, 1998), 262.

8. Grandin, *Empire's Workshop*, 3.

9. Harry Magdoff, *The Age of Imperialism: The Economics of U.S. Foreign Policy* (New York: Monthly Review Press, 1969), 14.

10. See Michio Kaku and Daniel Axelrod, *To Win a Nuclear War: The Pentagon's Secret War Plans* (Boston: South End Press, 1987).

11. David Sylvan and Stephen Majeski, *U.S. Foreign Policy in Perspective: Clients, Enemies, and Empire* (New York: Routledge, 2009), 33; David Vine, *Base Nation: How U.S. Military Bases Abroad Harm America and the World* (New York: Henry Holt, 2015), 3, 28–41; Michael E. Flynn, Carla Martinez Machain, and Michael A. Allen, "Why Does the U.S. Pay So Much for the Defense of Its Allies? 5 Questions Answered," *The Conversation*, December 1, 2019, https:// theconversation.com/why-does-the-us-pay-so-much-for-the-defense-of-its-allies-5-questions-answered-127683; and Kathy Gilsinan, "The War Machine Is Run on Contracts," *The Atlantic*, January 17, 2020, https://www.theatlantic.com/politics/archive/2020/01/us-contractors-and-hidden-costs-us-wars-iran/605068/.

12. This phrase first appeared in Charles Krauthammer, "The Unipolar Moment," *Foreign Affairs* (January 1991), https://www.foreignaffairs.com/articles/1990-01-01/unipolar-moment.

13. *Maafa* is a Swahili word. See Thomas Jerome Baker, *Black Lives Matter: From Holocaust to Lynching to Liberation* (San Bernardino, CA: Self-Published, 2016), 6.

14. *Oxford Dictionaries Online*, "holocaust," https://en. oxforddictionaries.com/definition/holocaust. The use of this word throughout the book is in no way intended to minimize the unique horrors of the *Shoah*, which claimed six million Jewish lives.

15. The World Health Organization uses this definition of violence. See its *World Report on Violence and Health: Summary* (Geneva: World Health Organization, 2002), 4.

16. Frederick Engels, *The Condition of the Working Class in England in 1844*, trans. Florence Kelley Wischnewetzky (London: Swan Sonnenschein and Co., 1892), 95.

17. The expression "wounded beast" is found in Marcelo Colussi, "U.S. Imperialism: The Wounded Beast Strikes Out for Oil," trans. Jordan Bishop, Latin America Information Agency, February 15, 2018, https://www.alainet.org/es/node/191047; and in Chris Hedges, "The World

292 NOTES TO PAGES 16–17

to Come," *Common Dreams,* January 28, 2019, https://www.commondreams.org/views/2019/01/28/world-come.

The Indigenous Peoples Holocaust

1. David Stannard, *American Holocaust: The Conquest of the New World* (New York: Oxford University Press, 1992), ix–x, 146.
2. Ward Churchill, *A Little Matter of Genocide: Holocaust and Denial in the Americas, 1492 to the Present* (San Francisco: City Lights Books, 1997), 97–98; and David Stannard, "Introduction," in *A Little Matter of Genocide,* xvi. See also Roxanne Dunbar-Ortiz, *An Indigenous Peoples' History of the United States* (Boston: Beacon Press, 2014). Some prominent scholars, though readily acknowledging various episodes of genocide against Indigenous peoples, frame Native depopulation over four centuries in terms of colonialism because more than wars, violence, and intentional destruction were involved. See, for example, Russell Thornton, *American Indian Holocaust and Survival: A Population History Since 1492* (Norman: University of Oklahoma Press, 1987), 44, 47–49, and 104–7.
3. Stannard, *American Holocaust,* x, 85–87, 146; Churchill, *A Little Matter of Genocide,* 1; Dunbar-Ortiz, *Indigenous Peoples' History,* 40; Thornton, *Indian Holocaust,* 42–43; and David S. Jones, *Rationalizing Epidemics: Meanings and Uses of American Indian Mortality Since 1600* (Cambridge, MA: Harvard University Press, 2004), 9.
4. Thornton, *Indian Holocaust,* xv–xvi, chaps. 3 and 4; Russell Thornton, "Population History of Native North Americans," in *A Population History of North America,* ed. Michael R. Haines and Richard H. Steckel (Cambridge: Cambridge University Press, 2000), 15–23; Suzanne Austin Alchon, *A Pest in the Land: New World Epidemics in a Global Perspective* (Albuquerque: University of New Mexico Press, 2003), 3–5, chaps. 4 and 5; Paul Kelton, Alan C. Swedlund, and Catherine M. Cameron, "Introduction," in *Beyond Germs: Native Depopulation in North America,* ed. Catherine M. Cameron, Paul Kelton, and Alan C. Swedlund (Tucson: University of Arizona Press 2015), 3–15; and David S. Jones, "Death, Uncertainty, and Rhetoric," in *Beyond Germs,* 16–28.
5. On Native American population recovery, see Thornton, *Indian Holocaust,* esp. chaps. 7 and 8, and "Native North Americans," 30–41. On the continuing Indigenous loss of life, see for example, Michael Parenti, *Democracy for the Few,* 9th ed. (Boston: Wadsworth Cengage Learning, 2011), 127; Teran Powell, "Native Americans Most Likely to Die from Police Shootings, Families Who Lost Loved Ones Weigh In," WUWM Radio, June 2, 2021, https:// www.wuwm.com/2021-06-02/ native-americans-most-likely-to-die-from-police-shootings-families-

NOTES TO PAGES 17-19 293

who-lost-loved-ones-weigh-in; Michelle Sarche and Paul Spicer, "Poverty and Health Disparities for American Indian and Alaska Native Children: Current Knowledge and Future Prospects," *Annals of the New York Academy of Sciences* (July 2008), https://www.ncbi.nlm.nih.gov/pmc/articles/PMC2567901/; and David K. Espey, Melissa A. Jim, Nathaniel Cobb, Michael Bartholomew, Tom Becker, Don Haverkamp, and Marcus Plescia, "Leading Causes of Death and All-Cause Mortality in American Indians and Alaska Natives," *American Journal of Public Health* 104, Supplement 3 (June 2014), https://www.ncbi.nlm.nih.gov/pmc/articles/PMC 4035872/.

6. Dunbar-Ortiz, *Indigenous Peoples' History*, 1, 46.
7. Ibid., 46.
8. Ibid., 10.
9. Ibid., 28-30.
10. Howard Zinn, *A People's History of the United States: 1492-Present*, 20th anniv. ed. (New York: HarperCollins, 1999), 21.
11. Ibid.
12. Lens, *Forging the American Empire*, chap. 1.
13. Gerald Horne, *The Apocalypse of Settler Colonialism: The Roots of Slavery, White Supremacy, and Capitalism in Seventeenth-Century North America and the Caribbean* (New York: Monthly Review Press, 2018), 8.
14. Dunbar-Ortiz, *Indigenous Peoples' History*, 42-44; and Zinn, *People's History*, 2-3, 11-12.
15. Karl Marx, *Capital*, vol. 1, trans. Ben Fowkes (New York: Penguin, 1990), 915.
16. Dunbar-Ortiz, *Indigenous Peoples' History*, 3, 198-99.
17. Some of the Spanish invaders mistakenly thought that millions lived on this island. A contemporary estimate of no more than 300,000 inhabitants is found in Andrés Reséndez, *The Other Slavery: The Uncovered Story of Indian Enslavement in America* (New York: Houghton Mifflin Harcourt, 2017), 16. However, recent DNA analysis indicates that the pre-contact population numbered in the low tens of thousands. See David Reich and Orlando Patterson, "Ancient DNA Is Changing the Way We Think About the Caribbean," *New York Times*, December 23, 2020.
18. Stannard, *American Holocaust*, 85-87; and Linda A. Newson, "The Demographic Collapse of Native Peoples of the Americas, 1492-1650," *Proceedings of the British Academy*, 81 (1993): 253-54.
19. Alfred L. Kroeber, "Cultural and Natural Areas of Native North America," *University of California Publications in American Archaeology and Ethnography* 38 (1939): 166, cited in Thornton, *Indian Holocaust*, 22-

24; Henry F. Dobyns, "Reassessing New World Populations at the Time of Contact," paper presented at Institute for Early Contact Studies, University of Florida, Gainesville, April 1988, cited in Stannard, *American Holocaust*, 342n23. Although Kroeber was a pioneer in U.S. anthropology, his collection of Indigenous peoples' remains and funerary objects from their graves without family or other consent, his mistreatment of a Native genocide survivor he employed, and other objectionable research practices led to the removal of his name from the anthropology building at the University of California at Berkeley in January 2021. See Melissa Gomez, "UC Berkeley Removes Kroeber Hall Name, Citing Namesake's 'Immoral' Work with Native Americans," *Los Angeles Times*, January 27, 2021.

20. Stannard, *American Holocaust*, 11, 151, 267–68; and Churchill, *A Little Matter of Genocide*, 1.

21. Thornton, *Indian Holocaust*, 25, 42, and "Native North Americans," 11; Russell Thornton, email to author, April 2, 2020.

22. Alexander Koch, Chris Brierly, Mark M. Maslin, and Simon L. Lewis, "Earth System Impacts of the European Arrival and Great Dying in the Americas After 1492," *Quaternary Science Reviews* 207 (March 1, 2019): 13–36.

23. Koch et al. demonstrate that massive Indigenous depopulation between 1492 and 1600 changed the atmosphere and temperature of the planet, but they likely underestimated the number of people living north of Mexico and in some other locations before the arrival of the Europeans. Interestingly, they provided an alternative statistical computation of the total pre-contact population which yields an estimate of more than 64 million. See "Earth System Impacts."

24. William Denevan, "The Pristine Myth: The Landscape of the Americas in 1492," *Annals of the Association of American Geographers* 82/3 (1992): 369–85.

25. Kroeber, "Cultural and Natural Areas," 166, cited in Thornton, *Indian Holocaust*, 26; and Dunbar-Ortiz, *Indigenous Peoples' History*, 10.

26. Douglas H. Ubelaker, "North American Indian Population Size, AD 1500–1985," *American Journal of Physical Anthropology* 77/ 3 (November 1988): 289–94.

27. Thornton, *Indian Holocaust*, 31–32, 43.

28. James Wilson, *The Earth Shall Weep: A History of Native America* (New York: Grove Press, 1998), 20; and Jeffrey Ostler, email to author, April 13, 2020. Wilson referred here to Thornton's estimate of more than five million Native people in the present-day coterminous United States and more than two million in what is now Canada, Alaska, and Greenland.

NOTES TO PAGES 19-20 295

29. James Mooney estimated the Indigenous population of Alaska to be 72,600 before European contact. See "The Aboriginal Population of America North of Mexico," in *Smithsonian Miscellaneous Collections* 80, ed. John R. Swanton (1928): 1–40, cited in Thornton, *Indian Holocaust*, 241. Thornton noted that this estimate may be low. Maria DaSilva-Gordon has estimated that the pre-contact Indigenous population of Puerto Rico was twenty to fifty thousand. See *Puerto Rico: Past and Present* (New York: Rosen Publishing Group, 2011), 16. The size of the Indigenous population of Hawai'i in 1492 is not known, but it was approximately 683,000 in 1778, when the British explorer James Cook made first contact. See David A. Swanson, "A New Estimate of the Hawaiian Population for 1778, the Year of First European Contact," paper presented at University of Hawai'i , February 2015, cited in Sara Kehaulani Goo, "After 200 Years, Native Hawaiians Make a Comeback," Pew Research Center, Fact Tank, April 6, 2015, http://www.pewresearch.org/fact-tank/2015/04/06/native-hawaiian-population/.

30. See, for example, Marvin Harris "Depopulation and Cultural Evolution: A Cultural Materialist Perspective," in *Columbian Consequences*, vol. 3: *The Spanish Borderlands in Pan-American Perspective*, ed. David Hurst Thomas, (Washington, DC: Smithsonian Institution Press, 1991), 584, cited in Stannard, *American Holocaust*, xii and 286nn7, 8. See also Gunter Lowy, "Were American Indians the Victims of Genocide?" *Commentary*, September 1, 2004, https://www.commentarymagazine.com/articles/were-american-indians-the-victims-of-genocide/; and Michael Medved, *The 10 Big Lies About America: Combatting Destructive Distortions About Our Nation* (New York: Three Rivers Press, 2008), 11–45.

31. Stannard, *American Holocaust*, xii.

32. Henry F. Dobyns, *Their Number Become Thinned: Native American Population Dynamics in Eastern North America* (Knoxville: University of Tennessee Press, 1983), 15–24, cited in Thornton, *Indian Holocaust*, 45; Douglas H. Ubelaker, "Patterns of Demographic Change in the Americas," *Human Biology* 64/3 (June 1992): 372; Jones, "Death, Uncertainty, and Rhetoric," 26–29; and George R. Milner, "Population Decline and Culture Change in the American Midcontinent: Bridging the Prehistoric and Historic Divide," in *Beyond Germs*, 63–65.

33. This language comes from Thornton, *Indian Holocaust*, 47. Different perspectives are found in Kelton, Swedlund, and Cameron, 6–8; and Jones, "Death, Uncertainty, and Rhetoric," 16–28.

34. Jones, "Death, Uncertainty, and Rhetoric," 28; and Jeffrey Ostler, "Genocide and American Indian History," *Oxford Research Encyclopedia of American History* (March 2015), https:// oxfordre.com/americanhis-

NOTES TO PAGES 21–22

tory/view/10.1093/acrefore/9780199329175.001.0001/acrefore-978
0199232975-e-3.

35. Jones, "Death, Uncertainty, and Rhetoric," 16. The same point is made in Thornton, *Indian Holocaust*, 47; and Alchon, *Pest in the Land*, 3–5, 79–80.

36. See, for example, Zinn, *People's History*, 1–8; Dunbar-Ortiz, *Indigenous Peoples' History*, 42–44. The description of the European invasion as "apocalyptic" is found in Horne, *Apocalypse of Settler Colonialism*.

37. Reséndez, *The Other Slavery*, chap. 1.

38. Bartolomé de Las Casas provided an account of the Spaniards' actions in *Brevísima Relación de la Destrucción de las Indias* (1542) and other works. See Kirkpatrick Sale, *The Conquest of Paradise: Christopher Columbus and the Columbian Legacy* (New York: Alfred A. Knopf, 1990), 155–61.

39. Gonzalo Fernández de Oviedo y Valdés, *Historia General y Natural de las Indias*, (1535), cited in Sale, 158.

40. Thornton, *Indian Holocaust*, 63–64; and Ethne Barnes, *Diseases and Human Evolution* (Albuquerque: University of New Mexico Press, 2005), 229.

41. Reich and Patterson, "Ancient DNA."

42. DaSilva-Gordon, *Puerto Rico*, 16.

43. This phrase appears in Stannard, *American Holocaust*, 85. The estimate of forty million deaths was made by Las Casas in 1560 and is cited in Denevan, "The Pristine Myth," 370. Stannard also concluded that about forty million Indigenous people had died in these regions by the late 1560s. See *American Holocaust*, 81–87.

44. Alchon, *Pest in the Land*, 78–79.

45. Koch et al., "Earth System Impacts," 13–36. The authors have noted that this sixteenth-century apocalypse was centered in the lands south of the present-day United States.

46. Ibid.; and Simon Lewis, Alexander Koch, Mark Maslin, and Chris Brierly, "Colonization of Americas Led to So Much Death It Caused a Period of Global Cooling," *Newsweek*, January 31, 2019, https://www.newsweek.com/americas-colonization-christopher-columbus-native-indigenous-death-global-1313097.

47. Douglas Hunter, "John Cabot," *The Canadian Encyclopedia*, May 19, 2017, https://encyclopediecanadienne.com/article/john-cabot.

48. Thornton, *Indian Holocaust*, 14, 50, 61–62; Jones, *Rationalizing Epidemics*, 23–24; Wilson, *Earth Shall Weep*, 72; Stannard, *American Holocaust*, 134–35; and Benjamin Madley, *An American Genocide: The United States and the California Indian Catastrophe* (New Haven: Yale University Press, 2016), 26.

NOTES TO PAGES 22-24

49. Charles C. Mann, *1491: New Revelations of the Americas Before Columbus*, 2nd ed. (New York: Vintage Books, 2006), 49.

50. Thornton, *Indian Holocaust*, 61; Rosemary Enright and Sue Maden, "JHS 100 Years: Narragansett Bay before the Europeans," *Jamestown Press*, January 12, 2012; and Eryn Dion, "What You Learned About the 'First Thanksgiving' Isn't True. Here's the Real Story," *Cape Cod Times*, November 23, 2021.

51. Thornton, *Indian Holocaust*, 61, 68.

52. Ibid., 68.

53. Ibid., 62, 76; and Alchon, *Pest in the Land*, 96–99.

54. Thornton, *Indian Holocaust*, 14, 61; Micheal Clodfelter, *Warfare and Armed Conflicts: A Statistical Encyclopedia of Casualty and Other Figures, 1494-2007*, 3rd ed. (Jefferson: McFarland and Company, 2008), 32; and T. Frederick Davis, *History of Juan Ponce De Leon's Voyages to Florida: Source Records* (1935), Wisconsin Historical Society, Digital Library and Archives, American Journeys Collection, Document No. AJ-095, (2003), 61.

55. Dobyns, *Their Number Become Thinned*, 254, cited in Thornton, *Indian Holocaust*, 63n3 and 64; Ostler, "Genocide and American Indian History"; and Paul Kelton, *Epidemics and Enslavement: Biological Catastrophe in the Native Southeast, 1492-1715* (Lincoln: University of Nebraska Press, 2007), 51–52.

56. Kelton, *Epidemics and Enslavement*, 55–56; and Gillian Brockell, "Before There Was 1619, There Was 1526: The Mystery of the First Enslaved Africans in What Became the United States," *Washington Post*, September 7, 2019.

57. See Douglas T. Peck, "Lucas Vásquez de Ayllón's Doomed Colony of San Miguel de Guadalpe," *Georgia Historical Quarterly* 85/2 (Summer 2001): 183–98.

58. Kelton, *Epidemics and Enslavement*, 58–59.

59. Ibid., 59; and Lawrence E. Aten, *Indians of the Upper Texas Coast* (New York: Academic Press, 1983), 55, cited in Thornton, *Indian Holocaust*, 76.

60. Thornton, *Indian Holocaust*, 129.

61. Clodfelter, *Warfare*, 32; and Donald E. Chipman, "Cabeza de Vaca, Álvar Núñez," *Handbook of Texas Online*, Texas State Historical Association, December 4, 2015, https://tshaonline.org/ handbook/online/ articles/fca06.

62. Mann, *1491*, 110–13; Wilson, *Earth Shall Weep*, 134–37; and Kelton, *Epidemics and Enslavement*, 59–60.

63. Kelton, *Epidemics and Enslavement*, 64.

64. Clodfelter, *Warfare*, 32.

298   NOTES TO PAGES 24–26

65. Jeffrey Ostler, *Surviving Genocide: Native Nations and the United States from the American Revolution to Bleeding Kansas* (New Haven: Yale University Pres, 2019), 13. Estimates of 2,500 Native deaths are found in Clodfelter, *Warfare*, 32; and in Kelton, *Epidemics and Enslavement*, 66.
66. Clodfelter, *Warfare*, 32; and Kelton, *Epidemics and Enslavement*, 66.
67. Clodfelter, *Warfare*, 32.
68. Kelton, *Epidemics and Enslavement*, 59–66; and Ostler, *Surviving Genocide*, 13.
69. Ostler, *Surviving Genocide*, 13–14.
70. Clodfelter, *Warfare*, 32; Carroll L. Riley, *Rio del Norte: People of the Upper Rio Grande from Earliest Times to the Pueblo Revolt* (Salt Lake City: University of Utah Press, 1995), 155, 180; and Gary Clayton Anderson, *Ethnic Cleansing and the Indian: The Crime That Should Haunt America* (Norman: University of Oklahoma Press, 2014), 33–34.
71. Riley, *Rio del Norte*, 224, 250, 266.
72. Clodfelter, *Warfare*, 32; and Riley, *Rio del Norte*, 251.
73. Riley, *Rio del Norte*, 252.
74. Ibid., 250, 266; and Daniel T. Reff, email to author, March 24, 2020.
75. Kelton, *Epidemics and Enslavement*, 74.
76. William W. Dewhurst, *The History of St. Augustine, Florida* (New York: G. P. Putnam's Sons, 1881), 53–67, 75–78; and Blake Beattie, "The Founding of St. Augustine, 1565: Interpretative Essay," in *What Happened? An Encyclopedia of Events That Changed America Forever,* vol. 1: *Through the Seventeenth Century*, ed. John E. Findling and Frank W. Thackeray (Santa Barbara: ABC-CLIO, 2011), 86–89.
77. Kelton, *Epidemics and Enslavement*, 75–76.
78. Ibid., 48, 82.
79. Thornton, *Indian Holocaust*, 66–68; and Kelton, *Epidemics and Enslavement*, 77–78.
80. Thornton, *Indian Holocaust*, 67; and Kelton, *Epidemics and Enslavement*, 80–82.
81. Ostler, *Surviving Genocide*, 15; and Dana Hedgpeth, "Powhatan and His People: The 15,000 American Indians Shoved Aside by Jamestown's Settlers," *Washington Post*, August 3, 2019.
82. James Mooney, "The Powhatan Confederacy, Past and Present," *American Anthropologist* 9 (1907): 142, cited in Thornton, *Indian Holocaust*, 68.
83. See, for example, Dobyns, *Their Number Become Thinned*, 15, 23; Stannard, *American Holocaust*, 107; Kelton, *Epidemics and Enslavement*, chaps. 2 and 3; and Ostler, "Genocide and American Indian History."
84. Brendan Wolfe, "First Anglo-Powhattan War (1609–1614)," *Encyclo-*

NOTES TO PAGES 26–28 299

pedia Virginia, May 30, 2014, http://www.encyclopediavirginia.org/first_anglo-powhatan_war_1609-1614#start_entry.

85. Dunbar-Ortiz, *Indigenous Peoples' History*, 60; and Wolfe, "First Anglo-Powhattan War."

86. Wolfe, "First Anglo-Powhattan War."

87. Ostler, *Surviving Genocide*, 15.

88. Dunbar-Ortiz, *Indigenous Peoples' History*, 60–61; Clodfelter, *Warfare*, 65.

89. Clodfelter, *Warfare*, 65.

90. Ibid.

91. Ibid.; and Thornton, *Indian Holocaust*, 69.

92. Clodfelter, *Warfare*, 65.

93. Thornton, *Indian Holocaust*, 69–70; and Ostler, *Surviving Genocide*, 15.

94. Clodfelter, *Warfare*, 68.

95. Kelton, *Epidemics and Enslavement*, 101–3.

96. Ibid., 103.

97. Ibid., 102.

98. Ibid., 101–2.

99. Ibid., chap. 3; and Ostler, *Surviving Genocide*, 16.

100. Thornton, *Indian Holocaust*, 70.

101. Peter H. Wood, "The Changing Population of the Colonial South: An Overview by Race and Region, 1685–1790," in *Powhatan's Mantle: Indians in the Colonial Southeast*, ed. Peter H. Wood, Gregory A. Waselkov, and M. Thomas Hatley (Lincoln: University of Nebraska Press, 1989), 38–39, cited in Catherine M. Cameron, "The Effects of Warfare and Captive-Taking on Indigenous Mortality in Post-Contact North America," in *Beyond Germs*, 181.

102. Ostler, *Surviving Genocide*, 17.

103. Ibid.

104. Thornton, *Indian Holocaust*, 72–75; and Ostler, *Surviving Genocide*, 18–19.

105. Ostler, *Surviving Genocide*, 18.

106. Thornton, *Indian Holocaust*, 74–75; and Ostler, *Surviving Genocide*, 19.

107. Ostler, *Surviving Genocide*, 26.

108. Ibid., 22.

109. Thornton, *Indian Holocaust*, 71; Jones, *Rationalizing Epidemics*, 21–32; Anderson, *Ethnic Cleansing*, 27; and Ostler, *Surviving Genocide*, 18. Some researchers have concluded that smallpox or other European diseases struck Native peoples in Maine and New Hampshire as early as 1584–86. See Ronda Roberts, "Maine," in Daniel S. Murphee, Editor, *Native America: A State-by-State Historical Encyclopedia*, vol. 1 (Santa Barbara: ABC-CLIO, 2012), 472–474; Peter C. Holloran, *Historical*

300 NOTES TO PAGES 28–30

Dictionary of New England, 2nd ed. (New York: Rowman and Little-field, 2017), xv; and Fletcher Haulley, *Primary Source History of the Colony of New Hampshire* (New York: Rosen Publishing Group, 2006), 10. Other investigators believe the first important epidemic was the one that erupted in 1616. See, for example, Dean R. Snow and Kim M. Lanphear, "European Contact and Indian Depopulation in the Northeast: The Timing of the First Epidemics," *Ethnohistory* 35/1 (Winter 1988): 20–25. This view has also been expressed by Ostler in email to author.

110. Jones, *Rationalizing Epidemics*, 31–32; and Ostler, *Surviving Genocide*, 18.

111. Dunbar-Ortiz, *Indigenous Peoples' History*, 62.

112. Ibid., 63. See also Alfred A. Cave, *The Pequot War* (Amherst: University of Massachusetts, 1996), 69.

113. Anderson, *Ethnic Cleansing*, 30; Ostler, *Surviving Genocide*, 20; and Clodfelter, *Warfare*, 66.

114. Clodfelter, *Warfare*, 67.

115. The phrase "wilderness warfare" came from Benjamin Church, the commander of the Plymouth militia. See Dunbar-Ortiz, *Indigenous Peoples' History*, 64.

116. David Sharp, "Penobscots Don't Want Ancestors' Scalping to Be Whitewashed," AP News, December 4, 2021, https://apnews.com/article/penobscots-indigenous-history-scalping-colonial-america-adf590d261599302207b8c377b711169.

117. Anthony Brandt, "Blood and Betrayal: King Philip's War," *HistoryNet.com*, October 30, 2014, http://www.history net.com/blood-and-betrayal-king-philips-war.htm. See also Clodfelter, 67.

118. Ostler, *Surviving Genocide*, 21.

119. Ibid., 22.

120. Jones, *Rationalizing Epidemics*, 32.

121. Anderson, *Ethnic Cleansing*, 37–38, and chap. 18.

122. Riley, *Rio del Norte*, 266; Alchon, *Pest in the Land*, 95–96; and Reff, email to author.

123. Riley, *Rio del Norte*, 268; Anderson, *Ethnic Cleansing*, 48; and Clodfelter, *Warfare*, 68.

124. Rick Hendricks, "Domingo Jironza Pétriz de Cruzate," New Mexico Office of the State Historian, *New Mexico History.com*, http://newmexicohistory.org/people/domingo-jironza-petriz-de-cruzate#_edn10.

125. Clodfelter, *Warfare*, 68.

126. Ibid.

127. Riley, *Rio del Norte*, 266.

128. Kelton, *Epidemics and Enslavement*, 82–87.

129. Ibid., 85–86.

NOTES TO PAGES 30–32   301

130. Ibid., 83, 85.
131. Ibid., 82–87, 99.
132. Ibid., 83–86; Alchon, *Pest in the Land*, 91–92; and Ostler, *Surviving Genocide*, 14.
133. Jerald T. Milanich, *Florida Indians and the Invasion from Europe* (Gainesville: University Press of Florida, 1995), 222–29.
134. Ibid., 230–31.
135. Ostler, *Surviving Genocide*, 22. Lower estimates of Haudenosaunee losses are found in Clodfelter, *Warfare*, 69; and in Howard Peckham, *The Colonial Wars: 1689–1762* (Chicago: University of Chicago Press, 1964), 53. Peckham's occasional depiction of Indigenous peoples as "savages" is racist and regrettable.
136. Clodfelter, *Warfare*, 68–69.
137. Mann, *1491*, 126.
138. Clodfelter, *Warfare*, 125.
139. Ibid.; Milanich, *Florida Indians and the Invasion from Europe*, 224–25; and Mark Frederick Boyd, Hale G. Smith, and John W. Griffin, *Here They Once Stood: The Tragic End of the Apalachee Missions* (Gainesville: University Press of Florida, 1951), 13.
140. Anderson, *Ethnic Cleansing*, 61.
141. Clodfelter, *Warfare*, 125; and Francis Jennings, *The Founders of America: From the Earliest Migrations to the Present* (New York: W. W. Norton, 1993), 270.
142. Clodfelter, *Warfare*, 125.
143. Ibid.
144. Ibid.
145. Kelton, *Epidemics and Enslavement*, 180–82.
146. Jennings, *Founders of America*, 277–79; Clodfelter, *Warfare*, 126; and Steven J. Oatis, *A Colonial Complex: South Carolina's Frontiers in the Era of the Yamasee War, 1680–1730* (Lincoln: University of Nebraska Press, 2004), cited in Kelton, *Epidemics and Enslavement*, 218.
147. Kelton, *Epidemics and Enslavement*, 220.
148. Ostler, *Surviving Genocide*, 28.
149. Jennings, *Founders of America*, 271.
150. Ostler, *Surviving Genocide*, 28.
151. Ibid.; and Clodfelter, *Warfare*, 125.
152. Clodfelter, *Warfare*, 125; and Jenkins, *Founders of America*, 271–72.
153. Brett Rushforth, "Slavery, the Fox Wars, and the Limits of Alliance," *William and Mary Quarterly* 63/1 (2006): 76, cited in Cameron, "The Effects of Warfare and Captive-Taking," 183–84.
154. Ostler, *Surviving Genocide*, 28.
155. Clodfelter, *Warfare*, 126.

302 NOTES TO PAGES 33-34

156. Dunbar-Ortiz, *Indigenous Peoples' History*, 66.
157. E. Wagner Stearn and Allen E. Stearn, *The Effect of Smallpox on the Destiny of the Amerindian* (Boston: Bruce Humphries, 1945), 38, cited in Thornton, *Indian Holocaust*, 78.
158. Thornton, *Indian Holocaust*, 81; and Donald J. Lehmer and David T. Jones, *Akira Archeology: The Bad River Phase*, Smithsonian Institution, River Basin Surveys, Publications in Salvage Archeology, no. 7 (1968), cited in Thornton, *Indian Holocaust*, 81.
159. Robert Thornton, *The Cherokees: A Population History* (Lincoln: University of Nebraska Press, 1990), 29-31.
160. Thornton, *Indian Holocaust*, 79-80.
161. Louis P. Towles, "Jenkins' Ear, War of," *Encyclopedia of North Carolina*, NCPedia, January 1, 2006, https://www.ncpedia.org/jenkins-ear-war.
162. This phrase appears in Jennings, *Founders of America*, 233. An estimate of fatalities in the conflict is found in Peckham, *Colonial Wars*, 117. However, it does not include Native deaths.
163. Ostler, *Surviving Genocide*, 29-35; and David G. Moore, "Catawba Indians," *Encyclopedia of North Carolina*, ed. William S. Powell, *NCPedia*, (2006), https://www.ncpedia.org/catawba-indians.
164. Ostler, *Surviving Genocide*, 31-35.
165. Ibid., 31.
166. This phrase appears in Ostler, *Surviving Genocide*, 34. Tsalagi deaths during the war(s) are discussed in Clodfelter, 130; and Ostler, *Surviving Genocide*, 32-34.
167. Ostler, *Surviving Genocide*, 34.
168. Ibid.; William B. Kessel and Robert Wooster, *Encyclopedia of Native American Wars and Warfare* (New York: Checkmark Books, 2005), 139; Anderson, *Ethnic Cleansing*, 75-77; Clodfelter, *Warfare*, 127-30; and *South Carolina Gazette*, quoted in John Duffy, "Smallpox and the Indians in the American Colonies," *Bulletin on the History of Medicine* 25 (1951): 338, cited in Thornton, *Indian Holocaust*, 79.
169. Kessel and Wooster, *Native American Wars*, 139; Clodfelter, *Warfare*, 129-30; and Ostler, *Surviving Genocide*, 31-35.
170. Ostler, *Surviving Genocide*, 36.
171. Clodfelter, *Warfare*, 131; and Kessel and Wooster, *Native American Wars*, 253. During the war, General Jeffrey Amherst approved efforts to spread smallpox among Native peoples fighting the British. As Ostler makes clear, another British military leader and a trader gave two Delaware emissaries blankets and a handkerchief infected with smallpox, but it is "impossible to say" if this led to new infections among Indigenous combatants. Still, the heinous intent is indisputable. See Ostler, *Surviving Genocide*, 36-37.

NOTES TO PAGES 34–35

172. Ostler, *Surviving Genocide*, 41–42.
173. Madley, *American Genocide*, 3, 36. An estimate of 300,000 is found in Albert L. Hurtado, *Indian Survival on the California Frontier* (New Haven: Yale University Press, 1988), 1. Both Madley and Hurtado drew on a similar estimate by Sherburne Cook in *The Population of the California Indians, 1769–1970* (Berkeley: University of California Press, 1976), 43–44, 59, 65.
174. Madley, *American Genocide*, chap. 1. The 1830 population estimate is found on page 36.
175. Ostler, "Genocide and American History." Different views on the possible transmission of European diseases to Northwest Pacific Native peoples are discussed in Robert Boyd, *The Coming of the Spirit of Pestilence: Introduced Infectious Diseases and Population Decline Among Northwest Coast Indians, 1774–1874* (Seattle: University of Washington Press, 1999), 21–39.
176. Elizabeth A. Fenn, *Pox Americana: The Great Smallpox Epidemic of 1775–82* (New York: Hill and Wang, 2001), 273–74.
177. Fenn, *Pox Americana*, 274; Thornton, *Indian Holocaust*, 79–81; and Mann, *1491*, 123.
178. Swanson, "Hawaiian Population."
179. Collin G. Calloway, "American Indians and the American Revolution," *The American Revolution: Stories from the Revolution*, U.S. Department of Interior, National Park Service, December 4, 2008, https://www.nps.gov/revwar/about_the_revolution/american_indians.html.
180. Anderson, *Ethnic Cleansing*, 90; and Ostler, *Surviving Genocide*, 56–57.
181. Anderson, *Ethnic Cleansing*, 96.
182. Dennis Zotigh, "A Brief Balance of Power—The 1778 Treaty with the Delaware Nation," *Smithsonian Magazine*, May 21, 2018, https://www.smithsonianmag.com/blogs/national-museum-american-indian/2018/05/22/1778-delaware-treaty/; and Dunbar-Ortiz, *Indigenous Peoples' History*, 142.
183. Rhiannon Koehler, "Hostile Nations: Quantifying the Destruction of the Sullivan-Clinton Genocide of 1779," *American Indian Quarterly* 42/4 (Fall 2018): 444. This estimate is based on a review of "never-before-examined unofficial accounts found in historical newspapers, military records, journal entries, and speeches to quantify the property, land, and lives lost in the campaign." See Koehler, "Hostile Nations," 428. An estimate of only two hundred violent deaths is found in Ostler, *Surviving Genocide*, 76.
184. Koehler, "Hostile Nations," 445–46; and Ron Soodalter, "Massacre and Retribution: The 1779–80 Sullivan Expedition," *HistoryNet.com*, http://www.historynet.com/massacre-retribution-the-1779-80-sullivan-expedition.htm.

304 NOTES TO PAGES 35-38

185. Ostler, *Surviving Genocide*, 67, 76.
186. An estimate of more than 4,500 Haudenosaunee deaths is found in Koehler, "Hostile Nations," 446. Ostler's estimate of no more than 1,500 Haudenosaunee fatalities in the war is much too low. However, he has estimated that at least one thousand Tsalagis died during the conflict, although the total number of deaths among the Lenapes, Shawnees, Wyandots, and Miamis is unknown. See Ostler, *Surviving Genocide*, 76–77. All told, an estimate of at least six thousand Indigenous deaths in the War of Independence appears prudent.
187. Dunbar-Ortiz, *Indigenous Peoples' History*, 78.
188. This phrase comes from Seymour Martin Lipset, *The First New Nation: The United States in Historical and Comparative Perspective* (New York: W. W. Norton, 1979), 2.
189. Ostler, *Surviving Genocide*, 85–90.
190. Ibid., 91–92.
191. Ibid., 91, 95.
192. Anderson, *Ethnic Cleansing*, 100.
193. Kristopher Maulden, "A Show of Force: The Northwest Indian War and the Early American State," *Ohio Valley History* 16/4 (2016): 20.
194. Clodfelter, *Warfare*, 145.
195. Ibid.
196. Dunbar-Ortiz, *Indigenous Peoples' History*, 83.
197. Clodfelter, *Warfare*, 145.
198. Ibid.; and Ostler, *Surviving Genocide*, 119.
199. Clodfelter, *Warfare*, 145; and Dunbar-Ortiz, *Indigenous Peoples' History*, 83.
200. Ostler, *Surviving Genocide*, 119.
201. Thornton, *Indian Holocaust*, 43.
202. Ibid., 91–94; and Boyd, *Spirit of Pestilence*, 22, 39–45.
203. Dunbar-Ortiz, *Indigenous Peoples' History*, 93.
204. Ibid., 132–46.
205. Spain had secretly returned the Louisiana Territory to France in 1801 after being defeated by Napoleon's forces in the War of the Pyrenees. On Jefferson's support for the forcible relocation of Indigenous people to areas west of the Mississippi River, see Zinn, *People's History*, 126; and Paul L. Atwood, *War and Empire: The American Way of Life* (London: Pluto Press, 2010), 63.
206. The "two parallel wars" are noted in Dunbar-Ortiz, *Indigenous Peoples' History*, 93. The expression "Wars of 1812" is found in Ostler, *Surviving Genocide*, chap. 5.
207. Ostler, *Surviving Genocide*, 145–46.
208. Ibid., 157.

NOTES TO PAGES 38–41

209. Ibid., 160–64.
210. Ibid., 162–64.
211. Ibid., 164–65.
212. Ibid., 165–66. The Seminoles were people who migrated in the previous century from Muscogee towns in southern Georgia to the lands in northern Florida formerly occupied by Apalachees and Timucuas.
213. Gregory A. Waselkov, *A Conquering Spirit: Fort Mims and the Red Stick War of 1813–1814* (Tuscaloosa: University of Alabama Press, 2006), 96–102, 110–15, 127–35, 190–93; and Frank Lawrence Owsley, Jr., *Struggle for the Gulf Borderlands: The Creek War and the Battle of New Orleans, 1812–1815* (Gainesville, University Press of Florida, 1981), 25–26, 30–32, 35–39; both cited in Ostler, *Surviving Genocide*, 167.
214. Ostler, *Surviving Genocide*, 169–70.
215. Ibid., 171.
216. Dunbar-Ortiz, *Indigenous Peoples' History*, 94.
217. Ostler, *Surviving Genocide*, 173–74; and Clodfelter, *Warfare*, 283.
218. An estimate of 7,500 Indigenous deaths is found in Donald R. Hickey, *The War of 1812: A Forgotten Conflict*, Bicentennial Edition (Urbana: University of Illinois Press, 2012), 306. An estimate of as many as 11,000 Native deaths appears in Clodfelter, *Warfare*, 263.
219. Ostler, *Surviving Genocide*, 174.
220. Ibid., 179.
221. Ibid., 274; Clodfelter, *Warfare*, 283; and Dunbar-Ortiz, *Indigenous Peoples' History*, 102.
222. Clodfelter, *Warfare*, 283.
223. Ibid.
224. Ibid.; Dunbar-Ortiz, *Indigenous Peoples' History*, 102; and Ostler, *Surviving Genocide*, 274.
225. Madley, *American Genocide*, 36–37.
226. Mexican forces killed hundreds of Indigenous people in California in the 1820s, 1830s, and early 1840s. See Madley, *American Genocide*, 39–40.
227. Dunbar-Ortiz, *Indigenous Peoples' History*, 102.
228. Ostler, *Surviving Genocide*, 248.
229. Ibid., 289.
230. Ibid., chap. 8, and 361. These two territories were combined to create the state of Oklahoma in 1907.
231. Ibid., chap. 9, and 361.
232. Ibid., 361. About eleven thousand Native people remained in the Southeast, but twenty-four thousand remained in the North.
233. Ibid.

234. History.com Editors, "Trail of Tears," *History*, February 21, 2020, https://www.history. com/topics/native-american-history/trail-of-tears.
235. Ostler, *Surviving Genocide*, 256. An estimate of 2,500 Choctaw deaths is also found in Anderson, *Ethnic Cleansing*, 157.
236. Clodfelter, *Warfare*, 275–76.
237. Ostler, *Surviving Genocide*, 263.
238. Clodfelter, *Warfare*, 284.
239. Ibid.
240. Ostler, *Surviving Genocide*, 286
241. Ibid., 273.
242. Thornton, *Indian Holocaust*, 114.
243. Ostler, *Surviving Genocide*, 273–74. See also Clodfelter, *Warfare*, 284.
244. Ostler, *Surviving Genocide*, 256.
245. Ibid., 256, 263, 273, 286, 361.
246. Ibid., 361–62.
247. Ibid., 363.
248. Ibid.
249. Ibid., 328; and Thornton, *Indian Holocaust*, 94.
250. Thornton, *Indian Holocaust*, 94.
251. Ibid., 94–99; and Alchon, *Pest in the Land*, 104–5.
252. Thornton, *Indian Holocaust*, 94–95; and Alchon, *Pest in the Land*, 104–5.
253. Thornton, *Indian Holocaust*, 95.
254. James Daschuk, *Clearing the Plains: Disease, the Politics of Starvation, and the Loss of Aboriginal Life* (Regina, CA: University of Regina Press, 2013), 67.
255. Ostler, "Genocide and American Indian History"; and Anderson, *Ethnic Cleansing*, 194–95.
256. Indigenous peoples in this area included Caddoans, Coahuiltecans, Karankawas, Tonkawas, Apaches, Nermernuhs, Wichitas, Tsalagis, Alabamas, Coushattas, Kickapoos, and scores of other peoples. David La Vere has estimated that in 1500, "Anywhere from 50,000 to several hundred thousand to maybe a million" lived here. See *The Texas Indians* (College Station: Texas A&M University Press, 2004), 28. In the centuries that followed, many Natives died or left Texas, and smaller numbers fleeing European and U.S. colonizers migrated there. For estimates for the Indigenous population in Texas in the 1830s, see Dunbar-Ortiz, *Indigenous Peoples' History*, 126; and Gary Clayton Anderson, *The Conquest of Texas: Ethnic Cleansing in the Promised Land, 1820–1875* (Norman: University of Oklahoma Press, 2005), 4.
257. John C. Ewers, "The Influence of Epidemics on the Indian Populations and Cultures of Texas," *Plains Anthropologist* 18 (1973): 107, cited in

NOTES TO PAGES 43–45 307

Thornton, *Indian Holocaust*, 128–31. Ewers estimated the Native population in present-day Texas to be about fifty thousand in 1690, but it was likely significantly higher.

258. Thornton, *Indian Holocaust*, 128, 131.
259. Anderson, *Ethnic Cleansing*, 275.
260. Ibid., 176.
261. Ibid.
262. Ibid.
263. Sherburne Cook, "Historical Demography," in *Handbook of North American Indians* 8, ed. Robert F. Heizer(Washington, DC: Smithsonian Institution, 1978), 92–93, cited in Madley, *American Genocide*, 39.
264. Cook, "Historical Demography," 92–93.
265. This phrase comes from John O'Sullivan, "Annexation," *The United States Magazine and Democratic Review* 17 (New York, 1845): 5–6, 9–10, cited in Zinn, *People's History*, 151. Zinn's discussion of "manifest destiny" is found in chap. 8.
266. Madley, *American Genocide*, 100.
267. Ibid., 300.
268. Ibid., 351.
269. Ibid., esp. 346–59.
270. Ibid., 3, 346.
271. Clodfelter, *Warfare*, 286.
272. Thornton, *Indian Holocaust*, 99.
273. Ibid., 285.
274. Clodfelter, *Warfare*, 276.
275. Thornton, *Indian Holocaust*, 99; Boyd, *Spirit of Pestilence*, 4; and Anderson, *Ethnic Cleansing*, 219–20.
276. E. A. Schwartz, "Rogue River War of 1855–1856," *The Oregon Encyclopedia* (February 19, 2019), https://oregonencyclopedia.org/articles/rogue_river_war_of_1855-1856/#.XpSWgEBFybh.
277. Clodfelter, *Warfare*, 276, 286–87. Most of these deaths occurred in the campaigns against the Nermenuh and Kiowa.
278. Anderson, *Ethnic Cleansing*, 237; and Ostler, "Genocide and American Indian History."
279. Clodfelter, *Warfare*, 287–88. These estimates do not include what Clodfelter described as "untold" Mexican civilian lives lost south of the U.S. border.
280. Kessel and Wooster, *Native American Wars*, 298.
281. Ibid., and Clodfelter, *Warfare*, 277–78.
282. Clodfelter, *Warfare*, 278.
283. Anderson, *Ethnic Cleansing*, 243.
284. Clodfelter, *Warfare*, 279.

308 NOTES TO PAGES 45–47

285. Kessel and Wooster, *Native American Wars*, 294; and Clodfelter, 278.
286. This estimate appears in Dana Hedgpeth, "This Was the Worst Slaughter of Native Americans in U.S. History— Few Remember It," *Washington Post*, September 26, 2021. See also Anderson, *Ethnic Cleansing*, 244; and Michael F. Dove, "Shoshone War," in *The Encyclopedia of North American Indian Wars, 1607–1890: A Political ,Social, and Military History*, vol. 2, ed. Spencer C. Tucker (Santa Barbara, CA: ABC-CLIO, 2011), 730–31.
287. Gregory Michno, *The Deadliest Indian War in the West: The Snake Conflict, 1864–1868* (Caldwell: Caxton Press, 2007), 5.
288. Michno, *Deadliest Indian War*, 345.
289. Clodfelter, *Warfare*, 276.
290. Kessel and Wooster, *Native American Wars*, 225.
291. Ibid.
292. Ibid.; Clodfelter, *Warfare*, 286; and Anderson, *Ethnic Cleansing*, 240.
293. Kessel and Wooster, *Native American Wars*, 80; and Clodfelter, *Warfare*, 289.
294. Clodfelter, *Warfare*, 289.
295. Ibid., 279.
296. Dunbar-Ortiz, *Indigenous Peoples' History*, 145–46.
297. Clodfelter, *Warfare*, 289–90.
298. Ibid., 280.
299. Ibid.
300. Ibid., 288.
301. Ibid.
302. Ibid., 291.
303. Ibid.
304. Robert Plocheck, "American Indians in Texas," *Texas Almanac* (1998–99), Texas State Historical Association, https://texasalmanac.com/topics/culture/american-indian/american-indian. As noted above, the Indigenous population in the area was approximately forty to fifty thousand in 1830. An estimate that perhaps four thousand Natives died in Texas between 1823 and 1875 is found in Anderson, *Conquest of Texas*, 11. However, the total number of violent deaths during this period was likely much higher. In addition, many Indigenous people perished from diseases, loss of food supplies, forced relocations, and other deadly features of colonialism. The Indigenous death toll in Texas in the nineteenth century probably runs into the tens of thousands, and similar numbers were undoubtedly driven out.
305. Kessel and Wooster, *Native American Wars*, 299.
306. Clodfelter, *Warfare*, 280.
307. Ibid.

NOTES TO PAGES 47–50 309

308. Ibid., 280–81.
309. Ibid., 281.
310. Ibid.
311. Ibid.; and "Today in History—October 5: Chief Joseph Surrenders," Library of Congress, https://www.loc.gov/item/today-in-history/october-05/.
312. Clodfelter, *Warfare*, 281.
313. Boyd, *Spirit of Pestilence*, 3.
314. Clodfelter, *Warfare*, 291.
315. Ibid., 288–89.
316. Kessel and Wooster, *Native American Wars*, 46.
317. This slogan originated with U.S. Army Captain Richard Henry Pratt, who established the Carlisle Indian Industrial School in Pennsylvania in 1879. See Dunbar-Ortiz, *Indigenous Peoples' History*, 151, 153, 211–14.
318. Ibid., 153.
319. Kessel and Wooster, *Native American Wars*, 300.
320. Ibid., 145.
321. Dunbar-Ortiz, *Indigenous Peoples' History*, 154.
322. Kessel and Wooster, *Native American Wars*, 145–46, 300; and Clodfelter, 281–82.
323. Clodfelter, *Warfare*, 282.
324. Dunbar-Ortiz, *Indigenous Peoples' History*, 155; Wounded Knee Museum Website/For Educators, http://www.woundedkneemuseum.org/; and Dana Lone Hill, "Wounded Knee Should Be a National Monument, Not a Profit Center," *Guardian*, May 1, 2013. Anderson has acknowledged that this incident was a massacre but estimated that about 150 Lakotas died. See *Ethnic Cleansing*, 336. Clodfelter has erroneously claimed that the Lakotas "resisted an attempt to disarm them" and provided an estimate of 153 Indigenous deaths while noting that 20 to 30 others may have also died. See Clodfelter, *Warfare*, 282.
325. Clodfelter, *Warfare*, 282.
326. U.S. Army Development and Readiness Command (DARCOM), *History of Fort Wingate Depot, Forts Fauntleroy, Lyon*, 29, https://www.ftwingate.org/docs/ pub/History_FortWingate. pdf.
327. Mel H. Bolster, "The Smoked Meat Rebellion," *Chronicles of Oklahoma* 31 (1953): 37–55; and Daniel F. Littlefield and Lonnie E. Underhill, "The 'Crazy Snake Uprising' of 1909: A Red, Black, or White Affair?," *Journal of the Southwest* 20/4 (Winter 1978): 307–24.
328. Clodfelter, *Warfare*, 282.
329. Mychel Matthews, "Hidden History: Bluff Indian War of 1915," *Magic Valley Times-News*, July 21, 2016.

330. H. B. Wharfield, "A Fight with the Yaquis at Bear Valley, 1918," *Arizoniana* 4/3 (Fall 1963): 1–8.

331. Jerry Spangler, "Last Indian War Not So Long Ago or Far Away: Paiute Remembered as Hero, Martyr," *Deseret News*, August 7, 1989.

332. U.S. Census Bureau, *Indian Population of the United States and Alaska, 1910* (Washington, DC: Government Printing Office, 1915), 10, cited in Thornton, "Population of Native North Americans," 32.

333. Carl Waldman, *Encyclopedia of Native American Tribes*, 3rd ed. (New York: Infobase Publishing, 2006), 19, 46, 73, 93–94, 127–28, 154, 168, 287, 291, 313, 321, 323, 327; Thornton, *Indian Holocaust*, 113; Milanich, *Florida Indians*, 230–35; and Stuart James Baldwin, "Tompiro Culture, Subsistence, and Trade" (PhD diss., University of Calgary, 1988), iii.

334. Mooney, "Aboriginal Population," 32; and Swanson, "Hawaiian Population."

335. Thornton, *Indian Holocaust*, 42; and Newson, "Demographic Collapse," 277.

336. Thornton, *Indian Holocaust*, xvi-xviii, chaps. 7–8, and "Native North Americans," 31–41; and Nancy Shoemaker, *American Indian Population Recovery in the Twentieth Century* (Albuquerque: University of New Mexico Press, 1999), esp. chap, 1.

337. U.S. Census Bureau, "Facts for Features: American Indian and Alaska Heritage Month: November 2018," (October 25, 2018), https://www.census.gov/newsroom/facts-for-features/ 2018/aian.html.

338. Goo, "Native Hawaiians."

339. Thornton, *Indian Holocaust*, xvi–xviii, chaps. 7 and 8, and "Native North Americans," 31–41, at 32.

340. An estimate of about 45 million Indigenous people in Latin America in 2010 is found in Economic Commission for Latin America and the Caribbean, United Nations, "Indigenous Peoples in Latin America" (September 22, 2014), https://www.cepal.org/en/infografias/los-pueblos-indigenas-en-america-latina. When the more than seven million Indigenous people in the present-day United States and almost two million more in Canada are added, the total is approximately 54 million. Even this appraisal is almost certainly too low because some countries' governments do not include all people of Indigenous descent in their estimates. On the Native population in Canada, see Government of Canada/Gouvernement du Canada, "Indigenous Peoples and Communities," June 11, 2021, https://www.rcaanc-cirnac.gc.ca/eng/110010001378 5/1529102490303.

341. Acknowledgment that some twentieth-century U.S. practices toward Indigenous peoples are genocidal is found in Ostler, "Genocide and American Indian History."

NOTES TO PAGE 50   311

342. See Thomas A. Britten, "Native American Soldiers in World War I," in *The Routledge Handbook of American Military and Diplomatic History: From 1865 to the Present*, ed. Antonio S. Thompson and Christos G. Frentzos (New York: Routledge, 2013), 88; Alison R. Bernstein, *American Indians and World War II: Toward a New Era in Indian Affairs* (Norman: University of Oklahoma Press, 1991), 61; and David A. Blum and Nese F. DeBruyne, Congressional Research Service, "American War and Military Operations Casualties: Lists and Statistics," CRS Report, July 29, 2020, https://fas.org/sgp/crs/natsec/RL32492.pdf.

343. David V. Baker, "American Indian Executions in Historical Context," *Criminal Justice Studies: A Critical Journal of Crime, Law, and Society* 20/4 (December 2007): 315–73; and "Registry of Known American Indian Executions, 1639–2006," in Death Penalty Information Center, "Native Americans," https://deathpenaltyinfo.org/stories/registry-of-known-american-indian-executions-1639-2006.

344. See David Grann, *Killers of the Flower Moon: The Osage Murders and the Birth of the FBI* (New York: Random House, 2017).

345. Dunbar-Ortiz, *Indigenous Peoples' History*, 183–86.

346. Parenti, *Democracy for the Few*, 127.

347. Teran Powell, "Most Likely to Die"; Elise Hansen, "The Forgotten Minority in Police Shootings," CNN, November 13, 2017, http://www.cnn.com/2017/11/10/us/native-lives-matter/ index.html; and Stephanie Woodard, "The Police Killings No One Is Talking About," *In These Times*, October 17, 2016, http://inthesetimes.com/features/ native_american_police_killings_ native_lives_matter.html. Hansen noted that police killed about twenty-two Indigenous people in 2016.

348. On the incarceration rate for Indigenous people, "Race and Justice News: Native Americans in the Justice System," The Sentencing Project, March 28, 2016, https://www.sentencingproject. org/news/race-justice-news-native-americans-in-the-justice-system/; and Roxanne Daniel, "Since You Asked: What Data Exists About Native American People in the Criminal Justice System," Prison Policy Initiative, April 22, 2020, https:www.prisonpolicy.org/blog/2020/04/22/native/. On the deaths of Native prisoners, see E. Ann Carson, Bureau of Justice Statistics, U.S. Department of Justice, *Mortality in Local Jails, 2000–2018—Statistical Tables*, April 2021, 13, Table 9, https://bjs.ojp.gov/content/pub/pdf/mlj0018st.pdf; and *Mortality in State and Federal Prisons, 2001–2018—Statistical Tables*, April 2021, 12, Table 10, https://bjs.ojp.gov/content/pub/pdf/ms fp0118st.pdf; and Nate Hegyi, "Indian Affairs Promised to Reform Tribal Jails—We Found Death, Neglect, and Despair," NPR, June 10, 2021, https://www.npr.org/2021/ 06/10/100245 1637/bureau-of-indian-affairs-tribal-detention-centers-deaths-ne-

312 NOTES TO PAGES 51–52

glect. Many Indigenous people who die in prison are not identified as such, so the annual number of fatalities is considerably higher than the scores reported each year.

349. Mose A. Herne, Alexandra C. Maschino, and Anita L. Graham-Phillips, "Homicide Among American Indians/Native Alaskans, 1999–2009: Implications for Public Health Interventions," *Public Health Reports* 1314 (July–August 2016): 597–604.

350. Alleen Brown, "Indigenous Women Have Been Disappearing for Generations. Politicians are Finally Starting to Notice," *The Intercept*, May 31, 2018, https://theintercept.com/2018/05/31/missing-and-murdered-indigenous-women/.

351. U.S. Department of Health and Human Services, National Institute of Mental Health, "Suicide," April 2019, https://www.nimh.nih.gov/health/statistics/suicide.shtml#part_154968.

352. Dunbar-Ortiz, *Indigenous Peoples' History*, 211.

353. David J. Hacker and Michael R. Haines, "AmerIndian Mortality in the Late 19th Century: The Impact of Federal Assimilation Policies on a Vulnerable Population," *Annales de Démographie Historique 2005* 110/2 (July 2005): 17–45.

354. Alleen Brown and Nick Estes, "As Untold Number of Children Disappeared at U.S. Boarding Schools, Tribal Nations Are Raising the Stakes in Search of Answers," *The Intercept*, September 25, 2018, https://theintercept.com/2018/09/25/carlisle-indian-industrial-school-indigenous-children-disappeared/; Mary Annette Pember, "Death by Civilization," *The Atlantic*, March 8, 2019, https://www.theatlantic.com/education/archive/2019/03/traumatic-legacy-indian-boarding-schools/584293/; and Brad Brooks, "Native Americans Decry Unmarked Graves, Untold History of Boarding Schools," Reuters, June 22, 2021, https://www.reuters. com/world/us/native-americans-decry-unmarked-graves-untold-history-boarding-schools-2021-06-22/.

355. U.S. Office of Indian Affairs, *Report of the Commissioner of Indian Affairs to the Secretary of the Interior for the Fiscal Year Ended June 30, 1916* (Washington, DC: Government Printing Office, 1916), cited in Brianna Theobald, "A 1970 Law Led to the Mass Sterilization of Native American Women. That Still Matters," *Time*, November 28, 2019, https://time.com/5737080/ native-american-sterilization-history/.

356. Pandemic deaths of 6,632 Indigenous people in the coterminous United States were reported in "Influenza Among the American Indians," *Public Health Reports (1896–1970)* 34/42 (October 17, 1919): 2298–2300. This was likely an undercount because officials frequently made broad estimates instead of surveying distant Indigenous households and because this figure did not include deaths in Native nations un-

NOTES TO PAGE 52 313

recognized by the U.S. government. Mikaela Morgane Adams, email to author, January 23, 2021. An estimate of at least 1,312 Native deaths in Alaska is found in Svenn-Erik Mamelund, Lisa Sattenspiel, and Jessica Dimka, "Influenza-Associated Mortality During the 1918–1919 Influenza Pandemic in Alaska and Labrador: A Comparison," *Social Science History* 37/2 (Summer 2013): 204, 210. Compelling evidence that the total number of Indigenous deaths surpassed eight thousand is found in the dramatic decline of the population between 1910 and 1920. Shoemaker has noted that the Census Bureau reported more than 21,000 fewer Native people in 1920 than in 1910, though she attributes part of the decrease to budget constraints that limited the agency's ability to identify Indigenous people. See Shoemaker, *Population Recovery*, 4.

357. Andrew Glass, "Indian Citizenship Act Signed, June 2, 1924," *Politico*, June 2, 2014, https://www.politico.com/story/2014/06/president-calvin-coolidge-signs-indian-citizenship-act-june-2-1924-107294.

358. Deborah Hastings, "Uranium Mining Leaves a Bitter Scar on Navajo Nation," *Los Angeles Times*, August 6, 2000; and Cheyanne M. Daniels, "The U.S. Nuclear Weapons Program Left 'a Horrible Legacy' of Environmental Destruction and Death Across the Navajo Nation," *Inside Climate News*, June 27, 2021, https://insideclimatenews.org/news/27062021/nuclear-weapons-navajo-nation-uranium-mining-environmental-destruction-health/.

359. Donald A. Grinde and Bruce E. Johansen, *Ecocide of Native America: Environmental Destruction of Indian Lands and Peoples* (Santa Fe: Clear Light Publishers, 1995); Daniel Brook, "Environmental Genocide: Native Americans and Toxic Waste," *American Journal of Economics and Sociology* 57/1 (January 1998): 105–13; and Dina Gilio-Whitaker, *As Long as Grass Grows: The Indigenous Fight for Environmental Justice, From Colonization to Standing Rock* (Boston: Beacon Press, 2019).

360. George St. J. Perrott and Margaret D. West, "Health Services for American Indians," *Public Health Reports (1896-1970)* 72/7 (July 1957): 565–70.

361. Vanessa Ho, "Native American Death Rates Soar as Most People Are Living Longer," *Seattle Post-Intelligencer*, March 11, 2009.

362. Espey et al., "All-Cause Mortality"; and Sela V. Panapasa, Marjorie K. Mau, David R. Williams, and James W. McNally, "Mortality Patterns of Native Hawaiians Across Their Lifespan," *American Journal of Public Health* 100/11 (November 2010): 2304–10.

363. Danielle M. Ely and Anne K. Driscoll, "Infant Mortality in the United States, 2017: Data from the Period Linked Birth/Infant Death File," Centers for Disease Control and Prevention, *National Vital Statistics Reports* 68/10 (August 1, 2019): 3–4.

364. Sarche and Spicer, "Health Disparities."

314 NOTES TO PAGES 52–54

365. D. E. Shalala, M. H. Trujillo, G. J. Hartz, and A. J. D'Angelo, *Regional Differences in Indian Health: 1998–1999* (Rockville: Indian Health Service, 1999), cited in Sarche and Spicer, "Health Disparities."

366. Engels, *Working Class in England*, 95.

367. See Shoemaker, *Population Recovery*, 8; Espey et al., "All-Cause Mortality"; and James A. Weed, "Vital Statistics in the United States: Preparing for the Next Century," *Population Index* 61/4 (Winter 1995): 527–39.

368. The concept of excess deaths was prominently used in U.S. Department of Health and Human Services, *Report of the Secretary's Task Force on Black and Minority Health*, vol. 1 (Washington, DC: Government Printing Office, 1985), 3, 62–85. Estimates of excess death rates of 25 percent for Native people under seventy and 43 percent for Native people under forty-five in 1979–81 are found on pages 79–80 of the *Report*.

369. The estimate of deaths for 1999–2019 is found in Centers for Disease Control and Prevention, National Center for Health Statistics, "Underlying Cause of Death 1999–2019," on CDC WONDER Online Database, 2020. Data are from the Multiple Cause of Death Files, 1999–2019, as compiled from data provided by the fifty-seven vital statistics jurisdictions through the Vital Statistics Cooperative Program, http://wonder.cdc.gov/ucd-icd10.html.

370. The 1930 population estimate is found in Thornton, "Native North Americans," 32. At the time, the average life expectancy of Indigenous peoples in the United States was fifty-two years, so most of this cohort was dead before 1999, when the Centers for Disease Control and Prevention began tracking Indigenous deaths. On life expectancy at the time, see C. Matthew Snipp, "The Size and Distribution of the American Indian Population: Fertility, Mortality, Migration, and Residence," in *Changing Numbers, Changing Needs: American Indian Demography and Public Health*, ed. Gary D. Sandefur, Ronald R. Rindfuss, and Barney Cohen (Washington, DC: National Academy Press, 1996), 19. This estimate of excess deaths between 1930 and 1999 is likely quite conservative because it uses the more recent 46 percent excess mortality rate and does not include the excess deaths of Native Hawaiians.

371. *Indian Child Welfare Program: Hearings Before the Subcomm. on Indian Affairs, 93rd Congress 1-3* (April 8–9, 1974), Opening Statement of Hon. James Abourezk, U.S. Senator from the State of South Dakota.

372. Ibid.

373. Theobald, "Mass Sterilization."

374. Ibid.

375. Nick Martin, "What's Lost When a Language Disappears?" *New Republic*, December 12, 2019, https://newrepublic.com/article/155913/na-

NOTES TO PAGES 54–55 315

tive-american-languages-disappearing-reauthorization-act-congress.

376. Justin Worland, "What to Know About the Dakota Access Pipeline Protests," *Time*, October 28, 2016, https://time.com/4548566/dakota-access-pipeline-standing-rock-sioux/; and Nina Lakhani, "'That's Genocide': Ancient Tribal Graves Threatened by Trump Border Wall," *Guardian*, December 16, 2019.

377. Virginia McLaurin, "Why the Myth of the 'Savage Indian' Persists," *Sapiens* (February 27, 2019), https://www.sapiens.org/culture/native-american-stereotypes/; "Ending the Era of Harmful 'Indian' Mascots," National Congress of American Indians, http://www.ncai.org/proud tobe; and Tom Lutz, "Indians, Braves, and Chiefs: What Now for U.S. Sports' Other Native American Names?," *Guardian*, July 13, 2020.

378. Worland, "Pipeline Protests."

379. Zack Budryk, "Here Are 16 Places Celebrating Indigenous Peoples Day for the First Time This Year," *The Hill*, October 14, 2019, https://thehill.com/homenews/state-watch/465701-here-are-the-16-states-and-cities-celebrating-indigenous-peoples-day-for; and Heather Murphy, "Maine Is the Latest State to Replace Columbus Day with Indigenous Peoples' Day," *New York Times*, April 28, 2019.

380. Jenni Fink, "79 Percent of College Students Support Getting Rid of Columbus Day for Indigenous Peoples' Day," *Newsweek*, October 7, 2019, https://www.newsweek.com/columbus-day-replace-indigenous-peoples-day-college-students-poll-1463610.

381. Tina Norris, Paula L. Vines, and Elizabeth M. Hoeffel, U.S. Census Bureau, "2010 Census Briefs: The American Indian and Alaska Native Population: 2010," January 2012, https://www.census.gov/prod/cen2010/briefs/c2010br-10.pdf.

382. Goo, "Native Hawaiians."

383. Wendy Wang, "Interracial Marriage: Who Is 'Marrying Out'?," Pew Research Center, Fact Tank: News in the Numbers, June 12, 2015, https://www.pewresearch.org/fact-tank/2015/06/12/ interracial-marriage-who-is-marrying-out/.

384. Timothy Williams, "Quietly, Indians Reshape Cities and Reservations," *New York Times*, April 13, 2013.

385. Russell Thornton, "Tribal Membership Requirements and the Demography of 'Old' and 'New' Native Americans," in *Changing Numbers, Changing Needs*, 14, cited in "Native North Americans," 41.

386. Thornton, *Indian Holocaust*, 43.

387. This is a multiplier of 2.4. Russell Thornton, email to author, December 4, 2015.

388. Twenty thousand to fifty thousand Tainos were wiped out in Puerto Rico within decades of the European invasion. Mooney estimated

316 NOTES TO PAGES 56-57

that the population loss in Alaska was at least 44,300 between 1492 and 1900. See "Aboriginal Population of America North of Mexico," 32. The application of Thornton's multiplier suggests that more than 106,000 Indigenous people in Alaska perished by the beginning of the twentieth century. The Native population of Hawai'i declined by about 659,000 between 1778 and 1920. It may not be possible to calculate the total number of lives lost or cut short in Hawai'i since 1778. David A. Swanson, email to author, March 27, 2016. However, it appears that the population losses in Puerto Rico, Alaska, and Hawai'i added up to a minimum of 785,000 by 1900 to 1920.

389. Koch et al., "Earth System Impacts," 13–36. The massive depopulation south of the present-day United States by 1600 must have significantly reduced the size of these new generations during the following centuries, rendering Thornton's multiplier for Native inapplicable to the Americas as a whole. Still, the additional deaths between 1600 and 1900 surely numbered in the millions.

390. On deaths in Mexico, Central America, and South America resulting from state violence and poor health conditions since 1900, see, for example, Stannard, *American Holocaust*, xiii–xiv; Alexander L. Hinton, *Annihilating Difference: The Anthropology of Genocide* (University of California Press, 2002), 57; Duncan Green and Sue Bradford, *Faces of Latin America*, 4th ed. (New York: Monthly Review Press, 2013), 164; Vanessa Barbara, "The Genocide of Brazil's Indians," *New York Times*, May 29, 2017; "Mexican Paramilitary Group That Killed 120 Indigenous People Reappears," *teleSUR*, December 28, 2015, https://www. telesurtv.net/english/ news/Mexican-Paramilitary-Group-that-Killed-120-Indigenous-Reappears-20151228-0011.html; and Bianca Jagger, "Stop the Murder of Environmental Defenders in Latin America," *Huffington Post*, September 11, 2017, https://www.huffingtonpost.com/ entry/stop-the-murder-of-environmental-defenders-in-latin-america_us_591345c4e4b0e3bb 894d5caf. For an earlier attempt to calculate the hemispheric loss of Indigenous lives since 1492, see David Michael Smith, "Counting the Dead: Estimating the Loss of Life in the Indigenous Holocaust, 1492–Present," *Representations and Realities: Proceedings of the Twelfth Native American Symposium*, ed. Mark B. Spencer (Durant: Southeastern Oklahoma State University, 2018), 7–17.

2. The African American Holocaust

1. Herbert S. Klein, *The Atlantic Slave Trade*, 2nd ed. (Cambridge: Cambridge University Press, 2010), 19–20; and Basil Davidson, *The African Slave Trade*, rev. ed. (Boston: Little, Brown, 1980), 63–66.

2. Marx, *Capital*, 915.

NOTES TO PAGES 57–58   317

3.   Sven Beckert, "How the West Got Rich and Modern Capitalism Was Born," *PBS News Hour*, February 13, 2015, http://www.pbs.org/newshour/making-sense/west-got-rich-modern-capitalism-born/; Edward E. Baptist, *The Half Has Never Been Told: Slavery and the Making of American Capitalism* (New York: Basic Books, 2014), xxi–xxiii, 322–23, 352–53, 359, 412–13; and Joseph R. Inikori, *Africans and the Industrial Revolution in England: A Study in International Trade and Economic Development* (Cambridge: Cambridge University Press, 2002). The expression "Great Divergence" was first used by Samuel P. Huntington in *Clash of Civilizations and the Remaking of World Order* (New York: Simon & Schuster, 1996), but his analysis differs significantly from that of Beckert, Baptist, and Inikori.

4.   David Brion Davis, Foreword, in David Eltis and David Richardson, *Atlas of the Transatlantic Slave Trade* (New Haven: Yale University Press, 2010), xvii. The United Nations World Conference against Racism, Racial Discrimination, Xenophobia, and Intolerance held in Durban, South Africa, in 2001 also recognized slavery and the transatlantic slave trade as a crime against humanity. See Nelly Schmidt, *Struggles Against Slavery: The International Year to Commemorate the Struggle Against Slavery and Its Abolition* (Paris: United Nations Educational, Social, and Cultural Organization, 2004), 61.

5.   Varying estimates of the total loss of life are found in Stannard, *American Holocaust*, 151, 317–18n9; W. E. B. Du Bois, *The Negro* (New York: Cosimo Classics, 2007), 93; Woodrow Borah, "America as Model: The Demographic Impact of European Expansion Upon the Non-European World," *Actas y Memorias del XXXV Congreso Internacional de Americanistsas, México, 1962*, vol. 3 (Mexico City, 1964), 379–87; and other works.

6.   See, for example, Frederick Douglass, *Narrative of the Life of Frederick Douglass, An American Slave, Written by Himself*, ed. John R. McKivigan IV, Peter P. Hinks, and Heather L. Kaufman (New Haven: Yale University Press, 2016); Theodore Dwight Weld, Angelina Grimké, and Sarah Grimké, Introduction, in *American Slavery as It Is: The Testimony of a Thousand Witnesses*, ed. Theodore Dwight Weld, Angelina Grimké, and Sarah Grimké (New York: American Anti-Slavery Society, 1839); Herbert Aptheker, *American Negro Slave Revolts*, 50th anniv. ed. (New York: International Publishers, 2013); W. Michael Byrd and Linda A. Clayton, *An American Health Dilemma: A Medical History of African Americans and the Problem of Race, Beginnings to 1900* (New York: Routledge, 2000); and Charles Johnson, Patricia Smith, and the WGBH Series Research Team, *Africans in America: America's Journey through Slavery* (New York: Harcourt International, 1998).

7. See, for example, James Downs, *Sick from Freedom: African American Illness and Suffering During the Civil War and Reconstruction* (Oxford: Oxford University Press, 2012); Douglas R. Egerton, *The Wars of Reconstruction: The Brief, Violent History of America's Most Progressive Era* (New York: Bloomsbury Press, 2014); Douglas A. Blackmon, *Slavery by Another Name: The Re-Enslavement of Black Americans from the Civil War to World War II* (New York: Anchor Books, 2008); Noel A. Cazenave, *Killing African Americans: Police and Vigilante Violence as a Racial Control Mechanism* (New York: Routledge, 2018); and Mary R. Jackman and Kimberlee A. Shauman, "The Toll of Inequality: Excess African American Deaths in the United States over the Twentieth Century," *Du Bois Review* 16/2 (2019), 291–340.

8. The estimate of 100 million is found in Zinn, *People's History*, 26; and in Patrick Manning, "African Connections with American Colonization," in *The Cambridge Economic History of Latin America*, vol. 1: *The Colonial Era and the Short Nineteenth Century*, ed. Victor Bulmer-Thomas, John H. Coatsworth, and Roberto Cortés-Conde (Cambridge: Cambridge University Press, 2006), 53. An estimate of 86 million is found in James D. Tarver, *The Demography of Africa* (Westport, CT: Prager, 1996), 26–27. In contrast, D. T. Niane has estimated the population of Africa in 1500 at 200 million. See "Conclusion," *General History of Africa, IV: Africa from the Twelfth to the Sixteenth Century*, ed. D. T. Niane (Paris: United Nations Educational, Social, and Cultural Organization; London: Heinemann; and Berkeley: University of California Press, 1984), 683–84.

9. Sydella Blatch, "Great Achievements in Science and Technology in Ancient Africa," *ASBAB Today: The Member Magazine of the American Society for Biochemistry and Molecular Biology*, February 1, 2013, https://www.asbmb.org/asbmb-today/science/020113/great-achievements-in-stem-in-ancient-africa.

10. Kwame Anthony Appiah, "Africa: The Hidden History," *New York Review of Books*, December 17, 1998, https://www.nybooks.com/articles/1998/12/17/africa-the-hidden-history/; and Lebo Matshego, "Great African Empires," Africa.com, https://africa.com/top-10-great-african-empires/.

11. Henry Louis Gates Jr., "African Civilizations Have Been Suppressed, Gates Says," NPR, February 27, 2017, https://www.npr.org/2017/02/27/517458892/africas-great-civilizations-have-been-suppressed-gates-says.

12. Zinn, *People's History*, 26.

13. Klein, *Atlantic Slave Trade*, 49–52; and John A. Garraty and Peter Gay, "Sub-Saharan Africa," *Columbia History of the World* (New York: Harper and Row, 1987), 297–306.

NOTES TO PAGES 58-59   319

14. Hakin Adi, "Africa and the Transatlantic Slave Trade," BBC, October 5, 2010, http://www.bbc.co.uk/history/british/abolition/africa_article_01.shtml.
15. See Ali A. Mazrui, "Dilemmas of African Historiography and the Philosophy of the UNESCO *General History of Africa*," *General History of Africa, Studies and Documents 8: The Methodology of Contemporary African History*, Report and Papers of the Meeting of Experts Organized by UNESCO at Ouagadougou, Upper Volta, from 17 to 22 May 1979 (Paris: United Nations Educational, Social, and Cultural Organization, 1984), 15-25; and Jan Vansina, *Oral Tradition: A Study in Historical Methodology*, trans. Selma Leydesdorff and Elizabeth Tonkin (Piscataway, NJ; Aldine Transaction, 2006).
16. Eric A. Powell, "Dawn of Egyptian Writing," *Archeology*, December 11, 2017, https://www.archaeology.org/issues/281-1801/features/6172-egypt-elkab-early-hieroglyphs; and Charles Q. Choi, "Nubian Stone Tablets Unearthed in African 'City of the Dead,'" Live Science, April 11, 2008, https://www.livescience.com/62272-oldest-meroe-inscriptions-sudan-africa.html.
17. Owen Jarus, "Timbuktu: History of Fabled Center of Learning," *Live Science*, October 21, 2013, http://www.livescience.com/26451-timbuktu.html.
18. Alexander Ives Bortolot, "The Transatlantic Slave Trade," Heilbrun Timeline of Art History, Metropolitan Museum of Art, October 2003, https://www.metmuseum.org/toah/hd/slav/hd_slav. htm. This point is developed in John K. Thornton, *Africa and Africans in the Making of the Atlantic World, 1400-1800*, 2nd ed. (Madison: University of Wisconsin Press, 1988), chap. 3.
19. John K. Thornton, *Africa and Africans*, chap. 3; Richard J. Reid, *Warfare in African History* (Cambridge: Cambridge University Press, 2012), 7; Erik Gilbert, email message to author, July 9, 2018.
20. Johnson et al., *Africans in America*, 2-5; and Paul Lovejoy, *Transformations in Slavery: A History of Slavery in Africa*, 2nd ed. (Cambridge: Cambridge University Press, 2000), chap. 1.
21. Lovejoy, *Transformations in Slavery*, 20.
22. Schmidt, *Struggles Against Slavery*, 48-49; Marcus Rediker, *The Slave Ship: A Human History* (New York: Viking, 2007), 77; and Silja Fröhlich, "East Africa's Forgotten Slave Trade," Deutsche Welle, August 22, 2019, https://www.dw.com/en/east-africas-forgotten-slave-trade/a-50126759.
23. Klein, *Atlantic Slave Trade*, 9.
24. Ibid., 10.
25. Bristol City Council, "Bristol and Transatlantic Slavery, Spain's Slavery

320   NOTES TO PAGES 59–60

Contract," http://discoveringbristol.org.uk/slavery/routes/places-involved/south-america/ Spain-slavery-contract/; and Margarita Gokun Silver, "The Town That Split the World in Two," BBC, June 16, 2017, https://www.bbc.com/travel/article/20170615-the-town-that-split-the-world-in-two.

26. Eltis and Richardson, *Transatlantic Slave Trade*, 21–22.

27. Ibid., 21.

28. A pronouncement by Pope Alexander VI in 1493 gave Portugal the exclusive right to trade with Africa, so Spanish colonizers in the Western Hemisphere had to buy captives from Portuguese or other, non-Catholic slave traders. See Bristol City Council, "Bristol and Transatlantic Slavery."

29. Eltis and Richardson, *Transatlantic Slave Trade*, 29; and Greta Weber, "Shipwreck Shines Light on Historic Shift in Slave Trade," *National Geographic*, June 5, 2015, http://news.national geographic.com/2015/06/150605-shipwreck-slave-trade-south-africa-18th-century-brazil/.

30. Eltis and Richardson, *Transatlantic Slave Trade*, 29.

31. Clodfelter, *Warfare*, 219–220; and John K. Thornton, *Warfare in Atlantic Africa, 1500–1800* (London: University College London Press, 1999), 100–104.

32. Eltis and Richardson, *Transatlantic Slave Trade*, 22–23.

33. Lovejoy, *Transformations in Slavery*, xxi, 9–12.

34. Martin Klein, "Slavery," in *The Oxford Encyclopedia of Economic History*, vol. 4, ed. Joel Mokyr (Oxford: Oxford University Press, 2003), 504.

35. Lisa Pierce Flores, *The History of Puerto Rico* (Santa Barbara, CA: Greenwood, 2009), xx, 35.

36. Brockell, "Before 1619"; Kelton, *Epidemics and Enslavement*, 55–56; and Peck, "Doomed Colony," 183–98.

37. Clodfelter, *Warfare*, 32; and Donald E. Chipman, "Cabeza de Vaca, Álvar Núñez," *Handbook of Texas Online*, Texas State Historical Association, n.d., https://www.tshaonline.org/handbook/ entries/ cabeza-de-vaca-lvar-nunez.

38. Mann, *1491*, 110–13; and Wilson, *Earth Shall Weep*, 134–37.

39. Nicole Johnson McGill, "Built on Slavery," *Florida Times-Union*, December 9, 2001.

40. Ariel Ron and Dael Norwood, "America Cannot Bear to Bring Back Indentured Servitude," *The Atlantic*, March 28, 2018, https://www.theatlantic.com/politics/archive/2018/03/american-immigration-service-slavery/555824/; and Kat Eschner, "The Horrible Fate of John Casor, the First Black Man to Be Declared Slave for Life, in America," *Smithsonian Magazine*, March 8, 2017, https://www.smithsonianmag.com/smart-news/horrible-fate-john-casor-180962352/.

NOTES TO PAGES 60-62   321

41. Leslie M. Harris, *In the Shadow of Slavery: African Americans in New York City, 1626–1863* (Chicago: University of Chicago Press, 2004), 18.

42. Steven Mintz and Sara McNeil, "The Origins of New World Slavery," *Digital History*, 2018, http://www.digitalhistory.uh.edu/disp_textbook_print.cfm?smtid=2&psid=449.

43. P. M. G. Harris, *The History of Human Populations*, vol. 2: *Migration, Urbanization, and Structural Change* (Westport, CT: Praeger, 2003), 140.

44. Lovejoy, *Transformations in Slavery*, 8.

45. Philip D. Curtin, *The Atlantic Slave Trade: A Census* (Madison: University of Wisconsin Press, 1969), 3–13.

46. Ibid., 86–87, 268.

47. Ibid., 275–86.

48. Herbert S. Klein, *Atlantic Slave Trade*, xviii.

49. See, for example, Herbert S. Klein, *Atlantic Slave Trade*, xviii–xvix; and James A. Rawley, Review of *The Atlantic Slave Trade: A Census* by Philip D. Curtin, *African Historical Studies* 3/2 (1970): 353–55.

50. Ibrahima Baba Kake, "Popularization of the History of the Slave Trade," in *From Chains to Bonds: The Slave Trade Revisited*, ed. Doudou Diène (Paris: United Nations Educational, Social, and Cultural Organization, and New York: Berghahn Books, 2001), xxii–xxiii.

51. Walter Rodney, *How Europe Underdeveloped Africa* (Baltimore: Black Classic Press, 2011), 96.

52. Joseph E. Inikori, "Measuring the Atlantic Slave Trade: An Assessment of Curtin and Anstey," *Journal of African History* 17/2 (1976): 197–223.

53. Eltis and Richardson, *Transatlantic Slave Trade*, 23, 89, 90.

54. Ibid., 2, 203.

55. Rediker, *Slave Ship*, 274–75; and Johannes Postma, *The Atlantic Slave Trade* (Gainesville: University Press of Florida, 2003), 24–25, 28–29.

56. David Richardson, "Shipboard Revolts, African Authority, and the Atlantic Slave Trade," *William and Mary Quarterly* 58/1 (January 2001): 74. Eric Robert Taylor has compiled information on almost 500 of these shipboard revolts and found that 5,500 deaths occurred in 170 of these revolts. See Eric Robert Taylor, *If We Must Die: Shipboard Insurrections in the Era of the Atlantic Slave Trade* (Baton Rouge: Louisiana State University Press, 2006), 3, 36–37, 172–73.

57. Max Guerout, "Submarine Archeology and the History of the Slave Trade," in *From Chains to Bonds*, 36–37; and Joseph E. Inikori, "The Unmeasured Hazards of the Atlantic Slave Trade: Sources, Causes, and Historiographical Implications," in *From Chains to Bonds*, 91.

58. See, for example, Henry Louis Gates Jr., "How Many Slaves Landed in the U.S.?," *The Root*, January 6, 2014, http://www.theroot.com/articles/

322 NOTES TO PAGES 62–64

history/2012/10/how_many_slaves_came_to_ america_fact_vs_fiction.html.

59. Schmidt, *Struggles Against Slavery*, 49; Joseph E. Inikori, "Slave Trade: West Africa," in *Encyclopedia of Africa: South of the Sahara*, vol. 4, ed. John Middleton (New York: Charles Scribner's Sons, 1997), 91; and Yves Benot, "From Slave Trade to Underdevelopment," in *From Chains to Bonds*, 80.

60. Paul E. Lovejoy, "The Impact of the Atlantic Slave Trade on Africa: A Review of the Literature," *Journal of African History* 30/3 (1989): 368.

61. Eltis and Richardson, *Transatlantic Slave Trade*, 17.

62. Ibid., 200. Table 6 lists a total of 391,060 Africans estimated to have landed in four major regions and unspecified areas of mainland North America.

63. Gregory E. O'Malley, "Beyond the Middle Passage: Slave Migration from the Caribbean to North America, 1619–1807," *William and Mary Quarterly* 66/1, Third Series (January 2009): 130.

64. An estimate of 26,700 Africans transported to Puerto Rico is in Eltis and Richardson, *Transatlantic Slave Trade*, 202, Table 6. However, Francisco Scarano estimated that the total was between 60,000 and 80,000 in *Sugar and Slavery in Puerto Rico: The Plantation Economy of Ponce, 1800–1850* (Madison: University of Wisconsin Press, 1984). More recently, Scarano revised his estimate to between 40,000 and 60,000. Email message to author, July 12, 2018.

65. These numbers add up to 513,000. See also Ira Berlin, "African Forced Migration to Colonial America," *History Now* 3 (March 2005), https://www.gilderlehrman.org/history-resources/essays/african-forced-migration-colonial-america.

66. Eltis and Richardson, *Transatlantic Slave Trade*, 17.

67. Curtin, *Atlantic Slave Trade: A Census*, 275.

68. Rodney, *How Europe Underdeveloped Africa*, 96.

69. Johannes Postma, *The Dutch in the Atlantic Slave Trade, 1600–1815* (Cambridge: Cambridge University Press, 2008), 240.

70. Du Bois, *The Negro*, 93.

71. Borah, "America as Model," 379–387.

72. Stannard, *American Holocaust*, 151, 317–18n9.

73. Curtin, *Atlantic Slave Trade: A Census*, 275.

74. Herbert S. Klein and Stanley L. Engerman, "Long-Term Trends in African Mortality in the Transatlantic Slave Trade," in *Routes to Slavery: Direction, Ethnicity, and Mortality in the Transatlantic Slave Trade*, ed. David Eltis and David Richardson (New York: Routledge, 1997), 38.

75. Herbert S. Klein, *Atlantic Slave Trade*, 156–61.

76. Zinn, *People's History*, 28; Johnson et al., *Africans in America*, 67; Tay-

NOTES TO PAGE 65 323

lor, *If We Must Die*, 17–19; and Thomas Fowell Buxton, *Abridgment of Sir T. Fowell Buxton's Work Entitled The African Slave Trade and Its Remedy*, 2nd ed. (London: John Murray, 1840, repr. Lexington: Leopold Classic Library, 2016), 14–15. As Taylor has noted, captives in certain locations were sometimes transported by boats part of the way to the West African coast.

77. Zinn, *People's History*, 28; Johnson et al., *Africans in America*, 67; Taylor, *If We Must Die*, 17–19; and Buxton, *Slave Trade and Remedy*, 14–15.

78. Zinn, *People's History*, 28; Johnson et al., *Africans in America*, 67; Taylor, *If We Must Die*, 17–19; Buxton, *Slave Trade and Remedy*, 14–15; and Linda A. Newson and Susie Minchin, *From Capture to Sale: The Portuguese Slave Trade to Spanish South America in the Early Seventeenth Century* (Leiden: Brill, 2007), 72.

79. Buxton, *Slave Trade and Remedy*, 15; and Du Bois, *Negro*, 94.

80. Ibid.,16; Taylor, *If We Must Die*, 19–23; and Postma, *Atlantic Slave Trade*, 21–22.

81. Patrick Manning, *Slavery and African Life: Occidental, Oriental, and African Slave* Trades (Cambridge: Cambridge University Press, 1990), 171. Manning's estimate apparently included the deaths associated with the Arab slave trade and the internal slave trade in Africa as well.

82. Buxton, *Slave Trade and Remedy*, 12; and Postma, *Atlantic Slave Trade*, 20–21.

83. Johnson et al., *Africans in America*, 7, 70.

84. Joseph C. Miller, "Mortality in the Atlantic Slave Trade: Statistical Evidence on Causality," *Journal of Interdisciplinary History* 11/3 (Winter 1981): 413, and *Way of Death: Merchant Capitalism and the Angolan Slave Trade, 1730–1830* (Madison: University of Wisconsin Press, 1988), 120, 153, 384–85.

85. Jan Hogendorn, "Economic Modelling of Price Differences in the Slave Trade Between the Central Sudan and the Coast," *Slavery and Abolition* 17/3 (December 1996): 213–15.

86. An estimate of 24 million captured Africans is found in Christine Hatt, *Slavery: From Africa to the Americas* (London: Evans Brothers, 2007), 14. Johnson et al. concluded that more than 20 million Africans were captured in *Africans in America*, 7.

87. The role of wars and raids in enslaving "the vast majority of Africans" is emphasized by John K. Thornton in *Warfare in Atlantic Africa*, 128–39. See also Lovejoy, *Transformations in Slavery*, chap. 4; and Adu Boahen with Jacob F. Ade Ajayi and Michael Tidy, *Topics in West African History*, new ed. (London: Longman Group, 1986), 108–9.

88. John K. Thornton, *Africa and Africans*, 73–75, and *Warfare in Atlan-*

324   NOTES TO PAGE 66

tic Africa, 128–39; Gilbert, email to author; and Sandra Elaine Greene, email to author, June 15, 2018.

89. Reid, *Warfare in African History*, 7, 69; Lovejoy, *Transformations in Slavery*, chap. 4; Boahen, Ajayi, and Tidy, *West African History*, 108–9; and Martin Klein, *Slavery and Colonialism in French West Africa* (New York: Columbia University Press, 1998), 4.

90. Boahen, Ajayi, and Tidy, *West African History*, 108–9; and W. A. Richards, "The Import of Firearms into West Africa in the Eighteenth Century," *Journal of African History* 21. 1 (1980): 43–59.

91. Ibid.,; and Reid, *Warfare in African History*, 11.

92. John K. Thornton, *Warfare in Atlantic Africa*, 4; Abiola Felix Iroko, "Africa: Economy and Society," in *History of Humanity*, vol. 5: *From the Sixteenth Century to the Eighteenth Century*, ed. Peter Burke and Halil Inalcik (New York: Routledge, 1999), 420; and Greene, email to author.

93. Lovejoy, *Transformations in Slavery*, 63.

94. Reid, *Warfare in African History*, 11–12; Robert S. Smith, *Warfare and Diplomacy in Pre-Colonial West Africa*, 2nd ed. (Madison: University of Wisconsin Press, 1976), 34–35; Gilbert, email to author; Greene, email to author; Richard Reid, email to author, June 17, 2018; and Joseph E. Inikori, email to author, July 10, 2018.

95. Miller has written that "although the mortality at this stage of the trade is virtually undocumented . . . the possible fatalities associated with enslavement may be speculatively estimated." See *Way of Death*, 381.

96. Thomas Cooper, *Letters on the Slave Trade* (Manchester, UK: C. Wheeler, 1787), 25.

97. John Newton, cited in Michaela Alfred-Kamara, *Recovered Histories: Reawakening the Narratives of Enslavement, Resistance, and the Fight for Freedom*, Anti-Slavery International (Horsham, UK: The Printed Word, October 2008), 17.

98. Buxton, *Slave Trade and Its Remedy*, 13–14.

99. Gustav Nachtigal, *Sahara and Sudan*, vol. 3: *The Chad Basin and Bagirmi*, trans. Allan G. B. Fisher and Humphrey J. Fisher (Amherst, MA: Humanity Books, 1987), cited in Jan Hogendorn, "Slave Acquisition and Delivery," in *West African Culture Dynamics*, ed. B. K. Swartz and Raymond E. Dumett (The Hague: Mouton, 1980), 486. See Miller, *Way of Death*, 381n5.

100. Dennis D. Cordell, *Dar Al-Kuti and the Last Years of the Trans-Saharan Slave Trade* (Madison: University of Wisconsin Press, 1985), 109–110, cited in Miller, 381n5.

101. Miller, *Way of Death*, 381, 440–41. The growth of enslavement for crime and debt in some parts of Africa has also been noted in John Iliffe, *Africans: The History of a Continent* (Cambridge: Cambridge University

NOTES TO PAGES 66–69 325

Press, 1995), 132–33. Other people were captured through kidnapping and trickery. Elsewhere on the continent, however, wars and raids tied to the transatlantic slave trade escalated during the eighteenth century. See John K. Thornton, *Africa and Africans*, 305–13.

102. Boahen, Ajayi, and Tidy, *West African History*, 109; and Alfred-Kamara, *Recovered Histories*, 17.

103. Martin Klein, email to author, May 15, 2020.

104. Milton Meltzer, *Slavery: A World History*, updated ed. (Cambridge: Da Capo Press, 1993), Part II, 50. Meltzer estimated that 4 or 5 percent died at this stage. Miller estimated that 4 to 10 percent of slaves arriving in Brazil died before they were sold, and an additional 10 to 15 percent who had to "continue on to other markets in the interior before final sale" also died. See also Miller, *Way of Death*, 438.

105. Lorena S. Walsh, "The African American Population of the Colonial United States," in *Population History*, 206.

106. Buxton, *Slave Trade and Its Remedy*, 20; Meltzer, *Slavery*, 50; Postma, *Atlantic Slave Trade*, 31; Miller, *Way of Death*, 440n221; Ira Berlin, *The Making of African America: The Four Great Migrations* (New York: Penguin, 2010), 77; and Vincent Brown, *The Reaper's Garden: Death and Power in the World of Atlantic Slavery* (Cambridge: Harvard University Press, 2008), 50.

107. Walsh, "African American Population," 206–7.

108. Edward Reynolds, "Human Commerce," in *Captive Passage: Transatlantic Slavery and the Making of the Americas*, ed. Beverly McMillan (Old Saybrook: Konecky and Konecky, 2002), 28. See also Miller, *Way of Death*, 438.

109. Laird W. Bergad, *The Comparative Histories of Slavery in Brazil, Cuba, and the United States* (Cambridge: Cambridge University Press, 2007), 98–101; and Steven Mintz and Sara McNeil, "American Slavery in Comparative Perspective," *Digital History*, 2018, http://www.digitalhistory.uh.edu/disp_textbook.cfm?smtid=2&psid=460.

110. Walsh, "African American Population," 206.

111. Ibid. Bergad makes the same point about slaves working in "southern tropical lowland regions" in the present-day United States in *Comparative Histories*, 101.

112. Walsh, "African American Population," 206–7.

113. Ibid., 207.

114. Ibid.

115. This estimate is 5 percent of the total loss of approximately 41.5 million African lives resulting from the transatlantic slave trade.

116. U.S. Census Bureau, "Colonial and Pre-Federal Statistics," in *The Statistical History of the United States: from Colonial Times to the Present*,

326   NOTES TO PAGES 69–71

with an Introduction and User's Guide by Ben J. Wattenberg (New York: Basic Books, 1976), 1168.

117. Ibid.

118. Ibid.; and Walsh, "African American Population," 198.

119. U.S. Census Bureau, *Historical Statistics of the United States* (Washington, DC: Government Printing Office, 1975), updated and corrected estimate included in Haines and Steckel, *Population History*, 694, Table 1A; and Robert William Fogel, *Without Consent or Contract: The Rise and Fall of American Slavery* (New York: W. W. Norton, 1989), 31–32.

120. Walsh, "African American Population," 198; and Bergad, *Comparative Histories*, 96–98.

121. Tom Costa, "Runaway Slaves and Servants in Colonial Virginia," *Encyclopedia Virginia*, Virginia Humanities, January 29, 2013, https://www.encyclopediavirginia.org/Runaway_Slaves_and_Servants_in_Colonial_Virginia.

122. Ibid.

123. Andrew Fede, "Legitimized Violent Slave Abuse in the American South, 1619–1865: A Case Study of Law and Social Change in Six Southern States," *American Journal of Legal History* 29/2 (April 1985): 93–150.

124. Johnson et al., *Africans in America*, 48.

125. Gary B. Nash, *The Forgotten Fifth: African Americans in the Age of Revolution* (Cambridge, MA: Harvard University Press, 2006), 23; and Derek N. Kerr, "Petty Felony, Slave Defiance, and Frontier Villainy: Crime and Criminal Justice in Spanish Louisiana, 1770–1803" (PhD diss., Tulane University, 1983), cited in Aptheker, *Slave Revolts*, 409.

126. Aptheker's classic work identified approximately 250 planned or actual revolts and demolished the long-standing racist depiction of enslaved people as docile. Subsequent scholarship has acknowledged the significance of their resistance and efforts to organize uprisings while noting various "flaws and exaggerations" in Aptheker's seminal research and emphasizing the limited number of large-scale rebellions. See Douglas R. Egerton, "Slave Resistance," in *The Oxford Handbook of Slavery in the Americas*, ed. Robert L. Paquette and Mark M. Smith (Oxford: Oxford University Press, 2010), 446–64. This chapter draws from Aptheker's work because it documents extensive resistance to enslavement by people of African descent, even though the number of major uprisings was limited.

127. Aptheker, *Slave Revolts*, 164–66.

128. Ibid., 169.

129. Ibid., 172–73.

130. Ibid., 174–75.

131. Ibid., 179–80.

132. Ibid., 181–82.

NOTES TO PAGES 71–73   327

133. Ibid., 188–89.
134. Clodfelter, *Warfare*, 125; and Eric Foner, *Gateway to Freedom: The Hidden History of the Underground Railroad* (New York: W. W. Norton, 2015), 29–30. Foner notes that the "contours" of this ostensible conspiracy "remain a matter of dispute among historians."
135. Aptheker, *Slave Revolts*, 198–99.
136. Ibid., 201.
137. Nash, *Forgotten Fifth*, chap. 1, and "The African Americans' Revolution," in *The Oxford Handbook of the American Revolution*, ed. Edward G. Gray and Jane Kamensky (Oxford: Oxford University Press, 2013), 254, 268–69n20.
138. See Howard H. Peckham, *The Toll of Independence: Engagements and Battle Casualties of the American Revolution* (Chicago: University of Chicago Press, 1974), ix.
139. An estimate of about 60,000 African Americans who escaped slavery is found in Ray Raphael, *People's History of the American Revolution: How Common People Shaped the Fight for Independence* (New York: HarperCollins, 2001), 330–31, 482n220. An estimate of no more than 40,000 is found in Nash, "African Americans' Revolution," 254, 260–61, 268–69n20.
140. Nash, *Forgotten Fifth*, 23.
141. Nash, "African Americans' Revolution," 261–62.
142. Raphael, *People's History of the American Revolution*, 482n220.
143. Ibid.
144. Nash, *Forgotten Fifth*, 42–45.
145. Sylviane A. Diouf, *Slavery's Exiles: The Story of the American Maroons* (New York: New York University Press, 2014), 190–206; and Walter J. Fraser, *Savannah in the Old South* (Athens: University of Georgia Press, 2005), 145.
146. Aptheker, *Slave Revolts*, 213.
147. Ibid., 215.
148. Ibid., 215–16.
149. Ibid., 217.
150. Ibid., 218–19.
151. "The ESPY List: U.S. Executions from 1608–2002," based on data compiled by M. Watt Espy Jr. and John Ortiz Smykla, Britannica ProCon. org, https://deathpenalty.procon.org/us-executions/#III.
152. Douglass, *Life*; Weld, Grimké, and Grimké, *American Slavery;* Aptheker, *Slave Revolts*; Byrd and Clayton, *American Health Dilemma*; and Johnson et al., *Africans in America*.
153. Walsh was right to note that reliable data from the eighteenth century is limited, but the "absence of reliable age-specific measures of life

328   NOTES TO PAGES 73–74

chances" need not prevent the development of informed and reasonable estimates of the minimum number of excess deaths among native-born enslaved people in the eighteenth century. See Walsh, "African American Population," 208–9.

154. This estimate for the nineteenth century is found in Richard H. Steckel, "The African American Population of the United States, 1790–1920," in *Population History*, 449, 453, and "Demography and Slavery," in *Handbook of Slavery*, 654. Steckel contrasted the mortality rate of enslaved people with that of the "entire free population," which was overwhelmingly white. Discussion of the poor health of both enslaved and free African Americans is found in Byrd and Clayton, *American Health Dilemma* 287, 346–47. Walsh has explained, "There is no reason to suppose that mortality levels were significantly lower in the colonial period." See "African American Population," 209.

155. Byrd and Clayton, *American Health Dilemma*, 287, 346–47.

156. U.S. Census Office, *Population of the United States in 1860: Eighth Census* (Washington, DC: Government Printing Office, 1864), cited in Steckel, "African American Population, 1790–1920," 435.

157. U.S. Census Bureau, *Population 1920: Fourteenth Census of the United States*, vol. 1 (Washington, DC: Government Printing office, 1921), cited in Steckel, "African American Population, 1790–1920," 435.

158. History.com Editors, "Slavery in America," *History*, August 23, 2021, https://www. history.com/topics/black-history/slavery; and "How Did Slavery Disappear in the North?," The Abolition Seminar, Library Company of Philadelphia, https:/www.abolitionseminar.org/ how-did-northern-states-gradually-abolish-slavery/.

159. Eric Foner, "Forgotten Step Toward Freedom," *New York Times*, December 30, 2007.

160. Sylvia R. Frey, "Slavery and Anti-Slavery," in *A Companion to the American Revolution*, ed. Jack P. Greene and J. R. Pole (Oxford: Blackwell, 2000), 411.

161. An estimate of about 50,000 illegal importations between 1808 and 1865, mainly to Texas and Louisiana, is found in Randy Sparks, *Africans in the Old South: Mapping Exceptional Lives Across the Atlantic World* (Cambridge: Harvard University Press, 2016), 80. An estimate of 46,000 between 1808 and 1860 is found in David Eltis, "The U.S. Transatlantic Slave Trade, 1644–1867: An Assessment," *Civil War History* 54/4 (December 2008): 353.

162. Allison Keyes, "The 'Clotilda,' the Last Known Slave Ship to Arrive in US, Is Found," *Smithsonian Magazine*, May 22, 2019, https://www. smithsonianmag.com/smithsonian-institution/clotilda-last-known-slave-ship-arrive-us-found-180972177/.

NOTES TO PAGES 74–75   329

163. Dale T. Graden, *Disease, Resistance, and Lies: The Demise of the Transatlantic Slave Trade to Brazil and Cuba* (Baton Rouge: Louisiana State University, 2014), 9, 12–39. See also Stephen Chambers, *No God but Gain: The Untold Story of Cuban Slavery, the Monroe Doctrine, and the Making of the United States* (London: Verso, 2015). The slave trade remained legal in Cuba and Brazil, but new federal legislation in the first decade of the nineteenth century prohibited U.S. citizens from participating in the trafficking of human beings.

164. Laird Bergad, *The Cuban Slave Market, 1790–1880* (Cambridge: Cambridge University Press, 1995), 38–39, 51, cited in Chambers, *No God but Gain*, 176n2.

165. Sidney Chalhoub, *A Forca da Escravidao: Ilegalidade e Costume no Brasil Oitocentista* (Sao Paulo: Companhia das Letras, 2012), 35, cited in Graden, *Disease, Resistance, and Lies*, 3, 235n16.

166. Graden, *Disease, Resistance, and Lies*, 38.

167. Ibid., 39.

168. Ibid., 20–23, 26–31, 36–39; and Chambers, *No God but Gain*, chaps. 3 and 8.

169. This assessment is based on the approach to calculating the total number of deaths in the entire transatlantic slave trade. For each of the more than one million people forcibly transported on U.S.-built ships to Cuba and Brazil in the first half of the nineteenth century, more than three people died in Africa, and close to 70 percent of those who arrived alive died within a decade and a half. The estimate of 3.7 million deaths in this illegal slave trade is conservative. The toll may well have been higher because of the harsher labor and climate conditions in Cuba and Brazil.

170. Chambers, *No God but Gain*, 159–170.

171. Berlin, *Making of African America*, 100; Walter Johnson, *Soul by Soul: Life Inside the Antebellum Slave Market* (Cambridge, MA: Harvard University Press, 1999), 5; and Edward Ball, "Retracing Slavery's Trail of Tears," *Smithsonian Magazine*, November 2015, https://www. smithsonianmag.com/history/slavery-trail-of-tears-180956968/.

172. Berlin, *Making of African America*, 100.

173. Ibid.

174. Baptist, *Half Has Never Been Told,* xxi, xxiii, 322–23, 352–53, 359, 412–13.

175. Berlin, *Making of African America*, 101.

176. Ibid., 101–2.

177. Ibid.; and Walter Johnson, *Soul by Soul*, 5–6.

178. Berlin, *Making of African America*, 111–116.

179. Ibid., 111–16; Walter Johnson, *Soul by Soul*, 49–50, 60–62; and Ball, "Slavery's Trail of Tears."

330 NOTES TO PAGES 75–81

180. Berlin, *Making of African America*, 111.
181. Berlin did not offer estimates of the lives lost but found that though "the mortality rate for the internal slave trade never approached that of the transatlantic transfer, it surpassed that of those who remained in the seaboard states." He also noted that "the slave mortality rate began increasing in the second and third decades of the nineteenth century." See *Making of African America*, 113. If even 1 percent of the African Americans forcibly transported during the "second Middle Passage" died in the process, this amounts to about 10,000 fatalities.
182. See Douglass, *Life*; Frederick Douglass, *My Bondage and My Freedom*, ed. John David Smith (New York: Penguin, 2003); and Frederick Douglass, *Life and Times of Frederick Douglass* (Mineola: Dover 2003). See also Sojourner Truth, *Narrative of Sojourner Truth* (New York: Penguin, 1998); Solomon Northup, *Twelve Years a Slave* (New York: Penguin, 2012); and Harriet Jacobs, *Incidents in the Life of a Slave Girl* (Mineola, NY: Dover, 2001).
183. Weld, Grimké, and Grimké, *American Slavery*, 9.
184. The firsthand reports in *American Slavery* made clear that large numbers of enslaved people died at the hands of slaveowners and overseers.
185. Harriet A. Washington, *Medical Apartheid: The Dark History of Medical Experimentation on Black Americans from Colonial Times to the Present* (New York: Anchor Books, 2006), esp. chap. 2.
186. Foner, *Gateway to Freedom*, 4.
187. Ibid., 15.
188. Even a conservative estimate of 10 percent fatalities, applied to the minimum estimate of 30,000 Black people escaping slavery between 1830 and 1860, suggests a rough estimate of 3,000 deaths. The actual loss of life may have been considerably higher.
189. Mary H. Moran, *Liberia: The Violence of Democracy* (Philadelphia: University of Pennsylvania Press, 2008), 2.
190. Ibid.
191. Antonio McDaniel, *Swing Low, Sweet Chariot: The Mortality Cost of Colonizing Liberia in the Nineteenth Century* (Chicago: University of Chicago Press, 1995), 89.
192. This estimate is based on the fatalities described in this section and other deaths reported in Aptheker, *Slave Revolts*.
193. Ibid., 222. A lower estimate of twenty-six executions is found in Egerton, "Slave Resistance," 451.
194. Aptheker, *Slave Revolts*, 230–31.
195. Ibid., 250–51.
196. Ibid.; and Baptiste, *Half Has Never Been Told*, 63.
197. PBS, "The War of 1812: Blacks in the War," https://www.pbs.org/video/

NOTES TO PAGES 78-79 331

the-war-of-1812-blacks-in-the-war/; and Oscar H. Blayton, "When Freed Africans Burned the White House," *Carolina Panorama*, June 14, 2018, https://www.carolinapanorama. com/opinion/editorials/when-freed-africans-burned-the-white-house/article_420fefee-6f80-11e8-956a-176d94e9a729.html.

198. Aptheker, *Slave Revolts*, 257–58.
199. Ibid., 258–59.
200. Clodfelter, *Warfare*, 283.
201. Aptheker, *Slave Revolts*, 263.
202. Ibid., 271.
203. Ibid., 276–77.
204. Ibid., 277–78.
205. Ibid., 281–82.
206. Ibid., 287.
207. Ibid., 289–90.
208. Ibid., 293–303.
209. Ibid., 301. Egerton has estimated that roughly thirty to forty slaves were killed without trial, in "Slave Resistance," 452.
210. Aptheker, *Slave Revolts*, 302. An estimate of seventeen executions is found in Egerton, "Slave Resistance," 452.
211. Aptheker, *Slave Revolts*, 330; and Junius P. Rodriguez, "Complicity and Deceit: Lewis Cheney's Plot and Its Bloody Consequences," in *Lethal Imagination: Violence and Brutality in American History*, ed. Michael A. Bellesiles (New York: New York University Press, 1999), 143–44.
212. Aptheker, *Slave Revolts*, 338.
213. Ibid., 340–41, 348.
214. Ibid., 346.
215. Anita S. Goldstein, "Slavery," *Tennessee Encyclopedia*, Tennessee Historical Society, March 1, 2018, http://tennesseeencyclopedia.net/entries/slavery/. An argument that there was more white panic than actual conspiracy by enslaved African Americans is found in Charles B. Dew, "Black Ironworkers and the Slave Insurrection Panic of 1856," *Journal of Southern History* 41/3 (August 1975): 321–38.
216. Aptheker, *Slave Revolts*, 351.
217. DeNeen L. Brown, "'Unflinching': The Day John Brown Was Hanged for His Raid on Harpers Ferry," *Washington Post*, December 2, 2017; and Fergus Bordewich, "John Brown's Day of Reckoning," *Smithsonian Magazine*, October 2009, http://www.smithsonianmag.com/ history/john-browns-day-of-reckoning-139165084/.
218. Brown, "Unflinching."
219. Aptheker, *Slave Revolts*, 357. Sixteen African Americans were executed in one of these towns, Pife Level. See "The Negro Plot in Alabama: Trial

332 NOTES TO PAGES 79–81

and Execution of Sixteen Negroes by a Committee at Pife Level, From the Montgomery (Ala.) Advertiser," *New York Times*, January 12, 1861.

220. Kathleen Jenkins, "No More Silence at Second Creek," *Natchez Democrat*, September 23, 2011.

221. Zinn, *People's History*, 193; and Downs, *Sick from Freedom*, 21.

222. Zinn, *People's History*, 194; and Paul D. Escott, "African Americans in the Civil War," History Net.com, http://www.historynet.com/african-americans-in-the-civil-war.

223. Abraham Lincoln, quoted in Associated Press, "Runaway Slave Who Joined Union Fight in U.S. Civil War and Lost Leg Finally Receives Recognition," *National Post*, June 8, 2015, https://nationalpost.com/news/world/runway-slave-who-joined-union-fight-in-u-s-civil-war-and-lost-leg-finally-receives-recognition.

224. Zinn, *People's History*, 194; Escott, "African Americans in the Civil War"; and Steven Mintz, "Historical Context: Black Soldiers in the Civil War," Gilder Lehrman Institute of American History, https://www.gilderlehrman.org/history-resources/teaching-resource/historical-context-black-soldiers-civil-war.

225. Egerton, *Wars of Reconstruction*, 46.

226. Andre Fleche and Peter C. Luebke, "The United States Colored Troops," *Encyclopedia Virginia*, Virginia Humanities, December 20, 2016, https://www.encyclopediavirginia.org/United_States_Colored_Troops_The#start_entry.

227. Linda Wheeler, "The New York Draft Riots of 1863," *Washington Post*, April 29, 2013; and Robert C. Kennedy, "On This Day: August 1, 1863," *New York Times*, August 1, 2001.

228. Brett M. Palfreyman, "The Boston Draft Riots," *New York Times*, July 16, 2013; and Adam Rozen-Wheeler, "Detroit Race Riot (1813)," *BlackPast.org*, January 8, 2018, https://www.black past.org/african-american-history/detroit-race-riot-1863/.

229. Downs, *Sick from Freedom*, 4.

230. Ibid.

231. Ibid.

232. James Downs, "Color Blindness in the Demographic Death Toll of the Civil War," *Oxford University Press Blog*, April 13, 2012, http://blog.oup.com/2012/04/black-white-demographic-death-toll-civil-war/; and email to author, February 23, 2018.

233. Downs has estimated that a total of about 500,000 African Americans died from disease during the Civil War and the years that followed. Email to author.

234. See Eric Foner, *The Second Founding: How the Civil War and Reconstruction Remade the Constitution* (New York: W. W. Norton, 2019).

NOTES TO PAGES 81-82

The Thirteenth Amendment abolished chattel slavery but permitted involuntary servitude "as a punishment for crime."

235. History.com, Editors, "Reconstruction," *History*, January 21, 2021, https://www.history. com/topics/american-civil-war/reconstruction.

236. Douglas R. Egerton, "Terrorized African Americans Found Their Champion in Civil War Hero Robert Smalls," *Smithsonian Magazine*, September 2018, https://www.smithsonianmag.com/history/terrorized-african-americans-champion-civil-war-hero-robert-smalls-180970031/.

237. On the deaths in Memphis, see Clodfelter, *Warfare*, 270; and Calvin Schermerhorn, "Civil Rights Laws Don't Always Stop Racism," *The Atlantic*, May 8, 2016, https://www.theatlantic.com/politics/archive/2016/05/the-memphis-massacre-of-1866-and-black-voter-suppression-today/481737/. On the deaths in New Orleans, see Calvin Schermerhorn, "When 'Taking Our Country Back' Led to a Massacre of Black Americans," *The Daily Beast*, June 3, 2020, https://www.the dailybeast.com/when-taking-our-country-back-led-to-a-massacre.

238. Lorraine Boissoneault, "The Deadliest Massacre in Reconstruction-Era Louisiana Happened 150 Years Ago," *Smithsonian Magazine*, September 28, 2018, https://www.smithsonianmag.com/history/story-deadliest-massacre-reconstruction-era-louisiana-180970420/.

239. Egerton, *Wars of Reconstruction*, 207–8, 285–309; and Khalil Gibran Muhammad, "The History of Lynching and the Present of Policing," *The Nation*, May 17, 2018, https://www.the nation.com/article/archive/the-history-of-lynching-and-the-present-of-policing/.

240. This was the estimate of delegates at the Southern States Convention in 1871. See Herbert Shapiro, "Afro-American Responses to Race Violence during Reconstruction," *Science and Society* 36/2 (Summer 1972): 158. This estimate far exceeds the estimate of nearly two thousand lynchings between 1865 and 1876 reported in Equal Justice Initiative, "Reconstruction in America: Racial Violence after the Civil War, 1865–1876," 2020, https://eji.org/report/ reconstruction-in-america/a-truth-that-needs-telling/#chapter-6.

241. Boissoneault, "The Deadliest Massacre"; and Clodfelter, *Warfare*, 270.

242. Equal Justice Initiative, "Reconstruction in America."

243. Brendan Wolfe, "Danville Riot (1883)," *Encyclopedia Virginia*, Virginia Humanities, December 7, 2020, https://encyclopediavirginia.org/entries/danville-riot-1883/.

244. Rick Ward, "The Carroll County Courthouse Massacre, 1886: A Cold Case File," *Mississippi History Now*, May 2012, https://www.mshistorynow.mdah.ms.gov/articles/381/the-carroll-county-courthouse-massacre-1886-a-cold-case-file.

245. Eric Foner, *Reconstruction: America's Unfinished Revolution, 1863–1877* (New York: W. W. Norton, 1988), 595.
246. David Smith, "Ida B. Wells: The Unsung Heroine of the Civil Rights Movement," *Guardian*, April 27, 2018.
247. Robert H. Zieger, *For Jobs and Freedom: Race and Labor in America Since 1865* (Lexington: University of Kentucky Press, 2007), 41.
248. Adrienne Lafrance and Vann R. Newkirk II, "The Lost History of an American Coup d'Etat," *The Atlantic*, August 12, 2017, https://www.theatlantic.com/politics/archive/2017/08/ wilmington-massacre/536457/; and David Zucchino, "The 1898 Wilmington Massacre Is An Essential Lesson in How State Violence Has Targeted Black Americans," *Time*, July 1, 2020, https://time.com/5861644/1898-wilmington-massacre-essential-lesson-state-violence/.
249. Egerton, "Terrorized African Americans," and *Wars of Reconstruction*, 287.
250. Egerton, "Terrorized African Americans."
251. Britannica ProCon.org, "The ESPY List: "U.S. Executions from 1608-2002"; Muhammad, "History of Lynching"; and National Association for the Advancement of Colored People, *Thirty Years of Lynching in the United States: 1889–1918*, *The African American Odyssey*, https://memory.loc.gov/ammem/aaohtml/ exhibit/aopart6b.html.
252. Blackmon, *Slavery by Another Name*.
253. Ibid., 7, 99, and Blackmon, email to author, April 8, 2018.
254. Blackmon, *Slavery by Another Name*, 7.
255. Ibid., 57, 73, 98, 109, 288–89, 320, 326–31, 334–335.
256. Blackmon, email to author.
257. Blackmon, in email to author, has estimated that at least six thousand prisoners perished in Alabama between the 1890s and the early 1920s and indicated that the total from the 1870s to almost 1930 would be even higher. He has also noted that Georgia and Florida had large prisoner populations and may have had substantial numbers of fatalities as well.
258. Egerton, "Terrorized African Americans," and *Wars of Reconstruction*, 21. See also Foner, *Reconstruction*, 425–59, 591–95.
259. Muhammad, "History of Lynching." See also Jamiles Lartney and Sam Morris, "How White Americans Used Lynchings to Terrorize and Control Black People," *Guardian*, April 26, 2018; and Cazenave, *Killing African Americans*, chap. 3.
260. Blackmon, *Slavery by Another Name*, 7, 358–59, and email to author.
261. Foner, *Second Founding*, 158–67; C. Vann Woodward, *The Strange Career of Jim Crow*, 3rd rev. ed. (Oxford: Oxford University Press, 1974); and Michele Alexander, *The New Jim Crow: Mass Incarceration in the*

NOTES TO PAGE 84 335

Age of Colorblindness, rev. ed. (New York: New Press, 2012), 29–35. Some new state constitutions that limited the franchise for African American men were written in the first decade of the twentieth century.

262. Again, on the limited life prospects of free African Americans during slavery, see Byrd and Clayton, *American Health Dilemma*, 287, 346–47. There is some controversy concerning the excess mortality rate of African American children in the decades following the end of the Civil War. Richard Steckel has argued that "the mortality of [African American] children was much lower" after slavery ended. In contrast, Samuel H. Preston and Michael R. Haines have found that there was no improvement in African American child mortality in the last two decades of the nineteenth century. Other researchers have also concluded that overall African American mortality did not significantly improve until the early twentieth century. See Steckel, "African American Population, 1790–1920," 473; and Samuel H. Preston and Michael R. Haines, *Fatal Years: Child Mortality in Late Nineteenth Century America* (Princeton: Princeton University Press, 1991), chap. 3. See also Reynolds Farley, *Growth of the Black Population* (Chicago: Markham, 1970); and Edward Meeker, "Mortality Trends of Southern Blacks, 1850–1910: Some Preliminary Findings," *Explorations in Economic History*, vol. 13 (1976): 13–42, both cited in Steckel, "African American Population, 1790–1920," 473.

263. U.S. Census Bureau, *Historical Statistics of the United States*, in "Population History," 694, Table A.1.

264. Ibid.; and Jesse McKinnon, U.S. Census Bureau, "Census 2000 Brief: Black Population 2000," August 2001, https://www.census.gov/ prod/2001pubs/c2kbr01-5.pdf, 1.

265. U.S. Census Bureau, "Facts for Features: National African American (Black) History Month: February 2021," January 7, 2021, https://www.census.gov/newsroom/facts-for-features/2021/ black-history-month.html.

266. Rashawn Ray, "Is the U.S. a Racist Country?" Brookings Institution, May 4, 2021, https://www.brookings.edu/blog/how-we-rise/2021/05/04/ is-the-united-states-a-racist-country/; Meilan Solly, "158 Resources to Understand Racism in America," *Smithsonian Magazine*, June 4, 2020, https://www.smithsonianmag.com/history/158-resources-understanding-systemic-racism-america-180975029/#sectionTwo; and Janelle Jones, John Schmitt, and Valerie Wilson, "50 Years after the Kerner Commission: African Americans Are Better Off in Many Ways but Are Still Disadvantaged by Racial Inequality," Economic Policy Institute, February 26, 2018, https:// www.epi.org/publication/50-years-after-the-kerner-commission/.

336 NOTES TO PAGES 85–86

267. *Times-Picayune*, "1900: One of the Bloodiest Episodes of the Jim Crow Era in New Orleans," October 4, 2011.
268. Blackmon, *Slavery by Another Name*, 275.
269. Ibid., 325.
270. David Martin Davies, "Should Texas Remember or Forget the Slocum Massacre?," Texas Public Radio, January 16, 2015, http://tpr.org/post/should-texas-remember-or-forget-slocum-massacre#stream/0; and E. R. Bills, *The 1910 Slocum Massacre: An Act of Genocide in East Texas* (Charleston, NC: History Press, 2014).
271. Doug Moore, "100 Years Later, East St. Louis Stops to Remember the Riots That Made Indelible Mark on City," *St. Louis Post-Dispatch*, June 28, 2017.
272. James Jeffrey, "A 100-Year-Old U.S. Riot Only Now Being Talked About," BBC, November 25, 2017, http://www.bbc.com/news/world-us-canada-42116688.
273. Vincent P. Franklin, "The Philadelphia Race Riot of 1918," *Pennsylvania Magazine of History and Biography* 99/3 (July 1975): 336–50.
274. Cameron McWhirter, *Red Summer: The Summer of 1919 and the Awakening of Black America* (New York: St. Martin's Griffin, 2011), 13.
275. Ibid., 1–11.
276. Peter Perl, "Race Riot of 1919 Gave Glimpse of Future Struggles," *Washington Post*, March 1, 1999.
277. McWhirter, *Red Summer*, 128–47.
278. This estimate came from a Tennessee National Guard officer. See Matthew Lakin, "'A Dark Night': The Knoxville Race Riot of 1919," *Journal of East Tennessee History* 72 (2000): 25. Twenty years after the massacre, a Knoxville newspaper stated that there had been hundreds of African American deaths. See "Colorful Career Closes," *Knoxville Journal*, March 10, 1939, cited in Lakin, 25n71.
279. Brandon Weber, "What Started the Arkansas Sharecropper Massacre of 1919? A Union," *The Progressive*, September 29, 2017, http://progressive.org/dispatches/what-started-the-arkansas-sharecropper-massacre-of-1919-a-uni/.
280. McWhirter, *Red Summer*, 13; and James S. Hirsch, *Riot and Remembrance: America's Worst Race Riot and Its Legacy* (Boston: Houghton Mifflin, 2002), 120.
281. Jesse J. Holland, Associated Press, "Hundreds of Black Deaths in 'Red Summer' of 1919 Are Being Remembered," *Chicago Sun-Times*, July 23, 2019.
282. Gabby Baquero, "Ocoee Debates Markers Memorializing 1920 Election Day Massacre," *West Orange Times and Observer*, September 5, 2017.
283. Hirsch, *Riot and Remembrance*, 2–6; and German Lopez, "An Eyewit-

NOTES TO PAGES 86–87 337

ness Account of the Horrific Attack that Destroyed Black Wall Street," *Vox*, June 1, 2016, https://www.vox.com/ 2016/6/1/11827994/tulsa-race-massacre-black-wall-street.

284. Monte Akers, *Flames After Midnight: Murder, Vengeance, and the Desolation of a Texas Community*, rev. ed. (Austin: University of Texas Press, 2011), 62–68, 77, 199–200.

285. Jeff Libby, "Rosewood Descendant Keeps the Memory Alive," *Orlando Sentinel*, February 1, 2004; and Heather Gilligan, "A White Mob Wiped This All-Black Florida Town Off the Map—60 Years Later, Their Story Was Finally Told," *Timeline*, April 3, 2018, https://timeline.com/all-black-town-rosewood-wiped-off-the-map-by-white-mob-73ca6630802b.

286. *The Detroit Independent* (1925), cited in Kevin Boyle, *Arc of Justice: A Saga of Race, Civil Rights, and Murder in the Jazz Age* (New York: Henry Holt, 2004), 24.

287. Joseph Boskin, ed., *Urban Racial Violence in the Twentieth* Century (Beverly Hills: Glencoe Press, 1969), Preface, chap.. 5 and 6.

288. Ibid., 52–61.

289. Detroit Historical Society, "Race Riot of 1943," *Encyclopedia of Detroit*, https://detroithistorical.org/learn/encyclopedia-of-detroit/race-riot-1943; and James S. Olson, "Beaumont Riot of 1943," *Handbook of Texas Online*, Texas State Historical Association, https://www.tshaonline.org/ handbook/entires/beaumont-riot-of-1943 .

290. Brad Schrade, "Moore's Ford Lynching: Years-Long Probe Yields Suspects—But No Justice," *Atlanta Journal-Constitution*, December 29, 2017.

291. Equal Justice Initiative, "Remembering Black Veterans Targeted for Racial Terror Lynchings," November 11, 2019, https://eji.org/news/remembering-Black-veterans-and-racial-terror-lynchings/.

292. This estimate is based on "Lynchings: By State and Race, 1882–1968," Tuskegee Archives, Tuskegee University, November 2020, http://archive.tuskegee.edu/repository/wp-content/ uploads/2020/11/Lynchings-Stats-Year-Dates-Causes.pdf.

293. Dara Lind, "The Ugly History of Racist Policing in America," *Vox*, July 7, 2016, https:// www.vox.com/michael-brown-shooting-ferguson-mo/2014/8/19/6031759/ferguson-history-riots-police-brutality-civil-rights.

294. Renee C. Romano, *Racial Reckoning: Prosecuting America's Civil Rights Murders* (Cambridge, MA: Harvard University Press, 2014), 2, 8–9.

295. Ben Brotemarkle, "Florida Frontiers: Christmas 1951 and the Bomb Heard Miles Away," *Florida Today*, December 22, 2014, https://www.floridatoday.com/story/news/local/2014/12/22/florida-frontiers-

338   NOTES TO PAGES 87–89

christmas-bomb-heard-miles-away/20767217/; and Southern Poverty Law Center, "Civil Rights Martyrs," https://www.splcenter.org/what-we-do/civil-rights-memorial/ civil-rights-martyrs.

296. Southern Poverty Law Center, "Civil Rights Martyrs."
297. Ibid.
298. Ibid.
299. Ibid.
300. Ibid.
301. Ibid.
302. "Harlem: Hatred in the Streets," *Newsweek*, August 3, 1964, in Boskin, *Urban Racial Violence*, 100–108; and "Rioting Follows a Common Pattern," *New York Times*, August 30, 1964.
303. Mark Hare, "Riots Still Haunt Rochester," *City Newspaper*, July 16, 2014.
304. Southern Poverty Law Center, "Civil Rights Martyrs."
305. In November 2021, a New York state judge vacated the convictions of two of the three people convicted of killing Malcolm X. See Shayna Jacobs, "They Served Decades in Prison for Killing Malcolm X. Now Their Names Are Cleared," *Washington Post*, November 18, 2021. On possible links between the real killers and the NYPD and FBI, see CBS New York News, "Daughters of Malcolm X, Civil Rights Attorney Say They Have Evidence That Proves NYPD, FBI Conspired to Have Him Assassinated," WLNY TV, February 22, 2021, https://newyork.cbs local.com/2021/02/22/ malcolm-x-death-investigation/; Zaheer Ali, "What Really Happened to Malcolm X?," CNN, February 17, 2015, https://www.cnn.com/2015/02/17/opinion/ali-malcolm-x-assassination-anniversary/index.html; and Garrett Felber, "Malcolm X Assassination: Fifty Years On, Mystery Still Clouds Details of the Case," *Guardian*, February 21, 2015.
306. Bayard Rustin, "The Watts 'Manifesto' and the McCone Report," *Commentary*, March 1966, in *Urban Racial Violence in the Twentieth Century*, 109–16.
307. Southern Poverty Law Center, "Civil Rights Martyrs."
308. Siddhartha Mitter, "The Newark Race Riots 50 Years On: Is the City in Danger of Repeating the Past?" *Guardian*, July 11, 2017.
309. DeNeen L. Brown, "In Detroit, the 'Rage of Oppression.' For Five Days in 1967, Riots Consumed a City," *Washington Post*, July 23, 2017.
310. Lorraine Boissoneault, "In 1968, Three Students Were Killed by Police. Today, Few Remember the Orangeburg Massacre," *Smithsonian Magazine*, February 7, 2018, https://www.smithsonianmag.com/history/1968-three-students-were-killed-police-today-few-remember-orangeburg-massacre-180968092/.
311. Alan Taylor, "The Riots that Followed the Assassination of Martin Lu-

NOTES TO PAGE 89

ther King, Jr.," *The Atlantic*, April 3, 2018, https://www.theatlantic.com/photo/2018/04/the-riots-that-followed-the-assassination-of-martin-luther-king-jr/557159/.

312. Molly Rubin, "Who Really Killed Martin Luther King, Jr.? His Family Says the Wrong Man Went to Prison," *Quartz*, April 3, 2018, https://qz.com/1243402/who-killed-martin-luther-king-jr-revisiting-his-assassination-on-the-50th-anniversary/; Tom Jackman, "Who Killed Martin Luther King, Jr.? His Family Believes James Earl Ray Was Framed," *Washington Post*, March 30, 2018; and Robert Scheer, "Did the FBI Play a Role in King's Death?" *Los Angeles Times*, July 15, 1997.

313. Parenti, *Democracy for the Few*, 126.

314. Virginia Postrel, "The Consequences of the 1960s' Race Riots Come into View," *New York Times*, December 30, 2004.

315. Alice Speri, "45 Years After Attica, Prisoners are Rebelling Again," *The Intercept*, October 3, 2016, https://theintercept.com/2016/10/03/45-years-after-attica-uprising-prisoners-are-rebelling-again/.

316. See Kenneth Robert Janken, *The Wilmington Ten: Violence, Injustice, and the Rise of Black Politics in the 1970s* (Chapel Hill: University of North Carolina Press, 2015).

317. "'Southern University Massacre' Victims Honored by University," *Louisiana Weekly*, April 10, 2017.

318. Joann Wypijewski, "Whitewash," *Mother Jones*, November 2005, https://www.motherjones.com/politics/2005/11/whitewash/.

319. "McDuffie Riots: Eerie Scene from Miami Race Riot of 1980," *Huffington Post*, May 29, 2013, http://www.huffingtonpost.com/2013/05/29/mcduffie-riots-miami_n_3353719.html.

320. Associated Press, "After 150 Years, Ku Klux Klan Sees Opportunities in U.S. Political Trends," *Los Angeles Times*, July 4, 2016.

321. Alan Yuhas, "Philadelphia's Osage Avenue Police Bombing, 30 Years On: 'This Story is a Parable,'" *Guardian*, May 13, 2015.

322. Associated Press, "Neo-Nazi Gets Life Sentence for Beating Black to Death," *New York Times*, June 6, 1989.

323. "Los Angeles Riots: Fast Facts," CNN, April 18, 2016, http://www.cnn.com/2013/09/ 18/us/los-angeles-riots-fast-facts/.

324. Lenny Flank, "The 1996 St. Petersburg, Florida Riots," *Daily Kos*, August 21, 2014, https://www.dailykos.com/ story/2014/8/21/1296361/-The-1996-St-Petersburg-FL-Riots.

325. Claire Cardona and the Associated Press, "Racist Killer Executed Decades After Dragging James Byrd, Jr., to His Death near Jasper," *Dallas Morning News*, April 24, 2019.

326. Michael Cooper, "Officers in Bronx Fire 41 Shots, and an Unarmed Man is Killed," *New York Times*, February 5, 1999.

327. Britannica ProCon.org, "The ESPY List: U.S. Executions from 1609-2002."
328. Cazenave, *Killing African Americans*, 104; Michael L. Radelet, Hugo Adam Bedau, and Constance E. Putnam, *In Spite of Innocence: The Ordeal of 400 Americans Wrongfully Convicted of Crimes Punishable by Death* (Boston: Northeastern University Press, 1992); and Charles J. Ogletree Jr. and Austin Sarat, eds., *From Lynch Mobs to the Killing State: Race and the Death Penalty in America* (New York: New York University Press, 2006).
329. Seanna Adcox, "Radio Host Tom Joyner Clears His Family's Name," *Seattle Times*, October 15, 2009.
330. *Washington Post*, "History of the Juvenile Death Penalty," July 19, 1988.
331. Ibid.
332. Kathy Lohr, "Georgia Woman Pardoned 60 Years After Her Execution," NPR, August 26, 2005, https://www.npr.org/templates/story/story.php?storyId=4818124.
333. Mary Mapes, "When Henry Wade Executed an Innocent Man," *D Magazine*, May 2016, https://www.dmagazine.com/publications/d-magazine/2016/may/henry-wade-executed-innocent-man/.
334. Molly Secours, "Is Tennessee Doomed to Repeat the Shame of Wrongful Execution?" *The Tennessean*, February 10, 2002.
335. Karl Keys, "Thirty Years of Executions with Reasonable Doubts: A Brief Analysis of Some Modern Executions," *Capital Defense Weekly*, March 10, 2007.
336. Nathan J. Robinson, "The Death of Ricky Ray Rector," *Jacobin*, November 5, 2016, https://www.jacobinmag.com/2016/11/bill-clinton-rickey-rector-death-penalty-execution-crime-racism/.
337. David Rose, "Death of Justice in Alabama," *Guardian*, June 19, 1999.
338. Elizabeth Nix, "Tuskegee Experiment: The Infamous Syphilis Study," *History*, December 15, 2020, https://www.history.com/news/the-infamous-40-year-tuskegee-study. See also James H. Jones, *Bad Blood: The Tuskegee Syphilis Experiment*, rev. ed. (New York: Free Press, 1993).
339. Washington, *Medical Apartheid*, 360–62.
340. Ibid., 244–57.
341. Ibid., 233–36.
342. Ibid., 272–79.
343. Alexander, *The New Jim Crow*, 109–11; Frank Baumgartner, "Forty Years of Experience with the 'New and Improved' Death Penalty, 1976–2016," *The American Prospect*, July 5, 2016, http://prospect.org/article/forty-years-experience-%E2%80%98new-and-improved%E2%80%99-death-penalty-1976%E2%80%932016; Matt Ford, "Racism and the Execution Chamber," *The Atlantic*, June 23, 2014, http://www.theatlan-

NOTES TO PAGES 91–92   341

tic.com/politics/archive/2014/06/race-and-the-death-penalty/ 373081; and Richard C. Dieter, "The Death Penalty in Black and White: Who Lives, Who Dies, Who Decides," Death Penalty Information Center, June 1998, http://www. deathpenaltyinfo.org/death-penalty-black-and-white-who-lives-who-dies-who-decides#Executive%20Summary.

344. Bianca Jagger, "A Day of Shame for the State of Georgia and the Justice System," *Huffington Post*, November 20, 2011.

345. Cazenave, *Killing African Americans*, chaps. 1 and 4; and Danielle Haynes, "Study: Black Americans 3 Times More Likely to Be Killed by Police," UPI, June 24, 2020, https://www.upi. com/Top_News/US/2020/06/24/Study-Black-Americans-3-times-more-likely-to-be-killed-by-police/6121592949925/.

346. Steve Martinot, "On the Epidemic of Police Killings," *Social Justice* 39/4 (2014): 52–75; Natasha Bach, "Police Violence Has Been Going on Forever. No Wonder People Are Fed Up With It," *Huffington Post*, August 24, 2014, https://www.huffpost.com/entry/police-brutality-michael-brown_n_5700970; Trymaine Lee, "Rumor to Fact in Tales of Post-Katrina Violence," *New York Times*, August 26, 2010; Daniel Funke and Tina Susman, "From Ferguson to Baton Rouge: Deaths of Black Men and Women at the Hands of Police," *Los Angeles Times*, July 12, 2016; Rachel Stockman, "Family Receives Settlement 12 Years after Teen Was Killed by Atlanta Police Officer," WSB-TV, September 2, 2014, https://www.wsbtv.om/news/local/ family-receives-settlement-12-years-after-teen-was/137961381/; "Family of Michael Pleasence Gets $3 Million Settlement: Unarmed Man Shot by Chicago Cop," *Huffington Post*, December 6, 2017, https://www.huffpost.com/entry/family-of-michael-pleasan_n_831308; Rich Juzwiak and Aleksander Chan, "Unarmed People of Color Killed by Police, 1999–2014," *Gawker*, December 8, 2014, http://gawker.com/unarmed-people-of-color-killed-by-police-1999-2014-1666672349; Latifah Muhammad, "Arkansas Cop Kills Wrongfully Suspected Man in Car Theft, Claims Self Defense," *HipHopWired*, July 17, 2013, https://hiphopwired.com/245907/arkansas-cop-kills-wrongfully-suspected-in-car-thief-claims-self-defense/; Rebecca R. Ruiz, "Baltimore Officers Will Face No Federal Charges in Death of Freddie Gray," *New York Times*, September 12, 2017; Richard Fausett, "Walter Scott Family Reaches a $6.5 Million Settlement for Police Shooting," *New York Times*, October 8, 2015; Kail Wright, "Why Alton Sterling and Philando Castile Are Dead," *The Nation*, July 7, 2016, https://www.the nation.com/article/why-alton-sterling-and-philando-castile-are-dead/; Frances Robles and Jose A. Del Real, "Stephon Clark Was Shot 8 Times, Primarily in Back, Family-Ordered Autopsy Finds," *New York Times*, March 30, 2018; Lucy Tompkins,

"Here's What You Need to Know About Elijah McClain's Death." *New York Times*, October 19, 2021; "Officer Did Not Identify Himself Before Firing Shot that Killed Fort Worth Woman, Police Say," KXAS-TV, October 14, 2019, https://www.nbcdfw.com/news/ local/fort-worth-police-to-hold-press-conference-after-shooting-killing-woman-in-home/196 5382/; Nicholas Bogel-Borroughs, "Indianapolis Police Face Growing Questions After Killing 3 People in 8 Hours," *New York Times*, May 7, 2020; Jennifer Emily and Tasha Tsiaperas, "Fired Cop Who Killed 15-Year-Old Jordan Edwards Indicted on Murder Charge," *Dallas Morning News*, July 17, 2017; Nicholas Bogel-Borroughs, "Months After Louisville Police Kill Woman in Her Home, Governor Calls for Review," *New York Times*, May 14, 2020; Evan Hill, Ainara Tiefenthäler, Christiaan Triebert, Drew Jordan, Haley Willis, and Robin Stein, "How George Floyd Was Killed in Police Custody," *New York Times*, April 20, 2021; Wil Gafney, "Jonathan Price's Shooting Was Not 'Reasonable.' Most Police Killings of Black People Aren't," NBC News, October 7, 2020, https://www.nbcnews.com/think/opinion/jonathan-price-s-shooting-was-not-reasonable-most-police-killings-ncna1242463; Jana Kadah, "'Person of Interest' in Gilroy Homicide Was Unarmed When SJ Police Killed Him," KTVU-TV, January 26, 2021, https:// www. ktvu.com/news/person-of-interest-in-gilroy-homicide-was-unarmed-when-sj-police-killed-him; Meredith Deliso and Will McDuffie, "Body Camera Footage Shows 'Horrific' In-Custody Death of Black Man in South Carolina Jail," ABC News, May 14, 2021, https://abcnews.go.com/US/body-camera-footage-shows-horrific-custody-death-black/story?id=77696809; and "What to Know About the Death of Daunte Wright," *New York Times*, April 23, 2021.

347. "Fatal Force," Police Shootings Database, *Washington Post*, https:// www.washingtonpost.com/graphics/investigations/police-shootings-database/.

348. The Mapping Police Violence Database includes people who died as a result of these interactions with police as well as police shootings. See Mapping Police Violence, "About the Data," https://mappingpoliceviolence.org/aboutthedata.

349. Mapping Police Violence, "2020 Police Violence Report," https://policeviolencereport.org.

350. Gafney, "Jonathan Price's Shooting Was Not 'Reasonable.'"

351. Although white mobs and vigilantes were responsible for most of the 53,000 African American deaths during the reign of terror against Reconstruction, racist law enforcement officers were likely responsible for thousands of these deaths. In addition, white police and corrections officials were complicit in the deaths of many Black people performing

NOTES TO PAGES 92–93

convict labor between the 1870s and the late 1920s. Law enforcement agents were also involved in many of the almost two thousand lynchings between 1900 and 1950 and in numerous other racist murders from the Red Summer of 1919 to the urban uprisings of the mid- and late-twentieth century. African Americans have always suffered disproportionately from routine police killings, and this loss of lives now exceeds two hundred each year.

352. Southern Poverty Law Center, "Terror from the Right: Archives," July 23, 2018, https:// www.splcenter.org/ terror-from-the-right-archives#2001; Anti-Defamation League, "A Dark and Constant Rage: 25 Years of Right-Wing Terrorism in the United States," 2017, 23, https:// www.adl.org/sites/default/files/documents/CR_5154_25YRS%20 RightWing%20Terrorism_V5.pdf; A. C. Thompson, "Katrina's Hidden Race War," *The Nation*, December 17, 2008, https:// www.thenation. com/article/archive/katrinas-hidden-race-war/; Matthew Stabley, Jim Lovino, and Andrew Greiner, "Slain Museum Guard's Kindness Repaid with Bullet," WRC-TV, June 12, 2009, https://www.nbcwashington. com/news/local/one-shot-at-holocaust-museum/1850620/; Renford Reese, "Double Tragedy of the Trayvon Martin Case," *San Bernadino Sun*, July 17, 2013; Terese Apel, "3 White Mississippi Men Sentenced for Hate Crimes, Including Running Over Black Man," *Huffington Post*, April 12, 2015, https://www.huffpost.com/entry/three-white-mississippi-men-hate-crimes_n_6655904; Matt Ford and Adam Chandler, "'Hate Crime': Mass Killing at a Historic Church," *The Atlantic*, June 19, 2015, http://www.theatlantic. com/ national/archive/2015/06/ shooting-emanuel-ame-charleston/396209/; "A Murder in College Park," *New York Times*, May 30, 2017; Katie Bernard and Max Londberg, "'True Definition of Evil': Alleged Shawnee Killer Is White Supremacist, Family Says," *Kansas City Star*, July 23, 2018; Adeel Hassan, "In Oregon, a Murder Conviction Adds to Calls for Tougher Hate Crime Punishments," *New York Times*, April 26, 2019; Bob Bauder and Tom Davidson, "Richard Baumhammers Still on Death Row 20 Years after Killing Spree," *Tribune-Review*, April 28, 2020; Khushbu Shah, "Ahmaud Arbery: Anger Mounts over Killing of Black Jogger Caught on Video," *Guardian*, May 6, 2020; and Quincy Walters, "'It's Another Racist Act': Vigil Held in Belmont for Black Man Killed in Road Rage Incident," WBUR Radio, January 22, 2021, https://www.wbur.org/ news/2021/01/21/belmont-road-rage-vigil.

353. Marc Mauer, *Race to Incarcerate*, rev. ed. (New York: The New Press, 2006), 33, cited in Alexander, *New Jim Crow*, 6.

354. Alexander, *New Jim Crow*, 48; James Cullen, "The History of Mass Incarceration," Brennan Center for Justice, July 20, 2018, https://www.

brennancenter.org/our-work/analysis-opinion/ history-mass-incarceration; and Tom LoBianco, "Report: Nixon's Aide Said War on Drugs Targeted Blacks, Hippies," CNN, March 24, 2016, http://www.cnn.com/2016/03/23/politics/ john-ehrlichman-richard-nixon-drug-war-blacks-hippie/.

355. Cullen, "History of Mass Incarceration."

356. Alexander, *New Jim Crow*, chaps. 1 and 2; and Cullen, "History of Mass Incarceration."

357. Alexander, *New Jim Crow*.

358. Ibid., esp. Introduction and chapter 1; Nathaniel Lewis, "Locking Up the Poor," *Jacobin*, January 30, 2018, https://jacobinmag.com/2018/01/mass-incarceration-race-class-peoples-policy-project; and Cedric Johnson, "The Panthers Can't Save Us Now," *Catalyst* 1/1 (Spring 2017), https://catalyst-journal.com/vol1/no1/panthers-cant-save-us-cedric-johnson. Although Johnson's call for anti-capitalist politics is welcome, his critique of racial affinity and anti-racism is problematic.

359. Michelle Ye Hee Lee, "Yes, U.S. Locks Up People at a Higher Rate than Any Other Country," *Washington Post*, July 7, 2015.

360. This rough estimate is based on reports of prisoner deaths in Carson, *Mortality in Local Jails, 2000–2014—Statistical Tables*, 12, Tables 8 and 13, Table 9, and *Mortality in State and Federal Prisons, 2001–2018—Statistical Tables*, 7, Tables 2 and 12, Table 10; Bureau of Justice Statistics, U.S. Department of Justice, *Sourcebook of Criminal Justice Statistics 1983*, ed. Edward J. Brown, Timothy Flanagan, and Maureen McLeod (Washington, DC: Government Printing Office, 1984), 601, Table 6.54; Bureau of Justice Statistics, U.S. Department of Justice, *Sourcebook of Criminal Justice Statistics 1991*, ed. Timothy Flanagan and Kathleen McGuire (Washington, DC: Government Printing Office, 1992), 619, Tables 6.44 and 701, Table 6.138; and Bureau of Justice Statistics, U.S. Department of Justice, *Sourcebook of Criminal Justice Statistics 1995*, ed. Kathleen McGuire and Ann Pastore (Washington, DC: Government Printing Office, 1996), 602, Table 6.72. Unfortunately, records of prisoner deaths have not always indicated the race of the deceased.

361. Eyal Press, "A Fight to Expose the Hidden Human Costs of Incarceration," *The New Yorker*, August 23, 2021, https://www.newyorker.com/magazine/2021/08/23/a-fight-to-expose-the-hidden-human-costs-of-incarceration; and Blake Ellis and Melanie Hicken, "CNN Investigation Exposes Preventable Deaths in Jails and Prisons," CNN, June 26, 2019, https://www.cnn.com/ interactive/2019/06/us/jail-health-care-ccs-invs/index.html.

362. Randolph Roth, *American Homicide* (Cambridge, MA: Harvard University Press, 2009), 387.

NOTES TO PAGES 93–94

363. Information on homicides between 1900 and 1997 is found in Douglas Eckberg, "Reported Homicides and Homicide Rates, by Sex and Mode of Death," in *Historical Statistics of the United States: Earliest Times to the Present, Millennial Edition*, vol. 5: *Part E: Governance and International Relations*, ed. Susan B. Carter, Scott Sigmund Gartner, Michael R. Haines, Alan L. Olmstead, Richard Sutch, and Gavin Wright (Cambridge: Cambridge University Press, 2006), 5-239, 5-240, Table Ec190–198. Data were not reported from all states until 1933. Information on homicides between 1998 and 2019 was published in successive issues of the National Center for Health Statistics's *National Vital Statistics Reports* between 2000 and 2021. These reports are available at https://www.cdc.gov/nchs/products/ nvsr.htm. For general discussion of the disproportionate impact of homicides in African American communities, see Roth, *American Homicide*, 387, 395–403, 414–443, chap. 9; and Robert J. Sampson and Janet L. Lauritsen, "Racial and Ethnic Disparities in Crime and Criminal Justice in the United States," *Crime and Justice* 21 (1997): 517.

364. Jeffrey Goldberg, "A Matter of Black Lives," *The Atlantic*, September 2015, http://www.theatlantic.com/magazine/archive/ 2015/09/a-matter-of-black-lives/399386/.

365. Matthew Cella and Alan Neuhauser, "Race and Homicide in America, by the Numbers," *U.S. News and World Report*, September 29, 2016, https://www.usnews.com/news/articles/2016-09-29/race-and-homicide-in-america-by-the-numbers; Centers for Disease Control and Prevention, "Leading Causes of Death—Males—Non-Hispanic Black—United States, 2016," Minority Health and Health Equity, September 27, 2019, https://www.cdc.gov/healthequity/lcod/men/ 2016/nonhispanic-black/index.htm; and Justin Wolfers, David Leonhardt, and Kevin Quealy, "1.5 Million Missing Black Men," *New York Times*, April 20, 2015.

366. Clodfelter, *Warfare*, 462; and "African Americans in World War I," Oxford African American Studies Center, https://oxfordaasc.com/page/focus-on-african-americans-in-world-war-i/african-americans-in-world-war-i.

367. Clodfelter, *Warfare*, 561.

368. Ibid., 710; and State of New Jersey, *Fact Sheet: The Beginnings of a New Era for African Americans in the Armed Forces*, 2000. http://www.nj.gov/military/korea/factsheets/afroamer.html.

369. Clodfelter, *Warfare*, 761.

370. Blum and DeBruyne, *American War Casualties*, 12, 16, 21.

371. An estimate of 83.000 annual excess Black deaths is found in David Satcher, George E. Fryer Jr., Jessica McCann, Adewale Troutman, Ste-

346   NOTES TO PAGE 95

ven H. Woolf, and George Rust, "What If We Were Equal? A Comparison of the Black-White Mortality Gap in 1960 and 2000," *Health Affairs* 24/2 (2005): 459–64. An approximate average of 76,470 annual excess Black deaths for the period 1970–2004 was advanced in Javier M. Rodriguez, Arline T. Geronimus, John Bound, and Danny Dorling, "Black Lives Matter: Differential Mortality and the Composition of the U.S. Electorate, 1970–2014," *Social Science and Medicine* 136–137 (2015): 193–99. A more recent estimate of 65,000 annual excess Black deaths is found in Gus Wezerek, "Racism's Hidden Toll," *New York Times*, August 11, 2020. See also David A. Ansell, *The Death Gap: How Inequality Kills* (Chicago: University of Chicago Press, 2017).

372. Linda Villarosa, "Why America's Black Mothers and Babies Are in a Life-or-Death Crisis," *New York Times*, April 11, 2018; and Danielle M. Ely and Anne K. Driscoll, National Center for Health Statistics, "Infant Mortality in the United States, 2017: Data from the Period Linked Birth/Infant Death File," *National Vital Statistics Reports* 68/10, August 1, 2019, https:// www.cdc.gov/nchs/data/nvsr/nvsr68/nvsr68_10-508. pdf.

373. Villarosa, "Black Mothers and Babies." Although the mortality rate for African American infants is higher today than in 1850, the overall mortality rate for African Americans from birth through their fifth year of life is lower. See Steckel, "African American Population, 1790–1920," 449, 453, and "Demography and Slavery," 654.

374. Villarosa, "Black Mothers and Babies"; and Centers for Disease Control and Prevention, "Reproductive Health: Pregnancy-Related Deaths," February 26, 2019, https://www.cdc.gov/reproductivehealth/maternalinfanthealth/pregnancy-relatedmortality.htm.

375. Satcher et al., "What If We Were Equal?"; Lisandro D. Colantonio, Christopher M. Gamboa, Joshua S. Richman, Emily B. Levitan, Elsayed Z. Soliman, George Howard, and Monika M. Safford, "Black-White Differences in Incident Fatal, Nonfatal, and Total Coronary Heart Disease," *Circulation* 136/2 (2017): 152–66; Office of Minority Health, U.S. Department of Health and Human Services, "Cancer and African Americans," February 28, 2020, https:// minorityhealth.hhs.gov/omh/browse. aspx?lvl=4&lvlid =16, "Diabetes and African Americans," December 19, 2019, https://minorityhealth.hhs.gov/omh/browse.aspx?lvl=4&lvlid=18, and "HIV/AIDS and African Americans," January 17, 2018, https://minorityhealth.hhs.gov/omh/   browse.aspx?lvl=4&lvlid=21; Jacey A. Loberg, R. David Hayward, Mary Fessler, and Elango Edhayan, "Associations of Race, Mechanisms of Injury, and Neighborhood Poverty with In-Hospital Mortality from Trauma," *Medicine (Baltimore)* 97/39 (September 2018), https:// www.ncbi.nlm.nih.gov/pmc/articles/

NOTES TO PAGES 95–96

PMC6181609/; and Cary P. Gross, Utibe R. Essien, Saamir Pasha, Jacob R. Gross, Shi-yi Wang, and Marcella Nunez-Smith, "Racial and Ethnic Disparities in Population Level COVID-19 Mortality," *Journal of General Internal Medicine* 35/10 (October 2020): 3097–99.

376. Satcher et al., "What If We Were Equal?", 462–63; Rodriguez et al., "Differential Mortality," 194–95; Oliver Milman, "Robert Bullard: 'Environmental Justice Isn't Just Slang, It's Real,'" *Guardian*, December 20, 2018; and Keeanga-Yamahtta Taylor, "The Black Plague," *The New Yorker*, April 16, 2020, https://www. new yorker.com/news/our-columnists/ the-black-plague.

377. Satcher et al., "What If We Were Equal?", 462–63; Rodriguez et al., "Differential Mortality," 194–95; Keeanga-Yamahtta Taylor, "The Black Plague"; Jamila Taylor, "Racism, Inequality, and Health Care for African Americans," Century Foundation, December 19, 2019, https://tcf.org/content/report/racism-inequality-health-care-african-americans/?agreed=1; Austin Frakt, "Race and Medicine: The Harm That Comes from Mistrust," *New York Times*, January 13, 2020; and Courtland Milloy, "The Cure for Racial Disparities in Health Care Is Known. It's the Willingness to Fix It That's Lagging," *Washington Post*, April 21, 2020.

378. Jackman and Shauman, "Toll of Inequality," 291–340.

379. Rodriguez et al., "Differential Mortality," 194–95. See also Arline T. Geronimus, Margaret Hicken, Danya Keene, and John Bound, "'Weathering' and Age Patterns of Allostatic Load Scores Among Blacks and Whites in the United States," *American Journal of Public Health* 96/5 (May 2006): 826–33; Arline T. Geronimus, Margaret T. Hicken, Jay A. Pearson, Sarah J. Seashols, Kelly L. Brown, and Tracey Dawson Cruz, "Do U.S. Black Women Experience Stress-Related Accelerated Biological Aging? A Novel Theory and First Population-Based Test of Black-White Differences in Telomere Length," *Human Nature* 21 (2010): 19–38; and Arline T. Geronimus, "Jedi Public Health: Leveraging Contingencies of Social Identity to Grasp and Eliminate Racial Health Inequality," in *Mapping 'Race' and Inequality: A Critical Reader on Health Disparities Research* (New Brunswick, NJ: Rutgers University Press, 2013).

380. Robert S. Levine, James E. Foster, Robert F. Fullilove, Mindy T. Fullilove, Nathaniel C. Briggs, Panela C. Hull, Baqar A. Husaini, and Charles H. Hennekens, "Black-White Inequalities in Mortality and Life Expectancy, 1933–1999: Implications for Healthy People 2010," *Public Health Reports* 116 (September–October 2001): 474–83.

381. Rodriguez et al., "Differential Mortality," 193–99.

382. Jackman and Shauman, "The Toll of Inequality," 291, 309.

348 NOTES TO PAGES 96–97

383. Ibid., 312.
384. Jackman and Shauman's estimate of more than one million excess deaths between 2000 and 2014 suggests an average of more than 66,000 deaths each year. If this average loss of life continued between 2015 and 2020, the total number of additional deaths was almost 400,000.
385. This rough estimate for the Western Hemisphere includes the total number of deaths associated with the transatlantic slave trade, the deaths of people of African descent born in the present-day United States examined in this chapter, and the countless violent deaths and social murders of people of African descent born in Brazil, the Caribbean, and other lands in the Americas. South of the United States, perhaps the most lethal mistreatment of Black people over time has occurred in Brazil. See, for example, Vinícius Lisboa, "Forum Reports Black Genocide in Brazil to UN," AgênciaBrasil, March 12, 2017, https://agenciabrasil.ebc.com.br/en/direitos-humanos/noticia/2017-12/forum-reports-black-genocide-brazil-un; Manuella Libardi, "Racial Cleansing in Brazil: A Twenty-first Century Genocide?," Open Democracy, September 27, 2019, https://www.opendemocracy.net/en/democraciaabierta/limpieza-racial-en-brasil-genocidio-versión-siglo-xxi-en/; and "How Many Acts of Genocide Will It Take to Call the Extermination of Black Brazilians a Genocide?, " RioOnWatch.org, October 31, 2019, https://www.rioonwatch. org/?p=56561. On the grave discrimination and disparities in health and access to health care still experienced by Blacks in Latin America and the Caribbean, see Economic Commission for Latin America and the Caribbean (ECLAC) and Office of the United Nations High Commissioner for Human Rights (OHCHR), *People of African Descent in Latin America and the Caribbean: Developing Indicators to Measure and Counter Inequalities*, LC/TS.2019/62, February 2020, https://www.cepal.org/en/publications/45202-people-african-descent-latin-america-and-caribbean-developing-indicators-measure. What this report calls "the persistent statistical invisibility of people of African descent" in Latin America and the Caribbean explains the traditional paucity of data on the violent deaths and social murders they have suffered in this region. See ECLAC and OHCHR, 5.

3. The Workers Holocaust

1. This use of Thomas Hobbes's language from *Leviathan* appears in Brendan Wolfe and Martha McCartney, "Indentured Servants in Colonial Virginia," *Encyclopedia Virginia*, Virginia Humanities, October 28, 2015, https://www.encyclopediavirginia.org/Indentured_Servants_in_Colonial_Virginia. See also Steven Mintz and Sara McNeil, "The Origins of New World Slavery," *Digital History*, 2018, http://www.digital-

NOTES TO PAGES 97-98 349

history.uh.edu/disp_textbook_print.cfm?smtid=2&psid=449.; Abbot Emerson Smith, *Colonists in Bondage: White Servitude and Convict Labor in America, 1607–1776* (Chapel Hill: University of North Carolina Press, 1947); David W. Galenson, "The Rise and Fall of Indentured Servitude in the Americas: An Economic Analysis," *Journal of Economic History* 44/1 (March 1984): 1–26; and Matthew Harris, "'A Mean and Brutal Business': Indentured Servitude in Early America," in *British Colonial America: People and Perspectives*, ed. John A. Grigg (Santa Barbara: ABC-CLIO, 2008), 21–40.

2. Eric Foner, *Give Me Liberty! An American History*, vol. 2, Seagull 3rd ed. (New York: W. W. Norton, 2012), chap. 16; and Fareed Zakaria, *From Wealth to Power: The Unusual Origins of America's World Role* (Princeton: Princeton University Press, 1998), 45–46.

3. Foner, *Give Me Liberty!*, 587; and John Fabian Witt, *The Accidental Republic: Crippled Workingmen, Destitute Widows, and the Remaking of American Law* (Cambridge, MA: Harvard University Press, 2004), 35–36.

4. Foner, *Give Me Liberty!*, 595; Witt, *Accidental Republic*, Introduction and chap. 1; John C. Waller, *Health and Wellness in 19th-Century America* (Santa Barbara, CA: Greenwood, 2014), chap. 7; *Industrial Relations: Final Report and Testimony Submitted to Congress by the Commission on Industrial Relations*, S. Doc. No. 64-415, (Washington, DC: Government Printing Office, 1916); U.S. Department of Labor and United States Department of Health, Education, and Welfare, *The President's Report on Occupational Safety and Health*, (Washington, DC: Government Printing Office, 1972); National Safety Council, *Accident Facts 1993* (Itasca. IL: National Safety Council, 1993), 26–27; Marc Linder, "Fatal Subtraction: Statistical MIAs on the Industrial Battlefield," *Journal of Legislation* 20/2 (1994): 99–145; and American Federation of Labor-Congress of Industrial Organizations, *Death on the Job: The Toll of Neglect*, 30th ed. (May 2021), 1–2, 5, 7, 9.

5. Philip Taft and Philip Ross, "American Labor Violence: Its Causes, Character, and Outcome," in *Violence in America*, ed. Hugh D. Graham and Ted R. Gurr (New York: Bantam, 1969), 281, cited in Robert Justin Goldstein, *Political Repression in Modern America: From 1870 to 1976* (Urbana: University of Illinois Press, 2001), 3.

6. Robert J. Schwendinger, *Ocean of Bitter Dreams; The Chinese Migration to the United States, 1850–1915* (San Francisco: Long River Press, 2015), 2, chaps 2–4; Walter LaFeber, *Inevitable Revolutions: The United States in Central America*, 2nd ed. (New York: W. W. Norton, 1993), 56–57; John Lindsay-Poland, *Emperors in the Jungle: The Hidden History of the U.S. in Panama* (Durham, NC: Duke University Press, 2003),

350 NOTES TO PAGES 98–99

14; John Tully, *The Devil's Milk: A Social History of Rubber* (New York: Monthly Review Press, 2011), chaps 5–6; Jules Marchal, *Lord Leverhulme's Ghosts: Colonial Exploitation in the Congo*, trans. Martin Thom (London: Verso, 2017); and Erik Loomis, *Out of Sight: The Long and Disturbing Story of Corporations Outsourcing Catastrophe* (New York: New Press, 2015).

7. Abbott Emerson Smith, *Colonists in Bondage*, chap. 1; Galenson, "Indentured Servitude," 1–13; Harris, "'Mean and Brutal Business,'" 23; Wolfe and McCartney, "Servants in Colonial Virginia"; and Mintz and McNeil, "Origins of New World Slavery."

8. Zinn, *People's History*, 42–43; Abbot Emerson Smith, *Colonists in Bondage*, 7; Galenson, "Indentured Servitude," 9, 10; Wolfe and McCartney, "Servants in Colonial Virginia"; and Mintz and McNeil, "Origins of New World Slavery."

9. Christopher Tomlins, "Reconsidering Indentured Servitude: European Migration and the Early American Labor Force, 1600–1775," *Labor History* 42/1 (2001): 5–43.

10. Wolfe and McCartney, "Servants in Colonial Virginia."

11. This estimate is found in Tomlins, "Reconsidering Indentured Servitude." Somewhat higher estimates are found in Zinn, *People's History*, 46; and in Abbott Emerson Smith, *Colonists in Bondage*, 336, cited in Galenson, "Indentured Servitude," 1–2.

12. Zinn, *People's History*, 44; Galenson, "Indentured Servitude," 4; Harris, "'Mean and Brutal Business,'" 24–25; and Wolfe and McCartney, "Servants in Colonial Virginia."

13. Mintz and McNeil, "Origins of New World Slavery."

14. Zinn, *People's History*, 41–46; Galenson, "Indentured Servitude," 4; Harris, "'Mean and Brutal Business,'" 25–26, 28; and Ron and Norwood, "America Cannot Bring Back Servitude."

15. Galenson, "Indentured Servitude," 2, 13.

16. Erik Loomis, "This Day in Labor History: October 26, 1825," *Lawyers, Guns, and Money*, October 26, 2013, http://www.lawyersgunsmoney-blog.com/2013/10/this-day-in-labor-history-october-26-1825; and Will Barclay, "A Look at History: The Erie Canal Celebrates 200 Years," *Oswego County News Now*, June 27, 2017. An estimate of about five hundred deaths is found in Gerard Koeppel, *Bond of Union: Building the Erie Canal and the American Empire* (Cambridge, MA: Da Capo Press, 2009), 319–20.

17. William E. Watson and J. Francis Watson, *Massacre at Duffy's Cut: Tragedy and Conspiracy on the Pennsylvania Railroad* (Charleston: History Press, 2018), 147; and Mary Helen Lagasse, "A Call to Remember the 8,000 Irish Who Died While Building the New Orleans

NOTES TO PAGES 99-100　　　　　351

Canal," *Irish Central*, November 7, 2013, https://www.irishcentral.com/news/8000-irish-died-while-building-the-new-basin-canal-in-new-orleans-231020191-237786681. Lower estimates for these deaths are found in Linder, "Fatal Subtraction," 144; and in Jay Dolan, *The Irish Americans: A History* (New York: Bloomsbury Press, 2008), 45.

18. Peter Way, *Common Labor: Workers and the Digging of North American Canals, 1780–1860* (Cambridge: Cambridge University Press, 1993), 148–57.

19. Ibid., 157–58.

20. Ibid., 158.

21. Ibid., 31.

22. Associated Press, "Divers Confirm Wreck Off North Carolina Coast Is 1830s Steamship," WFAE Radio, May 10, 2018, http://www.wfae.org/post/divers-confirm-wreck-north-carolina-coast-1830s-steamship#stream/0.

23. Amanda Beam, "New Albany Bicentennial: Lucy Walker Steamboat Disaster," (New Albany, Indiana) *News and Tribune*, May 15, 2013.

24. Kat Eschner, "This Civil War Boat Explosion Killed More People Than the 'Titanic,'" *Smithsonian Magazine*, April 27, 2017, https://www.smithsonianmag.com/smithsonianmag/ civil-war-boat-explosion-killed-more-people-titanic-180963008/.

25. Mark Aldrich, *Death Rode the Rails: American Railroad Accidents and Safety, 1828–1965* (Baltimore: Johns Hopkins University Press, 2006).

26. Mark Aldrich, *Safety First: Technology, Labor, and Business in the Building of American Work Safety, 1870–1939* (Baltimore: Johns Hopkins University Press, 1997), 9.

27. History.com Editors, "The First Railroad Accident," *History*, July 23, 2020, https://www. history.com/ this-day-in-history/the-first-railroad-accident.

28. Aldrich, *Death Rode the Rails*, 20.

29. Ibid., 19.

30. Ibid., 2.

31. Ibid.

32. Ibid., 35.

33. Aldrich, *Safety First*, 12.

34. Secretary of the Interior, *Statistics of the United States (Including Mortality, Property, and c.,) in 1860* (Washington, DC: Government Printing Office, 1866), 4, 52–55, Table 2. The new Census category is noted in Witt, *Accidental Republic*, 26.

35. Aldrich, *Death Rode the Rails*, 15–18.

36. Joseph Schott, *Rails Across Panama: The Story of the Building of the Panama Railroad* (New York: Bobbs-Merrill, 1967), 173; and David

352   NOTES TO PAGES 100–101

McCullough, *The Path Between the Seas* (New York: Simon & Schuster, 1977), 37, both cited in Lindsay-Poland, *Emperors in the Jungle*, 14.

37. Waller, *Health and Wellness*, 143.

38. M. T. Anderson, "Clothed in Misery," *New York Times*, April 29, 2013.

39. Charles Levenstein, Dianne Plantamura, and William Mass, "Labor and Byssinosis, 1941–1969," in *Dying for Work: Workers' Safety and Health in Twentieth-Century America*, ed. David Rosner and Gerald Markowitz (Bloomington: Indiana University Press, 1987), 208–9; William Moran, *The Belles of New England: The Women of the Textile Mills and the Families Whose Wealth They Wove* (New York: St. Martin's Press, 2002), 22–23; and Kathryn Walbert and James Leloudis, "Work in a Textile Mill," in *ANCHOR: A North Carolina History Online Resource*, https://www.ncpedia.org/anchor/work-textile-mill, accessed on December 9, 2021. See also Gerald N. Grob, *The Deadly Truth: A History of Disease in America* (Cambridge, MA: Harvard University Press, 2002), 160–61, 166–67.

40. Erik Loomis, "This Day in Labor History: July 3, 1835," *Lawyers, Guns, and Money*, July 3, 2012, https://lawyersgunsmon.wpengine.com/2012/07/this-day-in-labor-history-july-3-1835; and "This Day in Labor History: September 15, 1845," *Lawyers, Guns, and Money*, September 15, 2017, https://www.lawyersgunsmoneyblog.com/2017/09/day-labor-history-september-15-1845.

41. Erik Loomis, "This Day in Labor History: February 13, 1845," *Lawyers, Guns, and Money*, February 13, 2014, https://lawyersgunsmon.wpengine.com/2014/02/this-day-in-labor-history- february-13-1845.

42. "The Fall of the Pemberton Mill," *New York Times*, February 16, 1860.

43. Sean Patrick Adams, "The U.S. Coal Industry in the Nineteenth Century," *EH.Net Encyclopedia*, Economic History Association, ed. Robert Whaples, June 2003, https://eh.net/ encyclopedia/the-us-coal-industry-in-the-nineteenth-century-2/.

44. Centers for Disease Control and Prevention, National Institute for Occupational Safety and Health, "All Mining Disasters: 1839 to the Present," February 26, 2013, https://www.cdc.gov/niosh/mining/statistics/content/allminingdisasters.html.

45. Christopher C. Sellers, *Hazards of the Job: From Industrial Disease to Environmental Health Science* (Chapel Hill: University of North Carolina Press, 1997), 16.

46. Grob, *Deadly Truth*, 167, cited in Waller, *Health and Wellness*, 145.

47. "Tremendous Explosion in New York Today! Fifty Lives Lost!" *Newport Daily News*, February 5, 1850, cited in "New York City, NY Building Explosion, Feb 1850," *GenDisasters.com*, http://www.gendisasters.com/new-york/15132/new-york-city-ny-building-explosion-feb-1850?page=0,1.

NOTES TO PAGES 101–103 353

48. "Destructive Conflagration. Terrible Loss of Life," *New York Times*, November 14, 1851, cited in "Philadelphia PA Factories Destroyed, Nov 1851," *GenDisasters.com*, http://www.gendisasters.com/pennsylvania/11073/philadelphia-pa-factories-destroyed-nov-1851.

49. "Terrible Catastrophe—Great Explosion at Ravenswood," *New York Times*, January 30, 1854, cited in "Ravenswood NY Gun Cartridge Factory Explosion Jan 1854," *GenDisasters.com*, http://www.gendisasters.com/new-york/20950/ravenswood-ny-gun-cartridge-factory-explosion-jan-1854?page=0,0.

50. *New York Tribune*, August 5 and August 6, 1850; and *New York Herald*, August 6 and August 7, 1850; both cited in Sean Wilentz, *Chants Democratic: New York City and the Rise of the Working Class, 1788–1850*, 20th anniv. ed. (Oxford: Oxford University Press, 2004), 380–81; and Lockwood L. Doty, *A History of Livingston County, New York* (Geneseo, NY: Edward E. Doty, 1876), 449–50.

51. Schwendinger, *Bitter Dreams*, 2.

52. Hallet Abend, *Treaty Ports* (1944), 103, cited in Schwendinger, *Bitter Dreams*, 57.

53. Schwendinger, *Bitter Dreams*, 20. See also Shih-Shan Henry Tsai, *The Chinese Experience in America* (Bloomington: Indiana University Press, 1986), 4.

54. Schwendinger, *Bitter Dreams* 21.

55. Ibid., 22; and Tsai, *Chinese Experience*, 4–5.

56. Tsai, *Chinese Experience*, 6; and Schwendinger, 23.

57. Tsai, *Chinese Experience*, 5; and Schwendinger, *Bitter Dreams* 2, 22–24, 27.

58. Schwendinger has acknowledged that the United States was complicit in the deaths of tens of thousands, but the total was likely scores of thousands. See Schwendinger, *Bitter Dreams* 2, 22–23, 27; and Tsai, *Chinese Experience*, 5.

59. Schwendinger, *Bitter Dreams* 57–62.

60. Benjamin T. Arrington, National Park Service, "Industry and Economy During the Civil War," in *The Civil War Remembered, Official National Park Service Handbook* (Virginia Beach, VA: Eastern National, 2011), 106.

61. Ibid.

62. Ibid.

63. Ibid., 104–7, 111.

64. Witt, *Accidental Republic*, chap. 1; Waller, *Health and Wellness*, chap. 7; Michael K. Rosenow, *Death and Dying in the Working Class, 1865–1920* (Urbana: University of Illinois Press, 2015), chap. 1; and Richard F. Selcer, *Civil War America,1850–1875* (New York: Facts on File, 2006), 29.

65. Aldrich, *Death Rode the Rails*, 20.

354   NOTES TO PAGES 103–104

66. Aldrich, *Safety First*, 80.
67. Jean Pfaelzer, *Driven Out: The Forgotten War against Chinese Americans* (Berkeley: University of California Press, 2007), 168. See also Tsai, *The Chinese Experience in America*, 17.
68. Richard O. Boyer and Herbert M. Morais, *Labor's Untold Story* (New York: United Electrical, Radio, and Machine Workers of America, 1955), 44; and Michael J. Makley, *The Infamous King of the Comstock: William Sharon and the Gilded Age in the West* (Reno: University of Nevada Press, 2006), 73–74.
69. Francis A. Walker, U.S. Department of the Interior, *Vital Statistics of the United States*, (Washington, DC: Government Printing Office, 1872), xix, 18–21, cited in Witt, *Accidental Republic*, 26.
70. Contemporary critiques of class exploitation of workers in the United States include the denunciation of "capitalistic slavery" by the General Council of Labor in Baltimore in August 1866, cited in Marx, *Capital*, 414. See also the rejection of "the rapacity, extortion, and refusal to pay the laborer his just wages" in an article in the *New York Herald*, June 22, 1877, cited in Boyer and Morais, *Labor's Untold Story*, 46; and the condemnation of "wage slavery" in Eugene Debs, "The Outlook for Socialism in the United States," *International Socialist Review* 1/3 (September 1900): 129–35. On the country's emergence as a leading global economic power, see Zinn, *People's History*, 301; Zakaria, *From Wealth to Power*, 45–46; David Rosner and Gerald Markowitz, "Introduction: Workers' Health and Safety—Some Historical Notes," in *Dying for Work*, xi; and Iain Haddow, "When U.K. GDP Last Outstripped U.S.," BBC News (January 7, 2008), http://news.bbc.co.uk/2/ hi/ uknews/7174996.stm.
71. Witt, *Accidental Republic*, 22
72. Linder, "Fatal Subtraction," 102.
73. Grob, *Deadly Truth*, 168. Grob found that "major disasters" killed several thousand miners, but most deaths occurred from "roof and coal falls," explosions, and haulage.
74. Waller, *Health and Wellness*, 143.
75. Loomis, *Out of Sight*, 32.
76. Tsai, *Chinese Experience*, xi–xii.
77. Iric Nathanson, "Looking Back at the Washburn A Mill Explosion," *MinnPost*, June 6, 2013, https://www.minnpost.com/minnesota-history/2013/06/looking-back-1878-washburn-mill-explosion.
78. S. J. Kleinburg, *The Shadow of the Mills: Working-Class Families in Pittsburgh, 1870–1907* (Pittsburgh: University of Pittsburgh Press, 1989), 29, 74, 86, cited in Peter Krass, *Carnegie* (Hoboken: John Wiley and Sons, 2002), x.

NOTES TO PAGES 104–105 355

79. LaFeber, *Inevitable Revolutions*, 56–57.
80. Ohio Bureau of Labor Statistics, *Annual Report*, (1881), 102–5, and *Annual Report*, (1883), 103, cited in U.S. Department of Labor, "History: State Investigations," https://www.dol.gov/ general/aboutdol/history/ mono-regsafepart01.
81. Minnesota Bureau of Labor Statistics, *Annual Report*, (1892), 104, 107–16, cited in U.S. Department of Labor, "History: State Investigations."
82. Witt, *Accidental Republic*, 24.
83. Benjamin Harrison, *First Annual Message to Congress*, December 3, 1889, https://www.presidency.ucsb.edu/documents/first-annual-message-14, cited in Witt, *Accidental Republic*, 24.
84. *Thirteenth Annual Report of the Bureau of Statistics of Labor and Industries of New Jersey for the Year Ending October 31, 1890* (Trenton, NJ: Trenton Electric, 1891), 367, cited in Witt, *Accidental Republic*, 24.
85. Aldrich, *Safety First*, 17, 23, 42, 79; Waller, *Health and Wellness*, 151; and Witt, *Accidental Republic*, 26.
86. Linder, "Fatal Subtraction," 99, 100, 106; and Witt, *Accidental Republic*, 25.
87. Foner, *Give Me Liberty!*, 595. Even if a considerably smaller number of people died in workplace accidents around 1850 and the annual toll only gradually reached 35,000 by 1880, the total number of deaths in these three decades likely ran into the hundreds of thousands.
88. Walbert and Leloudis, "Textile Mill"; and Grob, *Deadly Truth*, 166–67.
89. Sellers, *Hazards of the Job*, 27.
90. See David Rosner and Gerald Markowitz, *Deadly Dust: Silicosis and the Politics of Occupational Disease in Twentieth-Century America* (Princeton: Princeton University Press, 1991).
91. Ibid.; and Sellers, *Hazards of the Job*, 16–17.
92. See Alan Derickson, *Black Lung: Anatomy of a Public Health Disaster* (Ithaca, NY: Cornell University Press, 1998).
93. Ibid., xii.
94. Anthony Robbins and Philip J. Landrigan, "Safer, Healthier Workers: Advances in Occupational Disease and Injury Prevention," in *Silent Victories: The History and Practice of Public Health in Twentieth-Century America*, ed. John W. Ward and Christian Warren (Oxford: Oxford University Press, 2007), 214.
95. Waller, *Health and Wellness*, 143; Sellers, *Hazards of the Job*, 15–16, 18–19, 22–26, 91–95; and George Rosen, "Urbanization, Occupation, and Disease in the United States, 1870–1920: The Case of New York City," *Journal of the History of Medicine and Allied Sciences* 43 (October 1988): 396–97.
96. Waller, *Health and Wellness*, 144; and Rosen, "Urbanization, Occupation, and Disease," 412–18, 422–24.

356 NOTES TO PAGES 106–107

97. Sellers, *Hazards of the Job*, 25.
98. Ibid., 18.
99. Steven Mintz and Sara McNeil, "The Great Railroad Strike," *Digital History*, http://www.digitalhistory.uh.edu/disp_textbook.cfm?smtID=2&psid=3189.
100. Kevin Kenny, "Ten Things to Understand About the Molly Maguires," *Oxford University Press Blog*, December 18, 2013, https://blog.oup.com/2013/12/ten-things-to-understand-about-the-molly-maguires/.
101. Boyer and Morais, *Labor's Untold Story*, 91–104; and Zinn, *People's History*, 269–72.
102. Alexander Trachtenberg, *The History of May Day* (New York: International Publishers, 1932).
103. Theresa Case, "Great Southwestern Strike," *Encyclopedia of Arkansas History and Culture* (2010), https://encyclopediaofarkansas.net/entries/great-southwestern-strike-4911/.
104. Foner, *Reconstruction*, 595.
105. Jeremy Brecher, *Strike!* (San Francisco: Straight Arrow Books, 1972), 58.
106. David Ray Papke, *The Pullman Case: The Clash of Labor and Capital in Industrial America* (Lawrence: University of Kansas Press, 1999), 35–37.
107. Witt, *Accidental Republic*, 2.
108. C. H. Mark, "Our Murderous Industrialism," *World Today* 12 (1907): 97, cited in Linder, "Fatal Subtraction," 102.
109. Nicolas A. Ashford and Charles C. Caldart, *Technology, Law, and the Working Environment*, rev. ed. (Washington, DC: Island Press, 1996), 8.
110. Carma Wadley, "The Scoville Disaster," *Deseret News*, April 27, 2000.
111. "Today in Labor History: The Johnstown Mine Disaster," *People's World*, July 10, 2012.
112. John B. Rehder, *Appalachian Folkways* (Baltimore: Johns Hopkins University Press, 2004), 185.
113. Tom Rea, "Thunder Under the House: One Family and the Hanna Mine Disasters," *WyoHistory.org*, Wyoming Historical Society, November 8, 2014, https://www.wyohistory.org/encyclopedia/thunder-under-house-one-family-and-hanna-mine-disasters.
114. "The Grover Shoe Factory Explosion Disaster Shakes the Nation in 1905," New England Historical Society, 2019, https://www.newenglandhistoricalsociety.com/grover-shoe-factory-disaster-shakes-nation-1905/.
115. Crystal Eastman, *Work Accidents and the Law* (New York: Russell Sage Foundation, 1910), 11.
116. Mine Safety and Health Administration, U.S. Department of Labor, "Mining Disasters 1839 to Present."

NOTES TO PAGES 107–108

117. Linda Hasco, "Here Are the Greatest Disasters in Pennsylvania History," (Harrisburg, Pennsylvania) *Patriot-News,* September 26, 2019.
118. Dana Bartholomew, "100 Years of Water: Los Angeles Aqueduct, William Mulholland Helped Create Modern LA," *Los Angeles Daily News,* August 28, 2017.
119. "Sixty-Seven Die by Fire and Water in Unprecedented Lake Disaster," *Chicago Examiner,* January 21, 1909, in "George W. Jackson Crib Fire," *Chicagology,* https://chicagology.com/notorious-chicago/jacksoncribfire/.
120. "This Week in Alabama History: May 3–May 9," Alabama Department of Archives and History, http://www.archives.alabama.gov/historythisweek/week19.html.
121. Clodfelter, *Warfare,* 397; Rosenow, *Death and Dying,* 38; and Loomis, *Out of Sight,* 2.
122. Nicole M. Christian, "A Landmark of the Unspeakable: Honoring the Site Where 146 Died in the Triangle Shirtwaist Fire," *New York Times,* March 26, 2003.
123. Adam Jones, "State's Larger Mining Accident Claimed 128 Men 100 Years ago," *Tuscaloosa News,* April 8, 2011.
124. Steve Lehto, "The Italian Hall Disaster: One More Reason to Observe a Silent Night This Christmas Eve," *Huffington Post,* January 23, 2014, https://www.huffpost.com/entry/the-italian-hall-disaster_b_1120771.
125. John Emeigh, "Looking Back at Butte's Most Deadly Mining Disaster," KPAX-TV, June 1, 2017, http://www.kpax.com/story/35568169/lookingback-at-buttes-most-deadly-mining-disaster.
126. Joe Ryan, "Looking Back: Explosions Shook Sayreville for Three Days," (Newark, New Jersey) *Star-Ledger,* October 4, 2007.
127. Alan Taylor, "On This Day: The Boston Molasses Disaster of 1919," *The Atlantic,* January 15, 2015, https://www.theatlantic.com/photo/2015/01/on-this-day-the-boston-molasses-disaster-in-1919/384573/.
128. Molly Larson Crook, "Miners Still Descend and Die in the Dark Heart of the Earth," *Seattle Times,* August 23, 2007; and "20 Killed, 100 Injured, 12 Missing in Nixon, NJ, Explosion Which Wrecks 40 Buildings and Is Felt 50 Miles Away," New York Times, March 2, 1924.
129. Efthimia K. Mihailidou, Konstantinos D. Antoniadis, and Marc J. Assael, "The 319 Major Industrial Accidents Since 1917," *International Review of Chemical Engineering* 4/6 (November 2012): 530–36.
130. Aldrich, *Death Rode the Rails,* 2, cited in Waller, *Health and Wellness,* 46.
131. Aldrich, *Safety First,* xvii.
132. Witt, *Accidental Republic,* 27.
133. Loomis, *Out of Sight,* 32; Jim Rasenberger, "Cowboys of the Sky," *New*

358 NOTES TO PAGES 108–109

York Times, January 28, 2001; and Alan Cornwell, "Chicago 1900: Pickled Hands and Much Worse," *Our Great American Heritage*, September 6, 2015, http://www.ourgreat americanheritage.com 2015/09/ disease-death-and-child-labor-the-birth-of-the-meatpacking-industry-in-chicago/.

134. I. M. Rubinow, *Social Insurance: With Special Reference to American Conditions* (New York: Henry Holt, 1913), 52, cited in Witt, *Accidental Republic*, 29.

135. Linder, "Fatal Subtraction," 103–5.

136. Arthur Reeve, "Our Industrial Juggernaut," *Everybody's Magazine* 16 (1907): 147, cited in Linder, "Fatal Subtraction," 103.

137. William H. Tolman, "Safety for American Life and Labor," *American Industries* 7/3 (March 15, 1908): 8–10. Tolman apparently counted all accidents, though his article focused on workplace accidents.

138. Waller, *Health and Wellness*, 144. These accidents involved at least one month of disability.

139. Ibid.; and Ellery Sedgwick, "The Land of Disasters, 1853–1904," *Leslie's Monthly Magazine* 59, January 1905: 350–51.

140. Witt, *Accidental Republic*, 38–39; Rosner and Markowitz, "Introduction" in *Dying for Work*; and Sellers, *Hazards of the Job*, chaps. 2 and 3.

141. Witt, *Accidental Republic*, 2–4.

142. American Public Health Association, "The Critical Need to Reform Workers Compensation," November 7, 2017, https://apha.org/policies-and-advocacy/public-health-policy-statements/ policy-database/2018/01/18/the-critical-need-to-reform-workers-compensation.

143. Elizabeth Nix, "7 Fascinating Facts about the Panama Canal," *History*, August 25, 2014, http://www.history.com/news/7-fascinating-facts-about-the-panama-canal. Nix noted that more than twenty thousand workers died during the previous phase of construction supervised by the French.

144. Louise Sherwood, "Brazil's Devil's Railway Gets New Lease of Life," BBC News, November 27, 2010, https://www.bbc.com/news/world-latin-america-11578463.

145. Tully, *Devil's Milk*, chaps. 4–6; Michael Edward Stanfield, *Red Rubber, Burning Trees: Violence, Slavery, and Empire in Northwest Amazonia, 1850–1933* (Albuquerque: University of New Mexico Press, 1998), chaps. 6–8; and Barbara Weinstein, *The Amazon Rubber Boom, 1850–1920* (Stanford, CA: Stanford University Press, 1983), 19–20. The estimate of thirty thousand deaths was made by contemporary investigator Roger Casement and is found in Tully, *Devil's Milk* 97; and in Stanfield, *Red Rubber*, 166. A Peruvian-British company was largely to blame for the ghastly loss of life, but the United States was complicit in the deaths.

NOTES TO PAGES 109–110 359

At least one U.S.-Peruvian company operated in the area, and much of the rubber produced there was shipped to the United States. U.S. officials initially refused to investigate reports of the mass deaths, though they subsequently had to do so.

146. Robert Wuliger, "America's Early Role in the Congo Tragedy," *The Nation*, October 10, 2017, https://www.thenation.com/article/archive/americas-early-role-congo-tragedy/; Georges Nzongola-Ntalaja, *The Congo from Leopold to Kabila: A People's History* (London: Zed Books, 2002), 32–33; Peter Duignan and L. H. Gann, *The United States and Africa: A History* (Cambridge: Cambridge University Press, 1984), 221–22; and Jerome Sternstein, "King Leopold II, Senator Nelson Aldrich, and the Strange Beginnings of American Economic Penetration of the Congo," *African Historical Studies* 2/2 (1969): 189–204.

147. On the genocide in King Leopold's Free State, see Nzongola-Ntalaja, *Congo*, 20–26; and Adam Hochschild, *King Leopold's Ghost: A Story of Greed, Terror, and Heroism in Colonial Africa* (Boston: Houghton Mifflin, 1999), 225–33.

148. Nzongola-Ntalaja, *Congo*, 26–54; and Marchal, *Lord Leverhulme's Ghosts*, 22, 35–37, 89, 92, 96, 126–27, 150–67, 186–87.

149. Duignan and Gann, *United States and Africa*, 222–24; "Partners in Apartheid: U.S. Policy on South Africa," *Africa Today* 11/3 (March 1964): 2–17; H. J. Simons, "Death in South African Mines," *Africa South* (1961): 41–55; and Kevin Danaher, *In Whose Interest? A Guide to U.S.-South Africa Relations* (Washington, DC: Institute for Policy Studies, 1985), 46–47.

150. Linder, "Fatal Subtraction," 106.

151. Ibid., 99, 100, 106; and Witt, *Accidental Republic*, 25.

152. Frederick L. Hoffman, "Industrial Accidents," *Bulletin of the United States Bureau of Labor* 17/78 (September 1908): 418, cited in Linder, "Fatal Subtraction," 107. Hoffman estimated that there were thirty to thirty-five thousand fatal accidents that year, and half of them occurred in workplaces.

153. Ashford and Caldart, *Technology, Law, and Working Environment*, 8.

154. Henry Rogers Seager, *Social Insurance: A Program of Social Reform* (New York: Macmillan, 1910), 15, 26.

155. National Safety Council, *Accident Facts 1998* (Itasca, IL: National Safety Council, 1998), in Centers for Disease Control and Prevention, *Morbidity and Mortality Weekly Report*, June 11, 1999, https://www.cdc.gov/mmwr/preview/mmwrhtml/mm4822a1.htm. See also Sellers, *Hazards of the Job*, 107.

156. E. H. Downey, *History of Work Indemnity in Iowa* (Iowa City: State Historical Society of Iowa, 1912), 2–5.

360 NOTES TO PAGES 110-111

157. Frederick L. Hoffman, *Bulletin of the U.S. Bureau of Labor Statistics: Industrial Accident Statistics* 157 (March 1915): 6, 17.
158. Carl M. Hansen, *Bulletin of the American Museum of Safety* (September 1914), cited in "Industrial Hygiene and Sanitation," *American Journal of Public Health* 4/ 12 (December 1914): 1251; and in David Rosner and Gerald Markowitz, "Labor Day and the War on Workers," *American Journal of Public Health* 89 (1999): 1320.
159. *Industrial Relations*, cited in Linder, "Fatal Subtractions," 107.
160. Carl Hookstadt, "Industrial Accidents and Hygiene," *Monthly Labor Review* 18/1 (January 1924): 142. Here "serious" accidents refer to those that produce disability for more than one week.
161. Downey, *Workmen's Compensation I* (1924), cited in Linder, "Fatal Subtractions," 100.
162. National Safety Council, *Accident Facts 1993*, 26–27, cited in Linder, "Fatal Subtractions," 114.
163. Rand School of Social Science, *American Labor Year Book 1929,* vol. 10 (New York: Rand School of Social Science, 1929), 85.
164. Grob, *Deadly Truth*, 165–67, 170–72; Levenstein, Plantamura, and Mass, "Labor and Byssinosis," 209–12; Arthur Reed Perry, United States Bureau of Labor, *Causes of Death Among Woman and Child Cotton-Mill Operatives* (Washington, DC: Government Printing Office, 1912); Rosner and Markowitz, *Deadly Dust*, chaps. 1–2; Derickson, *Black Lung*, xii, chaps. 2–4; and Sellers, *Hazards of the Job*, chap. 3.
165. See William Osler, "On the Study of Tuberculosis," *Philadelphia Medical Journal* (December 1, 1900), https://collections.nlm.nih.gov/ext/document/101743406X355/PDF/101 743406X355.pdf; and Emery R. Hayhurst, *Consumption and Preventable Deaths in American Occupations* (Columbus: F. J. Heer, 1913). See also George M. Price, *The Modern Factory: Safety, Sanitation, and Welfare* (New York: John Wiley and Sons, 1914), 439; and Susan Speaker, U.S. National Library of Medicine, "Revealing Data: Collecting Data about TB, Ca 1900," *Circulating Now*, January 31, 2018, https://circulatingnow.nlm.nih.gov/2018/01/31/collecting-data-about-tuberculosis-ca-1900/; and Levenstein, Plantamura, and Mass, "Labor and Byssinosis," 209.
166. David Kotelchuck, "Asbestos: 'The Funeral Dress of Kings'—and Others," in *Dying for Work*, 192–205; and Matt Mauney, "History of Asbestos," Mesothelioma Center, *Asbestos. com*, August 6, 2018, https://www.asbestos. com/ asbestos/history/.
167. Ashford and Caldart, *Technology, Law, and Working Environment*, 8.
168. Grob, *Deadly Truth*, 173.
169. Ibid., 172–73; and Josephine White Bates, *Mercury Poisoning in the In-*

NOTES TO PAGES 111-113   361

dustries of New York City and Vicinity (National Civic Federation, New York and New Jersey Section, 1912), chaps 1, 6, 7.

170. Grob, *Deadly Truth*, 175–76; and Bates, *Mercury Poisoning*, chaps. 1, 6, 7.

171. Price, *Modern Factory*, 440.

172. Angela Nugent, "The Power to Define a New Disease: Epidemiological Politics and Radium," in *Dying for Work*, 177–91; and Kate Moore, *The Radium Girls: The Dark Story of America's Shining Women* (Napierville, IL: Sourcebooks, 2017).

173. Ashford and Caldart, *Technology, Law, and Working Environment*, 8.

174. Grob, *Deadly Truth*, 178.

175. Price, *Modern Factory*, 439; and William G. Thompson, *The Occupational Diseases: Their Causation, Symptoms, Treatment, and Prevention* (New York: Appleton, 1914), 10–18.

176. Grob, *Deadly Truth*, 178–79; and U.S. Census Bureau, *Mortality Statistics 1910* (Washington, DC: Government Printing Office, 1913), 11.

177. Hayhurst, *Consumption and Preventable Deaths*, 10. The statistics examined by Hayhurst came from U.S. Census Bureau, *Mortality Statistics 1909* (Washington, DC: Government Printing Office, 1910).

178. Ibid., 3–7.

179. Between 1900 and 1930, the annual number of tuberculosis deaths declined from 150,000 to 81,000. However, the loss of life from other occupational diseases increased. See Osler, "Study of Tuberculosis," 2; and U.S. Census Bureau, *Mortality Statistics 1931* (Washington, DC: Government Printing Office, 1935), 25. On the increasing significance of other occupational diseases during this period, see Grob, *Deadly Truth,*" 165–67, 170–72; Levenstein, Plantamura, and Mass, "Labor and Byssinosis," 209–12; Perry, *Causes of Death*; Rosner and Markowitz, *Deadly Dust*, chaps. 1–2; Derickson, *Black Lung*, xii, chaps. 2–4; and Sellers, *Hazards of the Job*, chap. 3. The estimate of 100,000 annual deaths from occupational diseases in 1970 is found in *President's Report on Occupational Safety and Health*, 111.

180. This estimate assumes a roughly equal annual increase in the number of deaths between 1900 and 1930.

181. Boyer and Morais, *Labor's Untold Story*, 142.

182. David Witwer, "Unionized Teamsters and the Struggle over the Streets of the Early Twentieth-Century City," *Social Science History* 24/1 (Spring 2000): 183–222.

183. Adolfo Gilly, *The Mexican Revolution*, trans. Patrick Camiller (New York: New Press, 2005), 48–49.

184. Larry Rohter, "Cananea Journal; For Sale: Symbol of Nationalism; Inquire Within," *New York Times*, June 17, 1988.

185. Katie Dowd, "Today Marks 110 Years since SF's 'Bloody Tuesday,' One of America's Most Violent Streetcar Strikes," *SF Gate*, May 7, 2017, https://www.sfgate.com/bayarea/article/San-Francisco-Bloody-Tuesday-1907-streetcar-strike-11122082.php; and John N. Ingham, "A Strike in the Progressive Era: McKees Rocks, 1909," *Pennsylvania Magazine of History and Biography* 90/3 (July 1966): 366.

186. Christopher Waldrep, "Word and Deed: The Language of Lynching, 1820–1853," in *Lethal Imagination*, 228; and "Steel Strike of 1910," *Bethlehem Press*, September 12, 2012.

187. Edward M. Steel Jr., "Introduction," in *The Court-Martial of Mother Jones*, ed. Edward M. Steel Jr. (Lexington: University of Kentucky Press, 1995), 61.

188. Christopher Klein, "The Strike that Shook America," *History*, November 26, 2019, https://www.history.com/news/the-strike-that-shook-america.

189. Ben Mauk, "The Ludlow Massacre Still Matters," *The New Yorker*, April 18, 2014, https://www.newyorker.com/business/currency/the-ludlow-massacre-still-matters.

190. Clodfelter, *Warfare*, 397.

191. Ibid.

192. Goldstein, *Political Repression*, 95; and William M. Adler, *The Man Who Never Died: The Life, Times, and Legacy of Joe Hill, American Labor Icon* (New York: Bloomsbury, 2012).

193. Goldstein, *Political Repression*, 95–96; and "Symposium Commemorates 1916 East Youngstown Riots," *Business Journal*, February 15, 2016, https://businessjournaldaily.com/ symposium-commemorates-1916-east-youngstown-riots/.

194. Goldstein, *Political Repression*, 97–98; and Eric Stevick and Julie Muhlstein, "100 Years after Everett Massacre, We're Still Learning More," *Daily Herald*, November 3, 2016, https:// www.heraldnet.com / news/100-years-after-the-everett-massacre-were-still-learning-more/.

195. Rory Carroll, "The Mysterious Lynching of Frank Little: Activist Who Fought Inequality and Lost," *Guardian*, September 21, 2016.

196. "1919 Trolley Strike," Charlotte-Mecklenburg Story, Charlotte Mecklenburg Library, https://www.cmstory.org/exhibits/history-timeline-roaring-twenties-1919-1928/1919-trolley-strike; and Stephen H. Norwood, "Bogalusa Burning: The War Against Biracial Unionism in the Deep South, 1919," *Journal of Southern History* 63/3 (August 1997): 591–628.

197. Weber, "Arkansas Sharecropper Massacre."

198. Boyer and Morais, *Labor's Untold Story*, 205.

199. Brecher, *Strike!*, 111.

NOTES TO PAGE 114   363

200. Ronald L. Lewis, *Black Coal Miners in America: Race, Class, and Community Conflict, 1780–1980* (Lexington: University Press of Kentucky, 1987), 61; Ed Quillen, "Denver's Bloody Transit Strike," *Denver Post*, April 6, 2006; and Howard Kimeldorf, *Battling for American Labor: Wobblies, Craft Workers, and the Making of the Union Movement* (Berkeley: University of California Press, 1999), 60.

201. Brecher, *Strike!*, 136–38; Jerry White, *Death on the Picket Line: The Story of John McCoy* (Detroit: Labor Publications, 1990), 6; and Robert Shogan, *The Battle of Blair Mountain: The Story of America's Largest Labor Uprising* (Boulder, CO: Westview Press, 2004), 25, 117, 128–29, 131–32, 158–59, 208–9.

202. Alan Scher Zagier, Associated Press, "Illinois Town Honors Coal Miners Killed in 1922 Massacre," AP News, June 20, 2015, https://apnews.com/7054a0246e48419d8d605312928f2552.

203. Tiffany Hill, "A Massacre Forgotten," *Honolulu Magazine*, January 2010, http://www.honolulumagazine.com/ core/pagetools.php?pageid =7078&url=/Honolulu-Magazine/January-2010/A-Massacre-Forgotten /&mode=print.

204. Editors, "Columbine Mine Massacre," *Colorado Encyclopedia*, November 21, 2021, https://coloradoencyclopedia.org/article/columbine-mine-massacre-0.

205. Peter Chapman, *Bananas: How the United Fruit Company Changed the World* (Edinburgh: Canongate, 2007), 91; and Jorge Enrique Elías Caro and Antonino Vidal Ortega, "La Masacre de 1928 en la Zona Bananera—Magdalena, Colombia: Una Historia Sin Terminar," *Memorias: Revista Digital de Historia y Arqueología Desde El Caribe Colombiano* 9/18, Barranquilla (December 2012), http://www.scielo.org.co/pdf/ memor/n18/n18a03.pdf.

206. Goldstein, *Political Repression*, 205–6.

207. Ibid., 205.

208. Cal Winslow, "The Strike That Shook San Francisco and Rocked the Pacific Coast," *CounterPunch*, July 2, 2014, https://www.counterpunch.org/2014/07/02/the-strike-that-shook-san-ancisco-and-rocked-the-pacific-coast/.

209. Brecher, *Strike!*, 161, 173; Ehsan Alam, "Minneapolis Teamsters' Strike, 1934," *MNopedia*, Minnesota Historical Society, https://www.mnopedia.org/event/minneapolis-teamsters-strike-1934, February 6, 2019.

210. Steven Beda, "Timber Strike of 1935," The Great Depression in Washington State Project, University of Washington, https://depts.washington.edu/depress/timber_strike_intro.shtml.

211. Sidney Lens, *The Labor Wars* (Garden City, NY: Doubleday, 1974), 318, cited in Goldstein, *Political Repression*, 218.

212. Ahmed White, *The Last Great Strike: Little Steel, the CIO, and the Struggle for Labor Rights in New Deal America* (Berkeley: University of California Press, 2016), 2–4, 136; and John Wojcik, "Today in Labor History: The 1937 'Women's Massacre,'" *People's World*, June 19, 2013, https://peoplesworld.org/article/today-in-labor-history-the-1937-women-s-day-massacre/.

213. Josh Barbanel, "Joseph Curran, 75, Founder of National Maritime Union," *New York Times*, August 15, 1981.

214. Three coal miners were killed during a strike in southeastern Kentucky in 1959. One coal miner was shot to death during a strike in Harlan County, Kentucky in 1974. Another coal miner was murdered while picketing a non-union mine near Welch, West Virginia, in 1990. See White, *Last Great Strike*; F. Ray Marshall, *Labor in the South* (Cambridge, MA: Harvard University Press, 1967), 286; and "13-Month Strike Is Ended by Kentucky Mine Accord," *New York Times*, August 30, 1974.

215. Girard C. Steichen, "W. Va. Tunnel Spawned 'Town of Living Dead': Victims of Depression-Era Tragedy Win Recognition—But No Justice," *Los Angeles Times*, October 5, 1986. An admittedly conservative estimate of more than seven hundred deaths is found in Martin Cherniak, *The Hawk's Nest Incident: America's Worst Industrial Disaster* (New Haven: Yale University Press, 1986), 73, cited in Rosner and Markowitz, *Deadly Dust*, 98. An estimate of as many as two thousand deaths is advanced in Sandy Smith, "The Hawk's Nest Tunnel Tragedy: The Forgotten Victims of America's Worst Industrial Disaster," May 20, 2014, *EHS Today*, https://www.ehstoday.com/industrial-hygiene/media-gallery/21917466/the-hawks-nest-tunnel-tragedy-the-forgotten-victims-of-americas-worst-industrial-disaster-photo-gallery.

216. Henry Brean, "Father and Son Died on Same Day, 14 Years Apart While Working on Hoover Dam," *Las Vegas Review-Journal*, March 5, 2018.

217. Daniel Person, "Forgotten Sacrifices: Grand Coulee Dam Memorial Found in Colville," *Spokesman-Review*, May 25, 2014.

218. "Ten Die in Utah Blast," *Salt Lake Telegram*, March 7, 1935.

219. "The Ten Most Tragic Workplace Accidents in U.S. History," *Code Red Safety*, January 27, 2015, https://coderedsafety.com/blog/10-most-tragic-workplace-accidents/.

220. Cecilia Dolgan, "60 Years Ago Today, East Ohio Gas Fire Brought… Death, Destruction," (Willoughby, Ohio) *News-Herald*, October 20, 2004.

221. Tully, *Devil's Milk*, 83–84.

222. Mine Safety and Health Administration, U.S. Department of Labor, "Coal Fatalities for 1900 through 2019," https://arlweb.msha.gov/stats/centurystats/coalstats.asp.

NOTES TO PAGES 115–116 365

223. Tom Zoellner, "In Congo, Silence Surrounds Forgotten Mine That Fueled First Atomic Bombs," *Al Jazeera America*, July 23, 2015, http://america.aljazeera.com/articles/2015/7/23/in-congo-silence-surrounds-forgotten-mine-that-fueled-first-atomic-bombs.html.

224. Hastings, "Uranium Mining Leaves a Bitter Scar on Navajo Nation"; Daniels, "U.S. Nuclear Weapons Program Left 'A Horrible Legacy'"; and National Institute for Occupational Safety and Health, Centers for Disease Control and Prevention, "Research on Long-Term Exposure: Uranium Miners," 2000, https://www.cdc.gov/niosh/pgms/worknotify/uranium.html#Study% 20of%20Uranium%20.

225. Rob Hotakainen, Lindsay Wise, Frank Matt, and Samantha Ehlinger, "Irradiated: The Secret, Tragic Legacy of America's Nuclear Weapons Program," February 4, 2016, https://www.mcclatchydc.com/news/nation-world/national/article49186995.html; and Lawrence Wittner, "American Casualties of the U.S. Nuclear Weapons Program," *Huffington Post*, June 3, 2017, https://www.huffpost.com/entry/american-casualties-of-th_b_8908530.

226. Hugh W. Stephens, *The Texas City Disaster, 1947* (Austin: University of Texas Press, 1997), 100–101.

227. Ibid., xi.

228. Tim O'Neil, "March 25, 1947: 'Dear Wife. Goodbye.' 111 Die in Central Illinois Mine Disaster," *St. Louis Post-Dispatch*, March 25, 2017.

229. Clayton Ruminksi, "The South Amboy, New Jersey, Port Explosion of 1950," Hagley Museum and Library, October 23, 2017, https://www.hagley.org/librarynews/south-amboy-new-jersey-port-explosion-1950.

230. Jacqueline Corn, "Protective Legislation for Coal Miners, 1870–1900: Response to Safety and Health Hazards," in *Dying for Work*, 82n20.

231. Anton Riecher, "Sunray 1956," *Industrial Fire World* 21/6 (2016), https://web.archive.org/web/20100504162441/http://www.fireworld.com/ifw_articles/sunray.php.

232. Lauren Berger, "Death Underground: The Knox Mine Disaster," Pennsylvania Center for the Book, Pennsylvania State University, Fall 2009, https://www.pabook.libraries.psu.edu/literary-cultural-heritage-mappa/feature-articles/death-underground-knox-mine-disaster; and Associated Press, "List of Major Industrial Accidents along Texas Coast with PM Plant-Explosion," July 6, 1990, https://apnews.com/7d4c790380aa0972a2343691c32c9c67.

233. Hank Hayes, "Eastman Safety Expert Details 1960 Explosion," (Kingsport, Tennessee) *Times News*, August 31, 2015.

234. Jeannie Roberts, "Survivor Recalls 1965 Titan II Missile Silo Fire That Killed 53," *Arkansas Democrat-Gazette*, August 16, 2015.

366 NOTES TO PAGES 116–117

235. Douglas Fritz, "Farmington Mine Disaster Remembered," WVNS-TV, November 20, 2019, https://www.wvnstv.com/news/farmington-mine-disaster-remembered/.
236. Occupational Safety and Health Administration, U.S. Department of Labor, "About OSHA," https://www.osha.gov/aboutosha.
237. Linder, "Fatal Subtraction," 99–100, 117–23; and U.S. Bureau of Labor Statistics, "Survey of Occupational Injuries and Illnesses: History," July 16, 2018, https://www.bls.gov/opub/hom/ soii/history.htm.
238. National Safety Council, *Accident Facts 1993*, 26–27, cited in Linder, "Fatal Subtraction," 114; and *The President's Report*, 1, 111.
239. *The President's Report*, 111. Some analysts estimated the annual loss of life from occupational diseases to be much higher. See, for example, Les Boden's calculations for an unnamed panel for the National Institute of Health, ca. 1975, in Peter S. Barth with H. Allan Hunt, *Workers' Compensation and Work-Related Illnesses and Diseases* (Cambridge, MA: MIT Press, 1980), 17–18, 372n19.
240. National Safety Council, *Accident Facts* 1993, 26–27, cited in Linder, "Fatal Subtraction," 114. On problems with NSC statistics, see Linder, "Fatal Subtraction," 110–15.
241. This estimate assumes a roughly equal annual increase in the number of deaths between 1930 and 1970.
242. David Rosner, "When Does a Worker's Death Become Murder?," *American Journal of Public Health* 90/4 (April 2000): 538.
243. Ian Urbina, "No Survivors Found After West Virginia Mine Disaster," *New York Times*, April 9, 2010.
244. Albert Scardino, "A Tragedy in South Georgia," *New York Times*, July 20, 1986.
245. Vicki Smith, "DEP Orders Stability Test on Coal Slurry Dam," *Times West Virginian*, July 2, 2011.
246. Cory Carpenter, "The Sunshine Mine Disaster: Idaho's Worst Mining Disaster," *Spokane Historical*, https://spokanehistorical.org/items/show/461.
247. Kimberly Hegeman, "Looking Back at the World's Deadliest Construction Projects," *ForConstructionPros.Com*, August 27, 2015, https://www.forconstructionpros.com/blogs/ construction-toolbox/blog/12096401/looking-back-on-the-worlds-deadliest-construction-projects.
248. Pongphon Sarnasmak, "More Teenaged Girls Getting HIV Infection," *The Nation* (Thailand), November 25, 2008, https://web.archive.org/web/20141126122625/http://nationmultimedia.com/2008/11/25/national/national_30089295.php; Elizabeth Rho-Ng, "The Conscription of Asian Sex Slaves: Causes and Effects of U.S. Military Sex Colonialism in Thailand and the Call to Expand U.S. Asylum Law," *Asian American*

NOTES TO PAGES 117–118 367

Law Journal 7, article 4 (January 2000), https:// scholarship.law.berkeley.edu/cgi/viewcontent.cgi?article=1063& context=aalj; and James Petras and Tienchai Wongchaisuwan, "Free Markets, AIDS, and Child Prostitution," *Economic and Political Weekly* 28/11 (March 13, 1993): 440–42. https://www.jstor.org/stable/4399484 https://www.jstor.org/stable/4399484 https://www.jstor.org/stable/4399484.

249. "Fatal Industrial Accidents in Texas," *San Antonio Express-News*, April 18, 2013.

250. Ibid.

251. Iver Peterson, "51 Killed in Collapse of Scaffold at Power Plant in West Virginia," *New York Times*, April 28, 1978.

252. Dan George, "20 Indicted on Fireworks Charges," AP News, August 28, 1985, https://apnews.com/2ba7a215402728466a6803769e164ccb.

253. Charles Mount, "$29 Million Settlement in Refinery Blast," *Chicago Tribune*, March 2, 1989.

254. Loomis, *Out of Sight*, 83–84.

255. Apoorva Mandavilli, "The World's Worst Industrial Accident Is Still Unfolding," *The Atlantic*, July 10, 2018, https://www.theatlantic.com/science/archive/2018/07/the-worlds-worst-industrial-disaster-is-still-unfolding/560726/.

256. Caitlin Lilly, "5 Things to Know about the PEPCON Disaster, 28 Years Later," *Las Vegas Review-Journal*, May 4, 2016.

257. Terry Macalister, "Piper Alpha Disaster: How 167 Oil Rig Workers Died," *Guardian*, July 4, 2013; and Associated Press, "Judge Approves $172 Million Settlement in Refinery Blast," AP News, October 20, 1993, https://apnews.com/9946b0097f5ba880a423469c19f730fd.

258. J. Michael Kennedy, "Phillips Will Pay Record Fine After Refinery Blast," *Los Angeles Times*, August 23, 1991; and Associated Press, "USS *Iowa* Returns to Port," *New York Times*, December 8, 1989.

259. National Safety Council, *Accident Facts 1993*, 26–27, cited in Linder, "Fatal Subtraction," 114.

260. Ibid. Again, on problems with NSC statistics, see Linder, "Fatal Subtraction," 110-15.

261. Philip J. Landrigan and Steven Markowitz, "Current Magnitude of Occupational Disease in the United States: Estimates from New York State," *Annals of the New York Academy of Sciences* 572/1 (December 1989): 43; and J. Paul Leigh, Steven B. Markowitz, Marianne Fahs, Chinggak Shin, and Philip J. Landrigan, "Occupational Injury and Illness in the United States: Estimates of Costs, Morbidity, and Mortality," *Archives of Internal Medicine* 157/14 (July 28, 1997): 1564.

262. *Oversight on Occupational Disease Risk Assessment: Hearing Before the Subcomm. on Health and Safety and the Subcomm. on Labor Standards*

368   NOTES TO PAGE 119

of the Committee on Education and Labor, 99th Congress, 21 (July 17, 1985), (Testimony of Milan Stone, Vice President, Industrial Union Department, AFL-CIO); and *Occupational Illness and Injuries: Hearing Before the Human Resources and Intergovernmental Relations Subcomm.on Human Resources and Intergovernmental Relations, 101st Congress,* 1 (April 17, 1989), (Statement of Hon. Ted Weiss, Chairman of the Subcomm.).

263. Testimony of Milan Stone, 20–21.

264. This estimate probably does not include all deaths caused by workplace carcinogens and work-related stress. On the magnitude of work-related cancer, see Kurt Straif, "The Burden of Occupational Cancer," *Occupational and Environmental Medicine* 65/12 (December 2008): 787–88; and Mark P. Purdue, Sally J. Hutchings, Lesley Rushton, and Debra T. Silverman, "The Proportion of Cancer Attributable to Occupational Exposures," *Annals of Epidemiology* 25/3 (March 2015): 188–92. On the lethal impact of work-related stress, see Jeffrey Pfeffer, *Dying for a Paycheck: How Modern Management Harms Employee Health and Company Performance—and What We Can Do About It* (New York: HarperCollins, 2018), chaps. 1–2. Pfeffer has estimated that work-related stress contributed to almost sixty thousand preventable deaths each year. See also Joel Goh, Jeffrey Pfeffer, and Stefanos A. Zenios, "Workplace Stressors and Health Outcomes: Health Policy for the Workplace," *Behavioral Science and Policy* 1/1 (Spring 1995): 43–52; and Michael Kahn, "Work-Related Stress Can Kill, Study Finds," Reuters, January 22, 2008, https://www.reuters.com/article/us-heart-stress/work-related-stress-can-kill-study-finds-idUSL228 4632220080123.

265. Roberto Suro, "Explosion Kills 17 at Petrochemical Plant in Texas," *New York Times,* July 7, 1990.

266. Bryant Simon, *The Hamlet Fire: A Story of Cheap Food, Cheap Government, and Cheap Lives* (New York: New Press, 2017).

267. Associated Press, "Death Toll Reaches 8 in Louisiana Blast," *Los Angeles Times,* May 3, 1991.

268. Loomis, *Out of Sight,* 76.

269. Associated Press, "Kansas Grain Elevator Blast Likely Killed 6," CBS News, October 31, 2011, https://www.cbsnews.com/news/kansas-grain-elevator-blast-likely-killed-6/.

270. "Ford Settlement," Michigan Bureau of Safety and Regulation, *MIOSHA News* 3/3 (Fall 1999): 1, 17–18.

271. Terry Macalister, "BP Admits Blame for Texas Oil Disaster," *Guardian,* May 17, 2005.

272. Editorial, "The Sago Mine Disaster," *New York Times,* January 5, 2006;

NOTES TO PAGES 119-120

and Dave Wischnowsky, "Explosion at Milwaukee Plant Leaves 3 Dead and 46 Injured," *Los Angeles Times*, December 7, 2006.

273. Samira Jafari, "Five Killed in Mine Explosion," *Boston Globe*, May 21, 2006.

274. Carter Williams, "Looking Back at the Crandall Canyon Mine Collapse Ten Years Later," KSL-TV, August 6, 2017, https://www.ksl.com/?sid=45302392&nid=148.

275. Russ Bynum, "Burned Georgia Plant Worker Dies 6 Months After Explosion," *St. Augustine Record*, August 24, 2008; and Barbara Ross, "Construction Workers' Families Reach Settlement in Fatal 2008 Crane Accident in Manhattan," New York *Daily News*, January 20, 2012.

276. Jim Morris, "Death in the Oilfields," Center for Public Integrity, December 21, 2018, https://apps.public integrity.org/blowout/us-oil-worker-safety/.

277. Robert D. McFadden, "5 Dead, Dozens Injured in Connecticut Power Plant Blast," *New York Times*, February 7, 2010; and Ian Urbina, "No Survivors Found after West Virginia Mine Disaster," *New York Times*, April 9, 2010.

278. James Osborne, "10 Years after: The Tragedy of Deepwater Horizon," *Houston Chronicle*, April 16, 2020.

279. Joe Sutton, "Six Dead from Weekend Grain Elevator Explosion in Kansas," CNN, October 31, 2011, https://www.cnn.com/2011/10/31/us/kansas-grain-explosion/index.html.

280. Fernando Ramirez, "A Look Back at the Explosion Five Years Ago That Rocked a Small Texas Town," *Houston Chronicle*, April 22, 2018.

281. Loomis, *Out of Sight*, 8–22, 70–81.

282. Saad Hamadi and Matthew Taylor, "Workers Jump to Their Deaths as Fire Engulfs Factory Making Clothes for Gap," *Guardian*, December 14, 2010.

283. Pfeffer, *Dying for a Paycheck*, 9.

284. Vikas Bajaj, "Fatal Fire in Bangladesh Highlights the Dangers Facing Garment Workers," *New York Times*, November 25, 2012; and Zia ur-Rehman, Daclan Walsh, and Salman Masood, "More Than 300 Killed in Pakistani Factory Fires," *New York Times*, September 12, 2012.

285. Gillian B. White, "What's Changed Since More Than 1110 People Died in Bangladesh's Factory Collapse?," *Guardian*, May 3, 2017.

286. Loomis, *Out of Sight*, 126.

287. Amnesty International and AfreWatch (African Resources Watch), *"This Is What We Die For": Human Rights Abuses in the Democratic Republic of the Congo, The Global Trade in Cobalt* (London: Amnesty International, 2016), https://www.amnesty.org/download/ Documents/AFR6231832016ENG-LISH.PDF; CBS News, "The Toll of the Cobalt Mining Industry on Health

370 NOTES TO PAGES 120-121

and the Environment," March 6, 2018, https://www.cbsnews.com/news/the-toll-of-the-cobalt-mining-industry-congo/; and Annie Kelly, "Apple and Google Named in U.S. Lawsuit over Congolese Child Cobalt Mining Deaths," *Guardian*, December 16, 2019.

288. AFL-CIO, *Death on the Job*, 1, 5.

289. Bureau of Labor Statistics, U.S. Department of Labor, "News Release: National Census of Fatal Occupational Injuries in 2018," December 17, 2019, https://www.bls.gov/news.release/ pdf/cfoi.pdf; and "News Release: National Census of Fatal Occupational Injuries in 2017," December 18, 2018, https://www.bls.gov/news.release/archives/cfoi_12182018.pdf; Henry Reeve, Shane Stephens, Stephen Pegula, and Ryan Farrell, Bureau of Labor Statistics, U.S. Department of Labor, "25 Years of Worker Injury, Illness, and Fatality Data," March 2019, https://www.bls.gov/spotlight/2019/25-years-of-worker-injury-illness-and-fatality-case-data/ home.htm; National Safety Council, *Accident Facts 1993*, 26–27, cited in Linder, "Fatal Subtraction," 114. Estimates for 1990 and 1991 are from National Safety Council, *Accident Facts 1993*, 26–27, cited in Linder, "Fatal Subtraction," 114. Estimates for the remaining years are from the Bureau of Labor Statistics.

290. AFL-CIO, *Death on the Job*, 2, 9.

291. Robin Herbert and Philip Landrigan, "Work-Related Death: A Continuing Epidemic," *American Journal of Public Health* 90/4 (April 2000): 541–45; and J. Paul Leigh, Steven Markowitz, Marianne Fahs, and Philip Landrigan, *Costs of Occupational Injuries and Illnesses* (Ann Arbor: University of Michigan Press, 2000), 1–2, 6.

292. See, for example, AFL-CIO, *Death on the Job: The Toll of Neglect*, 26th ed. (April 2017), 1, 5.

293. An estimate of 95,000 annual deaths from occupational diseases in the United States is found in Jukka Takala, Päivi Hämäläinen, Kaija Leena Saarela, Loke Yoke Yun, Kathiresan Manickam, Tan Wee Jin, Peggy Heng, Caleb Tjong, Lim Guan Kheng, Samuel Lim, and Gan Siok Lin, "Global Estimates of the Burden of Injury and Illness at Work in 2012," *Journal of Occupational and Environmental Hygiene* 11/5 (2014): 326–37, Table 3. See also Carel B. Germain and Martin Bloom, *Human Behavior in the Social Environment: An Ecological View*, 2nd ed. (New York: Columbia University Press, 1999), 120–21.

294. AFL-CIO, *Death on the Job*, 30th ed., 1, 5, 7. These annual reports cite the findings in Takala et al., "Global Estimates." See also Straif, "Burden of Occupational Cancer," 787–88; Purdue et al., "Occupational Exposures," 188–192; Pfeffer, *Dying for a Paycheck*, chaps 1–2; Goh, Pfeffer, and Zenios, "Workplace Stressors and Health Outcomes," 43–52; and Kahn, "Work-Related Stress Can Kill."

NOTES TO PAGES 121–123 371

295. This estimate includes approximately 2.7 million fatal occupational injuries and approximately 10 million deaths resulting from occupational diseases.

4. From Colonial Wars to Global Holocausts

1. Atwood, *War and Empire: The American Way of Life*, (London: Pluto Press, 2010), 60–65; Lens, *Forging the American Empire* (Chicago: Haymarket Books, 2003), 17, 22–27, 35–39, and chap. 4; Hickey, *War of 1812: A Forgotten Conflict*, Bicentennial Edition (Urbana: University of Illinois Press, 2012); and Frank Lambert, *The Barbary Wars: American Independence in the Atlantic World* (New York: Hill and Wang, 2005).

2. Lens, *Forging the American Empire*, chaps. 5–7; William Earl Weeks, *Building the Continental Empire: American Expansion from the Revolution to the Civil War* (Chicago: Ivan Dee, 1996), chaps. 2–5; and Lloyd C. Gardner, Walter LaFeber, and Thomas J. McCormick, *Creation of the American Empire*, vol. 1: *U.S. Diplomatic History to 1901*, 2nd ed. (Chicago: Rand McNally, 1973), chaps. 5, 9.

3. Lens, *Forging the American Empire*, 155–157; Weeks, *Continental Empire*, 72–73, 78–79; and Gardner, LaFeber, and McCormick, *Creation of the American Empire*, 128–32, 167–69.

4. LaFeber, *New Empire*; Lens, *Forging the American Empire*, chap. 9; Atwood, *War and Empire*, chap. 5; Lars Schoultz, *Beneath the United States: A History of U.S. Policy Toward Latin America* (Cambridge: Harvard University Press, 1998), 99–105; and Barbara Salazar Torreon and Sofia Plagakis, Congressional Research Service, *Instances of Use of United States Armed Forces Abroad, 1798–2021*, CRS Report, September 8, 2021, 5–7, https://sgp.fas.org/ crs/natsec/R42738.pdf.

5. On the War of 1898 and the War against the Philippines, see Zinn, A *People's History of the United States: 1492–Present*, 20th anniv. ed. (New York: HarperCollins, 1999), chap. 12; Lens, *Forging the American Empire*, chap. 10; Atwood, *War and Empire*, chap. 6; and Luzvimenda Francisco, "The First Vietnam: The U.S.-Philippine War of 1899," *Bulletin of Concerned Asian Scholars* 5/4 (1973), https://doi.org/10.1080/1467271 5.1973.10406345. On the U.S. role in defeating the Boxer Rebellion in China, see Michael Parenti, *Against Empire* (San Francisco: City Lights Books, 1995), 38; V. G. Kiernan, *America: The New Imperialism, From White Settlement to World Hegemony* (London: Verso, 2005), 114, 151; and David J. Silbey, *The Boxer Rebellion and the Great Game in China* (New York: Hill and Wang, 2012). On the U.S. role in the creation of Panama, see Zinn, *People's History of the United States*; Lens, *Forging the American Empire*, 201–203; Schoultz, *Beneath the United States*, 175; and John Lindsay-Poland, *Emperors in the Jungle: The Hidden History*

372   NOTES TO PAGE 123

of the U.S. in Panama (Durham: Duke University Press, 2003), 25–27, 45. On U.S. intervention in the Mexican Revolution, see Lens, *Forging the American Empire*, 229–34; James D. Cockcroft, *Mexico's Hope: An Encounter with Politics and History* (New York: Monthly Review Press, 1998), 98–99, 101–7; and Dan La Botz, "¡Viva la Revolución!" *Against the Current*, no. 147 (July–August 2010), https://solidarity-us.org/atc/147/p2938/. On the U.S. occupation of Nicaragua, Haiti, and the Dominican Republic, see Lens, *Forging the American Empire*, 212–15, 222–27; Schoultz, *Beneath the United States*, chap. 12; Oliver Stone and Peter Kuznick, *The Untold History of the United States* (New York: Gallery Books, 2012), xxx–xxxiii; and Alan McPherson, *The Invaded: How Latin Americans and Their Allies Fought and Ended U.S. Occupations* (New York: Oxford University Press, 2014).

6. This description of the First World War is found in Seumas Milne, "First World War: An Imperial Bloodbath That's a Warning, Not a Noble Cause," *Guardian*, January 8, 2014. See also Zinn, *People's History*, chap. 14; Lens, *Forging the American Empire*, chap. 13; Atwood, *War and Empire*, chap. 7; and Jacques R. Pauwels, *The Great Class War, 1914–1918* (Toronto: James Lorimer, 2016), chap. 25.

7. On U.S. participation in the invasion of Soviet Russia, see Zinn, *People's History*, 408–9; Michael Parenti, *The Sword and the Dollar* (New York: St. Martin's Press, 2011), 136–40; Michael Sayers and Albert E. Kahn, *The Great Conspiracy: The Secret War Against Soviet Russia* (San Francisco: Proletarian Publishers, 1946), chaps. 6 and 7; and David S. Fogelsong, *America's Secret War Against Bolshevism: U.S. Intervention in the Russian Civil War, 1917–1920* (Chapel Hill: University of North Carolina Press, 1995). On U.S. support for the Guomindang regime in China, see Edgar Snow, *Red Star Over China* (New York: Bantam Books, 1978), 385–86; James Bradley, *The China Mirage: The Hidden History of American Disaster in Asia* (New York: Little, Brown, 2015), 109–10, 127–30, 156–57, 163–64; and Warren I. Cohen, *America's Response to China: A History of Sino-American Relations*, 5th ed. (New York: Columbia University Press, 2010), 110–12.

8. Atwood, *War and Empire*, chap. 8; David F. Schmitz, *Thank God They're on Our Side: The United States and Right-Wing Dictatorships, 1921–1965* (Chapel Hill: University of North Carolina Press, 1999), 30–45; Jacques R. Pauwels, *The Myth of the Good War: America in the Second World War*, 2nd ed. (Toronto: James Lorimer, 2015), chaps. 2–4; Charles Higham, *Trading with the Enemy: The Nazi-American Money Plot 1933–1949* (New York: Barnes and Noble Books, 1995); Edwin Black, *Nazi Nexus: America's Corporate Connections to Hitler's Holocaust* (Danvers: Dialog Press, 2009); Bradley W. Hart, *Hitler's Ameri-*

NOTES TO PAGES 123–125 373

can Friends: The Third Reich's Supporters in the United States (New York: Thomas Dunne Books, 2018), chap. 5; and Richard J. Smethurst, "Japan, the United States, and the Road to World War II in the Pacific," *The Asia-Pacific Journal 10/37* (September 10, 2012), http://apjjf.org/2012/10/ 37/Richard-J.-Smethurst/3825/article.html.

9. Peckham, *Colonial Wars*, 53; Ostler, *Surviving Genocide*, 22; and Clodfelter, *Warfare*, 68–69.

10. Clodfelter, *Warfare*, 125.

11. Ibid., 124–25; and Peckham, *Colonial Wars*, 74–75.

12. Clodfelter, *Warfare*, 125; Boyd, Smith, and Griffin, *Here They Once Stood*, 13; and Jennings, *Founders of America*, 269–70.

13. Louis P. Towles, "Jenkins' Ear, War of," *Encyclopedia of North Carolina*, NCPedia, January 1, 2006, https://www.ncpedia.org/jenkins-ear-war.

14. Clodfelter, *Warfare*, 79; and William Neuman, "A Hammer Comes Down in Colombia on an Honor for Britain," *New York Times*, November 19, 2014.

15. In addition to the 8,500 deaths of British and colonial troops at Cartagena, there were more than 1,600 other deaths among British colonists, approximately 2,850 deaths of French sailors and soldiers, and approximately 1,200 Spanish deaths. See Clodfelter, *Warfare*, 79, 81; Neuman, "A Hammer Comes Down"; and Peckham, *Colonial Wars*, 110–11, 117.

16. Clodfelter, *Warfare*, 130; and Ostler, *Surviving Genocide*, 28–35.

17. Approximately 13,400 British soldiers died in North America, and more than 6,700 British and colonial troops died during the siege of Havana. Thousands of British colonists died in battles and massacres on the frontier. The number of deaths of French and French colonial troops who perished is unknown but was likely in the low thousands. About ten thousand French colonists died when the British expelled them from Acadia. Spain lost 3,800 men during the siege of Havana alone. The number of Native people who perished in the French and Indian War, including the Anglo-Cherokee War, likely exceeded three thousand. See Clodfelter, *Warfare*, 89, 129–30; Kessel and Wooster, *Native American Wars*, 139; Ostler, *Surviving Genocide*, 31–35; and Fred Anderson, *Crucible of War: The Seven Years' War and the Fate of Empire in British North America, 1754–1766* (New York: Vintage Books, 2000), 637, and *The War That Made America: A Short History of the French and Indian War* (New York: Penguin Books, 2006), 223.

18. Zinn, *People's History*, chaps. 4 and 5; Atwood, *War and Empire*, 49–52; Ostler, *Surviving Genocide*, 44–51; and Gerald Horne, *The Counter-Revolution of 1776: Slave Resistance and the Origins of the United States of America* (New York: New York University Press, 2014), chaps 9 and 10.

374 NOTES TO PAGES 125–126

19. Zinn, *People's History*, 59–60, 74, 77; Atwood, *War and Empire*, 50–52.

20. On the continuing settlement of Indigenous peoples' lands west of the line drawn by the Proclamation of 1763, see Atwood, *War and Empire*, 49–50; and Ostler, *Surviving Genocide*, 44–51. On the egalitarian and democratic aspirations of some common people who supported independence, see Raphael, *People's History of the American Revolution*.

21. Zinn, *People's History*, 77; and John Adams, Letter to James Lloyd, January 1815, in *The Works of John Adams, Second President of the United States*, vol. 10, ed. Charles Francis Adams (Boston: Little, Brown, 1856), 108–14, cited in Edward Larkin, "Loyalism," in *Handbook of the American Revolution*, 292.

22. Calloway, "Indians and the American Revolution."

23. Raphael, *People's History of the American Revolution*, 330–31, 482n220; and Nash, "African Americans' Revolution," 254, 260–61, 268–69n20.

24. Edmund S. Morgan, *The Birth of the Republic, 1763–1789*, rev. ed. (Chicago: University of Chicago Press, 1977), 82–83.

25. Clodfelter, *Warfare*, 132–44; and Alice George, "The American Revolution Was Just One Battlefront in a Huge World War," *Smithsonian Magazine*, June 28, 2018, https://www.smithson ianmag.com/smithsonian-institution/American-revolution-was-just-one-battlefront-huge-world-war-180969444/.

26. Zinn, *People's History*, 77, 80; Clodfelter, *Warfare*, 132; Morgan, *Birth of the Republic*, 82–86; and Paul W. Mapp, "The Revolutionary War and Europe's Great Powers," in *Handbook of American Revolution*, 311–26.

27. Almost 26,000 members of the Continental army and militias died in combat, from injuries, or from disease. About 25,000 African Americans who escaped bondage and fled to British lines died, primarily from disease. It has been estimated that Britain lost 43,633 soldiers and sailors and that 11,843 troops from the German states died. About three thousand Loyalists and British Canadians perished. About ten thousand French military personnel died in combat. Spain lost about five thousand men in battle, and Holland lost about five hundred. At least six thousand Indigenous people died. The number of deaths from disease among Loyalist, British Canadian, French, Spanish, or Dutch fighters is unknown. See Howard H. Peckham, ed., *The Toll of Independence: Engagements and Battle Casualties of the American Revolution* (Chicago: University of Chicago Press, 1974), 130–32; Raphael, *People's History of the American Revolution*, 482n220; Clodfelter, *Warfare*, 141–42; Koehler, "Hostile Nations," 444–46; Soodalter, "Massacre and Retribution"; and Ostler, *Surviving Genocide*, 77.

28. Zinn, *People's History*, chap. 5; and Raphael, *People's History of the American Revolution*, chap. 7.

NOTES TO PAGES 126-128   375

29. Alexander Keyssar, *The Right to Vote: The Contested History of Democracy in the United States* (New York: Basic Books, 2000), 23–24.
30. Morgan, *Birth of the Republic*, 96.
31. Zinn, *People's History*, 90–102; and Parenti, *Democracy for the Few*, chap. 2.
32. These powers are enumerated in Article I of the United States Constitution. These phrases appear in Article I, Section 8, and Article IV, Section 4. See *The Constitution of the United States of America: Analysis and Interpretation*, U.S. Library of Congress, https://constitution.congress.gov/about/constitution-annotated/. See also Parenti, *Democracy for the Few*, chap. 2.
33. Zinn, *People's History*, 90–102; Parenti, *Democracy for the Few*, chap. 2; and Atwood, *War and Empire*, 52–56.
34. This is the title of chapter 2 in Parenti's *Democracy for the Few*.
35. George Washington, quoted in Niall Ferguson, "'Colossus,'" *New York Times*, July 25, 2004.
36. George Washington, quoted in Steven Newcomb, "A Brief Story about the American Empire," *Indian Country Today*, March 5, 2004, https://www.globalpolicy.org/us-military-expansion-and-intervention/north-korea/ 25973.html.
37. Alexander Hamilton, quoted in Robert Kagan, "Our 'Messianic Impulse,'" *Washington Post*, December 10, 2006.
38. Alexander Hamilton, *Federalist* No. 11, in *The Federalist Papers*, ed. Clinton Rossiter (New York: New American Library, 1961), 90–91.
39. Thomas Jefferson, quoted in Lens, *Forging the American Empire*, 2.
40. Ibid.
41. John Jay, *Federalist* Number 4, in *The Federalist Papers*, 48.
42. Ferguson, "'Colossus.'"
43. Lens, *Forging the American Empire*, 16, 22; and Atwood, *War and Empire*, 59–60.
44. Ibid., 22; ibid., 60.
45. Ibid., 17, 22–24; ibid.
46. Ibid., 22–24; ibid.
47. Ibid.; ibid.
48. Clodfelter, *Warfare*, 145–46; and Lens, *Forging of the American Empire*, 22–34.
49. Atwood, *War and Empire*, 62; Lens, *Forging the American Empire*, 35–39; and Lambert, *Barbary Wars,* chap. 5.
50. Lambert, *Barbary Wars*, 4–6, 42, 105–7, 199–201.
51. Lens, *Forging the American Empire*, 37–39; and Eric Scigliano, "Our Original Libyan Misadventure," *Salon*, April 17, 2011, http://www.salon.com/2011/04/17/Libya_jefferson_ scigliano/.

52. Lambert, *Barbary Wars*, 154–55.
53. An estimate of more than eight hundred deaths in the U.S. bombardment of Darnah is found in A. Houissa, "'To the Shores of Tripoli': America's Military Connection to Libya and Tripoli's Link to the U.S. Marines' Hymn," *Middle East and Islamic Studies Collection Blog: The Librarian's Blog About Current Issues*, Cornell University, September 14, 2011, https://blogs. cornell.edu/mideastlibrarian/2011/09/14/to-the-shores-of-tripoli/. Other deaths occurred in previous combat engagements. See Clodfelter, *Warfare*, 212.
54. Joseph A. Harriss, "How the Louisiana Purchase Changed the World," *Smithsonian Magazine*, April 2003, https://www.smithsonianmag.com/history/how-the-louisiana-purchase-changed-the-world-79715124/.
55. Ibid.
56. Ibid.
57. Ibid.; and Lens, *Forging the American Empire*, 35.
58. Harriss, "How the Louisiana Purchase Changed the World."
59. Atwood, *War and Empire*, 61.
60. Lens, *Forging the American Empire*, 2–3; and Peter J. Kastor, *The Nation's Crucible: The Louisiana Purchase and the Creation of America* (New Haven: Yale University Press, 2004), 55–56.
61. Atwood, *War and Empire*, 64–66; and Lens, *Forging the American Empire*, chap. 4.
62. Atwood, *War and Empire*, 61; Weeks, *Continental Empire*, 71–72; and Gardner, LaFeber, and McCormick, *Creation of the American Empire*, 84–85.
63. Lens, *Forging the American Empire*, 66–67.
64. Ibid., 62, 67–70, 74–75.
65. Ibid., 71–73; and Atwood, *War and Empire*, 65.
66. Lens, *Forging the American Empire*, 73–79; and Atwood, *War and Empire*, 65.
67. Lens, *Forging the American Empire*, 64–65, 77, 79.
68. Ibid., 77–80; and Atwood, *War and Empire*, 63–66.
69. Lens, *Forging the American Empire*, 80.
70. Ibid.
71. Ibid.
72. An estimate of 37,500 deaths, including 7,500 Indigenous fatalities, is found in Hickey, *War of 1812*, 306. An estimate of as many as 11,000 Native deaths appears in Clodfelter, *Warfare*, 263. Thus, the total loss of life may have been as high as 41,000.
73. Lambert, *Barbary Wars*, 188–202; and Clodfelter, *Warfare*, 213.
74. Lens, *Forging the American Empire*, 64–65, 92–95.
75. Eric J. Dolin, "How the China Trade Helped Make America," *Daily Beast*,

NOTES TO PAGES 130–132

November 4, 2012, http://www.thedailybeast.com/articles/2012/11/04/how-the-china-trade-helped-make-america.html; and Karl Meyer, "The Opium War's Secret History," *New York Times*, June 28, 1997.

76. Diana Ahmad, *The Opium Debate and Chinese Exclusion Laws in the Nineteenth-Century American West* (Reno: University of Nevada Press, 2007), 21.

77. Brandon Rottinghaus, *Inside Texas Politics: Power, Policy, and Personality of the Lone Star State* (Oxford: Oxford University Press, 2018), 7; and Margaret Swett Henson, "Anglo-American Colonization," *Handbook of Texas Online*, Texas State Historical Association, June 30, 2016, https://tshaonline.org/handbook/online/articles/uma01.

78. Alexander Barnes Dryer, "Our Liberian Legacy," *The Atlantic*, July 30, 2003, https://www.theatlantic.com/magazine/archive/2006/03/our-liberian-legacy/304821/.

79. James Monroe, quoted in Lens, *Forging the American Empire*, 98.

80. Atwood, *War and Empire*, 67.

81. Lens, *Forging the American Empire*, 154; and Chambers, *No God but Gain*, 103–5.

82. Torreon and Plagakis, *Use of Armed Forces*, 3; and Lens, *Forging the American Empire*, 154.

83. Lens, *Forging the American Empire*, 154.

84. Ibid.

85. Ibid.; Max Boot, *The Savage Wars of Peace: Small Wars and the Rise of American Power*, rev. ed. (New York: Basic Books, 2002), 42; Hezekiah Niles, ed., *Niles' Weekly Register* 42, August 25, 1832, 452–53; Robert W. Love, Jr., *History of the U.S. Navy*, vol. 1, *1775–1941* (Harrisburg, PA: Stackpole Books, 1992), 148; and James A. Wombwell, *The Long War Against Piracy: Historical Trends*, Occasional Paper 32 (Fort Leavenworth, KS: Combat Studies Institute Press, 2010), chaps 2–3.

86. Lens, *Forging the American Empire*, 154; Clodfelter, *Warfare*, 244; and Sabri Zain, "The United States Attack on Kuala Batu," in *Sejarah Melayu: A History of the Malay Peninsula*, http://sabrizain.org/malaya/. Lower casualty estimates are found in Boot, *Savage Wars*, 47–48; and Weeks, *Continental Empire*, 76–77.

87. Lens, *Forging the American Empire*, 54.

88. Ibid., 154–55; and Boot, *Savage Wars*, 50, 66.

89. Lens, *Forging the American Empire*, 155.

90. Ibid., 104–105; and Gary Clayton Anderson, *Conquest of Texas*, 78.

91. Emily McCullar, "How Leaders of the Texas Revolution Fought to Preserve Slavery," *Texas Monthly*, October 29, 2020, https://www.texasmonthly.com/being-texan/how-leaders-texas-revolution-fought-preserve-slavery/; James W. Russell, "Slavery and the Myth of the Alamo,"

NOTES TO PAGES 132–133

History News Network, May 28, 2012, https://historynewsnetwork. org/article/146405; and Lee Ballinger, "The Alamo: America's Shrine to White Supremacy," *CounterPunch*, November 6, 2015, https://www. counterpunch.org/2015/11/06/the-alamo-americas-shrine-to-white-supremacy/. See also Bryan Burrough, Chris Tomlinson, and Jason Stanford, *Forget the Alamo: The Rise and Fall of an American Myth* (New York: Penguin Press, 2021), chaps. 2–3.

92. McCullar, "How Leaders of the Texas Revolution Fought to Preserve Slavery"; Russell, "Slavery and the Myth of the Alamo"; Ballinger, "The Alamo: America's Shrine to White Supremacy"; and Burrough, Tomlinson, and Stanford, *Forget the Alamo*, chaps. 2–3.

93. McCullar, "How Leaders of the Texas Revolution Fought to Preserve Slavery"; Russell, "Slavery and the Myth of the Alamo"; Ballinger, "The Alamo: America's Shrine to White Supremacy"; Burrough, Tomlinson, and Stanford, *Forget the Alamo*, 111; and Clodfelter, *Warfare*, 265.

94. Ahmad, *Opium Debate*, 22; and Kiernan, *New Imperialism*, 18.

95. Lens, *Forging the American Empire*, 155–56.

96. Ibid.

97. Cohen, *America's Response,* 11; and Yoni Wilkenfeld, "The First U.S.-China Trade Deal," *JSTOR Daily*, (October 23, 2019), https://daily.jstor. org/the-first-us-china-trade-deal/.

98. Wilkenfeld, "The First U.S.-China Trade Deal."

99. Lens, *Forging the American Empire*, 155–56. In view of Cushing's actions in China, the suggestion that the treaty was achieved "without firing a shot and without issuing a threat" is unpersuasive. See Cohen, *America's Response*, 11.

100. Zinn, *People's History*, chap. 8.

101. O'Sullivan, "Annexation," 5–6, 9–10.

102. Estimates of approximately fifty thousand Mexican deaths are found in Atwood, *War and Empire*, 74; Weeks, *Continental Empire*, 135; and Cockcroft, *Mexico's Hope*, 68. Timothy J. Henderson has reported almost fourteen thousand U.S. deaths and estimates of Mexican deaths ranging from 25,000 to 50,000. See *A Glorious Defeat: Mexico and Its War with the United States* (New York: Hill and Wang, 2007), 179.

103. In 1853, Washington engineered the Gadsden Purchase and obtained additional Mexican lands which later became parts of Arizona and New Mexico. See Weeks, *Continental Empire*, 162.

104. Andrew Glass, "U.S. and Mexico Sign Treaty of Guadalupe Hidalgo, Feb. 2, 1848," *Politico*, February 2, 2019, https://www.politico.com/ story/2019/02/02/us-mexico-treaty-of-guadalupe-hidalgo-1137572.

105. Atwood, *War and Empire*, 74. This phrase is from the song "America

NOTES TO PAGES 133–136 379

the Beautiful," music composed by Samuel A. Ward in 1883 and lyrics written by Katharine Lee Bates.

106. Dryer, "Our Liberian Legacy"; Judson M. Lyon, "Informal Imperialism: The United States in Liberia, 1897–1912," *Diplomatic History* 5/3 (Summer 1981), 221–43; and Niels Stefan Cato Hahn, *Two Centuries of U.S. Military Operations in Liberia: Challenges of Resistance and Compliance* (Maxwell AFB, Montgomery, AL: Air University Press, 2020).

107. Roger Bell, *Last Among Equals: Hawaiian Statehood and American Politics* (Honolulu: University of Hawaii Press, 1984), 8–9.

108. Weeks, *Continental Empire*, 147–148.

109. Ibid., 148–149; and A. Filibustiero [pseudonym], *Life of General Narciso Lopez* (New York: Dewitt and Davenport, 1851), 13–27.

110. Weeks, *Continental Empire*, 148–49.

111. "The Bombardment of Johanna," *New York Times*, February 4, 1852.

112. Weeks, *Continental Empire*, 157–58.

113. Dan Vergano, "Bird Droppings Led to U.S. Possession of Newly Protected Pacific Islands," *National Geographic*, September 28, 2014, https://www.nationalgeographic.com/news/2014/ 9/140926-pacific-island-guano-national-monument-history/#close.

114. Kevin Underhill, "The Guano Islands Act," *Washington Post*, July 8, 2014.

115. Matthew Perry, quoted in Weeks, *Continental Empire*, 78.

116. Matthew Perry, quoted in Lens, *Forging the American Empire*, 156.

117. Weeks, *Continental Empire*, 78; and Lens, *Forging the American Empire*, 157.

118. Weeks, *Continental Empire*, 154–56.

119. Ibid., 158–59.

120. Ibid., 159–61; and Clodfelter, *Warfare*, 325–26.

121. An estimate of ten thousand deaths is found in Clodfelter, *Warfare*, 325–26.

122. Lens, *Forging the American Empire*, 156; and Cohen, *America's Response*, 17.

123. Boot, *Savage Wars*, 52; and David F. Long, *Gold Braid and Foreign Relations: Diplomatic Activities of the U.S. Naval Officers, 1798–1883* (Annapolis: Naval Institute Press, 1998), 224.

124. Cohen, *America's Response*, 17–21; Clodfelter, *Warfare*, 249; and Immanuel C. Y. Hsu, *The Rise of Modern China*, 6th ed. (Oxford: Oxford University Press, 2000), 203–5.

125. Cohen, *America's Response*, 21–22; and James Mason Hoppin, *Life of Andrew Hull Foote, Rear-Admiral U.S. Navy* (New York: Harper and Brothers, 1874), 120.

126. Cohen, *America's Response*, 23–24; and Love, *History of the U.S. Navy*, 238.

380 NOTES TO PAGES 136–138

127. Weeks, *Continental Empire*, 73.

128. Meyer, "The Opium War's Secret History"; John Langellier, *U.S. Armed Forces in China 1856–1941* (Oxford: Osprey Publishing, 2009); *China Offensive* (Washington, DC: U.S. Army Center of Military History), https://history.army.mil/html/books/072/72-39/CMH_Pub_72-39.pdf; and Henry I. Shaw, Jr., *The United States Marines in North China 1945–1949*, Marine Corps Historical Reference Pamphlet (Washington, DC: U.S. Marine Corps, 1960), https:// www.usmcu.edu/Portals/218/TheUnited StatesMarinesInNorthChina1945-1949.pdf.

129. Baptist, *Half Has Never Been Told*, xxi–xxiii, 322–23, 352–53, 359, 412–13.

130. Zinn, *People's History*, 188–98; Eric Foner, *Free Soil, Free Labor, Free Men: The Ideology of the Republican Party Before the Civil War* (Oxford: Oxford University Press, 1970); and James M. McPherson, "Civil War," in *The Reader's Companion to American History*, ed. Eric Foner and John A. Garrity (Boston: Houghton Mifflin, 1991), 182–85.

131. Foner, *Free Soil*, 9–10, chap. 1, 308–17.

132. Zinn, *People's History*, 190–91; and Foner, *Free Soil*, 315–16.

133. Quote is from "The Battle Hymn of the Republic," written by Julia Ward Howe in 1861. See Michael E. Ruane, "How Julia Ward Howe Wrote 'The Battle Hymn of the Republic'—Despite Her Husband," *Washington Post*, November 18, 2011. On the evolution of the national government's purpose during the Civil War, see Zinn, *People's History*, 189–92; and Atwood, *War and Empire*, 75–78.

134. J. David Hacker, "Recounting the Dead," *New York Times*, September 20, 2011.

135. Ibid.

136. Ibid.

137. Downs, "Color Blindness."

138. Ibid.

139. Clodfelter, *Warfare*, 250.

140. Ibid., and Boot, *Savage Wars*, 54.

141. Torreon and Plagakis, *Use of Armed Forces*, 5.

142. Sebastien Roblin, "That Time America Went to War in Korea (79 Years Before the Korean War)," *National Interest*, April 1, 2017, https://nationalinterest.org/blog/the-buzz/time-america-went-war-korea-79-years-before-the-korean-war-19977; and Ian Murray, "Seward's True Folly: American Diplomacy and Strategy During 'Our Little War with the Heathens,' Korea, 1871," *Penn History Review* 18/2 (Spring 2011): 55.

143. Torreon and Plagakis, *Use of Armed Forces*, 5.

144. Atwood, *War and Empire*, 88; and Robert Kagan, *Dangerous Nation:*

NOTES TO PAGES 138-140   381

America's Foreign Policy from its Earliest Days to the Dawn of the Twentieth Century (New York: Vintage, 2007), 277.

145. Zakaria, *From Wealth to Power*, 70–72.
146. Torreon and Plagakis, *Use of Armed Forces*, 5–6.
147. Zakaria, *From Wealth to Power*, 45.
148. LaFeber, *New Empire*, 9–10.
149. Ibid., 30.
150. Roblin, "That Time America Went to War in Korea"; Murray, "Seward's True Folly," 43; and Daniel Rolph, "The Other Korean War: A Little-Known Conflict in American History," Historical Society of Pennsylvania, August 29, 2013, https://hsp.org/blogs/hidden-histories/the-other-korean-war-a-little-known-conflict-in-american-history.
151. Kagan, *Dangerous Nation*, 331–32.
152. Torreon and Plagakis, *Use of Armed Forces*, 6; and Tom Correa, "King Kalākaua Needed U.S. Marines in 1874," *The Cowboy Chronicles*, June 19, 2011, http://www.americancowboy chronicles.com/2011/06/1874-king-kalakaua-and-us-marines.html.
153. Lens, *Forging the American Empire*, 164–65.
154. Clodfelter, *Warfare*, 217.
155. Torreon and Plagakis, *Use of Armed Forces*, 6; and Boot, *Savage Wars*, 54.
156. Torreon and Plagakis, *Use of Armed Forces*, 6; and Lindsay-Poland, *Emperors in the Jungle*, 19.
157. Linday-Poland, *Emperors in the Jungle*, 19–20.
158. Irving King, "The Occupation of Panama," *New York Tribune*, May 8, 1885, cited in Lindsay-Poland, *Emperors in the Jungle*, 20.
159. Pat Pitzer, "The Overthrow of the Monarchy," *Spirit of Aloha*, May 1994, https://www. Hawai'i-nation.org/soa.html.
160. Ibid.
161. Torreon and Plagakis, *Use of Armed Forces*, 6; Pitzer, "The Overthrow of the Monarchy"; Kagan, *Dangerous Nation*, 325; and David M. Pletcher, *The Diplomacy of Involvement: American Economic Expansion Across the Pacific, 1784–1900* (Columbia: University of Missouri Press, 2001), 235.
162. David Starr, "Robert Wilcox and the Revolution of 1895: Hawaiiian Revolutionary Honored," *Against the Current*, no. 57, July–August 1995, https://solidarity-us.org/atc/57/p2642/.
163. Torreon and Plagakis, *Use of Armed Forces*, 6.
164. LaFeber, *New Empire*, 137–38, 304.
165. "Typhoons and Hurricanes: The Storm at Apia, Samoa, 15–16 March 1889," Naval History and Heritage Command, September 14, 2017, https://www.history.navy.mil/research/library/online-reading-room/

382 NOTES TO PAGES 140–142

title-list-alphabetically/t/typhoons-and-hurricanes-the-storm-at-apia-samoa-15-16-march-1889.html.

166. LaFeber, *New Empire*, 138–40; and Boot, *Savage Wars*, 64–65.

167. Ibid., 127–28; and Brandon Byrd, "Frederick Douglass, Haiti, and Diplomacy," *Black Perspectives*, February 11, 2017, https://www.aaihs.org/frederick-douglass-haiti-and-diplomacy/.

168. Byrd, "Frederick Douglass, Haiti, and Diplomacy."

169. LaFeber, *New Empire*, 128–29.

170. Zakaria, *From Wealth to Power*, 46.

171. Ibid.

172. Haddow, "When U.K. GDP Last Outstripped U.S."

173. Zinn, *People's History*, 301; LaFeber, *New Empire*, 8–10, 18–19; and Douglas Irwin, "Explaining America's Surge in Manufactured Exports, 1880–1913," *Review of Economics and Statistics* 85/2 (May 2003): 364–76.

174. Zinn, *People's History*, 301; and LaFeber, *New Empire*, 9, 18.

175. Atwood, *War and Empire*, 91–92; and LaFeber, *New Empire*, chap. 2.

176. Atwood, *War and Empire*, 91; LaFeber, *New Empire*, 85–93; and Lens, *Forging the American Empire*, 166–68.

177. Torreon and Plagakis, *Use of Armed Forces*, 6.

178. Ibid.

179. Schoultz, *Beneath the United States*, 99–105.

180. Clodfelter, *Warfare*, 350.

181. Gardner, LaFeber, and McCormack, *Creation of the American Empire*, 203; and LaFeber, *New Empire*, 133–35.

182. Lens, *Forging the American Empire*, 164; LaFeber, *New Empire*, 144–46; and Steven Mintz and Sara McNeil, "The Annexation of Hawai'i," *Digital History*, 2018, https://www.digitalhistory.uh.edu/disp_textbook.cfm?smtid=2&psid=3159.

183. LaFeber, *New Empire*, 146.

184. Ibid., 147–49.

185. Grover Cleveland, cited in Mintz and McNeil, "The Annexation of Hawai'i."

186. LaFeber, *New Empire*, 365–70; and Noenoe K. Silva, *Aloha Betrayed: Native Hawaian Resistance to American Colonialism* (Durham, NC: Duke University Press, 2004), chap. 4.

187. LaFeber, *New Empire*, 210–18; and Gardner, LaFeber, and McCormack, *Creation of the American Empire*, 234–235.

188. Ibid.; and Hélio Alves Flores, *No Tempo das Degolas: Revolugões Imperfeitas* (Porto Alegre, Brazil: Martins Livreiro, 1996), 168, cited in Rodrigo Santos de Oliveira, "Os 120 Anos da Guerra Civil de 1893," *Historiae (Rio Grande)* 4/ 2 (2013): 142.

NOTES TO PAGES 142–144   383

189. Torreon and Plagakis, *Use of Armed Forces*, 6–7; LaFeber, *New Empire*, 228; and Gardner, LaFeber, and McCormack, *Creation of the American Empire*, 235–37.

190. LaFeber, *New Empire*, 226–29; and Gardner, LaFeber, and McCormack, *Creation of the American Empire*, 235–37.

191. Richard Olney, quoted in LaFeber, *New Empire*, 262. See also Atwood, *War and Empire*, 89–90.

192. Henry Cabot Lodge, "Our Blundering Foreign Policy," *Great Issues in American History: From Reconstruction to the Present Day, 1864–1981*, rev. ed., ed. Richard Hofstadter and Beatrice K. Hofstadter (New York: Random House, 1982), 182.

193. Stone and Kuznick, *Untold History*, xxii; Gardner, LaFeber, and McCormack, *Creation of the American Empire*, 244–51; Zinn, *People's History*, 302–6; and Kagan, *Dangerous Nation*, 378–99.

194. Zinn, *People's History*, 301–4; and Atwood, *War and Empire*, 96–102.

195. Editorial, *Washington Post*, 1898, quoted in Zinn, *People's History*, 299.

196. Stone and Kuznick, *Untold History*, xxii; Zinn, *People's History*, 306–8.

197. Clodfelter, *Warfare*, 273. An additional six crew members died later from their injuries. See "The Destruction of USS *Maine*," Naval History and Heritage Command, November 9, 2017, https://www.history.navy. mil/browse-by-topic/disasters-and-phenomena/ destruction-of-uss-maine.html.

198. Zinn, *People's History*, 304; Atwood, *War and Empire*, 102.

199. Clodfelter, *Warfare*, 273–74. See also Thomas Schoonover, *Uncle Sam's War of 1898 and the Origins of Globalization* (Lexington: University Press of Kentucky, 2003).

200. Zinn, *People's History*, 312; Atwood, *War and Empire*, 102–3; and Lens, *Forging the American Empire*, 204.

201. Zinn, *People's History*, 309.

202. Approximately a thousand Spaniards died in combat, and another fifteen thousand perished from diseases. The United States lost about 390 men in combat and 2,600 men to disease in the war zone. Another three thousand U.S. troops died of disease in training camps at home. See Clodfelter, *Warfare*, 274; Bob Wintermute, "Casualties," in *The Encyclopedia of the Spanish American and Philippine-American Wars: A Political, Economic, and Social History*, vol. 1, ed. Spencer C. Tucker (Santa Barbara, CA: ABC-CLIO, 2009), 105; and Donald H. Dyal, Brian B. Carpenter, and Mark A. Thomas, "Casualties," *Historical Dictionary of the Spanish American War* (Westport, CT: Greenwood Press, 1996), 67.

203. Marco Hewitt, "Philippine-American War," in *Spanish American and Philippine-American Wars*, 476–78.

384 NOTES TO PAGES 144–146

204. Stone and Kuznick, *Untold History*, xxv–xxvi; Zinn, *People's History*, 314–17; Lens, *Forging the American Empire*, 187–89; Francisco, "The First Vietnam"; and Jason Ditz, "The Philippines: Remembering a Forgotten Occupation," *Huffington Post*, August 18, 2013, https://www.huffingtonpost.com/jason-ditz/remembering-a-forgotten-o_b_3447598.html.

205. Zinn, *People's History*, 316; Lens, *Forging the American Empire*, 188; Francisco, "The First Vietnam"; and Ditz, "The Philippines."

206. Francisco, "The First Vietnam."

207. See, for example, Dunbar-Ortiz, *Indigenous Peoples' History*, 164–66.

208. Francisco, "The First Vietnam"; and Ditz, "The Philippines."

209. The estimate of one million Filipino deaths is found in Francisco, "The First Vietnam." A decrease of about one million in the Filipino population between 1898 and 1908 is noted in Ditz, "The Philippines." Ken De Bevoise has emphasized that U.S. soldiers were "agents of disease" and estimated the loss of life between 1899 and 1903, at about 775,000. See *Agents of Apocalypse: Epidemic Disease in the Colonial Philippines* (Princeton: Princeton University Press, 1995), x, 13. Much lower estimates of 200,000 deaths are found in Atwood, *War and Empire*, 103; and in Clodfelter, *Warfare*, 260.

210. Clodfelter, *Warfare*, 259.

211. Lens, *Forging the American Empire*, 165.

212. Zinn, *People's History*, 408.

213. Clodfelter, *Warfare*, 382–83.

214. Silbey, *Boxer Rebellion*, chaps. 7–8; and Robert Bickers, "Introduction," in *The Boxers, China, and the World*, ed. Robert Bickers and R. G. Tiedemann (Lanham, MD: Rowman and Littlefield, 2007), xiv.

215. Silbey, *Boxer Rebellion*, 218–19, 227–29; Bickers, "Introduction," xiv–xv; and John King Fairbank and Merle Goldman, *China: A New History* 2nd ed. (Cambridge, MA: Belknap Press, 2006), 231–32.

216. Clodfelter, *Warfare*, 382–83.

217. Bickers, "Introduction," xiv.

218. Torreon and Plagakis, *Use of Armed Forces,* 7; and Lindsay-Poland, *Emperors in the Jungle*, 23–24.

219. Lindsay-Poland, *Emperors in the Jungle*, 23.

220. Ibid., 23–24.

221. Ibid.; Alvaro Mendez, *Colombian Agency and the Making of U.S. Foreign Policy: Intervention by Invitation* (New York: Routledge, 2017), 50.

222. BBC News, "Colombia Timeline," August 14, 2012, http://news.bbc.co.uk/2/hi/americas/countryprofiles/ 1212827.stm. An estimate of "as many as 100,000" is found in Clodfelter, *Warfare*, 352.

223. Lens, *Forging the American Empire*, 201.

NOTES TO PAGES 146–148

224. Ibid.
225. Zinn, *People's History*, 408.
226. Lens, *Forging the American Empire*, 202; Lindsay-Poland, *Emperors in the Jungle*, 25; and Stone and Kuznick, *Untold History*, xxviii.
227. Schoultz, *Beneath the United States*, 168–69.
228. Ibid., 175.
229. Theodore Roosevelt, quoted in Foner, *Give Me Liberty*, 719. Different contemporary and subsequent accounts of precisely what Roosevelt said in his 1911 speech at the University of California at Berkeley are noted in James F. Vivian, "The 'Taking' of the Panama Canal Zone: Myth and Reality," *Diplomatic History* 4/1 (Winter 1980), https://www.jstor.org/stable/ 24910575.
230. Linday-Poland, *Emperors in the Jungle*, 27, 45.
231. Theodore Roosevelt, *Presidential Addresses and State Papers*, vol. 3: *Homebound* (New York: Review of Reviews Company, 1910), 176–77, cited in Serge Ricard, "The Roosevelt Corollary," *Presidential Studies Quarterly* 36/1 (March 2006): 18.
232. Ricard, "The Roosevelt Corollary."
233. Theodore Roosevelt to William Bayard Hale, February 26, 1904, *Letters of Theodore Roosevelt*, vol. 4, 740, cited in Schoultz, *Beneath the United States*, 183.
234. Schoultz, *Beneath the United States*, 182–89; and Niall Ferguson, *The Pity of War* (New York: Basic Books, 1999), 55.
235. Brett Wilkins, "The History—and Hypocrisy—of U.S. Meddling in Venezuela," *teleSur*, January 28, 2019, https://www.telesurenglish.net/opinion/The-History--and-Hypocrisy-of-US-Meddling-in-Venezuela-0190128-0016.html; and Eduardo Galeano, *Open Veins of Latin America: Five Centuries of the Pillage of a Continent*, 25th anniv. ed., trans. Cedric Belfrage (New York: Monthly Review Press, 1997), 168. When rumors of a revolution in Venezuela began to circulate in 1923, the United States sent a naval squadron to show support for the Gómez dictatorship. See Stone and Kuznick, *Untold History*, 39.
236. Schoultz, *Beneath the United States*, 210–19; and LaFeber, *Inevitable Revolutions*, 47–51.
237. Atwood, *War and Empire*, 103; Schoultz, *Beneath the United States*, 19; and Lens, *Forging the American Empire*, 197.
238. Lens, *Forging the American Empire*, 204; and Jana K. Lipman, "5 Things to Know about Guantánamo Bay on Its 115th Birthday," *The Conversation*, December 10, 2018, https:/ the conversation.com/5-things-to-know-about-guantanamo-bay-on-its-115th-birthday-108301.
239. Juan Gonzalez, *Harvest of Empire* (New York: Penguin, 2000), 64–65; Clodfelter, *Warfare*, 406; and Gabriel Molina Franchossi, "La Tercera

386 NOTES TO PAGES 148–150

Intervención de EE.UU. en Cuba," *Granma* 17/143, May 22. 2013, http://www.granma.cu/granmad/2013/05/22/nacional/ artic02.html.

240. Torreon and Plagakis, *Use of Armed Forces*, 7–8; LaFeber, *Inevitable Revolutions*, 47–50; and Alan McPherson, *Invaded*, chap. 1.

241. LaFeber, *Inevitable Revolutions*, 50.

242. Lens, *Forging the American Empire*, 222–23.

243. Edwidge Danticat, "The Long Legacy of Occupation in Haiti," *The New Yorker*, July 28, 2015, https://www.newyorker.com/news/news-desk/haiti-us-occupation-hundred-year-anniversary. An estimate of at least 11,500 Haitian deaths is found in Michel-Rolph Trouillot, *Haiti: State Against Nation, The Origins and Legacy of Duvalierism* (New York: Monthly Review Press, 1990), 106. Alternative estimates of at least two thousand deaths by Clodfelter and approximately 2,200 deaths by Alan McPherson significantly undercount the deaths in the armed resistance and ignore or minimize the deaths in the labor camps. See Clodfelter, *Warfare*, 406; and Alan McPherson, *Invaded*, 59, 94, 262.

244. Clodfelter, *Warfare*, 406; and Alan McPherson, *Invaded*, 69.

245. Alan McPherson, *Invaded*, 1–9.

246. Elizabeth Schmidt, *Foreign Intervention in Africa, From the Cold War to the War on Terror* (Cambridge: Cambridge University Press, 2013), 198. See also Dryer, "Our Liberian Legacy"; Lyon, "Informal Imperialism"; Hahn, *Military Operations in Liberia*; and Emily S. Rosenberg, "The Invisible Protectorate: The United States, Liberia, and the Evolution of Neocolonialism, 1909–1940," *Diplomatic History* 9/3 (Summer 1985), 191–214.

247. Dryer, "Our Liberian Legacy"; and Rosenberg, "The Invisible Protectorate," 202–7.

248. Stone and Kuznick, *Untold History*, 2.

249. William Howard Taft to Nellie Taft, October 17, 1909, William Howard Taft Papers, Series 2, Box 48, 3, Manuscript Division, Library of Congress, https://www.loc.gov/exhibits/mexican-revolution-and-the-united-states/us-involvement-before-1913.html.

250. Ibid.

251. La Botz, "¡Viva la Revolución!"

252. Ibid.

253. Ibid.; and Cockcroft, *Mexico's Hope*, 98–99.

254. Cockcroft, *Mexico's Hope*, 98–99.

255. Ibid., 101–3.

256. Ibid.; Stone and Kuznick, *Untold History*, 2–3.

257. Smedley Butler, Excerpt from Speech, 1933, Federation of American Scientists, https://www.fas.org/man/smedley.htm.

258. Cockcroft, *Mexico's Hope*, 104–5.

NOTES TO PAGES 150-152

387

259. Niall Ferguson, *Colossus: The Rise and Fall of the American Empire* (New York: Penguin, 2004), 59.
260. Ibid., 106.
261. Ibid., 106–7; and Friedrich Katz, *The Life and Times of Pancho Villa* (Stanford, CA: Stanford University Press, 1998), 774–82.
262. Cockcroft, *Mexico's Hope*, 107, 117; and Katz, *Pancho Villa*, 780–82.
263. Cockcroft, *Mexico's Hope*, 107. Other scholars estimate the death toll at about one million. See, for example, Clodfelter, *Warfare*, 405.
264. Cockcroft, *Mexico's Hope*, 103, 117.
265. Ibid.
266. Stone and Kuznick, *Untold History*, 3.
267. Ibid., 3–4; Lens, *Forging the American Empire*, 236–39; Zinn, *People's History*, 359, 363; Atwood, *War and Empire*, 105–6; and Pauwels, *Great Class War*, chaps. 6–7.
268. Lenin, "Preface to the French and German Editions," *Imperialism, the Highest Stage of Capitalism*, in *The Lenin Anthology*, ed. Robert C. Tucker (New York: W. W. Norton, 1975), 206.
269. Woodrow Wilson, quoted in Lens, *Forging the American Empire*, 239.
270. Atwood, *War and Empire*, 108.
271. Woodrow Wilson, Speech in St. Louis, Missouri, September 5, 1919, in *The Papers of Woodrow Wilson*, vol. 63, ed. Arthur S. Link (Princeton: Princeton University Press, 1990), 45–46.
272. Andrew Glass, "U.S. Proclaims Neutrality in World War I, August 4, 1914," *Politico*, August 4, 2009, https://www.politico.com/story/2009/08/us-proclaims-neutrality-in-world-war-i-august-4-1914-025751.
273. Lens, *Forging the American Empire*, 259.
274. Atwood, *War and Empire*, 104.
275. Ibid., 111.
276. Lens, *Forging the American Empire*, 241.
277. Ibid.
278. Ibid., 252; and Boyer and Morais, *Labor's Untold Story*, 194.
279. Lens, *Forging the American Empire*, 241; and Atwood, *Labor's Untold Story* 111.
280. Lens, *Forging the American Empire*, 259, 263; Atwood, *War and Empire*, 116–17; Pauwels, *Great Class War*, 443–44; and Zinn, *People's History*, 361.
281. Lens, *Forging the American Empire*, 259–60.
282. Walter Hines Page, quoted in Lens, *Forging the American Empire*, 260.
283. Lens, *Forging the American Empire*, 259–61; Atwood, *War and Empire*, 11, 104, 115–16; and Pauwels, *Great Class War*, 450–54.
284. Page, quoted in Lens, *Forging the American Empire*, 260.
285. Lens, *Forging the American Empire*, 253.

386. Stone and Kuznick, *Untold History*, 6–7; Atwood, *War and Empire*, 107–9, 116–17; and Pauwels, *Great Class War*, 448–50.

287. Lens, *Forging the American Empire*, 259–61; and Atwood, *War and Empire*, 116–17.

288. Woodrow Wilson, quoted in Lens, *Forging the American Empire*, 261; and in Atwood, *War and Empire*, 116.

289. Woodrow Wilson, quoted in Stone and Kuznick, *Untold History*, 7.

290. Zinn, *People's History*, 365–74; Atwood, *War and Empire*, 109; and Milne, "First World War."

291. Ferguson, *Pity of War*, 329.

292. Lens, *Forging the American Empire*, 263–65.

293. Ibid., 262–63; and Atwood, *War and Empire*, 117.

294. Lens, *Forging the American Empire*, 252; Gardner, LaFeber, and Mc-Cormick, *Creation of the American Empire*, 270; and Pauwels, *The Great Class War*, 452.

295. Lens, *Forging the American Empire*, 242.

296. The phrase is found in Milne. Estimates of ten million combatant deaths and twenty million civilian deaths are found in Zinn, *People's History*, 359; and in Stone and Kuznick, *Untold History*, 18. Clodfelter has estimated 8.6 million military deaths and 6.5 million noncombatant deaths but this number appears to exclude civilians who died from disease or starvation. See *Warfare*, 460.

297. Alain Badiou, "On the Russian October Revolution of 1917," trans. Frank Ruda, *Crisis and Critique* 4/ 2 (July 11, 2017): 23.

298. Parenti, *Sword and the Dollar*, 135–41. Churchill is quoted in Ronald E. Powaski, *Toward an Entangling Alliance: American Isolationism, Interventionism, and Europe, 1901–1950* (Westport, CT: Greenwood Press, 1991), 18.

299. Robert Lansing, "Memorandum on the Russian Situation," December 7, 1917, Lansing Papers, Library of Congress, cited in Parenti, *Sword and the Dollar*, 137; and in Fogelsong, *America's Secret War*, 43.

300. Parenti, *Sword and the Dollar*, 136, 139; Zinn, *People's History*, 408–9; Fogelsong, *America's Secret War*, 5–6, chaps. 6 and 7; and Sayers and Kahn, *Great Conspiracy*, chap. 6.

301. Parenti, *Sword and the Dollar*, 139; and Fogelsong, *America's Secret War*, 69–75.

302. Parenti, *Sword and the Dollar*, 138–39; Sayers and Kahn, *Great Conspiracy*, 107; Marcel Liebman, *The Russian Revolution* (New York: Random House, 1970), 336–40; and Evan Mawdsley, "International Responses to the Russian Civil War (Russian Empire)," in *1914–1918 Online: International Encyclopedia of the First World War*, ed. Ute Daniel, Peter Gatrell, Oliver Janz, Heather Jones, Jennifer Keene, Alan Kramer, and Bill

NOTES TO PAGES 154–155   389

Nasson, Free University, Berlin, October 8, 2014, DOI:10.15555463/ie1418.10489.

303. Parenti, *Sword and the Dollar*, 139.

304. Ibid., 136–39; and Clodfelter, *Warfare*, 369.

305. Michael R. Ebner, *Ordinary Violence in Mussolini's Italy* (Cambridge: Cambridge University Press, 2011), 28–29.

306. Ibid., 9.

307. Pauwels, *Myth of the Good War*, 30–31; and Schmitz, *Right-Wing Dictatorships*, 30–45.

308. The Italian Ambassador's language is quoted in Schmitz, *Right-Wing Dictatorships*, 37.

309. Schmitz, *Right-Wing Dictatorships*, 30–45; Pauwels, *Good War*, 30–31; and Stone and Kuznick, *Untold History*, 52.

310. Schmitz, *Right-Wing Dictatorships*, 43–44.

311. On political repression in fascist Italy, see Ebner, *Ordinary Violence*. On U.S. arms sales to Mussolini's regime, see Thomas G. Paterson, J. Garry Clifford, Shane J. Maddock, Deborah Kisatsky, and Kenneth J. Hagan, *American Foreign Relations: A History*, vol. 2: *Since 1895*, 7th ed. (Boston: Wadsworth, 2009), 136. An estimate of half a million deaths during the Italian conquest and colonization of Libya is found in Ali Abdullatif Ahmida, *The Making of Modern Libya: State Formation, Colonization, and Resistance*, 2nd ed. (Albany: State University of New York Press, 2009), 1, 155. Some of these deaths occurred in the decade before Mussolini came to power, but many of them occurred during his rule.

312. Stone and Kuznick, *Untold History*, 52.

313. Michael Parenti, *Blackshirts and Reds: Rational Fascism and the Overthrow of Communism* (San Francisco: City Lights Books, 1998), 10.

314. See Michael Schroeder, "The Sandino Rebellion Revisited: Civil War, Imperialism, Popular Nationalism, and State Formation Muddied Up Together in the Segovias of Nicaragua, 1926–1934," in *Close Encounters of Empire: Writing the Cultural History of U.S.-Latin American Relations*, ed. Gilbert M. Joseph, Catherine C. LeGrand, and Ricardo D. Salvatore (Durham, NC: Duke University Press, 1998), 208–68. Schroeder has estimated that between 3,600 and six thousand died in Las Segovias in northern Nicaragua between 1927 and 1934, with possibly as many wounded or injured; email to author, July 28, 2016. The loss of five thousand lives during this period would bring the total number of Nicaraguan fatalities during the U.S. occupation to seven thousand. A lower total estimate of five thousand deaths appears in Alan McPherson, *Invaded*, 16.

315. International Commission of Jurists, *Human Rights in Nicaragua: Yes-*

390 NOTES TO PAGES 155–157

terday and Today (Geneva: International Commission of Jurists, 1981), 5. See also Richard Grossman, "Nicaragua: A Tortured Nation," *Torture, American Style, Historians Against the War*, https://www.historiansagainstwar.org/resources/torture/grossman.html#N_1.

316. "A Century of U.S. Intervention in the Dominican Republic," *teleSur*, September 25, 2016, https://www.telesurenglish.net/analysis/A-Century-of-U.S.-Intervention-in-the-Dominican-Republic-20160921-0034.html. An estimate of more than 50,000 deaths is in Randal C. Archibold, "A Museum of Repression Aims to Shock the Conscience," *New York Times*, September 12, 2011. This estimate includes about 17,000 Haitians killed by the Trujillo regime in 1937. The U.S. government stopped supporting Trujillo only after he tried to assassinate the president of Venezuela in 1960. A year later, the CIA was complicit in Trujillo's assassination. See Gonzalez, *Harvest of Empire*, 73; and Nicholas M. Horrock, "CIA Is Reported to Have Helped in Trujillo Death," *New York Times*, June 13, 1975.

317. Gonzalez, *Harvest of Empire*, 133.

318. Schmitz, *Right-wing Dictatorships*, 78–82.

319. Elio Delgado Legon, "Massacres During Batista's Dictatorship," *Havana Times*, January 26, 2017. This estimate is for the number of deaths during Batista's rule between 1952 and 1958, so the total loss of life is certainly higher.

320. Cohen, *America's Response*, 110–12; Bradley, *China Mirage*, 109–10, 127–30, 156–57, 163–64; Snow, *Red Star Over China*, 385–86; and Fairbank and Goldman, *China: A New History*, 290–91.

321. Cohen, *America's Response*, 112; Bradley, *China Mirage*, 127–30, 156–57; and Snow, *Red Star Over China*, 385.

322. On Japanese expansionism, see Zinn, *People's History*, 410–11; and Lens, *Forging the American Empire*, 288–89, 303–4. On U.S. accommodation in the early 1930s, see Cohen, *America's Response*, 115–37; Bradley, *China Mirage*, 117–26; James C. Thomson Jr., *When China Faced West: American Reformers in Nationalist China, 1928–1937* (Cambridge, MA: Harvard University Press, 1969), 22–27; and Kiernan, *New Imperialism*, 246.

323. Bradley, *China Mirage*, 127–30; Snow, *Red Star Over China*, 385–86; and Guangqiu Xu, "Americans and Chinese Nationalist Military Aviation," *Journal of Asian History* 31/2 (1997): 155–80.

324. An estimate of more than one million combat deaths and one million civilian deaths is found in Clodfelter, *Warfare*, 390.

325. Schmitz, *Right-Wing Dictatorships*, 90.

326. Frederic Sackett, quoted in Bernard V. Burke, *Ambassador Frederic Sackett and the Collapse of the Weimar Republic, 1900–1933* (Stanford,

NOTES TO PAGES 157–158   391

CA: Stanford University Press, 1964), cited in Schmitz, *Right-Wing Dictatorships*, 90.

327. Schmitz, *Right-Wing Dictatorships*, 90. The language is Schmitz's.

328. George Gordon, "The Counselor of Embassy in Germany (Gordon) to the Secretary of State," March 23, 1933, U.S. Department of State, Foreign Service Institute, Office of the Historian, *Foreign Relations of the United States: Diplomatic Papers, 1933, The British Commonwealth, Europe, Near East and Africa*, vol. 2, cited in Schmitz, *Right-Wing Dictatorships*, 91.

329. Breckinridge Long, quoted in Schmitz, *Right-Wing Dictatorships*, 92.

330. Ibid..

331. Zinn, *People's History*, 409–10; Schmitz, *Right-Wing Dictatorships*, chap. 3; and Pauwels, *Good War*, chaps. 2–3.

332. Zinn, *People's History*, 409–10; Schmitz, *Right-Wing Dictatorships*, chap. 3; Pauwels, *Good War*, chap. 3; Arnold A. Offner, "Appeasement Revisited: The United States, Great Britain, and Germany, 1933–1940," *The Journal of American History* 64/2 (September 1977), 373–93; Frederick W. Marks III, "Six Between Roosevelt and Hitler: America's Role in the Appeasement of Nazi Germany," *Historical Journal* 38/ 4 (December 1985): 969–82; and Rafael Medoff, "Why FDR Wouldn't Condemn Hitler," History News Network, April 28, 2019, https://historynewsnetwork.org/article/171833. These researchers have divergent views on the origins of the Second World War but acknowledge the importance of U.S. accommodation and appeasement of the Nazi Reich.

333. Pauwels, *Good War*, 32.

334. Ibid.

335. Higham, *Trading with the Enemy*, xvi, cited in Pauwels, *Good War*, 35.

336. Pauwels, *Good War*, 32–36; Higham, *Trading with the Enemy*; Black, *Nazi Nexus*; and Hart, *Hitler's American Friends*, chap. 5.

337. Pauwels, *Good War*, 32–36; Higham, *Trading with the Enemy*, chap. 2; and Stone and Kuznick, *Untold History*, 81–82.

338. Hart, *Hitler's American Friends*, 123.

339. Ibid. See also Pauwels, *Good War*, 36–41, 46–48.

340. Hart, *Hitler's American Friends*, chaps 1, 2, 3, and 7; Pauwels, *Good War*, 37–39.

341. Parenti, *Blackshirts and Reds*, 11; Philip Olterman, "Revealed: How Associated Press Cooperated with the Nazis," *Guardian*, March 30, 2016; and Nina Strochlic, "The Nazi Who Infiltrated *National Geographic*," *National Geographic*, April 27, 2017, https://news.national geographic.com/2017/04/lost-found-douglas-chandler-nazi/?user. testname=lazyloading:1.

342. Schmitz, *Right-wing Dictatorships*, 95–97.

392 NOTES TO PAGES 158-159

343. Zinn, *People's History*, 409; G. Bruce Strang, "The Worst of All Worlds: Oil Sanctions and Italy's Invasion of Abyssinia, 1935-1936," in *Diplomacy and Statecraft* 19/2 (2008): 210-35, and William D. Baker, "Neutrality Debates," in *Encyclopedia of the United States Congress*, ed. Robert E. Dewhirst and John David Kausch (New York: Facts on File, 2007), 378.

344. Schmitz, *Right-Wing Dictatorships*, 96-97.

345. Spencer C. Tucker, "Second Italo-Ethiopian War, 1935-1936," in *Encyclopedia of African Colonial Conflicts*, vol. 2, ed. Timothy J. Stapleton (Santa Barbara, CA: ABC-CLIO, 2017), 375. An Ethiopian government memorandum to the Paris Peace Conference of 1946 estimated that 760,300 lives had been lost in the Italian invasion and occupation. A similar estimate is found in Brian R. Sullivan, "More than Meets the Eye: The Ethiopian War and the Origins of the Second World War," in *The Origins of the Second World War Reconsidered: A. J. P. Taylor and the Historians*, 2nd ed., ed. Gordon Martel (New York: Routledge, 1999), 188. A much lower estimate of 275,000 deaths is given in Clodfelter, *Warfare*, 382. However, this estimate includes only the number of Ethiopians killed in action in 1935-36 and omits the much larger number who perished during the subsequent occupation. See A. J. Barker, *The Civilizing Mission: A History of the Italo-Ethiopian War of 1935-1936* (New York: Dial Press, 1968), 316.

346. Schmitz, *Right-Wing Dictatorships*, 102-13.

347. U.S. State Department, "Memorandum for the Honorable Norman H. Davis; A Contribution to a Peace Settlement," February 16, 1937, Box 24, Davis Papers, Library of Congress, cited in Schmitz, *Right-Wing Dictatorships*, 91-92.

348. Pauwels, *Good War*, chaps. 2 and 3.

349. Schmitz, *Right-Wing Dictatorships*, 98-101.

350. Ibid.; and Stone and Kuznick, *Untold History*, 84-85.

351. Stone and Kuznick, *Untold History*, 84; and Clodfelter, *Warfare*, 362-63.

352. Stone and Kuznick, *Untold History*, 84; and Zinn, *People's History*, 409-10. The Neutrality Acts enacted by Congress in 1935-37 were largely in response to widespread public condemnation of war profiteering in the First World War. Ironically, a great deal of war profiteering occurred when U.S. companies aided and abetted Franco's insurgency.

353. Stone and Kuznick, *Untold History*, 84; John Hubbard, "How Franco Financed His War," *Journal of Modern History* 25/4 (December 1953): 404, cited in Antony Beevor, *The Battle for Spain: The Spanish Civil War, 1936-1939* (New York: Penguin, 2006), 138; and Adam Hochschild, *Spain in Our Hearts: Americans in the Spanish Civil War, 1936-1939*

NOTES TO PAGES 159–161 393

(New York: Houghton Mifflin Harcourt, 2016), 173.

354. Hubbard, "How Franco Financed His War," 404; and Hochschild, *Spain in Our Hearts*, chap. 10.

355. Beevor, *Battle for Spain*, 138; and Hochschild, *Spain in Our Hearts*, 281–82.

356. Stone and Kuznick, *Untold History*, 84–85; Zinn, *People's History*, 409–10; Pauwels, *Good War*, 36; Robert Whealey, "How Franco Financed His War—Reconsidered," *Journal of Contemporary History* 12/1 (January 1977): 145–46; Vicente Navarro, "They Worked for Franco," *Counter-Punch*, October 30, 2004; https://www.counterpunch.org/2004/10/30/they-worked-for-franco/; and Adam Hochschild, "How Texaco Helped Franco Win the Spanish Civil War," *Mother Jones*, March 29, 2016, https://www.motherjones.com/politics/2016/03/texaco-franco-span-ish-civil-war-rieber/.

357. Charles Foltz, *The Masquerade in Spain* (Boston: Houghton Mifflin, 1948), 46–48, cited in Beevor, *Battle for Spain*, 138.

358. Stone and Kuznick, *Untold History*, 84–85.

359. This estimate is found in Hugh Thomas, *The Spanish Civil War*, rev. ed. (New York: Modern Library, 1989), xviii, 900–901.

360. The widespread use of this expression has been noted by Pauwels, *Good War*, 7–17; and by Studs Terkel, *"The Good War": An Oral History of World War II* (New York: New Press, 1984).

361. On the imperialist nature of the war, see Zinn, *People's History*, 407–25; Atwood, *War and Empire*, chap. 8; Lens, *Forging the American Empire*, chaps 14–16; and Pauwels, *Good War*, chaps 1–6. On the Soviet view of what soon came to be known as the Great Patriotic War, see Joseph Stalin, Radio Broadcast, July 3, 1941, https://www.marxists.org/reference/ archive/stalin/works/1941/07/03.htm.

362. Pauwels, *Good War*, chaps 2–4; Schmitz, *Right-Wing Dictatorships*, 30–45; Higham, *Trading with the Enemy*; Black, *Nazi Nexus*; Hart, *Hitler's American Friends*, chap. 5; Bradley, *China Mirage*, 123; Smethurst, "Road to World War II"; and Kiernan, *New Imperialism*, 246.

363. Atwood, *War and Empire*, 125.

364. Zinn, *People's History*, 407–25; Atwood, chap. 8; Lens, *Forging the American Empire*, chaps. 14–16; and Pauwels, *Good War*, chaps. 1–6.

365. Zinn, *People's History*, 410–11; Atwood, *War and Empire*, 127–28, 136, 139; Lens, *Forging the American Empire*, 289–90, 303–4; 321–322; and Pauwels, *Good War*, 80–82.

366. Bradley, *China Mirage*, 123. See also Smethurst, "Road to World War II."

367. Kiernan, *New Imperialism*, 246.

368. Clodfelter, *Warfare*, 392.

369. Pauwels, *Good War*, 80–82.

394 NOTES TO PAGES 161–163

370. Smethurst, "Road to World War II"; *and* Foner, *Give Me Liberty*, 839.
371. Zinn, *People's History*, 411; and Lens, *Forging the American Empire*, 290.
372. Zinn, *People's History*, 410–11; Atwood, *War and Empire*, 127–28, 136, 139; Lens, *Forging the American Empire*, 289–90, 303–4; 321–22; and Pauwels, *Good War*, 80–82.
373. Atwood, *War and Empire*, 128; and Lens, *Forging the American Empire*, 311–12.
374. James O. Richardson, *On the Treadmill to Pearl Harbor: The Memoirs of Admiral James O. Richardson, USN* (Washington, DC: Naval History Division, Department of the Navy, 1973), 427. See Atwood, *War and Empire* 126–30; Lens, *Forging the American Empire*, 321–22; and Pauwels, *Good War*, 82–83.
375. Smethurst, "Road to World War II"; and Zinn, *People's History*, 410.
376. Atwood, *War and Empire*, 126–27, 130.
377. Ibid. Chapter 8 in Atwood's book is titled "Pearl Harbor: The Spark But Not the Cause." The estimate of U.S. deaths at Pearl Harbor is found in Clodfelter, *Warfare*, 531.
378. Pauwels, *Good War*, 35; Ben Aris and Duncan Campbell, "How Bush's Grandfather Helped Hitler's Rise to Power," *Guardian*, September 25, 2004.
379. Pauwels, *Good War*, 33, 40, 227–29; and Black, *Nazi Nexus*, chap. 4.
380. Ibid., 40, 78–79, 226–227; and Higham, *Trading with the Enemy*, chap. 3.
381. Higham, *Trading with the Enemy*, 99, cited in Pauwels, *Good War*, 227.
382. Ibid.
383. Pauwels, *Good War*, 226, 233–34; and Black, *Nazi Nexus*, chap. 5.
384. Black, *Nazi Nexus*, 143.
385. Pauwels, *Good War*, chap. 20; Stone and Kuznick, *Untold History*, 81–83; Higham, *Trading with the Enemy*; Black, *Nazi Nexus*; and Michael Dobbs, "Ford and GM Scrutinized for Alleged Nazi Collaboration," *Washington Post*, November 30, 1998.
386. Atwood, *War and Empire*, 140.
387. Ibid., 135–42, 149; and Lens, *Forging the American Empire*, 313–14. See also Pauwels, *Good War*, 59–62. Pauwels has recognized growing U.S. concerns about the prospects for Nazi autarky and the end of the Open Door in Europe but has not acknowledged Roosevelt's eventual willingness to go to war with the Reich because it threatened the U.S. Empire.
388. Atwood, *War and Empire*, 136–37; and Lens, *Forging the American Empire*, 313–15.
389. Atwood, *War and Empire*, 136–37, 141–42; and Lens, *Forging the American Empire*, 317–21.

NOTES TO PAGES 163–165 395

390. Gabriel Kolko, *The Politics of War: The World and United States Foreign Policy, 1943–1945* (New York: Vintage Books, 1968), 252, cited in Zinn, *People's History*, 413.

391. Atwood, *War and Empire*, 134–36, 142–43, 149–50; Zinn, *People's History*, 412–15; Lens, *Forging the American Empire*, 327–28; and Kolko, *Politics of War*, 245–77, 607–10.

392. Isaiah Bowen, Memorandum T-A21, January 16, 1942, Council on Foreign Relations, *War-Peace Studies*, Baldwin Papers, Yale University Library, cited in Kaku and Axelrod, *Nuclear War,* 64.

393. Minutes S-3 of the Security Subcommittee, Advisory Committee on Postwar Foreign Policy, May 6, 1942, Notter File, Box 77, R.G. 59, cited in Kaku and Axelrod, *Nuclear War*, 64.

394. Pauwels, *Good War*, 127; and Donny Gluckstein, *A People's History of the Second World War* (London: Pluto Press, 2012), 93.

395. Pauwels, *Good War*, 119; and Gluckstein, *People's History of the Second World War*, 143–44.

396. Atwood, *War and Empire*, 152–53; Pauwels, *Good War*, 16, 70–74; and Matthew Lenoe, "Why It's Time to Give the Soviet Union Its Due for World War II," *Washington Post*, December 5, 2018.

397. Pauwels, *Good War*, chaps. 8 and 11; and William Z. Foster, *The Second Front Now: For Speedy Victory* (New York: Workers Library Publishers, 1943), 1, 6–8. See also Stone and Kuznick, *Untold History*, 102–11; and Oleg A. Rzheshevsky, "D-Day/60 Years Later: For Russia, Opening of a Second Front in Europe Came Far Too Late," *New York Times*, June 8, 2004.

398. Joseph Stalin to Winston Churchill and Franklin D. Roosevelt, June 24, 1943, cited in Rzheshevsky, "D-Day/60 Years Later."

399. Pauwels, *Good War*, 103, 123–24; and Alan Woods, "D-Day and the Truth About the Second World War," *In Defense of Marxism*, July 21, 2004, https://www.marxist.com/wwii-anniversary -one210704.htm.

400. King George II had supported and collaborated with the fascist dictator Metaxas before the war but fled the country after Italian forces invaded in 1941.

401. Lens, *Forging the American Empire*, 330–31.

402. Lawrence S. Wittner, "American Policy Toward Greece During World War II," *Diplomatic History* 3/2 (Spring 1979): 129–49. U.S. officials eventually persuaded the British government that King George II should not return until a plebiscite on the monarchy could be held.

403. See, for example, Pauwels, *Good War*, 127–31; Gluckstein, *People's History of the Second World War,* chaps. 2, 6; and Kolko, *Politics of War*, 131–37, 345, 414–20.

404. Pauwels, *Good War*, 197–98; Atwood, *War and Empire*, 161; and San-

396 NOTES TO PAGES 165–166

dra Kollen Ghizoni, "Creation of the Bretton Woods System," Federal Reserve History, July 22, 2013, https://www.federalreservehistory.org/essays/bretton_woods_created.

405. Zinn, *People's History*, 415, 419.
406. Ibid.
407. See, for example, V. Carl Allsup, "Felix Longoria Affair," *Handbook of Texas Online*, Texas State Historical Association, February 21, 2020, http://www.tshaonline.org/handbook/online/ articles/vef01.
408. Stone and Kuznick, *Untold History*, 152–57; and Zinn, *People's History*, 416.
409. Stone and Kuznick, *Untold History*, 150.
410. Atwood, *War and Empire*, 144–45; Daniel A. Gross, "The U.S. Government Turned Away thousands of Jewish Refugees, Fearing They Were Nazi Spies," *Smithsonian Magazine*, November 18, 2015, https://www.smithsonianmag.com/history/us-government-turned-away-thousands-jewish-refugees-fearing-they-were-nazi-spies-180957324/; Zinn, *People's History*, 420; and Geoffrey R. Stone, *Perilous Times: Free Speech in Wartime from the Sedition Act of 1798 to the War on Terrorism* (New York: W. W. Norton, 2004), 255, 279.
411. Hermann Knell, *To Destroy a City: Strategic Bombing and Its Human Consequences in World War II* (Cambridge, MA: Da Capo Press, 2003), 1, 334. Estimates of 600,000 civilian deaths in Germany and almost 350,000 civilian deaths in Japan are found in John Keegan, *The Second World War* (New York: Penguin, 2005), 432–33, 576. A postwar German government estimate of 593,000 civilian deaths in Japan appears in J. A. S. Grenville, *A History of the World in the Twentieth Century* (Cambridge, MA: Belknap Press, 1994), 280. A much lower estimate of about 630,000 civilian deaths from these bombing campaigns, including the atomic attacks on Hiroshima and Nagasaki, is found in *The United States Strategic Bombing Surveys* (Maxwell AFB, Montgomery, AL: Air University Press, 1987), 6, 92, cited in John Tirman, *The Deaths of Others: The Fate of Civilians in America's Wars* (Oxford: Oxford University Press, 2011), 55.
412. Lens, *Forging the American Empire*, 331; and Reuters, "Algerians Remember Massacres of 1945," *Washington Post*, May 9, 2005.
413. This point was made by the head of the League of Arab States to U.S. Envoy Somerville Pinkney Tuck in Egypt. The language is Tuck's. See Somerville Pinkney Tuck, "The Minister in Egypt (Tuck) to the Secretary of State," June 21, 1945, U.S. Department of State, Foreign Service Institute, Office of the Historian, *Foreign Relations of the United States: Diplomatic Papers, 1945, The Near East and Africa*, vol. 3, https://history.state.gov/ historicaldocuments/frus1945v08/d14; and Marcel Vi-

NOTES TO PAGE 166   397

gneras, *United States Army in World War II, Special Studies, Rearming the French*, U.S. Army Center of Military History (Washington, DC: Government Printing Office, 1957), 1.

414. Clodfelter, *Warfare*, 559–60; Alex Wallerstein, "Counting the Dead at Hiroshima and Nagasaki," *Bulletin of the Atomic Scientists*, August 4, 2020, https://thebulletin.org/2020/08/ counting-the-dead-at-hiroshima-and-nagasaki/; and BBC News, "Hiroshima Bomb: Japan Marks 75 Years Since Nuclear attack," August 6, 2020, https://www.bbc.com/news/world-asia-533660059.

415. Clodfelter, *Warfare*, 560; and Erin O'Hara Slavick, "Hiroshima: A Visual Record," *Asia-Pacific Journal* 7/30 (July 27, 2009), https://apjjf.org/-elin-o'Hara-slavick/3196/article.html.

416. The U.S. government's own experts concluded less than a year later that "Japan would have surrendered even if the atomic bombs had not been dropped, even if Russia had not entered the war, and even if no invasion had been planned or contemplated." See *Strategic Bombing Surveys*, 107. On the Truman administration's actual rationale for the atomic bombings, see Pauwels, *Good War*, chap. 18; Stone and Kuznick, *Untold History*, chap. 4; Gar Alperovitz, *The Decision to Use the Atomic Bomb* (New York: Vintage Books, 1995); and Gar Alperowitz and Martin J. Sherwin, "U.S. Leaders Knew We Didn't Have to Drop Atomic Bombs on Japan to End the War. We Did It Anyway," *Los Angeles Times*, August 5, 2020.

417. Atwood, *War and Empire*, 178–81.

418. Kolko, *Politics of War*, 601.

419. The destruction of much of Europe and Asia is discussed in Margaret MacMillan, "Rebuilding the World after the Second World War," *Guardian*, September 11, 2009. Estimates of 80 million deaths are found in Alan Taylor, "World War II: After the War," *The Atlantic*, October 30, 2011, https://www.theatlantic.com/photo/2011/10/world-war-ii-after-the-war/1001 80/; Ben Wattenberg, "The First Measured Century: World War II, the Home Front," PBS, December 2000, https://www.pbs.org/fmc/segments/progseg8.htm; and Greg Dobbs, "The Parallels and Differences Between Pearl Harbor and 9/11," *Denver Post*, December 6, 2016. This includes tens of millions who died from famine and disease during the war. Estimates of 70 million deaths during the war are found in Stone and Kuznick, *Untold History*, 182; and Mary Kaldor, "Restructuring Global Security for the Twenty-first Century," in *The Quest for Security: Protection Without Protectionism and the Challenge of Global Governance* (New York: Columbia University Press, 2013), 120. The human toll of the Second World War included at least 27 million Soviet deaths and possibly more; at least 20 million

398   NOTES TO PAGES 166–169

Chinese deaths and possibly many more; millions of additional deaths in Asia, the Pacific, and Europe; six million deaths in the Shoah; and many other fatalities. See "Russia's Losses in World War II Estimated at Some 27 Million—Paper," May 6, 2010, https://sputniknews.com/ russia/2010050615889 6419/; Kyle Mizokami, "These Are the Five Wars That Changed History (and Killed Millions) Forever," *National Interest*, May 31, 2017, http://nationalinterest.org/ blog/the-buzz/these-are-the-5-wars-changed-history-killed-millions-forever-20926; Jeremy Bender, "This Chart Shows the Astounding Devastation of World War II," *Business Insider*, May 29, 2014, http://www.businessinsider.com/ percentage-of-countries-who-died-during-wwii-2014-5; and "Holocaust Facts: Where Does the Figure of 6 Million Victims Come From?," *Haaretz*, August 11, 2013.

420. Atwood, *War and Empire*, 149–50; Zinn, *People's History*, 425; Lens, *Forging the American Empire*, 336–40.

421. Atwood, *War and Empire*, 163; and MacMillan, "Rebuilding the World."

422. Kolko, *Politics of War*, 618; Lens, *Forging the American Empire*, 336–37; Atwood, *War and Empire*, 148–51; and Pauwels, *Good War*, 268–69.

423. Seymour Melman, *The Permanent War Economy: American Capitalism in Decline* (New York: Simon & Schuster, 1974), 15–17; Stone and Kuznick, *Untold History*, 182; Pauwels, *Good War*, 268–69; Lens, *Forging the American Empire*, 336–37 and Zinn, *People's History*, 425.

424. Stone and Kuznick, *Untold History*, 182.

425. Ibid.

426. Frederick James Marquis, First Earl of Woolton, quoted in Lens, *Forging the American Empire*, 337.

427. Walter Lippmann, quoted in Foner, *Give Me Liberty*, 876.

5. The Holocausts of Pax Americana I

1. Atwood, *War and Empire: The American Way of Life* (London: Pluto Press, 2010), 149–50, 159, 161–65, 174; Pauwels, *The Myth of the Good War: America in the Second World War*, 2nd ed. (Toronto: James Lorimer, 2015), 268–76; Zinn, *A People's History of the United States: 1492–Present*, 20th anniv. ed. (New York: HarperCollins, 1999), 429–30; William Appleman Williams, *The Tragedy of American Diplomacy* (New York: W. W. Norton, 2009), 229–39; and Richard J. Barnet, *Roots of War: The Men and Institutions Behind U.S. Foreign Policy* (New York: Penguin, 1973), chap. 6.

2. On the expanded US. economic penetration of other countries after the end of the Second World War, see Magdoff, *The Age of Imperialism: The Economics of U.S. Foreign Policy* (New York: Monthly Review Press, 1969), 40–66; Lens, The *Forging of the American Empire* (Chicago: Hay-

NOTES TO PAGES 170–171   399

market Books, 2003), chaps. 18 and 19; and Barnet, *Roots of War*, chap. 6. On the development of U.S. client states, see Parenti, *The Sword and the Dollar* (New York: St. Martin's Press, 2011, 46–47, 103; Sylvan and Majeski, *U.S. Foreign Policy in Perspective: Clients, Enemies, and Empire* (New York: Routledge, 2009); and David Sylvan and Stephen Majeski, "An Agent-Based Model of the Acquisition of U.S. Client States," Paper delivered at the 44th Annual Convention of the International Studies Association, Portland, February 25–March 1, 2003, https://faculty.washington.edu/majeski/isa03.pap.pdf. On the proliferation of U.S. military bases after 1945, see Vine, *Base Nation: How U.S. Military Bases Abroad Harm America and the World* (New York: Henry Holt, 2015), 3, 28–41.

3.   Lens, *Forging the American Empire*, 349.

4.   Atwood, *War and Empire*, chaps. 10 and 11; Parenti, *Sword and the Dollar*, and *Against Empire* (San Francisco: City Lights Books, 1995); Stone and Kuznick, *The Untold History of the United States* (New York: Gallery Books, 2012); Noam Chomsky and Edward S. Herman, *The Washington Connection and Third World Fascism: The Political Economy of Human Rights*, vol. 1 (Boston: South End Press, 1979); William Blum, *Killing Hope: U.S. Military and CIA Interventions Since World War II*, rev. ed. (Monroe, ME: Common Courage Press, 2004), and *Rogue State: A Guide to the World's Only Superpower* (Monroe, ME: Common Courage Press, 2005); and Andre Vltchek, *Exposing Lies of the Empire* (Jakarta: Badak Merah, 2015).

5.   Kaku and Axelrod, *To Win a Nuclear War: The Pentagon's Secret War Plans* (Boston: South End Press, 1987).

6.   A similar point is made by Chomsky and Herman, *Washington Connection*, 41.

7.   Kolko, *The Politics of War: The World and United States Foreign Policy, 1943–1945* (New York: Vintage Books, 1968), 266–79; and Phyllis Bennis, *Calling the Shots: How Washington Dominates Today's UN* (New York: Olive Branch Press, 1996), chap. 1.

8.   Bennis, *Calling the Shots*, chap. 1.

9.   Ibid., 2.

10.   Ibid., 4.

11.   Ibid.

12.   Ibid., 3–6.

13.   Kolko, *Politics of War*, 268.

14.   Daniel Immerwahr, *How to Hide an Empire: A History of the Greater United States* (New York: Farrar, Straus and Giroux, 2019), 229.

15.   Torreon and Plagakis, *Instances of Use of United States Armed Forces Abroad, 1798–2021*, CRS Report, September 8, 2021, 10, https://sgp.

400 NOTES TO PAGES 171–172

fas.org/ crs/natsec/R42738.pdf; Blum, *Killing Hope*, 21; and John Tirman, *The Deaths of Others: The Fate of Civilians in America's Wars* (New York: Oxford University Press, 2011), 70.

16. Henry I. Shaw, Jr., *The United States Marines in North China, 1945–1949*, Marine Corps Historical Reference Pamphlet (Washington, DC: Historical Branch, G-3 Division Headquarters, U.S. Marine Corps, 1968); Blum, *Killing Hope*, 21–22; and Micheal Clodfelter, *Warfare and Armed Conflicts: A Statistical Encyclopedia of Casualty and Other Figures, 1494–2007*, 3rd ed. (Jefferson: McFarland and Company, 2008), 670.

17. Blum, *Killing Hope*, 22–23.

18. Ibid.; and Lens, *Forging the American Empire*, 372.

19. Mao Zedong, "The Chinese People Have Stood Up!," Opening Address at the First Plenary Session of the Chinese People's Political Consultative Conference, September 21, 1949, in *Selected Works of Mao Zedong*, vol. 5, Marxists Internet Archive, https://www.marxists.org/ reference/ archive/mao/selected-works/volume-5/mswv5_01.htm.

20. An estimate of 1.2 million battle deaths is found in Clodfelter, *Warfare*, 673, but five million civilians in this second phase of the Chinese Civil War also perished. See Michael Lynch, *The Chinese Civil War, 1945–1949* (Oxford: Osprey Publishing, 2010), 91; and Milton Leitenberg, *Deaths in Wars and Conflicts in the 20th Century*, Cornell University Peace Studies Program Occasional Paper No. 29, 3rd ed. (2006), 76, https://ecommons.cornell.edu/bitstream/handle/1813/69395/29-Leitenberg-Deaths-in-Wars-3ed.pdf?sequence=1.

21. "Nationalists Claim Mainland Victory: Capture of Town and Slaughter of Reds," *West Australian*, March 20, 1950.

22. Blum, *Killing Hope*, 23–24.

23. Atwood, *War and Empire*, 179–81; and Kiernan, *New Imperialism*, 291.

24. William Stueck and Boram Yi, "'An Alliance Forged in Blood': The American Occupation of Korea, the Korean War, and the U.S.-South Korean Alliance," *Journal of Strategic Studies* 33/2 (2010): 180; and Jon Halliday and Bruce Cumings, *Korea: The Unknown War* (New York: Pantheon Books, 1988), 16.

25. Halliday and Cumings, *Korea*, 16, 23–24.

26. Kim Il Sung, "On the Establishment of the Workers' Party of North Korea and the Question of Founding the Workers' Party of South Korea," September 26, 1946, *Kim Il Sung: Collected Works*, vol. 1, 102–20, Marxists Internet Archives, 2008, https://www.marxists.org/ archive/kim-il-sung/1946/09/26.htm.

27. Halliday and Cumings, *Korea*, 19–20.

28. Ibid., 20.

NOTES TO PAGES 172–175   401

29. Atwood, *War and Empire*, 180. See also Bruce Cumings, *Origins of the Korean War*, vol. 1 (Princeton: Princeton University Press, 1980), xxvi, cited in Tirman, *Deaths of Others*, 83.
30. Blum, *Killing Hope*, 122–125; and Zinn, *People's History*, 469–70.
31. Blum, *Killing Hope*, 123; and Stone and Kuznick, *Untold History*, 266.
32. Blum, *Killing Hope*, 124; and Zinn, *People's History*, 471.
33. Blum, *Killing Hope*, 124.
34. Kaku and Axelrod, *Nuclear War*, 91–93; Blum, *Killing Hope*, 122–25; and Stone and Kuznick, *Untold History*, 266–68.
35. Timothy J. Lomperis, *From People's War to People's Rule: Insurgency, Intervention, and the Lessons of Vietnam* (Chapel Hill: University of North Carolina Press, 1996), 96.
36. Bradley R. Simpson, *Economists with Guns: Authoritarian Development and US-Indonesian Relations, 1960–1968* (Stanford, CA: Stanford University Press, 2008), 13–16; and Theodore Friend, *Indonesian Destinies*, (Cambridge, MA: Belknap Press, 2003), 35–38.
37. Friend, *Indonesian Destinies*, 37.
38. Simpson, *Economists with Guns*, 14.
39. Friend, *Indonesian Destinies*, 38.
40. Simpson, *Economists with Guns*, 14; and Friend, *Indonesian Destinies*, 37–38.
41. Adrian Vickers, *A History of Modern Indonesia* (Cambridge: Cambridge University Press, 2005), 100.
42. Douglas Little, "Cold War and Colonialism in Africa: The United States, France, and the Madagascar Revolution of 1947," *Pacific Historical Review* 59/4 (November 1990): 527–52.
43. Ibid., 539.
44. Ibid., 540.
45. Ibid., 541–42.
46. Ibid., 551.
47. Ibid., 527.
48. See, for example, Phillip Deery, "Malaya 1948: Britain's Asian Cold War?" *Journal of Cold War Studies* 9/1 (Winter 2007): 31–32.
49. Souchou Yao, *The Malayan Emergency: Essays on a Small, Distant War* (Copenhagen: Nordic Institute of Asian Studies, 2016), 14.
50. Deery, "Malaya 1948," 52.
51. Robert Tilman, "The Non-Lessons for the Malayan Emergency," *Asian Survey* 6/8 (August 1966): 408.
52. Kaku and Axelrod, *Nuclear War*, 32; and Stone and Kuznick, *Untold History*, 194–96.
53. *New York Times*, March 12, 1947, cited in Blum, *Killing Hope*, 41.
54. Blum, *Killing Hope*, 41.

402   NOTES TO PAGES 175–177

55. Chomsky and Herman, *Washington Connection*, 231–232; Lomperis, *People's War*, 179.
56. Blum, *Killing Hope*, 41.
57. Ibid., 41–44; and Craig A. Lockard, *Societies, Networks, and Transitions: A Global History,* vol. 2: *Since 1450*, 3rd ed. (Stamford, CT: Cengage, 2015), 802.
58. Ishaan Tharoor, "The Long History of the U.S. Interfering with Elections Elsewhere," *Washington Post*, October 13, 2016.
59. Lomperis, *People's War*, 182. This estimate does not include civilian deaths, which were likely numerous.
60. *New York Herald Tribune*, September 17, 1946, cited in Lens, *Forging the American Empire*, 355.
61. "Text of President Truman's Speech on New Foreign Policy," *New York Times*, March 13, 1947, cited in Stone and Kuznick, *Untold History*, 207.
62. Blum, *Killing Hope*, 37; and Zinn, *People's History*, 426.
63. Ibid.
64. Stone and Kuznick, *Untold History*, 208.
65. Ibid.
66. Lomperis, *People's War*, 160. This estimate includes deaths from 1944 to 1949.
67. Zinn, *People's History*, 438; Stone and Kuznick, *Untold History*, 209, 213–15; Sylvan and Majeski, *U.S. Foreign Policy*, 62–63; and Atwood, *War and Empire*, 165–67.
68. Blum, *Killing Hope*, 27–34; and Tharoor, "U.S. Interfering with Elections."
69. Tharoor, "Interfering with Elections."
70. Geoff Simons, *Colombia: A Brutal History* (London: Saqi Books, 2004), 42–50; and Robin Kirk, *More Terrible Than Death: Massacres, Drugs, and America's War in Colombia* (New York: Public Affairs, 2003), 22–23, 42–43.
71. Simons, *Colombia*, 41–42. Simons noted that most of the violence subsided after 1958 when the Liberals and Conservatives agreed to form a coalition government, but another 18,000 people died between 1958 and 1965.
72. Walter LaFeber, *Inevitable Revolutions: The United States in Central America* (New York: W.W. Norton, 1993), 102–4; "Venezuela," Global Policy Forum, https://www. globalpolicy.org/us-military-expansion-and-intervention/venezuela.html; and Larry Rohter, "Marco Pérez Jiménez, 87, Venezuela Ruler," *New York Times*, September 22, 2001.
73. The role of Zionist terrorism in the creation of Israel is examined in Thomas Suarez, *State of Terror: How Terrorism Created Modern Israel* (Northampton, MA: Interlink Publishing, 2016).

NOTES TO PAGES 177–178 403

74. Atwood, *War and Empire*, 202–3.
75. Ibid.; and Melvyn P. Leffler, *A Preponderance of Power: National Security, the Truman Administration, and the Cold War* (Stanford, CA: Stanford University Press, 1992), 239–46. See also Andrew Cockburn and Leslie Cockburn, *Dangerous Liaison: The Inside Story of the US-Israeli Covert Relationship* (New York: HarperCollins, 1991), 24–27.
76. An estimate of about 15,000 Arab deaths and over 6,000 Israeli deaths is found in Clodfelter, *Warfare*, 610. See also Atwood, *War and Empire*, 202–3.
77. This estimate is found in Project Ploughshares, Canadian Council of Churches, "Israel-Palestine (1948-First Combat Deaths)," https://ploughshares.ca/pl_armedconflict/israel-palestine-1948-first-combat-deaths/#. An estimate of 100,000 is provided by Dov Waxman, in *The Israeli-Palestinian Conflict: What Everyone Needs to Know* (Oxford: Oxford University Press, 2019), 66. Waxman's claim that these wars' "lethality is comparatively low" must be offensive to the Palestinians and other Arabs who have suffered most of the casualties.
78. "Douglas Little, "Cold War and Covert Action: The United States and Syria, 1945–1958," *Middle East Journal* 44/1 (Winter 1990): 55–57, cited in Stephen Rosskamm Shalom, *Imperial Alibis: Rationalizing U.S. Intervention After the Cold War* (Boston: South End Press, 1993), 7.
79. Pauwels, *Good War*, 260.
80. Ralf Beste, George Bönisch, Thomas Darnstaedt, Jan Friedmann, Michael Fröhlingsdorf, and Klaus Wiegrefe, "The Role Ex-Nazis Played in Early West Germany," *Der Spiegel*, March 6, 2012, https://www.spiegel.de/international/germany/from-dictatorship-to-democracy-the-role-ex-nazis-played-in-early-west-germany-a-810207.html.
81. Ibid.
82. Bruni de la Motte, "East Germany Did Face Up to Its Past," *Guardian*, March 28, 2007. The German Democratic Republic and allied socialist states convicted far more individuals involved in Nazi war crimes than the Federal Republic and allied capitalist states. See Clive Ponting, *Armageddon: The Reality Behind the Distortions, Myths, Lies, and Illusions of World War II* (New York: Random House, 1995), 341.
83. Pauwels, *Good War*, 260; Atwood, *War and Empire*, 169–70; and Stone and Kuznick, *Untold History*, 220. The most influential early public statement advocating the "containment" of the Soviet Union was made by George F. Kennan of the State Department, writing anonymously as "X" in "The Sources of Soviet Conduct," *Foreign Affairs*, 25/4 (July 1947), https://www. cvce.eu/ content/publication/1999/1/1/a0f03730-dde8-4f06-a6ed-d740770dc423/publishable_en. pdf.
84. Sylvan and Majeski, *U.S. Foreign Policy*, 90–91.

85. Stone and Kuznick, *Untold History*, 214; Blum, *Killing Hope*, 55–57; and Sylvan and Majeski, *U.S. Foreign Policy*, 189–91.
86. Halliday and Cumings, *Korea*, chaps. 1 and 2. This description of the war appears on page 74. See also Atwood, *War and Empire*, 178–88.
87. Halliday and Cumings, *Korea*, 88–90; and Atwood, *War and Empire*, 182–83.
88. Halliday and Cumings, *Korea*, 74–78.
89. Ibid., 84–88; and Atwood, *War and Empire*, 182–83.
90. Halliday and Cumings, *Korea*, 121–28; and Atwood, *War and Empire*, 183–84.
91. Halliday and Cumings, *Korea*, 121–23, 155; and Atwood, *War and Empire*, 184–85.
92. This estimate is found in Editors, "Korean War," *History.com*, May 7, 2021, https://www.history.com/topics/korea/korean-war; and in Mandy Baker, "5 Facts about the Korean War, a War Technically Still Being Fought 71 Years Later," *Insider*, June 25, 2021, https://www.businessinsider.com/facts-about-korean-war-still-being-fought-70-years-later-2020-6. Curiously, Halliday and Cumings suggested that the total loss of life was "almost certainly well over three million—possibly more like four million" but then estimated two million North Korean civilian deaths, half a million North Korean military deaths, at least one million Chinese deaths and possibly more, one million South Korean civilian deaths, and well under 200,000 South Korean, U.S., and allied military deaths. These estimates add up to close to five million total deaths. See Halliday and Cumings, *Korea*, 200–201.
93. Stone and Kuznick, *Untold History*, 259–60.
94. Ibid.; Blum, *Killing Hope*, 64–72; and Saaed Kamali Dehghan and Richard Norton-Taylor, "CIA Admits Role in 1953 Coup," *Guardian*, August 19, 2013.
95. Michael Zepezauer, *The CIA's Greatest Hits*, rev. 2nd ed. (Berkeley: Soft Skull Press, 2010), 13.
96. Stone and Kuznick, *Untold History*, 260.
97. Robert C. de Camara, "The Shah as Tyrant: A Look at the Record," *Washington Post*, March 23, 1980.
98. Sylvan and Majeski, *U.S. Foreign Policy*, 63–64.
99. "Foreign Policy Under Franco," in *Spain: A Country Study*, ed. Eric Solsten and Sandra W. Meditz, Library of Congress (Washington, DC: Government Printing Office, 1988), http://countrystudies.us/spain/24.htm.
100. Ibid.
101. Alex Thomson, *U.S. Foreign Policy Towards Apartheid South Africa, 1948–1994: Conflict of Interest* (New York: Palgrave, 2008), 6–10.

NOTES TO PAGES 180-181 405

102. Ibid., 20; and Peter J. Schraeder, *United States Foreign Policy Toward Africa: Incrementalism, Crisis, and Change* (New York: Cambridge University Press, 1994), 195.

103. Dia Kayyali, "EFF Files Amicus Brief in Case That Seeks to Hold IBM Responsible for Facilitating Apartheid in South Africa," Electronic Frontier Foundation, February 5, 2015, https://www.eff.org/deeplinks/2015/02/eff-files-amicus-brief-case-seeks-hold-ibm-responsible-facilitating-apartheid; Michael Kwet, "Apartheid in the Shadows: The U.S.A., IBM, and South Africa's Digital Police State," *CounterPunch*, May 3, 2017, https://www.counterpunch.org/ 2017/05/03/apartheid-in-the-shadows-the-usa-ibm-and-south-africas-digital-police-state/; and Alister Sparks, "Apartheid: How Resettlement works," *Washington Post*, August 7, 1982.

104. Associated Press, "Apartheid Abuse Cases Against Ford, IBM Go Ahead," *USA Today*, April 17, 2014; and David Smith, "General Motors Settles with Victims of Apartheid Regime," *Guardian*, March 2, 2012.

105. Getachew Metaferia, *Ethiopia and the United States: History, Diplomacy, and Analysis* (New York: Algora Publishing, 2009), 45–52.

106. Ibid.; Kiernan, *America: The New Imperialism, From White Settlement to World Hegemony* (London: Verso, 2005), 317; Baffour Agyeman-Duah, "The Horn of Africa: Conflict, Demilitarization, and Reconstruction," *Journal of Conflict Studies* 16/2 (1992), https://journals.lib.unb.ca/index.php/jcs/ article/view/11813/12632; and Lemmu Baissa, "United States Military Assistance to Ethiopia, 1953–1974: Reappraisal of a Difficult Patron-Client Relationship," *Northeast African Studies* 11/3 (1989): 51–70.

107. Kiernan, *New Imperialism*, 317.

108. Ibid.

109. Metaferia, *Ethiopia*, 47, 50.

110. Blum, *Killing Hope*, 72–83; and Stone and Kuznick, *Untold History*, 260–66.

111. Stone and Kuznick, *Untold History*, 262.

112. Ibid., 263; and Blum, *Killing Hope*, 75.

113. Stone and Kuznick, *Untold History*, 264; and Blum, *Killing Hope*, 73–77.

114. Stone and Kuznick, *Untold History*, 265; Blum, *Killing Hope*, 76; and Clodfelter, *Warfare*, 677.

115. Julio Castellanos Cambranes, "Guatemala: The Failure of a Counter-Revolutionary Strategic Model for Latin America," *Ibero-Americana—Nordic Journal of Latin American Studies* 14/1–2 (1985): 28.

116. Mike Allison, "Guatemala: Rios Montt Genocide Trial Ends with Historic Verdict," *Al Jazeera*, May 15, 2013, https://www.aljazeera.com/ opinions/2013/5/15/guatemala-rios-montt-genocide-trial-ends-with-

406 NOTES TO PAGES 181-183

historic-verdict; and Reuters, "Former Guatemala President, Mayor of Capital Arzu, Dies," April 27, 2018, https://www.reuters. com/article/us-guatemala-arzu/ former-guatemala-president-mayor-of-capital-arzu-dies-idUSKBN1HZ01F.

117. Atwood, *War and Empire*, 189–92; Stone and Kuznick, *Untold History*, 268–270.

118. Ibid..

119. Stone and Kuznick, *Untold History*, 269.

120. Ibid., 270; Atwood, *War and Empire*, 192; and Blum, *Killing Hope*, 126.

121. Atwood, *War and Empire*, 192; and Blum, *Killing Hope*, 126.

122. Kiernan, *New Imperialism*, 314; Martin Stone, *The Agony of Algeria* (New York: Columbia University Press, 1997), 228–29, 245; and Irwin M. Wall, *France, the United States, and the Algerian War* (Berkeley: University of California Press, 2001), chap. 1.

123. Miloud Barkaoui, "Managing the Colonial Status Quo: Eisenhower's Cold War and the Algerian War of Independence," *Journal of North African Studies* 17.1 (2011): 125.

124. Wall, *Algerian War*, 20–21.

125. Ibid., 23; and Matthew Connelly, "The French-American Conflict Over North Africa and the Fall of the Fourth Republic," *Revue Française d'Histoire d'Outre-Mer* 84.315 (1997): 13.

126. Kiernan, *New Imperialism*, 314. A $650 million U.S. loan in 1958 was ostensibly contingent on the withdrawal of about one-third of the French troops in Algeria, but this condition was never met. See Connelly, "French-American Conflict," 10, 18; and Wall, *Algerian War*, 282n56.

127. Wall, *Algerian War*, 174–75, 207, 228.

128. Nabila Ramdani, "Fifty Years After Algeria's Independence, France Is Still in Denial," *Guardian*, July 5, 2012; and "France Admits Torture During Algeria's War of Independence," *Al Jazeera*, September 13, 2018, https://www.aljazeera.com/news/2018/09/france-admits-torture-algeria-war-independence-180913140641963.html. An estimate of 800,000 deaths is found in Stone, *Agony of Algeria*, 41. This undercounts the numerous deaths of civilians and Algerians who fought for the French.

129. Clodfelter, *Warfare*, 613–14; Kiernan, *New Imperialism*, 310–11; and Kaku and Axelrod, *Nuclear War*, 168.

130. Associated Press, "Casualties of Mideast Wars," *Los Angeles Times*, March 8, 1991.

131. Blum, *Killing Hope*, 60–61; and Herbert Aptheker, *The Truth About Hungary* (New York: Mainstream Publishers, 1957).

132. Blum, *Killing Hope*, 61; and Aptheker, *Hungary*, chap. 9.

133. Ibid.

NOTES TO PAGES 183–184

134. Clodfelter, *Warfare*, 576–77.
135. Michael Parenti, "Friendly Feudalism: The Tibet Myth," rev. ed., January 2007, http://www.michaelparenti.org/Tibet.html#notes.
136. Ibid.
137. Kenneth Conboy and James Morrison, *The CIA's Secret War in Tibet* (Lawrence: University of Kansas Press, 2002); William Leary, "Secret Mission to Tibet," *Air & Space*, December 1997/January 1998; and Jim Mann, "CIA Gave Aid to Tibetan Exiles in '60s, Files Show," *Los Angeles Times*, September 15, 1998, all cited in Parenti, "Friendly Feudalism."
138. Parenti, "Friendly Feudalism."
139. Ibid.
140. Estimates of approximately 40,000 deaths in 1956 and approximately 90,000 deaths in 1959 are found in Clodfelter, *Warfare*, 674. Additional violent deaths occurred in subsequent years. See Mark J. Mullenbach, "China/Tibet (1950–Present)," Dynamic Analysis of Dispute Management Project, Department of Political Science, University of Central Arkansas, https://uca.edu/politicalscience/dadm-project/asiapacific-region/chinatibet-1950-present/.
141. Clodfelter, *Warfare*, 674.
142. Blum, *Killing Hope*, 145–46; and Kiernan, *New Imperialism*, 324.
143. Blum, *Killing Hope*, 145–46. See also Richard A. Haggerty, ed., "Francois Duvalier 1957–1971" and "Jean-Claude Duvalier 1971–1986," in *Haiti: A Country Study*, Library of Congress (Washington, DC: Government Printing Office, 1989), http://countrystudies.us/haiti/; and Amy Wilentz, *The Rainy Season* (New York: Simon & Schuster, 1989), 328.
144. Jon Henley, "Haiti: A Long Descent to Hell," *Guardian*, January 14, 2010; and Yves Colon, "Duvalier Secret Police Chief Convicted of Murder," AP News, July 16, 1986, https://apnews.com/b6495e5ac-86cf6a410a32958 89f1c4b8.
145. Blum, *Killing Hope*, 94–95.
146. Ibid.
147. Alasdair Soussi, "Legacy of U.S.' 1958 Invasion," *Al Jazeera*, July 15, 2013, https:/www.aljazeera.com/indepth/features/2013/07/2013714111605 25538.html.
148. Soussi, "1958 Invasion"; and Maurice Labelle Jr., "A New Age of Empire? Arab 'Anti-Americanism,' U.S. Intervention, and the Lebanese Civil War of 1958," *International History Review* 35/1 (2013), https://www.tandfonline.com/doi/full/10.1080/07075332.2012.707134? need-Access= true.
149. Blum, *Killing Hope*, 98.
150. Ibid.

408   NOTES TO PAGES 185–186

151. Ibid., 101–3.
152. Ibid.
153. Ibid., 103.
154. Ömer Aslan, "U.S. Involvement in Military Coups D'Etat in Turkey and Pakistan During the Cold War: Between Conspiracy and Reality" (PhD diss., İhsan Doğramacı Bilkent University, 2016), 142. See also Hasan Kösebalaban, *Turkish Foreign Policy: Islam, Nationalism, and Globalization* (London: Palgrave Macmillan, 2011), 89–91; and Christopher Gunn, "The 1960 Coup in Turkey: A U.S. Intelligence Failure or a Successful Intervention?," *Journal of Cold War Studies* 17/2 (Spring 2015), 106, 123–24, 138.
155. Sylvan and Majeski, *U.S. Foreign Policy*, 39.
156. *East African Standard*, December 20, 1960, cited in Christopher Clapham, "The Ethiopian Coup d'Etat of December 1960," *Journal of Modern African Studies* 6/4 (December 1968): 497.
157. Blum, *Killing Hope*, 155–59; Georges Nzongola-Ntalaja, *Patrice Lumumba* (Athens: Ohio University Press, 2014), 130, and *The Congo from Leopold to Kabila: A People's History* (London: Zed Books, 2002), chap. 4; Stephen R. Weissman, "What Really Happened in Congo: The CIA, the Murder of Lumumba, and the Rise of Mobutu," *Foreign Affairs* (July/August 2014), https://www.foreignaffairs.com/articles/democratic-republic-congo/2014-06-16/what-really-happened-congo.
158. Blum, *Killing Hope*, 159–63; and Weissman, "Murder of Lumumba."
159. Weissman, "Murder of Lumumba"; Jacob Bercovich and Richard Jackson, *International Conflict: A Chronological Encyclopedia of Conflicts and Their Management, 1945–1995* (Washington, DC: Congressional Quarterly, 1997), 97. An estimate that hundreds of thousands died between 1961 and 1965 is found in Carole J. L. Collins and Steve Askin, "The Man Who Stole a Country,"(South Africa) *Mail and Guardian*, September 12, 1997, https://mg.co.za/article/1997-09-12-the-man-who-stole-a-country
160. Gonzalez, *Harvest of Empire* (New York: Penguin, 2000), 119; and Blum, *Killing Hope*, 175–77.
161. Bercovich and Jackson, *International Conflict*, 86.
162. "Bay of Pigs: Forty Years After, Chronology," National Security Archive, George Washington University, https://nsarchive2.gwu.edu/bayofpigs/chron.html.
163. Elizabeth Borrego, "60th Anniversary of *La Coubre*: U.S. Terrorism in Cuba," *The Havana Reporter* 10/33, March 4, 2020.
164. Yenia Silva Correa, "60 Years since *La Coubre* Bombing," *Granma*, March 5, 2020.
165. Paul K. Drain and Michele Barry, "Fifty Years of U.S. Embargo: Cuba's

NOTES TO PAGES 186-188

Health Outcomes and Lessons," *Science* 328/5978 (April 30, 2010): 572-73; Richard Garfield and Sarah Santana, "The Impact of the Economic Crisis and the U.S. Embargo on Health in Cuba," *American Journal of Public Health* 87/1 (January 1997): 17-18; and Jack Nelson, "Embargo of Cuba Exacts a 'Tragic Human Toll,' Health Report Says," *Los Angeles Times*, March 3, 1997.

166. Zinn, *People's History*, 440-41; and Stone and Kuznick, *Untold History*, 291-94.

167. Ibid.; Bercovich and Jackson, *International Conflict*, 103; and Parenti, *Sword and the Dollar*, 110-11.

168. Kiernan, *New Imperialism*, 316.

169. Ibid., 316-17.

170. Ibid., 316.

171. Ibid.

172. Ibid., 316-17; and Blum, *Killing Hope*, 250-51.

173. This estimate is found in Clodfelter, *Warfare*, 599. However, it does not include fatalities from starvation, malnutrition, disease, and related causes.

174. Blum, *Killing Hope*, 250.

175. Stone and Kuznick, *Untold History*, 305; and "Operation Farm Gate Combat Missions Authorized," This Day in History: December 6, 1961, *History.com*, August 21, 2018, https:// www.history.com/this-day-in-history/operation-farm-gate-combat-missions-authorized.

176. Blum, *Killing Hope*, 110-14.

177. Ibid.

178. Stone and Kuznick, *Untold History*, 303-13; and Kaku and Axelrod, *Nuclear War*, 142-44.

179. Raymond L. Garthoff, "The Cuban 'Contras' Caper," *Washington Post*, October 25, 1987; Noam Chomsky, "Cuba in the Cross-Hairs: A Near Half-Century of Terror," excerpt from *Hegemony or Survival* (New York: Metropolitan Books, 2003), http://www.chomsky.info/ books/ hegemony02.htm.

180. Andrew Cockburn, "A Loophole in U.S. Sanctions Against Pretoria," *New York Times*, October 13, 1986.

181. Kenneth Mokoena and Sipho Shezi, "Introduction: U.S. Policy Toward Southern Africa: An Overview," *South Africa and the United States: The Declassified History*, ed. Kenneth Mokoena (New York: New Press, 1993), xxi.

182. Ibid.

183. Ibid.; and Thomson, *Apartheid South Africa*, 41-42.

184. Cockburn, "Sanctions Against Pretoria."

185. South African History Online, "1960-1966: The Genesis of the

410 NOTES TO PAGES 188–189

Armed Struggle," November 16, 2016, https://www.sahistory.org.za/article/1960-1966-genesis-armed-struggle; and "Political Executions in South Africa by the Apartheid Government, 1961–1989," August 10, 2017, https://www.sahistory.org.za/topic/political-executions-south-africa-apartheid-government-1961-1989.

186. John F. Kennedy, Commencement Address at American University, Washington, DC, June 10, 1963, John F. Kennedy Presidential Library and Museum, Boston, www.jfklibrary.org/archives/other-resources/john-f-kennedy-speeches/american-university-19630610.

187. Lloyd C. Gardner, *Three Kings: The Rise of an American Empire in the Middle East After World War II* (New York: New Press, 2009), 193–201.

188. Ibid., 195–96.

189. Sylvan and Majeski, *U.S. Foreign Policy*, 185; and Chalmers Johnson, *The Sorrows of Empire: Militarism, Secrecy, and the End of the Republic* (New York: Owl Books, 2005), 223.

190. Gardner, *Three Kings*, 196; and Blum, *Rogue State*, 173.

191. Blum, *Killing Hope*, 153–56; and Philip Agee, *Inside the Company: CIA Diary* (New York: Stonehill, 1975), Part Two.

192. Mark J. Mullenbach, "Ecuador (1905–Present)," Dynamic Analysis of Dispute Management Project, Department of Political Science, University of Central Arkansas, https://uca.edu/ politicalscience/dadm-project/western-hemisphere-region/ecuador-1905-present/.

193. *Time*, June 30, 1975, cited in Blum, *Killing Hope*, 128; and Atwood, *War and Empire*, 93.

194. Ashley Byrne, "50 Years Ago This Week, Riots Determined the Future of the Panama Canal," *The World*, Public Radio International, January 10, 2014, https://www.pri.org/stories/ 2014-01-10/50-years-ago-week-riots-determined-fate-panama-canal; and George Lauderbaugh, "Panama Canal Treaty, 1977," *Encyclopedia of the Developing World*, vol. 3, ed. Thomas M. Leonard (New York: Routledge, 2006), 1238.

195. Byrne, "Panama Canal."

196. Blum, *Killing Hope*, 200–206; and Clodfelter, *Warfare*, 692.

197. Ibid., 163–71; Stone and Kuznick, *Untold History*, 343–45; Kiernan, *New Imperialism*, 327; and National Security Archive, George Washington University, "Brazil Marks 40th Anniversary of Military Coup: Declassified Documents Shed Light on U.S. Role," ed. Peter Kornbluh, March 31, 2004, https://nsarchive2.gwu.edu/NSAEBB/NSA EBB118/index.htm.

198. Jonathan Watts, "Brazil's President Weeps as She Unveils Report on Military Dictatorship's Abuses," *Guardian*, December 10, 2014; and Dom Phillips, "Brazil: Tortured Dissidents Appalled by Bolsonaro's Praise for Dictatorship," *Guardian*, March 30, 2019.

NOTES TO PAGES 189–190 411

199. Atwood, *War and Empire*, 193, Stone and Kuznick, *Untold History*, 327; and Lens, *Forging the American Empire*, 425.
200. Atwood, *War and Empire*, 193–94; and Stone and Kuznick, *Untold History*, 328.
201. Lens, *Forging the American Empire*, 425.
202. Ibid.
203. John A. Farrell, "Nixon's Vietnam Treachery," *New York Times*, December 31, 2016; and Jason Daley, "Notes Indicate Nixon Interfered with 1968 Peace Talks," *Smithsonian Magazine*, January 2, 2017, https://www.smithsonianmag.com/smart-news/notes-indicate-nixon-interfered-1968-peace-talks-180961627/. Anna Chennault conveyed Nixon's promise to the South Vietnam government officials.
204. Discussion of U.S. nuclear threats and related plans during the Vietnam War is found in Stone and Kuznick, *Untold History*, 360–64, 386–87, and 393.
205. Zinn, *People's History*, 493–501; Katie Mettler, "The Day Anti-Vietnam War Protesters Tried to Levitate the Pentagon," *Washington Post*, October 19, 2017; and Derek Seidman, "Vietnam and the Soldiers' Revolt: The Politics of a Forgotten History," *Monthly Review* 68/2 (June 2016), https://monthlyreview.org/2016/06/01/vietnam-and-the-soldiers-revolt/.
206. Socialist Republic of Vietnam officials provided this estimate on the twentieth anniversary of the end of the war. See Agence France-Presse concerning the Vietnamese Government's release of official figures of dead and wounded during the Vietnam War, April 4, 1995, cited in Bob Ostertag, *People's Movements, People's Press: The Journalism of Social Justice Movements* (Boston: Beacon Press, 2007), 209n5; and Myron Allukian and Paul L. Atwood, "The Vietnam War," in *War and Public Health*, 2nd ed., ed. Barry S. Levy and Victor W. Sidel (Oxford: Oxford University Press, 2008), 313–16. Former Secretary of Defense Robert McNamara estimated the loss of life at 3.8 million during a lecture to Peter Kuznick's class at American University, October 21, 1999, cited in Stone and Kuznick, *Untold History*, 387.
207. Blum, *Killing Hope*, 140–45; and Zepezauer, *CIA's Greatest Hits*, 44–45.
208. Blum, *Killing Hope*, 141–44.
209. Ibid., 143–45.
210. John Tirman, "Why Do We Ignore the Civilians Killed in America's Wars?," *Washington Post*, January 6, 2012; John Dower, "Why Can't Americans Remember Anyone's Death Other than Those of Their Own?," *The Nation*, May 4, 2017, https://www.thenation.com/article/why-cant-americans-remember-anyones-deaths-other-than-their-own/.

412   NOTES TO PAGE 191

211. Blum, *Killing Hope*, 133–36.
212. Ibid., 137.
213. Sihanouk himself blamed the CIA for his ouster, but Ben Kiernan has argued that there is no evidence of the agency's involvement, though acknowledging that "a good deal of evidence points to a role played by sections of the U.S. military intelligence establishment and the Army Special Forces." Seymour M. Hersh reported that Green Beret reconnaissance units in Cambodia had made the overthrow of Sihanouk "a high priority" for years, and U.S. military intelligence agents asked prime minister Lon Nol to depose him in 1969. Lon Nol became the new head of state after the coup. U.S. Navy intelligence officer Samuel R. Thornton later reported that approval of plans to overthrow Sihanouk came from "the highest level of government." Kiernan, however, has written that this claim remains uncorroborated. See Norodom Sihanouk and Wilfred Burchett, *My War with the CIA: The Memoirs of Prince Norodom Sihanouk* (New York: Pantheon, 1973); Ben Kiernan, *The Pol Pot Regime: Race, Power, and Genocide in Cambodia Under the Khmer Rouge, 1975–1979*, 3rd ed. (New Haven: Yale University Press, 2008), 300–301; and Seymour M. Hersh, *The Price of Power: Kissinger in the Nixon White House* (New York: Simon & Schuster, 1983), 176–83.
214. Atwood, *War and Empire*, 198; Chalmers Johnson, *Blowback: The Costs and Consequences of American Empire* (New York: Henry Holt, 2004), 12; and Ben Kiernan, *Pol Pot Regime*, 16–25. See also William Shawcross, *Sideshow: Kissinger, Nixon, and the Destruction of Cambodia* (New York: Simon & Schuster, 1979).
215. An estimate of as many as 800,000 is found in Tirman, "Why Do We Ignore the Civilians Killed in America's Wars?" An estimate of 750,000 is provided by Chalmers Johnson in *Blowback*, 12.
216. This estimate is advanced in Ben Kiernan, *Pol Pot Regime*, ix. An assessment of 1.5 million deaths appears in Chalmers Johnson, *Blowback*, 12. See also Atwood, *War and Empire*, 198; Shawcross, *Sideshow*, esp. chap. 24 and Afterword; and Alex De Jong, "Inside the Khmer Rouge's Killing Fields," *Jacobin*, April 27, 2019, https://jacobinmag.com/2019/04/khmer-rouge-james-tyner-cambodia-violence.
217. Sylvan and Majeski, *U.S. Foreign Policy*, 55, 85, 170, 192; and V. G. Kiernan, *New Imperialism*, 290, 300–301.
218. V. G. Kiernan, *New Imperialism*, 301; Clodfelter, *Warfare*, 663; and Arne Kislenko, "A Not So Silent Partner: Thailand's Role in Covert Operations, Counter-Insurgency, and the Wars in Indo-China," *Journal of Conflict Studies* 24/1 (June 2004), https://journals.lib.unb.ca/index.php/JCS/article/view/292.

NOTES TO PAGES 191–193 413

219. Blum, *Rogue State*, 176
220. Ibid.
221. Clodfelter, *Warfare*, 662–63.
222. Sarnasmak, "HIV Infection"; Rho-Ng, "Sex Colonialism"; and Petras and Wongchaisuwan, "AIDS and Child Prostitution," 440–42. https:// www.jstor.org/stable/4399484 https://www.jstor.org/stable/4399484 https://www.jstor.org/stable/4399484.
223. Galeano, *Open Veins*, 77–78.
224. Ibid., 78; and Tim Shenk, "1965 Revolution Shaped Resistance in Dominican Republic and U.S.," *TeleSur*, April 24, 2015, https://www. telesurenglish.net/opinion/1965-Revolution-Shaped-Resistance-in-Dominican-Republic-and-US-20150424-0001.html.
225. David N. Gibbs, *The Political Economy of Third World Intervention: Mines, Money, and U.S. Policy in the Congo Crisis* (Chicago: University of Chicago Press, 1991), 194.
226. Stone and Kuznick, *Untold History*, 279; Nzongola-Ntalaja, *Congo*, 171–72; and Tim Weiner, "Mobutu's Thievery Propped Up by the U.S.," *Seattle Times*, November 3, 1991.
227. Helen C. Epstein, *Another Fine Mess: America, Uganda, and the War on Terror* (New York: Columbia Global Reports, 2017), 116. See also Nzongola-Ntalaja, *Congo*, chap. 5.
228. Blum, *Rogue State*, 177; Nzongola-Ntalaja, *Congo*, chap. 5; and Sean Kelly, *America's Tyrant: The CIA and Mobutu of Zaire* (Washington, DC: American University Press, 1993), ix–xi, chaps. 12–15.
229. George H. W. Bush, quoted in *Washington Post*, May 21, 1997, cited in Blum, *Rogue State*, 177.
230. Stone and Kuznick, *Untold History*, 348–50; Blum, *Killing Hope*, 193–97; Sylvan and Majeski, *U.S. Foreign Policy*, 186; and Simpson, *Economists with Guns*, chap. 6.
231. Stone and Kuznick, *Untold History*, 350; Blum, *Killing Hope*, 196–97; Simpson, *Economists with Guns*, chap. 6.
232. Stone and Kuznick, *Untold History*, 350; Blum, *Killing Hope*, 194–97; Sylvan and Majeski, *U.S. Foreign Policy*, 186; Hamish McDonald, "Indonesia's Coup Remains a Mystery 50 Years On," Australian Broadcasting Corporation News, September 30, 2015, https://www.abc.net.au/news/2015-10-01/mcdonald-the-indonesian-coup-remains-a-mystery/6818682; and Simpson, *Economists with Guns*, 173–74.
233. A survey authorized by the Indonesian army's operations command estimated that one million people died. The same estimate appears in Tariq Ali, *The Clash of Fundamentalisms: Crusades, Jihads, and Modernity* (London: Verso, 2002), 382; and Michael Parenti, *The Face of Imperialism* (Boulder, CO: Paradigm Publishers, 2011), 79. Simpson

414 NOTES TO PAGES 193-195

estimated that "perhaps half a million" perished. See *Economists with Guns*, 1, 192. A similar estimate is found in V. G. Kiernan, *New Imperialism*, 302.

234. Blum *Killing Hope*, 193–97; Sylvan and Majeski, *U.S. Foreign Policy*, 187; and Simpson, *Economists with Guns*, chap. 6.

235. Blum, *Killing Hope*, 194; and Ali, *Clash of Fundamentalisms*, 380.

236. Howard Federspiel, quoted in Stone and Kuznick, *Untold History*, 351.

237. Max Frankel, "U.S. Aides Are Cautious on Indonesia Power Shift," *New York Times*, March 12, 1966, cited in Stone and Kuznick, *Untold History*, 350.

238. Parenti, *Face of Imperialism*, 79.

239. *Guardian*, December 12, 1983, cited in Blum, *Killing Hope*, 194.

240. Blum, *Killing Hope*, 172–74; Clodfelter, *Warfare*, 694.

241. Blum, *Killing Hope*, 198–200; John Stockwell, *In Search of Enemies: A CIA Story* (New York: W. W. Norton, 1978), 201n; Seymour M. Hersh, "CIA Said to Have Aided Plotters Who Overthrew Nkrumah in Ghana," *New York Times*, May 9, 1978.

242. David J. Finlay, "The Coup in Ghana . . . One Year Later," *Trans-Action* 4 (1967): 16.

243. Blum, *Killing Hope*, 221–26; and V. G. Kiernan, *New Imperialism*, 326–27.

244. Mark J. Mullenbach, "Bolivia (1917–Present)," Dynamic Analysis of Dispute Management Project, Department of Political Science, University of Central Arkansas, https://uca.edu/politicalscience/dadm-project/western-hemisphere-region/bolivia-1917-present/.

245. Blum, *Killing* Hope, 225–26; and Michael Ratner and Michael Steven Smith, *Who Killed Che Guevara? How the CIA Got Away with Murder* (New York: OR Books, 2011).

246. Simons, *Colombia*, 42–44, 48–50, and chap. 10; Kirk, *America's War in Colombia*, 48–51, 54–56, 187–88, 240–48, 252, 256–57.

247. Jonathan Watts and Sibylla Brodzinsky, "Colombia Closes in on a Peace Deal that Could End World's Longest Civil War," *Guardian*, March 16, 2014.

248. Blum, *Killing Hope*, 215–21, and *Rogue State*, 184–85; and Chalmers Johnson, S*orrows of Empire*, 205–6.

249. Chalmers Johnson, *Sorrows of Empire*, 204–5.

250. Ibid., 206. See also Blum, *Killing Hope*, 218.

251. V. G. Kiernan, *New Imperialism*, 331–32.

252. On mass imprisonment and torture by the Greek dictatorship, see Blum, *Killing Hope*, 219–21. Approximately fifty people died at the hands of the junta's forces during the uprising at the Athens Polytechnic School in 1973. See "George Papadopoulos Dies," *Washington Post*,

NOTES TO PAGES 195–196

June 28, 1999. An estimate of the number of deaths resulting from torture is not available.

253. Clodfelter, *Warfare*, 580.

254. Gardner, *Three Kings*, 215–20; and Zaki Shalom, "Lyndon Johnson's Meeting with Abba Eban, 26 May 1967, An Introduction," *Israel Studies* 4/2 (Fall 1999): 221–36.

255. Moti Bassok, "Hellfire in Perspective: U.S. Military Aid to Israel Exceeds $100 Billion," *Haaretz*, August 18, 2014.

256. Associated Press, "Casualties of Mideast Wars."

257. Clodfelter, *Warfare*, 616.

258. Stephen Zunes, "Why the U.S. Supports Israel," Institute for Policy Studies, May 1, 2002, https://ips-dc.org/why_the_us_supports_israel/.

259. This description of the PLO comes from "PLO: Palestine Liberation Organization," Embassy of Palestine, https://www.ambasciatapalestina.com/en/p-l-o/.

260. V. G. Kiernan, *New Imperialism*, 317; Clodfelter, *Warfare*, 590.

261. Godfrey B. Warren, "Petroleum and the Nigerian Civil War, 1966–1970," *The Fletcher Forum* 3/2 (Summer 1979): 67–68.

262. Ibid., 68–70, 73–75.

263. Ibid., 79–80.

264. Ibid., 79.

265. Ibid., 80; and Stephen Rosskamm Shalom, *Imperial Alibis*, 118.

266. Stephen Rosskamm Shalom, *Imperial Alibis*, 118–19; and David Callahan, *Unwinnable Wars: American Power and Ethnic Conflict* (New York: Hill and Wang, 1997), 135.

267. Stephen Rosskamm Shalom, *Imperial Alibis*, 118; and Warren, "Nigerian Civil War," 80.

268. Stephen Rosskamm Shalom, *Imperial Alibis*, 119–22; and Noo Saro-Wiwa, review, "*There Was a Country: A Personal History of Biafra*, by Chinua Achebe," *Guardian*, October 5, 2012.

269. Estimates of one to three million deaths, largely from starvation, are in Chigbo Arthur Anyaduba, "Nigerian Writers Compare Genocide of Igbos to Holocaust," *The Conversation*, February 12, 2019, https://theconversation.com/nigerian-writers-compare-genocide-of-igbos-to-the-holocaust-110766; and in "Biafra War," GlobalSecurity.org, https://www.global security.org/military/world/war/biafra.htm. An estimate of two million deaths is in Cebiloan Hyacint, "Nigeria, Biafra, and Oil," *Socialist Standard*, no. 1246, June 2008, https:// www.worldsocialism.org/spgb/socialist-standard/2000s/2008/no-1246-june-2008/nigeriabiafra-and-oil/. An estimate of more than three million deaths is in Saro-Wiwa, review of *There Was a Country*.

270. Stephen Rosskamm Shalom, *Imperial Alibis*, 117–22; Hyacint, "Nigeria, Biafra, and Oil"; and Warren, "Nigerian Civil War," 79–80.

416 NOTES TO PAGES 196–198

271. Chalmers Johnson, *Sorrows of Empire*, 223.
272. Neil MacFarquhar, "Saddam Hussein, Defiant Dictator Who Ruled Iraq With Violence and Fear, Dies," *New York Times*, December 30, 2006.
273. Ibid.
274. Chalmers Johnson, *Sorrows of Empire*, 210–11; Raymond Bonner, "Attach Ropes to U.S. Aid to Marcos," *New York Times*, February 17, 1985; and Felix Chang, "U.S. Military Returns to the Philippines," *RealClearWorld*, October 9, 2013, https://www.realclearworld.com/2013/10/09/us_military_returns_to_the_philippines_152293.html.
275. Bonner, "Aid to Marcos."
276. Rhonda Ramiro and Azadeh Shahshahani, "America's Indefensible Alliance with the Philippines," *Huffington Post*, February 23, 2018, https://www.huffpost.com/entry/opinion-ramiro-duterte-philippines_n_5a8f3c57e4b01e9e56b9cae1.
277. Estimates of 40,000 NPA deaths and 150,000 Muslim deaths are found in Thomas Lum and Ben Dolven, *The Republic of the Philippines and U.S. Interests—2014*, Congressional Research Service (Washington, DC: May 15, 2014), 20–21, https://fas.org.sgp/crs/row/R43498. pdf. This total does not include the deaths of insurgents or other victims of the government since 2014.
278. Bradley J. Pierson, "The Power of Presence: Nixon, Israel, and the Black September Crisis," *Primary Source: The Indiana University Undergraduate History Journal* 4/1 (Fall 2013): 35–36, http://www.indiana.edu/~psource/archive.html.
279. Ibid., 36.
280. Ibid., 37.
281. Adam M. Garfinkel, "U.S. Decision-Making in the Jordan Crisis: Correcting the Record," *Political Science Quarterly* 100/1 (Spring 1985): 124–36.
282. Pierson, "Power of Presence," 38; Garfinkel, "Jordan Crisis," 135–36; and "From the Archive, 29 September 1970: President Nasser Dies of Heart Attack," *Guardian*, September 29, 2014.
283. Clodfelter, *Warfare*, 618.
284. Middle East Research and Information Project, "Armed Struggle in North Yemen," *MERIP Reports* 22 (November 1973): 24–26.
285. Bercovitch and Jackson, *International Conflict*, 145; and Clodfelter, *Warfare*, 618.
286. Some Turkish politicians publicly criticized the role of the CIA in the coup. See V. G. Kiernan, *New Imperialism*, 332; Kösebalaban, *Turkish Foreign Policy*, 104; and Interview with Jurgen Roth, "Turkish Fascism as NATO Democracy," *Counterspy* 6/2 (February-April 1982), 20.
287. Associated Press, "Turkish Regime Is Ousted by the Military Leaders," *New York Times*, March 31, 1971.

NOTES TO PAGES 198–199 417

288. "Timeline: A History of Turkish Coups," *Al Jazeera*, July 15, 2016, https://www.aljazeera. com/news/europe/2012/04/20124472814687973.html; and Marvine Howe, "A Day in the Political Life of Turkey: Shootings and Reprisals by Left and Right," *New York Times*, October 30, 1979.

289. ANF (Firat News Agency), "History of U.S. Military Support for Turkey," ANF News, April 20, 2018, https://anfenglish.com/news/history-of-us-military-support-for-turkey-26207.

290. *San Francisco Chronicle*, September 1, 1971, cited in Blum, *Killing Hope*, 228; Ken Silverstein, "A Trip Down Memory Lane: U.S. Financed 1971 Bolivian Coup," *Harper's Magazine*, June 2, 2010; and Stephen Zunes, "U.S. Intervention in Bolivia," *Huffington Post*, May 25, 2011, https://www.huffingtonpost.com/stephen-zunes/us-intervention-in-bolivi_b_127528.html.

291. Silverstein "Bolivian Coup"; and Zunes, "Intervention in Bolivia."

292. Charles Mohr, "Ugandan President to Curb Nationalization Plans," *New York Times*, May 2, 1971; and Pat Hutton and Jonathan Bloch, "How the West Established Idi Amin and Kept Him There," in *Dirty Work 2: The CIA in Africa*, ed. Ellen Ray, William Schaap, Karl Van Meter, and Louis Wolf (London: Zed Press, 1980), 145–46.

293. Mohr, "Ugandan President"; and Hutton and Bloch, "Idi Amin," 149.

294. Hutton and Bloch, "Idi Amin," 150–51; and Roger Mann, "Libya's Military Largesse Feeds Idi Amin's Anti-Zionism," *Washington Post*, February 27, 1977.

295. Hutton and Bloch, 150–53; and "Paper Cites CIA Aid to Amin's Army in 1970s," *New York Times*, December 17, 1986.

296. Michael T. Kaufman, "Murderous and Erratic Ruler of Uganda in 1970s, Dies in Exile," *New York Times*, August 17, 2003.

297. V. G. Kiernan, *New Imperialism*, 305.

298. Lorraine Boissoneault, "The Genocide the U.S. Can't Remember but Bangladesh Can't Forget," *Smithsonian Magazine*, December 16, 2016) https://www.smithsonianmag.com/ history/genocide-us-cant-remember-bangladesh-cant-forget-180961490/.

299. This expression is from Sir Olaf Caroe, the British former governor of the North-west Frontier Province in India, cited in V. G. Kiernan, *New Imperialism*, 305.

300. Boissoneault, "Genocide Bangladesh Can't Forget."

301. Ibid.

302. Ibid.; V. G. Kiernan, *New Imperialism*, 307; and Dexter Filkins, "Collateral Damage," *New York Times*, September 27, 2013.

303. Boissoneault, "Genocide Bangladesh Can't Forget"; V. G. Kiernan, *New Imperialism*, 307; and Filkins, "Collateral Damage."

304. Ibid.

418   NOTES TO PAGES 199–200

305. An estimate of one million deaths was advanced by journalists from *Time* at the end of the war. See Ishaan Tharoor, "Keeping Dhaka's Ghosts Alive," *Time*, September 24, 2008, http:// content.time.com/ time/world/article/0,8599,1843844,00.html. The government of Bangladesh has long claimed a total of about three million deaths, and similar estimates are found in Boissoneault, "Genocide Bangladesh Can't Forget"; and in Michael Peck, "The War That Made India a Great Power (and Destroyed Pakistan)," *The National Interest*, December 16, 2016, https://nationalinterest.org/blog/the-buzz/the-war-made-india-great-power-destroyed-pakistan-18761. A challenge to the estimate of three million deaths appears in David Bergman, "The Politics of Bangladesh's Genocide Debate," *New York Times*, April 5, 2016, https:// www.nytimes.com/2016/04/06/opinion/the-politics-of-bangladeshs-genocide-debate.html. An estimate of 500,000 deaths is found in George T. Curlin, Lincoln C. Chen, and Sayed Babur Hussain, "Demographic Crisis: The Impact of the Bangladesh Civil War on Births and Deaths in a Rural Area of Bangladesh," *Population Studies* 30/1 (March 1976): 87–105. Other analysts have suggested that the number of deaths could be between 300,000 and three million. See, for example, Anam Zakaria, "Remembering the War of 1971 in East Pakistan," *Al Jazeera*, December 16, 2019, https://www.aljazeera.com/indepth/ opinion/ remembering-war-1971-east-pakistan-191216054546348. html; and Mark Dummett, "Bangladesh War: The Article that Changed History," BBC News, December 16, 2011, https://www.bbc. com/ news/world-asia-16207201.

306. Gerald Horne, *From the Barrel of a Gun: The United States and the War Against Zimbabwe, 1965–1980* (Chapel Hill: University of North Carolina Press, 2001), 143, 150–53.

307. Ibid., chaps. 4–5.

308. Ibid., 157–59, 187–98, and chap. 6.

309. Ibid., 138, 142.

310. *Weekly Mail and Guardian*, August 1–7, 1997; and *Zimbabwe Mirror*, May 19–25, 2000, cited in Horne, *From the Barrel of a Gun*, 289n8.

311. Callahan, *Unwinnable Wars*, 3.

312. Ibid., 4–5.

313. An estimate of more than 100,000 deaths is found in Callahan, *Unwinnable Wars*, 3, 5. An estimate of 200,000 deaths is found in Warren Weinstein, "Conflict and Confrontation in Central Africa: The Revolt in Burundi, 1972," *Africa Today* 19/4 (Autumn 1972): 23.

314. Juan De Onis, "Uruguay's Military Leaders Angry Over Congressional Cutoff on Aid for Arms," *New York Times*, October 5, 1976.

315. Ibid.

NOTES TO PAGES 201–202

316. "Uruguay's Ex-President Arrested," BBC News, November 17, 2006, http://news.bbc.co.uk/ 2/hi/ americas/6157418.stm.
317. Stone and Kuznick, *Untold History*, 372–78; and Blum, *Killing Hope*, 209–15.
318. Stone and Kuznick, *Untold History*, 372; Blum, *Killing Hope*, 206–8.
319. Stone and Kuznick, *Untold History*, 374; and Blum, *Killing Hope*, 210.
320. Senan Fox, "Remembering Salvador Allende," Open Democracy, August 21, 2013, https://www.opendemocracy.net/en/remembering-salvador-allende/.
321. Stone and Kuznick, *Untold History*, 375–76.
322. Stone and Kuznick, *Untold History*, 372–78; and Blum, *Killing Hope*, 209–15.
323. This language is the CIA's, quoted in Stephen Kinzer, *Overthrow: America's Century of Regime Change from Hawai'i to Iraq* (New York: Henry Holt, 2006), 190, and cited in Stone and Kuznick, *Untold History*, 377.
324. Estimates of more than three thousand deaths are in Stone and Kuznick, *Untold History*, 377–78; and in Blum, *Rogue State*, 183–184. Approximately one thousand other Chileans disappeared and are presumed dead. See Maryrose Fison, "Chileans Honor Those Tortured, Killed after 1973 Military Coup," *Los Angeles Times*, September 12, 2013.
325. Zunes, "Why the U.S. Supports Israel."
326. Ibid.; Abraham Rabinovich, "The War That Nearly Was," *Jerusalem Post*, October 2, 2012; and John L. Scherer, "Soviet and American Behavior During the Yom Kippur War," *World Affairs* 141/1 (Summer 1978): 4, 17.https://www.jstor.org/stable/20671755.
327. Rabinovich, "The War That Nearly Was"; and Scherer, "Yom Kippur War," 3–23.
328. Kaku and Axelrod, *Nuclear War*, 169–70.
329. Ibid., 170–71.
330. Henry Kissinger quoted in "Memorandum of Discussion at the 174th Meeting of the NSC," Top Secret—Eyes Only, FRUS 1952-4, vol. 15, Part 2, 1984, 1654, cited in Kaku and Axelrod, *Nuclear War*, 171.
331. Associated Press, "Casualties of Mideast Wars."
332. Chalmers Johnson, *Sorrows of Empire*, 75–76; Blum, *Rogue State*, 188–89.
333. Blum, *Rogue State*, 188.
334. Chalmers Johnson, *Sorrows of Empire*, 76; Blum, *Rogue State*, 188.
335. Blum, *Killing Hope*, 251–57; Stephen R. Weissman, "CIA Covert Action in Zaire and Angola: Patterns and Consequences," *Political Science Quarterly* 94/2 (Summer 1979): 282–84; and Howard W. French, "From Old Files, a New Story of U.S. Role in Angolan War," *New York Times*, March 31, 2002.

336. Weissman, "CIA Covert Action," 284; and Charles Mohr, "Panel Links CIA to Arms Shipment," *New York Times*, March 25, 1982, cited in Blum, *Killing Hopes*, 253–54.
337. Clodfelter, *Warfare*, 603–4.
338. As'ad AbuKhalil, "Lebanon: Key Battleground for Middle East Policy," Institute for Policy Studies, October 12, 2005, https://ips-dc.org/lebanon_key_battleground_for_middle_east_ policy/.
339. John Gershman and Stephen Zunes, "The U.S. and Lebanon: A Meddlesome History," *Foreign Policy in Focus,* April 6, 2006, https://fpif.org/the_united_states_and_lebanon_ a_ meddlesome_history/.
340. AbuKhalil, "Lebanon"; and Gershman and Zunes, "U.S. and Lebanon."
341. Ibid.
342. Ibid.
343. Ibid.
344. Clodfelter, *Warfare*, 625.
345. National Security Archive, Carlos Osorio and Thomas Blanton, "Press Release: Argentine Military Believed U.S. Gave Go-Ahead for Dirty War," George Washington University, August 21, 2002, http://nsarchive.gwu.edu/NSAEBB/NSAEBB73/index3.htm; Duncan Campbell, "Kissinger Approved Argentinian 'Dirty War,'" *Guardian*, December 5, 2003; Jorge E. Taiana, "Foreign Powers, Economic Support, and Geopolitics," in *The Economic Apprentices to the Argentine Dictatorship: Outstanding Debts*, ed. Horacio Verbitsky and Juan Pablo Bohoslavsky (Cambridge: Cambridge University Press, 2016), 67–69.
346. Cynthia J. Arnson, "The U.S. Congress and Argentina: Human Rights and Military Aid," in *Argentina-U.S. Bilateral Relations*, ed. Cynthia J. Arnson, (Washington, DC: Woodrow Wilson International Center for Scholars, 2003), 83–96.
347. Campbell, "Argentinian 'Dirty War.'"
348. Roger Burbach and Jim Tarbell, *Imperial Overstretch: George W. Bush and the Hubris of Empire* (London: Zed Books, 2004), 69.
349. J. Patrice McSherry, "Operation Condor: Deciphering the U.S. Role," *Global Policy Forum* (July 2001), https://www.globalpolicy.org/component/content/article/168/28173.html.
350. Stone and Kuznick, *Untold History*, 378.
351. Blum, *Killing Hope*, 263–67.
352. Ibid., 264.
353. Ibid., 264–66.
354. Ibid., 267.
355. Vijay Prashad, *The Darker Nations* (New York: New Press, 2007), 238.
356. LaFeber, *Inevitable Revolutions*, 229–42.
357. Ibid., 230–31.

NOTES TO PAGES 205–206   421

358. Ibid., 233; Blum, *Killing Hope*, 291; and Charles H. Roberts, "U.S.-Sponsored Genocide," *Harvard Crimson*, October 25, 1978.
359. LaFeber, *Inevitable Revolutions*, 238.
360. Ibid., 241; and Blum, *Killing Hope*, 291.
361. Stone and Kuznick, *Untold History*, 411; and Andrew Glass, "This Day in Politics: Carter Lauds Shah of Iran, Dec. 31, 1977," *Politico*, December 31, 2018, https://www.politico.com/ story/2018/12/30/this-day-in-politics-december-31-1077103.
362. Stone and Kuznick, *Untold History*, 411.
363. Reuters, "Timeline of the Iranian Revolution," February 11, 2019, https://www.reuters.com/article/us-iran-revolution-anniversary-timeline/timeline-of-the-iranian-revolution-idUSKCN1 Q017W.
364. Zein Basravi, "Iran's Referendum and the Transition to the Islamic Republic," *Al Jazeera*, March 30, 2019, www.aljazeera.com/features/2019/3/30/irans-referendum-and-the-transforma tion-to-the-islamic-republic.
365. Stone and Kuznick, *Untold History*, 410.
366. Ken Menkhaus, "U.S. Foreign Assistance to Somalia: Phoenix from the Ashes?" *Middle East Policy* 5/1 (January 1997), https://www.mepc.org/node/4743; and Stephen Zunes, "The Long and Hidden History of the U.S. in Somalia," *AlterNet*, January 21, 2002, http://www.thirdworldtraveler.com/North_Africa/Hx_US_Somalia.html.
367. Menkhaus, "U.S. Foreign Assistance to Somalia."
368. Ismail Einashe and Matt Kennard, "In the Valley of Death: Somaliland's Forgotten Genocide," Pulitzer Center on Crisis Reporting, October 22, 2018, https://pulitzercenter.org/ reporting/valley-death-somalilands-forgotten-genocide.
369. Menkhaus, "Foreign Assistance to Somalia."
370. Ibid.
371. Ibid., and Zunes, "The U.S. in Somalia."
372. Mark Fineman, "The Oil Factor in Somalia: Four American Petroleum Giants Had Agreements with the African Nation Before Its Civil War Began. They Could Reap Big Rewards If Peace Is Restored," *Los Angeles Times*, January 18, 1993, cited in Parenti, *Against Empire*, 122–23.
373. Blum, *Killing Hope*, 340; and Beverly Male, *Revolutionary Afghanistan* (London: Palgrave Macmillan, 1982), chap. 6.
374. Blum, *Killing Hope*, 340–41; and Male, *Revolutionary Afghanistan*, chap. 6.
375. Blum, *Killing Hope*, 343–52; Stone and Kuznick, *Untold History*, 412–16; Chalmers Johnson, *Blowback*, xii–xiv; Gabriel Kolko, *Another Century of War?* (New York: New Press, 2002), 45–50; and John Trumpbour, "Epilogue: The American Imperium from the Cold War to the Age of Bin Laden," in V. G. Kiernan, *New Imperialism*, 367–72.

422   NOTES TO PAGES 207–208

376. "Les Révélations d'un Ancien Conseilleur de Carter: 'Oui, la CIA Est Entrée en Afghanistan avant les Russes,'" *Le Nouvel Observateur* (January 15–21, 1998), 76, trans. William Blum and David N. Gibbs, cited in David N. Gibbs, "Afghanistan: The Soviet Invasion in Retrospect," *International Politics* 37/2 (2000): 241–42.

377. The estimate of 1.5 million deaths is in Nake M. Kamrany, "Ending the 30-Year War in Afghanistan," Middle East Institute, April 19, 2012, https://www.mei.edu/publications/ending-30-year-war-afghanistan. The estimate of 1.8 million deaths appears in M. Siddieq Noorzoy, "Afghanistan's Children: The Tragic Victims of 30 Years of War," Middle East Institute, April 20, 2012, https://www.mei.edu/publications/afghanistans-children-tragic-victims-30-years-war. Estimates of more than one million dead are found in Blum, *Rogue State*, 201; and in Alan Taylor, "The Soviet War in Afghanistan, 1979–1989," *The Atlantic*, August 4, 2014, https://www.theatlantic.com/photo/2014/08/the-soviet-war-in-afghanistan-1979-1989/100786/.

378. Chalmers Johnson, *Blowback*, xii–xv; and Trumpbour, "Epilogue," in Kiernan, 369–72.

379. Blum, *Rogue State*, 194.

380. Clodfelter, *Warfare*, 627. This estimate reflects combat deaths only.

381. Blum, *Rogue State*, 194.

382. Aslan, "U.S. Involvement in Military Coups," 143–51; Kösebalaban, *Turkish Foreign Policy*, 111–12; Dorian Jones, "Turkey's Failed Coup Stokes Historical U.S.-Turkish Tensions," *Voice of America*, August 22, 2016, https://www.voa news.com/a/turkey-failed-coup-shakes-historical-us-turkish-relations/3475235.html; and Reuters, "Factbox—Turkey's 1980 Coup and Its Aftermath," April 4, 2012, https://www.reuters. com/article/uk-turkey-trial-1980/fact box-turkeys-1980-coup-and-its-aftermath-idUKBRE8330F320120404.

383. Blum, *Rogue State*, 195; and Johnson, *Blowback*, 112–19.

384. Niels Hahn, "U.S. Covert and Overt Actions in Liberia, 1970s–2003," *Air and Space Power Journal: Africa and Francophonie* 5/3 (Fall 2014): 20–21.

385. Ibid., 21.

386. Ibid., 21, 23–24.

387. Ibid., 22; Bill Berkeley, "Liberia," *The Atlantic*, December 1992, http://www.theatlantic.com/magazine/ archive/1992/12/liberia/376354/; and Michael Massing, "How Liberia Held 'Free' Elections," *The Nation*, October 13, 2005, https://www.thenation.com/article/how-liberia-held-free-elections/.

388. Hahn, "U.S. Actions in Liberia," 23–24.

389. Jimmy Carter, "State of the Union Address 1980," January 23, 1980,

NOTES TO PAGES 208–210 423

Jimmy Carter Presidential Library and Museum, https://www.jimmy-carterlibrary.gov/assets/documents/ speeches/su80jec.phtml; Thanassis Cambanis, "The Carter Doctrine: A Middle East Strategy Past Its Prime," *Boston Globe*, October 14, 2012; and Daniel L. Davis, "Don't Take the Oil: Time to Ditch the Carter Doctrine," *The National Interest*, February 3, 2017, https://national interest.org/feature/dont-take-the-oil-time-ditch-the-carter-doctrine-19310.

390. Carter, "State of the Union Address 1980," cited in Josh Cohen, "The U.S. Commitment to the Persian Gulf Is Outdated," Reuters, July 7, 2016, https://www.reuters.com/article/us-persian-gulf-commentary/commentary-the-u-s-commitment-to-the-persian-gulf-is-outdated-idUSKC N0ZN2DB.

391. Cambanis, "Carter Doctrine"; Cohen, "U.S. Commitment to the Persian Gulf"; Andrew J. Bacevich, *America's War for the Greater Middle East: A Military History* (New York: Random House, 2016); and Marwan Bishara, review of *America's War for the Greater Middle East*, by Andrew J. Bacevich, *Al Jazeera*, August 4, 2016, https://www.aljazeera.com/indepth/opinion/2016/08/america-war-greater-middle-east-160803141910584.html.

6. The Holocausts of Pax Americana II

1. Parenti, *The Sword and the Dollar* (New York: St. Martin's Press, 2011, chaps. 1–3, and *Against Empire* (San Francisco: City Lights Books, 1995), chap. 2; Sylvan and Majeski, "An Agent-Based Model of the Acquisition of U.S. Client States," Paper delivered at the 44th Annual Convention of the International Studies Association, Portland, February 25–March 1, 2003, 19, https://faculty.washington.edu/majeski/isa03.pap.pdf; and David Vine, "The Imperialist Lie That Won't Die: America Is Making the Planet Safer," *Salon*, September 20, 2015, https://www.salon.com/2015/09/20/garrisoning_the_globe_how_u_s_military_bases_abroad_undermine_our_national_security_and_harm_us_all_partner/.

2. Parenti, *Democracy for the Few*, 9th ed. (Boston: Wadsworth Cengage Learning, 2011), 150; Eric Hobsbawm, Preface, in V.G. Kiernan, *America: The New Imperialism, From White Settlement to World Hegemony* (London: Verso, 2005), xii; Alfred W. McCoy, *In the Shadows of the American Century: The Rise and Decline of U.S. Global Power* (Chicago: Haymarket Books, 2017), 15, 21; Ferguson, *Colossus: The Rise and Fall of the American Empire* (New York: Penguin, 2004), Introduction and chap. 1; and Daniel Bessner, "America Has No Duty to Rule the World," *New Republic*, October 21, 2020, https://newrepublic.com/article/159672/tomorrow-world-wertheim-book-review-birth-america-world-power.

424   NOTES TO PAGES 210-211

3. Quoted in Grandin, *Empire's Workshop: Latin America, the United States, and the Rise of the New Imperialism* (New York: Henry Holt), 181. See also Stone and Kuznick, *The Untold History of the United States* (New York: Gallery Books, 2012), chap. 11.

4. Atwood, *War and Empire:The American Way of Life* (London: Pluto Press, 2010), 209–28; Parenti, *Sword and the Dollar*, chaps. 1–2, and *Against Empire*, chaps. 6–7; Blum, *Killing Hope: U.S. Military and CIA Interventions Since World War II*, rev.ed. (Monroe, ME: Common Courage Press, 2004), chaps. 41–56, and *Rogue State: A Guide to the World's Only Superpower* (Monroe, ME: Common Courage Press, 2005), chap. 17; Stone and Kuznick, *Untold History*, chaps. 11–14; Grandin, *Empire's Workshop*; Stephen Rosskamm Shalom, *Imperial Alibis: Rationalizing U.S. Intervention After the Cold War* (Boston: South End Press, 1993); and Vltchek, *Exposing Lies of the Empire* (Jakarta: Badak Merah, 2015).

5. On the catastrophe resulting from the collapse of most socialist states, see Parenti, *Blackshirts and Reds: Rational Fascism and the Overthrow of Communism* (San Francisco: City Lights Books, 1998), chaps. 6 and 7; Seumas Milne, "Catastroika Has Not Only Been a Disaster for Russia," *Guardian*, August 15, 2001; Nancy Holstrom and Richard Smith, "The Necessity of Gangster Capitalism: Primitive Accumulation in Russia and China," *Monthly Review* 51/9 (February 2000); Stephen F. Cohen, *Failed Crusade: America and the Tragedy of Post-Communist Russia* (New York: W.W. Norton, 2001); and Michael Parenti, *To Kill a Nation: The Attack on Yugoslavia* (London: Verso, 2000).

6. On the decline of the U.S. Empire, see McCoy, *American Century*, esp. 22–24 and chap. 8; Charles Kupchan, "The Decline of the West: Why America Must Prepare for the End of Dominance," *The Atlantic*, March 20, 2012, https://theatlantic.com/international/archive/2012/ 03/the-decline-of-the-west-why-america-must-prepare-for-the-end-of-dominance/254779/; Christopher Layne, "What Comes after U.S. Primacy," *The National Interest*, September 8, 2016, https://nationalinterest.org/ feature/what-comes-after-us-primacy-17631; Nathan P. Freier, Christopher M. Bado, Christopher J. Bolan, Robert S. Hume, and J. Matthew Lissner, *At Our Own Risk: DoD Risk Assessment in a Post-Primacy World*, U.S. Army War College, Strategic Studies Institute, June 29, 2017, https://ssi.armywarcollege.edu/pubs/display.cfm?pubID=1358; and Victor Bulmer-Thomas, *Empire in Retreat: The Past, Present, and Future of the United States* (New Haven: Yale University Press, 2018), chaps. 11, 12, and Epilogue.

7. McCoy, *American Century*, 240–43; Bulmer-Thomas, *Empire in Retreat*, 305; John Campbell, *American Discontent: Donald Trump and Decline of the Golden Age* (Oxford: Oxford University Press, 2018); Dilip Hiro,

NOTES TO PAGES 211-212

425

"Trump Is Accelerating America's Decline," *The Nation*, July 2, 2019, https://www.thenation.com/ article/archive/tom-dispatch-trump-is-accelerating-americas-decline-china-russia/; and Jon Henley, "Majority of Europeans Fear Biden Unable to Fix 'Broken' U.S.," *Guardian*, January 19, 2021.

8. Lou Cannon, "Reagan: Action to Rescue Hostages 'Long Overdue,'" *Washington Post*, May 1, 1980.

9. Stone and Kuznick, *Untold History*, 420.

10. Ibid. Two congressional investigations later found "no credible evidence" to support this account, but this conclusion was mistaken. See Barbara Honiger, *October Surprise* (New York: Tudor Publishing, 1989); Gary Sick, *October Surprise: America's Hostages in Iran and the Election of Ronald Reagan* (New York: Times Books, 1991); Robert Parry, *Trick or Treason: The October Surprise Mystery* (New York: Sheridan Square Press, 1993); Nicholas Schou, "The 'October Surprise' Was Real, Legendary Spymaster Hints in Final Interview," *Newsweek*, April 24, 2016, https://www.newsweek.com/duane-dewey-clarridge-october-surprise-spies-cia-451611; Kai Bird, "Some 'October Surprise' Conspiracies Turn Out to Be True," *Los Angeles Times*, June 20, 2017; and *The Outlier: The Unfinished Presidency of Jimmy Carter* (New York: Crown, 2021), 551–63, 572–73, 625.

11. Bird, "'October Surprise' Conspiracies."

12. Stone and Kuznick, *Untold History*, 420; and Seymour M. Hersh, "U.S. Secretly Gave Aid to Iraq Early in Its War Against Iran," *New York Times*, January 26, 1992.

13. Stone and Kuznick, *Untold History*, 439. See also Hersh, "U.S. Secretly Gave Aid to Iraq."

14. Ibid."

15. Stone and Kuznick, *Untold History*, 420.

16. Atwood, *War and Empire*, 209–10; Hersh, "U.S. Aid to Iraq"; and Bruce Riedel, "Lessons from America's First War with Iran," *The Fletcher Forum of World Affairs* 37/2 (Summer 2013): 102.

17. Ibid., 209; Stone and Kuznick, *Untold History*, 439–40; Rosskamm Shalom, *Imperial Alibis*, 67–86; and Chalmers Johnson, *The Sorrows of Empire: Militarism, Secrecy, and the End of the Republic* (New York: Owl Books, 2005), 224–25.

18. Atwood, *War and Empire*, 209; Stone and Kuznick, *Untold History*, 439–40; Hersh, "U.S. Aid to Iraq"; and Chalmers Johnson, *Sorrows of Empire*, 224.

19. Atwood, *War and Empire*, 209–10; Stone and Kuznick, *Untold History*, 439–40; Chalmers Johnson, *Sorrows of Empire*, 224–25; and Julian Borger, "Rumsfeld 'Offered Help to Saddam,'" *Guardian*, December 31, 2002.

426   NOTES TO PAGES 212-213

20. Borger, "Rumsfeld 'Offered Help.'"
21. Doug Noble, "Assassination Nation," *CounterPunch*, July 19, 2012, https://www.counterpunch.org/2012/07/19/assassination-nation/.
22. Stone and Kuznick, *Untold History*, 455–59.
23. Ibid., 457.
24. Riedel, "First War with Iran," 101.
25. John H. Cushman, Jr., "U.S. Strikes Two Iranian Oil Rigs and Hits Six Warships in Battles Over Mining Sea Lanes in Gulf," *New York Times*, April 19, 1988; and David B. Crist, "Gulf of Conflict: A History of U.S.-Iranian Confrontation at Sea," Policy Focus #95, Washington Institute for Near East Policy, June 2009, https://www.washingtoninstitute.org/media/3423.
26. James Pasley, "Inside the U.S. Navy's Mistaken Shooting of Iran Air Flight 655 in 1988, Which Killed 290 People," *Insider*, January 9, 2020, https://www.businessinsider.com/iran-air-flight-655-us-navy-shot-down-1988-photos-2020-1.
27. Atwood, *War and Empire*, 209–10; Rosskamm Shalom, *Imperial Alibis*, 67–68.
28. Grandin, *Empire's Workshop*, 71, 92, 108–10; Stone and Kuznick, *Untold History*, 426–34, 455–59; LaFeber, *Inevitable Revolutions: The United States in Central America* (New York: W.W. Norton, 1993), 321–23, 359–61; Juan Blanco Prada, "Reagan's Legacy in Latin America Marked by Obsession, Failure," *The Progressive*, June 16, 2004, https://progressive.org/op-eds/reagan-s-legacy-latin-america-marked-obsession-failure/; Cynthia J. Arnson, "The U.S. Congress and Argentina: Human Rights and Military Aid," in *Argentina—US Bilateral Relations*, ed. Cynthia J. Arnson (Washington, DC: Woodrow Wilson International Center for Scholars, 2003), 83–96; and Joakim Kreutz, "Colombia (1978-Present)," in *Civil Wars of the World: Major Conflicts Since World War II*, vol. 1, ed. Karl DeRoven, Jr. and Uk Heo (Santa Barbara, CA: ABC-CLIO, 2007), 275, 284–85.
29. Stone and Kuznick, *Untold History*, 428.
30. Joel Brinkley, "Administration Seeks to Double Aid for Peru," *New York Times*, January 30, 1985.
31. Blum, *Killing Hope*, 291–305.
32. Ibid., 292–94; and LaFeber, *Inevitable Revolutions*, 300–310, 325–30, 333–53.
33. Stone and Kuznick, *Untold History*, 455–59.
34. Blum, *Killing Hope*, 303–4.
35. Kevin Sullivan and Mary Jordan, "In Central America, Reagan Remains a Polarizing Figure," *Washington Post*, June 10, 2004. An estimate of 43,000 deaths is in LaFeber, *Inevitable Revolutions*, 339.

NOTES TO PAGES 214–215 427

36. Blum, *Rogue State*, 113; and LaFeber, *Inevitable Revolutions*, 310–12, 330–32.
37. Blum, *Rogue State*, 70–71.
38. Blum, *Killing Hope*, 352–69; LaFeber, *Inevitable Revolutions*, 312–18, 353–58.
39. Sullivan and Jordan, "Reagan Remains a Polarizing Figure"; and Stone and Kuznick, *Untold History*, 431–32.
40. Raymond Bonner, "Time for a U.S. Apology to El Salvador," *The Nation*, April 15, 2016, https://www.thenation. com/article/time-for-a-us-apology-to-el-salvador/.
41. Nina Lakhani, "El Salvador Issues Warrants for Guerrilla Who Killed U.S. Soldiers During Civil War," *Guardian*, July 25, 2017.
42. An estimate of eighty thousand dead and eight thousand missing is found in Lakhani, "Warrants for Guerrilla." An estimate of between 70,000 and 94,000 deaths appears in Grandin, *Empire's Workshop*, 108. An estimate of 75,000 civilian deaths is found in Blum, *Killing Hope*, 369.
43. Blum, *Killing Hope*, 283.
44. Ibid., 195–96; and Richard Keeble, "Crimes Against Humanity in Chad," *ZNet*, December 4, 2006, https://zcomm.org/znetarticle/crimes-against-humanity-in-chad-by-richard-keeble/.
45. AbuKhalil, "Lebanon"; and Gershman and Zunes, "The U.S. and Lebanon."
46. Associated Press, "History of the Lebanese-Israeli Conflict," *New York Times*, July 17, 2006; and Associated Press, "Casualties of Mideast Wars."
47. Stone and Kuznick, *Untold History*, 434.
48. Ibid., 688; and Blum, *Killing Hope*, 276.
49. Igbal Athas, "Sri Lanka's Endless War," *Jane's Defense Weekly*, January 12, 2000, reproduced in Center for Public Integrity, May 19, 2014, https://publicintegrity.org/accountability/sri-lankas-endless-war/; and Peter Layton, "How Sri Lanka Won the War," *The Diplomat*, April 9, 2015, https://thediplomat.com/2015/04/how-sri-lanka-won-the-war/.
50. "The Fear Inside Us: Confronting Sri Lanka's Past," *Al Jazeera*, February 4, 2018, https://www.aljazeera.com/indepth/features/fear-confronting-sri-lanka-180204081422288.html.
51. Shreerupta Mitra-Jha, "Tamils Continue to Face Racial Discrimination in Sri Lanka, Says UN Committee Post Review," *Firstpost*, August 25, 2016, https://www.firstpost.com/world/ tamils-continue-to-face-racial-discrimination-in-sri-lanka-says-un-committee-post-review-2976326. html.
52. Thomson, *U.S. Foreign Policy Towards Apartheid South Africa, 1948–*

428 NOTES TO PAGES 215–216

1994: Conflict of Interest (New York: Palgrave, 2008), 11–12, 114–15; and Justin Elliot, "Reagan's Embrace of Apartheid South Africa," *Salon*, February 5, 2011, https://www.salon.com/2011/02/05/ronald_ reagan_ apartheid_south_ africa.

53. Blum, *Killing Hope*, 256–57; Horne, *From the Barrel of a Gun: The United States and the War Against Zimbabwe, 1965–1980* (Chapel Hill, University of North Carolina Press, 2001), 268–69; Kent Somerville, "It's 30 Years Since Cuito Canavale. How the Battle Redefined Southern Africa," *The Conversation*, May 29, 2017, https://theconversation.com/its-30-years-since-cuito-cuanavale-how-the-battle-redefined-southern-africa-78134; Laurent C. W. Kaela, "The United States and the Decolonization of Namibia: The Reagan Years," *Transafrican Journal of History* 22 (1993): 122–41; Horace Campbell, "The Military Defeat of the South Africans in Angola," *Monthly Review* (April 1989), reprinted in *Monthly Review* 64/11 (April 2013), https://monthlyreview.org/2013/04/01/the-military-defeat-of-the-south-africans-in-angola/; and Paul Lewis, "Angola and Namibia Accords Signed," *New York Times*, December 23, 1988.

54. Blum, *Killing Hope*, 256.

55. Robert Pear with James Brooke, "Rightists in U.S. Aid Mozambique Rebels," *New York Times*, May 22, 1988.

56. Rosskamm Shalom, *Imperial Alibis*, 146; and Joseph Hanlon, *Mozambique: Who Calls the Shots?* (London: James Currey, 1991), chaps 1–4.

57. Steven V. Roberts, "Senate, 78 to 21, Overrides Reagan's Veto and Imposes Sanctions on South Africa," *New York Times*, October 3, 1986.

58. See Max Coleman, ed., *A Crime Against Humanity: Analyzing the Repression of the Apartheid State* (Cape Town: David Philip Publishers, 1998), 12, 42, 163. The total number of people who were killed by agents of the apartheid regime may be considerably larger. See Mahmood Mamdani, "Amnesty or Impunity? A Preliminary Critique of the Report of the Truth and Reconciliation Commission of South Africa (TRC)," *Diacritics* 32/3–4 (Autumn–Winter 2002), https://www.jstor.org/stable/1566444.

59. Clodfelter, *Warfare and Armed Conflicts: A Statistical Encyclopedia of Casualty and Other Figures, 1494–2007*, 3rd ed. (Jefferson: McFarland and Company, 2008), 601.

60. An estimate of 1.2 million dead in Angola appears in Tirman, *The Deaths of Others: The Fate of Civilians in America's Wars* (New York: Oxford University Press, 2011), 188–89. An estimate of one million fatalities is found in Jon Jeter, "Angolan Rebel Reported Killed," *Washington Post*, February 23, 2002. Assessments of one million deaths in Mozambique are in Hanlon, *Mozambique*, 5; and in Alan Cowell,

NOTES TO PAGES 216–217   429

"Afonso Dhlakama, Mozambique's Opposition Leader, Dies at 65," *New York Times*, May 6, 2018. However, Hanlon more recently estimated the total loss of life in Mozambique to be approximately two million. Email to author, November 22, 2015.

61. Jack Shepherd, "Ethiopia: The Use of Food as an Instrument of U.S. Foreign Policy," *Issue: A Journal of Opinion* 14 (1985): 6–7; and Edmund J. Keller, "Drought, War, and the Politics of Famine," *Journal of Modern African Studies* 30/ 4 (December 1992): 609–24.

62. Keller, "Politics of Famine," 609–24; and Clifford Krauss, "Ethiopia and 3 Rebel Groups Look Toward U.S.-Led Peace Talks," *New York Times*, May 14, 1991.

63. An estimate of one million deaths by 1986 is found in Keller, "Politics of Famine," 616; and in Metaferia, *Ethiopia*, 63.

64. Barry Riley, *The Political History of American Food Aid: An Uneasy Benevolence* (Oxford: Oxford University Press, 2017), 441–42.

65. Ibid.

66. Vijay Prashad, "Bad Aid," *CounterPunch*, March 29, 2010, http://www.counterpunch.org/ 2010/03/29/bad-aid/; and Nicolas Perpitch and Debbie Guess, "How Bob Geldof's Live Aid Funds Went to Ethiopian Rebels," *The Australian*, March 5, 2010.

67. Metaferia, *Ethiopia*, 69; and Patrick E. Tyler, David B. Ottaway, and Joe Pichirallo, "Ethiopian Security Police Seized, Tortured CIA Agent," *Washington Post*, April 25, 1986.

68. Metaferia, *Ethiopia*, 69–70.

69. Jerry Tinker and John Wise, "A Misguided Policy on Ethiopia," *New York Times*, August 16, 1986; and Sylvan and Majeski, *U.S. Foreign Policy*, 198–99.

70. Metaferia, *Ethiopia*, 64, 77, 84–85, 125. Sylvan and Majeski have argued that Washington did not aid these insurgents. But they have acknowledged that U.S. officials "groomed" the Tigrayan guerrilla leader during the last year of the conflict and that a former CIA and National Security Council staff person met with him after his soldiers arrived in Addis Ababa. See Sylvan and Majeski, *U.S. Foreign Policy*, 198–99.

71. This phrase was used by an unnamed U.S. official and quoted in Sylvan and Majeski, *U.S. Foreign Policy*, 199. See also Metaferia, *Ethiopia*, 78.

72. Metaferia, *Ethiopia*, 78; and Krauss, "U.S.-Led Peace Talks."

73. Clodfelter, *Warfare*, 591.

74. Stone and Kuznick, *Untold History*, 438–39, 443–44; C. Raja Mohan, "Waiting for the Nuclear Winter: Breakdown of Nuclear Arms Control," *Social Scientist* 12/1 (January 1984): 30–52; and William Drozdiak, "More than a Million Protest Missiles in Western Europe," *Washington Post*, October 23, 1983.

75. Blum, *Killing Hope*, 285.
76. Ibid., 280–82; and Rosskamm Shalom, *Imperial Alibis*, 141–45.
77. Blum, *Killing Hope*, 281.
78. Michael J. Berlin, "Raid on Libya Condemned by UN General Assembly," *Washington Post*, November 21, 1986.
79. Blum, *Killing Hope*, 289; and Torreon and Plagakis, *Instances of Use of United States Armed Forces Abroad, 1798-2021*, CRS Report, September 8, 2021, 10, https://sgp.fas.org/ crs/natsec/R42738.pdf , 13.
80. Clodfelter, *Warfare*, 632.
81. Einashe and Kennard, "Somaliland's Forgotten Genocide."
82. This estimate by Africa Watch is cited in Clodfelter, *Warfare*, 595.
83. Zunes, "The U.S. in Somalia."
84. Ibid.
85. Clodfelter, *Warfare*, 595. An estimate of 300,000 deaths is found in Zunes, "The U.S. in Somalia."
86. Hahn, "U.S. Actions in Liberia," 24–28; David Model, *From Slaves to Oil: United States Role in the Plunder of Africa* (Bloomington, IN: AuthorHouse, 2014), xxi–xxii, 186–87; and T. Christian Miller and Jonathan Jones, "Firestone and the Warlord: The Untold Story of Firestone, Charles Taylor, and the Tragedy of Liberia," *ProPublica*, in collaboration with PBS *Frontline*, November 18, 2014, https://www.propublica.org/article/firestone-and-the-warlord-intro.
87. Chris Arsenault, "Accused War Criminal Taylor 'Worked with CIA,'" *Al Jazeera*, January 21, 2012, http://www.aljazeera.com/indepth/features/2012/01/2012120194243233526.html; Nick Allen, "Liberian Despot Charles Taylor Worked with U.S. Intelligence," *The Telegraph*, January 17, 2012; and Jon Lee Anderson, "Charles Taylor and the Killing Tree," *The New Yorker*, April 26, 2012, https://www.newyorker.com/news/news-desk/charles-taylor-and-the-killing-tree.
88. Owen Bowcott and Monica Mark, "Charles Taylor Found Guilty of Abetting Sierra Leone War Crimes," *Guardian*, April 26, 2012.
89. Arsenault, "Accused War Criminal."
90. Stone and Kuznick, *Untold History*, 471–72; Blum, *Killing Hope*, 305–14; and Rosskamm Shalom, *Imperial Alibis*, 177–83.
91. Rosskamm Shalom, *Imperial Alibis*, 180.
92. Stone and Kuznick, *Untold History*, 472.
93. Ibid.
94. Chalmers Johnson, *Sorrows of Empire*, 69.
95. Thomas C. Hayes, "Confrontation in the Gulf; The Oil Field Lying Below the Iraq-Kuwait Dispute," *New York Times*, September 3, 1990.
96. Stone and Kuznick, *Untold History*, 474.
97. Ibid., 474–81.

NOTES TO PAGES 219–220 431

98. Ibid.; Atwood, *War and Empire*, 218–20; Tirman, *Deaths of* Others, 199–200; and Larry Everest, *Oil, Power, and Empire: Iraq and the U.S. Global Agenda* (Monroe, ME: Common Courage Press, 2004), chap. 5.

99. Atwood, *War and Empire*, 218; Clodfelter, *Warfare*, 633; and Paul D'Amato, "U.S. Intervention in the Middle East: Blood for Oil," *International Socialist Review* 15 (December 2000–January 2001), http://www.isreview.org/issues/15/blood_for_oil.shtm.

100. Clodfelter, *Warfare*, 632.

101. Stone and Kuznick, *Untold History*, 481; Beth Osborne Daponte, "A Case Study in Estimating Casualties from War and Its Aftermath: the 1991 Persian Gulf War," *PSR Quarterly* 3/2 (June 1993): 65; and Paul Magnusson, "Toting the Casualties of War," Bloomberg, February 5, 2003, https://www.bloomberg.com/news/articles/2003-02-05/toting-the-casualties-of-war. Daponte's estimate included Iraqi soldiers and civilians killed during the conflict, Iraqi Shia and Kurdish people killed in the postwar rebellions against Hussein which Washington had encouraged, and Iraqi deaths caused by war-related damage to the water system, medical facilities and supplies, and the electric power grid.

102. Barbara Crossette, "Iraq Sanctions Kill Children, UN Reports," *New York Times*, December 1, 1995; Anthony Arnove, "Iraq Under Siege: Ten Years On," *Monthly Review* 52/7 (December 2000), http://monthlyreview.org/2000/12/01/iraq-under-siege/; and Edward Herman and David Peterson, *The Politics of Genocide* (New York: Monthly Review Press, 2010), 29–33.

103. Blum, *Killing Hope*, 371–74; and Parenti, *Against Empire*, 129.

104. Ibid., 373–76; Jim Mann, "Congress to Probe CIA-Haiti Ties: Intelligence: Members of Both Houses Say They Will Investigate. Reports Say Agency Financed Some Leaders Involved in Coup," *Los Angeles Times*, November 2, 1993; Mark Weisbrot, "Undermining Haiti," *The Nation*, November 23, 2005, https://www.thenation.com/article/under mining-haiti/; and Peter Hallward, *Damming the Flood: Haiti and the Politics of Containment* (London: Verso, 2007), 39–42.

105. Hallward, *Damming the Flood*, 42–50; and Parenti, *Against Empire*, 130.

106. Hallward, *Damming the Flood*, 50–58; and Parenti, *Against Empire*, 130–31.

107. Chalmers Johnson, *Blowback: The Costs and Consequences of American Empire* (New York: Henry Holt, 2004), 14–16; Parenti, *To Kill a Nation*, 10–11; and Carl Boggs, *Imperial Delusions: American Militarism and Endless War* (Lanham, MD: Rowman and Littlefield, 2005), 186.

108. Parenti, *To Kill a Nation*, 11.

109. Kevin McKiernan, "Turkey's War on the Kurds," *Bulletin of the Atomic*

Scientists 55/ 2 (March 1, 1999), https://journals.sagepub.com/doi/abs/10.2968/055002008; and Laura Poitras, Marcel Rosenbach, Michel Sontheimer, and Holger Stark, "How the NSA Helped Turkey Kill Kurdish Rebels," *The Intercept*, August 3, 2014, https://theintercept.com/2014/08/31/nsaturkeyspiegel/.

110. *New York Times* News Service, "Peru's Military to Get U.S. Aid," *Chicago Tribune*, April 22, 1990; and Michael L. Evans, "U.S. Drug Policy and Intelligence Operations in the Andes," Institute for Policy Studies (October 6, 2005), https://ips-dc.org/us_drug_policy_intelligence_operations_ in_the_andes/.

111. Charles Lane, "'Superman' Meets Shining Path: Story of a CIA Success," *Washington Post*, December 7, 2000.

112. BBC News, "Peru Admits 'Shining Path' Rebels Have Not Been Exterminated," August 6, 2015, https://www.bbc.com/news/world-latin-america-33813695; and Peter J. Meyer, *U.S. Foreign Assistance to Latin America and the Caribbean: FY 2018 Appropriations*, Congressional Research Service, May 9, 2018, 9, 11, https://fas.org/sgp/crs/row/R45089.pdf; and Álvaro Vargas Llosa, "Peru's Dim Future from Shining Path," *Wall Street Journal*, September 21, 2021.

113. Juan Forero, "Peru Report Says that 69,000 Died in 20 Years of Rebel War," *New York Times*, August 29, 2003.

114. Parenti, *Blackshirts and Reds*, chaps. 4 and 5; Bahman Azad, *Heroic Struggle, Bitter Defeat: Factors Contributing to the Dismantling of the Socialist State in the Soviet Union* (New York: International Publishers, 2000); and Roger Kieran and Thomas Kenny, *Socialism Betrayed: Behind the Collapse of the Soviet Union* (Bloomington, IN: iUniverse, 2010).

115. An estimate of more than 120,000 deaths is found in Robert E. Hamilton, "The Post-Soviet Wars, Part I," Foreign Policy Research Institute, December 18, 2017, https://www.fpri.org/article/2017/12/post-soviet-wars-part-i/. However, Hamilton acknowledged that this appraisal is not comprehensive. See also Nikola Budanovic, "War and Conflict After the Fall of the USSR," *War History Online*, June 3, 2017, https://www.warhistoryonline.com/cold-war/7-conflicts-happened-fall_ussr-xc.html.

116. Parenti, *Blackshirts and Reds*, chaps 6 and 7; Holstrom and Smith, "Gangster Capitalism"; Milne, "Catastroika"; Stephen F. Cohen, *Failed Crusade;* and James Galbraith, "Shock Without Therapy," *The American Prospect*, August 12, 2002, http://prospect.org/article/shock-without-therapy.

117. Milne, "Catastroika."

118. Ibid.

NOTES TO PAGES 222-223   433

119. Elizabeth Brainerd and David M. Cutler, "Autopsy on an Empire: Understanding Mortality in Russia and the Former Soviet Union," *Journal of Economic Perspectives* 19/1 (Winter 2005), https://www.jstor.org/stable/4134995.

120. Tamara Men, Paul Brennan, Paolo Boffetta, and David Zaridze, "Russian Mortality Trends for 1991–2001: Analysis by Cause and Region," *BMJ* 327/7421: (October 25, 2003): 964, https://www.ncbi.nlm.nih.gov/pmc/articles/PMC259165/.

121. Masha Gessen, "The Dying Russians," *New York Review of Books Daily*, September 2, 2014, https://www.nybooks.com/daily/2014/09/02/dying-russians/.

122. Brainerd and Cutler, "Autopsy on an Empire," 107–110.

123. Neli Espova and Julie Ray, "Former Soviet Countries See More Harm from Breakup," Gallup poll, December 19, 2013, http://gallup.com/poll/166538/former-soviet-countries-harm-breakup.aspx; David Masci, "In Russia, Nostalgia for Soviet Union and Positive Feelings About Stalin," Pew Research Center, Fact Tank, June 29, 2017, https://www.pewresearch.org/fact-tank/2017/06/29/in-russia-nostalgia-for-soviet-union-and-positive-feelings-about-stalin/; "Many Eastern Europeans Feel Nostalgia for the Communist Era," *The Economist*, October 12, 2017, https://www.economist.com/europe/2017/10/12/many-eastern-europeans-feel-nostalgia-for-the-communist-era; and Richard Wike, Jacob Poushter, Laura Silver, Kat Devlin, Janell Fetterolf, Alexandra Castillo, and Christine Huang, "Political and Economic Changes Since the Fall of Communism," Pew Research Center, October 14, 2019, https://www.pewresearch.org/global/2019/10/14/political-and-economic-changes-since-the-fall-of-communism/?utm_source=newsletter&utm_medium=email&utm_campaign=sendto_newslettertest&stream=top.

124. Daniel Goodkind and Lorraine West, "The North Korean Famine and Its Demographic Impact," *Population and Development Review* 27/2 (June 2001): 219–38. https://www.jstor.org/stable/2695207 https://www.jstor.org/stable/2695207 https://www.jstor.org/stable/2695207.

125. Fineman, "Oil Factor in Somalia"; and Parenti, *Against Empire*, 122–24.

126. Zunes, "The U.S. in Somalia."

127. Parenti, *Against Empire*, 124; and Lee Wengraf, "Making Somalia's Nightmare Worse," *Socialist Worker*, April 14, 2011, https://socialistworker.org/2011/04/14/making-somalias-nightmare-worse.

128. Parenti, *To Kill a Nation*, 18–19, 25–28.

129. Ibid., 19–22.

130. Ibid., 23–25.

131. Ibid., 29–31; Herman and Peterson, *Politics of Genocide*, 46–47; and Clodfelter, *Warfare*, 582.

434 NOTES TO PAGES 223–224

132. Herman and Peterson, *Politics of Genocide*, 49.
133. Ibid., 50–51; Parenti, *To Kill a Nation*, chaps. 10–14.
134. Parenti, *To Kill a Nation*, 122, 171.
135. "More U.S. Troops Enter Kosovo," CNN, June 15, 1999, http://www.cnn.com/US/9906/ 15/us.kosovo.01/index.html; Julie Kim and Steven Woehrel, "Kosovo and U.S. Policy: Background to Independence," Congressional Research Service Report to Congress, June 20, 2008, 2–3, 10, https://sgp.fas.org/crs/row/RL31053.pdf; and Peter Beaumont, "U.S. Backs Kosovo Independence Regardless of UN Ruling," *Guardian*, July 22, 2010.
136. George H. W. Bush, "The Other 9/11: George H. W. Bush's 1990 New World Order Speech," *Dallas Morning News*, September 8, 2017.
137. John Bellamy Foster, "The New Imperialism," *Monthly Review* 55/3 (July–August 2003), https://monthly review.org/2003/07/01/the-new-age-of-imperialism/.
138. Helen C. Epstein, *Another Fine Mess: America, Uganda, and the War on Terror* (New York: Columbia Global Reports, 2017), 21–22.
139. Ibid., 21–22, 25–26, 71–72; and Robin Philpot, *Rwanda and the New Scramble for Africa: From Tragedy to Useful Imperial Fiction* (Montreal: Baraka Books, 2013), 23, 38–42.
140. Clodfelter, *Warfare*, 606; and Epstein, *Another Fine Mess*, 22, 27, 96.
141. Philpot, *New Scramble for Africa*, 49; Dan Glazebrook, "The Real Lesson of the Rwandan Tragedy," *CounterPunch*, March 21, 2014, https://www.counterpunch.org/2014/03/21/the-real-lesson-of-the-rwandan-tragedy/; and Epstein, *Another Fine Mess*, 108.
142. Philpott, *New Scramble for Africa*, 48–50; and Glazebrook, "Rwandan Tragedy."
143. Epstein, *Another Fine Mess*, 28–29; and Philpot, *New Scramble for Africa*, 33.
144. Philpot, *New Scramble for Africa*, Part 1; and Herman and Peterson, *Politics of Genocide*, 51–68. On the U.S. training of Tutsis in the Ugandan army who became commanders of the Rwandan Patriotic Front, see Philpot, *New Scramble for Africa*, 40.
145. Epstein, *Another Fine Mess*, 25–26, 71; Philpot, *New Scramble for Africa*, 23, 38–42; and Herman and Peterson, *Politics of Genocide*, 61.
146. Philpot, *New Scramble for Africa*, 40, 42, 47. Philpot noted that the Belgians soon turned against the Rwandan government.
147. Hermann and Peterson, *Politics of Genocide*, 55.
148. Philpot, *New Scramble for Africa*, 40; and Nzongola-Ntalaja, *Congo*, 222.
149. Epstein, *Another Fine Mess*, 29, 106.
150. Ibid., 29.

NOTES TO PAGES 225-226

435

151. Philpot, *New Scramble for Africa*, 59–61; Herman and Peterson, *Politics of Genocide*, 54.

152. Clodfelter, *Warfare*, 603.

153. Herman and Peterson, *Politics of Genocide*, 54–56, 59–60; and Judi Rever, *In Praise of Blood: The Crimes of the Rwandan Patriotic Front* (Toronto: Random House Canada, 2018), 61–63.

154. Alan C. Stam, "Coming to a New Understanding of the Rwanda Genocide," lecture at the Gerald Ford School of Public Policy, University of Michigan, February 18, 2009, cited in Herman and Peterson, *Politics of Genocide*, 56.

155. Epstein, *Another Fine Mess*, 110–11; and Herman and Peterson, *Politics of Genocide*, 52–55

156. Rever, *In Praise of Blood*, 200, 232, 266–67.

157. Herman and Peterson, *Politics of Genocide*, 53, 56, 63.

158. Reuters, "U.S. Recognizes New Government in Rwanda," July 29, 1994, and "200 US Troops Going to Kigali to Open Airport," July 29, 1994, both cited in Herman and Peterson, *Politics of Genocide* 56; Epstein, *Another Fine Mess*, 130.

159. Rever, *In Praise of Blood*, 150–52; and John Ryle, "A Sorry Apology from Clinton," *Guardian*, April 13, 1998.

160. Boutros Boutros-Ghali, cited in Philpot, *New Scramble for Africa*, 13, 118.

161. Rever, *In Praise of Blood*, 4.

162. Ibid., 200, 232, 266–67.

163. Epstein, *Another Fine Mess*, 30, 117.

164. Rever, *In Praise of Blood*, 95–96, 153; and Herman and Peterson, *Politics of Genocide*, 67.

165. Epstein, *Another Fine Mess*, 30, 117.

166. Ibid., 30–31, 120, 130; and Rever, *In Praise of Blood*, 143. In view of U.S. complicity in the Rwandan holocaust, Epstein's claim that "there is no evidence that the Americans knew what the commandos were about to do" before attacking the Hutu refugee camps in Zaire is unconvincing.

167. Epstein, *Another Fine Mess*, 116–17.

168. Ibid., 25–26, 71; Rever, *In Praise of Blood*, 8, 41–44; Philpot, *New Scramble for Africa*, 39–42, 225–26; and Herman and Peterson, *Politics of Genocide*, 61, 66–68.

169. Epstein, *Another Fine Mess*, 71, 132–33; and Philpot, *New Scramble for Africa*, 39–40.

170. Philpot, *New Scramble for Africa*, 223.

171. Epstein, *Another Fine Mess*, 29, 130–31.

172. Ibid., 130–31; Rever, *In Praise of Blood*, 25, 41; and Philpot, *New Scramble for Africa*, 217.

436 NOTES TO PAGES 227–228

173. Several other African countries also supported the ouster of Mobutu. See Nzongola-Ntalaja, *Congo*, 225–27.
174. Rever, *In Praise of Blood*, 25.
175. Ibid., 22.
176. Herman and Peterson, *Politics of Genocide*, 67.
177. Epstein, *Another Fine Mess*, 128; and Nzongola-Ntalaja, *Congo*, 227–33.
178. Epstein, *Another Fine Mess*, 128; Nzongola-Ntalaja, *Congo*, 227–33; and Thomas Turner, "War in the Congo," Institute for Policy Studies, February 1, 1999, https://ips-dc.org/war_in_ the_congo/.
179. Colette Braeckman, "The Looting of the Congo," *New Internationalist*, May 2, 2004, https://newint.org/features/2004/05/01/congo.
180. Richard Boudreaux, "Congo War Widens as Angolan Jets Bomb Rebel Stronghold," *Los Angeles Times*, August 26, 1998.
181. Epstein, *Another Fine Mess*, 31–32, 128–29; Nzongola-Ntalaja, *Congo*, 235–38; Herman and Peterson, *Politics of Genocide*, 67–68; and Helen C. Epstein, "Congo for the Congolese," *New York Review of Books*, February 19, 2018, https://www.nybooks.com/daily/2018/02/19/ congo-for-the-congolese/.
182. Rory Carroll, "Multinationals in Scramble for Congo's Wealth," *Guardian*, October 21, 2002.
183. Epstein, "Congo for the Congolese"; and Jeffrey Gettleman, "The World's Worst War," *New York Times*, December 15, 2012.
184. Epstein, *Another Fine Mess*, 129–30, and "Congo for the Congolese"; John Prendergast, "Congo's Looting and Killing Machine Moves into High Gear," *Daily Beast*, June 6, 2018, https://www.thedailybeast.com/congos-looting-and-killing-machine-moves-into-high-gear; and Eric Lipton and Dionne Searcey, "How the U.S. Lost Ground to China in the Contest for Clean Energy," *New York Times*, November 21, 2021.
185. Stanis Bujakera, "Congo Election Runner-Up to Press Fraud Dispute in Court," Reuters, January 11, 2019, https://af.reuters.com/article/topNews/idAFKCN1P51C8-OZATP.
186. Peter Moszynski, "5.4 million People Have Died in Democratic Republic of Congo Since 1998 Because of Conflict, Report Says," *BMJ* 336/7638, February 2, 2008, https://www. ncbi. nlm.nih.gov/pmc/articles/PMC2223004/; and "Congo's War Was Bloody. It May Be About to Start Again," *The Economist*, February 15, 2018, https://www.economist.com/briefing/2018/02/15/congos-war-was-bloody-it-may-be-about-to-start-again.
187. *The Monitor* (Kampala), July 3, 2000, cited in Nzongola-Ntalaja, *Congo*, 232–33.
188. Glen Ford, "16 Years of U.S. Genocide in Congo," Black Agenda Report, December 12, 2012, https://blackagendareport.com/content/16-years-us-genocide-congo.

NOTES TO PAGES 228–230 437

189. Dan Connell, "Sudan," Institute for Policy Studies, August 1, 1997, https://ips-dc.org/sudan/; and Anna Martín, "Moving Stones and Speaking Trees: The War in South Sudan," *Counter Punch*, August 15, 2016, https://www.counterpunch.org/2016/08/15/moving-stones-and-speaking-trees-the-war-in-south-sudan/.
190. Ibid.
191. Epstein, *Another Fine Mess*, 26–27.
192. Connell, "Sudan"; and "Sudan People's Liberation Army (SPLA), Sudan People's Liberation Movement (SPLM)," Federation of American Scientists, Intelligence Resource Program, January 5, 2000, https://fas.org/irp/world/ para/spla.htm.
193. Helen C. Epstein, "The U.S. Turns a Blind Eye to Uganda's Assault on Democracy," *The Nation*, July 20, 2018, https://www.thenation.com/article/us-turns-blind-eye-ugandas-assault-democracy/; and Ken Opalo, "Why Is Uganda's Army in South Sudan?," *Christian Science Monitor*, February 3, 2014, https://www.csmonitor.com/World/Africa/Africa-Monitor/2014/0203/Why-is-Uganda-s-Army-in-South-Sudan.
194. Federation of American Scientists, "Sudan People's Liberation Army (SPLA), Sudan People's Liberation Movement (SPLM)."
195. Jeremy Scahill, *Dirty Wars: The World Is a Battlefield* (New York: Nation Books, 2013), 125.
196. Ibid., 126; and Nathan J. Robinson, "Bill Clinton's Act of Terrorism," *Jacobin*, October 12, 2016, http://www. jacobinmag.com/2016/10/bill-clinton-al-shifa-sudan-bombing-khartoum/.
197. Robinson, "Act of Terrorism."
198. Chalmers Johnson, *Blowback*, 80–83; and Noam Chomsky, *Rogue States: The Rule of Force in World Affairs* (Cambridge, MA: South End Press, 2000), 3.
199. Chalmers Johnson, *Blowback*, 80–83.
200. Ibid.
201. Ibid., 81–82.
202. Chomsky, *Rogue States*, 2; and Blum, *Rogue State*, 189.
203. Sudanese president Hassan Abdullah al-Turabin made this observation in *Africa Confidential* 39/11 (May 1998): 1, cited in Metaferia, *Ethiopia*, 92.
204. Metaferia, *Ethiopia*, 97, 122.
205. Clodfelter, *Warfare*, 637.
206. William Arkin, "Desert Fox: The Difference Was in the Details," *Washington Post*, January 17, 1999.
207. Kirk, *America's War in Colombia*, 260–61; Simons, *Colombia*, 229–41, 257–81; and Steven Cohen, "Rewriting the History of Plan Colombia," North American Committee on Latin America, *NACLA Report on the*

438   NOTES TO PAGES 230–231

Americas, July 17, 2015, https://nacla.org/news/2015/07/17/ rewriting-history-plan-colombia.

208. Martin Pengelly, "U.S. Confirms Death of Jamal al-Badawi, Al-Qaida Militant in USS *Cole* Bombing," *Guardian*, January 6, 2019.

209. Michael Muskal, "Bill Clinton: 'I Could Have Killed' Osama bin Laden in 1998," *Los Angeles Times*, August 1, 2014.

210. "The Second Intifada," *Al Jazeera*, December 4, 2003, http://www.aljazeera.com/archive/2003/12/20084101554875168.html; and Bodour Youssef Hassan, "The Second Intifada Put Holes in Israel's Wall of Fear," *Electronic Intifada*, October 4, 2013, https://electronic intifada.net/content/second-intifada-put-holes-israels-wall-fear/12826.

211. Clodfelter, *Warfare*, 632; and BBC News, "Intifada Toll, 2000–2005," February 8, 2005, http://news.bbc.co.uk/2/hi/middle_east/3694350.stm. The statistics in the BBC report were compiled by B'tselem, an Israeli human rights group.

212. Robert W. Merry, "How Bill Clinton Made America More Ambitious—and More Dangerous," *National Interest*, August 17, 2016, https://nationalinterest.org/feature/how-bill-clinton-made-america-more-ambitious%E2%80%94-dangerous-17387.

213. Ibid.

214. Stone and Kuznick, *Untold History*, 492–96; Harvey Wasserman, "The Unelected President," Common Dreams, January 20, 2001, http://www.commondreams.org/views01/0120-04.htm; and David A. Graham, "What Happens When a President Is Declared Illegitimate?," *The Atlantic*, January 18, 2017, https://www.theatlantic.com/politics/archive/2017/01/what-happens-when-a-president-is-declared-illegitimate/513473/.

215. Atwood, *War and Empire*, 223–24; Stone and Kuznick, *Untold History*, 490–92, 497; and James McCartney with Mary Sinclair McCartney, *America's War Machine: Vested Interests, Endless Conflicts* (New York: St. Martin's Press, 2015), 56–62, 65–67.

216. McCartney, *America's War Machine*, 59; and Richard W. Behan, "Jeb Bush and His Brother's Wars," *CounterPunch*, July 10, 2015, https://www.counterpunch.org/2015/07/10/jeb-bush-and-his-brothers-wars/.

217. CNN, "O'Neill: Bush Planned Iraq Invasion Before 9/11," January 14, 2004, http://www.cnn.com/2004/ALLPOLITICS/01/10/oneill.bush/; and Dilip Hiro, "How Bush's Oil Grab Went Awry," *The Nation*, September 26, 2007, https://www.thenation.com/article/how-bushs-iraqi-oil-grab-went-awry/.

218. Jean-Charles Brisard and Guillaume Dasquié, *Forbidden Truth: U.S.-Taliban Secret Oil Diplomacy and the Failed Hunt for Bin Laden*, trans. Lucy Rounds with Peter Fifield and Nicholas Greenslade (New York: Thunder's Mouth Press/Nation Books, 2002), 42–43.

NOTES TO PAGES 231–232 439

219. Ibid., 44–46; CNN, "U.S. Terrorist Attacks Fast Facts," September 2, 2019, https://www.cnn.com/2013/04/18/us/u-s-terrorist-attacks-fast-facts/index.html.

220. International Physicians for the Prevention of Nuclear War, Physicians for Social Responsibility, and Physicians for Global Survival, eds. *Body Count: Casualty Figures After 10 Years of the "War on Terror": Iraq, Afghanistan, Pakistan*, trans. Ali Fathollah-Nejad (Berlin: Internationale Ärzte für die Verhütung des Atomkrieges, March 2015), 81–82; and Rupert Stone, "Has Pakistan Come Out on Top in the War in Afghanistan?," *TRT World*, January 21, 2019, https://www.trtworld.com/ opinion/has-pakistan-come-out-on-top-in-the-war-in-afghanistan-23484.

221. IPPNW, PSR, and PGS, *Body Count*, 15–18.

222. Blum, *Rogue State*, 216; and Ed Vulliamy, "Venezuelan Coup Linked to Bush Team," *Guardian*, April 21, 2002.

223. Blum, *Rogue* State, 217; and Julian Borger and Alex Bellos, "U.S. 'Gave the Nod' to Venezuelan Coup," *Guardian*, April 17, 2002.

224. Predictably, the State Department insisted there was no connection between U.S. aid to the coup plotters and the coup. See U.S. Department of State and Broadcasting Board of Governors, Office of Inspector General, *A Report on US Policy Toward Venezuela, November 2001–April 2002, Report Number 02-OIG-003*, July 2002, 3, cited in Mark Weisbrot and Robert Naiman, "Correct the Facts on US-Venezuelan Relations: Remember the Attempted Coup?," *Huffington Post*, May 25, 2011, https://www.huffpost.com/entry/correct-the-facts-on-usve_b_31612.

225. Duncan Campbell, "American Navy 'Helped Venezuelan Coup,'" *Guardian*, April 29, 2002.

226. Vulliamy, "Venezuelan Coup"; and Blum, *Rogue State*, 216.

227. Chalmers Johnson, *Sorrows of Empire*, 213–14.

228. Ibid., 214; and Adam Hudson, "U.S. Wages 'War on Terror' in the Philippines," *Truthout*, April 9, 2015, http://www.truth-out.org/news/item/30061-us-wages-war-on-terror-in-the-philippines.

229. Atwood, *War and Empire*, 221–23; and Valerie Plame Wilson and Joe Wilson, "How the Bush Administration Sold the War—and How We Bought It," *Guardian*, February 27, 2013.

230. Atwood, *War and Empire*, 223–28; Blum, *Killing Hope*, 390–91; Stone and Kuznick, *Untold History*, 518–19; and Everest, *Oil, Power, and Empire*, chaps. 9 and 10.

231. Atwood, *War and Empire*, 222; Blum, *Killing Hope*, 390–91; and Stone and Kuznick, *Untold History*, 512–24.

232. Barbara Epstein, "Notes on the Anti-War Movement," *Monthly Review* 55/3 (July–August 2003), http://monthlyreview.org/2003/07/01/notes-

440 NOTES TO PAGES 233–234

on-the-antiwar-movement/; and Phyllis Bennis, "February 15, 2003: The Day the World Said No to War," Institute for Policy Studies, February 15, 2013, http://www.ips-dc.org/february_15_2003_the_day_the_world_ said_no_to_war/.

233. Ewan MacAskill and Julian Borger, "Iraq War Was Illegal and Breached UN Charter, Says Annan," *Guardian*, September 15, 2004; Stephen Zunes, "The Democrats' War," *Huffington Post*, May 25, 2011, https://www.huffpost.com/entry/the-democrats-war_b_712379; and John Haltiwanger, "Joe Biden's Vote for the 2003 Iraq War Is Coming Back to Bite Him With 2020 Voters," *Business Insider*, May 16, 2019, https://www.businessinsider.com/ joe-bidens-iraq-war-vote-is-coming-back-to-bite-him-with-2020-voters-2019-5.

234. Stone and Kuznick, *Untold History*, 530; and Ahmed Rashed, "Iraq Throws Open Door to Foreign Oil Firms," Reuters, June 30, 2008, https://www.reuters.com/article/us-iraq-oil/iraq-throws-open-door-to-foreign-oil-firms-idUSL301894212 0080630.

235. Missy Ryan, "Who Made the Decision to Withdraw U.S. Troops from Iraq?," *Washington Post*, September 26, 2016.

236. IPPNW, PSR, and PGS, *Body Count*, 15–18; Tirman, *Deaths of* Others, 266; and Dahr Jamail, "Report Shows U.S. Invasion, Occupation of Iraq Left 1 Million Dead," *Truthout*, April 13, 2015, https://truthout.org/articles/report-shows-us-invasion-occupation-of-iraq-left-1-million-dead/. IPPNW, PSR, and PGS, and Jamail have provided robust critiques of investigations which have reported much lower numbers of deaths in Iraq.

237. Micah Zenko, "Obama's Embrace of Drone Strikes Will Be a Lasting Legacy," *New York Times*, January 12, 2016.

238. Ibid.

239. Markus Virgil Hoehne, "Counter-Terrorism in Somalia: How External Interference Helped to Produce Militant Islam," Social Science Research Council, Crisis in the Horn of Africa, December 17, 2009, 8–11, http://hornofafrica.ssrc.org/somalia/.

240. Ibid.

241. Blum, *Rogue State*, 219–20; Hallward, *Damning the Flood*, 232–49; Paul Farmer, "Who Removed Aristide?," *London Review of Books*, April 15, 2004, http://www.lrb.co.uk/v26/n08/ paul-farmer/who-removed-aristide; and Lydia Polgreen and Tim Weiner, "Haiti's President Forced Out; Marines Sent to Keep Order," *New York Times*, February 29, 2004.

242. Polgreen and Weiner, "Haiti's President Forced Out."

243. Athena R. Kolbe and Royce A. Hutson, "Human Rights Abuse and Other Criminal Violations in Port-au-Prince, Haiti; A Random Survey of Households," *The Lancet* 368/9538 (September 2, 2006), https://

NOTES TO PAGES 234–235   441

www.thelancet.com/journals/lancet/article/PIIS0140673606692118/
fulltext.

244. Ibid.

245. Stone and Kuznick, *Untold History*, 537–38; and John J. Mearsheimer,
"Why the Ukraine Crisis Is the West's Fault," *Foreign Affairs*, (September–October 2014), 1–12.

246. Ian Traynor, "U.S. Campaign Behind the Turmoil in Kiev," *Guardian*,
November 25, 2004; and Gerald Sussman, "The Myths of 'Democracy
Assistance': U.S. Political Intervention in Post-Soviet Eastern Europe,"
Monthly Review 58/7 (December 1, 2006), https://monthly review.
org/2006/12/01/the-myths-of-democracy-assistance-u-s-political-intervention-in-post-soviet-eastern-europe/.

247. Dan Connell, "Rethinking Sudan," Institute for Policy Studies, August
1, 2001, https://ips-dc.org/rethinking_sudan/; and Rebecca Hamilton,
"U.S. Played Key Role in South Sudan's Long Journey to Independence," *The Atlantic*, July 9, 2011, http://www.theatlantic.com/international/ archive/2011/07/us-played-key-role-in-southern-sudans-long-journey-to-independence /241660/.

248. Rebecca Hamilton, "South Sudan's Long Journey."

249. Ibid.

250. Mark Landler, "U.S. Is Facing Hard Choices in South Sudan," *New York
Times*, January 3, 2014.

251. Rebecca Hamilton, "South Sudan's Long Journey"; and "Sudan: The
Quick and the Terrible," PBS, January 2005, https://www.pbs.org/frontlineworld/stories/sudan/facts.html.

252. Hoehne, "Counter-Terrorism in Somalia," 9–10; Epstein, *Another Fine
Mess,* 157–58; and Mark Mazzetti, "Efforts by CIA Fail in Somalia, Officials Charge, *New York Times,* June 8, 2006.

253. Hoehne, "Counter-Terrorism in Somalia," 11.

254. Jeremy Scahill, "Blowback in Somalia," *The Nation*, September 7, 2011,
https://www.thenation.com/article/blowback-somalia/.

255. David Smith, "Ethiopia's Meles Zenawi Dies of Undisclosed Illness,"
Guardian, August 21, 2012; William Easterly and Laura Freschi,
"Why Are We Supporting Repression in Ethiopia?," *New York Review of Books*, November 15, 2010, http://www.nybooks.com/blogs/
nyrblog/2010/nov/15/why-are-we-supporting-repression-ethiopia/;
Amitabh Pal, "Obama Eulogizes Ethiopian Dictator," *The Progressive*,
August 24, 2012, http://www.progressive.org/ obama_eulogizes_ethiopian-dictator; and Robert Wachter, "Bush's Strategy Enables an Ethiopian Despot," *The Nation*, February 17, 2007, https://www.thenation.
com/ article/bushs-somalia-strategy-enables-ethiopian-despot/.

256. Michael R. Gordon and Mark Mazzetti, "U.S. Used Base in Ethiopia

442   NOTES TO PAGES 235–236

to Hunt for Al Qaeda," *New York Times*, February 23, 2007; and Eric Schmitt and Jeff Gettleman, "Qaeda Agent Reportedly Killed in Somalia," *New York Times*, May 2, 2008.

257. Xan Rice, "How U.S. Forged an Alliance with Ethiopia Over Invasion," *Guardian*, January 12, 2007; and Nadia Prupis, "U.S. Confirms Years-Long 'Secret' Military Presence in Somalia," *MintPress News*, July 4, 2014, https://www.mintpressnews.com/us-confirms-years-long-secret-military-presence-somalia/193497/.

258. Gordon and Mazzetti, "U.S. Used Base in Ethiopia"; and Metaferia, *Ethiopia*, 103.

259. Epstein, *Another Fine Mess*, 158–63.

260. Rob Prince, "Wikileaks Reveals U.S. Twisted Ethiopia's Arm to Invade Somalia," Foreign Policy in Focus, December 8, 2010, https://fpif.org/wikileaks_reveals_us_twisted_ethiopias_ arm_to_invade_somalia/. An estimate of at least 16,000 civilian deaths during the invasion and occupation is found in Xan Rice, "Ethiopia Ends Somalia Occupation," *Guardian*, January 26, 2009.

261. Hoehne, "Counter-Terrorism in Somalia," 24–26; and Scahill, "Blowback in Somalia."

262. William I. Robinson, "Latin America's Left at the Crossroads," *Al Jazeera*, September 14, 2011, http://www.aljazeera.com/indepth/opinion2011/09/2011913141540508756.html.

263. Roger Burbach, "Orchestrating a Civic Coup in Bolivia," *CounterPunch*, November 18, 2008, http://www.counterpunch.org/2008/11/18/orchestrating-a-civic-coup-in-bolivia/; and Stephen Zunes, "U.S. Intervention in Bolivia," *Huffington Post*, May 25, 2011, https://www.huffington post.com/stephen-zunes-us-intervention-in-bolivi_b_127528.html.

264. Ellie Mae O'Hagan, "The U.S. May Have Blood on Its Hands in Mexico," *Guardian*, October 8, 2014; and Cora Currier and Jesse Franzblau, "Mexican Authorities Implicated in Violence, but U.S. Security Aid Still Flows," *The Intercept*, May 8, 2015, https://theintercept.com/2015/05/08/ayotzinapa-mexico-u-s-security-aid-keeps-flowing/.

265. O'Hagan, "Blood on Its Hands"; Currier and Franzblau, "Mexican Authorities Implicated"; Nina Lakhani and Erubiel Tirado, "Mexico's War on Drugs: What Has It Achieved and How Is the U.S. Involved?," *Guardian*, December 8, 2016; and Brianna Lee, Danielle Renwick, and Rocio Caro Labrador, "Mexico's Drug War," Council on Foreign Relations, October 22, 2019, https://www.cfr.org/backgrounder/mexicos-drug-war.

266. Ted Galen Carpenter, "How Will the Growing U.S. European Split Affect NATO?," *National Interest*, March 17, 2019, https://nationalinterest.org/feature/how-will-growing-us-european-split-affect-nato-47667.

267. Stone and Kuznick, *Untold History*, 537; Atwood, *War and Empire*,

NOTES TO PAGES 236–237 443

235–37; Timothy Heritage, "Georgia Started War with Russia: EU-Backed Report," Reuters, September 30, 2009, https://www.reuters.com/article/us-georgia-russia-report/georgia-started-war-with-russia-eu-backed-report-idUSTRE58T4MO0090930; and Stephen Zunes, "U.S. Role in Georgia Crisis," Foreign Policy in Focus, August 14, 2008, https://fpif.org/us_role_in_georgia_crisis/.

268. Noam Chomsky, "Exterminate All the Brutes: Gaza 2009," *Chomsky. Info*, June 6, 2009, http://chomsky.info/ 20090119/; and Palestinian Centre for Human Rights, "Confirmed Figures Reveal the True Extent of the Destruction Inflicted Upon the Gaza Strip," March 12, 2009, http://www.pchrgaza.org/files/PressR/English/2008/36-2009.html.

269. Stone and Kuznick, *Untold History*, 547–48; and Gary C. Jacobson, "George W. Bush, the Iraq War, and the Election of Barack Obama," *Presidential Studies Quarterly* 40/10 (June 2010): 207–24.

270. Stone and Kuznick, *Untold History*, 551; Editors, "Restoring America's Reputation," *Los Angeles Times*, October 18, 2008; and Ellen Hallams, "From Crusader to Exemplar: Bush, Obama, and the Reinvigoration of America's Soft Power," *European Journal of American Studies* 6/1 (2011), https://journals.openedition.org/ejas/9157#text.

271. Jack Serle, "More Than 2,400 Dead as Obama's Drone Campaign Marks Five Years," Bureau of Investigative Journalism, January 23, 2014, https://www.thebureauinvestigates.com/stories/ 2014-01-23/more-than-2-400-dead-as-obamas-drone-campaign-marks-five-years.

272. Jessica Purkiss and Jack Serle, "Obama's Covert Drone War in Numbers: Ten Times More Strikes Than Bush," Bureau of Investigative Journalism, January 17, 2017, https://www.the bureauinvestigates.com/stories/2017-01-17/obamas-covert-drone-war-in-numbers-ten-times-more-strikes-than-bush.

273. Micah Zenko, "Obama's Final Drone Strike Data," Council on Foreign Relations, January 20, 2017, https://www.cfr.org/blog/obamas-final-drone-strike-data. This is probably a very conservative estimate.

274. Mollie Reilly, "Obama Told Aides He's 'Really Good at Killing People,' New Book 'Double Down' Claims," *Huffington Post*, November 3, 2013, http://www.huffingtonpost.com/2013/11/ 03/obama-drones-double-down_n_ 4208815.html.

275. "Q & A: U.S. Targeted Killings and International Law," Human Rights Watch, December 19, 2011, https://www.hrw.org/news/2011/12/19/q-us-targeted-killings-and-international-law#11.% 20Was%20the%20targeted %20killing%20of%20Anwar%20al-Awlaki%20in%20Yemen%20 lawful?

276. Ibid.; Spencer Ackerman, Jason Burke, and Julian Borger, "Eight-Year-Old American Girl 'Killed in Yemen Raid Approved by Trump,'" *Guardian*, February 1, 2017.

277. Mark Landler, "The Afghan War and the Evolution of Obama," *New York Times*, January 1, 2017.
278. IPPNW, PSR, and PGS, *Body Count*, 74–78.
279. Wesley Morgan, "Whatever Happened to Al Qaeda in Afghanistan?," *Politico*, August 15, 2018, https://www.politico.com/story/2018/08/15/Al-Qaeda-afghanistan-terrorism-777511; and Najim Rahim and Mujib Mashal, "Afghan Forces Fail to Turn Back Taliban Gains," *New York Times*, July 28, 2016.
280. Ashley Jackson, "The Taliban's Fight for Hearts and Minds," *Foreign Policy*, September 12, 2018, https://foreignpolicy.com/2018/09/12/the-talibans-fight-for-hearts-and-minds-afghanistan/; and Franz-Stephan Gady, "Afghanistan to Start Peace Talks with Taliban by the End of February," *The Diplomat*, February 8, 2016, https://thediplomat.com/2016/02/ afghanistan-to-start-peace-talks-with-taliban-by-the-end-of-february/.
281. Eric Draitser and Ramiro Funez, "Honduras Bleeding," *CounterPunch*, June 29, 2015, http://www.counterpunch.org/ 2015/06/29/honduras-bleeding/; Jake Johnston, "How Pentagon Officials May Have Encouraged a Coup in Honduras," *The Intercept*, August 29, 2017, https://theintercept.com/2017/08/ 29/honduras-coup-us-defense-departmetnt-center-hemispheric-defense-studies-chds/; and Dana Frank, *The Long Honduran Night: Resistance, Terror, and the United States in the Aftermath of the Coup* (Chicago: Haymarket Books, 2018), 18–19.
282. Johnston, "Coup in Honduras"; and Frank, *Long Honduran Night*, 18–19.
283. Frank, *Long Honduran Night*, 18.
284. Ibid., 17–19, 245–46.
285. Stephen Zunes, "The U.S. Role in the Honduran Coup and Subsequent Violence," *National Catholic Reporter*, May 14, 2016, https://www.ncronline.org/blogs/ncr-today/us-role-honduras-coup-and-subsequent-violence.
286. Mark Weisbrot, "Ecuador's Correa Haunted by Honduras," *Guardian*, October 1, 2010.
287. Madeline Bunting, "Somalia Was a Sideshow in the War on Terror—and Is Paying a Colossal Price," *Guardian*, September 11, 2011.
288. Ibid.; and Elizabeth Dickinson, "Arming Somalia," *Foreign Policy*, September 10, 2009, https://foreignpolicy.com/2009/09/10/arming-somalia.
289. Bunting, "Somalia Was a Sideshow."
290. Ibid.; and Robyn Dixon, "Report: Nearly 260,00 Died in Somalia Food Crisis," *Los Angeles Times*, May 2, 2013.
291. Mark Mazzetti, Jeff Gettleman, and Eric Schmidt, "In Somalia, U.S. Escalates a Shadow War," *New York Times*, October 16, 2016.

NOTES TO PAGE 239 445

292. Alan J. Kuperman, "A Model Humanitarian Intervention? Reassessing NATO's Libyan Campaign," *International Security* 38/1 (Summer 2013), https://www.mitpressjournals.org/ doi/10.1162/ISEC_a_00126; and Ted Rall, "Obama Destroyed Libya," *Common Dreams*, February 17, 2015, http://www.commondreams.org/ views/2015/02/17/obama-destroyed-libya.

293. Steve Chapman, "Did Obama Avert a Bloodbath in Libya?," *Chicago Tribune*, April 3, 2011.

294. Micah Zenko, "The Big Lie About the Libyan War," *Foreign Policy*, March 22, 2016, https://foreignpolicy.com/2016/03/22/libya-and-the-myth-of-humanitarian-intervention/; and Seumas Milne, "If the Libyan War Was About Saving Lives, It Has Been a Catastrophic Failure," *Guardian*, October 26, 2011.

295. Mark Hosenball, "Exclusive: Obama Authorizes Secret Help for Libya Rebels," Reuters, March 30, 2011, https://www.reuters.com/article/us-libya-usa-order/exclusive-obama-authorizes-secret-help-for-libya-rebels-idUSTRE72T6H220110330; and John Barry, "America's Secret Libya War: U.S. Spent $1 Billion on Covert Ops Helping NATO," *Daily Beast*, August 30, 2011, https://www.thedailybeast.com/americas-secret-libya-war-us-spent-dollar1-billion-on-covert-ops-helping-nato.

296. Barry, "America's Secret Libya War."

297. Scott Shane and Jo Becker, "A New Libya, 'With Very Little Time Left,'" *New York Times*, February 27, 2016.

298. Nick Turse, Henrik Moltke, and Alice Speri, "Secret War," *The Intercept*, June 20, 2018, https://theintercept. com/2018/06/20/libya-us-drone-strikes/.

299. Ibid.

300. An estimate of more than 21,000 deaths in 2011 alone is found in Mohamed A. Daw, Abdallah H. El-Bouzedi, and Aghnyia A. Dau, "Libyan Armed Conflict 2011: Mortality, Injury, and Population Displacement," *African Journal of Emergency Medicine* 5/3 (September 2015): 101–7. An estimate of more than 16,000 deaths between 2012 and 2017 was provided by Mohamed A. Daw, Abdallah H. El-Bouzedi, and Aghnyia A. Dau in "Trends and Patterns of Deaths, Injuries, and Intentional Disabilities within the Libyan Armed Conflict: 2012-2017," *PLOS One* 14/5 (May 10, 2019), https://doi.org/10.1371/journal.pone.0216061. An estimate of four thousand deaths in 2018 appears in "Human Rights Solidarity: About 4000 People Were Victims of Armed Fighting in Libya in 2018," *Libya Observer*, February 12, 2019, https://www.libyaobserver.ly/news/human-rights-solidarity-about-4000-people-were-victims-armed-fighting-libya-2018. A conservative estimate of at least 2,200 deaths in 2019–20 is found in Patrick Wintour and agen-

446   NOTES TO PAGES 239–240

cies, "Libya Peace Talks Go Ahead in Berlin Despite Ceasefire Setback," *Guardian*, January 14, 2020.

301. "'Deadly Sea Crossings': 41 Migrants Drown in the Mediterranean," *Al Jazeera*, February 24, 2021, https://www.aljazeera.com/news/2021/2/24/un-says-41-europe-bound-migrants-drown-in-mediterranean. See also "Dozens Missing as Migrant Boat Sinks Off Tunisia's Mediterranean Coast," CBS News, May 10, 2019, https://www.cbsnews.com/news/migrant-boat-sinks-off-tunisia-coast-left-libya-dozens-missing-feared-dead-today-2019-05-10/.

302. Yochi J. Dreazen, "U.S. Troops Are Leaving Because Iraq Doesn't Want Them There," *The Atlantic*, October 21, 2011, http://www.theatlantic.com/politics/archive/2011/10/us-troops-are-leaving-because-iraq-doesnt-want-them-there/247174/; and David S. Cloud and Ned Parker, "U.S. Willing to Leave 10,000 Troops in Iraq Past Year's End, Officials Say," *Los Angeles Times*, July 6, 2011.

303. The quote from Obama appears in Rick Brennan, "Withdrawal Symptoms: The Bungling of the Iraq Exit," *Foreign Affairs* (November/December 2014), https://www.foreignaffairs.com/ articles/united-states/withdrawal-symptoms.

304. Tirman, *Deaths of Others*, 266–67; Joshua Holland, interview with Raed Jarrar, "An Iraqi Perspective: How America's Destruction of Iraq Led to Today's Crisis," *Moyers and Company*, June 20, 2014, http://billmoyers.com/2014/06/20/an-iraqi-perspective-how-americas-destruction-of-iraqi-society-led-to-todays-chaos/; Nicolas J. S. Davies, *The American Invasion and Destruction of Iraq* (Ann Arbor, MI: Nimble Books, 2010); Jacopo Ottaviani, "The Iraq War Never Ended," *Foreign Policy*, February 10, 2014, http://foreignpolicy.com/2014/02/10/the-iraq-war-never-ended/; and Gareth Porter, "Why the U.S. Owns the Rise of the Islamic State and the Syria Disaster," *Truthdig*, October 8, 2015, https://www.truthdig.com/articles/why-the-u-s-owns-the-rise-of-islamic-state-and-the-syria-disaster/.

305. Stephen Collinson, "Obama Sends 1500 Troops to Iraq," CNN, November 7, 2014, https://www.cnn.com/2014/11/07/politics/obama-sends-troops-to-iraq/index.html.

306. Kevin Liptak, "How Obama Came to Launch Strikes in Syria," CNN, September 23, 2014, https://www.cnn.com/2014/09/23/politics/obama-syria-strikes-policy/index.html; Nora Kelly and Marina Koren, "Obama's View of ISIS Two Years into Air Strikes," *The Atlantic*, August 14, 2016, https://www.theatlantic.com/politics/archive/2016/08/obama-isis-iran-transfer/494624/.

307. Juan Cole, "How the United States Helped Create the Islamic State," *Washington Post*, November 23, 2015; and Medhi Hassan and Dina

NOTES TO PAGES 240-241   447

Sayedahmed, "Blowback: How ISIS Was Created by the U.S. Invasion of Iraq," *The Intercept*, January 29, 2018, https://theintercept.com/2018/01/29/isis-iraq-war-islamic-state-blowback.

308. Porter, "Rise of the Islamic State"; and BBC News, "Mid-East Unrest: Syrian Protests in Damascus and Aleppo," March 15, 2011, https://www.bbc.com/news/world-middle-east-12749674.

309. Porter, "Rise of the Islamic State"; and Nicholas Blanford, "Can the Syrian Regime Divide and Conquer Its Opposition?," *Time*, April 9, 2011, https://content.time.com/time/world/article/ 0,8599,2064214,00.html.

310. Stephen Gowans, *Washington's Long War on Syria* (Montreal: Baraka Books, 2017), 11–13, and chap. 2; Ariel Zirulnick, "Cables Reveal Covert U.S. Support for Syria's Opposition," *Christian Science Monitor*, April 18, 2011, https://www.csmonitor.com/World/terrorism-security/2011/0418/Cables-reveal-covert-US-support-for-Syria-s-opposition; and Scott Wilson and Joby Warrick, "Assad Must Go, Obama Says," *Washington Post*, August 18, 2011.

311. Gowans, *Long War on Syria*, chap. 4.

312. Porter, "Rise of the Islamic State."

313. Ibid.; Kareem Fahim, "Syria Blames Al Qaeda After Bombs Kill Dozens in Damascus," *New York Times*, December 23, 2011; and Rania Abouzaid, "Interview with Official of Jabhat al-Nusra, Syria's Islamist Militia Group," *Time*, December 25, 2012, http://world.time.com/2012/ 12/25/interview-with-a-newly-designated-syrias-jabhat-al-nusra/.

314. Porter, "Rise of the Islamic State"; and Gareth Porter, "How America Armed Terrorists in Syria," *The American Conservative*, June 22, 2017, https://www.theamericanconservative.com/ articles/how-america-armed-terrorists-in-syria/; and Seymour M. Hersh, "The Red Line and the Rat Line," *London Review of Books*, April 17, 2014, https://www.lrb.co.uk/v36/n08/seymour-m-hersh/the-red-line-and-the-rat-line.

315. Porter, "America Armed Terrorists in Syria."

316. U.S. Department of Defense, "Department of Defense Information Report, Not Finally Evaluated Intelligence, Country: Iraq," 14-L-0552/DIA/287, August 2012, cited in Seumas Milne, "Now the Truth Emerges: How the U.S. Fueled the Rise of ISIS in Syria and Iraq," *Guardian*, June 3, 2015.

317. Ibid.

318. David S. Cloud and Raja Abdulrahim, "U.S. Has Secretly Provided Arms Training to Syrian Rebels Since 2012," *Los Angeles Times*, June 21, 2013.

319. Aron Lund, "The Free Syrian Army Doesn't Exist," *Syria Comment*, March 16, 2013, https://www.joshualandis.com/blog/the-free-syrian-army-doesnt-exist/.

320. Gowans, *Long War on Syria*, 142–46; and Daniel Wagner, "The Dark Side of the Free Syrian Army," *Huffington Post*, March 2, 2013, https://www.huffpost.com/entry/dark-side-free-syrian_b_2380399.

321. Gowans, *Long War on Syria*, 142–46; Rania Abouzaid, "The Jihad Next Door," *Politico*, June 23, 2014, https://www.politico.com/magazine/story/2014/06/Al-Qaeda-iraq-syria-108214_full.html#.hWKZCsbzIV; and Souad Mekhennet, "The Terrorists Fighting Us Now? We Just Finished Training Them," *Washington Post*, August 18, 2014.

322. Porter, "Rise of Islamic State," and "America Armed Terrorists in Syria"; and David Ignatius, "Al-Qaeda Affiliate Playing Larger Role in Syria Rebellion," *Washington Post*, November 30, 2012.

323. Porter, "Rise of Islamic State," and "America Armed Terrorists in Syria."

324. Ibid.; Tom O'Connor, "How ISIS Got Weapons from the U.S. and Used Them to Take Iraq and Syria," *Newsweek*, December 14, 2017, https://www.news week.com/how-isis-got-weapons-us-used-them-take-iraq-syria-748468; and Mona Mahmood and Ian Black, "Free Syrian Army Rebels Defect to Islamist Group Jabhat al-Nusra," *Guardian*, May 8, 2013.

325. "The Rise and Fall of ISIL Explained," *Al Jazeera*, June 20, 2017, https://www.aljazeera.com/indepth/features/2017/06/rise-fall-isil-explained-170607085701484.html.

326. Liptak, "Strikes in Syria."

327. Porter, "Rise of Islamic State," and "America Armed Terrorists in Syria."

328. Liptak, "Strikes in Syria"; Kelly and Koren, "Obama's View of ISIS."

329. Associated Press, "A Timeline of the U.S. Involvement in Syria's Conflict," January 11, 2019, https://www.apnews.com/96701a254c5a448 cb253f14ab697419b; and Barbara Starr and Jeremy Diamond, "Syria: Obama Authorizes Boots on the Ground to Fight ISIS," CNN, October 30, 2015, https://www.cnn.com/2015/10/30/politics/syria-troops-special-operations-forces/index.html.

330. Brian Murphy, "Official: Over 20,000 Foreign Fighters Lured by Militant Factions in Syria," *Washington Post*, February 11, 2015.

331. Porter, "America Armed Terrorists in Syria"; Gareth Porter, "Behind the Real U.S. Strategic Blunder in Syria," *Middle East Eye*, December 27, 2016, https://www.middleeasteye. net/opinion/behind-real-us-strategic-blunder-syria; and Ishaan Tharoor, "Russia Stays in the Driver's Seat in Syria," *Washington Post*, July 10, 2018.

332. Tharoor, "Driver's Seat in Syria"; and Mara Karlin, "After 7 Years of War, Assad Has Won in Syria. What's Next for Washington?," Brookings Institution, February 13, 2018, https://www. brookings.edu/blog/order-from-chaos/2018/02/13/after-7-years-of-war-assad-has-won-in-syria-whats-next-for-washington/.

NOTES TO PAGES 242–243 449

333. Rodi Said, "U.S.-Backed Syrian Alliance Declares Attack on Islamic State in Raqqa," Reuters, November 6, 2016, https://www.reuters.com/article/us-mideast-crisis-syria-raqqa-idUSKBN1310GX; and Eric Schmitt, "U.S. to Send 200 More Troops to Syria in ISIS Fight," *New York Times* (December 10, 2016), https://www.nytimes.com/2016/12/10/us/politics/us-adds-200-troops-syria-isis.html.

334. Jeffrey Sachs's estimate of 600,000 deaths in Syria is found in Tim Hains, "Jeffrey Sachs to President Trump: Please Get U.S. Out of Syria, We've Done Enough Damage," *RealClearPolitics*, April 13, 2018, https://www.realclearpolitics.com/video/2018/04/13/jeffrey_sachs_to_president_trump_please_get_us_out_of_syria_weve_done_enough_damage.html. The same estimate is found in Seth J. Frantzman, "Northern Exposure: Israel's Stability in Question Amid Russia's Offer," *Jerusalem Post*, July 28, 2018.

335. Jon Donnison, "Gaza Baby 'Only Knew How to Smile,'" BBC News, November 26, 2012, https://www.bbc.com/news/world-middle-east-20466027.

336. Reuters, "Timeline: Major Events in Egypt since Arab Spring Uprisings," March 26, 2018, https://in.reuters.com/article/egypt-election-timeline/timeline-major-events-in-egypt-since-arab-spring-uprisings-idINKBN1H2188.

337. David D. Kirkpatrick, Kareem Fahim, and Ben Hubbard, "By the Millions, Egyptians Seek Morsi's Ouster," *New York Times*, June 30, 2013.

338. David D. Kirkpatrick and Mayy El Sheikh, "Morsi Spurned Deals, Seeing Military as Tamed," *New York Times*, July 6, 2013.

339. Ibid.

340. David D. Kirkpatrick, "That Time Obama Wouldn't Call a Coup a Coup," *The Atlantic*, September 2018, https://www.theatlantic.com/magazine/archive/2018/09/obama-egypt-coup/565733/.

341. Elise Labott, "U.S. Suspends Significant Military Aid to Egypt," CNN, October 9, 2013, https://www.cnn.com/2013/10/09/world/meast/us-egypt-aid/index.html; Mark Thompson, "U.S. Resumes Weapons Flow to Egypt," *Time*, March 31, 2015, http://time.com/3766224/ united-states-weapons-ban-lifted-egypt/; and Kyle Rempfer, "U.S. Training and Security Assistance May Be Empowering Egyptian War Crimes, Says Human Rights Group," *Military Times*, May 28, 2019, https://www.militarytimes.com/news/your-military/2019/05/28/us-training-and-security-assistance-may-be-empowering-egyptian-war-crimes-says-human-rights-group/.

342. Michelle Dunne and Scott Williamson, "Egypt's Unprecedented Instability by the Numbers," Carnegie Endowment for International Peace, March 24, 2014, https://carnegieendowment.org/2014/03/24/egypt-s-unprecedented-instability-by-numbers-pub-55078.

450 NOTES TO PAGES 243-244

343. An estimate of more than eight thousand deaths since 2013, mostly at the hands of the regime, is found in Tahir Institute for Middle East Policy, *Egypt Security Watch: Five Years of Egypt's War on Terror*, July 24, 2018, 7, 9, 11, https://timep.org/esw/five-years-of-egypts-war-on-terror/.
344. John Kerry, quoted in Martín, "War in South Sudan."
345. Nick Turse, "Ghost Nation," *Harper's*, July 2017, https://harpers.org/archive/2017/07/ ghost-nation/.
346. Ibid.
347. United Nations Panel of Experts on South Sudan, *Letter to the President of the Security Council on South Sudan*, April 13, 2017, cited in Edward Hunt, "How the United States Kept Arms Flowing into South Sudan," *Foreign Policy in Focus*, December 12, 2018, https://fpif.org/ how-the-united-states-kept-arms-flowing-into-south-sudan/.
348. Hunt, "Arms into South Sudan"; Edward Hunt, "With Nearly 400,000 Dead in South Sudan, Will the U.S. Change Policy?," *Foreign Policy in Focus*, November 15, 2018, https://fpif.org/ with-nearly-400000-dead-in-south-sudan-will-the-u-s-change-policy/; Turse, "Ghost Nation"; and Epstein, *Another Fine Mess*, 19.
349. Ilya Gridneff, "Exxon Ends Oil Search with Total in South Sudan as War Rages," Bloomberg, August 14, 2014, https://www.bloomberg.com/news/articles/2014-08-13/exxon-abandons-oil-search-with-total-in-south-sudan-as-war-rages; and Sudarshan Varadhan, "South Sudan to Return to Pre-War Oil Production Levels by Mid-2020: Minister," Reuters, February 10, 2019, https://www.reuters.com/article/us-south-sudan-oil/south-sudan-to-return-to-pre-war-oil-production-levels-by-mid-2020-minister-idUSKCN1PZ09W.
350. Hunt, "Arms into South Sudan"; and "U.S. Targets South Sudan Oil Companies over Civil War," *Sudan Tribune*, March 21, 2018, http://www.sudan tribune.com/spip.php?article 64996.
351. Siobhán O'Grady, "A New Report Estimates that More Than 380,000 People Have Died in South Sudan's Civil War," *Washington Post*, September 26, 2018; and "South Sudan Rivals to Hold Talks to Salvage Stalled Peace Deal," *Al Jazeera*, May 2, 2019, https://www.aljazeera.com/ news/2019/05/south-sudan-rivals-hold-talks-salvage-stalled-peace-deal-190502061304207.html.
352. Mearsheimer, "Ukraine Crisis," 1–12; Seumas Milne, "The Clash in Crimea Is the Fruit of Western Expansion," *Guardian*, March 5, 2014; Seumas Milne, "It's Not Russia That Pushed Ukraine to the Brink of War," *Guardian*, April 30, 2014; Robert Parry, "The Mess That Nuland Made," Consortium News, July 13, 2015, https://consortiumnews.com/2015/07/ 13/the-mess-that-nuland-made/; and Douglas Val-

NOTES TO PAGES 244–245

entine, *The CIA as Organized Crime: How Illegal Operations Corrupt America and the World* (Atlanta, GA: Clarity Press, 2016), chap. 9.

353. Milne, "Clash in Crimea," and "It's Not Russia"; Mearsheimer, "Ukraine Crisis," 4; Harriet Salem, "Who Exactly Is Governing Ukraine?" *Guardian*, March 14, 2014; Olga Rudenko and Jennifer Collins, "As Many as 100 Killed in New Ukraine Clashes," *USA Today*, February 20, 2014; and Ian Traynor, "Ukraine's Bloodiest Day: Dozens Dead as Kiev Protesters Regain Territory from Police," *Guardian*, February 21, 2014.

354. Milne, "It's Not Russia"; and Parry, "Mess That Nuland Made."

355. Robyn Dixon and Natalie Gryvnyak, "Ukraine's Zelensky Wants to End a War in the East. His Problem? No One Agrees How to Do It," *Washington Post*, March 19, 2020; and Derek Saul, "Russia-Ukraine's War's Mounting Death Toll: Latest Estimates Suggest Russian Troops Have Been Hit Harder," *Forbes*, April 26, 2022, https://www.forbes.com/sites/dereksaul/2022/04/26/russia-ukraine-wars-mounting-death-toll-latest-estimates-suggest-russian-troops-have-been-hit-harder/?sh=43d4c93e4549.

356. Mairav Zonszein, "Israel Killed More Palestinians in 2014 Than in Any Other Year Since 1967," *Guardian*, March 27, 2015.

357. Medea Benjamin and Nicolas J.S. Davies, "The U.S. is Complicit in the Atrocities Israel Commits," *Fair Observer*, May 18, 2021, https://www.fairobserver.com/region/middle_east_north_africa/medea-benjamin-nicolas-js-davies-gaza-conflict-us-weapons-israel-palestine-world-news-74304/. See also David Corn, "How America Finances the Destruction in Gaza—and the Cleanup," *Mother Jones*, July 23, 2014, http://www.motherjones.com/politics/2014/07/israel-gaza-united-states-assistance-unrwa/#.

358. Mark Spetalnick, "U.S., Israel Sign $38 Billion in Military Aid Package," *Reuters*, September 14, 2016, https://www.reuters.com/article/us-usa-israel-statement/u-s-israel-sign-38-billion-military-aid-package-idUSKCN11K2CI; and Emma Green, "Why Does the U.S. Give So Much Money to Israel?," *The Atlantic*, September 15, 2016, https://www.theatlantic.com/international /archive/2016/09/united-states-israel-memorandum-of-understanding-military-aid/500192/.

359. Ashish Kumar Sen, "A Brief History of Sanctions on Iran," Atlantic Council, May 8, 2018, https://www.atlanticcouncil.org/blogs/new-atlanticist/a-brief-history-of-sanctions-on-iran; and Sasan Fayazmanesh, *Containing Iran: Obama's Policy of "Tough Diplomacy"* (Newcastle upon Tyne, UK: Cambridge Scholars Publishing, 2013), 5–8, chaps 5–9, 452–54.

360. James Risen and Mark Mazzetti, "U.S. Agencies See No Move by Iran to Build a Bomb," *New York Times*, February 24, 2012. See also "IAEA Saw

452 NOTES TO PAGES 245–246

No 'Credible Evidence' Iran Was Working on Nuclear Weapon after 2009," Radio Free Europe/Radio Liberty, May 1, 2018, https://www.rferl.org/a/iaea-saw-no-credible-evidence-iran-was-working-on-nuclear-weapon-after-2009/29201840.html.

361. Thomas Erdbrink, "Iran's Aging Airliner Fleet Seen as Faltering Under U.S. Sanctions," *New York Times*, July 13, 2012; and Ali Gorji, "Sanctions Against Iran: The Impact on Health Services," *Iranian Journal of Public Health* 43/3 (March 2014), https://www.ncbi.nlm.nih. gov/pmc/articles/PMC4419179/.

362. Missy Ryan, "Post Nuclear-Deal: Carter Says Military Option Against Iran Remains on Table," *Washington Post*, July 19, 2015; and Doug Bandow, "Washington Should Take War Off the Table Against Iran: Americans Not Anointed to Kill at Will," *The World Post*, May 15, 2015, http://www.huffingtonpost.com/doug-bandow/washington-should-take-wa_b_7290250.html.

363. Jeff Mason and Roberta Rampton, "U.S. Declares Venezuela a National Security Threat, Sanctions Top Officials," Reuters, March 9, 2015, https://www.reuters.com/article/us-usa-venezuela-idUSK-BN0M51NS20150310; and Teresa Walsh, "Venezuela Sanctions Backfire on Obama," *U.S. News and World Report*, April 10, 2015, https://www.usnews.com/news/articles/2015/04/10/venezuela-sanctions-backfire-on-obama.

364. BBC News, "Yemen Crisis: Why Is There a War?," June 19, 2020, https://www.bbc.com/ news/world-middle-east-29319423; and John R. Allen and Bruce Riedel, "Ending the Yemen War Is Both a Strategic and Humanitarian Imperative," Brookings Institution, November 16, 2020, https://www.brookings.edu/blog/order-from-chaos/2020/11/16/ending-the-yemen-war-is-both-a-strategic-and-humanitarian-imperative/.

365. Jeff Bachman, "U.S. Complicity in the Saudi-Led Genocide in Yemen Spans Obama, Trump Administrations," *The Conversation*, November 26, 2018, https://theconversation.com/us-complicity-in-the-saudi-led-genocide-in-yemen-spans-obama-trump-administrations-106896; Missy Ryan and Ann Gearan, "Trump Administration Looks to Resume Saudi Arms Sale Criticized as Endangering Civilians in Yemen," *Washington Post*, March 8, 2017; and Samuel Oakford and Peter Salisbury, "Yemen: The Graveyard of the Obama Doctrine," *The Atlantic*, September 23, 2016, https://www.theatlantic.com/international /archive/2016/09/yemen-saudi-arabia-obama-riyadh/501365/.

366. Missy Ryan, "With Small Changes, U.S. Maintains Military Aid to Saudi Arabia Despite Rebukes Over Yemen Carnage," *Washington Post*, December 13, 2016.

NOTES TO PAGES 246-247 453

367. Azad Essa, "Cornel West: Obama Was Never the Revolutionary That Mandela Was," *Al Jazeera*, July 16, 2018, https://www.aljazeera.com/news/2018/07/cornel-west-obama-revolutionary-mandela-180715195817422.html.

368. Eric Draitser, "America's Imperial Footprint in Africa," *CounterPunch*, September 9, 2015, at http://www.counterpunch.org/2015/09/09/americas-imperial-footprint-in-africa/; Nick Turse, *Tomorrow's Battlefield: U.S. Proxy Wars and Secret Ops in Africa* (Chicago: Haymarket Books, 2015), and "U.S. Military Says It Has a 'Light Footprint' in Africa—These Documents Show a Vast Network of Bases," *The Intercept*, December 1, 2018, https://theintercept.com/2018/12/ 01/u-s-military-says-it-has-a-light-footprint-in-africa-these-documents-show-a-vast-network-of-bases/.

369. Kyle Mizokami, "Obama Administration Cuts Back Size of Nuclear Arsenal," *Popular Mechanics*, January 12, 2017, https://www.popularmechanics.com/military/weapons/a24739/ obama-administration-unilateral-nuclear-arms-cuts/; and Jonathan Weisman and Peter Spiegel, "U.S. Keeps First-Strike Strategy," *Wall Street Journal*, April 6, 2010, https://www.wsj.com/ articles/SB1000142405270230462030457516626 3632513790.

370. Adam Mount, "A Pivotal Moment for U.S. Nuclear Arsenal," Council on Foreign Relations, October 9, 2014, https://www.cfr.org/expert-brief/pivotal-moment-us-nuclear-arsenal; and Hans M. Christensen, "Nuclear Weapons Modernization: A Threat to the NPT?" *Arms Control Today*, May 1, 2014, https://www.armscontrol.org/act/2014_05/Nuclear-Weapons-Modernization-A-Threat-to-the-NPT.

371. Glen Ford, "Foreword: Obama: Imperialism's Second Wind," in Jeremy Kuzmarov, *Obama's Unending Wars: Fronting the Foreign Policy of the Permanent Warfare State* (Atlanta, GA: Clarity Press, 2019), 9.

372. Thomas Meaney and Stephen Wertheim, "When the Leader of the Free World Is an Ugly American," *New York Times*, March 9, 2018; and Doug Stokes, "Trump, American Hegemony, and the Future of the Liberal International Order," *International Affairs* 98/1 (January 5, 2018): 135–36.

373. Meany and Wertheim, "Ugly American"; Stokes, "Liberal International Order"; Parenti, *Democracy for the Few*, chap. 16; and Atwood, *War and Empire*, chap. 1.

374. Rosie Gray, "Trump Declines to Affirm NATO's Article 5," *The Atlantic*, May 25, 2017, https://www.theatlantic.com/international/archive/2017/05/trump-declines-to-affirm-natos-article-5/528129/; Nicholas Burns, "Does the U.S. Need NATO?," *Quartz*, April 4, 2019, https://qz.com/1585911/does-the-us-need-nato/; Peter Wittig, "Hope for the Future of American Leadership Dies Hard," *Foreign*

Affairs, October 16, 2020, https://www.foreignaffairs.com/ articles/ europe/2020-10-16/hope-future-american-leadership-dies-hard; Robin Emmott, "Germany and France Vie for European Leadership at NATO," Reuters, November 20, 2019, https://www.reuters.com/article/ us-nato-future/germany-and-france-vie-for-european-leadership-at-nato-idUSKBN1XU1FR; and Peter Rough, "Europe Is Thinking Hard About Divorcing America," *Foreign Policy*, February 26, 2020, https:// foreignpolicy.com/2020/02/26/europe-is-thinking-harder-about-divorcing-america-macron-merkel-trump/.

375. Igor Bobic, "Trump Repeatedly Asked Why We Couldn't Use Nukes," *Huffington Post*, August 3, 2016, https://www.huffpost.com/entry/scarborough-trump-nukes_n_57a1e47ae4 b0693164c347d0; and Adam Withnall, "Trump Refuses to Rule Out Using Nuclear Weapons against Europe," *The Independent*, March 31, 2016.

376. Julian Borger, "Ex-Intelligence Chief: Trump's Access to Nuclear Codes Is 'Pretty Damn Scary,'" *Guardian*, August 23, 2017.

377. "Treaty to Ban Nuclear Weapons Made Official with 50th UN Signatory," *Guardian*, October 25, 2020; and Rick Gladstone, "Treaty to Prohibit Nuclear Weapons Passes Important Threshold," *New York Times*, October 25, 2020.

378. Courtney Kube, Kristen Welker, Carol E. Lee, and Savannah Guthrie, "Trump Wanted Tenfold Increase in Nuclear Arsenal, Surprising Military," *NBC News*, October 11, 2017.

379. William Lambers, "Trump Ignores the History of Nuclear Weapons at Our Peril," *Washington Post*, July 16, 2020; "A Critical Evaluation of the Trump Administration's Nuclear Weapons Policies," Arms Control Association, July 29, 2019, https://www.armscontrol.org/ events/2019-07/ critical-evaluation-trump-administrations-nuclear-weapons-policies; and David E. Sanger, "Trump Budget Calls for New Nuclear Warheads and 2 Types of Missiles," *New York Times*, February 10, 2020.

380. Lambers, "Trump Ignores History at Our Peril"; Julian Borger, "Donald Trump Confirms U.S. Withdrawal from INF Nuclear Treaty," *Guardian*, February 1, 2019; and David E. Sanger, "Trump Will Withdraw from Open Skies Arms Control Treaty," *New York Times*, May 21, 2020.

381. Donald Trump, quoted in Ramin Skibba, "How Trump's 'Space Force' Could Set Off a Dangerous Arms Race," *Politico*, June 22, 2018, https:// www.politico.com/magazine/ story/2018/06/22/how-trumps-space-force-could-set-off-a-dangerous-arms-race-218888. See also Gbenga Oduntan, "Donald Trump's Space Force: The Dangerous Militarization of Outer Space," *The Conversation*, June 25, 2018, http://theconversation.com/donald-trumps-space-force-the-dangerous-militarisation-of-outer-space-98588.

NOTES TO PAGE 248   455

382. Skibba, "Trump's 'Space Force'"; Simon Tisdale, "The Nuclear Arms Race Is Back . . .and Ever More Dangerous Now," *Guardian*, August 17, 2019; Simon Tisdale, "Trump Is Creating a Nuclear Threat Worse than the Cold War," *Guardian*, October 23, 2018; Joe Cirincione, "Nuclear Nuts: Trump's New Policy Hypes the Threat and Brings Us Closer to War," *Defense One*, February 2, 2018, https://www.defenseone.com/ideas/2018/02/trumps-new-nuclear-policy-hypes-threat-and-bring-war-nearer/145703/; and Editors, "Trump Is Trashing Arms Control Treaties and Making the World More Dangerous," *Los Angeles Times*, June 11, 2020.

383. Louis Jacobson and John Kruzel, "Has Donald Trump Been 'Much Tougher on Russia' than Barack Obama?," *PolitiFact*, February 20, 2018, https://www.politifact.com/truth-o-meter/   statements/2018/feb/20/donald-trump/has-donald-trump-been-much-tougher-russia-barack-o/#; David A. Graham, "Trump's Pattern of Deference to the Kremlin Is Clear," *The Atlantic*, January 15, 2019, https://www.theatlantic.com/politics/archive/2019/01/trump-russia-putin-burden/580 477/; and John Haltiwanger and Sonam Sheth, "Here's a Glimpse of Trump's Decades-Long History of Business Ties to Russia," *Business Insider*, March 22, 2019, https://www.businessinsider.com/trump-russia-business-financial-ties-2018-11.

384. Glenn Thrush and Peter Baker, "Trump's Threat to North Korea Was Improvised," *New York Times*, August 9, 2017.

385. Donald Trump, quoted in Aaron Blake, "Why Trump's Threat to 'Totally Destroy' North Korea is Extraordinary—Even for Him," *Washington Post*, September 19, 2017.

386. Jonathan Martin and Mark Sandler, "Bob Corker Says Trump's Recklessness Threatens 'World War III,'" *New York Times*, October 8, 2017.

387. Alex Ward, "How Trump Made the North Korea Crisis Worse," *Vox*, December 12, 2018, https://www.vox.com/2018/12/12/18130628/north-korea-trump-nuclear-war-jackson. See also Van Jackson, *On the Brink: Trump, Kim, and the Threat of Nuclear War* (Cambridge: Cambridge University Press, 2018); Tom O'Connor, "Russia Says U.S. War with North Korea Could Kill 'Millions' of Innocent People," *Newsweek*, February 28, 2018, https://www. newsweek.com/russia-says-us-war-north-korea-could-kill-millions-innocent-people-824226; Alex Lockie, "The U.S. Can Survive a Nuclear North Korea—But a First Strike Could Start World War III," *Business Insider*, June 6, 2017, https://www.businessinsider.com/north-korea-icbm-world-war-iii-2017-6;   and Alex Lockie, "Reckless Game Over the Korean Peninsula Runs Risk of Real War," *Global Times*, August 10, 2017, http://www.globaltimes.cn/content/1060791.shtml.

388. Roberta Rampton, "We Fell in Love," Reuters, September 29, 2018, https://www.reuters.com/article/us-northkorea-usa-trump/we-fell-in-love-trump-swoons-over-letters-from-north-koreas-kim-idUSKC-N1MA03Q.

389. Tim Shorrock, "Why Are Democrats Trying to Torpedo the Korea Peace Talks?," *The Nation*, February 22, 2019, https://www.thenation.com/article/north-korea-democrats-peace-talks/.

390. BBC News, "Trump Accuses China of 'Raping' U.S with Unfair Trade Policy," May 2, 2016, https://www.bbc.com/news/election-us-2016-36185012.

391. Zachary Karabell, "Trump's China Tariffs Failed—Why Isn't Biden Dropping Them?," *Washington Post*, December 4, 2020; Michael T. Klare, "The U.S. Is Already at War with China," *The Nation*, February 18, 2019, https://www.the nation.com/article/the-us-is-already-at-war-with-china/; and Helen Davidson, "Trump's U.S. Investment Ban Aims to Cement Tough-on-China Policy," *Guardian*, November 23, 2020.

392. Karabell, "Trump's China Tariffs"; and Sam Meredith, "China Accuses the U.S. of Launching the 'Largest Trade War in Economic History,'" CNBC, July 9, 2018, https://www. cnbc.com/2018/07/06/china-implements-new-tariffs-on-us-products-state-media-says.html.

393. Klare, "Already at War"; James Reinl, "Is a U.S.-China War in Asia Inevitable?," *Al Jazeera*, October 29, 2018, https://www.aljazeera.com/news/2018/10/china-war-asia-inevitable-1810291 95111603.html; and Jane Perlez and Steven Lee Myers, "U.S. and China Are Playing 'Game of Chicken' in South China Sea," *New York Times*, November 8, 2018.

394. Ted Galen Carpenter, "Forget the U.S.-China Trade War: Is a Conflict over Taiwan the Real Threat?," *The National Interest*, June 8, 2019, https://nationalinterest.org/feature/forget-us-china-trade-war-conflict-over-taiwan-real-threat-61627; Lily Kuo, "Whether Trump or Biden Wins, U.S.-China Relations Look Set to Worsen," *Guardian*, October 25, 2020; and Associated Press, "China Condemns New U.S. Hong Kong Sanctions, Taiwan Arm Sales," December 8, 2020, https://apnews.com/article/joe-biden-legislature-beijing-hong-kong-china-1dd40f1c0b084b10cdaa563e129fcbf8.

395. Reinl, "Is War Inevitable?"; Carpenter, "Conflict over Taiwan"; Caitlin Talmadge, "Beijing's Nuclear Option: Why a U.S.-Chinese War Could Spiral Out of Control," *Foreign Affairs* (November/December 2018), https://www.foreign affairs.com/articles/china/2018-10-15/ beijings-nuclear-option; and Christopher Layne, "Coming Storms: The Return of Great-Power War," *Foreign Affairs* (November/December 2020), https://www.foreignaffairs.com/articles/united-states/2020-10-13/coming-storms.

NOTES TO PAGE 250

396. Davidson, "Tough-on-China Policy"; Associated Press, "New Sanctions, Arm Sales"; and Patrick Wintour and Julian Borger, "Trump Attacks China over COVID 'Plague' as Xi Urges Collaboration in Virus Fight," *Guardian*, September 22, 2020.

397. John Haltiwanger, "Trump Inherited Obama's Drone War and He's Significantly Expanded It in Countries Where the U.S Is Not Technically at War," *Business Insider*, November 27, 2018, https://www.businessinsider.com/trump-has-expanded-obamas-drone-war-to-shadow-warzones-2018-11.

398. Dan De Luce and Sean D. Naylor, "The Drones Are Back," *Foreign Policy*, March 26, 2018, https://foreignpolicy.com/2018/03/26/the-drones-are-back/; David Sterman, "Pakistan Set to Mark One Year with No U.S. Drone Strikes: Is the War Over?," *New America*, July 3, 2019, https://www.newamerica.org/international-security/blog/pakistan-set-mark-one-year-no-drone-strikes-war-over/; and David Sterman, "Drone Warfare," Bureau of Investigative Journalism, https://www.thebureauinvestigates.com/projects/drone-war.

399. Human Rights Watch, "Somalia: Events of 2017," *World Report* (2018), https://www. hrw.org/world-report/2018/country-chapters/somalia#; Associated Press, "One U.S. Soldier Killed, Four Wounded in Somalia Attack," June 9, 2018, https://www.nbc news.com/news/world/one-u-s-soldier-killed-four-wounded-somalia-attack-n881671; Michael Phillips, "America's Other Endless War: Battling Al-Shabaab in Somalia," *Wall Street Journal*, January 17, 2019; and Melissa Salyk-Virk, "The Hidden Damage of Trump's Secret War in Somalia," *Defense One*, October 3, 2019, https://www.defenseone.com/ideas/2019/10/hidden-damage-trumps-secret-war-somalia/160339.400.   Wesley Morgan, "Behind the Secret U.S. War in Africa," *Politico*, July 2, 2018, https://www.politico.com/story/2018/07/02/secret-war-africa-pentagon-664005; Phillip Carter and Andrew Swick, "Why Were U.S. Soldiers Even in Niger? America's Shadow Wars in Africa, Explained," *Vox*, October 26, 2017, https://www.vox.com/world/2017/10/26/16547528/us-soldiers-niger-johnson-widow-africa-trump; and Ibram X. Kendi, "The Day 'Shithole' Entered the Presidential Lexicon," *The Atlantic*, January 13, 2019, https://www.theatlantic.com/politics/archive/2019/01/shithole-countries/580054/.

401. Reuters, "Nigeria Says U.S. Agrees Delayed $593 Million Fighter Plane Sale," December 27, 2017, https://www.reuters.com/article/us-nigeria-usa/nigeria-says-u-s-agrees-delayed-593-million-fighter-plane-sale-idUSKBN1EL1EN; Meghann Myers, "Army Troops, Special Forces Train Nigerian Infantry for Fight Against Boko Haram, ISIS," *Army Times*, February 23, 2018, https://www.armytimes.com/news/your-

army/2018/02/23/special-forces-troops-train-nigerian-infantry-for-fight-against-boko-haram-isis/; Lauren Ploch Blanchard and Tomas F. Husted, *Nigeria: Current Issues and Policy*, Congressional Research Service, Report to Congress, February 1, 2019, 12–15, 20–22, https://fas.org/sgp/crs/row/RL33964.pdf; and Annika Lichtenbaum, "U.S. Military Operational Activity in the Sahel," *Lawfare*, January 25, 2019, ttps://www.lawfareblog.com/us-military-operational-activity-sahel.

402. Reuters, "Northeast Nigeria's Insurgency Has Killed Almost 350,000—UN," June 24, 2021, https://www.reuters.com/world/africa/northeast-nigeria-insurgency-has-killed-almost-350000-un-2021-06-24/.

403. Marc-Antoine Pérouse de Montelos, "The Nigerian Military Response to Boko Haram: A Critical Analysis," *African Conflict and Peacebuilding Review* 102 (Fall 2020): 69, 74–76; and Sam Olukoya, "10,000 Nigerians Died in Military Custody, Alleges Amnesty," Associated Press, December 8, 2020, https://abcnews.go.com/International/wireStory/10000-nigerians-died-military-custody-alleges-amnesty-74606130.

404. On U.S. intervention in these countries, see Carter and Swick, "U.S. Soldiers in Niger"; and Wesley Morgan, "Behind the Secret U.S. War in Africa," *Politico*, July 2, 2018, https://www. politico.com/story/2018/07/02/secret-war-africa-pentagon-664005. On regime, ethnic, or gender violence in these countries, see Epstein, "Uganda's Assault on Democracy"; Philip Obaji Jr., "The U.S.-Backed Military Slaughters Women and Children in Cameroon," *Daily Beast*, August 1, 2018, https://www.thedailybeast.com/ the-us-backed-military-slaughters-women-and-children-in-cameroon; "Killing Kenya," *Al Jazeera*, September 23, 2015, https://www.aljazeera. com/programmes/peopleandpower/2015/09/killing-kenya-150923092758366.html; Agence France-Presse, "Ethnic Violence Leads to Fall of Mali's Government," *New York Times*, April 19, 2019; Johanna Higgs, "Surviving Violence in the Sahara: The Women of Mauritania," *Huffington Post*, February 17, 2018, https://www.huffingtonpost.co.uk/johanna-higgs/ surviving-violence-in-the_b_14807932.html; Tristan Guéret, "Niger and the Fight Against Violent Extremism in the Sahel," Royal United Services Institute, April 13, 2017, https:// rusi.org/ commentary/niger-and-fight-against-violent-extremism-sahel; and Rikke Hostrup Haugbølle and Ahlam Chemlali, "Everyday Violence and Security in Tunisia," Middle East Institute, February 19, 2019, https://www.mei.edu/publications/every day-violence-and-security-tunisia.

405. Hilary Matfess, "In Partnering with Nigeria's Abusive Military, the U.S. Is Giving Boko Haram a Lifeline," *World Politics Review*, October 24, 2017, https://www.worldpolitics review.com/insights/23447/in-partnering-with-nigeria-s-abusive-military-the-u-s-is-giving-boko-ha-

NOTES TO PAGES 250-251

ram-a-lifeline; Hampton Stevens, "The Truth About the U.S. Military in Africa," *World Politics Review*, April 1, 2019, https://www.worldpoliticsreview.com/insights/26330/the-truth-about-the-us-military-in-africa; and Nathaniel Powell, "The Destabilizing Dangers of U.S. Counterterrorism in the Sahel," *War on the Rocks*, February 8, 2018, https://warontherocks.com/2018/02/the-destabilizing-dangers-of-american-counterterrorism-in-the-sahel/.

406. Lichtenbaum, "Military Activity in the Sahel"; Mark Landler and Edward Wong, "Bolton Outlines a Strategy for Africa That's Really About Countering China," *New York Times*, December 13, 2018; and Ryan Brown, "Top U.S. General in Africa Warns of Growing Threats as Trump Administration Weighs Cutting Troop Numbers," CNN, February 2, 2020, https:// www.cnn.com/2020/02/02/politics/africa-threats-trump-troops/index.html.

407. Declan Walsh, Eric Schmitt, and Julian E. Barnes, "A CIA Fighter, A Somali Bomb-Maker, and a Faltering Shadow War," *New York Times*, October 24, 2021; and Helene Cooper, "Trump Orders All American Troops Out of Somalia," *New York Times*, December 4, 2020.

408. Glenn Kessler, "Trump's $110 Billion in Arms Sales to Saudi Arabia: Still Fake," *Washington Post*, October 11, 2018.

409. Reuters, "Trump to Resume Precision Munitions Deliveries to Saudis: Officials," June 13, 2017, https://www.reuters.com/article/us-usa-saudi-arms-congress/trump-to-resume-precision-munitions-deliveries-to-saudis-officials-idUSKBN1942GG; and Declan Walsh and Eric Schmitt, "Arms Sales to Saudis Leave American Fingerprints on Yemen's Carnage," *New York Times*, December 25, 2018.

410. Helene Cooper, Thomas Gibbons-Neff, and Eric Schmitt, "Army Special Forces Secretly Help Saudis Combat Threat From Yemen Rebels," *New York Times*, May 3, 2018.

411. Sudarsan Raghavan, "Still Fighting Al-Qaeda," *Washington Post*, July 6, 2018; and "Report: Saudi-UAE Coalition 'Cut Deals' with Al-Qaeda in Yemen," *Al Jazeera*, August 6, 2018, https:// www.aljazeera.com/news/2018/08/report-saudi-uae-coalition-cut-deals-Al-Qaeda-yemen-1808 06074659521.html.

412. *Al Jazeera*, "Coalition 'Cut Deals' with Al-Qaeda."

413. Josh Dawsey, Shane Harris, and Karen DeYoung, "Trump Calls Saudi Arabia a 'Great Ally,' Discounts Crown Prince's Responsibility for Khashoggi's Death," *Washington Post*, November 20, 2018.

414. Lauren Gambino and Julian Borger, "Yemen War: Congress Votes to End U.S. Military Assistance to Saudi Arabia," *Guardian*, April 4, 2019.

415. Mark Landler and Peter Baker, "Trump Vetoes Measure to Force End to U.S. Involvement in Yemen War," *New York Times*, April 16, 2019.

460 NOTES TO PAGES 251–252

416. United Nations, "UN Humanitarian Office Puts War Dead at 233,000 in Yemen, Mostly from 'Indirect Causes,'" *UN News*, December 1, 2020, https://news.un.org/en/story/2020/ 12/1078972.

417. Annell R. Sheline and Bruce Riedel, "Biden's Broken Promise on Yemen," Brookings Institution, September 16, 2021, https://www.brookings.edu/blog/order-from-chaos/2021/09/16/ bidens-broken-promise-on-yemen/.

418. Greg Myre, "Under Trump, U.S. Troops in War Zones on the Rise," NPR, December 1, 2017, https://www.npr.org/sections/parallels/2017/12/01/566798632/under-trump-u-s-troops-in-war-zones-are-on-the-rise.

419. Dan Spinelli, "After Trump Loosened the Rules of Engagement, Civilian Casualties in Afghanistan Rose by 95 Percent," *Mother Jones*, December 7, 2020, https://www.motherjones. com/politics/2020/12/after-trump-loosened-the-rules-of-engagement-civilian-casualties-in-afghanistan-rose-by-95-percent/.

420. James Mackenzie, "The Victor, the Spoils? Trump Eyes Afghanistan's Elusive Mineral Riches," Reuters, August 20, 2017, https://www.reuters.com/article/us-usa-afghanistan-minerals-idUSKCN1B102L; and Ben Dangl, "Profiting from America's Longest War: Trump Seeks to Exploit Mineral Wealth of Afghanistan," *CounterPunch*, October 16, 2017, https://www.counterpunch.org/2017/10/16/profiting-from-americas-longest-war-trump-seeks-to-exploit-mineral-wealth-of-afghanistan/.

421. Mackenzie, "The Victor, the Spoils?"; Dangl, "Mineral Wealth"; and Antony Loewenstein, "Peace in Afghanistan? Maybe—But a Minerals Rush Is Already Underway," *The Nation*, January 30, 2019, https://www.the nation.com/article/afghanistan-war-peace-talks-minerals/.

422. *Business Wire*, "CENTAR Announces Signing of Historic Afghan Gold and Copper Mining Agreements," October 5, 2018, https://www.businesswire.com/news/home/20181005005243/en/CENTAR-Announces-Signing-Historic-Afghan-Gold-Copper.

423. Erin Banco, "The U.S. Isn't Leaving Afghanistan Anytime Soon," *Daily Beast*, January 28, 2019, https://www.thedailybeast.com/the-us-isnt-leaving-afghanistan-anytime-soon?ref= scroll.

424. Ashley Jackson, "The Taliban's Fight for Hearts and Minds," *Foreign Policy*, (September 12, 2018), https://foreignpolicy.com/2018/09/12/the-talibans-fight-for-hearts-and-minds-afghanistan/ ; Jerrod A. Laber, "America Can't Solve Afghanistan's Corruption Problems," *National Interest*, April 17, 2019, https://nationalinterest.org/blog/middle-east-watch/america-cant-solve-afghanistans-corruption-problems-52977; Rod Nordland, Ash Ngu, and Fahim Abed, "How the U.S. Government Misleads the Public on Afghanistan," *New York Times*, September 8,

NOTES TO PAGE 252   461

2018; and Tony Walker, "Trump and Turnbull Have Little Cause for Satisfaction Over Progress in Afghanistan," *The Conversation*, February 6, 2018, http://theconversation.com/trump-and-turnbull-have-little-cause-for-satisfaction-over-progress-in-afghanistan-90918.

425. Dan De Luce, Mushtaq Yusufzai, Courtney Kube, and Josh Lederman, "Trump's Envoy 'Tests All Channels' with Afghan Taliban in Bid to Launch Peace Talks," *NBC News*, November 28, 2018, https://www.nbcnews.com/news/ world/trump-s-envoy-tests-all-channels-afghan-taliban-bid-launch-n940846; Mujib Mashal, Fahim Abed, and Fatima Faizi, "After Deadly Assault on Afghan Base, Taliban Sit for Talks With US Diplomats," *New York Times*, January 21, 2019; and Mujib Mashal, "Taliban and U.S. Strike Deal to Withdraw American Troops from Afghanistan," *New York Times*, February 29, 2020.

426. Clayton Thomas, *Afghanistan: Background and U.S. Policy: In Brief*, Congressional Research Service, Report to Congress, November 10, 2020, 2, 4, 8, https://fas.org/sgp/crs/ row/R45122.pdf; and Ryan Pickrell, "Taliban Cheers Trump's Decision to Pull Thousands of American Troops Out of Afghanistan," *Business Insider*, November 18, 2020, https://www. businessinsider.com/taliban-cheers-trump-decision-on-afghanistan-troop-withdrawal-2020-11.

427. In January 2019, Afghan President Ashraf Ghani told the World Economic Forum that 45,000 soldiers and police had been killed since he took office in September 2014. The total loss was likely considerably higher. About eight thousand government security forces were dying annually by 2016 and more than twelve thousand dying annually by 2018. More than three thousand civilians have been killed each year since 2013. Although Ghani probably exaggerated when he claimed that as many Taliban fighters had died as soldiers and police, the insurgents' losses likely ran into the tens of thousands since 2014. See BBC, "Afghanistan's Ghani Says 45,000 Security Personnel Killed Since 2014," January 25, 2019, https://www.bbc.com/news/ world-asia-47005558; Rod Nordland, "The Death Toll of Afghan Security Forces Is Secret, Here's Why," *New York Times*, September 21, 2018; *Al Jazeera*, "Afghanistan Civilian Deaths Hit Record High in 2018," February 24, 2019, https://www. aljazeera.com/news/2019/02/ afghanistan-civilian-deaths-hit-record-high-2018-190224071129307.html; and Human Rights Service, UN Assistance Mission in Afghanistan, *Afghanistan: Protection of Civilians in Armed Conflict, Annual Report 2020*, Kabul, February 2021, 11–12, https://unama.unmissions.org/sites/default/files/afghanistan_protection_of_civilians_report_2020_revs3.pdf. A much lower, less comprehensive estimate of fewer than 175,000 deaths since October 2001 has been advanced by the Costs of War Project, Watson Institute for Interna-

tional and Public Affairs, Brown University, April 2021, https://watson.brown.edu/costsofwar/figures/2021/ human-and-budgetary-costs-date-us-war-afghanistan-2001-2021.

428. On the continuity between Obama's and Trump's policies toward the Islamic State, see Brian Glyn Williams, "Who Really Defeated the Islamic State—Obama or Trump?," *The Conversation*, October 16, 2020, https://theconversation.com/who-really-defeated-the-islamic-state-obama-or-trump-148066; and John Haltiwanger, "Trump's Secret War? U.S. Military's Presence in Middle East Has Grown 33 Percent in Past Four Months," *Newsweek*, November 21, 2017, https://www.newsweek.com/trumps-secret-war-us-militarys-presence-middle-east-has-grown-33-percent-past-718089.

429. On the deaths of Islamic State fighters in Iraq and Syria, see Williams, "Who Really Defeated the Islamic State?"; Christopher Woody, "U.S. Special Operations Command Chief Claims '60,000 to 70,000' ISIS Fighters Have Been Killed," *Business Insider*, July 24, 2017, https://www.businessinsider.com/gen-raymond-thomas-socom-60000-to-70000-isis-fighters-killed-2017-7; and Jane Arraf, "More Civilians Than ISIS Fighters Are Believed Killed in Mosul Battle," NPR, December 19, 2017, https://www.npr.org/sections/parallels/2017/12/19/570483 824/more-civilians-than-isis-fighters-are-believed-killed-in-mosul-battle. On the deaths of civilians caused by U.S. forces, see Arraf, "More Civilians Killed"; Karen McVeigh, "'Crazy Numbers': Civilian Deaths from Airstrikes Almost Double in a Year," *Guardian*, January 8, 2018; Samuel Oakford, "Counting the Dead in Mosul," *The Atlantic*, April 5, 2018, https://www. theatlantic. com/international/archive/2018/04/counting-the-dead-in-mosul/556466/; and Sune Engel Rasmussen, "U.S.-Led Coalition Captures Last ISIS Bastion in Syria, Ending Caliphate," *Wall Street Journal*, March 23, 2019.

430. Jonathan Swan and Alayna Treene, "Trump to Iraqi PM: How about That Oil?," *Axios*, November 25, 2018, https://www.axios.com/trump-to-iraqi-pm-how-about-that-oil-1a31cbfa-f20c-4767-8d18-d518ed9a6543.html.

431. Ibid.

432. Falih Hassan and Rick Gladstone, "Angered at Trump's Visit, Some Iraqi Lawmakers Want U.S. Troops Out," *New York Times*, December 27, 2018, https://www.nytimes.com/2018/12/ 27/12/27/world/middleeast/trump-iraq-visit.html.

433. David Brunnstrom and Idrees Ali, "U.S. Says Signs Syria May Be Using Chemical Weapons, Warns of Quick Response," *U.S. News and World Report*, May 21, 2019, https://www.usnews.com/news/world/articles/2019-05-21/us-says-sees-signs-syrian-government-may-be-using-chemical-weapons.

NOTES TO PAGE 253

434. Maria Tsvetkova, "Russian Toll in Syria Battle Was 300 Killed and Wounded: Sources," Reuters, February 15, 2018, https://www.reuters.com/article/us-mideast-crisis-syria-russia-casualtie-idUSKCN1FZ-2DZ.

435. Michael R. Gordon, "White House Accepts 'Political Reality' of Assad's Grip on Power in Syria," *New York Times*, March 31, 2017; and Greg Jaffe and Adam Entous, "Trump Ends Covert CIA Program to Arm Anti-Assad Rebels in Syria, A Move Sought by Moscow," *Washington Post*, July 19, 2017.

436. Scott Ritter, "Iran Deserves Credit for the Ruin of ISIS," *American Conservative*, October 17, 2018, https://www.theamericanconservative.com/articles/iran-deserves-credit-for-the-ruin-of-isis/; Araz Muhmanad Arash and Sylvain Mercadier, "The Militias in Iraq: From Popular Mobilization to Political Interference," *OrientXXI*, February 6, 2018, https://orientxxi.info/magazine/the-militias-in-iraq-from-popular-mobilization-to-political-interference; Mike Giglio, "The Flash Point Between America and Iran Could Be Iraq's Militias," *The Atlantic*, May 8, 2019, https://www.theatlantic.com/politics/archive/2019/05/iraq-militias-flash-point-between-united-states-and-iran/589003/; and "Kurds Slam Abadi's Peshmerga Snub in ISIL Speech," *Al Jazeera*, December 10, 2017, https://www.aljazeera.com/news/2017/12/ kurds-slam-abadi-peshmerga-snub-isil-speech-171210100538711.html.

437. Ritter, "Iran Deserves Credit"; Tharoor, "Russia Stays in the Driver's Seat"; Reuters, "Syrian Government Forces Enter Palmyra, Drive Back Islamic State: Monitors," March 1, 2017, https://www. reuters.com/article/us-mideast-crisis-syria-palmyra/syrian-government-forces-enter-palmyra-drive-back-islamic-state-monitors-idUSKBN16847B; and Max Blumenthal, *The Management of Savagery: How America's National Security State Fueled the Rise of Al Qaeda, ISIS, and Donald Trump* (London: Verso, 2019), 202–4, 292–93.

438. More than 86,000 civilians died as a result of the conflicts during this period. More than 26,000 Iraqi government troops, approximately 8,000 Popular Mobilization forces, and about 1,800 Kurdish Peshmerga fighters perished during the struggle against the Islamic State between 2014 and 2017. See Arraf, "More Civilians Killed"; "Kurds Slam Abadi's Snub," *Al Jazeera*; Leith Aboufadel, "Over 26,000 Iraqi Soldiers Killed in 4 Year War with ISIS, *Al-Masdar News,* December 13, 2017, https://www.almasdarnews.com/article/26000-iraqi-soldiers-killed-4-year-war-isis/; Hélène Sallon, "L'Intégration des Milices, un Défi pour l'Etat Irakien," *Le Monde*, December 27, 2017; and Statista Research Department, "Number of Documented Civilian Deaths in the Iraq War from 2003 to October 20, 2021," *Statista*, October 31, 2021, https://www.

statista.com/statistics/269729/documented-civilian-deaths-in-iraq-war-since-2003. This total does not include combatant deaths in 2012–13.

439. Rasmussen, "Coalition Captures Last ISIS Bastion"; and Wilson Center, "Timeline: The Rise, Spread, and Fall of the Islamic State," October 28, 2019, https://wilsoncenter.org/article/timeline-the-rise-spread-and-fall-the-islamic-state.

440. Mark Landler, Helene Cooper, and Eric Schmitt, "Trump to Withdraw U.S. Forces from Syria, Declaring, 'We Have Won Against ISIS,'" *New York Times*, December 19, 2018, https://www.nytimes.com/2018/12/19/us/politics/trump-syria-turkey-troop-withdrawal.html; Daniel Flatley, "Senate Rebukes Trump on Syria Policy Hours Before State of the Union," Bloomberg, February 5, 2019, https://www.bloomberg.com/news/articles/2019-02-05/senate-rebukes-trump-on-syria-policy-hours-before-state-of-union; and Ellen Mitchell, "Trump Backs Off Total Syria Withdrawal," *The Hill*, February 23, 2019, https://thehill.com/policy/defense/431289-trump-backs-off-total-syria-withdrawal.

441. Alissa J. Rubin and Eric Schmitt, "Trump's Plan for U.S. Forces in Iraq Met with Unified Rejection in Baghdad," *New York Times*, February 4, 2019.

442. Peter Wehner, "Trump Betrayed the Kurds. He Couldn't Help Himself," *The Atlantic*, October 15, 2019, https://www.theatlantic.com/ideas/archive/2019/10/trump-betrayed-kurds-whos-next/600004/; and James Longman, "For Many Kurds, the U.S. Is All They Have Left," *ABC News*, February 13, 2020, https://abcnews.go.com/International/kurds-us-left-reporters-notebook/story?id=68966991.

443. Tom O'Connor, "Syria Says Donald Trump 'Stealing' Its Oil, After U.S. Company Makes Deal to Drill," *Newsweek*, August 20, 2020, https://www.newsweek.com/syria-trump-stealing-oil-us-confirms-deal-1526589; "Syria: U.S. Continues to Steal Oil through Iraq," *Middle East Monitor*, September 21, 2020, https://www.middleeastmonitor.com/20200921-syria-us-continues-to-steal-oil-through-iraq/; and Aamer Madhani, Associated Press, "Biden Ending Trump Ok for U.S. Oil Company in Syria," *Military Times*, May 27, 2021, https://www.military times.com/news/pentagon-congress/2021/05/27/biden-ending-trump-ok-for-us-oil-company-in-syria-says-official/.

444. Alex Rogers, "McConnell Opposed Removing U.S. Troops from Middle East, Saying Terrorists 'Would Love' It," CNN, November 16, 2020, https://www.cnn.com/2020/11/16/ politics/mitch-mcconnell-opposes-troop-withdrawal-middle-east/index.html.

445. "Read the Full Transcript of Trump's Speech on the Iran Nuclear Deal," *New York Times*, May 8, 2018.

NOTES TO PAGE 254

446. Mark Landler, "Trump Abandons Iran Nuclear Deal He Long Scorned," *New York Times*, May 8, 2018.
447. Medhi Hassan, "The Corona Virus Is Killing Iranians. So Are Trump's Brutal Sanctions," *The Intercept*, March 17, 2020, https://theintercept.com/2020/03/17/coronavirus-iran-sanctions/; Seyed Hossein Mousavian, "Sanctions Make Iran's Coronavirus More Deadly," *Al Jazeera*, May 8, 2020, https://www.aljazeera.com/opinions/2020/5/8/sanctions-make-irans-coronavirus-crisis-more-deadly/; and "Iran Passes Grim Milestone of 40,000 Deaths from COVID-19," *Al Jazeera*, November 12, 2020, https://www.aljazeera.com/news/2020/11/12/ iran-passes-grim-milestone-of-40000-deaths-from-coronavirus.
448. "TV Report: White House Tells Russia It Backs Israeli Strikes in Syria," *Times of Israel*, June 2, 2019, https://www.timesofisrael.com/tv-report-white-house-tells-russia-it-backs-israeli-strikesin-syria/; Tom O'Connor, "Donald Trump Defends Saudi Arabia, Attacks Iran, and Doubts U.S. Intelligence in Extraordinary Khashoggi Statement," *Newsweek*, November 20, 2018, https:// www.newsweek.com/donald-trump-saudi-arabia-iran-khashoggi-1224878; and Jackson Diehl, "Trump's Overarching Middle East Strategy Reaches a Disastrous Dead End," *Washington Post*, November 22, 2020.
449. Robert Mackey, "Here's John Bolton Promising Regime Change in Iran by the End of 2018," *The Intercept*, March 23, 2018, https://theintercept.com/2018/03/23/heres-john-bolton-promising-regime-change-iran-end-2018/.
450. David McKean and Patrick Granfield, "Trump Is Moving Us Closer to War with Iran," *Washington Post*, February 7, 2019; and Chas Danner, "Trump Makes Needless Threat to 'End' Iran," *New York*, May 19, 2019, http://nymag.com/intelligencer/2019/05/trump-makes-needless-threat-to-end-iran.html.
451. Michael Crowley, Falih Hassan, and Eric Schmitt, "U.S. Strike in Iraq Kills Qassim Suleimani, Commander of Iranian Forces," *New York Times*, July 9, 2020, https://www. nytimes.com/2020/01/02/world/middleeast/qassem-soleimani-iraq-iran-attack.html; and Eliza Relman, "World Leaders Largely Condemn the Deadly U.S. Drone Strike on an Iranian General as a 'Dangerous Escalation,' While the UN Says the Move is Likely Unlawful," *Business Insider*, January 3, 2020, https:// www.businessinsider.com/ world-leaders-condemn-deadly-us-drone-strike-on-the-iranian-general-2020-1.
452. Eric Schmitt, Maggie Haberman, David E. Sanger, Helene Cooper, and Lara Jakes, "Trump Sought Options for Attacking Iran to Stop Its Growing Nuclear Program," *New York Times*, December 2, 2020.
453. Ibid.; Medea Benjamin and Ariel Gold, "Trump Risks War Again: Will

466   NOTES TO PAGE 255

the World Condemn the Murder of Iran's Top Nuclear Scientist?," *Salon*, November 30, 2020, https:// www.salon.com/2020/11/30/trump-risks-war-again-will-the-world-condemn-the-murder-of-irans-top-nucle-ar-scientist/.

454. An estimate of 29,000 fatalities is found in Emmanuel Tupas, "29,000 Deaths Probed Since Drug War Launched," *Philippine Star*, March 6, 2019, https://www.philstar. com/nation/2019/03/06/1898959/29000-deaths-probed-drug-war-launched. An estimate of at least 27,000 deaths appears in "Rodrigo Duterte's Lawless War on Drugs Is Wildly Popular," *The Economist*, February 20, 2020, https://www.economist. com/briefing/ 2020/02/20/rodrigo-dutertes-lawless-war-on-drugs-is-wildly-popular.

455. Nancy A. Youssef, Vivian Salama, and Michael C. Bender, "Trump, Awaiting Egyptian Counterpart at Summit, Called Out for 'My Favorite Dictator,'" *Wall Street Journal*, May 13, 2019.

456. Kevin Liptak, "Trump Declares Himself a 'Big Fan' of Turkey's Strongman Leader Erdogan," CNN, November 13, 2019, https://www.cnn. com/2019/11/13/politics/donald-trump-recep-tayyip-erdogan-turkey-impeachment/index.html.

457. Agence France-Presse, "Honduras Post-Election Crisis Leaves Dozens Dead," *Yahoo News,* January 10, 2018, https://www.yahoo.com/news/honduras-post-election-crisis-leaves-dozens-dead-184114627.html.

458. Luis Jaime Acosta, "Murder of Hundreds of Colombian Activists Casts Shadow over Peace Process," Reuters, August 25, 2019, https:// www.reuters.com/article/us-colombia-peace-feature/murder-of-hundreds-of-colombian-activists-casts-shadow-over-peace-process-idUSKCN1VF0IK; Associated Press, "'Staggering Number' of Human Rights Activists Killed in Colombia, UN Reports," *Guardian*, January 14, 2020; and Joe Parkin Daniels, "'We're Being Massacred': Colombia Accused of Failing to Stop Murders of Activists," *Guardian*, October 8, 2020.

459. Marjorie Cohn, "The U.S. Is Orchestrating a Coup in Venezuela," *Truthout*, February 2, 2019, https://truthout.org/articles/the-us-is-orchestrating-a-coup-in-venezuela/; Mark Weisbrot and Jeffrey Sachs, *Economic Sanctions as Collective Punishment: The Case of Venezuela*, Center for Economic and Policy Research, April 2019, http://cepr.net/publications/reports/economic-sanctions-as-collective-punishment-the-case-of-venezuela; Uri Friedman and Kathy Gilsinan, "The U.S. Is Running Low on Options to Force Maduro Out," *The Atlantic*, March 22, 2019, https://www.theatlantic.com/politics/archive/2019/03/united-states-weights-limited-options-venezuela/ 585541/; Rachael Boothroyd Rojas, "U.S. Donates Almost USD $1 Million to Pro-Venezuelan Opposition

NOTES TO PAGES 255–266   467

Think Tank," *Venezuelanalysis.com*, December 13, 2017, https://venezuelanalysis.com/news/13550; Jefferson Morley, "CIA in Venezuela: Seven Rules for Regime Change," *Salon*, February 1, 2019, https://www.salon.com/2019/02/01/cia-in-venezuela-7-rules-for-regime-change_partner/; and Jon Queally, "Fear of U.S.-Backed Coup in Motion as Trump Recognizes Venezuela Opposition Lawmaker as 'Interim President,'" *Common Dreams*, January 23, 2019, https://www.commondreams.org/news/2019/01/23/fears-us-backed-coup-motion-trump-recognizes-venezuela-opposition-lawmaker-interim.

460. Sarah Westwood and Devan Cole, "Trump Says Use of Military Force in Venezuela Is Still on the Table," CNN, February 3, 2019, https://www.cnn.com/2019/02/03/politics/trump-nicolas-maduro-military-force/index.html.

461. "Notes from the Editors," *Monthly Review* 71/2 (June 2019), https://monthlyreview.org/ 2019/06/01mr-071-02-2019-06_0/#lightbox/0/; and Ana Vanessa Herrero, "In Fight for Venezuela, Who Supports Maduro and Who Backs Guaidó?," *New York Times*, February 4, 2019.

462. Weisbrot and Sachs, *Sanctions as Collective Punishment*, 1, 14–16; CBS News, "Death Toll in Venezuela Unrest Soars Past 100, According to AP," July 27, 2017, https://www.cbsnews.com/ news/ venezuela-unrest-death-toll-soars-past-100-protesters-nicolas-maduro/; Deutsche Welle, "Venezuela: A Country in Meltdown," January 14, 2018, https://www.dw.com/en/venezuela-a-country-in-meltdown/a-42137133; and Vasco Cotovio and Emanuella Grinberg, "At Least 40 Venezuelans Have Been Killed in Recent Protests," CNN, January 29, 2019, https://www.cnn. com/2019/01/29/americas/venezuela-protests-deaths/index.html.

463. Glenn Greenwald, "The New York Times Admits Key Falsehoods That Drove Last Year's Coup in Bolivia: Falsehoods Peddled by the US, Its Media, and the Times," *The Intercept*, June 8, 2020, https://theintercept.com/2020/06/08/the-nyt-admits-key-falsehoods-that-drove-last-years-coup-in-bolivia-falsehoods-peddled-by-the-u-s-its-media-and-the-nyt/; "Trump Lifts Restrictions on Aid Delivery to Bolivia," teleSur, January 7, 2020, https://www.telesurenglish. net/news/Trump-Lifts-Restriction-on-Aid-Delivery-to-Bolivia-20200107-0011.html; and Cindy Forster, "Bolivia's Post-Coup President Has Unleashed a Campaign of Terror," *Jacobin*, May 30, 2020, https://www.jacobinmag.com/2020/05/bolivia-coup-jeanine-anez-evo-morales-mas.

464. Mark Weisbrot, "Silence Reigns on the U.S.-Backed Coup against Evo Morales in Bolivia," *Guardian*, September 18, 2020; Tom Phillips, "How Bolivia's Left Returned to Power Months after Morales Was Forced Out," *Guardian*, October 23, 2020.

468   NOTES TO PAGE 259

7. Other Holocausts at Home and Abroad

1. David A. Blum and Nese F. DeBruyne, *American War Casualties*; Office
    of Public Affairs, Veterans Administration, "America's Wars," November
    2020, https://www.va.gov/opa/publications/ factsheets/fs_americas_wars.pdf;
    and Paul Waldman, "American War Dead, By the Numbers,"
    American Prospect, May 26, 2014, https://prospect.org/power/
    american-war-dead-numbers/.

2. Parenti, *Democracy for the Few*, 9th ed. (Boston: Wadsworth Cengage
    Learning, 2011), chaps 9 and 10; Goldstein, *Political Repression*; Joshua
    D. Rothman, "Mobs of White Citizens Rioting Have Been Commonplace
    in the United States for Centuries," *The Hechinger Report*,
    January 8, 2021, https://hechingerreport.org/mobs-of-white-citizens-
    rioting-have-been-commonplace-in-the-united-states-for-centuries/;
    Katie Nodjimbadem, "The Long, Painful History of Police Brutality in
    the U.S.," *Smithsonian Magazine*, July 27, 2017, https://www.smithso-
    nianmag.com/smithsonian-institution/long-painful-history-police-
    brutality-in-the-us-180964098; Michael Sainato, "Why Are So Many
    People Dying in U.S. Prisons and Jails?," *Guardian*, May 26, 2019; and
    Jeff Gammage, "Hundreds of Migrants Die Every Year Trying to Cross
    the Southwest Border into the U.S.," *Philadelphia Inquirer*, October 29,
    2019.

3. Michael A. Bellesiles, "Introduction," in *Lethal Imagination*, 1, 10; Erin
    Grinshteyn and David Hemenway, "Violent Death Rates: The U.S.
    Compared to Other High-Income OECD Countries 2010," *American
    Journal of Medicine* 129/3 (March 2016): 266–73; and Kieran Healy,
    "America Is a Violent Country," *Washington Post*, November 8, 2018.

4. Anti-Defamation League, "A Dark and Constant Rage: 25 Years of
    Right-Wing Terrorism in the United States," 2017, 23, https:// www.
    adl.org/sites/default/files/documents/CR_5154_25YRS%20Righ-
    tWing%20Terrorism_V5.pdf; National Consortium for the Study of
    Terrorism and Responses to Terrorism, "Far-Right Violence in the
    United States, 1990–2010," University of Maryland, August 8, 2012,
    https://www.start.umd.edu/sites/default/files/files/publications/br/
    ECDB_FarRight_FactSheet.pdf; and Nadia Khomami, "Terrorist At-
    tacks by Violent Jihadis in the U.S. Since 9-11," *Guardian*, December 5,
    2015.

5. Dolin, "How the China Trade Helped Make America," *Daily Beast*,
    November 4, 2012, http://www.thedailybeast.com/articles/2012/11/04/
    how-the-china-trade-helped-make-america.html; John Kamp, "Over-
    dose Deaths Likely to Fall for First Time Since 1990," *Wall Street Jour-
    nal*, June 26, 2019; Robert N. Proctor, *Golden Holocaust: Origins of the
    Cigarette Catastrophe and the Case for Abolition* (Berkeley: University

NOTES TO PAGE 259 469

of California Press, 2011), Parts 2 and 3; Catherine Lutz and Anne Lutz Fernandez, *Carjacked: The Culture of the Automobile and Its Effect on Our Lives* (New York: Palgrave Macmillan, 2010); Susan Brink, "Why the Breastfeeding Vs. Formula Debate is Especially Critical in Poor Countries," NPR, July 13, 2018, https://www.npr.org/sections/goatsandsoda/2018/07/13/628105632/is-infant-formula-ever-a-good-option-in-poor-countries; and *Oversight of the Consumer Product Safety Commission: Hearing Before the Subcomm. on Consumer Affairs, Insurance, and Automotive Safety, of the Senate Comm. on Commerce, Science, and Transportation, 110th Congress, 3,* March 21, 2007 (Testimony of Rachel Weintraub, Consumer Federation of America).

6. Washington, *Medical Apartheid: The Dark History of Medical Experimentation on Black Americans from Colonial Times to the Present* (New York: Anchor Books, 2006) ; Eileen Welsome, *The Plutonium Files: America's Secret Medical Experiments in the Cold War* (New York: Dell, 1999); David A. Grimes with Linda G. Brandon, *Every Third Woman in America: How Legal Abortion Transformed Our Nation* (Carolina Beach, NC: Daymark Publishing, 2014), chap. 1; Allen White, "Reagan's AIDS Legacy/ Silence Equals Death," *San Francisco Chronicle,* June 8, 2004; Ed Vulliamy, "How Drug Giants Let Millions Die of AIDS," *Guardian,* December 19, 1999; Jorge L. Ortiz, "'Blood on His Hands': As U.S. Surpasses 400,000 COVID-19 Deaths, Experts Blame Trump for a 'Preventable' Loss of Life," *USA Today,* January 19, 2021; Alison P. Galvani, Alyssa S. Parpia, Eric M. Foster, Burton H. Singer, and Meagan C. Fitzpatrick, "Improving the Prognosis of Health Care in the U.S.A.," *The Lancet* 395/10223, (February 15, 2020): 524–33; John T. James, "A New, Evidence-based Estimate of Patient Harms Associated with Hospital Care," *Journal of Patient Safety* 9/3 (September 2013): 122–28; and Peter C. Gøtzsche, *Deadly Medicines and Organized Crime: How Big Pharma Has Corrupted Healthcare* (London: Radcliffe Publishing, 2013).

7. Devra Davis, *When Smoke Ran Like Water: Tales of Environmental Deception and the Battle Against Pollution* (New York: Basic Books, 2002) and *The Secret History of the War on Cancer* (New York: Basic Books, 2007); Benjamin Bowe, Yan Xie, Yan Yan, and Ziyad Al-Aly, "Burden of Cause-Specific Mortality Associated with PM. Air Pollution in the United States," *JAMA Network Open* 2/11 (November 20, 2019), https://jamanetwork.com/ journals/jamanetworkopen/fullarticle/2755672; Keith Meyers, "Some Unintended Fallout from Defense Policy: Measuring the Effect of Atmospheric Nuclear Testing on American Mortality Patterns," March 7, 2019, 20, 22, https: https://static1.squarespace.com/static/59262540b3db2b0d0d6d7d2b/t/5c81809a419202f922f0cfa4/1551990940274/FalloutMortDraft_3-5-2019.pdf; Bruce P. Lamp-

hear, Stephen Rauch, Peggy Auinger, Ryan W. Allen, and Richard W. Hornung, "Low-Level Lead Exposure and Mortality in U.S. Adults: A Population-Based Cohort Study," *The Lancet: Public Health* 3/4 (March 12, 2018): E177-E184; and David Wallace-Wells, *The Uninhabitable Earth: Life After Warming* (New York: Penguin Random House, 2019).

8. Peckham, *The Toll of Independence: Engagements and Battle Casualties of the American Revolution* (Chicago: University of Chicago Press, 1974), 130–32.

9. Hickey, *War of 1812: A Forgotten Conflict*, Bicentennial Edition (Urbana: University of Illinois Press, 2012), 306.

10. Henderson, *A Glorious Defeat: Mexico and Its War with the United States* (New York: Hill and Wang, 2007), 179.

11. Downs, "Color Blindness in the Demographic Death Toll of the Civil War," *Oxford University Press Blog*, April 13, 2012, http://blog.oup.com/2012/04/black-white-demographic-death-toll-civil-war/.

12. U.S. Census Bureau, "Indian Wars and Their Costs, and Civil Expenditures for Indians," *Eleventh Census*, vol. 10: *Report on Indians Taxed and Not Taxed in the United States, Except Alaska*, (1890), 637–38.

13. Wintermute, "Casualties," in *The Encyclopedia of the Spanish American and Philippine-American Wars: A Political, Economic, and Social History*, vol. 1, ed. Spencer C. Tucker (Santa Barbara, CA: ABC-CLIO, 2009), 105; Dayl, Carpenter, and Thomas, "Casualties," *Historical Dictionary of the Spanish American War* (Westport, CT: Greenwood Press, 1996), 67; and Clodfelter, *Warfare and Armed Conflicts: A Statistical Encyclopedia of Casualty and Other Figures, 1494–2007*, 3rd ed. (Jefferson: McFarland and Company, 2008), 274.

14. Clodfelter, *Warfare*, 260.

15. Ibid., 462.The description of this war is found in Milne, "First World War."

16. Clodfelter, *Warfare*, 561.

17. Ibid., 710.

18. U.S. National Archives and Records Administration, "Vietnam War U.S. Military Fatal Casualty Statistics," April 30, 2019, https://www.archives.gov/research/military/vietnam-war/casualty-statistics.

19. Fred A. Wilcox, *Scorched Earth: Legacies of Chemical Warfare in Vietnam* (New York: Seven Stories Press, 2011), 69–71, 103, and email to author, July 9, 2019.

20. Stone and Kuznick, *Untold History*, 395.

21. Blum and DeBruyne, *American War Casualties*, 3.

22. Sommer Brokaw, "U.S. Soldier Killed 'In Action' in Afghanistan," UPI, July 13, 2019, https:// www.upi.com/Top_News/US/2019/07/13/US-soldier-killed-in-action-in Afghanistan/96615630 30676/.

NOTES TO PAGES 260-261   471

23. Blum and DeBruyne, *American War Casualties*, 15.

24. Almost eight thousand mercenaries and other military contractors died in these two wars by November 2019. U.S. nationals have constituted about 33 percent of these groups, but Washington does not maintain a record of their deaths. See Nita C. Crawford and Catherine Lutz, "Human Cost of Post-9/11 Wars: Direct War Deaths in Major War Zones," Watson Institute for International and Public Affairs, Brown University, November 13, 2019, https://watson.brown.edu/costsofwar/figures/2019/direct-war-death-toll-2001-801000; and Sean McFate, "America's Addiction to Mercenaries," *The Atlantic*, August 12, 2016, https://www.theatlantic.com/inter national/archive/2016/08/iraq-afghanistan-contractor-pentagon-obama/495731/.

25. PBS, *American Experience: Anti-Mormon Violence*, https://www.pbs.org/wgbh/americanexperience/features/mormons-opposition/.

26. Paul Simon, *Freedom's Champion: Elijah Lovejoy*, rev. ed. (Carbondale: Southern Illinois University Press, 1994), chap. 7.

27. Sandy Hingston, "Bullets and Bigots; Remembering Philadelphia's 1844 Anti-Catholic Riots," *Philadelphia*, December 17, 2015, https://www.phillymag.com/news/2015/12/17/philadelphia-anti-catholic-riots-1844/; and Tim O'Neil, "A Look Back: Irish Immigrants Fight Back in 1854 Nativist Riots," *St. Louis Post-Dispatch*, August 8, 2019.

28. Martin Ford, "Gangs of Baltimore," *Humanities* 29/3, May–June 2008, https://www.neh.gov/humanities/2008/mayjune/feature/gangs-baltimore.

29. Dale E. Watts, "How Bloody Was Bleeding Kansas? Political Killings in Kansas Territory, 1854–1861," *Kansas History: A Journal of the Central Plains* 18/2 (Summer 1995): 116–29.

30. William D. Carrigan and Clive Webb, *Forgotten Dead: Mob Violence Against Mexicans in the United States, 1848–1928* (New York: Oxford University Press, 2013), 1, 5, and "When Americans Lynched Mexicans," *New York Times*, February 20, 2015; Simon Romero, "Lynch Mobs Killed Latinos Across the West: The Fight to Remember These Atrocities Is Just Starting," *New York Times*, March 2, 2019.

31. Pfaelzer, *Driven Out: The Forgotten War against Chinese Americans* (Berkeley: University of California Press, 2007), 39–41, 47–51, 54, 69–70, 74, 125, 172–75, 209–15, 224, 255, 309.

32. Marilynn S. Johnson, *Street Justice: A History of Police Violence in New York City* (Boston: Beacon Press, 2003), 17.

33. Paul Reeve and Patrick Mason, "Mormons Know What It's Like to Be a Persecuted Minority—So Pass a Hate Crimes Law for Utah," *Salt Lake Tribune*, February 25, 2018.

34. Erin Blakemore, "The Grisly Story of America's Largest Lynching,"

472 NOTES TO PAGES 261–262

History, September 1, 2018, https://www.history.com/news/the-grisly-story-of-americas-largest-lynching; and Alan G. Gauthreaux, "An Inhospitable Land: Anti-Italian Violence in Louisiana, 1891–1924," *Louisiana History: The Journal of the Louisiana Historical Association* 51/1 (Winter 2010): 41–68.

35. Steve Oney, "A Distant Mirror: The Leo Frank Lynching," *The New Republic*, August 16, 2015, https://newrepublic.com/article/122542/distant-mirror-leo-frank-lynching.

36. Nodjimbadem, "History of Police Brutality"; Gary Potter, "The History of Policing in the United States, Part 1," Eastern Kentucky Police Studies Online, June 25, 2013, https://plsonline. eku.edu/insidelook/history-policing-united-states-part-1; and Sidney L. Harring, *Policing a Class Society: The Experience of American Cities, 1865–1915*, 2nd ed. (Chicago: Haymarket Books, 2017), 1–34.

37. Potter, "History of Policing"; Victor E. Kappeler, A Brief History of Slavery and the Origins of Policing," Eastern Kentucky Police Studies Online, January 7, 2014, https://plsonline. eku.edu/insidelook brief-history-slavery-and-origins-american-policing.

38. Gary Potter, "The History of Policing in the United States, Part 2," Eastern Kentucky Police Studies Online, July 2, 2013, https://plsonline.eku. edu/insidelook/history-policing-united-states-part-2.

39. Marilynn S. Johnson, *Street Justice*, 17–21; and Ralph Blumenthal, "Police Killing of Unarmed Man Agitated New York . . . in the 1850s," *New York Times*, April 24, 2015.

40. *New York Tribune*, August 5 and August 6, 1850, and *New York Herald*, August 6 and August 7, 1850, both cited in Wilentz, *Chants Democratic: New York City and the Rise of the Working Class, 1788–1850*, 20th anniv. ed. (Oxford: Oxford University Press, 2004), 380–81; and Doty, *A History of Livingston County, New York* (Geneseo, NY: Edward E. Doty, 1876), 449–450.

41. Harring, *Policing a Class Society*, 33; and Blumenthal, "Police Killing Agitated New York."

42. *Chicago Daily Tribune*, "Police Brutality—A Prisoner Was Shamefully Beaten by Officers, He Was Kicked and Pounded in a Cell—Probably Fatally Injured," October 12, 1872.

43. Most of those murders were committed by vigilantes in the countryside, but racist police, constables, and deputies killed African Americans in Memphis; New Orleans; Opelousas, Louisiana; Wilmington, North Carolina; and other locations. On the involvement of law enforcement officers in these killings, see Schermerhorn, "Civil Rights Laws Don't Always Stop Racism," *The Atlantic*, May 8, 2016, https://www.theatlantic. com/politics/archive/2016/05/the-memphis-massacre-of-1866-and-black-

NOTES TO PAGES 262–263

voter-suppression-today/481737/ and "When 'Taking Our Country Back' Led to a Massacre of Black Americans," *The Daily Beast*, June 3, 2020, https://www.the dailybeast.com/when-taking-our-country-back-led-to-a-massacre;Boissoneault, "The Deadliest Massacre in Reconstruction-Era Louisiana Happened 150 Years Ago," *Smithsonian Magazine*, September 28, 2018, https://www.smithsonianmag.com/history/story-deadliest-massacre-reconstruction-era-louisiana-180970420/; and Zucchino, "The 1898 Wilmington Massacre Is An Essential Lesson in How State Violence Has Targeted Black Americans," *Time*, July 1, 2020, https://time.com/5861644/1898-wilmington-massacre-essential-lesson-state-violence/. How many of the rural murderers were current or former law enforcement agents may never be known.

44. Carrigan and Webb, *Forgotten Dead*, 1, 5, and "When Americans Lynched Mexicans"; and Romero, "Mobs Killed Latinos."

45. Boyer and Morais, *Labor's Untold Story* (New York: United Electrical, Radio, and Machine Workers of America, 1955), chaps. 1–5; Lens, *The Labor Wars* (Garden City, NY: Doubleday, 1974), chaps. 1–7, Brecher, *Strike!* (San Francisco: Straight Arrow Books, 1972), chaps. 1–3; Goldstein, *Political Repression in Modern America: From 1870 to 1976* (Urbana: University of Illinois Press, 2001), chaps. 1 and 2; and Clodfelter, *Warfare*, 397.

46. Lawrence W. Sherman and Robert H. Langworthy, "Measuring Homicide by Police Officers," *Journal of Criminal Law and Criminology* 70/4 (Winter 1979): 546–50; Wesley Lowery, "How Many Police Shootings a Year? No One Knows," *Washington Post*, September 8, 2014; and U.S. Commission on Civil Rights, *Police Use of Force: An Examination of Modern Policing Practices* (Washington, DC, November 2018), 1–4, 12–20, https://www.usccr.gov/pubs/2018/ 11-15-Police-Force.pdf.

47. Jeffrey S. Adler, "The Killer Behind the Badge: Race and Police Homicide in New Orleans 1925–1945," *Law and History Review* 30/2 (May 2012): 499.

48. Livia Gershon, "A History of Police Violence in Chicago," *JSTOR Daily*, October 3, 2018, https://daily.jstor.org/a-history-of-police-violence/; Jeffrey S. Adler, "Shoot to Kill: The Use of Deadly Force by the Chicago Police, 1875–1920," *Journal of Interdisciplinary History* 38/2 (Autumn 2007): 240; and Gerald D. Robin, "Justifiable Homicide by Police Officers," *Journal of Criminal Law and Criminology* 54/2 (June 1963): 226.

49. Adler, "Killer Behind the Badge," 505.

50. Goldstein, *Political Repression*, 156–61; and Ahmed White, "100 Years Ago the First Red Scare Tried to Destroy the Left," *Jacobin*, December 23, 2019, https://www.jacobinmag.com/ 2019/12/ red-scare-industrial-workers-of-the-world-iww.

474   NOTES TO PAGES 263–264

51. Benjamin Heber Johnson, *Revolution in Texas: How a Forgotten Rebellion and Its Bloody Suppression Turned Mexicans into Americans* (New Haven: Yale University Press, 2003), 2–3, 120. Johnson concluded that it is "probable" that two to three thousand people of Mexican descent died but acknowledged that the number might have been as high as five thousand.

52. Carrigan and Webb, "When Americans Lynched Mexicans," and Romero, "Mobs Killed Latinos."

53. McWhirter, *Red Summer: The Summer of 1919 and the Awakening of Black America* (New York: St. Martin's Griffin, 2011), 13; and Khalil Gibran Muhammad, "The History of Lynching and the Present of Policing," *The Nation*, May 17, 2018, https://www.the nation.com/article/archive/the-history-of-lynching-and-the-present-of-policing.

54. Boyer and Morais, *Labor's Untold Story*, chaps. 6–9; Lens, *Labor Wars*, chaps. 8–15; Brecher, *Strike!*, chaps. 4–5; Goldstein, *Political Repression*, chaps. 3–7; and Clodfelter, *Warfare*, 397–99.

55. Nodjimbadem, "History of Police Brutality"; and National Commission on Law Observance and Enforcement, *Records of the Wickersham Commission on Law Observance and Enforcement, Part One: Records of the Committee on Official Lawlessness*, 1931, http://www.lexisnexis.com/documents/academic/upa_cis/1965_WickershamCommPt1.pdf.

56. Nodjimbadem, "History of Police Brutality"; and Sarah Brady Siff, "Policing the Police: A Civil Rights Story," *Origins: Current Events in Historical Perspective* 9/8 (May 2016), http://origins.osu.edu/article/policing-police-civil-rights-story.

57. Olivia B. Waxman, "Sacco and Vanzetti Were Executed Ninety Years Ago, Their Deaths Made History," *Time*, August 22, 2017, https://time.com/4895701/sacco-vanzetti-90th-anniversary/.

58. Goldstein, *Political Repression*, 203.

59. Ibid.

60. Ibid., 198–99.

61. Nelson A. Denis, *War Against All Puerto Ricans: Revolution and Terror in America's Colony* (New York: Bold Type Books, 2015), 43–48.

62. For the official numbers in the 1950s, see Eckberg, "Reported Homicides and Homicide Rates, by Sex and Mode of Death," in *Historical Statistics of the United States: Earliest Times to the Present, Millennial Edition*, vol. 5: *Part E: Governance and International Relations*, ed. Susan B. Carter, Scott Sigmund Gartner, Michael R. Haines, Alan L. Olmstead, Richard Sutch, and Gavin Wright (Cambridge: Cambridge University Press, 2006), 5–239, 5–240, Table Ec190–198. A more realistic estimate for the 1950s is found in Lawrence W. Sherman, "Execution Without Trial: Police Homicide and the Constitution," *Vanderbilt Law Review* 33/1 (January 1980): 71–100.

NOTES TO PAGES 264–266   475

63. Sherman, "Execution Without Trial," 71.
64. For the official numbers in the first half of the 1970s, see Eckberg, 5–239, 5-240, Table Ec190–198. For a more accurate appraisal, see Lawrence W. Sherman and Robert H. Langworthy, "Measuring Homicide by Police Officers," *Journal of Criminal Law and Criminology* 70/4 (Winter 1979): 551–53.
65. Romano, *Racial Reckoning: Prosecuting America's Civil Rights Murders* (Cambridge, MA: Harvard University Press, 2014), 2, 8–9; and Parenti, *Democracy for the Few*, 126.
66. Postrel, "The Consequences of the 1960s' Race Riots Come into View," *New York Times*, December 30, 2004.
67. Denis, *War Against All Puerto Ricans*, chaps. 18–21.
68. See Ellen Schrecker, *Many Are the Crimes: McCarthyism in America* (New York: Little, Brown, 1998), and "McCarthyism: Political Repression and the Fear of Communism," *Social Research* 71/4 (Winter 2004): 1041–86.
69. Schrecker, *Many Are the Crimes*, 361.
70. Stone and Kuznick, *The Untold History of the United States* (New York: Gallery Books, 2012), 370; and Dave Davis, "Kent State University Shootings: Four Students Killed in Anti-War Protests Forty Years Ago This Week," *Cleveland Plain Dealer*, May 2, 2010.
71. Mario T. García, "An Important Day in U.S. History: The Chicano Moratorium," *National Catholic Reporter*, August 27, 2015.
72. Parenti, *Democracy for the Few*, 127.
73. Tony Mazzochi, "Karen Silkwood Remembered," *Labor Party Press*, November 1999, https://web.archive.org/web/20121130081633/http://lpa.igc.org/lpv46/lpp46_silkwood.html.
74. Michael Marriott, "Diplomat's Assassin to Be Freed," *Washington Post*, July 26, 1983.
75. Wypijewski, "Whitewash," *Mother Jones*, November 2005, https://www.motherjones.com/politics/2005/11/whitewash/.
76. *New York Times*, "Puerto Ricans Vow to Avenge Death in U.S. Prison," November 18, 1979.
77. Yuhas, "Philadelphia's Osage Avenue Police Bombing, 30 Years On: 'This Story is a Parable,'" *Guardian*, May 13, 2015.
78. Melissa Chan, "The Real Story Behind the Waco Siege: Who Were David Koresh and the Branch Davidians?," *Time*, January 24, 2018, https://time.com/5115201/waco-siege-standoff-fbi-david-koresh/.
79. A total of 866 officer-involved deaths in 2000 is reported in Fatal Encounters, https://docs.google.com/spreadsheets/d/1dKmaV_JiWc-G8XBoRgP8b4e9Eopkpgt7FL7nyspvzAsE/edit#gid=0.
80. Dianne Solis, "40 Years after the Murder of Santos Rodriguez, Scars

476 NOTES TO PAGES 266–267

Remain for Family, Neighbors, and Dallas," *Dallas Morning News*, July 21, 2013; Marialuisa Rincon, "40 Years Ago, Police Killed Joe Campos Torres, Sparking Massive Moody Park Riots," *Houston Chronicle*, May 10, 2017; Joseph P. Fried, "Police Ruled Not Liable in Killing," *New York Times*, November 21, 1979; Jared Jacang Maher, "Target Practice: Racism and Police Shootings Are No Game," *Westword*, April 3, 2008, https://www.westword.com/news/target-practice-racism-and-police-shootings-are-no-game-5098269; George Stein, "Teenagers Shot by Officer in Chase; Patrolman Slipped Over a Pile of Wood, Police Say," *Los Angeles Times*, February 22, 1987; Jesus Rangel, "Violence Erupts After a Slaying by Police," *New York Times*, June 11, 1988; Marilynn S. Johnson, *Street Justice*, 292; Brooklyn Dance, "'It Woke Longmont Up': Community Remembers 40-Year Anniversary of Police Shooting of Two Latino Men," *Times-Call*, August 14, 2020; Julie Chao, "Cop Won't Face Charges for Killing Drunken Man," *San Francisco Examiner*, June 19, 1997; and "History of Recent Cases of Cops Charged with Murder," *San Francisco Chronicle*, February 15, 2009.

81. Eckberg, "Homicides and Homicide Rates," 5-239, 5-240, Table Ec190–198.

82. Parenti, *Democracy for the Few*, 127; and Abby Goodnough, "Killing of Militant Raises Ire in Puerto Rico," *New York Times*, September 28, 2005.

83. Brian Contreras and Paige Cornwell, "Armed Man Attacking Tacoma's ICE Detention Center Killed in Officer-Involved Shooting," *Seattle Times*, July 13, 2019.

84. Evan Hill, Mike Baker, Derek Knowles, and Stella Cooper, "'Straight to Gunshots': How a U.S. Task Force Killed an Antifa Activist," *New York Times*, December 4, 2020.

85. Ulysses Torassa, "$1.8 Million Settlement in Killing by Police Officer: 4-Foot-9-Inch Troubled Mother Fatally Shot in Kitchen While Holding a Vegetable Peeler," *San Francisco Chronicle*, December 1, 2005; Patrick Smith, "The War on Terror: Miami," *Salon*, December 9. 2005, https://www.salon.com/2005/12/09/askthepilot165/; "DOJ Study: Excessive Stun Gun Use Increases Risk of Death," *Salt Lake Tribune*, May 27, 2011; H. G. Reza, "Korean Americans Angered by Killing," *Los Angeles Times*, February 11, 2008; Kevin Canfield, "City Council OKs Settlement in Officer-Involved Shooting Death Lawsuits," *Tulsa World*, August 31, 2012; Hunter Stuart, "Houston Officer Cleared of Wrongdoing in Killing of Brian Claunch, Double Amputee," *Huffington Post*, November 5, 2013, https://www.huffpost.com/entry/brian-claunch-houston-shot-matthew-marin-police-cleared-disabled-amputee_n_4218889; Rebecca Solnit, "Death by Gentrification: The Killing That Shamed San

NOTES TO PAGE 267   477

Francisco," *Guardian*, March 21, 2016; Nita Johnson, "Constable Guilty of Reckless Homicide," (Kentucky) *Sentinel Echo*, March 22, 2017; Eli Rosenberg, "A Couple Were Killed During a Botched Drug Raid. Now an Officer Has Been Charged with Murder," *Washington Post*, August 23, 2019; "Bodycam Footage Shows Fatal Officer-Involved Shooting Inside Chino Home," KABC-TV, August 24, 2019, https:// abc7.com/bodycam-footage-shows-chino-police-fatally-shoot-man-in-home/5489712/; Mario Koran, "'We're Suffering the Same Abuses': Latinos Hear Their Stories Echoed in Police Brutality Protests," *Guardian*, June 12, 2020; Elisha Fieldstadt, "Idaho Man in His Own Backyard Fatally Shot by Officer Who Mistook Him for Armed Suspect, Police Say," NBC News, February 9, 2021, https://www.nbcnews.com/news/us-news/idaho-man-his-own-backyard-fatally-shot-officer-who-mistook-n1257131.

86. Lowery, "How Many Police Shootings?"; and U.S. Commission on Civil Rights, *Police Use of Force*.

87. See Mapping Police Violence, https://www.mappingpoliceviolence.org; and Fatal Encounters database, https://fatal encounters.org.

88. Police Shootings Database, "Fatal Force," *Washington Post*, https:// www.washingtonpost.com/graphics/investigations/police-shootings-database/; and Database, "The Counted: People Killed by Police in the U.S.," *Guardian*, https://www.the guardian.com/us-news/ng-interactive/2015/jun/01/the-counted-police-killings-us-database.

89. Jamiles Lartey, "U.S. Police Killings Undercounted by Half, Study Using *Guardian* Data Finds," *Guardian*, October 11, 2017; Carl Bialik, "The Government Finally Has a Realistic Estimate of Killings by Police," *Five Thirty-Eight*, December 15, 2018, https://fivethirtyeight. com/features/the-government-finally-has-a-realistic-estimate-of-killings-by-police/; and Jerome Karabel, "Police Killings Surpass the Worst Years of Lynching, Capital Punishment, and a Movement Responds," *Huffington Post*, December 6, 2017, https://www.huffpost.com/entry/ police-killings-lynchings-capital-punishment_b_8462778.

90. Bialik, "Estimate of Killings by Police"; and Duren Banks, Paul Ruddle, Erin Kennedy, and Michael G. Planty, "Arrest-Related Deaths Program Redesign Study, 2015–2016: Preliminary Findings," Bureau of Justice Statistics, U.S. Department of Justice, December 15, 2016, https:// bjs.ojp.gov/library/publications/arrest-related-deaths-program-redesign-study-2015-16-preliminary-findings.

91. John Sullivan, Liz Weber, Julie Tate, and Jennifer Jenkins, "Four Years in a Row, Police Nationwide Fatally Shoot Nearly 1000 People," *Washington Post*, February 12, 2019.

92. Mapping police violence reported 8,768 police killings between 2013 and 2020. See "Police Scorecard," https://policescorecard.org/.

478   NOTES TO PAGES 267–268

93. Fatal Encounters Database, https://docs.google.com/spreadsheets/
    d/1dKmaV_JiWcG8XBoRgP8b4e9Eopkpgt7FL7nyspvzAsE/
    edit#gid=0; and D. Brian Burghart, email to author, January 8, 2020.
94. Jamiles Lartey, "U.S. Police Kill More in Days Than Other Countries
    Do in Years," *Guardian*, June 9, 2015; and German Lopez, "Ameri-
    can Police Shoot and Kill Far More People Than Their Peers in Other
    Countries," *Vox*, November 14, 2018, https://www.vox.com/ identi-
    ties/2016/8/13/17938170/us-police-shootings-gun-violence-homicides.
95. Mapping Police Violence, "2020 Police Violence Report"; Gafney, "Jon-
    athan Price's Shooting Was Not 'Reasonable.' Most Police Killings of
    Black People Aren't," NBC News, October 7, 2020, https://www.nbc-
    news.com/think/opinion/jonathan-price-s-shooting-was-not-reason-
    able-most-police-killings-ncna1242463; Haynes, "Study: Black Ameri-
    cans 3 Times More Likely to Be Killed by Police," UPI, June 24, 2020,
    https://www.upi. com/Top_News/US/2020/06/24/Study-Black-Amer-
    icans-3-times-more-likely-to-be-killed-by-police/6121592949925/;
    Seth Stoughton, "Police Shouldn't Ask If a Shooting Is Justified But
    If It's Avoidable," *New York Times*, April 9, 2015; Editors, "Justified
    Shooting?," *Houston Chronicle*, July 14, 2016; German Lopez, "Police
    Can Use Deadly Force if They Merely Perceive a Threat," *Vox*, Novem-
    ber 14, 2018, https://www. vox.com/identities/2016/8/13/179 38226/
    police-shootings-killings-law-legal-standard-garner-graham-connor;
    Jonathan Blanks, "Another Unnecessary Police Killing," CATO Insti-
    tute, October 15, 2019, https://www.cato.org/blog/another-unneces-
    sary-police-killing; and David D. Kirkpatrick, Steve Eder, Kim Barker,
    and Julie Tate, "Why Many Police Traffic Stops Turn Deadly," *New York
    Times*, November 30, 2021.
96. Mapping Police Violence, "2020 Police Violence Report."
97. *Houston Chronicle* Editors, "Justified Shooting?"
98. Chris Wilson, "Every Execution in U.S. History in a Single Chart,"
    Time, April 25, 2017, https://time.com/82375/every-execution-in-u-
    s-history-in-a-single-chart/; Radelet, Bedau, and Putnam, *In Spite of
    Innocence*; and Ogletree, Jr., and Sarat, *From Lynch Mobs to the Killing
    State*. This total does not include the thousands of lynchings and other
    extrajudicial killings involving government officials.
99. Ostler, *Surviving Genocide*, 273; Kessel and Wooster, *Native American
    Wars*, 225; Clodfelter, *Warfare*, 286; and Anderson, *Ethnic Cleansing
    and the Indian*, 240.
100. Blackmon, email to author.
101. Tetsuden Kashima, "Homicide in Camp," *The Densho Encyclopedia*, ed.
    Brian Niiya (2020), http://encyclopedia.densho.org/about/.
102. Louis Fiset, "Health Care in Camp," *The Densho Encyclopedia*; and

NOTES TO PAGES 268–269

Japanese American Citizens League, *Lesson in American History: The Japanese American Experience, Curriculum and Resource Guide*, 5th ed. (2011), 12; and Gwenn M. Jensen, "System Failure: Health-Care Deficiencies in the World War II Japanese American Detention Centers," *Bulletin of the History of Medicine* 73/4 (Winter 1999): 602–28.

103. Gwendolyn M. Jensen, "The Experience of Injustice: Health Consequences of the Japanese American Internment" (PhD diss., University of Colorado, 1997), cited in PBS, "Children of the Camps: Internment History," 1999, http://www.pbs.org/childofcamp/history/ index.html.

104. A 1993 survey of nearly five hundred third-generation Japanese Americans who had at least one parent interned during the Second World War found that twice as many fathers who were interned died before the age of sixty as fathers who were not incarcerated. See Donna K. Nagata, Jackie H. J. Kim, and Teresa U. Nguyen, "Processing Cultural Trauma: Intergenerational effects of the Japanese American Incarceration," *Journal of Social Issues* 71/ 2 (2015): 361–62; and Corinne Purtill, "Japanese American Internment Camps Taught Us What Happens to the Health of Separated Families," *Quartz*, June 23, 2018, https://qz.com/1311736/japanese-american-internment-camps-taught-us-what-happens-to-the-health-of-separated-families/.

105. Mauer, *Race to Incarcerate*, rev. ed. (New York: The New Press, 2006), 33, cited in Alexander, *The New Jim Crow: Mass Incarceration in the Age of Colorblindness*, rev. ed. (New York: New Press, 2012), 6.

106. Michelle Ye Hee Lee, "Yes, U.S. Locks Up People at a Higher Rate than Any Other Country," *Washington Post*, July 7, 2015.

107. This estimate is based on reports of prisoner deaths in Brown, Flanagan, and McLeod, *Criminal Justice Statistics 1983*, 601, Table 6.54; Flanagan and McGuire, *Criminal Justice Statistics 1991*, 619, Table 6.44, and 701, Table 6.138; and McGuire and Pastore, *Criminal Justice Statistics 1995*, 602, Table 6.72.

108. This estimate is based on reports of prisoner deaths in Carson, *Mortality in Local Jails*, 12, Table 8, and 13, Table 9, and *Mortality in Prisons*, 7, Table 2, and 12, Table 10; and Christopher J. Mumola, U.S. Department of Justice, Bureau of Justice Statistics, *Suicide and Homicide in State Prisons and Local Jails*, August 2005, http://www.bjs.gov/content/pub/pdf/shsplj.pdf, 2, 9–10.

109. Press, "Human Costs of Incarceration"; Ellis and Hicken, "Deaths in Jails and Prisons"; Michael Sainato, "Dying in Prisons and Jails," *Guardian*, May 26, 2019; and Christine Willmsen and Beth Healy, "When Inmates Die of Poor Medical Care, Jails Often Keep It Secret," WBUR Radio, March 30, 2020, https://www.wbur.org/news/2020/03/23/county-jail-deaths-sheriffs-watch.

480 NOTES TO PAGES 269–270

110. Joe Russo, Dulani Woods, John S. Shaffer, and Brian A. Jackson, "Caring for Those in Custody: Identifying High-Priority Needs to Reduce Mortality in Correctional Facilities," RAND Corporation, 2017, 3, 17, https://www.rand.org/pubs/research_reports/RR1967.html.

111. Richard A. Boswell, "Racism and U.S. Immigration Law: Prospects for Reform After 9/11?," *Journal of Gender, Race, and Justice* 7/ 2 (2003), http://repository.uchastings.edu/faculty_scholarship/58.

112. César Cuauhtémoc García Hernández, "Ellis Island Welcomed Thousands to America—But It Was Also a Detention Center," *Time*, January 1, 2020, https://time.com/5752116/ellis-island-immigration-detention-center/; and PBS, "Immigration and Deportation at Ellis Island," https://www.pbs.org/wgbh/americanexperience/features/goldman-immigration-and-deportation-ellis-island/.

113. Francisco E. Balderrama and Raymond Rodriguez, *Decade of Betrayal: Mexican Repatriation in the* 1930s, rev. ed. (Albuquerque: University of New Mexico Press, 2006), 140–51, 195, 265–66.

114. Ibid., 266.

115. As Balderrama and Rodriguez observed in *Decade of Betrayal*, "Deaths occurred daily along the way and in repatriation centers at the border." They cited the Mexican newspaper *Excélsior*'s report that twenty-five children and adults died on one repatriation train alone (140–41). Balderrama has indicated that he does not have an estimate of casualties, email to author, June 12, 2017. Yet with about one million deportees, hundreds of deaths are likely.

116. Amy B. Wang, "A Ship Full of Refugees Fleeing the Nazis Once Begged the U.S. for Entry—They Were Turned Back," *Washington Post*, January 29, 2017.

117. Dara Lind, "How America's Rejection of Jews Fleeing Nazi Germany Haunts Our Refugee Policy Today," *Vox,* January 27, 2017, https://www.vox.com/policy-and-politics/2017/1/27/144 12082/refugees-history-holocaust.

118. Wang, "A Ship Full of Refugees"; and Kelly Lytle Hernandez, "The Crimes and Consequences of Illegal Immigration: A Cross-Border Examination of Operation Wetback, 1943–1955," *Western Historical Quarterly* 37/4 (Winter 2006): 421–44.

119. Eighty-eight deportees died from heat stroke in one incident in July 1955, and there were other reports of fatalities. See Wang, "A Ship Full of Refugees"; and Hernandez, "Crimes and Consequences," 437–40.

120. Gammage, "Hundreds Die Every Year." See also Pedro Rios, "For 25 Years, Operation Gatekeeper Has Made Life Worse for Border Communities," *Washington Post*, October 1, 2019.

121. Alex Nowrasteh, "People Died in Immigration Detention in 2019,

NOTES TO PAGE 270   481

193 Since 2004," Cato Institute, Cato at Liberty, January 8, 2020, https://www.cato.org/blog/8-people-died-immigration-detention-2019-193-2004; Sarah Stillman, "When Deportation Is a Death Sentence," *The New Yorker*, January 8, 2018, https://www.newyorker.com/magazine/2018/01/15/when-deportation-is-a-death-sentence; Nicole Acevedo and Adiel Kaplan, "Hundreds Deported from U.S. to El Salvador Have Been Killed or Abused, New Report Says," NBC News, February 5, 2020, https://www.nbcnews.com/news/latino/hundreds-deported-u-s-el-salvador-have-been-killed-or-n126906.

122. Bellesiles, "Introduction," in *Lethal Imagination*, 1, 10; Grinshteyn and Hemenway, "Violent Death Rates", 266–73; Healy, "America Is a Violent Country"; Roth, *American Homicide* (Cambridge, MA: Harvard University Press, 2009), Introduction; Roxanne Dunbar-Ortiz, *Loaded: A Disarming History of the Second Amendment* (San Francisco: City Lights Books, 2018); Rebecca Solnit, "Our Forever War: How the White Male Hegemony Uses Violence to Cling to Power," *Guardian*, August 8, 2019; and Kevin Quealy and Margot Sanger-Katz, "Comparing Gun Deaths by Country: The U.S. Is in a Different World," *New York Times*, June 13, 2016.

123. Gun Violence Archive, https://www.gunviolencearchive.org/. GVA defines mass shootings as incidents in which "a minimum of four victims [are] shot, either injured or killed, not including any shooter who may also have been killed or injured in the incident." See also Jack Brewster, "More Than One Mass Shooting Per Day Has Occurred in 2021," *Forbes*, April 16, 2021, https://www.forbes.com/sites/jackbrewster/2021/04/16/more-than-one-mass-shooting-per-day-has-occurred-in-2021/?sh=102590536493; and Jason Silverstein, "There Have Been More Mass Shootings Than Days This Year," CBS News, September 1, 2019, https://www.cbsnews.com/news/mass-shootings-2019-more-mass-shootings-than-days-so-far-this-year/.

124. Mark Follman, Gavin Aronsen, and Deanna Pan, "A Guide to Mass Shootings in America," *Mother Jones*, May 26, 2021, https://www.motherjones.com/politics/2012/07/mass-shootings-map/.

125. Ibid.

126. Ibid.

127. Ibid.

128. Rio Lacanlale, "Sheriff Admits 'Failure to Recognize' Route 91 Victims, Increases Death Toll," *Las Vegas Review-Journal*, October 21, 2020.

129. Follman, Aronsen, and Pan, "Mass Shootings in America."

130. Gun Violence Archive; Brewster, "Mass Shooting Per Day"; and Silverstein, "More Mass Shootings Than Days."

131. John Gramlich, "What the Data Says About Gun Deaths in the U.S.,"

482 NOTES TO PAGES 270–271

Pew Research Center, August 16, 2019, https://www.pewresearch.org/fact-tank/2019/08/16/what-the-data-says-about-gun-deaths-in-the-u-s/.

132. Gun Violence Archive; Reis Thebault and Danielle Rindler, "Shootings Never Stopped During the Pandemic: 2020 Was the Deadliest Gun Violence Year in Decades," *Washington Post*, March 23, 2021.

133. Goldberg, "*A* Matter of Black Lives," *The Atlantic*, September 2015, http://www.theatlantic.com/magazine/archive/ 2015/09/a-matter-of-black-lives/399386/; Cella and Neuhauser, "Race and Homicide in America, by the Numbers," *U.S. News and World Report*, September 29, 2016, https://www.usnews.com/news/articles/2016-09-29/race-and-homicide-in-america-by-the-numbers; and Wolfers, Leonhardt, and Quealy, "1.5 Million Missing Black Men," *New York Times*, April 20, 2015.

134. Sheila Kaplan, "Congress Quashed Research into Gun Violence. Since Then, 600,000 People Have Been Shot," *New York Times*, March 12, 2018; and Nicole Wetsman, "After a 20-Year Drought, U.S. Lawmakers Fund Gun Violence Research," *The Verge*, December 19, 2019, https://www. theverge.com/2019/12/19/21028779/gun-violence-research-funding-20-year-freeze-congress-bill-cdc-nih-dickey.

135. Adequate data are lacking for much of the late eighteenth and nineteenth centuries, but criminal homicide was a regular feature of life in the United States throughout this period. Roth has reported that thousands of men died in fights in railroad and mining camps during the 1850s, and the nation's homicide rates dramatically increased in the second half of the nineteenth century. The *Chicago Tribune* estimated that there were 6,971 homicides in 1892, 10,500 homicides in 1895, and 10,652 in 1896. A contemporary publication offered an estimate of almost 49,000 criminal homicides between 1886 and 1895, excluding executions and lynchings. See Roth, *American Homicide*, 15; Charles A. Ellwood, "Has Crime Increased in the United States Since 1880?," *Journal of the American Institute of Criminal Law and Criminology* 1/3 (May 1910–March 1911): 381; and *World Almanac and Encyclopedia, The World Monthly Edition* 4/40 (January 1897): 216.

136. More than 1.5 million homicides occurred in the United States between 1900 and 2019. For information on homicides between 1900 and 1997, see Eckberg, "Homicides and Homicide Rates," 5-239, 5-240, Table Ec190–198. Data were not reported from all states until 1933. For information on homicides since 1998, see successive issues of the NCHS's *National Vital Statistics Reports* between 2000 and 2021. These *Reports* are available at https://www.cdc.gov/nchs/products/ nvsr.htm.

137. Caitlin Owens, "The U.S. Suicide Rate Is Exceptionally High Among

NOTES TO PAGES 271–272 483

Wealthy Nations," *Axios*, January 30, 2020, https://www.axios.com/us-suicide-rate-comparison-f513c699-3b78-4a23-aebd-f96d126f7fd2.html; Kirsten Weir, "Worrying Trends in U.S. Suicide Rates," American Psychological Association, *Monitor on Psychology* 50/3, March 2019: 24; and Claudia Wallis, "Another Tragic Epidemic: Suicide," *Scientific American*, August 1, 2020, https://www.scientificamerican.com/article/another-tragic-epidemic-suicide/.

138. Roni Caryn Rabin, "U.S. Suicides Declined Over All in 2020 But May Have Risen Among People of Color," *New York Times*, April 15, 2021.

139. Gramlich, "Gun Deaths in the U.S."

140. Alia E. Dastagir, "Suicide Rates for Native American Women Is Up 139%," *USA Today*, June 22, 2019; and Jennifer Steinhauer, "VA Officials, and the Nation, Battle an Unrelenting Tide of Veteran Suicides," *New York Times*, April 14, 2019.

141. Anne Case and Angus Deaton, "Mortality and Morbidity in the 21st Century," *Brookings Papers on Economic Activities*, Spring 2017: 397–439.

142. Ibid.

143. Hilary Brueck and Shayanne Gal, "Suicide Rates Are Climbing in Young People from Ages 10 to 24. Here's How to Support the People You Love," *Insider*, September 12, 2020, https://www.insider.com/cdc-suicide-rate-in-young-people-10-24-continues-climb-2020-9.

144. For information on suicides between 1900 and 1997, see Douglas Eckberg, "Reported Suicides and Suicide Rates, by Sex and Mode of Death, 1900–1997" in *Historical Statistics of the United States: Earliest Times to the Present, Millennial Edition*, vol. 5: *Part E: Governance and International Relations*, ed. Susan B. Carter, Scott Sigmund Gartner, Michael R. Haines, Alan L. Olmstead, Richard Sutch, and Gavin Wright (Cambridge: Cambridge University Press, 2006), 5-237, 5-238, Table Ec182–189. However, accurate data on suicides were not reported until 1907, and data from all states were not reported until 1933. Information on suicides between 1998 and 2018 was published in successive issues of the NCHS's *National Vital Statistics Reports* between 2000 and 2020. These reports are available at https://www/cdc/ gov/nchs/products/nvsr.htm. The number of suicides for 2019 and 2020 are found in Rabin, "U.S. Suicides."

145. Joel Dyer, "The Perils of Forgotten History," *Boulder Weekly*, August 29, 2019.

146. Kimberly Yam, "Asian-American's Fatal Beating Over U.S. Job Loss 35 Years Ago Resonates Today," *Huffington Post*, June 19, 2017, https://www.huffpost.com/entry/vincent-chin-murder-detroit_n_59440e71e4b0f15cd5bafe14.

147. Parenti, *Democracy for the Few*, 127; and Stephen Singular, "Alan Berg:

Talked to Death," *Rolling Stone*, January 31, 1985, https://www.rollingstone.com/music/music-news/alan-berg-talked-to-death-71920/.

148. Steve Grossman, "Vietnamese Death Squads: Is This the End?," *Indochina Newsletter*, May–June 1988, cited in Parenti, *Democracy for the Few*, 126; and A. C. Thompson, "Terror in Little Saigon: An Old War Comes to a New Country," *ProPublica* in Partnership with PBS *Frontline*, November 3, 2015, https://www.propublica.org/article/terror-in-little-saigon-vietnam-american-journalists-murdered.

149. Jason Wilson, "Ruby Ridge, 1992: The Day the American Militia Movement Was Born," *Guardian*, August 26, 2017.

150. William Claiborne, "Two Killed at Clinic in Florida," *Washington Post*, July 30, 1994.

151. Andrew Gumbel, "Oklahoma City Bombing: 20 Years Later, Key Questions Remain Unanswered," *Guardian*, April 13, 2015.

152. Dan Eggen, "Rudolph to Plead Guilty to Bombings," *Washington Post*, April 9, 2005.

153. Anti-Defamation League, "Dark and Constant Rage," 23.

154. Dakin Andone, "Matthew Shepard Finally Laid to Rest 20 Years After He Was Killed for Being Gay," CNN, October 27, 2018, https://www.cnn.com/2018/10/26/us/matthew-shepard-washington-service/index.html.

155. Kim Smith, "Neo-Nazi Charged in Slaying of Anti-Racist Activists," *Las Vegas Sun*, November 24, 2000.

156. Anti-Defamation League, "Dark and Constant Rage," 19.

157. Ibid., 18–19.

158. Ibid., 16–17.

159. Ibid., 16.

160. Ibid., 15–16.

161. Ibid., 15.

162. Ibid., 14.

163. Ibid., 13.

164. Ibid., 12.

165. Ibid., 11.

166. Ibid., 9.

167. Ibid., 10.

168. Sarah Kaplan, "FBI Releases Video, Explains How Oregon Police Fatally Shot Refuge Occupier," *Washington Post*, January 28, 2016.

169. Christine Hauser, "Oklahoma Man Charged With Killing Lebanese-American Neighbor," *New York Times*, August 23, 2016.

170. Medhi Hassan, "After El Paso, We Can No Longer Ignore Trump's Role in Inspiring Mass Shootings," *The Intercept*, August 4, 2019; Vanessa Williamson and Isabella Gelfand, "Trump and Racism: What Do

NOTES TO PAGES 273–274   485

the Data Say?" Brookings Institution, August 14, 2019, https://www.brookingsedu/blog/fixgov/2019/08/14/trump-and-racism-what-do-the-data-say/; and Daniel Villarreal, "Hate Crimes under Trump Surged Nearly 20 Percent Says FBI Report," *Newsweek*, November 16, 2020, https://www.newsweek.com/hate-crimes-under-trump-surged-nearly-20-percent-says-fbi-report-1547870.

171. John Eligon, Alan Blinder, and Nada Najar, "Hate Crime Is Feared as 2 Indian Engineers Are Shot in Kansas," *New York Times*, February 24, 2017.

172. Jonah Engel Bromwich, "Man in Florida Told Police He Killed Neo-Nazi Roommates for Disrespecting His Muslim Faith," *New York Times*, May 24, 2017; and Matthew Haag and Jacey Fortin, "Two Killed in Portland While Trying to Stop Anti-Muslim Rant, Police Say," *New York Times*, May 27, 2017.

173. E. J. Dickson, "Man Who Killed Heather Heyer at Charlottesville Sentenced to Life in Prison, Plus 419 Years," *Rolling Stone*, July 15, 2019, https://www.rollingstone.com/culture/culture-news/heather-heyer-james-fields-charlottesville-murderer-859182/.

174. Kyle Swenson, "Suspects in Five Killings Reportedly Linked to Macabre Neo-Nazi Group," *Washington Post*, January 29, 2018.

175. Anti-Defamation League, *Murder and Extremism in the United States in 2018*, January 2019, 24, https://www.adl.org/media/12480/download.

176. Ibid.

177. Ibid.

178. Ibid.

179. Ibid., 23.

180. Ibid.

181. Michael Kunzelman, "Report: Domestic Extremists Killed at Least 42 in 2019," AP News, February 26, 2020, https://apnews.com/article/patrick-crusius-tx-state-wire-omar-mateen-new-york-race-and-ethnicity-73adb64ec29bfd75e99302cf258adc92.

182. Reuters and Kelly McLaughlin, "A Suspected Neo-Nazi and His Wife Are on the Run after Overpowering Security Guards Holding Them on Murder Charges," *Insider*, August 28, 2019, https://www.insider.com/blane-susan-barksdale-murder-suspectshave-escaped-2019-8.

183. Jill Cowan, "What to Know About the Poway Synagogue Shooting," *New York Times*, April 29, 2019.

184. Jessica Kwong, "Gilroy Gunman Cited White Supremacist Manifesto on Instagram Just Before Shooting," *Newsweek*, July 29, 2019, https://www.newsweek.com/gilroy-shooter-white-supremacist-manifesto-instagram-1451586.

485\. Angela Kocherga, "Two Years After Walmart Mass Shooting, El Paso Leaders See Inaction and Betrayal by Texas Officials," *Texas Tribune,* August 3, 2021, https://www.texastribune.org/2021/08/03/el-paso-wal mart-mass-shooting-legislature/.

186\. Anti-Defamation League, "White Supremacist Charged with Murder of Alabama Police Officer," March 17, 2020, https://www.adl.org/blog/white-supremacist-charged-with-capital-murder-of-alabama-police-officer.

187\. Jeff German, "Emerging Extremists Bring New Concerns for Law Enforcement," *Las Vegas Review-Journal,* February 21, 2021.

188\. Editor, "2 'Boogaloo' Members Charged in Drive-by Shooting of Federal Officer in Oakland," *Times of San Diego,* June 17, 2020, https://timesofsandiego.com/crime/2020/06/17/2-boogaloo-members-charged-in-drive-by-shooting-of-federal-officer-in-oakland/.

189\. Tracey Tully, "Judge Whose Son Was Killed by Misogynistic Lawyer Speaks Out," *New York Times,* August 3, 2020.

190\. Lois Beckett, "White Supremacists Behind Majority of U.S. Domestic Terror Attacks in 2020," *Guardian,* October 22, 2020.

191\. Haley Willis, Muyi Xiao, Christiaan Triebert, Christoph Koettl, Stella Cooper, David Botti, John Ismay, and Ainara Tiefenthäler, "Tracking the Suspect in the Fatal Kenosha Shootings," *New York Times,* April 22, 2021.

192\. Peter Hermann and Steve Thompson, "DC Medical Examiner Releases Cause of Death for Four People Who Died During Capitol Riot," *Washington Post,* April 7, 2021.

193\. Jan Wolfe, "Four Officers Who Responded to U.S. Capitol Attack Have Died by Suicide," Reuters, August 2, 2021, https://www.reuters.com/world/us/officer-who-responded-us-capitol-attack-is-third-die-by-suicide-2021-08-02/.

194\. *New York Times,* "8 Dead in Atlanta Spa Shootings, with Fears of Anti-Asian Bias," March 26, 2021.

195\. Ashley Collman, "The Gunman in the FedEx Shooting Browsed White Supremacist Websites a Year before His Attack, Which Killed Four Sikhs, Police Say," *Insider,* April 20, 2021, https:// www.insider.com/indianapolis-fedex-shooting-suspect-visited-white-supremacist-web-sites-police-2021-4.

196\. Robert O'Harrow, Andrew Ba Tran, and Derek Hawkins, "The Rise of Domestic Extremism in America," *Washington Post,* April 12, 2021; and Jenny Gross, "Far-Right Groups Are Behind Most U.S. Terrorist Attacks, Report Finds," *New York Times,* October 24, 2020.

197\. An estimate of 348 deaths between 1990 and 2010 is found in National Consortium for the Study of Terrorism and Responses to Terrorism, "Far-Right Violence in the United States." An estimate of 330 deaths

NOTES TO PAGES 275–276 487

from 2010 through 2019 appears in Anti-Defamation League, "ADL Report: Right-Wing Extremists Killed 38 People in 2019, Far Surpassing All Other Murderous Extremists," February 26, 2020, https:// www. adl.org/news/press-releases/adl-report-right-wing-extremists-killed-38-people-in-2019-far-surpassing-all. An estimate of sixteen additional murders by far-right extremists in 2020 is found in Anti-Defamation League, *Murder and Extremism in the United States in 2020*, February 2021, https://www.adl.org/murder-and-extremism-2020, but it does not include the two killings in Kenosha, Wisconsin.

198. This language appears in bin Laden's *fatwa*, "Declaration of War Against the Americans Occupying the Land of the Two Holy Places," which appeared in the London newspaper *Al-Quds Al-Arabi*, in 1996 and was immediately shared with adherents around the world. See Dominic Tierney, "The Twenty Years' War," *The Atlantic*, August 23, 2016, https://www. theatlantic.com/international/archive/2016/08/twenty-years-war/496736/.

199. Alan Dowd, "Al-Qaida's First Attack on the World Trade Center: A Quarter-Century of War," *Providence*, February 26, 2018, https://providencemag.com/2018/02/al-qaedas-first-attack-world-trade-center-quarter-century-war-1993/.

200. CNN, "Pakistani Man Executed for CIA Killings," November 15, 2002, http://edition.cnn.com/2002/LAW/11/14/cia.killings.execution/index.html.

201. Dowd, "Al-Qaida's First Attack."

202. Tierney, "Twenty Years' War."

203. Dowd, "Al-Qaida's First Attack."

204. Ibid.

205. Brisard and Dasquié, *Forbidden Truth*, 42–46.

206. CNN, "US Terrorist Attacks Fast Facts," September 2, 2021, https:// www.cnn.com/2013/04/18/us/u-s-terrorist-attacks-fast-facts/index.html.

207. Levi Pulkinnen, "Jury Finds Haq Guilty in Jewish Federation Center Shootings," *Seattle Post-Intelligencer*, December 14, 2009.

208. Khomami, "Terrorist Attacks."

209. Ibid.

210. Ben Finley, "Prosecutor: Man Charged with Killing 4 Was on Terrorism Watch List," *Seattle Times*, January 20, 2016.

211. Kristina Sgueglia, "Chattanooga Shootings 'Inspired' by Terrorists, FBI Chief Says," CNN, December 16, 2015, https://www.cnn.com/2015/12/16/us/chattanooga-shooting-terrorist-inspiration/index.html.

212. Khomami, "Terrorist Attacks."

488   NOTES TO PAGES 276–277

213. Jane Coaston, "New Evidence Shows the Pulse Nightclub Shooting Wasn't About Anti-LGBT Hate," *Vox*, April 5, 2018, https://www.vox.com/policy-and-politics/2018/4/5/17202026/ pulse-shooting-lgbtq-trump-terror-hate.

214. Benjamin Mueller, William K. Rashbaum, and Al Baker, "'Terror Attack Kills 8 and Injures 11 in Manhattan," *New York Times*, October 31, 2017.

215. Sarah N. Lynch and Mark Hosenball, "FBI Phone Probe Links al-Qaeda to Saudi Who Killed Three at Florida Base, Barr Says," Reuters, May 18, 2020, https://www.reuters.com/article/us-florida-shooting-alqaeda/fbi-phone-probe-links-al-qaeda-to-saudi-who-killed-three-at-florida-base-barr-says-idUSKBN22U1WL.

216. Charles Kurzman, *Muslim American Involvement with Violent Extremism, 2001–2020*, Duke University Triangle Center on Terrorism and Homeland Security, January 14, 2021, https://duke.app.box.com/s/pfbtxnvjxyou4g978atolj9axfeptuzm.

217. Ahmad, *Opium Debate*, 21–22; and V. G. Kiernan, *New Imperialism*, 18.

218. Dolin, "China Trade"; and Schwendinger, *Ocean of Bitter Dreams: The Chinese Migration to the United States, 1850–1915* (San Francisco: Long River Press, 2015), 2.

219. On the scope of opium use in China, see Editors, "An Opioid Crisis Foretold," *New York Times*, April 21, 2018; and United Nations Office on Drugs and Crime, *World Drug Report 2008*, 18, https://www.unodc.org/documents/wdr/WDR_2008/WDR_2008_eng_web.pdf. On the number of related deaths by the end of the nineteenth century, see General Manager, Soochow Salt Gabelle, Introduction, in *Opinions of Over 100 Physicians on the Use of Opium in China*, comp. William Hector Park (Shanghai: American Presbyterian Mission Press, 1899), vi, https://archive.org/details/39002055095831.med.yale.edu/page/vi/mode/2up.

220. Karen Berger, "Pharmacy's Past: The Soothing Syrup Known for Causing Death in Thousands of Babies," *Pharmacy Times*, March 21, 2019, https://www.pharmacytimes.com/ contributor/karen-berger/2019/03/pharmacys-past-the-soothing-syrup-known-for-causing-death-in-thousands-of-babies.

221. David Courtright, *Dark Paradise: A History of Opiate Addiction in America*, rev. ed.(Cambridge, MA: Harvard University Press, 2001), 54–55.

222. Ibid., 36–40, 55; and Erick Trickey, "Inside the Story of America's 19th-Century Opiate Addiction," *Smithsonian Magazine*, January 4, 2018, https://www.smithsonianmag.com/history/inside-story-americas-19th-century-opiate-addiction-180967673/.

NOTES TO PAGE 277 489

223. Courtright, *Dark Paradise*, chap. 4; and Trickey, "Inside the Story of America's 19th-Century Opiate Addiction."
224. Ibid., 9, 28; Clinton Lawson, "America's 150-Year Opioid Epidemic," *New York Times*, May 19, 2018; and Christina Tkacik, "'The Laudanum Evil': Maryland's 19th-Century Opiate Epidemic," AP News, January 13, 2019, https://apnews.com/910654effffe 42f985ebe01f2 99407f5.
225. Trickey, "Inside the Story of America's 19th-Century Opiate Addiction"; Nick Miroff, "From Teddy Roosevelt to Trump: How Drug Companies Triggered an Opioid Crisis a Century Ago," *Washington Post*, October 17, 2017; Mike Stobbe, Associated Press, "Opioid Epidemic Shares Chilling Similarities with Past Drug Crises," *Stat*, October 29, 2017, https://www.statnews.com/2017/10/29/opioid-epidemic-shares-chilling-similarities-with-past-drug-crises/.
226. Deborah Blum, "The Chemist's War," *Slate*, February 19, 2010, https://slate.com/technol ogy/2010/02/the-little-told-story-of-how-the-u-s-government-poisoned-alcohol-during-prohibition.html.
227. Julian G. West, "The Accidental Poison That Founded the Modern FDA," *The Atlantic*, January 16, 2018, https://www.theatlantic.com/technology/archive/2018/01/the-accidental-poison-that-founded-the-modern-fda/550574/.
228. Joel Fort, "The Problem of Barbiturates in the United States of America," UN Office on Drugs and Crime, January 1, 1964, https://www.unodc.org/unodc/en/data-and-analysis/bulletin/bulletin_1964-01-01_1_page004.html.
229. Stobbe, "Opioid Epidemic"; Fort, "Problem of Barbiturates"; James M. Markham, "Mixing of Mind-Altering Drugs Rises as Spread of Heroin Addiction Slows," *New York Times*, March 25, 1973; and Mark E. Wallace, "Fatal Massive Amphetamine Ingestion Associated with Hyperprexia," *Journal of the American Board of Family Practice* 13/4 (July–August 2000), https://www. abfm.org/content/jabfp/13/4/302.full.pdf. Most fatalities during this period were associated with the use or abuse of barbiturates.
230. See Stobbe, "Opioid Epidemic." An estimate of just under 68,000 opiate-related deaths from 1970 through 1978 is found in Judith S. Samkoff and Susan P. Baker, "Recent Trends in Fatal Poisoning by Opiates in the United States," *American Journal of Public Health* 72/11 (1982): 1251–56. Data indicating a total of more than 86,000 drug-related deaths in the 1980s is found in U.S. Department of Justice, Bureau of Justice Statistics, *Technical Appendix: Drugs, Crime, and the Justice System* (Washington, DC: Government Printing Office, 1993), 7. It is likely that numerous other drug-related deaths were not identified as such during the 1970s and 1980s.

490 NOTES TO PAGES 277–279

231. Stephen Rosskamm Shalom, *Imperial Alibis*, chap. 8; Alexander Cockburn and Jeffrey St. Clair, *Whiteout: The CIA, Drugs, and the Press* (London: Version, 1998); and Alfred W. McCoy, *The Politics of Heroin: CIA Complicity in the Global Drug Trade*, 2nd rev. ed. (Chicago: Lawrence Hill Books, 2003).

232. Stobbe, "Opioid Epidemic." See also Centers for Disease Control and Prevention, "Opioid Basics," https://www.cdc.gov/drugoverdose/ epidemic/index.html, accessed December 8, 2021; and Abby Goodnough, "A New Drug Scourge: Deaths Involving Meth Are Rising Fast," *New York Times*, December 17, 2019.

233. Centers for Disease Control and Prevention, "Drug Overdose Deaths in the U.S. Top 100,000 Annually," National Center for Health Statistics, November 17, 2021, https://www.cdc.gov/nchs/pressroom/nchs_press_releases/2021/20211117.htm; Lenny Bernstein and Joel Achenbach, "Drug Overdose Deaths Soared to a Record 93,000 Last Year," *Washington Post*, July 14, 2021.

234. Steven Reinberg, "Among Rich Nations, US Has Highest Rate of Fatal Drug ODs," *U.S. News and World Report*, February 21, 2019, https:// www.usnews.com/news/health-news/articles/ 2019-02-21/among-rich-nations-us-has-highest-rate-of-fatal-drug-ods.

235. Case and Deaton, "Mortality and Morbidity."

236. Proctor, *Golden Holocaust*.

237. Ibid., 11.

238. Estimates of more than 20.8 million deaths between 1965 and 2014 and 480,000 annual deaths are found in U.S. Department of Health and Human Services, *The Health Consequences of Smoking—Fifty Years of Progress: A Report of the Surgeon General, Executive Summary* (Atlanta, GA: National Center for Chronic Disease Prevention and Health Promotion, Office on Smoking and Health, 2014), 1–2. However, Proctor has estimated that 25 million tobacco-related deaths occurred in this country by 2015, email to author, September 6, 2015. When the loss of life between 2015 and 2021 is added to Proctor's estimate, the total number of deaths approaches 28 million.

239. Proctor, email to author.

240. World Health Organization, "Tobacco," May 27, 2020, https://www.who.int/news-room/fact-sheets/detail/tobacco.

241. Parenti, *Democracy for the Few*, 87–89; and Catherine Lutz, "The U.S. Car Colossus and the Production of Inequality," *American Ethnologist* 41/2 (2014): 232–45.

242. John Pucher and Christian Lefèvre, *The Urban Transport Crisis in Europe and North America* (London: Palgrave Macmillan, 1996), chap. 10.

243. Parenti, *Democracy for the Few*, 87–89; Lutz, "U.S. Car Colossus"; and

NOTES TO PAGE 279 491

Margaret J. Douglas, Stephen J. Watkins, Dermot R. Gorman, and Martin Higgins, "Are Cars the New Tobacco?," *Journal of Public Health* 33/2 (June 2011): 160–69.

244. Ralph Nader, *Unsafe at Any Speed* (New York: Grossman Publishers, 1965).

245. Ibid., chap. 1; Mark Dowie, "Pinto Madness," *Mother Jones*, September–October 1977, https://www.motherjones.com/politics/1977/09/pinto-madness/; Robert Sherefkin, "Lee Iacocca's Pinto: A Fiery Failure," *Automotive News*, June 16, 2003, https://www.autonews.com/article/20030616/SUB/306160770/lee-iacocca-s-pinto-a-fiery-failure; "History of the GM Side Saddle Gas Tank Defect," Center for Auto Safety, https://www.autosafety.org/history-gm-side-saddle-gas-tank-defect/; Myron Levin, "GM's Exploding Pickup Problem," *Mother Jones*, April 6, 2010, https://www.motherjones.com/environment/2010/04/gm-ck-exploding-pickup/; Chris Isidore, "Safety Group Claims 303 Deaths Linked to Recalled GM Cars," CNN, March 14, 2014, https://money.cnn.com/2014/03/14/news/companies/gm-recall-crash-deaths/; Hillary Stout, Danielle Ivory, and Rebecca R. Ruiz, "Regulator Slow to Respond to Deadly Vehicle Defects," *New York Times*, September 14, 2014; CNBC, "Automakers Recall 1.7 Million Cars with Fatal Airbags," February 8, 2019, https:// www.cnbc.com/2019/02/08/automakers-recall-1point7-million-cars-with-fatal-airbags. html; and "Five Deadliest Defects in History," *AutoInsurance.com*, https://www. auto insurance.org/5-deadliest-vehicle-defects/.

246. Kimberly Leonard, "Why the U.S. Is a Leader in Car Crash Deaths," *U.S. News and World Report*, July 6, 2016, https://www.usnews.com/news/articles/2016-07-06/the-us-is-a-world-leader-in-car-crash-deaths?

247. Ibid.; Ryan Beene, "Traffic Deaths in U.S. Exceed 40,000 for Third Straight Year," Bloomberg, February 12, 2019, https://www.bloomberg.com/news/articles/2019-02-13/traffic-deaths-in-u-s-exceed-40-000-for-third-straight-year.

248. National Highway Traffic Safety Administration, U.S. Department of Transportation, "Motor Vehicle Traffic Fatalities and Fatality Rates, 1899–2019," *Traffic Safety Facts Annual Report*, May 2021, https://cdan.nhtsa.gov/tsftables/Fatalities%20and%20Fatality%20Rates.pdf.

249. In 1981, Dr. Stephen Joseph estimated that use of infant formula led to the deaths of about one million infants each year. In 1991, the United Nations Children's Fund concluded that the aggressive marketing of this product caused 1.5 million deaths annually. In 2016, a study found that more than 800,000 infants' lives could be saved each year if breastfeeding replaced the use of infant formula and other kinds of nutrition in low- and medium-income countries. Not all of these annual deaths

492 NOTES TO PAGE 280

can be attributed to the use of infant formula, but many can. See Brink, "Breastfeeding vs. Formula Debate"; Stephen Solomon, "The Controversy Over Infant Formula," *New York Times*, December 6, 1981; Michelle Faul, "Improper Formula Feeding Spreads Malnutrition, Death in Third World: Babies: More than 1.5 Million Die Each Year Because of Campaigns That Discourage Mothers from Nursing, Health Officials Say," *Los Angeles Times*, May 19, 1991; and Cesar G. Victora, Rajiv Bahl, Aluísio J. D. Barros, Giovanny V. A. França, Susan Horton, Julia Krasevec, Simon Murch, Mari Jeeva Sankar, Neff Walker, Nigel C. Rollins, "Breastfeeding in the 21st Century: Epidemiology, Mechanisms, and Lifelong Effect," *The Lancet* 387/10017 (January 30, 2016), 475–90.

250. Solomon, "Controversy Over Infant Formula"; and Sudeep Chakravarty, "World's Top 10 Infant Formula Manufacturers," *MarketResearchReports*, https://www.marketresearchreports.com/blog/2019/04/09/world%E2%80%99s-top-10-infant-formula-manufacturers. In 2017, Mead Johnson was acquired by the British company Reckitt Benckiser.

251. Weintraub, Testimony; Hubert Humphrey, Remarks at the Swearing-in Ceremony of the Commissioners of the National Commission on Product Safety, Executive Office Building, Washington, DC, May 15, 1968, in Minnesota Historical Society, http://www2.mnhs.org/ library/findaids/00442/pdfa/00442-02547.pdf; and Tom Christoffel and Katherine K. Christoffel, "The Consumer Product Safety Commission's Opposition to Consumer Product Safety: Lessons for Public Health Advocates," *American Journal of Public Health* 79/3 (March 1989): 336–39.

252. An estimate of 29,000 annual deaths is found in Christoffel and Christoffel, "Opposition to Consumer Product Safety," 336. The U.S. Consumer Product Safety Commission reported 21,600 deaths in 1992 but has stopped disclosing total annual fatalities, largely because of undue industry influence and inadequate congressional oversight. See U.S. Consumer Product Safety Commission, *1992 Annual Report to Congress* (Washington, DC: Consumer Product Safety Commission, 1992), 5, Appendix A; Christoffel and Christoffel, "Opposition to Consumer Product Safety," 336–39; and Myron Levin, "Lawmakers Question Industry Influence at Consumer Product Safety Commission," *FairWarning,* April 11, 2019, https://www.fairwarning.org/2019/04/lawmakers-question-influence-of-industry-at-cpsc/. A 2007 estimate of more than 27,000 deaths is found in Weintraub, Testimony, 3.

253. Centers for Disease Control and Prevention, "Estimates of Foodborne Illness in the United States," https://www.cdc.gov/foodborneburden/index.html; and Melanie Warner, "Our Unsafe Food Supply Is Killing Us," *Daily Beast*, July 12, 2017, https://www.thedaily beast.com/our-unsafe-food-supply-is-killing-us?ref=scroll.

NOTES TO PAGES 280-281 493

254. Warner, "Our Unsafe Food Supply." See also Robert Lustig, "Ultraprocessed Food: Addictive, Toxic, and Ready for Regulation," *Nutrients* 12/11 (November 5, 2020), https://doi.org/ 10.3390/nu12113401.

255. The number of fatalities resulting from the infamous Tuskegee experiment and the University of Cincinnati radiation experiment alone likely total about two hundred. See Nix, "Tuskegee Experiment"; and Washington, *Medical Apartheid*, 233–36.

256. Susan E. Lederer, *Subjected to Science: Human Experimentation in America Before the Second World War* (Baltimore: Johns Hopkins University, 1995), chaps. 4–6.

257. Mike Mariani, "The Guatemala Experiments," *Pacific Standard*, May 3, 2017, https:// psmag.com/news/the-guatemala-experiments.

258. Ibid.

259. Welsome, *Plutonium Files*; Philip J. Hilts, "Panel Urges U.S. to Apologize for Radiation Testing and Pay Damages," *New York Times*, October 3, 1995; and Rebecca Leung, "A Dark Chapter in Medical History," CBS News, February 9, 2005, https://www.cbsnews.com/news/a-dark-chapter-in-medical-history-09-02-2005/.

260. Welsome, *Plutonium Files*, chaps. 24–33; and Clyde Haberman, "Veterans of Atomic Test Blasts: No Warning, and Late Amends," *New York Times*, May 29, 2016.

261. Haberman, "Veterans of Atomic Test Blasts." Scores of thousands of other U.S. troops occupied Hiroshima and Nagasaki after the Japanese surrender, cleaned up the Marshall Islands following nuclear tests, and flew in military airplanes monitoring the nuclear tests in Nevada. Many troops also experienced health problems in the following decades. See Welsome, *Plutonium Files*, 269, and chaps. 29–30.

262. Welsome, *Plutonium Files*, 267–69; Haberman, "Veterans of Atomic Test Blasts"; Vincent J. Intondi, "Justice for the Atomic Veterans," *Huffington Post*, March 15, 2014, https://www.huffpost.com/entry/justice-for-the-atomic-veterans_b_4582004; and Jennifer LaFleur, "America's Atomic Vets: 'We Were Used as Guinea Pigs—Every One of Us,'" *Reveal*, May 27, 2016, https://www.revealnews.org/article/us-veterans-in-secretive-nuclear-tests-still-fighting-for-recognition/.

263. Intondi, "Justice for the Atomic Veterans."

264. Claudia Grisales, "Conspiracy of Silence: Veterans Exposed to Atomic Tests Wage Final Fight," *Stars and Stripes*, June 16, 2019.

265. Patricia Kime, "Lawmakers Want Medals, Not Certificates, to Honor Veterans Involved in Nuclear Testing," *Military.com*, July 16, 2020, https://www.military.com/daily-news/2020/07/ 16/lawmakers-want-medals-not-certificates-honor-veterans-involved-nuclear-testing.html.

494 NOTES TO PAGES 281–282

266. Complications from illegal abortions resulted in many women's deaths in the early twentieth century, but the total for the first two decades of the century remains unknown. By the late 1920s, approximately 15,000 women were dying each year. In the 1930s, it was estimated that between five and ten thousand women died each year. The annual death rate in the 1940s was more than one thousand, perhaps many more. Deaths from illegal abortions declined in the years preceding *Roe*, but the human toll during the twentieth century may be conservatively estimated to exceed 100,000. See Christopher Tietze and Sarah Lewit, "Abortion," *Scientific American* 220/1 (January 1969): 21–27; Katha Pollitt, "Abortion in American History," *The Atlantic*, May 1997, https://www.theatlantic.com/ magazine/archive/1997/05/abortion-in-american-history/376851/; David A. Grimes with Linda G. Brandon, *Every Third Woman in America: How Legal Abortion Transformed Our Nation* (Carolina Beach, NC: Daymark Publishing, 2014), 8–9; and Glenn Kessler, "Planned Parenthood's False Stat: 'Thousands' of Women Died Every Year Before Roe," *Washington Post*, May 29, 2019.

267. Tasleem Padamsee, "Fighting an Epidemic in Political Context: Thirty-Five Years of HIV/AIDS Policy Making in the United States," *Social History of Medicine* 33/3 (August 2020): 1001–28. See also White, "Reagan's AIDS Legacy."

268. See "HIV/AIDS: Snapshots of An Epidemic," amfAR, the Foundation for AIDS Research, https://www.amfar.org/thirty-years-of-hiv/aids-snapshots-of-an-epidemic/; and Centers for Disease Control and Prevention, "First 500,000 AIDS Cases—United States, 1995, "*Morbidity and Mortality Weekly Report* 44/46 (November 24, 1995): 849–53, https://www.cdc.gov/mmwr/preview/mmwrhtml/00039622.htm.

269. Vulliamy, "Drug Giants Let Millions Die"; Rachel Swarns, "Drug Makers Drop South Africa Suit Over AIDS Medicine," *New York Times*, April 20, 2001; Dylan Gray, "Big Pharma's Excuses for the Monopolies on Medicine Won't Wash," *Guardian*, February 22, 2013; and Donald G. McNeil, Jr., "Drug Companies Are Focusing on the Poor After Decades of Ignoring Them," *New York Times*, June 24, 2019.

270. Andrea Bernstein, "Rudy Giuliani and Air Quality After 9/11: Part 1," WNYC Radio, January 22, 2008, https://www.wnyc.org/story/78448-rudy-giuliani-and-air-quality-after-911-part-1/; and Joanna Walters, "Former EPA Head Admits She Was Wrong to Tell New Yorkers Post 9/11 Air was Safe," *Guardian*, September 10, 2016.

271. Adriana Diaz, "New York City Residents Battling Illnesses After 9-11," CBS News, September 11, 2019, https://www.cbsnews.com/news/911-related-illness-former-nyc-students-raise-the-alarm-2019-09-11/; Tim Povtak, "9/11 Cancer Deaths Continue to Rise," The Mesothelioma

NOTES TO PAGE 282 495

Center, Asbestos.com, September 10, 2018, https://www.asbestos.com/news/2018/09/10/september-11-cancer-deaths-rise/.

272. German Lopez, "Hurricane Katrina, in Seven Essential facts," *Vox*, August 28, 2015, https://www.vox.com/ 2015/8/23/9191907/hurricane-katrina.

273. Jenny Staletovich, "Maria Death Toll Likely Topped 4,000 in Puerto Rico, 70 Times Official Count, Study Finds," *Miami Herald*, May 29, 2018; Maegan Vasquez, "San Juan Mayor Says the Trump Administration Killed Thousands Through Neglect During Hurricane Maria," CNN, August 29, 2018, https://www.cnn.com/2018/08/29/politics/san-juan-mayor-carmen-yulin-cruz-death-toll-cnntv/ index.html; and Editors, "How Can the U.S. Atone for 4,600 Dead in Puerto Rico After Hurricane Maria?," *Houston Chronicle*, June 1, 2018.

274. Editors, "An Opioid Crisis Foretold," *New York Times*, April 21, 2018; and Leah Kuntz, "Biden Administration Plan Tackles Drug Addiction Crisis," *Psychiatric Times*, March 31, 2021, https://www.psychiatrictimes.com/view/biden-administration-plan-narrows-in-on-drug-addiction-crisis.

275. Adeel Hassan, "The U.S. Surpasses 1 Million COVID Deaths, The World's Highest Known Total," *New York Times*, May 9, 2022.; and Elizabeth Gamillo, "COVID-19 Surpasses 1918 Flu to Become Deadliest Pandemic in American History," *Smithsonian Magazine*, September 24, 2021, https://www.smithsonianmag. com/smart-news/the-covid-19-pandemic-is-considered-the-deadliest-in-american-history-as-death-toll-surpasses-1918-estimates-180978748/.

276. See Ortiz, "Blood on His Hands"; Gamillo, "COVID-19 Surpasses 1918 Flu"; Adam Gellar and Janie Har, "'Shameful': U.S. Virus Deaths Top 400K as Trump Leaves Office," AP News, January 19, 2021, https://apnews.com/article/donald-trump-pandemics-public-health-coronavirus-pandemic-f6e976f34a6971c889ca8a4c5e1c0068; and Carol Leonnig and Philip Rucker, *I Alone Can Fix It: Donald J. Trump's Catastrophic Final Year* (New York: Penguin Press, 2022), Part 1.

277. An estimate of more than 550,000 homeless people in 2018 is in U.S. Department of Housing and Urban Development, *The 2018 Annual Homeless Assessment Report (HAR) to Congress, Part 1: Point-in Time Estimates of Homelessness*, December 2018, 1, 10, https:// files.hudexchange.info/resources/documents/2018-AHAR-Part-1.pdf. The estimate of 13,000 annual deaths is found in "Remembering Those Lost to Homelessness," National Coalition for the Homeless, December 21, 2018, https://nationalhomeless.org/category/ mortality/. Between 2014 and 2018, 3,612 homeless people died in Los Angeles County alone. See "Anna Gorman and Harriet Blair Rowan, "LA County's Homeless

Population Is Growing—but Not as Fast as They're Dying," *Los Angeles Times*, April 22, 2019.

278. Howard Waitzkin, "The Commodification of Health Care and the Search for a Universal Health Care Program in the United States," Robert Wood Johnson Foundation, October 11, 2012), https://www.rwjf.org/en/blog/2012/10/the_commodification.html.

279. Roosa Tikkanen and Melinda K. Abrams, "U.S. Health Care from a Global Perspective, 2019: Higher Spending, Worse Outcomes?," Commonwealth Fund, January 30, 2020, https://www.commonwealthfund.org/publications/issue-briefs/2020/jan/us-health-care-global-perspective-2019.

280. Galvani et al., "Improving the Prognosis of Health Care." This number is up from an annual loss of 45,000 lives in 2009. See Andrew P. Wilper, Steffie Woolhandler, Karen E. Lasser, Danny McCormick, David H. Bor, and David U. Himmelstein, "Health Insurance and Mortality in U.S. Adults," *American Journal of Public Health* 99/12 (December 2009), http://www.pnhp.org/excessdeaths/health-insurance-and-mortality-in-US-adults.pdf.

281. Galvani et al., "Improving the Prognosis of Health Care."

282. Ken Alltucker, "Fear and Health Care: Gallup Survey Finds Americans Skipped Treatment, Borrowed $88B to Pay for Costs," *USA Today*, April 2, 2019.

283. Scottie Andrew, "13% of Americans Say They Know Someone Who Died After They Couldn't Afford Health Care, Survey Says," CNN, November 23, 2019, https://www.cnn.com/ 2019/11/12/health/us-cant-afford-health-care-trnd. See also Michael Sainato, "The Americans Dying Because They Can't Afford Medical Care," *Guardian*, January 7, 2020; and Ken Alltucker, "Struggling to Stay Alive: Rising Insulin Prices Cause Diabetics to Go to Extremes," *USA Today*, March 27, 2019.

284. Carolyn Y. Johnson, "The Real Reason the U.S. Spends Twice as Much on Health Care as Other Wealthy Countries," *Washington Post*, March 13, 2018; Gerard F. Anderson, Peter Hussey, and Varduhi Petrosyan, "It's Still the Prices, Stupid: Why the U.S. Spends So Much on Health Care, and a Tribute to Uwe Reinhardt," *Health Affairs* 38/1 (January 2019), https://www.healthaffairs.org/doi/pdf/10.1377/hlthaff.2018.05144; and National Research Council, *U.S. Health in International Perspective: Shorter Lives, Poorer Health*, ed. Steven H. Woolf and Laudan Aron (Washington, DC: The National Academies Press, 2013), chaps. 1 and 2.

285. Woolf and Aron, *Shorter Lives, Poorer Health*, chaps. 1 and 2; Roosa Tikkanen and Melinda K. Abrams, "U.S. Health Care from a Global Perspective, 2019: Higher Spending, Worse Outcomes?," Common-

NOTES TO PAGE 283

wealth Fund, January 30, 2020, https://www.commonwealth fund. org/publications/issue-briefs/2020/jan/us-health-care-global-perspective-2019; Carolyn Y. Johnson, "U.S. Spends Twice as Much"; Case and Deaton, "Mortality and Morbidity"; and Gabby Galvin, "The U.S. Has a Maternal Mortality Rate Again. Here's Why That Matters," *U.S. News and World Report*, January 30, 2020, https://www. usnews.com/news/healthiest-communities/articles/2020-01-30/why-the-new-us-maternal-mortality-rate-is-important.

286. Donald A. Barr, *Health Disparities in the United States: Social Class, Race, Ethnicity, and the Social Determinants of Health*, 3rd ed. (Baltimore: Johns Hopkins University Press, 2019); Paula Braveman, "Health Inequalities by Class and Race in the U.S.: What Can We Learn from the Patterns?," *Social Science and Medicine* 74/5 (March 2012): 665–67, https://www.sciencedirect.com/science/article/abs/pii/S0277953611007052?via%3Dihub; Celine Gounder, "How Long Will You Live? That Depends on Your ZIP Code," *Guardian*, December 14, 2016; Jamie Ducharme and Elijah Wolfson, "Your ZIP Code Might Determine How Long You Live—and the Difference Could Be Decades," *Time*, June 17, 2019, https://time.com/5608268/ zip-code-health/; and Todd Ackerman, "Texans' Life Expectancy Varies Wildly Depending on ZIP Code," *San Antonio Express-News*, February 27, 2019.

287. James, "Estimate of Patient Harms," 122–28; Niki Carver, Vikas Gupta, and John E. Hipskind, "Medical Error," National Center for Biotechnology Information, U.S. National Library of Medicine, February 16, 2021, https://www.ncbi.nlm.nih.gov/books/NBK430763; John T. James, "Deaths from Preventable Adverse Events Originating in Hospitals," *BMJ Quality & Safety* 26/8 (July 20, 2017): 692–93; and Martin A. Makary and Michael Daniel, "Medical Error—the Third Leading Cause of Death in the U.S.," *BMJ* 353/2139 (May 3, 2016), https://doi.org/10.1136/bmj.i2139.

288. Carver, Gupta, and Hipskind, "Medical Error"; Ann Carrie, "The 8 Most Common Roots of Medical Errors," Always Culture, March 16, 2021, https://alwaysculture.com/hcahps/ communication-medications/8-most-common-causes-of-medical-errors/.

289. James G. Anderson and Kathleen Abrahamson, "Your Health Care May Kill You," *Studies in Health Technology and Informatics* 234 (2017), 13–17, https://pubmed.ncbi.nlm.nih.gov/2818 6008/.

290. Mainul Haque, Massimo Sartelli, Judy McKimm, and Muhamad Abu Bakar, "Health Care-Associated Infections—An Overview," *Infection and Drug Resistance* 11 (November 2018): 2321–33; and Jayne O'Donnell, "As COVID-19 Spread, the Feds Relaxed Rules, and Hospitals Tried to Contain the Outbreak, Other Infections May Have Risen,"

USA Today, August 5, 2020.

291. Gøtzsche, *Deadly Medicines*, 1; Donald W. Light, Joel Lexchin, and Jonathan J. Darrow have also blasted "the myth of safe and effective drugs" and the often deadly "institutional corruption" in the pharmaceutical industry, Congress, the FDA, and the medical community. See "Institutional Corruption of Pharmaceuticals and the Myth of Safe and Effective Drugs," *Journal of Law, Medicine, & Ethics* (Fall 2013): 590–600.

292. Gøtzsche, *Deadly Medicines* 126, 260.

293. Ibid., 100, 260.

294. Ibid., 160–62, 260. An estimate of 60,000 deaths, which arguably fails to account for the different ways in which this drug fatally injured people, is found in Damian Garde, "The Return of Vioxx: Can a Drug Once Deemed Deadly Be Relaunched to Treat Rare Disease?," *Stat*, October 9, 2019, https://www.statnews.com/2019/10/09/vioxx-relaunched-treat-hemophilia-rare-disease/.

295. Gøtzsche, *Deadly Medicines*, 232, 260.

296. Ibid., 167, 260.

297. "Overdose Deaths Top 100,000 Annually"; Bernstein and Joel Achenbach, "Drug Overdose Deaths"; Sarah DeWeerdt, "Tracing the Opioid Crisis to Its Roots," *Nature*, September 11, 2019, https://www.nature.com/articles/d41586-019-02686-2; Andrew Kolodny, "How FDA Failures Contributed to the Opioid Crisis," *AMA Journal of Ethics* 22/8 (2020): E743-E750, https:// journalofethics.ama-assn.org/article/how-fda-failures-contributed-opioid-crisis/2020-08; and Ronald Hirsch, "The Opioid Epidemic: It's Time to Place Blame Where It Belongs," *Missouri Medicine* 114/2 (March-April 2017): 82–83, 90.

298. The estimate of 22.000 annual deaths is found in Benjamin A. Rodman, Victor P. Bilan, Naseema B. Merchant, Catherine G. Steffens, Alyssa A. Grimshaw, Lori A. Bastian, and Craig G. Gunderson, "Rate of Preventable Mortality in Hospitalized Patients," *Journal of General Internal Medicine* 35/7 (July 2020): 2099–2116, https://pubmed.ncbi.nlm.nih.gov/ 31965 525/. The estimate of more than 780,000 annual deaths is found in Introduction to Gary Null, Martin Feldman, Debora Rasio, and Carolyn Dean, *Death by Medicine* (Mount Jackson, VA: Praktikos Books, 2011). A review of the related literature during the past two decades suggests that both of these estimates are outliers. Barbara Starfield advanced an estimate of between 230,000 and 284,000 annual deaths in "Is U.S. Health Really the Best in the World?," *JAMA* 284/4 (July 26, 2000), https://jamanetwork.com/journals/jama/article-abstract/192 908. James provided an estimate of as many as 440,000 annual deaths in "Estimate of Patient Harms," 122–28. An estimate of 250,000 annual deaths is found in Makary and Daniel, "Medical Error."

NOTES TO PAGES 284–285 499

299. Gøtzsche, *Deadly Medicines*, 259–60. An estimate of 200,000 annual deaths is also found in Donald L. Barlett and James B. Steele, "Deadly Medicine," *Vanity Fair*, January 2011, https://www.vanityfair.com/news/2011/01/deadly-medicine-201101. An estimate of 180,000 annual deaths appeared in Miles Hacker, "Adverse Drug Reactions," in *Pharmacology: Principles and Practice*, ed. Miles Hacker, Kenneth Bachmann, and William Messer (Burlington: Academic Press, 2009), 327. An estimate of 128,000 annual deaths from the use of prescription drugs is found in Donald W. Light, "New Prescription Drugs: A Major Health Risk with Few Offsetting Advantages," Edmond J. Safra Center for Ethics, Harvard University, June 27, 2014, https://ethics.harvard.edu/blog/new-prescription-drugs-major-health-risk-few-offsetting-advantages.

300. This appraisal is based on estimates of 200,000 annual deaths from the use of prescription drugs, 100,000 annual deaths from medical errors unrelated to prescription drugs, and 100,000 annual deaths from iatrogenic infections.

301. The conclusion that millions have died is found in Milton Silverman, Philip R. Lee, and Mia Lydecker, *Prescriptions for Death: The Drugging of the Third World* (Berkeley: University of California Press, 1982), 86. See also Christopher Scanlan, "Dangerous Exports—Drugs Banned in the U.S. Find Overseas Markets," *Seattle Times*, June 11, 1991. An estimate that 223,000 people die each year from adverse drug reactions in low- and medium-income countries is found in National Academies of Sciences, Engineering, and Medicine, *Crossing the Global Quality Chasm: Improving Health Care Worldwide* (Washington, D.C.: National Academies Press, 2018), 2, 135. U.S. corporations produced many of the drugs involved in these deaths.

302. An estimate of between 200,000 and 300,000 deaths is found in Grob, *Deadly Truth*, 108. An estimate of approximately 200,000 deaths is found in Joseph P. Byrne, ed., *Encyclopedia of Pestilence, Pandemics, and Plagues*, vol. 1: *A–M* (Westport, CT: Greenwood Publishing Group, 2008), 99, 107.

303. David A. Keiser, Catherine L. Kling, and Joseph S. Shapiro, "The Low But Uncertain Benefits of U.S. Water Quality Policy," *Proceedings of the National Academy of Sciences* 116/12 (March 19, 2019): 5262.

304. Waller, *Health and Wellness*, 97–98; and Rachel Snyder, Sarah Tran, Scott Saunders, and Jay Pandya, "Who Died of Consumption? Race and Disease in the United States," *Perspectives on History*, American Historical Association, September 12, 2016, https://www.historians.org/publications-and-directories/perspectives-on-history/september-2016/who-died-of-consumption-race-and-disease-in-the-united-states.

500   NOTES TO PAGE 285

305. David Cutler and Grant Miller, "The Role of Public Health Improvements in Health Advances: The Twentieth Century United States," *Demography* 42/1 (February 2005): 1–2.

306. Gerald Markowitz and David Rosner, *Lead Wars: The Politics of Science and the Fate of America's Children* (Berkeley: University of California Press, 2013), 8.

307. Davis, *When Smoke Ran Like Water*; David Stradling and Peter Thorsheim, "The Smoke of Great Cities: British and American Efforts to Control Air Pollution 1860–1914," *Environmental History* 4/1 (January 1999): 8, 12–14, 16–19; Jim Dwyer, "Remembering a City Where the Smog Could Kill," *New York Times*, February 28, 2017; and Jack Williams, "U.S. Once Had Air Pollution to Match China's Today," *Washington Post*, October 25, 2013.

308. Loomis, *Out of Sight*, 83; Jen Carlson, "Flashback: The City's Killer Smog," *The Gothamist*, November 24, 2009, https://gothamist.com/news/flashback-the-citys-killer-smog; and "Clean Air Timeline," American Lung Association, April 23, 2019, https://www.lung.org/our-initiatives/ healthy-air/outdoor/fighting-for-healthy-air/about-fighting-for-healthy-air/clean-air-timeline. html.

309. See Meyers, "Some Unintended Fallout," 20, 22. He estimated that between 145,300 and 429,400 excess deaths occurred, yielding a mid-range calculation of more than 280,000. A much lower and less reliable estimate of approximately 11,000 deaths from nuclear testing was advanced in Centers for Disease Control and Prevention and National Cancer Institute, *Report on the Feasibility of a Study of the Health Consequences to the American Population from Nuclear Weapons Tests Conducted by the United States and Other Nations*, vol. 1: Technical Report, January 25, 2006, 115–16, https://www.cdc.gov/nceh/radiation/fallout/default.htm. Challenges to the CDC/NCI estimate are noted in Editors, "When It Comes to Nuclear Tests in Nevada, Numbers Just Don't Add Up," *Las Vegas Sun*, August 9, 2020.

310. Hastings, "Bitter Scar on Navajo Nation"; Daniels, "'Horrible Legacy'"; Grinde and Johansen, *Ecocide of Native America*; Brook, "Environmental Genocide," 105–13; and Gilio-Whitaker, *As Long as Grass Grows*.

311. Davis, *When Smoke Ran Like Water*, xviii, 156–58. Davis's appraisal is based on her estimate of 60,000 to 120,000 annual air pollution deaths during this period.

312. See Bowe, Xie, Yan, and Al-Aly, "Air Pollution in the United States"; and Fabio Caiazzo, Akshay Ashok, Ian A. Waitz, Steve H. L. Yim, and Steven R. H. Barrett, "Air Pollution and Early Deaths in the United States: Quantifying The Impact of Major Sectors in 2005," *Atmospheric Environment* 79 (November 2013): 198–208. This estimate is almost

NOTES TO PAGES 285-286   501

certainly conservative because it does not include all deaths caused by exposure to lead in the atmosphere.

313. Kacy Burdette, "See Aerial Photos of the Worst Hazardous Waste Sites in the U.S.," *Fortune*, October 30, 2018, https://fortune.com/2018/10/30/aerial-photos-superfund-sites-usa/.

314. Burdette, "Worst Hazardous Waste Sites"; and David Johnson, "Do You Live Near Toxic Waste? See 1317 of the Most Polluted Spots in the U.S.," *Time*, March 22, 2017, https://time. com/4695109/superfund-sites-toxic-waste-locations/; Alexander Kirpich and Emily Leary, "Superfund Locations and Potential Associations with Cancer Incidence in Florida," *Statistics and Public Policy* 4/1 (February 6, 2017), 1–9, DOI: 10.10 80/2330443X.2016.1267599; and Raid Amin, Arlene Nelson, and Shannon McDougall, "A Spatial Study of the Location of Superfund Sites and Associated Cancer Risk," *Statistics and Public Policy* 5/1 (January 25, 2018), 1-9, DOI: 10.1080/2330443X.2017.1408439.

315. Mitch Smith, Julie Bosman, and Monica Davey, "Flint's Water Crisis Started 5 Years Ago—It's Not Over," *New York Times*, April 25, 2019; and David Rosner—"Newark's Lead-Water Crisis Is a National Problem," *Columbia News*, October 31, 2019, https://news.columbia.edu/news/lead-newark-flint-water.

316. Lanphear, Rauch, Auinger, Allen, and Hornung, "Lead Exposure and Mortality"; Honor Whiteman, "Over 400,000 U.S. Deaths Per Year Caused by Lead Exposure," *Medical News*, March 13, 2018,https://www. medicalnewstoday.com/articles/321203.php#1; and Bruce Lanphear, email to author, December 4, 2019.

317. David Andrews and Bill Walker, "'Erin Brockovich' Carcinogen in Tap Water of More Than 200 Million Americans," Environmental Working Group, September 20, 2016, https://www. ewg.org/research/chromium-six-found-in-us-tap-water; David Andrews, "Report: Up to 110 Million Americans Could Have PFAS-Contaminated Drinking Water," Environmental Working Group, May 22, 2018, https://www.ewg.org/research/report-110-million-americans-could-have-pfas-contaminated-drinking-water; and Laura Santhanam, "Even If Your Drinking Water Gets a 'Passing Grade,' It May Not Be Safe," PBS, October 25, 2019, https://www.pbs.org newshour/ health/even-if-your-drinking-water-gets-a-passing-grade-it-may-not-be-safe.

318. Santhanam, "Even If Your Drinking Water May Not Be Safe"; News21 Staff, Jasmine Spearing-Bowen, and Karl Schneider, "Industrial Waste Pollutes America's Drinking Water," The Center for Public Integrity, August 22, 2017, https://publicintegrity.org/environment/industrial-waste-pollutes-americas-drinking-water/; and Charles Duhigg, "Millions of Americans Drink Dirty Water, Records Show," *New York Times*, December 7, 2009.

502   NOTES TO PAGE 286

319. Lanphear, Rauch, Auinger, Allen, and Hornung, "Lead Exposure and Mortality"; and Lanphear, message to author.
320. The conclusion that millions have died because of water and soil pollution is also found in Robert H. Weiss, "Nothing Super About Superfund Sites," *Forbes*, April 28, 2010, https:// www.forbes.com/2010/04/28/superfunds-environment-pollution-toxic-opinions-contributors-robert-h-weiss.html#17880b647db8.
321. See Devra Davis, *Secret History of the War on Cancer*; McKay Jenkins, *ContamiNation: My Quest to Survive in a Toxic World* (New York: Penguin Random House, 2011); E.G. Vallianatos with McKay Jenkins, *Poison Spring: The Secret History of Pollution and the EPA* (New York: Bloomsbury Press, 2014); and Michelle Mart, *Pesticides, A Love Story: America's Enduring Embrace of Dangerous Chemicals* (Lawrence: University Press of Kansas), 2018.
322. Devra Davis, *Secret History of the War on Cancer*, 430.
323. Davis, *Secret History of the War on Cancer*; Jenkins, *ContamiNation*, "Prologue"; Vallianatos with Jenkins, *Poison Spring*, xii–xv; The President's Cancer Panel, *2008-2009 Annual Report: Reducing Environmental Cancer Risk, What We Can Do Now*, U.S. Department of Health and Human Services, National Cancer Institute, April 2010, https:// deainfo.nci.nih.gov/ advisory/pcp/ annualReports/pcp08-09rpt/PCP_Report_08-09_508.pdf; and David Servan-Schreiber, "We Can Stop the Cancer Epidemic," *New York Times*, September 19, 2008.
324. Ashley Perez, "8 Foods We Eat in the US that Are Banned in Other Countries," *BuzzFeed*, June 19, 2013, https://www.buzzfeed.com/ashleyperez/8-foods-we-eat-in-the-us-that-are-banned-in-other-countries; and Roni Caryn Rabin, "What Foods Are Banned in Europe but Not Banned in the US?" *New York Times*, December 28, 2018.
325. Davis, *Secret History of the War on Cancer*, 363–79; Markowitz and Rosner, *Deceit and Denial*, esp. chap. 6; and National Cancer Institute, "Cancer-Causing Substances: Vinyl Chloride," December 28, 2018, https://www.cancer.gov/about-cancer/causes-prevention/ risk/substances/vinyl-chloride.
326. State of California, "Phthalates," Proposition 65 Warnings, September 2017, https://www.p65warnings.ca.gov/fact-sheets/phthalates; Sai Sandeep Singh Rowdhwal and Jiaxiang Chen, "Toxic Effects of Di-2-ethylhexyl Phthalate: An Overview," *BioMed Research International* 2018/1750368 (February 22, 2018), DOI: 10.1155/2018/1750368. See also Amy Westervelt, "Phthalates Are Everywhere, and the Health Risks Are Worrying: How Bad Are They Really?," *Guardian*, February 10, 2015.
327. The estimate for the total number of deaths in 2019 is found in Centers

NOTES TO PAGES 286–287   503

for Disease Control and Prevention, *An Update on Cancer Deaths in the United States* (Atlanta, GA: U.S. Department of Health and Human Services, Division of Cancer Prevention and Control, 2021), https://www.cdc.gov/cancer/dcpc/research/update-on-cancer-deaths/index.htm. The estimate for the number of deaths resulting from exposure to phthalates appears in Amanda Holpuch, "Chemicals Used in Packaging May Play Role in 100,000 U.S. Deaths a Year—Study," *Guardian*, October 14, 2021.

328. Davis, *Secret History of the War on Cancer*, 4.

329. Philip J. Landrigan et al., "The *Lancet* Commission on Pollution and Health," *The Lancet* 391/10119 (February 3, 2018): 462–512.

330. The significance of transboundary pollution is discussed in Laura Naranjo, "On the Trail of Global Pollution Drift," EarthData, National Aeronautics and Space Administration, July 23, 2020, https://earthdata.nasa.gov/learn/sensing-our-planet/on-the-trail-of-global-pollution-drift; Global Alliance on Health and Pollution, and Pure Earth, *Pollution Knows No Boundaries: How the Pollution Crisis in Low- and Middle-Income Countries Affects Everyone's Health and What We Can Do About It*, January 2019, https://www.pure earth.org/wp-content/uploads/2019/01/ PE_PollutionKnowsNoBordersFinal.pdf; and National Research Council, *Global Sources of Local Pollution: An Assessment of Long-Range Transport of Key Air Pollutants To and From the United States* (Washington, DC: National Academies Press, 2010), https://doi.org/10.17226/12743.

331. Loomis, *Out of Sight*, chap. 3; and Vandana Shiva, "Outsourcing Pollution and Energy-Intensive Production," in *The Energy Reader: Overdevelopment and the Delusion of Endless Growth*, ed. Tom Butler, Daniel Lerch, and George Wuerthner (Healdsburg, CA: Watershed Media, 2012), 256–63.

332. The important role of U.S. production in China is discussed in Shiva, "Outsourcing Pollution and Production"; and in "Why Many U.S. Companies Have Kept Production in China and Have No Plans of Moving," National Public Radio, August 30, 2019, https://www.npr.org/ 2019/08/30/756034624/why-many-u-s-companies-have-kept-production-in-china-and-have-no-plans-of-moving. An estimate of 1.1 million annual air pollution deaths in China is found in Jonathan Tirone and Bloomberg News, "Air Pollution," *Washington Post*, October 3, 2019.

333. Tammy Webber and Katy Daigle, Associated Press, "U.S. Exporting Dirty Fuel to Already Pollution-Choked India," Fox News, December 1, 2017, https://www.foxnews.com/world/us-exporting-dirty-fuel-to-already-pollution-choked-india.

334. Anna Bruederle and Roland Holder, "The Effect of Oil Spills on Infant

Mortality: Evidence from Nigeria," *CESifo Working Papers* no. 6653, September 2017, https://www.ifo.de/DocDL/ cesifo1_wp6653.pdf; Conor Gaffey, "Oil Spills in Nigeria Could Kill 16,000 Babies a Year," *Newsweek*, November 6, 2017, https://www.newsweek.com/nigeria-oil-oil-spills-neonatal-mortality-702506; Anamesere Igboeroteonwu, "Exxon Mobil Oil Spill Hits Communities in Southeast Nigeria: Local Leader," Reuters, December 2, 2016, https://www.reuters.com/article/us-nigeria-exxon-mobil-spill-idUSKBN14A1RC; and Drew Hinshaw, "Chevron Faces Fire in Nigeria," *Wall Street Journal*, March 6, 2012.

335. United Nations General Assembly, *Report of the Special Rapporteur on the Right to Food*, January 24, 2017, 3–8, https://www.pan-uk.org/site/wp-content/uploads/United-Nations-Report-of-the-Special-Rapporteur-on-the-right-to-food.pdf; and Ryan Rifai, "UN: 200,000 Die Each Year from Pesticide Poisoning," *Al Jazeera*, March 8, 2017, https://www.aljazeera.com/news/2017/03/200000-die-year-pesticide-poisoning-170308140641105.html.

336. Lynn Peeples, "Lead Paint, Other Toxic Products Banned in U.S. Still Exported to Unsuspecting Customers Abroad," *Huffington Post*, March 25, 2013, https://www.huffpost. com/entry/lead-paint-exports-pesticides_n_2949694; Erin McCormick, Bennett Murray, Carmela Fonbuena, Leonie Kijewski, Gökçe Saraçoğlu, Jamie Fullerton, Alastair Gee, and Charlotte Simmonds, "Where Does Your Plastic Go? *Guardian* Investigation Reveals America's Dirty Secret," *Guardian*, June 17, 2019; David Biello, "Trashed Tech Dumped Overseas: Does the U.S. Care?," *Scientific American*, September 19, 2008, https://www.scientificamerican.com/ article/trashed-tech-dumped-overseas/; Ken Christensen and Katie Campbell, "The U.S. Is Still Dumping Some of Its Toxic E-Waste Overseas," Public Radio International, June 2, 2016, https://www.pri.org/stories/2016-06-02/us-still-dumping-some-its-toxic-e-waste-overseas.

337. Justin Gillis and Nadja Popovich, "The U.S. Is the Biggest Carbon Polluter in History—It Just Walked Away from the Paris Climate Deal," *New York Times*, June 1, 2017. Gillis and Popovich acknowledge that China overtook the United States as the largest single emitter of carbon pollution around 2007.

338. World Meteorological Organization, *WMO Statement on the State of the Global Climate in 2019* (Geneva: World Meteorological Organization, 2020) 18–26; "Heat Waves Are Killing People," *The Economist*, July 27, 2019, https://www.economist.com/leaders/2019/07/27/heatwaves-are-killing-people; Alejandra Borunda, "The Science Connecting Wildfires to Climate Change," *National Geographic*, September 17, 2020, https://www.nationalgeographic. com/science/article/

NOTES TO PAGE 288

climate-change-increases-risk-fires-western-us; Ajit Niranjan, "Extreme Weather Explained: How Climate Change Makes Storms Stronger," *Deutsche Welle*, November 6, 2020, https://www.dw.com/en/climate-storms-cyclones-hurricanes-typhoons-explained/a-55521226; and Matthew Daly and Ellen Knickmeyer, "U.S. Needs to Brace Itself for More Deadly Storms, Experts Say," AP News, February 18, 2021, https://apnews.com/article/us-deadly-winter-storms-2021-df7d37d12 ef13633bb5666e1151bcf9e.

339. World Meteorological Organization, *State of the Global Climate*, 27–34; Jessica Elise and Kenneth Foster, "World Hunger Has Risen for Three Straight Years, and Climate Change Is a Cause," *The Conversation*, October 22, 2018, https://theconversation.com/world-hunger-has-risen-for-three-straight-years-and-climate-change-is-a-cause-103818; Tedros Adhanom Ghebreyesus, "Climate Change Is Already Killing Us," *Foreign Affairs*, September 23, 2019, https://www.foreignaffairs.com/ articles/2019-09-23/climate-change-already-killing-us; and Associated Press, "A Warmer World Is an Unhealthier Place for Children, New Study Finds," NBC News, November 13, 2019, https://www.nbcnews.com/health/health-news/warmer-world-unhealthier-place-children-new-study-finds-n1081951.

340. An estimate of more than 300,000 deaths a year is found in Global Humanitarian Forum, *Human Impact Report—Climate Change: The Anatomy of a Silent Crisis* (Geneva: Global Humanitarian Forum, 2009), 1–3, https://ghf-ge.org/human-impact-report.pdf. An estimate of 400,000 deaths a year is found in DARA and the Climate Vulnerable Forum, *Climate Vulnerability Monitor*, 2nd ed., *A Guide to a Cold Calculus of a Hot Planet* (Madrid: Fundación DARA Internacional, 2012), 17, https://daraint.org/wp-content/uploads/2012/09/CVM2ndEd-FrontMatter.pdf.

341. David Wallace-Wells, "The Uninhabitable Earth," *New York*, July 10, 2017, https://nymag.com/intelligencer/2017/07/climate-change-earth-too-hot-for-humans.html.

342. Ibid.; Timothy M. Lenton, Johan Rockström, Owen Gaffney, Stefan Rahmstorf, Katherine Richardson, Will Steffen, and Hans Joachim Schellnhuber, "Climate Tipping Points—Too Risky to Bet Against," *Nature* 575 (April 9, 2020): 592–95; Christopher Flavelle, "Climate Change Threatens the World's Food Supply, United Nations Warns," *New York Times*, August 8, 2019; Sarah Azau, "1 Billion People Threatened by Climate Change Risks to Oceans, Polar and Mountain Regions, UN Report Warns," *Phys.org*, September 25, 2019, https://phys.org/news/2019-09-billion-people-threatened-climate-oceans.html; Alexander C. Kaufman, "Climate Change Could Threaten Up to 2 Bil-

lion Refugees by 2100," *Huffington Post*, June 26, 2017, https://www.
huffpost.com/entry/ climate-change-refugees_n_59506463e4b0 da2c-
731c5e73; and Jonathan Tirone, "Pentagon Fears Confirmed: Climate
Change Leads to More Wars and Refugees," Bloomberg, January 23,
2019, https://www.bloomberg.com/news/articles/2019-01-23/penta-
gon-fears-confirmed-climate-change-leads-to-war-refugees.

343. This includes more than 1.8 million war-related deaths and close to
100,000 fatalities from mob, vigilante, police, and extremist violence,
not including most of the related Indigenous and African American
deaths surveyed in chapters 1 and 2. This also includes scores of thousands of other deaths resulting from incarceration and more than four
million homicides and suicides since 1900, many of which were among
Indigenous and Black people.

344. This includes well over one million drug overdose deaths since the
mid-twentieth century, almost 28 million tobacco-related deaths since
1965, almost four million automobile deaths since 1899, more than one
million deaths related to defective or dangerous consumer products in
the United States since 1968, thousands from medical experimentation, close to one million deaths from government failures to address
public health crises, more than one million deaths resulting from limited access to medical care since 2000, eight million deaths from all
iatrogenic causes since 2000, eight million deaths from air pollution
since 1980, and eight million deaths from water and soil pollution since
1980. Deaths from cholera and tuberculosis are not included here. Nor
are deaths partly caused by the consumption of processed foods.

345. The number of deaths resulting from use of U.S. tobacco products
abroad is likely much higher but difficulty to quantify. Proctor, email
to author. The total number of climate deaths since 2010 is based on
the Global Humanitarian Forum's estimate of three hundred annual
deaths.

Index

al-Abadi, Haider, 253
Abdul-Mahdi, Adil, 253
abuse, of enslaved people, 76
Act of Union (1707), 30
Adams, John, 125
Adams, John Quincy, 131
Adler, Jeffrey S., 262
Afghanistan, 206–7, 209, 230–31, 251–52
Africa: before Europeans, 58–59; intervention in, 223–24
African American participation, in War of Independence, 71–72
African American population: in eighteenth century, 69–73; in nineteenth century, 73–84; since 1900, 84–85
African American service, in Civil War, 80
African farmers, skill of, 58
African oral tradition, 48

Africans imported, number of, 61–63
Africans transported, from Caribbean to North America, 62
Agent Orange, 260
Alaska, 36, 50, 123, 137–38
Alaska Natives, 50
Alcatraz Island, occupation of, 51
Aldrich, Mark, 99–100
Aleutian Islands, 141
Alexander, Michelle, 93
Alexandria (Louisiana), 79
Algeria, 182
Allende Gossens, Salvador, 201
Alliance of Democratic Forces for the Liberation of Congo-Zaire, 226–27
de Almagro, Diego, 21–22
American Colonization Society, 77, 131

508 INDEX

The American Federation of Labor and Congress of Industrial Organizations (AFL-CIO), 120
The American Labor Year Book (government document), 111
American Samoa, 10, 144–45
Amin, Idi, 198–99
amphetamines, 277
ancient Egypt, 58
Anderson, Gary Clayton, 31
Anderson, M. T., 100
Anglo-Cherokee War, 33–34
Angola, 186, 202, 215–16
Anishinaabe people, 32, 49
annihilation, large-scale, 14
anthrax, 212
anti-labor violence, 106–7, 112–15
Anti-Slavery Society, 76
Apalachee people, 30
apartheid, 180, 187–88
aplastic anemia, 111
Appy, Christian, 9
Aquino, Benigno, 197
Arab slave trade, 59
Arapaho people, 46
Arbenz, Jacobo, 181
Argentina, 141, 203–4
Arizona Rangers, 112–13
armed forces, Indigenous people in, 51
Army, United States, 90
Arrington, Benjamin T., 102
asbestos, 111
al-Assad, Bashar, 240–41, 253
The Atlantic Slave Trade (Curtin), 61
attack, on Sikhs, 275

Atwood, Paul L., 131, 151, 162
Augusta (Georgia), 78
automobile accidents, 279
automobile-centered transportation, 279
automobiles, 278–79
al-Awlaki, Anwar, 237
Axis Powers, 12, 162–63

Baath Party, 196–97
Bacon, Nathaniel, 27
Bangladesh, 199
Bao Bai, 181–82
Baptist, Edward E., 75
Barbary States, 128
Barkaoui, Miloud, 182
barracoons, 102
Barre, Mohammed Siad, 205–6
al-Bashir, Omar, 234–35
Batista y Zaldívar, Fulgencio, 155
Battalion 316, 214
Battle of Blair Mountain, 114
Battle of Fallen Timbers, 37
battle of Two Lakes, 24
the Bay of Pigs, 186
Bear River, 45
Belgium, 109–10
Bennis, Phyllis, 170
Berg, Alan, 272
Berlin, Ira, 75
Biden, Joseph, 251–52, 256–57
Biennio Rosso, 154
bin Laden, Osama, 206–7, 230–31, 275–76
Black Hawk (chief), 41
Black people, police and, 264–65
Black September, 197

INDEX 509

Blackmon, Douglas A., 82–83
Blum, William, 191
boarding schools, 48–49, 51–52, 54
boiler, in hat manufacturing plant, 101
Boko Haram, 250
Bolivia, 194, 198, 256
Boogaloo, 274
Borah, Woodrow, 67
Bortolot, Alexander Ives, 59
Bosch, Juan, 192
Boskin, James, 86–87
Bosque Redondo Reservation, 46
Boxer Rebellion, 123, 145
Bradley, David, 161
Brazil, 189
Brazilian Civil War, 142
Bretton Woods agreement, 165, 170
Britain: China and, 135–36; trade with, 127–28
British Guiana, 187
Brown, John, 79
Brown, Michael, 267
Bureau of Justice Statistics, 267
Bureau of Labor Statistics, U.S., 110–11
Bureau of State Security, 188
Burundi, 200–201
Bush, George H. W., 218–19
Bush, George W., 230–31, 236–37
business dealings, in Germany, 157–58
Buxton, Thomas Fowel, 65, 66
Byrd, James, 89
byssinosis (brown lung disease), 100, 118–19

Cabeza de Vaca, Álvar Núñez, 23
Cabot, John: see Caboto, Giovanni
Caboto, Giovanni, 22
California, 43, 135
Calusa people, 23
Cambodia, 190–91
cancer rates, 286
Capital (Marx), 18, 57
capital crimes, conviction of African Americans of, 89–90
capitalists, 98, 102, 109, 162
the Caribbean, 21–22, 133–34, 147
Carranza de la Garza, José Venustiano, 149–50
Carroll County (Mississippi), 82
Carson, Kit, 45
Carswell Grove (Georgia), 85–86
Cartagena (Colombia), 124
Carter, Jimmy, 205, 208, 211
Case, Anne, 271
Castillo Armas, Carlos, 181
Castro, Fidel, 185–86, 210
Cazenave, Noel A., 90
Celebrex, 284
Census Bureau, U.S., 259–60, 264; Census (1860), 100; Census (1870), 103; Census (2010), 54–55
Centers for Disease Control and Prevention, 53
Central Intelligence Agency (CIA), 90, 173, 179, 183, 187–88
César Sandino, Augusto, 123
Chad, 214
Chambers, Stephen, 75
de Champlain, Samuel, 27–28
Charleston (South Carolina), 78

510 INDEX

Charlottesville (Virginia), 273–74
chemical plant explosions, 116, 117, 118, 119
Cherry Mine coal fire, 107
Chesapeake and Ohio Canal, 99
Chesapeake Bay colonies, 98
Chickasaw people, 42
Chile, 141, 201
China, 130, 132, 135–36, 156, 171–72; Trump and, 249–50
Chinese Civil War, 171
Chinese Communist Party, 156
Chinese laborers, 101–3
Choctaw people, 41
cholera, 284–85
Churchill, Ward, 19
Churchill, Winston, 153–54, 164
Ciudad Juarez (Mexico), 120
Civil Rights Act (1964), 88
civil rights activists, 87
Civil War, 123, 136–37; African American service in, 80; convict labor after, 82–83; deaths in, 137, 167; escapes from slavery before, 76–77; increased industrial development during, 102–3; Indigenous participation in, 44–45
Clapper, James, 247–48
Cleveland, Grover, 142
Cleveland Citizen (newspaper), 107
client states, 12, 210
climate change, 287–88
Clinton administration, 281
Clodfelter, Micheal, 47, 123–24
Coahuiltecan people, 24

coal mine explosions, 107–8, 117, 119
coal miner strikes, 113, 114
coal mining, 101
coal pollution, 285
cocaine, 277
Cockcroft, James, 150
Cold War, 180
collective action, 106
Colombia, 139, 145–46, 176, 194, 229–30
Colón (Panama), 145
Colón, Cristóbal, 17, 21
colonialist, United States as, 10
colonist attitude, toward War of Independence, 125
Colorado, 46
Colorado Cavalry, 46
Colorado County (Texas), 79
Columbus, Christopher: see Colón, Cristóbal
communism, 12, 180–93
concessionary treaties, 36
Confederate States of America, 136–37
Continental Army, 125–26
continental expansion, 130–31
convict labor, 82–83
Cook, James, 35
Cook, Sherburne, 43
Cooper, Thomas, 66
copper mine, in Sonora, 113
Cordell, Dennis D., 66
Corte-Real, Gaspar, 22
Cortés, Hernan, 21–22
Costa, Tom, 70
Costa Rica, 104, 176

INDEX

coterminous United States, 37
cotton, 75
La Coubre (ship), 185
Council on Foreign Relations,
193;, 163–64
counter-hegemonic literature,
13–14
coup, in Greece, 194–95
COVID-19, 282
Crandall Canyon (Utah), 119
Crazy Horse: *see* Tasunke Witco
(chief)
Creek War, 38–39
criminal homicides, 93–94
Cuba, 134, 138, 147–48, 185–86;
pirates in, 131
Cuban Missile Crisis, 187
cultural genocide, 54–55
Cumberland River Iron Works, 79
Cumings, Bruce, 178
Curtin, Philip, 61–63
Cushing, Caleb, 132–33
Custer, George Armstrong, 46–47

da Verrazano, Giovanni, 22
Dakota Access Pipeline, 54
Dale, USS (ship), 134
dangerous medicines, 283–84
Darden, Willie, 90
Darlan, Francois, 164
Darr Mine disaster, 107
Davis, David Brion, 58
Davis, Devra, 285
Death on the Job (AFL-CIO),
120–21
deaths: of African Americans
total, 73, 84, 95–96; of captive

Africans before leaving ships,
67; in Civil War, 137, 167;
from colonialism number of,
13, 55–56; from drugs and
tobacco, 288; of enslaved people
in Caribbean, 69; in First and
Second World Wars, 167–68;
from medicines and pollution,
288–89; from racist violence,
288; in raids, 65–66; in transatlantic slave trade, 63–71; in U.S.
wars, 259–60; in wars between
1775-1898, 167; in wars
between 1945-1980, 208–9; in
wars between 1980-2020, 256–
57; from workplace accidents,
110–11, 116–17, 121
Deaton, Angus, 271
Deep South, 75
Deepwater Horizon drilling rig,
120
Deery, Phillip, 174
Delawares: *see* Lenape people
Democratic Republic of the
Congo, 109–10, 185, 227–28
Democratic Republic of Vietnam
(DRV), 189
demonstration, in Greensboro,
North Carolina, 89
Denevan, William, 19
Department of Labor, U.S., 104,
116
deportation, of prisoners, 98
derailed train, in Burlington (New
York), 100
descendants, of enslaved people,
72–73

512 INDEX

Dhaka (Bangladesh), 120
Diallo, Amadou, 89
Díaz Mori, José de la Cruz Porfirio, 148
dictators, Trump and, 255
dictatorships, in the Americas, 155
Diné people, 44, 45–46, 49, 52, 115–16; internment of, 268
diseases, 20–24, 65, 80–81, 100–101, 105–6
Dobyns, Henry, 19, 20
doctors, unequal treatment by, 95
Doctrine of Discovery, 18, 59–60
Doe, Samuel, 207–8
Dole, Stanford, 142
Dominican Republic, 148, 155, 192
Donald, Michael, 89
Dorsey, George W., 87
Dorsey, Mae Murray, 87
Douglass, Frederick, 57
Downey, E. H., 110
Downs, James, 80–81, 137
Drake, Francis, 26
drone strikes, 237
drugs, 276–78
Du Bois, W. E. B., 63
Dunbar-Ortiz, Roxanne, 17, 19, 28, 36, 37; on expansion of U.S. Empire, 40
Dunmore (Lord), 71, 125
Dutch settlers, 28–29
Duterte, Rodrigo, 255
Duvalier, Francois "Papa Doc," 184
Duvalier, Jean-Claude "Baby Doc," 184

E. I. du Pont de Nemours company (firm), 152
East Timor, 202
economic expansion, 97–98, 138
Ecuador, 188
Edwards, Willie, Jr., 87
Egerton, Douglas R., 81, 82, 83–84
Egypt, 58, 139, 182–83, 242–43
Eisenhower, Dwight, 173, 181–82, 184–86
El Salvador, 214, 219
election (2000), 230–31
Ellis Island, 269
Eltis, David, 62, 65
embargo, against Cuba, 186
Embargo Act, 129–30
empire, United States as, 10, 15, 122–23, 169–70
Engels, Frederick, 14, 53
Engerman, Stanley L., 63–64
England, 30–31, 34
English settlements, permanent, 25
English settlers, 98–99
enslaved Africans, transportation to Puerto Rico of, 60
enslaved people: abuse of, 76; forced marches of, 64–65; labor of, 11, 57–58; resistance of, 70–71; seasoning of, 67–68
enslaved women, experimental surgery on, 76
Entente Powers, 11–12, 123, 151–52
Erdogan, Recep Tayyip, 255
Erie Canal, 99
escapes from slavery, before Civil War, 76–77

INDEX

Ethiopia, 158–59, 180, 185, 216–17, 229; Somalia and, 235–36
European colonization, environmental effect of, 22
Evers, Medgar, 87
exceptionalism, U.S., 9
excess deaths: of African Americans, 73, 84, 95–96; of Native people, 53
executions, of African Americans, 89–90
expansion, economic, 97–98, 138
experimental surgery, on enslaved women, 76
explosion: at ammunitions manufacturing plant, 101; at munitions depot in New Jersey, 107–8
expropriation, of Indigenous lands, 18
extremist violence, 275–76

factory fires, 119, 120
Fajardo (Puerto Rico), 131
far-right violence, 271–72
fascism, 15, 154–55, 158–59
fascists in Spain, U.S. support of, 159–60, 179–80
Fatal Encounters project, 267
fatal occupational injuries, 105
fatal train disasters, frequent, 100
Federal Republic of Germany (FRG), 177–78
Federspiel, Howard, 193
Fenfluramine, 91
Ferguson, Fortune, 90
Ferguson, Niall, 127, 153

fireworks factory explosion, 117
Flint, Michigan, 286
Foner, Eric, 73–74
Food and Drug Administration, 277
force, by police officers, 88–89, 91–92
forced marches, of enslaved people, 64–65
Ford, Gerald, 202
Ford, Glen, 247
Forminière (firm), 109
Forrest, Nathan Bedford, 80
Fort Defiance (Arizona), 49
Fort Logan, 85
Fort Mims, 38–39
Fort Pillow (Tennessee), 80
Fort Ross, 40
Fort Sumter (South Carolina), 136
France, 125–26, 127–28, 172–74, 181–82
Franco, Francisco, 159
Frank, Leo, 260
Franz Ferdinand, 151
Free Syrian Army, 241
French and Indian War, 33
French colonizers, 32
French Revolution, 127
Friend, Theodore, 173

Gabriel's Rebellion, 77
garlic festival shooting, 274
garment sweatshops, 105
Garner, Eric, 267
gas explosions, 116, 118
Gaza, 245
General Motors, 162

514 INDEX

General Sherman (ship), 138–39
genocide: cultural, 54–55; against
  Indigenous people, 13–50; in
  Rwanda, 225–26
George III (King), 124–25
Georgia, 74, 124
Georgia Colony, 32–33
German Democratic Republic, 178
Germany, 151–53, 156–57, 162–63
Ghana, 194
Ghani, Ashraf, 252
Ghost Dance, 48–49
Giáp, Võ Nguyên, 169
Gnadenhütten (Ohio), 35
gold: discovery of, 43, 47; quest
  for, 18, 24–25
Gomes, Estêvão, 22
Gómez, Juan Vicente, 147
Gordon, George, 157
Graden, Dale T., 74
Grand Coulee Dam, 115
Grandin, Greg, 11
Grant, Ulysses, 138
the Great Depression, 114, 269
great disaster (*Maafa*), 13, 58, 64,
  69
Great Divergence, between
  wealthy and poor nations,
  57–58
Great Southeastern Smallpox
  Epidemic, 27
Great Steel Strike of 1919, 113
Greece, 164, 175–76, 194–95
Grenada, 215
Grob, Gerald N., 112
Grover Shoe Factory, 107
growth, industrial, 11

Guale people, 30
guano, 134
Guantánamo Bay, 147–48
Guatemala, 181
Guggenheim, Daniel, 109
Guomindang regime, 123, 156,
  170–71

Hacker, J. David, 137
Haiti, 140, 184, 220, 233–34
Haitian Revolution, 77
Halliday, Jon, 172, 178
Hamilton, Alexander, 127–28
Hansen, Carl M., 110
Harlan County (Kentucky), 114
Harpers Ferry (Virginia), 79
Harrison, Benjamin, 104
hatmakers, 111
Haudenosaunee confederacy, 28,
  30–31, 35, 36, 123
Hawai'i, 123, 134, 139–42
Hawkins, Howie, 258
Hawk's Nest Tunnel, 115
Hayer, Heather, 273–74
Hayhurst, Emery R., 112
health care, unequal access to, 95,
  259, 282–83
Helen McGregor (steamboat), 99
Hernández Martínez,
  Maximiliano, 155
heroine, 277, 278
Hickory Ground, Oklahoma, 49
Higham, Charles, 162
high-profile police killings, 90–91
Hiroshima, Nagasaki and, 166
Hispaniola, 21
Hitler, Adolf, 156–57, 165–66

INDEX   515

HIV/AIDS, 281, 289
Ho Chi Minh, 181–82
Hoffman, Frederick L., 110
Hogendorn, Jan, 65
Holland, Jesse I., 86
holocaust, 14; *see also specific topics*
homicide, 259, 270–71
Honduras, 213–14, 237–38
Hookstadt, Carl, 110–11
Horne, Gerald, 18
hostages, in Iran, 211
The Houston Chronicle (newspaper), 267–68
Huerta, Victoriana, 149, 150
Hukbalahap movement, 175
Hungary, 183
Huron: *see* Wendat people
Hurricane Katrina, 282
Hurricane Maria, 282
Hussein, Saddam, 188, 196–97, 212, 219, 231
Hutu people, 225–26

iatrogenic infections, 283
IBM, 162
Igbo people, 196
illegal trafficking, diplomatic cover for by U.S., 74–75
Illinois: *see* Inoca people
imperialism, modern, 11, 12, 14, 15
imperium, American, 12, 14, 15, 127, 210
incarceration deaths, 268
indentured servitude, 98–99
Indian Health Service, 52

Indian Removal Act (1830), 40
Indigenous armed resistance, end of, 49–50
Indigenous participation: in Civil War, 44–45; in War of Independence, 125
Indigenous people: genocide against, 13, 14–15, 16–17, 20–50; police and, 51
Indigenous People's Day, 54
Indigenous population: of present-day Mexico, 19; size of, 18–19; in United States decline in, 16–17
indigenous resistance, suppression of, 39
Indigenous societies, diverse, 17
Indigenous struggle for sovereignty, of 1970s, 20
Indigenous struggles, public awareness of, 54–55
Indochina, 161–62
Indonesia, 173, 184–85m 192–193, 229
industrial accident rate, of U.S., 108–9
industrial growth, 11, 98–99, 167
Industrial Revolution, 13, 97–99
Industrial Union Department, 118
Industrial Workers of the World (IWW), 113
infant formula, 279–80
Inikori, Joseph E., 61–62
Inoca people, 28
institutionalized racism, 84–85
international industrial supremacy, 107

516 INDEX

invaders, Spanish, 19, 20–30
invasion, of Russia, 153–54
Iowa (battleship), 118, 145–46
Iran, 174–75, 179, 188, 205, 254
Iraq, 184–85, 195–96, 219–20, 229–30, 252–54
Irish immigrants, 99
iron, 101
Islamic Republic, 212
Islamic State, 239–40, 252–53, 276
Israel, 245; creation of, 177; Six-Day War and, 195; Yom Kippur War and, 201–2
Italian elections, 176

J. P. Morgan and Company (firm), 151–52
Jackman, Mary R., 95–96
Jackson, Andrew, 39, 40, 130, 131–32
Jackson, Jimmie Lee, 88
Jaggan, Cheddi, 187
Jamaica, 204
Jamestown, 26
January insurrection, by Trump supporters, 274–75
Japan, 134–35, 156, 161
Japanese internment, 165, 268
Jay, John, 127
Jefferson, Thomas, 37, 127, 128–29
Jemez, 30
Jewish Federation Attack, 276
Jewish refugees, refusal to accept, 165, 269–70
Jiang, Jieshi, 156, 171
Johnson, Charles, 70
Johnson, James Weldon, 85–86

Johnson, Lyndon, 189, 195
Joint Comprehensive Plan of Action, 254
Jones, David S., 20–21
Jordan, 197, 203
Joseph (chief), 48

Kabila, Joseph, 227–28
Kabila, Laurent Désiré, 226–27
Kagame, Paul, 224–26
Kagan, Robert, 138
Kake, Ibrahima Baba, 61
Kalākaua (King), 139
Karachi (Pakistan), 120
Karankawa people, 24, 43
Keaton, Paul, 25
Kelton, Paul, 25, 27
Kennedy, John, 186, 187–88
Kenosha (Wisconsin), 274
Kerr, Derek N., 70
Khashoggi, Jamal, 251
Khmer Rouge, 191, 209
Kiernan, V. G., 161, 180, 182, 186
Kim, Il Sung, 172
Kim, Jong Un, 248–49
King, Martin Luther, Jr., 88–89
King, Rodney, 89
King George's War, 33
King Philip's War, 29
King Williams's War, 30–31, 123
Kinsport (Tennessee), 116
Kirven (Texas), 86
Kissinger, Henry, 202
Klein, Herbert S., 63
Klein, Martin, 60
the Klu Klux Klan, 83, 86, 87–89
known slave traders, 74

INDEX 517

Knoxville (Tennessee), 86
Kolko, Gabriel, 163
Korea, 138–39, 166, 172, 178–79
Koresh, David, 265
Kristallnacht (massacre), 157
Kroeber, Alfred, 19
Kuala Batu (Sumatra), 131
Kuwait, 212–13, 219–20
Kuznick, Peter, 151, 176, 211

La Florida, 29–30, 130
labor, of enslaved people, 11,
   57–58
labor activists, 116
Lakota people, 44, 47, 49, 54
Lamar, Mirabeau, 43
land concessions, 36
Landler, Mark, 234–35
Laos, 190
large-scale annihilation, 14
de Las Casas, Bartolomé, 21
Latin America, 213–14
Lawrence Textile Strike, 113
lead, 286
Lebanon, 184, 203, 214
Lee, George, 87
Lee, Herbert, 87
Lenape people, 28–29, 35
Lend-Lease Act, 163
Lenin, Vladimir, 151
Lens, Sidney, 9, 129, 151–52, 170
de Leon, Solon, 97
Leopold (King), 109
Levine, Robert S., 96
Liberia, 10, 77, 131, 133–34,
   207–8; U.S. support for repres-
   sion in, 218

Libya, 217–18, 238–39
Liliʻuokalani (Princess), 140
Liliʻuokalani (Queen), 141–42
Lincoln, Abraham, 45, 80, 136, 137
Linder, Marc, 110
literature, counter-hegemonic,
   13–14
Little, Douglas, 174
Little, Frank, 113
Little Steel Strike, 114
Lodge, Cabot, 142
Long, Breckinridge, 157
López, Narciso, 134
López de Santa Anna, Antonio, 132
Los Angeles Aqueduct, 107
Louisiana Purchase, 129
Louisiana Territory, 37, 128–29
Lovejoy, Paul, 62, 66
Lowell (Massachusetts), 100–101
low-wage countries, production
   in, 120
Loyalists, 125–26
Ludlow (Colorado), 113
Ludlow Massacre, 113
Lumumba, Patrice, 185
lynchings, 83–84, 85–89

Maafa: *see* great disaster
Madagascar, 173–74
Madeira-Mamore railroad, 109
Madero González, Francisco
   Ignacio, 149
Madison, James, 130
Madley, Benjamin, 43–44
Maduro, Nicolás, 255–56
Magdoff, Harry, 12
Maine (ship), 143

518 INDEX

malaria, 25, 42, 43
Malaya, 173–74
Malcolm X, 88
Malcom, Dorothy, 87
Malcom, Roger, 87
Mandela, Nelson, 187
manifest destiny, 43
Manley, Michael, 204
Manning, Patrick, 65
Mao, Zedong, 171
Mapping Police Violence project,
    267–68
Marcos, Ferdinand, 196–97
marginalized people, resistance by,
    15, 54–55
Mark, C. H., 107
Markowitz, Gerald, 105
Marshall Plan, 176
Marx, Karl, 18, 57
mascots for sports teams, racist, 54
Mascouten people, 32
mass deaths, 14
mass incarceration, 82–83, 93,
    268–69
mass shootings, 270
Massachusetts Bay Colony, 28
Massacre at Wounded Knee, 49
La Matanza (massacre), 155
Matewan Massacre, 114
McCormick Harvester Works
    (firm), 106
McKinley, William, 142, 143
McNeil, Sara, 98
McVeigh, Timothy, 272
medical errors, 283–84
medical experiments, 90–91,
    280–81

Menéndez de Avilés, Pedro, 25
Menominee people, 34
mercury poisoning, 111
Mesquakie people, 32
Metacom (chief), 29
Metaxas, Ioannis, 158
Mexican Revolution, 11, 148–50
Mexico: acquisition of half of by
    U.S., 131–32; independence
    of Spain from, 40; Mérida
    Initiative of, 236
Mianning (emperor), 132
The Middle Passage, 61, 67, 68
Midway Island, 138
migrants, government action
    against, 269–70
Mi'kmaq people, 28
military: intervention, 131; pres-
    ence, in Thailand, 117, 191–92
mill workers, 100–101
Miller, Joseph C, 65, 66
Milne, Seumas, 221–22
miners, 103–4
miner's asthma, 101
Minnesota Bureau of Labor
    Statistics, 104
Mintz, Steven, 98
Mobile Bay, Alabama, 74
Mobile people, 24
Mobutu, Joseph-Désiré, 185, 192,
    226–27
Monongah (West Virginia), 107
Monroe, James, 131
the Monroe Doctrine, 11, 131, 147
Moore, Henriette, 87
Moore, Henry, 87
Morales, Evo, 256

INDEX

morality, myth of, 9, 17–18
morphine, 277
Morsi, Mohamed, 242–43
mortality rates: of African
    Americans, 63–64, 69–70, 84,
    95; of Native people, 51–53
Mossadegh, Mohammad, 179
Mozambique, 215–16
Mrs. Winslow's Soothing Syrup,
    277
munitions explosion, 115
murder: of African Americans by
    white mobs, 85, 260–61; social,
    14, 52–53, 56, 72–73, 85, 94–96
Muscogee people, 31, 38, 39, 41
Mussolini, Benito, 154–55, 158
myth, of morality, 9

Nachtigal, Gustav, 66
nadir, of Native population, 50
Namibia, 215–16
Napoleon, 129
Napoleonic Wars, 129
de Narváez, Pánfilo, 23
Nash, Gary B., 71–72
Nasser, Gamal, 182–83
Nat Turner's Rebellion, 78–79
National Conference on Industrial
    Diseases, 112
National Guard, 264–65
National Liberation Front (NLF),
    187, 189
National Maritime Union, 115
National Safety Council, 110, 118
Native deaths, number of, 55–56
Native Hawaiians, 50
Native languages, 54

Native people, support for British
    of, 35
Native population, recovery in, 50
natural reproduction, 69
naval vessels, of U.S., 131
Nazism, 156–57
Negro Fort, 39, 78
Nermernuh population, 42
The Netherlands, 173
New Amsterdam, 28
new constitution, of United States,
    126
New Jersey Bureau of Statistics,
    104–5
New Jim Crow, 93
New Mexico Territory, 44
New Orleans (Louisiana), 77, 85
New York City, rebellion in, 71, 80
Newark, New Jersey, 286
Newton (Long Island), 71
Newton, John, 66
Ngo Dinh Diem, 182
Nicaragua, 135, 138, 142, 147,
    204–5; Reagan and, 213
Nichols, Terry, 272
Nigeria, 195–96, 250
Nimi'ipuu people, 47–48
Nixon, Isaiah, 87
Nixon, Richard, 93, 116, 189–91,
    197, 199–200
nomadic hunters, 17
Norfolk County (Virginia), 78
Normandy, 164
North Africa, 164
North America, colonial wars in,
    17, 124
North Atlantic Treaty

520 INDEX

Organization (NATO), 178, 230, 233–34
North Korea, 172, 248–49
Northampton County (Virginia), 72
Northeast, 27–28
The Northern Mariana Islands, 171
Nova Scotia, 27–28
nuclear weapons testing, 285
Nuevo México, 29–30
Al-Nusra, Jabhat, 240–41

Oak Creek (Wisconsin), 273
Obama, Barack, 237–47
Obregón, Alvaro, 150
Obwandiyag (chief), 34
occupational diseases, 105–6, 111–12, 115–16
Occupational Safety and Health Act (1970), 116–17
October Revolution, 153–54
Oglethorpe, James, 32–33
Ohio Bureau of Labor Statistics, 104
oil well explosion, 115
Ojeda Ríos, Filiberto, 266
Old Northwest Territory, 36
Olney, Richard, 11, 142
de Oñate, Juan, 25
Oneida people, 35
Opechancanough (chief), 26–27
Open Door Policy, 161
Operation Condor, 203–4
opioids, 277–78, 284
opium trade, 130, 276–77, 288

oppressed people seeking freedom, English settlement as, 17–18
Oregon Territory, 133
Organization of the Petroleum Exporting Countries, 188
Osage people, 51
Ostler, Jeffrey, 39, 42
O'Sullivan, John, 133
overseers, violence by, 70
de Oviedo, Fernández, 21

Pacific Northwest, Native population of, 34, 44, 48
Pacific Northwest Lumber Strike, 114
Pact of Madrid, 179–80
Page, Walter Hines, 152
Paiute people, 49–50
Pakistan, 199, 250
Palestine, 177, 230
Palestine Liberation Organization (PLO), 197, 203
Pamunkey people, 26–27
Panama, 189, 218–19
Panama Canal, 121, 146
Panama Canal Zone, 189
Panama Railroad, 100, 139, 145–46
Papadopoulos, George, 194–95
Parenti, Michael, 126, 258
Pathet Lao, 190
Pauwels, Jacques R., 157
peace treaty, with Lenape people, 35
Pearl Harbor, 162
Pemberton textile mill, 101
People's Grocery, attack at, 82

INDEX

521

People's Liberation Army, 171, 183
People's Republic of China,
   83–84
Pequot people, 28
Perdue Pharma, 284
Perry, Matthew, 134
Persian Gulf Doctrine, 208
Peru, 194, 220–21
pesticides, 286
Philadelphia, riot in, 95
the Philippines, 10, 143–44, 174–
   75, 196–97, 231–32
Piegan War, 46–47
Pierce, Franklin, 135
Pinochet, Augusto, 201
pirates, in Cuba, 131
Pizarro, Francisco, 21–22
Planned Parenthood attack, 273
Plymouth Colony, 28
pneumoconiosis, 105
police brutality, 262–66
police killings, tracking of, 267
police murders, 261–67
police officer use, of force, 88–89,
   91–92
police records, 92
Polk, James K., 79, 133–34
pollution, 284–87
Ponce de León, Juan, 21, 23
Popular Front for the Liberation of
   Palestine (PFLP), 197
Popular Mobilization forces, 253
Popular Movement for the
   Liberation of Angola (MPLA),
   202
Portuguese: colonialism, 186;
   traders, 59

post-slavery oppression, of African
   Americans, 96
Potter, Gary, 261–62
Pount Coupee Parish (Louisiana),
   72
power plant explosion, 119
the Powhatan Confederacy, 26
*The President's Report on
   Occupational Safety and Health*
   (government document),
   116–17
prevention of lynching, attempt
   to, 86
Prince William County (Virginia),
   72
prisoner uprising, in Attica, New
   York, 89
prisoners, deportation of, 98
Proclamation of 1763, 125
profits, pursuit of, 109
progressive reforms, following
   War of Independence, 126
Prohibition, 277
Prosser, Gabriel, 77
protests, at Standing Rock, 54
proxy wars, 12
public health crises, 281–82
Pueblo population, 25, 29–30, 44
Pueblo Revolt, 44
Puerto Rico, 144, 282
Pulaski (steamboat), 99
Pulse nightclub shooting, 276
Putin, Vladimir, 255

Qaddafi, Muammar, 238–39
Al Qaida, 206–7, 230–31, 241, 251,
   275

522   INDEX

QAnon, 274
Qasim, Abd al-Karim, 184, 188
Quebec, 27–28
Queen Anne's War, 31

racial caste system, mass incarceration as, 93
racism: institutionalized, 84–85; poor health conditions and, 94–95; during Second World War, 165
racist mascots, for sports teams, 54
racist violence, 87–89; in twenty-first century, 91–92
radium poisoning, 111
railroad employees, accidents of, 99–103, 110
Ramadier regime, 174
Rana Plaza building, 120
Reagan, Ronald, 93, 210–14
rebellion, in New York City, 71
reconstruction period, 81–82
recovery, of Native population, 50
Red River War, 47
Red Scare, 264
Red Sticks, 38–39
Red Summer, 85–86
Reeves, Arthur, 108
refinery fire, 116
Reinoehl, Michael, 266
religious extremists, 276
Report on Lawlessness in Law Enforcement (government document), 263
repression, of workers, 106, 112–13
Republic of Texas, 43, 132

resistance, by marginalized people, 15, 54–55, 70–71
Rhodesia, 200
Rice, Tamir, 267
Richardson, David, 62, 65
riot: following assassination of King, M., 89; in Philadelphia, 95
Roanoke Island, 26
Rodney, Walter, 61
Roe v. Wade (1973), 281
Roosevelt, Franklin, 157, 163–65
Roosevelt, Theodore, 109, 146–47
Rosewood (Florida), 86
Rosner, David, 105, 117
Roth, Randolph, 93
Roxas, Manuel, 175
Rubinow, I. M., 108
Russia, 12, 36; invasion of, 153–54
Rwanda, 224
Rwandan Patriotic Front (RPF), 224
Ryan, Thomas Fortune, 109

Sackett, Frederic, 157
Samoza García, Anastasio, 155
San Bernadino (California), 276
San Diego mission, 34
San Miguel de Gualdape, 23
Sandinista government, 213
Sandino, Augusto, 155
Sankofa, Shaka, 91
Santa Fe de Nuevo México, 29
Saudi Arabia, 251
Sauk people, 32, 41
scalps, bounty for, 29
Schmitz, David F., 156–57
Schwendinger, Robert J., 102

INDEX

Second Continental Congress, 125

Second Seminole War, 41

Security Council, of United Nations, 171

segregation, 87–88

Selassie, Haile, 180, 185

Sellers, Christopher C., 105–6

Seminole people, 39–40, 41

September 11, 2001, 230–31, 275, 281–82

Seraw, Mulugeta, 89

Serbia, 223

settler colonialism, 13, 16

Seven Years' War, 33–34

Shah, of Iran, 179, 205

sharecropping, 83–84, 113

Shauman, Kimberlee A., 95–96

Shays's Rebellion, 126

Shepard, Matthew, 272

shingle-makers, 113

Sierra Leone, 218

Sihanouk, Norodom, 190–91

silicosis, 105, 115

Silkwood, Karen, 265

silver, discovery of, 46

Simpson, Bradley R., 173

Sims, J. Marion, 76

Sioux War, 46–47

Sitting Bull: see Tatanka Yotanka (chief)

sixteenth century, 22

Sixteenth Street Baptist Church, 87–88

slave forts, 65

slave trade, in Cuba Brazil and, 74–75

slave trade, outlawing of, 74; in Mexico, 132; In U.S., 81

Slave Trail of Tears, 75

slaveholders: removal of indigenous people and, 40; War of Independence and, 125

Slocum Massacre, 85

smallpox, 21–22, 25, 28, 30, 33; in California, 43; French and Indian War and, 34–35; on Missouri River, 42

Smalls, Roberts, 82

Snake War, 45

social murder, 14, 52–53, 56, 72–73, 84; since 1900, 94–96

social violence, 13, 15

Socialist Republic of Vietnam, 190

soil pollution, 286

sole superpower, United States as, 12

Somalia, 205–6, 218, 222–23, 233, 235–36; civil war in, 238; Trump and, 250

de Soto, Hernando, 24

South Africa, 180, 187–88, 215–16

South America, 21–22

South Carolina, 74

South Dakota, 47

South Korea, 172, 207

South Sudan, 234–35, 243–44

Southern States Convention of Colored Men, 81–82

Southwest Railroad Strike, 106

sovereignty, 1970s Indigenous struggle for, 20

Soviet Union, 159, 164, 166–67; collapse of, 221–22; Yom Kipper

524 INDEX

War and, 159, 164, 166–67, 169–70, 178

Spain, 128–29, 143–44, 159

Spaniards, 18; in Florida, 30; as invaders, 19, 29–30; permanent settlements of, 25; slave trade of, 59–60; in War of Independence, 125–26

Spanish flu, 52

Spanish settlements, permanent, 25

Special Plan Green, 150

Springfield (Illinois), 85

Sri Lanka, 215

stampede, at Italian Hall, 107

Standing Rock, South Dakota, 49

Stannard, David, 16, 19, 20, 63

State Department, U.S., 158–59

state violence, 56

state-sponsored piracy, 128

steel mills, 103–4, 113

sterilization, of Indigenous women, 54

Stone, Milan, 118–19

Stone, Oliver, 151, 176, 211

Stono Rebellion, 71

streetcar strike, 113, 114

strikes: of mill workers, 100–101; railroad, 113

Sudan, 228–29

Suez Canal, 182–83

sugar workers, 82, 114

Suharto, 193, 202

suicide, 259, 271

Sukarno, 185, 192–93

Suleimani, Qassim, 254

Sullivan, John, 35

Sultana (steamboat), 99

Susquehannock people, 27

Syria, 240–41, 252–54

Taft, William Howard, 149

Taino people, 18–19, 21

Taiping Rebellion, 135

the Taliban, 207, 252, 275

Tampa Bay (Florida), 23

Taoyetaduta (chief), 45

Tascalusa (chief), 24

Tasunke Witco (chief), 47

Tatanka Yotanka (chief), 47, 49

Tecumseh (chief), 16, 38

tenant farming, 83–84

Tennessee, 79

territories, of U.S., 10

Texas, 43, 130–32, 133, 263

Texas City (Texas), 116

Texas Rangers, 43

textile mills, 100–101, 120

Thailand military presence in, 117, 191–92

Theobald, Brianna, 54

Thornton, Russell, 19, 55–56

Tibet, 183–84

Till, Emmett, 87

Timuca people, 24, 30

Tines, William, 90

Tinney, George, Jr., 90

Tippecanoe Creek, 38

tobacco, 278

Tohopeka (Alabama), 39

Toledo (Ohio), 114

Tolman, William H. T, 108

Tonkawa people, 43

total body radiation, 90–91

INDEX

525

toxic air inversions, 285
trade: with Britain, 127–28; with settlers, by Powhatans, 26–27
traders, Portuguese, 59
Trail of Tears, 40–41
train derailment, near Angola (New York), 103
transatlantic slave trade, 14–15, 57–60, 96
transport of Chinese workers to America, outlawing of, 102
Treaty of Paris (1783), 36
Tree of Life Synagogue, 274
Triangle Shirtwaist Factory fire, 107
Tripoli, 128
Trujillo, Rafael, 155, 185
Truman, Harry, 166, 172–73, 175
Truman Administration, 173
Truman Doctrine, 175–76
Trump, Donald, 247–56, 273
Tsalagi people, 32–33, 41–42, 268
Tsetchestahase people, 46, 47–48
Tsiya (village in Nuevo México), 29–30
tuberculosis, 105–6, 111–12, 285
Tulsa, Oklahoma, 86
Turkey, 185, 198, 207, 220–21
Turner, Frederick Jackson, 141
Turner, Nat, 79
Tuscarora people, 31
Tuscarora War, 31
Tuskegee experiment, 90
Tutsi people, 225–26
Tyler, John, 132
typhoid, 285
typhus, 26

Ubelaker, Douglas, 19
Uganda, 198–99, 224
Ukraine, 244–45
unarmed Black men, killed by police, 92
Underground Railroad, 77
Union Carbide (firm), 117–18
United Fruit Company (firm), 181
United Nations (UN), 170–71
United States (U.S.): as colonialist, 10, 122–23, 126–28; exceptionalism of, 9; in First World War, 152–53; as sole superpower, 12; territories of, 10
University of Sankore, 58
unsafe consumer products, 279–80
Upper South, 75
uranium mining, 52, 115–16
Uruguay, 189, 200–201

Vanderbilt, Cornelius, 135
Vázquez de Ayllón, Lucas, 23, 60
Vázquez de Coronado, Francisco, 24–25
Venezuela, 147, 176, 231–32
Vesey, Denmark, 78
Vietnam, 172–73, 181–82, 187, 188; war in, 189–90, 210
vigilantes, white supremacist, 92, 259, 260–61
Villa, Francisco "Pancho," 149, 150
Villarosa, Linda, 95
vinyl chloride, 286
violence: by overseers, 70; social, 13, 15; white supremacist, 82, 85–93, 272–75
La Violencia war, 176

Vioxx, 284
Virginia, 70
Voice of America radio program, 217
voting rights: of African American men, 81; of Indigenous people, 52
Voting Rights Act (1965), 88

Wabash and Erie Canal, 99
Walker, Tommy Lee, 90
Walker, William, 135
Walker County (Alabama), 114
Wallace-Wells, David, 288
Walmart (firm), 120
Walsh, Lorena S., 67–68
war: in Afghanistan, 230–31, 251–52; Algerian War of Independence, 182; Anglo-Cherokee War, 124; Bangladesh War, 199; Biafran War, 195–96; Cold War, 180; colonial wars in North America, 123–24; First Barbary War, 128; First Opium War, 132; First Seminole War, 130; First War in Iraq, 219–20; First World War, 94, 150–51, 260; French and Indian War, 124; between Iraq and Iran, 211–13; King Williams's War, 30–31, 123; Korean War, 94, 178–79, 260; Quasi War, 127–28; Queen Anne's War, 123–24; Second Opium War, 136, 276; Second Seminole War, 41; Second War in Iraq, 232–33, 260; Second World

War, 12, 94, 122, 123, 160–67, 260; Vietnam War, 189–90; War in the Philippines, 143–44; War of 1812, 38, 77–78, 128–30; War of 1898, 123, 143–44; War of Independence, 35, 71–72, 73–74, 124–27; War of Jenken's Ear, 33, 124; war on drugs, 83; War on Terror, 231, 233, 236–37, 250; see also Civil War
Washburn flour mill, 103–4
Washington, George, 36–37, 126–28
Washington Post (newspaper), 143
watchmakers, 111
water intake tunnel, for Chicago, 107
Wayne, Anthony, 37
Wendat people, 28
West, Cornel, 246
West Coast Waterfront Strike, 114
White House, burning of, 78, 130
white mobs, 260–61
white supremacist: vigilantes, 92, 259, 260–61; violence, 82, 85–93, 272–75
white supremacy, 58, 81, 83–84
Wilson, James, 19
Wilson, Woodrow, 149, 151–53
Witt, John Fabian, 103, 108
workers, repression of, 106, 112–13
Workmen's Compensation Bureau, 110
workplace deaths, estimates of, 110–11, 116–17

INDEX

workplace injuries, 15, 98–107, 115–16

World Trade Towers, 117

wounded beast, U.S. ruling class as, 15, 257

Wovoka (mystic), 48–49

Wyoming, USS (ship), 137–38

Xi, Jinping, 249

Yamasee War, 32

yellow fever: epidemic at

Pontchartrain Canal, 99; mosquitoes, 90–91

Yemen, 198, 207, 233, 245–46, 251

Younge, Samuel Leamon, Jr., 88

Zaire, 192, 226–27

Zakaria, Fareed, 138

Zapata Salazar, Emiliano, 150

Zelaya, Jose Manuel, 237–38

Zinn, Howard, 17–18, 146

Zionist State, creation of, 177

Printed in the USA
CPSIA information can be obtained
at www.ICGtesting.com
JSHW021926080324
58872JS00007B/67